The Rise and Decline
of the Zairian State

The
Rise and Decline
of the
Zairian State

Crawford Young
Thomas Turner

THE UNIVERSITY OF WISCONSIN PRESS

Published 1985

The University of Wisconsin Press
114 North Murray Street
Madison, Wisconsin 53715

The University of Wisconsin Press, Ltd.
1 Gower Street
London WC1E 6HA, England

First printing

Printed in the United States of America

For LC CIP information see the colophon

ISBN 0-299-10110-X

Contents

Illustrations and Figures   vii

Maps   ix

Tables   xi

Preface   xiii

Acronyms   xvii

1   The State in Zaire: An Introductory Perspective   3

2   Zaire in the Mobutu Years: An Overview, 1965–1980   47

3   The State and Civil Society: Capital, Town, and Countryside   78

4   The Dynamics of Inequality: Class Formation   100

5   The Ethnic Dimension of Civil Society   138

6   The Patrimonial State and Personal Rule   164

7   In Pursuit of Legitimacy: Party and Ideology   185

8   Regional Administration   221

9   The Seventh Scourge: The Security Forces   248

10   Economic Policy during the Mobutu Years   276

11   Zairianization and Radicalization: Anatomy of a Disaster   326

12   Zaire in the International Arena   363

13   Conclusion: Crisis of the Zairian State   396

Notes   409

Index   469

Illustrations and Figures

Illustrations

Colonie Belge   4
Etat Indépendant du Congo   5

Figures

4.1   Real Wage Movements, 1910–1978   134
10.1 Copper Price Movements, 1950–1977   308
12.1 Relations of Major Powers with Zaire, 1965–1978   394

Maps

Map 1. Zaire: Political Sub-Divisions   9
Map 2. Major Events, 1965–1970   48
Map 3. Language Distribution and Ethnic Groups   141

Tables

3.1	Urban Population Growth	81
3.2	Per Capita Income Changes, 1957–1970	82
3.3	Government-Approved Investment Projects, by Region, 1969–1972	83
3.4	Power Consumption by Region, 1972	83
3.5	Demand Bank Deposits by Region, 1971–1974	84
3.6	Zairian Wage Employment, 1915–1970	85
3.7	Sectoral Employment, 1958–1970	86
3.8	Public Sector Employment of Zairians, 1960–1978	86
3.9	Sex Ratios of Adult Zairians in Kananga, 1955–1972	89
3.10	Index of Government-Fixed Agricultural Prices, 1960–1974	94
3.11	Consumer Goods Prices, Kikwit (Bandundu), 1968–1976	95
3.12	Income per Month by Sex, Rural Bandundu Sample, 1973–1975	97
4.1	Stratification and Class in Zaire	103
4.2	Length of Service as Minister and/or Political Bureau Member, 1965–1975	118
4.3	Changes in Remuneration Level within the Sub-Bourgeoisie, 1960–1965	124
4.4	Indices of Wages, Prices, and Real Wages, Kinshasa, at Official Minimum Wage (UNTZA data)	132
4.5	Indices of Nominal and Real Wages and Salaries, 1974–1977 (IBRD data)	133
5.1	Regional Origins of Second Republic Political Elite, 1965–1975	151
5.2	Comparison of Secondary School Populations, 1962 and 1978	156
6.1	The CELZA Plantation Empire	180
6.2	CELZA Share of Total Zairian Production, Agricultural Commodities, 1976	180

6.3	Cattle Holdings in Zaire, 1975 Estimates	181
7.1	Occupational Distribution of Legislative Candidates, Mongala Subregion, 1970	203
8.1	Position, Rank, and Salary of Regional Administrators, Lisala, 1974	229
8.2	Rural Collectivities by Type and by Region, 1972	235
10.1	Government Budgets, 1964–1966	278
10.2	Inflation Rate, 1960–1967	279
10.3	Primary Commodity Production, 1959–1980	282
10.4	Ownership of UMHK, End of 1965	289
10.5	Leverage in the Zaire-UMHK Conflict	292
10.6	Taxation and Profits of Gécamines	294
10.7	Africanization of Gécamines Management, 1967–1980	296
10.8	Zairian Terms of Trade, 1967–1975	309
10.9	Returns to Peasant Farm Labor, Northern Zaire, 1973–1974	313
10.10	Comparative State Cotton Prices, 1970	317
10.11	Returns to Peasants on Main Cash Crops, Gandajika, 1974	318
10.12	Cotton Prices	319
10.13	Public Finance, 1970–1977	323
10.14	State Consumption Levels	324
10.15	Inflation, 1970–1978	324
11.1	Effects of Zairianization in Lubumbashi	341
11.2	Effects of Zairianization in Bumba	342
11.3	Radicalization: The Ten Scourges and Their Remedies	352
12.1	Zaire's External Public Debt, 1972–1977	386
12.2	Debt Service Obligations, 1978–1983	387

Preface

A tortuous trail stretched between commencement and completion of this work. When we embarked upon our journey, the distance and difficulty of the path were mercifully concealed from us. Had we anticipated either the length of the odyssey or the greatly altered circumstances at its conclusion, we wonder whether we would have had the fortitude to set forth.

The idea for the venture took form more than a decade ago, in early 1973. At that time we were both afforded the opportunity to return to Zaire for two-year teaching assignments at the Faculty of Social Science of the then-Université Nationale du Zaire Lubumbashi campus. Those were times of relative optimism concerning the future of Zaire, both within the country and among those outside who followed its affairs. Some problems were apparent, yet the New Regime, which under President Mobutu Sese Seko had seized power in November 1965, seemed to have a number of achievements to its credit. There was no shortage of critics, but seeming success muted the intensity of their attacks. We recollect no prophets who foretold that Zaire was on the verge of sudden descent into the maelstrom of unending crises. Certainly we had no such premonitions. Nor would we have ever imagined that state decline would become a central theme of our book.

Our initial decision to undertake the study was primarily motivated by a more mundane sense that there was as yet no sustained, comprehensive study of the Mobutu era, which had brought many changes to the political life of the country. The First Republic years had fostered an abundant literature, but only the very beginning phases of the New Regime had been treated (in particular in the excellent 1972 study by Jean-Claude Willame, *Patrimonialism and Political Change in the Congo*). Both of us had already devoted years of study to Zaire. Young had first visited Zaire in 1958, then carried out dissertation research there in 1962. In 1963, 1965, and 1967 he undertook study missions for the Department of State. In 1969 he headed a survey team of the Overseas Liaison Committee of the American

Council on Education, which carried out a study of the educational system for the U.S. Agency for International Development. In 1965 he had published a study of decolonization and the early independence period, *Politics in the Congo*. Turner had taught at the former Université Libre du Congo in Kisangani from 1969 to 1971, while carrying out research which led to his University of Wisconsin–Madison dissertation, "A Century of Conflict in Sankuru" (1972). Both authors had published a number of other articles and chapters dealing with the 1960–65 period.

In the course of our stay in Zaire from 1973 to 1975 we witnessed the first phases of what was to become a crisis of the state itself. During vacation periods we were able to pursue our inquiry in a number of areas of the country. Subsequently, Young spent the summer of 1976 collecting additional material in Brussels, and Turner was able to return to Zaire for several additional months of interviewing in 1978.

Drafting of the manuscript began in 1978, with the first version completed in 1980. We then placed the draft in circulation, eliciting comments from a number of Zairian and American scholars. The work has enormously benefitted from the candid, searching comments of its numerous critics, whom we can reward only with our heartfelt thanks, and the customary absolution from any responsibility for remaining blemishes. Those who criticized the work in its entirety include Bakonzi Agayo, Bianga Waruzi, Bifuko Baharanyi, Edouard Bustin, David Gould, Bogumil Jewsiewicki, Ngoma Ngambu, Nzongola Ntalaja, Michael Schatzberg, Jan Vansina, and Yamvu Makasu. Those who offered critiques of portions of the manuscript include Stephen Morrison, Patrick Riley, Saroja Reddy, Harlan Robinson, Herbert Weiss, the members of the Institute for Advanced Study (Princeton) 1980 seminar on comparative colonialism, and the Woodrow Wilson International Center for Scholars 1983 colloquium on power and authority.

The manuscript underwent three comprehensive revisions. In the process, it shed 500 of its initial 1,200 typescript pages, and five of the original eighteen chapters. Its conceptual framework also experienced major alteration. Initially, our theme was authoritarianism; as time went by and patterns of decline became more pronounced, this theoretical vantage point seemed increasingly irrelevant. In mid-passage—after toying, in one draft, with the possibility of dropping the theoretical framework altogether—we shifted to the nature of the state as a unifying concept.

After 1976, the authors were always separated by several hundred miles. We divided primary responsibility by chapter, with subsequent mutual editing, and several meetings to integrate the work. Whether we have wholly succeeded in unifying the style is a verdict to be pronounced by the jury of readers. In the final version, Turner was the initial author of chapters 7, 8, and 9, and Young the remainder. However, we present the book as a fully joint undertaking for which we share equal responsibility.

Any undertaking so long in gestation has accumulated along the way innumerable debts to the many individuals and organizations who were of assistance. They, like our critics, enjoy total absolution from any defects in the work. Our instructional service in Zaire was supported by the Rockefeller Foundation, as part of its program of university development. We should record our particular gratitude to James Coleman, a scholar of quite extraordinary dedication, whose commitment and skill was primarily responsible for whatever success this program had. His colleagues R. K. Davidson and Joseph Black, and his talented assistant Mvemba Makessa, were also of signal assistance.

Other financial assistance, at different stages, came from the National Endowment for the Humanities, the Guggenheim Foundation, and the University of Wisconsin Graduate School Research Committee. Some of the editorial work on the manuscript was completed while Young enjoyed the superb hospitality of the Institute for Advanced Study in Princeton in 1980–81, and the Woodrow Wilson International Center for Scholars in 1983–84.

Our particular gratitude goes to our colleagues at the Lubumbashi campus of the Université Nationale du Zaire: the campus officials (especially the dynamic vice-rector, Koli Motukua), our associates in the Faculty of Social Science, and our students. We particularly cherish those associations—the mood of intellectual encounter, the ethos of collegial solidarity, the will to cope and overcome in the face of already difficult material circumstances—and look upon them as emblematic of the future resurrection of Zaire. Young had the privilege to serve as dean of the faculty during that period; special tribute is due to those whose collaboration, both academic and intellectual, was most valuable: Ilunga Kabongo, Munzadi Babole, Payanzo Ntsomo, Mwabila Malela, Lubadika Botha, Ileka Nkiere, Manoni Ngongo, Lobho Lwa Djugu Djugu, Johannes and Ilona Fabian. Turner would like to acknowledge in particular the hospitality and assistance of Kasongo Owandji Okenge and Sokolua Lubanzadio. Our heartfelt thanks as well to the many others we are unable to name individually.

The Centre de Recherches et de Documentation Africaine (CEDAF) in Brussels was as hospitable to us as this marvelous research center is to all wandering scholars. We express our thanks to those former graduate students who helped us in one way or another as research assistants: Darab

Aram, Bakonzi, Bianga, Larry German, Guy Gran, Vwakyanakazi Mukohya. Dorothy Berg, Mary Reardon, and Marilyn Henry rendered yeoman service in deciphering and typing the manuscript at different stages. For the index, we are indebted to Eva Young, Kathleen Laughlin, and Elizabeth Diez.

Some years ago, a colleague examining Young's collection of Tshibumba paintings—two of which begin the first chapter—remarked upon the tragic view of history they conveyed. The publication of this volume will coincide with the centennial of the foundation of the Leopoldian colonial state in Zaire. This unintended commemoration serves to underline the cogency of that observation; the fates have not smiled upon Zaire for much of the last century. In the closing paragraph of the book, we evoke the African proverb "No condition is permanent." May that prophecy serve as dedication to this volume.

January 1984
Crawford Young   Thomas Turner
Madison, Wisconsin   Wheeling, West Virginia

Acronyms

ABAKO	Alliance des Bakongo
AID	Agency for International Development
ANEZA	National Association of Business
AZAP	Agence Zairoise du Presse
BCK	Compagnie du Chemin de Fer du Bas-Congo au Katanga
BRITMOND	British Diamond Distributors
CELZA	Cultures et Elevages du Zaire
CFL	Chemin de Fer du Congo Supérieur aux Grands-Lacs
CIPEC	International Council of Copper Exporting Countries
CIZA	Cimenteries du Zaire
CND	Centre National de Documentation
CNKi	Comité National du Kivu
CNRI	Centre National de Recherche et d'Investigation
COGERCO	Parastatal marketing board
CONACO	Convention Nationale Congolaise
COTONCO	Compagnie Cotonnière Congolaise
CPP	Convention People's Party (of Ghana)
C.R.I.S.P.	Centre de Recherche et d'Information Socio-Politiques
CSK	Comité Special du Katanga
CSLC	Confédération des Syndicats Libres du Congo
CVR	Corps des Volentaires de la République
DITRAC	Paracommando Division, Forces Armées Zairoises
ENA	National School of Administration
FAZ	Forces Armées Zairoises
FDC	Front Democratique Congolais
FGTK	Fédération Générale des Travailleurs Kongolais
FLEC	Frente de Libertação do Enclave de Cabinda
FLNA	Frente Nacional de Libertação de Angola

FLNC	Front pour la Libération Nationale du Congo
Forminière	Société Internationale Forestière et Minière
Gécamines	Générale les Carrières et des Mines
IBRD	International Bank for Reconstruction and Development
IMF	International Monetary Fund
JMPR	Jeunesse du Mouvement Populaire de la Révolution
LDC	Less developed country
MIBA	Minière du Bakwanga
MNC	Mouvement Nationale Congolaise
MNC/L	Mouvement Nationale Congolaise, Lumumba wing
MPLA	Movimento Popular de Libertação de Angola
MPR	Mouvement Populaire de la Révolution
OAU	Organization of African Unity
OCAM	Organisation Commune Africaine et Malgache
ONACER	Office National de Céréales
ONAFITEX	Office National des Fibres Textiles
ONC	Office National du Café
OTRAG	Orbital Transport and Raketen A. G.
PDG	Parti Démocratique de Guinée (of Guinea)
PNP	Parti National du Progrès
PSA	Parti Solidaire Africain
SADCC	Southern African Development Coordination Conference
SCAM	Société Commerciale et Agricole du Mayombe
SGA	Société Générale d'Alimentation
SIBEKA	Société d'Enterprise et d'Investissement du Bécéka
SICAI	Italian industrial consulting firm
SMTF	Société Minière de Tenke-Fungurume
SNCZ	Société Nationale des Chemins de Fer Zairois
SOBAKI	Société Belgo-Africaine du Kivu
SOCOBANQUE	Société Congolaise du Banque
SODEMAZ	Zairian Upkeep and Maintenance Co.
SODIMIZA	Société de Developpement Industriel et des Mines du Zaire
SOGEMIN	Société Générale des Minerais
SONAS	Société Nationale d'Assurance
SOZACOM	Société Zairoise pour la Commercialisation des Minerais
UDI	Unilateral Declaration of Independence

UDPS	Union pour la Démocratie et le Progrès Social
UGEC	Union Générale des Etudiants Congolais
UMHK	Union Minière du Haut-Katanga
UN	United Nations
UNARCO	Union of Nationalists of Revolutionary Africa
UNAZA	Université Nationale du Zaire
UNITA	União Nacional para a Independência Total de Angola
UNTZA	Union Nationale des Travailleurs Zairois
UTC	Union des Travailleurs Congolais
WIGMO	Western International Ground Maintenance Organization

The Rise and Decline
of the Zairian State

I

The State in Zaire: An Introductory Perspective

Part One

"Colonie belge"

On the walls of hundreds of Zairian homes in southern Shaba, some of them quite modest, hang oil paintings.[1] This urban folk art is truly syncretic. The medium is European in origin, although the "canvas" typically is flour-sacking; the motifs are African, chosen to appeal to a local audience. The themes are varied—mermaids, leopards, villages, cities—but unquestionably one of the most popular is "Colonie belge" ("Belgian colony"). Virtually all Zairian urban folk artists have this theme in their repertory; we reproduce two paintings on "Colonie belge" by Tshibumba Kanda-Matula, one of the most prolific urban artists. Graphically portrayed are a number of the political themes we wish to develop in our search for understanding of the Zairian state.[2]

In both paintings the most striking attribute of the colonial state is force, present in several vectors. Dominating the center of the canvas is the African soldier, coercive backbone of the state. *Colonie Belge* depicts the soldier in a pose which vividly communicates both the strength and brutality of the system. The prominent number 3011 on his uniform perhaps symbolizes the highly impersonal, bureaucratized, inhuman state. All state personnel are uniformed, a further association with force and military might. Stretched helpless on the ground is the colonial subject, who suffers the wrath of the state for some nameless transgression of the web of regulation which surrounds him. The source of power and authority in the colonial state, the Belgian administrator, savors his pipe with the calm self-assurance of total command over the situation. Further in the background is the ubiquitous public works department, or "T.P.M."—a familiar agency to most rural men, who had been required during much of the colonial period to provide it with service, often unremunerated. The concrete, physical presence of the state was most visible in its administrative out-

3

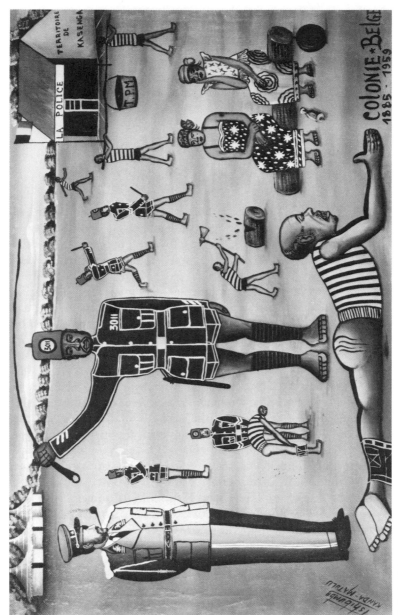

Colonie Belge

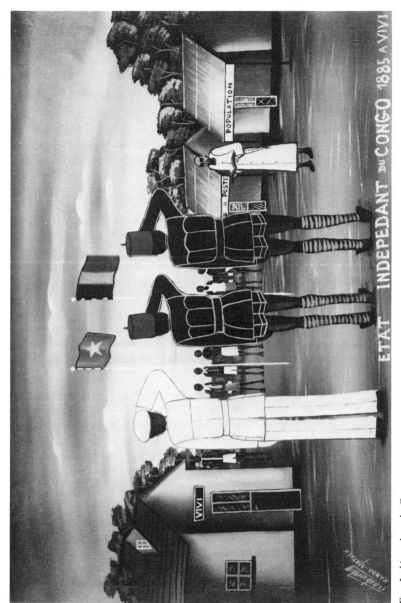

Etat Indépendant du Congo

posts; here Tshibumba selects the prison to visually represent the state. The two women, who have brought food for the prisoner, gaze directly at us in forlorn entreaty, inviting our further contemplation of the many meanings in this portrait. The Fabians, students of Zairian urban art, spell out one of these meanings, suggesting continuing colonial residues in the contemporary state:

> Colonial experience, although chronologically a thing of the past, remains an active element of present consciousness. Paintings of *Colonie belge* express the omnipresence of powerful, organized, and bureaucratic oppression of the little man as he feels it now, in a system whose decolonization remains imperfect and which constantly uses the former oppressor as a negative counterimage.[3]

The companion painting, *Etat Indépedant du Congo*, refers to the initial version of the colonial state, which was a personal fiefdom of King Leopold II (Congo Free State, 1885–1908). However, its imagery is of broader application. Buildings of a distinctive, stereotypical architecture are the physical manifestation of the state, while the twin flags—the Congo colonial banner with yellow star on blue field, and the black-red- and yellow-banded Belgian flag—are its icons. Its human agents are again impersonal; thus their backs are toward us in this portrait. The emaciated, skeletal African subjects are in the background, incongruous neckties offering a striking metaphor of cultural subordination. The state is a soldier, and its subjects are prisoners.

In this study, we wish to step behind the portraits and to seek out the state in post-colonial Zaire. We want to grasp its nature, peer beyond its ideological images and public metaphors to perceive its realities. Formal structure imperfectly mirrors its inner mechanism; publicly asserted purposes bear little resemblance to its actual behavior. Through the prism of the state, projected upon our own flour-sacking, we hope to compose a portrait of politics in the Mobutu era, from 1965 to 1980.

In our representation of the state, embodying politics as process over time, we must incorporate one dimension missing from the Tshibumba imagery: state decline. *Colonie Belge* and *Etat Indépedant du Congo* depict state ascendancy; its hegemony over the recumbent prisoner, the grieving women, and the bare-chested but necktied subjects is unmistakable and unchallengeable. Yet embedded within every state is the latent possibility of deflation of its power and authority, of loss of its legitimacy, of decay of its institutional structure. The Tshibumba prisoners may abscond, and the seemingly docile subjects may cast off their neckties; the center may not hold.

Since the formal creation of the Congo Free State, ancestor to contemporary Zaire, on 1 July 1885, there have been two cycles of rise and decline. The colonial era, from 1885 until 1958, was a period of nearly uninterrupted state construction; the hegemony of the Belgian colonial apparatus steadily deepened. In its final two years, the colonial edifice progressively lost control over civil society to a tumultuous and fragmented nationalist movement, which was unable to capture intact the colonial infrastructure. The result was five years of turbulent state deflation, generally known as the "Congo crisis." The Mobutu coup in 1965 inaugurated a new cycle, with eight years in which a rising tide of state ascendancy seemed to dominate the political process. After 1974 currents of decline again began to flow strongly, progressively eroding the superstructure of hegemony. It is this second cycle of rise and decline which serves as the central theme for our study.

Before turning to the particulars of the Zairian state, our understanding of the complex concept of "state" should be made clear. Although in the six thousand years of human history since the first known emergence of state forms many different types of state have existed, contemporary discourse on this topic has been overwhelmingly concerned with one particular form: the territorial, sovereign "nation-state" which became dominant from the sixteenth century on in Europe. Its domination has been not only political, but philosophical, ideological, and analytical; discourse, whether normative reflection, political exhortation, or social science theory construction, is deeply rooted in a notion of state whose model is the modern, primarily Western, political entity.

We will begin by considering the contemporary concept of state as it is universally used, with its implicit point of reference in the Western nation-state. Zaire, however, is not simply an African example of such a state; contemporary state formation in Africa has been mediated through the intrusive erection of the colonial state by European occupants. We must examine the particular characteristics of the colonial state. In part two we turn to the Zairian state to identify both its individuality, as manifest in its unusual historical experiences, and those dimensions of its evolution which are broadly comparable to general African patterns. In part two we will present a succinct recapitulation of the first cycle of rise and decline of the Zairian state. The remainder of the volume will focus upon the second (and current) cycle.

Historic concepts of "state"

"State," in truth, proves to be an elusive quarry. In everyday discourse it is commonly understood to refer to the 156-odd political entities whose sovereignty is recognized by United Nations membership. Scholars who have examined the etymology of the term "state" discovered that its present meaning, as autonomous political territory, emerged at roughly the same moment as the modern state system in sixteenth century Europe.[4] The state has experienced many adventures since that time: reduction in numbers in its European heartland from five hundred to fewer than two dozen;[5] globalization, through imperial expansion; marriage with the idea of nation after the French Revolution; evolution through absolutist, constitutionalist, welfare, and socialist forms. The unit, however, is recognizably the same.

Until the nineteenth century, the creation of meanings for the concept of state was in the hands of the political philosophers. Before the seventeenth century the state was not clearly distinguished from its ruler. Machiavelli contributed the notion of "reason of state," a distinctive logic of survival and security which was the object of the prince's statecraft. With the construction of the doctrine of sovereignty, and its fusion with the unfolding concept of state, by degrees the notion entered the abstract realm. For Bodin, immanent in the kingdom was a "high, perpetual, and absolute" power—though he did not clearly distinguish between crown and state. Hobbes, in his geometrical, psychological, and secular reasoning, portrayed the state as "leviathan," a "mortal God," constituted by its subjects' willing surrender to its omnipotent authority as the sole escape from a "nasty, brutish, and short" existence. His vision of the state is graphically represented in the frontispiece to the 1651 edition of *Leviathan*: a huge figure towers over the lilliputian subjects, sword in one hand, scepter of justice in the other; the anthropomorphic sovereign, closely scrutinized, proves to be composed of tiny people.[6]

With Rousseau, sovereignty was reconceptualized to embody a different nexus between state and civil society; sovereignty now originated in civil society, which transmitted it to the state as "general will." Hegel elevated the state to the level of an ideal, the highest accomplishment of the human spirit: at once an instrument for securing common ends, and, on a higher plane, an expression of reason and solidarity.[7]

The state was now, in intellectual discourse, firmly constituted as an impersonal abstraction. This transformation was reflected in its symbolic expressions, such as flags and anthems, and in its institutional emblems:

Map 1. Zaire: Political Sub-Divisions

bureaucracy, the military, and magistrature on the continent; Crown-in-Parliament in Britain; the constitution in the United States. Its further theoretical development was hastened by the timely appearance of the new architects of abstraction, social scientists.

From the encounter between the state and social science came a family of contrasting concepts. Marx and Engels defined the modern state, in a celebrated phrase, as "but a committee for managing the common affairs of the whole bourgeoisie."[8] Weber, in an equally famous passage, characterized the state as "a human community that (successfully) claims the *monopoly of the legitimate use of physical force* within a given territory."[9] The "ideal-typical" modern state, for Weber, was institutionally embodied in the "rational-legal" bureaucracy.

Woodrow Wilson, speaking for the Anglo-American political thought of his age, described the higher evolutionary (Anglo-American) form of the state as organized force, limited by law and constitution, sanctioned by representative government, and directed toward social convenience and individual advancement.[10] The Wilsonian definition was echoed in that of R. M. MacIver: "The state is an association which, acting through law as promulgated by a government endowed to this end with coercive power, maintains within a community territorially demarcated the universal external conditions of social order."[11]

Conceptualization about the state then experienced a long period of hibernation in both Marxist thought and Anglo-American social science (though not in continental European legal philosophy). The legal-institutional optimism of Wilson was an easy target for "realists" such as Arthur Bentley, who defined politics as a group process, with the state simply one interest group among others.[12] For a time the "behavioral revolution" held sway, with its renunciation of state as a dignified object of inquiry; David Easton, in his classic exposition of this paradigm, managed to completely shun even the use of the word in the five hundred pages of *A Systems Analysis of Political Life*.[13] "Political system," of course, is a surrogate for "state," and "authoritative allocation of values" is, in effect, the Eastonian definition of "state."

By the late 1960s, both Marxist and non-Marxist schools of analysis rediscovered the state. The reasons for this resurgence are not difficult to identify; the mystery is why it did not occur earlier. The conditions of armed peace punctuated by frequent regional conflicts within the global framework of American-Soviet rivalry yielded a phenomenal increase in the military dimension of modern states. A vast expansion in state functions occurred in all corners of the world. State socialist regimes ruled a third of the world, with an ideologically-prescribed comprehensiveness of state purpose. In advanced capitalist states, the postwar emergence of the "welfare state" produced a rapid enlargement of state outlays, exceeding 50 percent of the gross national product in such exemplary cases as Sweden and the Netherlands; at the turn of the century state outlays everywhere were only 5 to 10 percent of the GNP. In the developing world, the creed of "development" was absorbed into state ideologies as a central legitimating element; in execution of the creed construction of a comprehensive state framework was imperative.

Contradictions between the public ideologies of contemporary states and their empirical operation also played an important part in resurrecting the concept of state. For the United States, for example, the folly of Vietnam without, the destruction of the environment within, among other developments, called into question the comfortable assumptions of liberal pluralism, in whose penumbra the advanced capitalist state had shrunk into a harmless black box between "inputs" and "outputs." "The end of liberalism" was proclaimed, and a new search undertaken to understand the pathology of the state.[14] Marxists sought explanations for its persistence in spite of its contradictions; non-Marxists hunted for reasons for its contradictions in the face of its apparent liberal modernity.[15] State socialist forms of state invited reconsideration as well; they stubbornly refused to wither, but also no longer corresponded to the totalitarian models of the Stalin era. Their further evolution was blocked by a self-reproducing ruling political class, building new patterns of privilege onto a ponderous bureaucratic autocracy.

On the neo-Marxist side, the inadequacy of classical Marxist representations of state as an epiphenomenal instrument of class dictatorship was conceded. This school, which deployed its analytical energies mainly upon advanced Western states, saw that the state at times appeared in conflict with the immediate claims of its capitalist class. Setting aside the complex typologies which have been developed to classify the nuances of conceptual logic, we may discern a common claim that, to serve the long-term interests of capitalism, the state required "relative autonomy" from the dominant class.[16] Various arguments are offered as to how the "relatively autonomous" state services the ultimate needs of the capitalist order. Miliband perceives the state as ruled by an elite with old school, family, and ideological ties with the capitalist class;[17] for Poulantzas the state itself is a condensation of class relations and constitutive of relations of production, equipped with "ideological instances" which reconstitute dominated classes as individual citizens collectivized as "nation";[18] for others the state is an instrumentality of accumulation, regulation of capital formation processes, or supply of social overhead capital (the welfare infrastructure).[19]

The reawakened concern with state in other analytical schools reflected a recognition of its complexity.[20] The formal-legal thrust and disposition to idealization of the state embedded in earlier approaches were set aside as generative of a "pathetic fiction."[21] Particularly useful are the conceptualizations by Poggi, Skocpol, and Dyson. Poggi defines the modern state as "a complex set of institutional arrangements for rule operating through the continuous and regulated activities of individuals acting as occupants of offices." The state seeks monopoly in law and fact over all "faculties and facilities" pertaining to rule. Internally, these pivot upon "authoritative allocations of values," and externally they hinge upon self-interested defense and expansion of the state's domain against outside adversaries.[22]

A parallel stress upon the fundamental duality of the state as internal aggregation of power and external actor in an international system is central to the influential conceptualization of Skocpol. The state, she insists, is much more than an arena for socioeconomic struggle; it is "a set of administrative, policing, and military organizations headed, and more or less well coordinated by, an executive authority." These structures stand at an intersection between internal socioeconomic structures, over which domination must be maintained and from which resources must be extracted, and a world geopolitical environment which provides both opportunities and dangers that condition state needs and behavior.[23]

A more complex and elaborated conceptual statement is provided by Dyson, who concludes a masterful recapitulation of the history of theoretical concepts of state with his own definition: "Besides referring to an entity or actor in the arena of international politics, state is a highly generalizing, integrating and legitimating concept that identifies the leading values of the political community with reference to which authority is to be exercised; emphasizes the distinctive character and unity of the 'public power' compared with civil society; focuses on the need for the depersonalization of the exercise of that power; finds its embodiment in one or more public purposes which thereby acquire a special ethos and prestige and an association with the public interest or general welfare; and produces a socio-cultural awareness of (and sometimes disassociation from) the unique and superior nature of the state itself."[24] The state, for Dyson, is a many-splendored thing: international actor, legitimating idea, impersonal institutional frame, teleological construct.

Conceptualization of the state

In our view, the complexity of state as a concept makes impossible its reduction to a single dimension, or its definition in a parsimonious phrase. The state must be understood in terms of its essential, irreducible attributes, its behavioral regularities, and its relationships with both the civil society over which it exercises rule and the international environment which conditions its existence. Cumulatively, these define a framework for grasping "state."

The state, to begin with, is a territorially demarcated entity. Normatively, within its boundaries the state lays claim to exclusive authority. Weaker states within the international system only imperfectly succeed in maintaining this value, as external political forces and economic actors intrude, directly or indirectly. Frequent transgression, however, does not annul the norm. The territoriality of the state is iconographically portrayed in the ubiquitous national map, where firm, broad lines enclose its domain.

Sovereignty is a second defining characteristic. However numerous the hidden ambiguities of this concept may be when closely examined, the philosophers of absolutism who erected the notion built better than they knew.[25] The power and authority of the state over its territorial domain are theoretically absolute, indivisible, and unlimited. They may be circumscribed by law or constitution, but these are ultimately self-imposed limitations, hypothetically subject to repeal. The practical constraints of its own scope, penetration, and resources likewise restrict the orbit of sovereignty. Yet over time the state tends to increase its resources and acquire new technologies of control. The doctrine of sovereignty is a powerful ideological weapon of the state in its pursuit of hegemony. The idea of sovereignty is the silent underpinning of the Weberian definition of state as a "legitimate" monopoly of the exercise of coercion.

Thirdly, since the emotionally powerful concept of nation became married to the state in the nineteenth century, this warm, vibrant, living notion has invested the state with a moral personality absent from the more arid and juridical concept of state. In its classic definitions, "nation" is asserted to constitute the citizenry as a community "with which men most intensely and most unconditionally identify themselves, even to the extent of being prepared to lay down their lives for it."[26] It is "a political creed that underlies the cohesion of modern societies, and . . . centers the supreme loyalty of the overwhelming majority of the people upon the nation-state."[27] The idea of nation, globalized through its role in legitimizing the anticolonial struggle which brought the political liberation of Third World states, serves as the vocation of the state, a central part of its *telos*. Its homogenizing, unitarian connotations may well sharply conflict with the cultural pluralism of civil society; "one nation, indivisible" has nonetheless nearly universal currency as state ideology. However far a given state may fall short of the ideal, nation is a generally accepted normative model of what a modern state should be.

Fourthly, the state is, as Poggi and Skocpol insist, a set of institutions of rule, an organizational expression of hegemony. The frame of governance includes the state's bureaucratic apparatus for the routine implementation of its tasks; its political, legislative, and executive agencies (parties, parliaments, presidents and ministers) for the expression of choice and decision; the police and judicial structures for the enforcement of its commands and adjudication of disputes among its citizens; its military forces, for repression of large-scale disorders and for expressing its will and capacity to resist external adversaries. Its institutions include as well a broader set of quasi-public agencies for the instruction and socialization of its young, for the conduct of economic functions brought within the state realm (transport, energy, public industries, for example), and for the supply of services to its populace (health, water, and the like).

Fifthly, the state is a legal system. It commands are systematized as impersonal, predictible, uniform rules, applied by legal professionals. A public law defines the structure and exercise of authority; a criminal code establishes boundaries of permissible behavior by its subjects. The state as well administers a web of private law, regulating transactions and relationships between individuals and legal persons. For Weber, a legal order represented the highest form of state, whose domination was legitimated "by virtue of the belief in the validity of legal statute and functional 'competence' based on rationally created rules."[28] For legal philosopher Hans Kelsen, the state was a King Midas whose touch turned everything to law.[29]

Finally, the state is an idea. It exists in the minds of its officials and citizens as an entity, abstract yet personal, above and beyond the formal institutions of governance. There is, at once, veneration by most of its majesty, frustration among those who reproach it for failure to alleviate their misfortune, and rage among those who experience oppression at its hands. As Gramsci noted, even though its hegemony serves a ruling class, others generally defer to the state's power and consent to its authority because its domination is clothed in some legitimating ideology.[30] The generally diffused image of the state includes affective symbols, legitimating myths, a theory of its origins, processes, and ultimate ends. Its authoritative acts are projected as an embodiment of the public interest. The specific content of its ideology may vary widely: Marxism–Leninism, populist socialism, liberal democracy, Islam. Its legitimating myth may falter because the economic system fails to supply enough consumable goods, its administrative system falls short of expectations of rationality, its legitimation system fails to generate sufficient supportive motivations, or the sociocultural system is hostile to the state ideology.[31] Still, the state is founded upon some form of public ideology.

The state is also identifiable through certain regularities in its behavior. Several observable types of imperatives govern its responses to stimuli arising from within its realm or within the international arena. Cumulatively, these imperatives constitute the autonomous reason of state which shapes its action.

The state seeks to uphold its hegemony over the territory it rules. In another lapidary Weberian definition, the modern state "is a compulsory association which organizes domination."[32] States bristle at overt resistance to the supremacy of their laws or dispute of their ultimate authority over territory and populace. Like the Hobbesian image, the state towers over its subjects, imposes oaths of fealty upon them, requires them to bear its identification and render unto it material sustenance and armed service. Segments of the populace may successfully evade its rules, but will provoke a speedy reaction if they openly deny its hegemony.

The state seeks to uphold and advance its security. This imperative is shaped by the incorporation of the state in an international system politically dominated by nation-state actors, and lacking any higher authoritative institutions. The patterned anarchy of the world system, and the disposition of each state to unilaterally define its own interests within it, mean that force, actual or threatened, is an important component of interstate relationships. States thus arm themselves, within limits imposed by their material resources and internal political structures, to meet individually calculated quantums of security. This congealed power is deemed necessary for preserving sovereignty, for averting territorial dismemberment, and for defending material interests. For the larger and more powerful states, the logic of security may include the predatory expansion of interests at the expense of weaker units. Security includes internal imperatives as well: deterring challenges to state hegemony, enforcing laws, forestalling secessionist claims. The magnitude of the commitment to security is measured by the extraordinary scope of global arms expenditures: $600 billion annually by the early 1980s.[33] The imperative of security is historically documented in the determinative role of warfare in the rise of the modern state.[34]

Related to the imperative of security is that of autonomy. Basic to the concept of sovereignty, externally viewed, is the premise that a state is independent of the dictation of any other authority. The fact that full enjoyment of unabridged autonomy is not possible in the contemporary world system does not diminish the force of the norm. Dependency theory acquires its moral and passionate dimensions not only through the discovery of asymmetrical relationships between industrial capitalist powers and Third World states, but through the conviction that such domination contravenes the normative premise of autonomy. States likewise assert and pursue autonomy with respect to their civil societies. They claim to embody and represent the entire society, and to pursue a "national" or "public" interest distinct from that of any particular group. The notion of interest invoked by the state is of course affected by the claims of civil society; however, it is, as Krasner argues, "a fundamental error to identify the goals of the state with some summation of the desires of specific individuals or groups."[35] Nordlinger defines the autonomy of the contemporary state as policy by "public elites," determined by their interpretation, as state executors, of a general interest.[36] Intersecting here as well is the important "relative autonomy" debate in neo-Marxist conceptualizations of the state.[37]

States also pursue an imperative of legitimation. The hegemony of the state rests in part on ultimate coercive power, but the currency of force is devalued if it must be constantly applied.[38] A state seeks rule by consent, and to secure habitual acquiescence to its authority. This makes legitimacy a requisite for the state. In part, legitimacy is assured through constitutionalizing authority, which casts it in the form of a solemn compact between state and civil society. To the extent that constitutions are living documents, as they generally are in democratic states, they provide a powerful source for legitimacy by establishing some boundaries to state hegemony, guaranteeing individual rights, and prescribing the processes of state operation. Legitimacy is also rooted in the public ideology associated with the state: liberal capitalism in the United States, Marxism–Leninism in the Soviet Union, social democracy in Sweden, Shiite Islamic theology in Iran. Public ideologies, however divergent in content, provide a charter for state actions against which its fidelity to the "public interest" may be appraised. From one perspective such ideologies may well be, as Marx argued long ago, merely the "ideas of the ruling class . . . The class which is the ruling *material* force of society, is at the same time its *ruling intellectual* force."[39] Ideology is in part mystification; it is no less a crucial aspect of the legitimation imperative. Performance as well enters into the legitimacy equation. The state needs to be seen as upholding its external interests, meeting in part the material expectations of civil society, and assuring the security of the realm. The contemporary state also must ground its legitimacy in its effective management of the national economy. In meeting the legitimacy imperative it can no longer, as Habermas observes, "rely on residues of tradition that have been undermined and worn out during the development of capitalism."[40]

Undergirding the other components of reason of state is the revenue imperative. State action in response to other imperatives invariably requires material resources. Closely linked with the role of warfare in expanding the modern state has been the necessity of a fiscal base which

could sustain it. Structural-functional analysis has referred to this imperative as the "extractive capability" of the political system: the "performance
in drawing material and human resources from the domestic and international environments" sets the limits for "attaining various goals for the system."[41] Meeting the revenue imperative decisively orients many of the policy pursuits of given states; Bates elegantly shows how agricultural policy
has been largely dictated by this concern in the case of African states.[42] For
the contemporary state, the revenue imperative goes beyond simply meeting state consumption needs; the state itself in nearly all modern economies, socialist or capitalist, is a direct participant in the broader process of
accumulation. The inherent reticence of civil society to yield to the state
sufficient resources to service state-defined needs for security, hegemony,
autonomy, legitimation, and state-directed accumulation is a veritable
mainspring of politics.[43]

To suggest this array of vectors of state behavior, which cumulatively
form a code of reason of state, leaves unstated how particular regimes or
leaders will deduce state interests in given circumstances. Charles de Gaulle
evidently interpreted French state interests with greater perspicacity than
did Idi Amin those of Uganda. States may also vary widely in their capacity for effective application of reason of state. States in a phase of decline
may progressively lose their ability for autonomous rationality in responding to these imperatives. As we shall see, such indeed has been the drama
of the Zairian state in the latter stages of the Mobutu era.

To complete our conceptual portrayal of the state, we need to add three
types of relationships: state linkages with civil society, with its own diverse
institutions of rule, and with the external system of nation-states. The
state, in some way, is an emanation of civil society, which we understand as
the human aggregate enclosed within the territorial boundaries of the
state.[44] In some form, not necessarily determinate, such primary cleavages
within civil society as class and cultural pluralism are reflected in the state.
In turn, the state itself may play a constitutive role in defining these categories of division and conflict. Class relations are likely to influence both recruitment patterns for state personnel and the public ideology of the state.
Cultural pluralism is likely to affect the personified image of the state in the
concept of nation. At the same time, in pursuit of its legitimation imperative, the state presumes the individuality of civil society in constituting its
members as "citizens," and collectivizes them through the unitary "one
people, one nation" connotations of the national idea.[45]

The state's intimate linkage with the civil societies over which it rules is
textured by the enduring fact of hegemony; states, usually successfully, lay

claim to authority, expressed in legal ideology as sovereignty. Ideologically, states tend to represent civil society as an amalgam of individuals, joined to it by the concept of citizenship. In an important sense, civil society is itself constituted by the state, as its boundaries are supplied by the jurisdictional limits of the state.

The state relationship with civil society is partly conflictual. The contours of the modern state have been shaped in protracted and continuing battle over the boundaries of its hegemony, and the imposition of limits, processual conditions, and predictability on its exercise of sovereign power.[46] This partial shackling of its hegemony becomes in turn a powerful component in the state's legitimating myths through the doctrines of constitutionalism, democracy, and civil liberties.

The notion of civil society as a singular and united entity proves on closer inspection to be a serviceable fiction, whose *dharma* (accumulated merit) is demonstrated in its unending cycle of virtuous rebirth after each analytical destruction. In reality, civil society is fractured into innumerable component parts, whose three fault lines may be identified as class, cultural pluralism (differences of religion, race, ethnicity, caste, or region), and interest.

Class, however murky and controversial its definition may be, divides a civil society in structured patterns of inequality. These may be rooted in mode of production, status, or power; they may be expressed in varying degrees of class consciousness, and the categorical definitions used to describe them vary. The historical contribution of the many strands of Marxist analysis lies in their focus upon this cleavage and its impact upon the state. The state is in part a reflection of class relationships within civil society, although not in so mechanical a fashion as classical Marxism would suggest. The state may be viewed as a congealed representation of class relations, provided that no exclusive determinism is attributed to this factor, and that the ongoing flux and change produced by processes of social conflict remain within the analytical field of vision.

Cultural pluralism constitutes a second crucial sphere of social conflict. Only a handful of contemporary states are culturally homogeneous. In many instances, the cleavages of cultural pluralism are more apparent than class divisions in civil society; ethnic affiliation or religious identification have the capacity to generate intense emotional commitments.[47] Cultural affinities often provide the most efficacious framework for collective mobilization to secure access to power or state-allocated resources.

In its ideological projection as nation, in which its symbolic personality is associated with one or more particular cultural groupings, the state may institutionalize relationships of domination and subordination. It may, through legally created differentiations among groups, entrench variant treatment for certain populations (native Americans and blacks, in the United States case). The civil society called into being by the jurisdictional domain of a state provides the authoritative arena within which the self, confronted with the other, achieves a consciousness generative of cultural solidarity and mobilization takes place. In its daily action, the state is prone to recognize or even create cultural classifications which acquire heightened social meaning through these publicly enshrined codes of differentiation (the enormous importance of colonial censuses in politicizing caste, language, and tribe in India is an example).[48]

Civil society divides and crosscuts into many distinct social and economic interests, latent or manifest. A quarter-century ago the discovery and analysis of these groups was presumed to be the central mission of political science; the state, in advanced industrial democracies, merely registered their preferences. The theoretical supremacy of the liberal pluralist state model has passed, but the importance of the segmentation of civil society into interest formations of unequal strength endures. Its significance is reflected in the revival of corporatist theories of the contemporary state, based on the premise that the primary interest groupings (big capital, labor, commerce, agriculture) tend to establish institutionalized linkages with the state. In their most statist forms, these relationships take the form of state-chartered interest associations, hierarchically ordered and regulated by the state (contemporary Mexico).[49]

The divisions of class, cultural pluralism, and interest which segment civil society are analytically distinct, but practically interrelated. Most contemporary analysts detect a class bias in state action, reflecting the aims of the dominant strata. This bias partly reflects the superior power and organizational resources of economically advantaged classes, whose claims are efficaciously transmitted through the associational network of interest groups and through political parties to officials often recruited from those classes. Not infrequently, class and cultural pluralism cumulate, as in racial hierarchies in South Africa and the United States; in their relationship with the state, the divergent nature of these two types of cleavage must be borne in mind.[50] Neither can be viewed as a mere derivative of the other. Finally, in delineating the state-civil society nexus, one must avoid reification of class, cultural pluralism, or interest. The groups defined by each of these patterns of cleavage have important internal conflicts, and are not fixed, immutable entities.[51]

One crucial paradox of the contemporary state is the contradiction between its ideological unity and its institutional fragmentation. In legal theory, the state speaks with a single voice; its commands are codified in a unified system of law. Ideologically, it is not only through the fervently inculcated concept of "one nation indivisible," but also through the daily ritual of portraying its acts as the authoritative undertakings of a singular authority that the state represents itself as a single actor. This legal fiction is just as regularly undermined by the living reality of dispersed authority and institutional complexity. In a contemporary state, innumerable agencies and individuals, exercising some function clothed with the authority of the state, carry out its tasks. They may be guided by different understandings of the public ideology, and interpret its rules in quite divergent ways. Competition and conflict among different institutional segments of the state may well be constitutionally created, as in the United States. The unitary mirage is not dissipated by the rivalries among its different components; each fragment acts in the name of the whole. Those occupying roles at the state's summit are engaged in relentless efforts to sustain an overall coherence to its acts, which are just as continuously subverted at its periphery.

The immense expansion and ramification of the state in recent decades have accentuated the importance of its fragmentation. The entry of the modern state into such novel realms as the creation of technology, and the multiplication of parastatal economic agencies, produces institutional spheres loosely linked to the state's executive core. The diversification of the state, in turn, renders more multistranded its interactions with private interests or social groups in civil society. As the state's different parts acquire interests and autonomous reasons of their own and are fortified by clientage relations with groups external to the state, it becomes far more than an arena for the enactment of societal conflict; the state is a stage for ceaseless struggle among its component parts for the fleeting possession of its mythological unitary will.[52]

The institutional complexity of the modern state leads to a corollary point: state action is carried out by a large number of human agents. The state is an impersonal institutional order, but abstractions lack the capacity to act. The skilled and knowledgeable human agents who, clothed with the authority of the state, execute in the name of its will, are constrained in their official behavior by institutional requirements of their role. But an element of individual autonomy remains, which may become of particular importance for those commanding separate state agencies, or serving as chief ruler. In the American case, one may recollect the idiosyncratic fashion in which J. Edgar Hoover long ran the Federal Bureau of Investigation. As we shall see on many occasions in Zaire, the singular dominance of the presidency over the state apparatus offers wide latitude to Mobutu in the interpretation of reason of state.[53]

The third type of relationship crucial to a conceptual portrayal of the state is the state's linkage to other nation-states. The state forms part of a system of nominally equal political entities, symbolized by the entitlement of each to a single vote at the world forum of states, the United Nations. A state acquires an international juridical personality through its recognition by the world system; without such anointment, its existence as a state is in doubt—as illustrated by the ambiguous standing of the black "homelands" pushed into an unrecognized "independence" by South Africa. It is above all in its externally directed conduct that the state appears to behave as a unitary actor. While sovereign states are in theory equal, and some widely acknowledged rules of behavior exist, the absence of effective sanctions for their contravention and of any higher authority means that disparities of power and resources have a major influence on interstate relationships. With each state engaged in self-interested maximization of advantage, the world system of states is characterized by frequent tension and periodic violent conflict.

As a conceptual field the state is thus rich and variegated. Before considering the particular form of this genus which arose in Africa as a consequence of colonial conquest, we need again remind ourselves that most of the corpus of state theory derives from the Western industrial states, for several reasons: the classical philosophical foundations of debate on the state are found in Western thought; the empirical model of the modern state was diffused to the formerly colonized regions of the world through imperial imposition; and the most influential contemporary theories of the state—liberal pluralist, corporatist, neo-Marxist—all have the advanced Western states as their primary field of analysis, whether these are positively or negatively evaluated.

It is worth remarking that these states have generally enjoyed a steady expansion of their ascendancy; this is especially true of those which have been the most salient exemplars—France, Great Britain, the United States, Prussia—Germany, and a few others. Some recent analyses have stressed crises of revenue, legitimacy, or even governability in these exemplary states, but none have experienced phases of prolonged decline. Catastrophic military defeats have occurred, but these have not produced an enduring deflation of state power. Dominant understandings of state have absorbed the premise of inevitable progress which has so profoundly permeated modern Western thought.[54]

The colonial state in Africa

To complete our introductory portrait of the state, we must consider the special characteristics of the African state, and of Zaire in particular. We turn first to the colonial state, chrysalis for the post-1960 configuration of polities. Its origins lie in the swift and brutal transformation of earlier forms of "informal empire," based on coastal footholds, into full-scale territorial conquest in the final quarter of the nineteenth century.

Well-established models of colonial dominion existed from earlier phases of European imperial expansion in Asia and the Western hemisphere. However, the African environment for colonial state construction was quite different from those in which extant models of domination had been fashioned. While states existed in parts of Africa, most of these lacked the accumulated wealth found in the Mughal, Inca, or Aztec states; nor did they have institutionalized mechanisms for extracting resources from slash-and-burn cultivators. In many areas political structures were small-scale, dispersed, and diffuse. With few exceptions (southern Africa, Algeria), colonization could not be primarily consolidated through settlements of European populations on the North American or Australian models. Creation of a production system based upon slave labor was not politically, economically, or ideologically feasible, as it was in the Caribbean model. Except for gold and diamonds in South Africa, there was initially no viable basis for extractive industries.

Imperial partition had some economic roots in the European rivalries which provided its peculiar dynamic, in the extravagant claims of its apostles in Europe, in the greed of some mercantile houses which sought to place upon the metropolitan states the political costs of their aggressive strategies, and in the grandiose schemes of buccaneering individual artisans of imperialism (such as Cecil Rhodes or Leopold II). In Africa, however, the initial visions of swift and rich returns, assumed as gospel by such early critics of imperialism as Hobson and Lenin, were largely illusory. Instead, those charged with implementing the partition, which in good part occurred through diplomatic maneuver and intrigue in Europe, found themselves mandated to achieve the subjugation of vast territories and substantial populations at little or no cost to the metropolitan treasuries.

In the task of institutionalizing European domination through the erection of state structures, they did enjoy one important advantage over their predecessors in other imperial domains: new technologies of domination. The machine gun permitted relatively small armed expeditions to defeat much larger African armies. Organizational techniques developed and perfected in India by France and Britain showed the way to the rapid composition of indigenous military formations under a handful of European officers.[55] New medical knowledge reduced the mortality rates of European cadres in the African disease environment. The steam engine turned Africa's inland plateau river system into so many roadways of penetration; the motor vehicle was not far behind. Telegraphic means of communication created novel possibilities for central direction and control.

The challenge remained of imposing upon African populations the full cost of an apparatus of conquest and subjugation. As well, they were expected to amortize the heavy burden, in many areas, of railway lines into the interior. At the Berlin Congress of 1884–85—symbolic if not actual apogee of the scramble for Africa—the adoption of the doctrine of "effective occupation" as confirmation of territorial claims placed upon the colonial powers a self-created imperative to quickly establish the skeletal framework of a military presence throughout their new domains.

These circumstances shaped the reason of state governing the erection of colonial institutions. Initial efforts to delegate the functions of occupation to private agencies, in the form of chartered or concessionary companies, quickly failed (with the partial exception of the British South Africa Company). Short-lived stores of natural wealth such as ivory or wild rubber provided only temporary answers to the revenue imperative in colonial state construction.

Basically, Africa was called upon to organize and finance its own subjugation and exploitation. The only reproductive resource for accomplishing this purpose was African labor. Very quickly, colonial states directed their attention to self-financing means for its expropriation.

The primary instrument for accomplishing this end was direct taxation. Although its revenue yield was not great, in the early stages it made a significant contribution to colonial budgets. More important, the fiscal obligation coerced rural populations into cash crop production, the exported portion of which could be taxed again. In addition, young men were driven into the labor market.

The revenue imperative likewise induced embryonic colonial states to solicit economic entry by metropolitan interests. Their trade and production would generate customs and excise returns to the state, and consolidate the preeminence of the colonial system. Concessionary terms were frequently accorded, in the form of land or mineral rights and a state-assured labor supply, to entice their participation. In the process, vested privileges were created and potent economic interests spawned to which the colonial state was peculiarly vulnerable during much of its life.

Intimately linked to the revenue imperative was the vocation of domination. Beginning with the assertion of effective occupation to preempt suspected latent expansionist lusts of rival predators, the preoccupation with hegemony was continuous. Domination—pervasive, systematic, comprehensive—characterized all aspects of what Balandier has termed the "colonial situation."[56]

Yet the resources of the colonial enterprise were extremely limited. In 1937, the sprawling domain of Afrique Occidentale Française had only 385 French administrators; the comparably vast realm of Afrique Equatoriale Française had only 250 on post in 1928.[57] Nigerian state expenditures were a minuscule £2.9 million in 1913, and only 7.4 million in 1937.[58]

Statecraft, for the colonial occupant, was the art of maximal domination and minimal cost; only Italy was willing to continuously subsidize the nurture of hegemony from the metropolitan budget.[59] In addition to the creation of cost-effective coercion through African military forces under small cadres of European officers, the colonial state required intermediaries. These were available, usually at bargain rates, either through the incorporation of extant sociopolitical hierarchies (the Lugardian doctrine of "indirect rule"), or through the investiture of clients of the colonial state with chiefly status underwritten by the colonizer ("direct rule"). Monitored by the colonial state, gradually reformed to more efficiently serve its purposes, this layer of intermediary infrastructure sufficed to meet the revenue and hegemony requirements. The reserve striking force of the colonial constabulary protected intermediaries from rebellion. The rewards of derivative power, relative status, and a small cut in the resources extracted were sufficient to maintain an ample supply of intermediaries should any be cashiered for recalcitrance, excessive independence, or inability to fulfill the performance criteria of the colonial state. Some intermediaries were supple and subtle in the adroit manipulation of their dependent role, and buffered their subjects from the more extravagant claims of the hegemon. Others, such as the generation of Buganda chiefs at the time of the 1900 Agreement, accumulated a higher fraction of the proceeds of authority than the colonial state had intended. All were essential to the consolidation of the colonial order. To the rural subject of the colonial state they were the most visible personification of its authority.

The ideological and legitimizing functions of the state were profoundly marked by its quintessentially alien character. The state was in conception and reality white, even if a few blacks—often of Western-hemisphere provenience—might serve in its apparatus. Colonialism was European rule; its grass roots application was "native administration." Africans were mere subjects; the colonial state did not recognize the notion of an autonomous civil society, defined by citizenship. Sharply distinct, the European society which grew up under the shelter of the colonial state was legally and socially entirely separate, even if in some instances a handful of Africans had won entry to its ranks.

Until World War II the primary audiences for the legitimating myths of the colonial state were European; the internal currency of colonialism was force (the Tshibumba soldier). The juridical concepts of state organization were derived from the metropolitan model, stripped of their representational and constitutional aspects. The judicial structures and bureaucracies which were introduced applied metropolitan notions of the supremacy of law as the rationalized and predictable expressions of the will of the state. The professional ethos of the magistrature did impose some restraints upon the arbitrary behavior of the colonial bureaucracy. But Africans had no constitutional rights which they could oppose to state power. However, litigation was occasionally a fruitful avenue for pursuit of African claims, particularly in British West African territories. In a few cases, such as Lesotho, Swaziland, or southern Ghana, African rulers fought off colonial administrative intrusions by invoking original treaty undertakings in British courts. Even in these rare instances the issue was the binding force of treaty commitments, and not the inherent rights of the subjugated population.

The central themes in colonial ideologies were "trusteeship," *mise en valeur* (development) and "civilizing mission." European rulers claimed to bring good government to their colonial territories; their dominion was portrayed as the very incarnation of the Weberian legal-rational order. The paternalistic office of the colonial state created a beneficent framework within which the long-term interests of the subjects would find fulfillment: *dominer pour servir*, in the phrase of the greatest Belgian proconsul, Pierre Ryckmans.[60]

Economically, Africa was portrayed as a virgin land whose resources belonged to all humanity. By this logic no people had a right to let its resources lie fallow. As the renowned French colonial minister Albert Sarraut put it, "Should a colonial power be able to hold immense areas of territory out of cultivation, mines without exploitation or waterways unimproved? Is her economic sovereignty totally unlimited by the rights of all and the general utility?" France served herself, her African subjects and the world at large by organizing the exploitation of African resources.[61]

The civilizing mission doctrine departed from the premise that African cultures were without redeeming value. Uplift was available through transmission of European culture, in its assorted national forms. The colonial state delegated this cultural function in large measure to the Christian missions, except where Islam was too firmly rooted to make this strategy safe (and, in the French case, where it was affected by the laic, anti-clerical component of French state ideology). Schools, over time recognized by African subjects as the primary avenue for social mobility, were a crucial instrument for the socialization mission. Status rewards in the form of differentiated treatment were available to those who mastered the linguistic code and external behavioral norms of the colonizer ("African gentlemen," *évolués, assimilados*).

In its final phases, after World War II, the African colonial state was compelled to reembroider its legitimating myth to counter the swelling nationalist challenge to European domination. At this stage "welfare" became an important theme. One may discern distant echoes of the absorption of welfare into the ideological arsenal of the liberal capitalist state in Europe. This new thrust was also stimulated by increasing demands from the African populace, and from the nascent political class that articulated its aspirations, for basic amenities—schools, clinics, safe water, roads. Dramatically increased state revenues generated by the long postwar primary commodity boom, and the first substantial public investments in colonial development from metropolitan treasuries, provided the empirical substance to support the defensive claims of a retreating colonialism to the efficacious provision of its subjects' welfare needs.

The post-colonial African state

African nationalism, whose claim to self-determination could not be contained at a cost acceptable to the metropolitan states in the profoundly altered geopolitical climate after 1945, found no alternative to the territorial grid of the colonial partition. In a handful of exemplary cases armed struggle carried the day (particularly in Algeria, Guinea-Bissau, Mozambique, Zimbabwe). In most instances, decolonization was a negotiated settlement whereby the bureaucratic core of the colonial state was Africanized and initially augmented by a constitutional array of representative institutions faithfully replicating the metropolitan model.[62] The territorial framework of the African state system was entrenched and sanctified as irrevocable and unchallengeable at the first summit conference of the Organization of African Unity (OAU), in 1963.

The colonial state continued to cast a long shadow over the postindependence landscape, and not only in its territorial legacy. Its doctrines, laws, mentalities, and routines exhibited a powerful inertial persistence. The post-colonial state's disposition to a command style of operation; its distance from a populace only passively transformed into citizens (epitomized by retention of a European language of discourse not understood by most of the population); its permeation by attitudes and unconscious premises emblematic of its former vocation of alien domination: these qualities suggest that the ironic hidden message of Tshibumba's *Colonie belge* was applicable to the post-colonial state in general.

Not all was continuity. A new kind of political domain was constructed, fused to and somewhat altering the bureaucratic core of the colonial state.[63] The hasty transplant of metropolitan representative institutions generally did not survive. Incumbent rulers were loath to accept displacement, and constrained or eliminated political competition. The imperative of unity required to make anti-colonial agitation and struggle effective supplied one argument for the imposition of monopolistic forms of political organization (single parties). The vulnerability of new states to politicized cultural pluralism was another. Within a few years of independence, the coup d'etat had become the normal form for political succession. The military groups who frequently organized these often, in turn, sought long-term legitimation by creating their own single parties.

The essence of the new authoritarian state was the centrality of personal rule and clientelization of state-society relationships. Authoritarianism was not in itself novel; the colonial state is a paradigmatic case of authoritarian rule. But colonial authoritarianism was exercised through an autonomous, impersonal bureaucracy. The African authoritarian state was not only distinctive from its colonial predecessor, it also differed from authoritarian state formulas in other regions. It bore little resemblance to the Latin American bureaucratic-authoritarian model, with its technocratic, statist project of capitalist construction under bureaucratic direction with military tutelage.[64] Neither the military nor the bureaucratic establishments in Africa exhibited the self-confident claim to technocratic mastery, much less the ideological commitment to a national capitalist development strategy, as, say, their Brazilian counterparts. Nor did they confront politicized "popular sectors" of the magnitude found in the more industrial Latin American economies. There was also relatively little corporatist content to African authoritarianism. The essential ingredients of hierarchically organized, comprehensive interest associations were only weakly present, if at all. Least of all was there much common ground between the post-colonial authoritarian state in Africa and the totalitarian model, sometimes loosely applied to all regimes of a leftward ideological hue. African states, even those espousing Marxism–Leninism, lacked the institutional capacity as well as the ideological compulsions which marked the Stalinist era in the Soviet Union.

The institutional character of the African state is best portrayed by the Jackson–Rosberg model of personal rule, defined as "a system of relations linking rulers not with the 'public' or even with the ruled (at least not directly), but with patrons, associates, clients, supporters, and rivals, who constitute the 'system.' If personal rulers are restrained, it is by the limits of their personal authority and power and by the authority and power of patrons, associates, clients, supporters, and—of course—rivals. The system is 'structured,' so to speak, not by institutions, but by the politicians themselves."[65]

The patrimonialization of state power at the summit carries as a logical corollary its clientelization at the base. Access to the state on the part of civil society is more efficaciously secured by penetrating its softened shell by means of a patron-client net, in pursuit of immediate, particularized advantage, rather than by assaulting its bastions through formal pursuit of the general interest. Affinities of kinship and ethnicity supply the ideological cement for clientage links between state and society.[66] In Hyden's terms, the reciprocities of social exchange, albeit asymmetrical, and the security which individuals find in these networks, constitute an "economy of affection," characteristic of a "peasant mode of production," which infiltrates the state and defines the terms of its relationships with society.[67]

The post-colonial state alters its legitimating charter in important ways. State doctrine must constitute a civil society, and construct an ideological organic relationship between civil society and the state. The primary means for accomplishing this goal is to transform the idea of nationalism from an anti-colonial rejection of alien rule into a positive assertion that the human collectivity enclosed within the territorial boundaries of the state is a historically ordained community, and not a mere accidental juxtaposition of individuals or microgroupings of residence and descent. "Nation" is a warm, living, anthropomorphic consciousness, a higher form of collectivity, associated with "progress" and "modernity." The rapid assimilation of the doctrine of nation by the fragmented sovereignties of Africa was the ultimate fulfillment of the Friedrich prophecy: "Such is the dialectic of the political that the state seeks and must seek to foster the growth of a nation, indeed must posit its potential coming into being."[68]

"Developmentalism" is a second component new to African state ideology. In about half the African states this is expressed through one or another form of socialist orientation. The idea of development, of course, has distant echoes of *mise en valeur*, and more immediate traces of the terminal imperial decade. But it more directly embodies a teleological link between state and society. The extraction and high consumption of the state, as well as its hegemony, are justified in terms of the economic progress they promise to bring.

The character of the state is also altered by its full entry into the international arena as a nominally autonomous actor possessing national interests. Fundamental to the newly acquired membership in the "anarchical society" of world politics is the asymmetrical nature of relationships to the more powerful nation-states. Under international norms, colonized territories were represented in the global arena by the colonizing power, whose legal dependencies they were. The end of legal dependency is the beginning of new forms of patterned inequality in the external relations of African states. In the political realm, they face the global rivalries of the superpowers and efforts of the former metropole to retain a privileged position as external patron. Eddying and deepening currents of regional conflict within or adjoining Africa bring perceptions of threatened security (Southern Africa, the Horn, the Middle East, the Western Sahara). The inherent impulse of the state to protect its sovereignty occurs within an anxiety-laden environment; insecurities are only partly mitigated by collective diplomacy at an African or Third World level.

In the economic realm as well dependency is a pervasive condition which constrains the behavior of the post-colonial state, although in a more complex, indeterminate, and relative way than the initial purveyors of dependency theory would suggest.[69] African states confront a global economic arena populated not only by the industrialized nation-states of both capitalist and state socialist orientation, but also powerful international economic agencies such as the International Monetary Fund and the World Bank, and the private realm of international banks and multinational corporations.

The asymmetry of its incorporation into the international arena has been felt by the African state in a number of ways. Politically, its pursuit of its security imperative leads to a search for added military technologies: exotic weapons, training, organizational skills for its internal security organs. Acquisition of these technologies provides the global power supplying the resource with a platform for further penetration: logistical control over advanced weapons, a perch and clientele within the state's security agencies. The expanded state consumption which results from its security investment and its developmentalist doctrine is prone to engender both a fiscal crisis and balance of payments difficulties. Add to these internal pressures to expand state employment opportunities (magnified by the permeation of the state with clientelist networks), deteriorating terms of trade, and the inherent vulnerability of primary commodity exporters, and one brings into focus the fatal cycle of deficits, indebtedness, and, for some, virtual bankruptcy which has afflicted African states.

Part Two

The state in Zaire: genesis and growth

In colonial times an especially powerful instrument of alien hegemony was constructed in Zaire, whose durable image of crushing force is well captured in Tshibumba's *Colonie belge*. Its appearance of omnipotence was shattered in the first years of independence when its central instruments of rule—bureaucracy and armed forces—decomposed after an abrupt and improvised decolonization foundered. The juridical and institutional shell of the colonial state served as a vessel for the construction of a seemingly plausible replica of *Colonie belge* in the first years of the reign of President Mobutu Sese Seko. A new ideological discourse claimed to provide a legitimating myth, and a theoretically monolithic single party reinforced the bureaucratic-military architecture bequeathed by the colonial state. Beneath this institutional facade, power was steadily patrimonialized. From 1974 on the Mobutist construction foundered, enveloped in a crisis whose first symptoms were economic, but which soon permeated state and society. The state entered a phase of decline, the end-point of which is not in sight, and the implications of which are incalculable. Sustained in part by external powers and economic interests that find its fictions convenient or even necessary, and by a narrowing ruling group that benefits from its action and has good reason to dread its demise, the Mobutu state persists despite its declining capacity to exercise rule or to maintain the conditions for the operation of its eroding productive infrastructure. This is the state we wish to portray.

A profoundly revealing metaphor is embodied in the term Bula Matari (or Bula Matadi) by which the colonial state was widely known. This label was first applied to Leopoldian agent Henry Stanley, reflecting the impression created by his feat of moving a large caravan bearing dismantled steamers around the rapids of the lower Zaire River, over a new and tortuous route from Vivi to Kinshasa in 1879–80. The expression means, literally, "he who breaks rocks"; by metaphorical extension it came to convey the image of a force which crushes all resistance. While initially attached to Stanley as imperial agent of the unfolding colonial state, it was soon transferred to the state as an abstraction, or to its European representatives as impersonal agents of domination. "For all Bakongo," N'kanza writes, "the name of Bula Matadi signified terror."[70] Though of Kongo origin, it soon became a common term throughout the territory.

Colonial officialdom found this image irresistible. It was widely used in the colonial literature as an alternative, informal designation for the state. "Tell X," the local European administrator would instruct his messenger, "that Bula Matari wants to see him." In this expression we find the same themes that are recorded in the paintings of Tshibumba. Bula Matari was white; no one would have considered an African chief or clerk to be Bula Matari. Bula Matari was alien, outside of society but irresistibly superimposed upon it.[71]

Another important example of popular cognitions of the quintessential alien nature of Europeans and the state they created is found in the collective terms applied to whites. In most Zairian languages, "bantu" (or a related word) is the term for "people." Yet Europeans were never referred to as "bantu." A special vocabulary applied to them; a white was a "mondele" (Kongo, Lingala), or a "muzungu" (Swahili).

What, then, were the central attributes of the Bula Matari state? To begin with, the territorial dimensions of the state were vast—905,000 square miles, or in real terms Africa's largest (if one discounts the large parts of Sudan and Algeria, which have slightly bigger land surfaces, that are uninhabited desert). This scale is a tribute to the diplomatic cunning of Leopold II, who in 1885 succeeded without the direct backing of a sovereign state in acquiring a personal mandate over the domain, under the cover of the fiction of the "Congo Free State." The details of Leopoldian scheming need not detain us; the enduring legacy was the extraordinary dimensions of the political unit he created, and its juridical portrayal as a single entity. In the early stages of colonial rule, obstacles of distance and communication imposed a degree of administrative decentralization.

De facto autonomy and the emergence of particular regional interests, particularly in Katanga province, brought some pressures for an administrative partition of the colonial domain. However, the ideological vision of a unified colonial state easily prevailed, and as practical resources for centralized control enlarged, autonomist tendencies were suppressed (definitively in the centralizing reforms of 1933).[72]

The Leopoldian interlude left its mark on the dependent sovereign personality of the territory as well. In defining the conditions by which Belgium acceded to colonial sovereignty in 1908, the Belgian state took unusual care, by the *séparation des patrimoines*, to ensure that the territory might be an asset but never a burden.[73] The Colonial Charter served as a constitutional instrument carefully delineating the separation between Belgium and the Congo. It assigned full responsibility for financing colonial administration, including military services and expenses in Belgium, to the colonial territory itself. It provided separate legal cover for colonial corporations (with a more favorable fiscal regime). It enshrined the untrammeled executive authority of the central institutions of colonial rule, whose power was limited only by the authority of the Colonial Ministry (which was dominated by the Catholic party), by rarely exercised parliamentary oversight of the colonial budget, and by review of proposed legislation by a colonial council composed of European notables from colonial milieux.

The Bula Matari state, at its peak, was a veritable leviathan. In relation to most African colonial states, its assertion of hegemony was comprehensive. Its relatively large cohort of European cadres penetrated farther down into African society than was normally the case. In its regulation of agriculture, particularly from the 1930s on;[74] its energetic recruitment of labor for mines and plantations; its tight control over population movement, and intricate web of restrictions upon African subjects; its vigorous promotion of Christian (especially Catholic) evangelism: in all these respects the Belgian colonial behemoth stands out.[75]

Initially, Leopold II held personal liability for financing his African barony. The potential cost was daunting; with encroachment possible by powerful and predatory colonial neighbors (Britain in Shaba and the northeast, France along the northern rim, Germany in the east, and, to a lesser degree, Portugal in the south), effective occupation was an urgent but expensive necessity. A railway around the rapids on the lower Zaire River was a categorical imperative, to consolidate colonial control; in the oft-cited Stanley phrase, absent the rail link, "the Congo is not worth a penny."[76] The problem was circular: in order to coerce any revenues from the Congo population, an apparatus of control was required.[77]

The initial solution—state expropriation of natural commodities, in particular ivory and wild rubber—was at first beyond the capacity of the embryonic colonial state acting alone; it also necessitated evasion of the diplomatic commitments to free trade which Leopold had used adroitly to win European acceptance of his huge estate. Resolution of the dilemma required recruitment of private allies who were vested with delegated sovereignty in large rubber-bearing tracts, while the Crown itself reconstituted a hefty swath of territory into a mercantile enterprise. Imposition of wild rubber collection on the populace as a tributary obligation to these concessionary companies, with the state sharing in the proceeds, led directly to the spiralling atrocities known to the outside world as "red rubber."

The rubber regime, and a reluctantly granted Belgian state loan for the railway, did see the Congo Free State over its initial revenue crisis. Leopold in his last years derived handsome dividends from his investment, which he devoted partly to monumental architecture in Brussels. The railway from the port of Matadi to Kinshasa at the navigational terminus of the vast inland waterway system was completed in 1898. Although Leopold had to abandon his dream of a foothold on the upper Nile, the remaining boundaries were effectively secured by 1900, even if full administrative control over some regions was not consolidated till the 1920s. In particular, the rich mineral zones of Katanga—whose mineral potential was documented by the mid-1890s—were retained within the Leopoldian empire, at the cost of cutting British interests into the exploitive organization.[78]

Wild rubber, however, was a temporary expedient; the long-run fiscal viability of the state required a productive infrastructure. The security imperative of the colonial state dictated that the capital needed to develop the mineral resources be predominantly Belgian. By the turn of the century, Belgian capital began to show interest, but the risks were substantial, and infrastructure was costly. The large financial groups finally came in, but used their leverage to secure exceedingly generous terms.

The Empain group was brought in, in 1902, with the establishment of a railway for the eastern zones, the Chemin de Fer du Congo Supérieur aux Grands Lacs (CFL). The state inducement: four million hectares of land and mineral rights, including the power to cede these claims to third parties; a guarantee of amortization of capital and 4 percent interest; an additional four million hectares for each additional investment of 25 million gold francs.[79] In 1906 the powerful financial giant Société Générale de Belgique, later to become the dominant corporate power, was brought in with the launching of three major undertakings: the Union Minière du Haut-Katanga (UMHK), the Société Internationale Forestière et Minière (Forminière), and the Compagnie du Chemin de Fer du Bas-Congo au Katanga (BCK). The enticements offered were seductive indeed. UMHK was granted the mineral rights to already-prospected ore bodies of south Shaba. Forminière received the right to a ninety-nine year monopoly on any mineral deposits it could identify within a six-year period in a 140-million hectare tract—equivalent to half the land surface of the colony. BCK was endowed with mineral rights to 21 million hectares in the zone traversed by the prospective rail line; the state dowry further included provision of essentially all the capital for the building of the line. BCK assumed only the responsibility for managing the construction and operation of the railway. These benefactions were enhanced by state action to induce a labor supply at wages far below those which might have motivated a voluntary flow.

Production of tin in Maniema and north Shaba, gold in the northeastern frontier soon followed, and by the 1920s a rich mineral base had been established. Simultaneously, a process of corporate concentration went forward; by 1928 the Société Générale had consolidated its hegemonic status among the several large financial groups that dominated the colonial capitalist economy. The state itself laid claim to a significant share in the ownership of a number of corporations in the extractive and infrastructure sectors. As majority shareholder in the charter company Comité Special du Katanga, the state potentially had a determinant voice in UMHK; it retained 55 percent of the shares in Forminière. This state capitalism, however, did not extend to active involvement in the operation of the enterprises; the administration passively collected its dividends.[80]

In the agricultural sphere the collapse of the wild rubber market and shrinking production led to a search for a policy which would produce an exportable surplus, a low-cost food supply for the work force, and a revenue flow for the state. King Leopold had been much attracted by Dutch formulas in Indonesia, where forced cultivation generated not only a bountiful fiscal harvest for the colonial administration, but, from 1862 to 1871, a surplus for the Dutch treasury. The Dutch model and the *dirigisme* which pervaded colonial thought pointed inexorably toward a rural policy characterized by coercive state paternalism, and a division of labor between peasant production and private monopolies in processing and marketing.

It was not until World War I that agricultural policy instruments became established. By this time it was clear that basic production could only come from peasant smallholders. In some areas, and for a narrow range of crops, the plantation formula might have been viable; but until World War II the only major export crop tied to plantations was palm oil—and even then a substantial fraction of the output of Lever and other palm oil exporters came from peasant-gathered wild palm fruits and kernels. The legal basis for coercion was created by the decree of 20 February 1917, which obligated the peasant to devote at least sixty days to the cultivation of crops prescribed by the administration, and was enforced by penal sanctions. Local administrators were informed in a 1917 circular that the "ordinance of 20 February 1917 placed at their disposition the means necessary to induce cultivators to expand their crops." These means, Mulambu notes in a penetrating analysis of colonial agricultural policy, "were nothing other than military or police occupation."[81] As early as 1915 officials of the newly created agricultural service were equipped with the authority of *officiers de police judiciaire*, giving them plenary power to impose fines or prison sentences upon those who contravened the agricultural regulations of the state. Thus in various ways the subject populace met the revenue imperative of the colonial state: as laborers in the mines and on plantations and as producers of export crops which yielded customs proceeds to the state. In addition, the head tax on rural heads of households was a significant source of state revenue until the 1930s. In 1921 it provided 21 percent of government receipts, and in 1939 still provided 13 percent.

While the economic space of the country was being structured and organized on the basis of highly concentrated corporate power, the administrative penetration of the territory was extended and elaborated during the latter decades of Belgian rule. Although financial retrenchment in the 1930s and manpower shortages during the Second World War slackened bureaucratic penetration for a time, it was decisively strengthened in the postwar years. The administrative occupation of Bula Matari was visibly accompanied by military force; local European administrators had directly available a small detachment of soldiers.

The state apparatus was completed through the bureaucratization of the African capillaries of the system. The medallioned chiefs first created in 1891 were gradually organized into a microadministrative grid extending into the farthest village. A decree of 3 June 1906 provided the legal sanction for this; its purpose was clearly described in the official annotations to the colonial code:

> [Sanction] no longer was limited to recognition of customary groupings or chiefs; [the decree] made of the chieftaincy an administrative subdivision of the organization of the State, and conferred upon the chiefs a segment of the authority exercised within this framework. If a chief thereby acquired privileged treatment, he was also bound by a series of new obligations in the administrative sphere.[82]

These duties to the state included tax collection, mobilization of labor for portage (and subsequently for road building), execution of the obligatory cultivation requirements after 1917, forcible recruitment of workers for mines and plantations, and, until World War II, meeting administration quotas for army levies.

The system was rationalized and placed under growing administrative tutelage in the 1920s. Smaller chieftaincies were regrouped into "sectors" in the many areas where traditional structures were very fragmented, or where they had been destroyed by the corrosive impact of Bula Matari. Rural local administration was given definitive form in a crucial decree of 5 December 1933, which provided for indigenous structures more or less uniform in scale throughout the country; these totaled somewhat fewer than one thousand (the precise number constantly fluctuated as endless tinkering with local circumscriptions continued throughout the colonial era). "While respecting traditional administration," the judicial theory ran, "the legislator wanted to establish a single administrative system; he made of the chieftaincy (or sector) the lowest echelon of the administrative organization, and of the chief a functionary integrated into the system without prejudice to his traditional role."[83] An analogous structure was created for African populations in the new towns.

Beneath the Cartesian logic of colonial public law there was, in practice, a significant range of variation in the local operations of this cellular structure of the state. Bustin documents the important impact of individual Belgian administrators, who had diverse views of modalities of tutelage ranging from the concept of a simple command hierarchy to more Lugardian notions of nurture of customary structures.[84] Vansina offers compelling evidence that in such solidly institutionalized historic states as the Kuba the ruler had some room for maneuver, which could be exploited by a crafty incumbent provided he had some legitimacy beyond the force of the Bula Matari superstructure.[85] None, however, could escape the overarching uniformities imposed by the nature of the state, its vocation of total control of the subject population, and its productionist orientation.

To undergird its far-reaching action, an ideological rationale was indispensable to the state. Initially, the primary concern was to provide an international legitimation for throwing upon Leopold's domains the blanket of sovereignty; no justification other than force was deemed necessary for the newly subjugated populations. By the time that Belgium assumed sovereignty over Zaire in 1908 the ideology of the state had become the *mission civilisatrice*, or civilizing mission; the "heart of darkness" was to be illuminated by the kindly beams of European culture. At first this *bonne nouvelle* was directed above all at Europe and America to quench the flames of the Congo reform campaign and extinguish memories of Leopoldian excesses; it also played no small part in persuading a skeptical Belgian public that its new colonial responsibilities were not only materially attractive but morally imperative. As time went on, the message of the *mission civilisatrice* was increasingly directed to the growing nucleus of Zairians incorporated into subaltern niches of the system. Finally, in the terminal phase of colonial rule, social welfare and economic advantage for the subjects of Bula Matari became central themes in state ideology.

The principal instrument of the *mission civilisatrice* was the Christian mission, upon which, until the 1950s, much of the cultural policy and welfare function of the state also devolved.[86] The Catholic mission infrastructure was particularly well developed; all told, on the eve of independence, there were 8,000 white missionaries in Zaire, 6,000 of them Catholic, and 966 mission stations. The mission establishment had virtually as many expatriate personnel as the state, and more than three times as many outposts. The sheer scope of the Christian evangelical effort was remarkable; it is no accident that in *Etat Indépedant du Congo* Tshibumba places the familiar, ubiquitous figure of the Catholic father among the other symbols of Bula Matari, armed with the book and its mysterious force.

The very nature of the mission enterprise brought the populace into much more intimate contact with pastor and priest than with the state or company; the latter sought only to use the body, while the church needed to capture the soul. Yet Tshibumba's symbolism is no accident; the representatives of the Catholic church in particular were partly absorbed into the Bula Matari concept. A Zairian anthropologist, recalling his village boyhood, describes the difficulty he and his companions had in distinguishing between the itinerant delegates of Caesar and Christ; both were white, and the orders of each were the irresistable commands of Bula Matari.[87] Douglas makes the same observation: while the foreign observer could readily distinguish between state, company, and church, to the Lele "they were as one. . . . The administration ensured security of life and property, transport, and communications. Without it neither commerce nor missionary development would have been possible. The commercial interest subsidized the missions, who trained their staff in schools and gave extensive medical services. The state supported the missionaries in the course of their normal enforcement of the laws of the colony, some of which were framed in response to missionary demands."[88]

The colonial state under stress: toward decolonization

The ideology of the state began to move beyond the *mission civilisatrice* in the postwar period as it found itself confronted with new challenges, domestic and foreign. Within the colony a nascent African elite began to ask about its status: "What will be our place in the world of tomorrow?" was the famous query of Paul Lomami-Tshibamba in the second issue of *La Voix du Congolais*. Abroad, anticolonialism was becoming a significant international force; the inclusion of Article 73 in the United Nations Charter, obliging colonial powers to "develop the capacity [of subject populations] to administer themselves, in accordance with the political aspirations of the populations," was a profound shock.[89] Belgian proconsul Pierre Ryckmans set the tone in a 1946 speech, declaring that "the days of colonialism are over"; the hour was at hand, he argued, to lead colonial populations toward an ill-defined emancipation. Only the European enterprises prospered; the indigenous sector was stagnant.[90]

The pathway thus traced led to the welfare state. The perpetuity of the Belgian edifice in Africa could only be assured if it could demonstrate its ability to bring material well-being to the populace. If social mobility and economic prosperity were freely available within the colonial framework to the African population, the ultimate emancipation could occur within a Belgian-established context. This reasoning assumed a central place in the state ideology of the terminal colonial era.

This policy was carried out with real vigor. The educational system, which had been a very modest undertaking before the Second World War, was rapidly expanded. What had been a system primarily serving the needs of Christian evangelism became a vast network which, by 1959, enrolled 70 percent of the children between six and eleven years old—though more than 70 percent of these were in the first two grades. The pyramid narrowed sharply beyond the primary level, but a secondary infrastructure was taking shape beyond the seminaries, which had been practically the sole postprimary channel available to earlier generations. Universities were founded in 1954 and 1956 in Kinshasa and Lubumbashi. By this time, the intimate link between school and social mobility was universally perceived, and the opening of this avenue of social promotion fostered growing hopes and ambitions—expectations far beyond, in fact, what the colonial system was able or willing to satisfy.

Social amenities were also swiftly expanded. Clinics, hospitals, and rural dispensaries pushed from the major centers out into the remote hinterland. Whereas it could be said in 1920 that "African medical service does not exist," by the late 1950s the Belgians could justifiably claim that their health service "was without doubt the best in the whole tropical world."[91] The mortality rate dropped from 30 to 40 per thousand in the interwar period to 20 per thousand in 1957.

The welfare thrust had important implications for the character of the state itself. While a significant fraction of the expanded services—particularly schools and dispensaries—was implemented through the missions or corporations, nonetheless this new range of activities vastly enlarged the domain of the state. Administrative services at the various echelons of governance were increased by a new wave of officials—specialists in health, education, public works, agriculture, veterinary medicine, and other fields. State expenditures grew remarkably. In 1939 outlays for the operating and investment budgets totalled only 788 million Congo francs, while by 1950 these outlays had risen to 11,473 million, a fifteen-fold increase in eleven years. With buoyant revenues generated by the postwar and Korean War commodity booms, this process continued until the copper recession of the late 1950s. Expenditures tripled during the final decade of colonial rule.[92] Throughout the 1950s, government expenditure hovered around the figure of 30 percent of the GDP (gross domestic product), or twice the more normal figure of 15 percent.

Another sea change in the self-concept of the state appeared in the 1950s when the colony was confronted with the issues of nationalism, nationality, and nation. For the earlier colonial state these issues did not arise; no one viewed Bula Matari as a nation, but only as an alien superstructure whose domination was justified by theories of state and sovereignty. But if, as Ryckmans declared in 1946, "the days of colonialism" are over, how could one conceptualize a polity which conformed to the nation-state model yet perpetuated the Belgian connection and the privileged status of the growing European community in Africa?

In the early postwar years the debate remained largely confined to Belgian circles. For the metropole, the predominant concern was a formula for the perpetuation of Belgian dominion in Africa. For the European community in the colony, the more crucial goal was guaranteeing their privileged role, sanctioned by adequate political power in whatever polity emerged to preserve their situation.

One of the first to address the issue of transforming Bula Matari into a nation-state was a progressive Belgian colonial, who articulated the new concerns in 1945:

> The issue is, during the coming years, to show that we are capable of transforming this country and fusing the fragments of the country, of clans, of groups, of races into a living unit, conscious of the bonds existing between all its members. . . . Those who fear this policy of cohesion and national and social content among the natives are completely mis-

> taken. . . . We have made this country, we have conquered it and we have assembled it. A social policy will complete this task of unification, will substitute for the actual fragmentation a united and conscious people . . . far from risking elimination of Belgium from the Congo, this will associate Belgium more intimately to its colony. The Congo will remain Belgian if we move forward.[93]

Generally confined to European milieux, the low-intensity debate over the future transformation of the alien Bula Matari hegemony into a Eurafrican state organically linked to its civil society proceeded in leisurely fashion until the open emergence of African nationalism in 1956. A singular conception of the populace of civil society undergirded the Eurafrican projects: Europeans (1%) and Africans (99%) were conceived of as separate but equal constitutive segments. Such notions eroded rapidly after 1956, and vanished entirely after the massive Kinshasa riots in January 1959. Thereafter the decolonization dialogue concerned exclusively a swiftly decomposing Bula Matari and the emergent African political class.

Debate subsequently focussed upon the nature of African civil society. Two major views emerged, which stamped their imprint upon political divisions throughout the first years of independence: "unitarism" and "federalism." The primary line of cleavage was articulated in the first major political manifestoes of 1956. The unitarist theses were stated by the Conscience Africaine group, which evolved into the major nationalist party, Mouvement National Congolais (MNC):

> We have only a single chance to assure the triumph of our causes: to be and to remain united.
> If we allow ourselves to divide we will never realize the ideal of a great Congolese nation.[94]

The Alliance des Bakongo (ABAKO), initially the most aggressively anticolonial group, set forth the alternative view:

> We have said that it is pure utopianism to rally all Congolese to a single opinion. . . . since the true union of Congolese peoples cannot be realized other than through political evolution, this evolution in the direction of democratic progress must first begin on the basis of what exists. That is to say that groups which are historically, ethnically, and linguistically united or linked must organize themselves to form political parties.[95]

In 1959–60 the competing plural and unitary visions of Zaire constituted the major aligning focus in the tumultuous competition among the burgeoning political parties. The constitutional slogans of "federalism" and "unitarism" gave content to this battle, whose most conspicuous leaders were Joseph Kasavubu and Patrice Lumumba. As time went on, other ideological connotations were added to the positions; federalists tended to be "moderate," unitarists "radical." Federalism was viewed as a realistic means of allaying fears and insecurities while preserving the territorial unity of the country. Unitarism drew some of its inspiration from the pan-African visions of the more radical African leaders of the age, such as Kwame Nkrumah of Ghana or Sékou Touré of Guinea. Federalism, for the unitarist nationalists, was thinly disguised separatism, promoted by political factions from the wealthier regions (especially Shaba and Bas-Zaire).

First Republic crises: the state as *pagaille*

The unitarist and pluralist paradigms of the nation-state remained locked in combat throughout the First Republic period (1960–65). In many respects the plural nation was the dominant vision during this period, but the victory was never complete. Nonetheless, the peculiar pathology of the First Republic utterly discredited the pluralist formula, and set the stage for the powerful reassertion of the unitary nation-state model as New Regime ideology.

The 1960 provisional constitution and its 1964 successor avoided a characterization of the system as pluralist or unitary. In fact, they represented a major retreat from the centralizing tradition of the colonial state by reserving a number of significant powers exclusively to the provinces, and above all by creating responsible, elected provincial governments. More important than the formal constitutional provisions, however, were the de facto institutionalization of a pluralized state through the incapacity of the central government to exercise its theoretical powers, and the fragmentation of the six provincial units into twenty-one through a process tantamount to ethnic or local self-determination. The decomposition of central authority was reflected in the total loss of budgetary and fiscal control. Provinces spent with little restraint in the first years of independence by simply debiting a central government's account. Provinces also acquired de facto control over the territorial administrations and the police forces within their frontiers.

Above all, First Republic politics at all levels were saturated with ethnicity. While it was generally not the sole or even the major factor in particular events, ethnicity was nearly always present in the perceptions of the actors and in the understandings of the spectators as well. Political conflict was at a high level of intensity throughout the crises of the First Republic years—breakdown of central authority and its aftermath in 1960–61, provincial fragmentation in 1962–63, rebellions in 1964–65. Social disharmony was frequently violent, beginning with the anti-Luba riots in Kananga in October 1959. By 1965, pluralism had run amok. There was a widespread desire to find release from the intense insecurities and endemic communal threats which ethnic mobilization had created. It was no small irony to find that in the last days of the First Republic the two contenders for presidential power were Kasavubu and Moise Tshombe, the two most outspoken partisans of the federalist paradigm in 1960, and both now would-be artisans of a more centralized state. The impasse of their struggle paved the way for the seizure of power by Mobutu Sese Seko (Joseph-Désiré), who found overwhelming support for the unitary concept of nation for which Lumumba had died in 1961.

Beyond the particular issue of ethnicity, the state itself in the First Republic had come to be viewed as a zone of disorder. The authoritarian order of Bula Matari had degenerated into *la pagaille* (a shambles). The operational definition of *la pagaille* was offered by Mobutu in his first major speech justifying the seizure of power:

> The very existence of the Nation was threatened. Threatened on all sides, from the interior and exterior.
>
> From the interior, by the sterile conflicts of politicians who sacrificed the country and their compatriots to their own interests.
>
> Nothing counted for them but power . . . and what the exercise of power could bring them. Fill their own pockets, exploit the Congo and the Congolese, this was their trademark.
>
> Given such examples, both national and provincial administrations were mired in inertia, inefficiency, and worse yet, corruption.
>
> At all levels, many of those in our country who held a morsel of public power allowed themselves to be corrupted, served individuals and companies who paid bribes and neglected the others. . . .
>
> . . . certain politicians, to maintain themselves in power or to regain it, did not hesitate to seek help from foreign powers. . . .
>
> . . . the social, economic and financial situation of the country is catastrophic.[96]

The Mobutu era: rise and decline of the Zairian state

In the collective self-consciousness, the First Republic had become associated with the gloomy vision of a Hobbesian state of nature. With nation a sphere of unlimited ethnic conflict, and state a zone of *pagaille*, the dismal skepticism of the English philosopher was a faithful enough rendering of the general Zairian self-image.

The Hobbesian diagnosis led necessarily to the Hobbesian remedy, the leviathan state and the unitary nation. The ideological model and institutional heritage of the centralized, authoritarian state were at hand in the machinery bequeathed by Bula Matari. Added to these was a new moral imperative—the nation—whose painful birth seemed to require as midwife the leviathan state. The image of *pagaille* and ethnicity unchained in popular consciousness served as an antithesis to the Bula Matari state which had collapsed in the face of the nationalist challenge in 1959–60. The nation-state model proposed by Mobutu in 1965 as a synthesis enjoyed at its genesis a remarkably broad consensus of approval as a political formula. Mobutu as a leader was privately contested by some, but the centralized, strong nation-state vision of the polity seemed to most the only salvation.

Worthy of note at this juncture is the largely negative and reactive character of this consensus. A product of sheer exhaustion with the torments of the *pagaille* years, the initial legitimacy of the Mobutu formula had an underlying fragility. But neither this nor the institutional fraility of a revived Leopoldian autocracy was generally apparent at the time.

The early Mobutu years appeared to reflect a progressive implementation of the leviathan state project. The centralized authority of the state was reasserted. Its hegemonical thrust eclipsed not only institutional autonomy at lower echelons of the state apparatus, but also claimed tutelary control over all spheres of corporate interest: the colonial corporations, unions, youth and student associations, the churches. An exclusionary political monopoly was asserted through the creation of a sole political organism, the Mouvement Populaire de la Révolution (MPR). In the ideological realm, the unitary concept of nation was fused with the personal creeds of "authenticity" and ultimately with "Mobutism," enshrined as constitutionally binding doctrine in 1974. In its ascendant phase, from 1965 to 1974, the New Regime appeared to be fashioning a modernized version of Leopoldian absolutism.

Dominant images of the Zairian state rapidly altered in the prolonged and seemingly permanent crisis whose onset was signaled by the break in world copper prices in April 1974. By 1977 Mobutu himself spoke of the state as "one vast marketplace" whose authority was monetized by an "invisible tax" levied by the state's agents on all its daily transactions.[97] In an anguished and angry pastoral letter in 1981, the permanent commission of Zairian bishops portrayed the state as "organized pillage for the profit of the foreigner and his intermediaries."[98] It gradually became apparent that the crisis was more than a momentary hiatus on a journey toward progress. Far-reaching processes of decline affected the very nature of the state.

The problematic of state decline

At this point, in the theoretical realm, we find ourselves suddenly upon an uncharted sea. An inarticulate major premise running through conceptualizations of the state becomes apparent: its functionalist logic. From the structural-functionalism of Almond to the functionalist structuralism of Poulantzas, from the bureaucratic rationality of Weber to the class rationality of Marx, state paradigms presume that ends are related to means in some ordered fashion. Embedded in the state is an ultimate rationality, whether it be that of the relatively benign neutral arbitrator of contending group interests (for liberal theorists), the relatively autonomous protection of the long-term interests of capitalism (for instrumentalist or structuralist neo-Marxists), the direct agency of capitalism, as its executive committee (for classical Marxists), or the engine of underdevelopment in the service of international capitalism (for dependency theorists). None of these models seriously entertains the possibility that the state loses its capacity for rational behavior, whoever the theoretically specified beneficiaries of its action might be. The aberrations of Zaire in its crisis phase make necessary a contemplation of the nature of state decay and the implications of decline.

Some recent contributions begin to map this theoretical terrain. A dawning consciousness of the possibility of the decaying, irrational state in Africa was first stimulated by the Amin regime in Uganda.[99] Shaw, from a dependency-flavored perspective, suggests that a new type of "anarchic state" may be emerging which is unable to supply the orderly conditions "conducive to the extraction of surplus," and which may simply "become expendable, at least for major interests in the metropole."[100] Jackson and Rosberg argue that weak states, whose "empirical" qualities erode, nonetheless persist because their "juridical" appearance is sustained by the international state system.[101] Some monographs have been devoted to particular instances of sustained decay, but invariably within a configurative context.[102]

The most illuminating and theoretically powerful inquest into state decay is Chazan's study of Ghana, which contains many parallels to the Zairian case.[103] She dissects the state deflation process, examining the anatomy of the recession of power, authority, autonomy, and legitimacy of the

Ghanaian state. Revealed is a progressive loss of control over resource flows, and a sharp contraction of the real revenue base of the state. Its ability to deliver valued services steadily corrodes, and its institutional structure grows increasingly irrelevant. It ceases to be a significant source of social stratification; wealth, prestige, and power are no longer sought within its framework. Chazan concludes,

> By the early 1980s it was apparent that Ghana had forfeited its elementary ability to maintain internal or external order and to hold sway over its population. Although its existence as a *de jure* political entity on the international scene was unquestionable, these outward manifestations did raise doubts as to its *de facto* viability. The Ghanaian state thus seemed to be on the brink of becoming less distinctive and relevant. Indeed, some kind of disengagement from the state was taking place. This withdrawal was only minimally directed at physical removal from the Ghanian context. Much more rampant was an emotional, social, and political detachment from the state element.[104]

In the face of state deflation, there was a resurgent vitality to Ghanaian civil society which revalidated old institutions and created new associations to fill, in a fragmented way, the growing void created by state decay.

We hope in this work to contribute to a comparative understanding of these processes. In Zaire, the central feature is the shrinkage in the competence, credibility, and probity of the state. It has progressively lost its capacity to relate means to ends, bringing about a loss of belief, within civil society, that the state can be expected to perform its accustomed functions. The ubiquity of corruption reinforces the skepticism of the citizenry, and undermines the legitimacy of the state apparatus. Worse than a mere *pagaille*, the state risks becoming an irrelevancy, as well as a mechanism of predatory accumulation by those associated with its eroding power.

Decay, however, is not a simple process occurring uniformly throughout state institutions. It affects the periphery more extensively than the center, agencies supplying technical or social services not essential for state survival (health, for example) more than the inner security core. Episodic efforts at reform may bring at least momentary rejuvenation to particular institutions. Some, like the educational system, may continue to process units (students) through the system even though the organizational superstructure is badly eroded. Secreted within the institutional infrastructure of the Zairian state today is a large reservoir of very able human talent, whose individual efforts at state rationality are largely defeated by the systemic aspects of its operation.

Yet the state persists as an important concept in the social imagination;

the image of a powerful, efficient, and rational state serves as a normative counterpoint to the derelict "empirical state." Thus the moral entitlement of the state to hegemony is not challenged, even while its regulations are widely ignored. The possibility of a resurrection around the normative image remains present.

Certainly the international system plays an important role in sustaining the state in crisis. In a widespread popular metaphor, the incumbent state authorities are "propped up" by external forces. Zaire provides valued services in the international arena: to Israel, through the resumption of relations in 1982; to the United States at the beginning of the 1980s, as a Security Council member responsive to American concerns; to Africa, as a member of the ill-starred OAU peace-keeping force in Chad in 1982. In return, diverse supports are provided to sustain the state in its hour of need: presidential security (Israel); officers for elite military units (Belgium and France); recognition as a visible member of the African community of states (OAU). Economically, the creditors of the Zairian state have a vital interest in its sustenance; repayment—or at least the friction that it may ultimately occur—can only come through the state.

This summary sketch of salient characteristics of the contemporary Zairian state suggests the task which lies ahead. We first provide an overview of the major political events of the Mobutu era, then turn to an examination of the changing nature of civil society: the differing evolution of its urban and rural components, the lines of cleavage affecting social class and cultural pluralism, and the relationship of these to the state. We next explore the institutional and ideological dimensions of the Mobutist state. The operation of the state and the cycle of rise and decline are scrutinized, with particular focus upon economic policy. Finally, the dependent linkages of the Zairian state to the international system are examined. It is our hope that this analysis will provide insight into Zaire in the Mobutu era, and a modest contribution to comparative understanding of the contemporary state.

2

Zaire in the Mobutu Years: An Overview, 1965–1980

This man has spoken; he has written, set forth orientation and decrees.
The sum total of his actions constitutes Mobutism, just as the sum total
of Mao's teachings constitute Maoism . . . The President and Founder of
the MPR repeats incessantly that a people aiming for greatness should
neither repudiate other nations nor copy them.

Mpinga Kasenda[1]

This homage to President Mobutu captures crucial characteristics of the
Zairian state at the apogee of the New Regime: its personalism, its presidentialism, its relentless quest for an elusive grandeur. At the beginning of
the 1980s, the hollow ring of these adulatory words reflects the distance
traveled from the zenith of success to the trough of despond in the years
of crisis and state decline. In this overview of the first fifteen years of
the Mobutu regime we follow its fortunes through five distinct stages:
(1) power seizure, (2) consolidation, (3) ascendancy, (4) state expansion,
(5) crisis and state decay.

Power seizure

Conditions propitious for power seizure were created by the deterioration
of the precarious constitutionalism of the First Republic from 1963 on.
The political compromise of 1961, by which, under United Nations (UN)
and Western sponsorship, near-unanimous parliamentary approval was
achieved for Cyrille Adoula, slowly unraveled. UN military forces, introduced in July 1960 to hold the ring and forestall external military interventions, were committed to withdraw by 30 June 1964. From the end of
1963, a wave of rebellions spread through an important part of the country. In July 1964 the enfeebled Adoula regime gave way to a government
led by Tshombe, who from July 1960 until January 1963 had led his

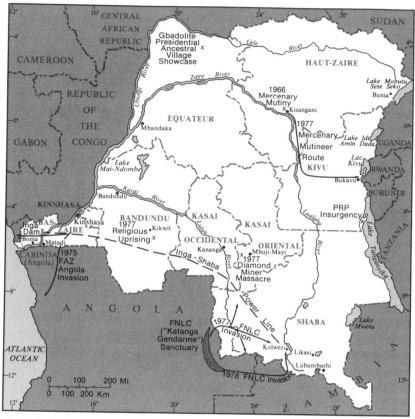

Map 2. Major Events, 1965–1970

copper-rich province of Katanga into secession. In an astonishing come-
back after the UN had crushed his secession only eighteen months earlier,
from his Madrid exile Tshombe had stitched together an improbable coalition. Building upon his regional base and shadowy support from certain
Belgian financial interests, as well as a demimonde of mercantile adventurers, he succeeded in persuading some discontented opposition elements
that he would combat American influence and negotiate a political settlement with the insurgents, who had eliminated Kinshasa's authority in the
northeastern third of the country.[2]

The Tshombe theatrics and the new hopes created by any novel political formula won for the coalition some transitory popularity in the capital. The efforts to strike a bargain with insurgent groups soon foundered, and Tshombe brought in new military resources to cope with rebellions. Thousands of his former secessionist gendarmes were incorporated into the national army and several hundred foreign mercenaries were recruited, as well as Belgian advisors; these forces were backed with American logistical support. Thus reinforced, mercenary and national army units began pushing the insurgents back by September 1964. On 24 November Belgian paratroopers with American air force support captured the insurgent capital of Kisangani in an operation whose official purpose was the rescue of European hostages. The rebel leadership fled and fell apart, though a number of pockets of resistance remained for many months.

The new Kananga constitution, adopted in 1964, stipulated as the prime tasks of the transitional government the organization of national elections and summoning of a new parliament, whose first undertaking was to be the election of a president. By early 1965 attention had shifted to the electoral scene. Tshombe, eager to extend his hold on power, launched a new national political movement in February, the Convention Nationale Congolaise (CONACO); this was an expensive and superficial alliance of 49 of the 223 political parties which arose to contend in the elections. Control of the state machinery was evidently an enormous asset.

CONACO was the apparent victor in the national elections, winning 122 of 167 seats. However, by the time Parliament actually met, in September 1965, the artificiality of the CONACO bloc was already clear. Battlelines were taking shape around the presidency, with Kasavubu, who had been initially elected president in 1960, anxious for reelection, and Tshombe determined to garner the top post himself. (The 1964 Zairian constitution established the president as chief executive officer, with a prime minister responsible for the daily conduct of governmental affairs, in a manner roughly analogous to the French Fifth Republic.) The Lumumbist bloc, which had been the pivot of opposition in the 1960–64 parliament, was supplanted by an anti-Tshombe group whose most active leaders were Kamitatu Massamba (Cléophas), former minister of the interior, and security agent head Nendaka Bika (Victor), a charter member of the Binza group which had formed the inner core support for the Adoula government.[3]

The deepening struggle between Kasavubu and Tshombe, and the shifting alignments it provoked, well illustrate the complex crosscurrents of First Republic politics. While both protagonists had favored a federal structure in 1959–60, and each had distrusted the aggressive, unitarist nationalism of Lumumba, their personalities were incompatible. Kasavubu was distant, mysterious, legalistic, lacking in charisma, and disposed to allow conflicts to seek their own resolution—and in important aspects politically naive. Tshombe was skilled in the art of constructing alliances of convenience, uninhibited by ideological conviction, open to diverse influences, charming personally, and captivating to crowds. Though Kasavubu had relied heavily on Western, especially American, support in 1960, he was never a client of external interests; neither a mercantile nor a venal politician, he died a pauper in 1969, unable to pay for his own medical care. Tshombe, who entered politics with modest family wealth, squirreled away large sums abroad, as evidenced by the expensive court he kept in Madrid during his periods of political exile in 1963–64 and 1965–67. He always maintained close and profitable ties to foreign financial milieux, especially those of Belgium.

The final crisis of the first republic began with the first meeting of the new parliament on 13 October 1965. To the surprise of most, President Kasavubu declared that the transitional tasks of the Tshombe government had been completed, and named a leading figure of the anti-Tshombe bloc, Evariste Kimba, to form a government in place of Tshombe. During a month of political maneuvering in an increasingly tense atmosphere both blocs viewed the struggle for investiture of a Kimba government as a surrogate for the presidental balloting to come, in which the two houses of Parliament and the provincial assemblies were to serve as the electoral college. The removal of Tshombe from the premiership was seen by his opponents as indispensable to denying him the resources of the state itself in the eventual competition.

The Tshombe–Kasavubu contest took on greater international visibility when President Kasavubu, leading the Zairian delegation to the Organization of African Unity annual summit at Accra in October, adopted a surprisingly firm tone close to the mainstream of African nationalism. In particular he pledged early removal of the white mercenaries from the national army. This promise, on the heels of the removal of the widely distrusted Tshombe, earned Kasavubu a personal triumph at the OAU, and a partial readmission of Zaire to respectable membership in the African concert of nations.[4] At the same time, these signs of a Zairian realignment in African affairs were unsettling to Western chanceries, and especially to the United States.

The month of maneuvering following Kimba's nomination for the premiership was the final demonstration of the virtual impossibility of founding legitimacy and consensus upon the parliamentary institution. The vote of confidence took place on 14 November 1965; the Tshombe coalition succeeded in blocking investiture by a vote of 121 to 134 (72 to 76 among lower house members, and 49 to 58 in the upper house). Examination of the voting alignments reveals the incurable fluidity of the parliament. Although the 16 parties included in the proposed Kimba government (of 39 represented in the new parliament) had a comfortable majority, numerous defections were recorded; these are attributable to the crosscurrents of individual ambition, personal incompatibility, external influence, and simple venality.[5]

The flavor of the parliamentary maneuvering is well conveyed in an incident recounted by Kamitatu which details the competition for the three votes apparently controlled by former student leader Moju'ongway Untuube (then Joseph Nsinga):

> The deputy Delvaux [subsequently Mafuta Kizola] and I were charged with negotiating with the deputy Joseph Nsinga, whose position remained vague. During the discussion we had with him at Delvaux's home, Nsinga told us that he was prepared to join us on condition that we help him overcome some financial difficulties . . . he had just rented a house, whose furnishing had cost him 60,000 francs. I gave him at once the sum requested. He then promised to vote for the *Front Democratique Congolais* [the anti-Tshombe coalition]. A little later I learned that the same Nsinga had used the same blackmail on the Conaco group, and that he had received 100,000 francs . . .
>
> . . . the day Parliament was to meet to pronounce its verdict on the Kimba government, deputy Nsinga, in excellent health that very morning, claimed to fall ill about 10 A.M., and thus missed the session, thereby betraying both camps which had bribed him.[6]

Following the 14 November vote Nendaka sought designation as premier, while others in the anti-Tshombe alliance vehemently opposed his selection, including both Mobutu and Kamitatu.[7] The next day Kasavubu renominated Kimba, amid a growing sense of impasse. The last days of the First Republic were now at hand.

It was in this last month that the Mobutu coup took form. From the time of the suppression of the Katanga secession in January 1963 it was evident that his relative control over the armed forces and his external CIA backing made Mobutu a potent arbiter—a role he first essayed in September 1960 when he "neutralized" Lumumba and Kasavubu and installed a "College of Commissioners," which held power in the capital till February 1961. He then became a pivotal member of the Binza group. In

October 1962, when the Adoula Regime seemed to falter, Mobutu seriously contemplated a military coup, and approached his American patrons for support. The United States remained committed to the Adoula formula, and was apprehensive as to negative repercussions in Africa and elsewhere should Mobutu seize power. He was discouraged from acting at that juncture.[8] During the first months of the Tshombe regime the state itself was held at bay by insurgent challenges in many areas, and the army in particular was in no condition to lay claim to power. The absorption of approximately 18,000 Katanga gendarmes as units, the influx of white mercenaries, and the operational role played by Belgian councillors who were not personal instruments of Mobutu made military intervention in these months inconceivable.

The failure of the Kimba government to obtain a vote of confidence opened the way for the Mobutu coup. The most careful study of the period concludes that Mobutu did not directly plan the coup before 16 November.[9] As late as 21 November Mobutu, in an astute dissimulation, reprimanded his close relative Litho Maboti for the surprise defection of seven northern Equateur deputies in the confidence vote, and in the company of Kimba met veteran Equateur politician Jean Bolikango to solicit his participation in the new Kimba cabinet.

On 24 November the fourteen members of the army high command were summoned to Kinshasa for an emergency session. It was this body—whose members were later designated by Mobutu as "Companions of the Revolution—which formally decided on the power seizure by its commander. In a proclamation read the following day it was announced that Kasavubu and Kimba were ousted as president- and prime-minister-designate, that Mobutu was designated as chief of state, and that Parliament and other institutions created by the constitution would continue to function.

The First Republic, in total disarray, surrendered itself without a whimper. Parliament, summoned on 25 November, by acclamation approved the power seizure, which Mobutu now specified would endure for five years. Kasavubu, after a brief hesitation, publicly accepted the coup on 29 November "in the higher interest of the country," and retired to his rural home in Bas-Zaire the following week. On 25 November Tshombe declared his support for Mobutu, expressing the thanks of CONACO for the removal of Kasavubu. The parliamentary vote was beyond any doubt representative of the public mood. "Politicians" had destroyed the First Republic, created the *pagaille* state, exposed it to sundry external machinations, and defaced its institutions with opportunism and venality. When the state later entered its phase of decline many would wonder whether this verdict was not too harsh. But at the time so dreary was the image of the present that virtually any new departure carried at least the hope of improvement.

Important to the immediate success of the coup were the strong support it enjoyed in the West and its acceptance elsewhere in Africa. We explore the external ties of the Mobutu regime in chapter 12; it is sufficient to note at this juncture that the American embassy certainly had advance knowledge of the coup and encouraged the takeover. Weissman, the most assiduous and thorough student of the U.S. Central Intelligence Agency (CIA) role in Zaire, concludes that the agency was "involved" in the coup, but without specifying in exactly what way or to what degree.[10] CIA Kinshasa station chief Lawrence Devlin, who had developed an intimate relationship with Mobutu in 1959 when both were in Brussels, had played a crucial covert role in Zairian affairs through the Binza group in 1960–62, and had returned for a second tour of duty in Zaire not long before the coup—a fact which many observers saw as circumstantial evidence of American complicity in the coup.[11] Though Tshombe had his supporters among American diplomats (particularly Ambassador McMurtrie Godley), his leadership was crippled by an inability to gain sufficient African legitimacy.[12] To Washington the Kasavubu group seemed embarked on a dangerous opening to the left. The Mobutu alternative thus appeared to promise both stability and reliability.

For Belgium the picture was complicated by the important cluster of interests, especially in the private sector, committed to support Tshombe. It was not at first clear that the new regime would swiftly develop an anti-Tshombe animus. Few Belgian interests were attracted to the path which the pro-Kasavubu forces seemed intent on pursuing.

The surprising degree of initial acceptance of the Mobutu regime by other African states can be explained by its apparent incorporation of a broad political spectrum, and sheer fatigue with Zairian political divisions. Mobutu also quickly moved to appropriate symbols of Zairian nationalism cherished elsewhere in Africa, particularly those associated with the name of Lumumba. As well, a spate of almost simultaneous coups (in Algeria, Togo, Benin, Ghana, Nigeria, and the Central African Republic) left Africa dazed by a continental drift toward military intervention.

Mobutu's initial strategy was to pour a new set of institutions into the mold set by the old, while incorporating within this framework the bulk of the political personnel of the first republic. As prime minister he designated Colonel Mulamba Nyunyi (Leonard), a widely respected officer with a distinguished combat record who had connections with both political factions. A cabinet of twenty-two persons was announced; one member was to be nominated by each province and by Kinshasa. A broad range of the political elite was thus coopted. Both the Front Démocratique Congolais (FDC) and CONACO were represented, though the latter only weakly so. The Binza group was present in force with two of its leading members, Bomboko Lokumba (Justin) and Nendaka. More radical nationalist voices included Mungul-Diaka (Bernardin) and Kande Zamulata (Jean-Jacques). Parliamentarians were assured of their formal powers and prerogatives (including material perquisites). Provincial presidents and assemblies were initially confirmed. Constitutionally guaranteed civil liberties were to be upheld. The major institutional and political forces were thus assured of their continuity and their interests. Kamitatu, one of the major losers in the coup, cogently explains the parliamentary acquiescence:

> All the assurances provided in the proclamation of the military high command, submitted to the special parliamentary session on 25 November 1965, gave to the deputies the most formal guarantees that, under the new regime, democratic institutions would continue to function normally. The problem then became simply an issue of individuals: Kasavubu and Tshombe were in conflict; Mobutu removed them, and despite the regret that each deputy might have for his leader's fall from office, all had tranquil consciences as they had only been neutralized, not arrested or killed.[13]

Consolidation of the regime

The consolidation phase extended from late 1965 to the adoption of a new constitution in June 1967 and the creation of the comprehensive regime party, the MPR, shortly before. During this period the First Republic machinery was progressively dismantled, the institutional framework of the New Regime was created, and the most dangerous opposition dispersed or coopted. At the outset many skeptics gave the regime no more than six months to survive; by the end of 1967 it was clear that the new order was entrenched for the foreseeable future.

While the Regime's initial proclamation seemed to pledge institutional continuity, it was accomplished by the declaration of a *Régime d'exception* for the entire country for a five-year period. This provision, which had no constitutional sanction, by itself created a reservoir of unlimited power vested in the presidency. On 30 November, again by extra-constitutional presidential edict, full legislative authority was attributed to the chief of state; although parliamentary review was provided for, this in turn was eliminated in March 1966. Parliament did continue to meet during 1966—indeed, its labors generated 1,400 pages of proceedings—but both legally and practically the New Regime had rendered it powerless. Ironically, Parliament itself had plebiscited its extra-constitutional emasculation by supporting the initial proclamation of the army high command by acclamation, and by unanimously approving the list of ministers submitted by Mobutu on 28 November 1965.[14]

The rich growth of political parties produced by the first republic was another early target. In his first major public address as president, Mobutu told a large crowd at the Kinshasa stadium that "it took five years for the politicians to lead the country to its ruin . . . This is why, on 24 November 1965, the stupid struggle for influence in which political parties were engaged was ended. For five years, there will be no more political party activity in the country."[15]

The extant provincial institutions enjoyed more of a respite, but by the end of 1966 this domain as well had been restructured and subdued. In April 1966 Mobutu signed a law reducing the number of provinces from twenty-one to twelve. This initial reorganization was achieved simply by fusing the political institutions of the provinces in question. In December 1966 a more far-reaching restructuring was imposed, further reducing the number to eight, in addition to the capital district of Kinshasa.[16] More important, the provincial governors were to become functionaries of the central state and the provincial assemblies mere consultative organs, before the latter disappeared entirely under the constitution of 1967.

From the beginning, the nature of the presidency was transformed. Although both the *Loi Fondamentale* and the Kananga constitution endowed the chief of state with significant powers as the ultimate custodian of sovereignty, government affairs had always been managed by the prime minister. The usually passive and self-effacing style of Kasavubu (except at a few moments of crisis) further reflected the subdued institutional role of the president. But when Mobutu designated Colonel Mulamba as his prime minister for the first months of the New Regime, the premiership became a very secondary office. To begin with, Mulamba was a military subordinate of the president. He had no political background, nor did his new office awaken a dormant will for power. Political decision, policy initiative, and its public presentation were firmly seated in the presidency.[17] Yet however modest his role, Mulamba did become the target of diverse criticisms—he was too conciliatory with the Belgians, too accessible to Catholic influence, and above all too tender with unruly military units he was sent to pacify in July 1966.[18] These charges provided ample pretext not only for dismissing Mulamba in October 1966, but also for abolishing the premiership. Executive powers were now de jure as well as de facto concentrated in the office of the president.

Power consolidation required not only conquest and the transformation of institutions, but dispersal of the numerous forces ready to fill the political space left vacant by the neutralization of the First Republic parties. This was partly accomplished by sealing off the familiar terrain by rendering Parliament functionless and freezing party activity. Cooptation, a device used with remarkable effect throughout the Mobutu era, was early developed into a fine art, as the far-flung apparatus of the state offered a large reservoir of positions for those willing to pledge faithful service. University graduates were the object of particular solicitation; a number were absorbed into the ramifying services of the presidency itself, including several who as student leaders had been articulate spokesmen for intransigent nationalism. The powerful post of general secretary at the presidency was held by Kamanda wa Kamanda (Grégoire), fresh from the leadership ranks of the Union Générale des Etudiants Congolais (UGEC), which had become the most articulate voice of the left in the final phase of the First Republic. The importance of this group in disarming potential critics of the regime among the small but influential intelligentsia can scarcely be overstated.

The other side of the cooptation coin was the threat of political disgrace. The credibility of this sanction was also quickly established; the first major victim was Bolikango, summarily dismissed in April 1966 for failure to execute presidential orders. Though he was brought back into the Political Bureau of the MPR from 1968 to 1970, the cavalier revocation in 1966 was a clear message to the older generation of political figures. A Second Republic ministry was a hostel for courtiers in transit, not a baronial fief.

Beyond the genteel seductions of cooptation, the regime chose an early occasion to demonstrate its ruthlessness in holding onto power. On 30 May 1966 four former cabinet ministers of First Republic vintage—Prime Minister-designate Kimba, Defense Minister Jérôme Anany, Finance Minister Emmanuel Bamba, and Minister of Mines and Energy Alexandre Mahamba—were arrested on treason charges, tried at once before a military tribunal, and publicly hanged before fifty thousand spectators three days later. The four had been in contact with Colonel Alphonse Bangala, then military governor of the capital, and Major Pierre Efomi concerning the possibility of overthrowing the regime. The officers, double agents or agents provocateurs in differing versions of their roles, had lured them to a final meeting at which they were arrested. This affair, which became known as the Pentecost Plot, had a tremendous psychological effect on the political world; opposition, it was now clear, carried mortal perils. Mobutu, who had warned politicians in January that secret meetings would lead to prosecution before military tribunals and in April had forbidden them to travel in the interior, now raised the ante of intimidation. A new theme began to develop in the regime's ideology of leadership: a chief—decisive, authoritarian, peremptory—will brook no cabals. As Mobutu put it, "One had to strike through a spectacular example, and create the conditions of regime discipline. When a chief takes a decision, he decides—period. I have decided, in the name of the high command, that we will be in power for five years—full stop. A group of politicians therefore has no business playing the game of the financiers to provoke further disorders and troubles in the country. They [the plotters] did it, and it was necessary to make an example of them."[19]

Probably the least dangerous opposition came from the rebel remnants within and without the country. The Chinese had provided significant military supplies to rebels through Tanzania during 1965, but were losing interest. Ernesto "Che" Guevara, who fought with one rebel band with a few hundred Cuban colleagues for several months in 1965, also gave up the struggle as hopeless.[20] A number of pockets of insurgent resistance continued into the early part of the Mobutu era in the northeast quadrant, and were only slowly brought under administrative control. The Fizi-Baraka bastion in south Kivu, which was still active in 1980, was isolated in a remote mountainous area, ethnically encapsulated, and no longer constituted a significant threat.

Apart from the actual threat posed by Tshombe's scheming, there was evident advantage to the regime in brandishing a Tshombe menace. To students and the residual Lumumbist group, Tshombe was the worst enemy of nationalism; this opinion was shared by a large segment of political Africa.[21] The focus on Tshombe as chief enemy of the regime provided invaluable legitimation in milieux suspicious of the close American ties of Mobutu, who was prone to be seen as "a running dog of imperialism."[22]

The first indication of the regime's anti-Tshombe orientation came in the composition of the Mulamba cabinet, in which Tshombe's followers carried little weight. Tshombe had left for Europe on 23 December 1965; by March 1966 the regime had begun attacking the financial accords Tshombe had negotiated with Belgium in February 1965 to settle economic conflicts (*contentieux*) arising out of Zairian independence. The Tshombe settlement came to be described as "high treason" on the part of Tshombe and not binding on the country. Beginning in April 1966, the epithet "traitor" came into official circulation. The following month Mobutu asked Parliament to expel Tshombe. The expulsion, which also removed Tshombe's parliamentary immunity, was unanimous.

By mid-1966 there was no doubt that Tshombe was actively engaged in conspiratorial activity. His admiring biographer, *London Daily Telegraph* correspondent Ian Colvin, notes that by this time, the Tshombe entourage was dominated by dubious adventurers, and that he was losing touch with reality.[23] In March 1967 Tshombe was tried in absentia for treason, and condemned to death.

In June 1967 the Tshombe threat was eliminated by an intelligence operation whose full ramifications remain to be explained. Tshombe was lured aboard a small chartered plane by Francis Bodenan, recently released from a twelve-year prison sentence on a murder charge, and a new recruit for the entourage.[24] The plane was hijacked to Algiers, where Tshombe was imprisoned. Though Algerian authorities turned down Zairian overtures for Tshombe's extradition to face treason charges, in June 1969 his death in prison was announced. The medical certificate attributed his demise to a heart attack, but this account was not believed by many in Zaire.[25]

The Tshombe dissidence was tied to unrest among the mercenaries and Katanga gendarme units, which first broke out in 1966 (on the mercenary mutinies, see chapter 9). A more serious mutiny in 1967 was unambiguously part of a plot orchestrated by Tshombe to overthrow Mobutu. The kidnapping of Tshombe on the eve of the operation preempted its success, but the machinery was already in motion. More than four months were required for the national army to flush the mutineers out of their final redoubt in Bukavu in November.

By late 1967 the heavyweights of the First Republic had been coopted, neutralized, or jailed. Nendaka, Bomboko, and Mungul-Diaka were key figures in the New Regime. Tshombe was jailed in Algiers, Godefroid Munongo and Kamitatu were imprisoned in Zaire. Kasavubu was in docile isolation in his home village, and Adoula was ambassador in Washington.

Completion of the consolidation phase of the regime was symbolized by the creation of its own political machinery and constitutional framework in 1967. After a brief period of ambiguity when the possibility of a second party was hinted at (it was explicitly permitted by the 1967 consti-

tution), Mobutu made clear that the newly created MPR intended to occupy all political space. As the MPR was to represent all Zairians, there
was no need for a second party (on the MPR, see chapter 7). The constitution of 1967, drafted by the New Regime, formally enshrined the presidential system which had already been created through metamorphosis of
the First Republic institutions; presidential hegemony was assured both
with respect to the ministers, whose function was simply to execute the
decisions and policies of the president, and the legislature, whose role was
circumscribed by the concurrent power of the president to make laws.

Adoption of a new constitution permitted disbanding of the old parliament. The country, Mobutu said, "has a revolutionary people and government, but a Parliament composed of retrograde politicians elected under
debatable circumstances."[26] In March 1967 Parliament was dissolved; a
new one would not be constituted until 1970, at the end of the initial five-
year period of Mobutu rule.

Though the national referendum on the new constitution, held in June
1967, showed apparently spectacular margins of approval, it also revealed
some of the regime's weaknesses. In Bas-Zaire, a sub rosa campaign was
carried out against the constitution; Mobutu himself publicly denounced
opposition by the Kongo ethnic community, and threatened to strike
without mercy at all those who sought to torpedo his regime.[27] In Matadi,
the yes vote was only 60 percent of the total, and in the nearby zone of
Songololo it was a mere 51 percent—astonishingly low totals in view of
the vigor with which approval was promoted by the state apparatus. In
Kinshasa, so much negative sentiment was encountered that the balloting
had to be called off, though official figures reported an 81 percent majority
for approval.[28] In Shaba, on the other hand, what government organs described as "revolutionary enthusiasm" yielded a 99 percent vote of approval.
Kasongo modestly suggests an additional explanation: "The presence of
Manzikala at the head of Katanga province, and the fear he inspired, had a
favorable impact on the vote results."[29]

Whatever clouds were discernible here and there, by 1967 the regime
was remarkably well established. On the economic front, though the
UMHK struggle wound up with a compromise solution, Zairian sovereignty over the mineral industry was at least nominally established through
the nationalization of UMHK in early 1967 (see chapter 10). The well-
executed 1967 financial stabilization plan eliminated inflation until 1973,
and projected an image of both strength and competence. In September
1967 Kinshasa successfully hosted an OAU summit conference, symboliz-

ing the full acceptance of Zaire by the African family of nations. Almost no one, in 1965, could have imagined that any regime in Zaire would achieve such unchallenged authority.

New Regime ascendancy

This phase in the fortunes of the regime, which stretched from late 1967 to 1970, was marked by the achievement by Mobutu of a personal ascendancy over the state and the patrimonialization of the state. One by one the key First Republic leaders who had their own clientele were shunted aside and were replaced by figures whose promotion depended upon presidential grace. The personalistic nature of the regime became increasingly salient. This process was accompanied by a steady reduction in spheres of autonomous activity.

Illustrative of the dynamic of personal ascendancy was the fate of the once-potent Binza group. Intimate associates since 1960, their relations were bound to become ambiguous as Mobutu increasingly asserted his individual hegemony. In the first years, Bomboko, Nendaka, and Ndele played crucial roles of influence within the regime. Bomboko remained a fixture as minister of foreign affairs. Nendaka, though removed at once by Mobutu from the Interior Ministry, retained his links with the security agency through his client and co-ethnic Singa Boyenge (Alexandre), who was named security chief on the day of the coup. (The security agency itself was renamed the Centre National de Documentation [CND].) Ndele initially retained his post as head of the central bank; in 1967 his term was extended for five years.

Bomboko and Nendaka were both ousted from their ministerial positions on 1 August 1969. Bomboko, who had also served in the MPR Political Bureau since its creation, ranked number two in both hierarchies at the time of his ouster. The initial demotion was cushioned by appointment as ambassador to Washington. However significant this embassy, Bomboko was evidently neutralized by removal from the sources of power in Kinshasa. In June 1970 he was suddenly dismissed as ambassador, accused of forming a Mongo ethnic combine with then-CND chief Efomi, and of excessive ambition. In October 1971 he was charged with organizing a league of conspirators who were plotting the assassination of Mobutu, and remained under house arrest for a year. He was then released to devote full time to a flourishing mercantile empire in his native Equateur. (Bomboko later enjoyed a spectacular second ascension, winning election to the Political Bureau in 1977, returning to the Foreign Ministry in 1980, and becoming deputy prime minister in 1981.)

The Nendaka trajectory was quite similar. There is some evidence of distrust of Nendaka at the time of the coup; it will be recalled that Mobutu urged Kasavubu not to name him premier-designate in mid-November 1965, after Kimba failed to win confirmation. Also, Mobutu assigned him to the relatively unimportant Ministry of Transport and Communication after the coup. In 1967 Nendaka was moved up to the Ministry of Finance, from which he was removed in August 1969 and posted as ambassador to Bonn. In June 1970 he was recalled and placed under house arrest in Kinshasa; in October 1971 he was accused, with Bomboko, of plotting the assassination of the president. After a year of rustication he resurfaced as a coffee baron, also eventually reentering politics as an elected member of the Political Bureau in 1977. Like Bomboko, he was a major participant in the fraudulent coffee export traffic of 1976–77, which was so costly to the then-bankrupt state.

Ndele, financial specialist of the Binza group, remained in the presidential entourage a little longer. He was shifted to the Ministry of Finance in September 1970, but removed two months later, ostensibly for his reluctance to attend the funeral of de Gaulle as Mobutu's representative. Ndele had close ties to the *Société Générale* group, and was identified as a supporter of the unsuccessful UMHK copper concession bid in 1970. Ndele left for the United States in 1973, and in 1975 was condemned in absentia to twenty years imprisonment on subversion charges.

The pattern suggested by these examples may be observed in many other careers. By 1969–70 such crucial figures on the initial Mobutu team as Tshisekedi, Manzikala, and Mungul-Diaka had all gone through periods of arrest and disgrace. Some, like Tshisekedi, reappeared in leading state organs; others were quietly released and encouraged to pursue profitable mercantile careers.[30] None were permitted to claim political roles on the basis of autonomous political power.

A comparable trend was observable in the presidential staff. The team of young university graduates initially assembled as a technocratic brain trust for the regime enjoyed considerable influence during the power-consolidation phase. There were daily briefings for the president, who listened carefully to policy arguments they had developed. By 1968 these sessions were less frequent, and the task of the presidential staff became the faithful interpretation of presidential thought rather than participation in the definition of policy. Independent-minded councillors, such as General Secretary Kamanda, were transferred to other jobs—in Kamanda's case to the OAU staff in Addis Ababa, and later to the UN. During the ascendancy stage the key figures in the presidential secretariat were technician-courtiers.

A small but by no means insignificant milestone on the trail of ascendancy was the death of Kasavubu in April 1969. With his demise vanished the last person who could oppose Mobutu in the name of a residual First Republic legality—which Kasavubu had never chosen to do.[31]

The regime's ascendancy was also expressed through the expansion of the state into organizational spheres having well-established traditions of autonomy—in particular, the trade unions and the student associations. The three major existing national trade union organizations were forced in 1967 to fuse into a single labor ancillary of the MPR. The 1967 party charter, the N'sele Manifesto, declared that the union role was no longer to function as a "force of confrontation, but [as] an organ of support for government policy."[32]

The student associations were more troublesome and establishment of full hegemony over them was a far more difficult task, leading to major confrontations in 1969 and 1971.[33] In April 1969 Lovanium University students sent an audacious note to the government, announcing their determination to defend their rights "by any means necessary, including revolutionary violence."[34] When the regime did not respond to their demands for a student share in university governance, a demonstration was called for 4 June 1969. The student march was dispersed by military units; several dozen deaths resulted.

In the aftermath, the Political Bureau dissolved all student organizations except the party youth wing, the Jeunesse du Mouvement Populaire de la Révolution (JMPR)—up to this point very weak at the university. But the task of subduing the students was only partly accomplished at this stage. Two years later a ceremony commemorating the second anniversary of the demonstration led to another violent encounter with the army. This time all Lovanium students were conscripted into the military, and two months later a radical reform of higher education was decreed, with all campuses and advanced institutes assimilated into the Université Nationale du Zaire (UNAZA). With this drastic surgery total political hegemony over both the university and the students was achieved.

The apotheosis of ascendancy came in mid-1970 with the convening of an extraordinary congress of the MPR, whose main tasks were the "institutionalization" of the party as the central organ of the state and nomination of Mobutu as president. Despite the artificiality of an unopposed contest, a presidential campaign was used as the occasion for a triumphant progress through the countryside during which the achievements of the regime were extolled. The themes were simple: "Now . . . political stability has returned, . . . peace, calm, tranquillity reign; we have in the Congo a people cured from the malady of youth, a people . . . that has become disciplined, a people which has become hard-working, a people that has become creative . . ."[35]

The insecurity, the dislocations, the sufferings of the First Republic were indeed fresh in the popular recollection, and 1970 was a better year for nearly all than 1965. Not only was the nightmare of the past behind, but dazzling prospects for the future were promised. "Objectif 80" was a major campaign theme, a rendezvous with abundance to be accomplished by a doubling of copper output and a flood of investments directed toward three "development poles"—Kinshasa, Kisangani, and southern Shaba. Viewed through the prism of subsequent economic calamities, these promises have a hollow ring. But as they fell upon the ears of enthusiastic crowds in 1970 they carried conviction. If the miraculous restoration of the state and the economy had been accomplished, why was "Objectif 80" beyond the state's capacity?

While the administration, the party, and the army deployed all their energies for some weeks to assure a massive voter turnout, and 99-percent majorities are always suspect, the consecration by plebiscite of Mobutu's ascendancy was thus more than simply a measure of a capacity for coercive mobilization by state organs. The new order was solidly constructed, and we believe that Mobutu at that juncture could have bested any competitor in an open contest.

A final mark of the ascendancy of the New Regime was the remarkably successful royal visit of King Baudouin in June 1970—the Belgian king's first visit since the disagreeable episodes of independence day in 1960, when the eulogies to colonialism and nationalism delivered respectively by Bauduoin and Lumumba each gave offense to the other camp. No such mishaps clouded the 1970 visit, which was continuous euphoria. The large contingent of foreign journalists attracted by this event made it a public relations masterpiece for the second republic; their rapturous dispatches added a valuable gloss to the now widely accepted image of success.

State expansion

The regime's fourth stage, which we term expansion, spanned the period 1970–74. With ascendancy assured, Mobutu was free to pursue his ambi-

tions *tous azimuts*: externally, by active pursuit of African leadership; ideologically, by staking a claim to philosophical innovation with the creed of
"authenticity"; economically, by luring a diverse assortment of (mostly
loan) capital to the country, while simultaneously capturing "economic independence" through Zairianization; domestically, through the MPR's
ever-enlarging hegemonical claims, now extended to the church and the
army. The promulgation of a new constitution in 1974, describing the
state as unparalleled personal power, was the zenith of this phase.

Intimately intertwined were the vision of a manifest destiny of greatness for Zaire, bestowed by the fates as the corollary to the country's vast
dimensions and colossal resources, and the ordination of Mobutu as the
instrument of this beneficent historic design. "Congolization" was only a
bad memory; the time had come to transcend mere respectability by reaching for greatness.

Grandeur, to be meaningful, required international credibility. Thus
these years of regime expansion were marked by a vast deployment of diplomatic energies (assessed in greater detail in chapter 12). Throughout this
phase Mobutu traveled extensively; President Nixon embraced him in the
Rose Garden in August 1970, and extolled the virtues of investment in
Zaire. Chairman Mao accorded him an audience in January 1973, and
chuckled at the ineffectiveness of the rebels on whom he had once squan-
dered a few arms, sending Mobutu back to Zaire with a $100-million
blessing in the form of a credit line for rural development.

Presidential travel and Zairian diplomatic action were particularly intense within Africa, where Zaire could grasp not merely respect for, but
for continental leadership. A modest clientele of junior partners was created (especially Togo, Chad, and Burundi). Mobutu regularly offered his
services as mediator of African conflicts outside Zaire. To demonstrate its
Third World credentials, Zaire spoke out more strongly on southern Africa, north-south matters. Mobutu used the forum of the United Nations
to announce a surprising rupture with Israel in October 1973. At the Algiers summit meeting of nonaligned nations in September 1973, he had
private audiences with seventeen heads of state and five prime ministers.
One commentator offered these lyrical words: "In effect, both in the
domestic field and in the pan-African and international arenas, General
Mobutu exhibits an extraordinary energy and dynamic activity, which
leaves one wondering what its outer limits might be . . . This enormous
energy . . . can well derive from the legitimate pride which he finds in giving his country a place in the concert of nations in keeping with its scale
and its potential wealth."[36]

In the ideological realm Mobutu embarked on a new course. In April 1971 he unveiled the concept of "authenticity," henceforward to serve as the centerpiece of state ideology. This catchword was offered as both a remedy for cultural alienation and a rhetorical passe-partout, a distinctively Zairian contribution to contemporary moral discourse (see chapter 3).

In the economic sphere, an array of projects of breathtaking scale was promised: the doubling of copper production; completion of the second stage of the Inga dam development; construction of a 1,200-mile, direct current high-tension power line to transport the dam's energy to the Shaba mines; completion of the national rail line from Shaba to Kinshasa, and its extension to a new deep-water port at Banana (with a huge bridge at Matadi), development of coastal and offshore oilwells, a steel mill near Kinshasa, an aluminum mill and a uranium enrichment plant near the Inga dam; promotion of a third "development pole" at Kinsangani, linked by rail to the national network. The scope of these visions was truly staggering, and the potential capital requirements were immense, available only out side the country.

At the same time, fulfillment of the state autonomy imperative through economic independence was a critical goal of the New Regime. While at the beginning of the expansion phase Mobutu claimed that economic independence had already been achieved through the triumphant struggle with colonial monopolies, by 1972 the emerging theme, repeated with growing insistence, was that this battle was yet to be won.[37] The apparent contradiction was resolved by making a distinction between old capital— legacy of colonialism, almost exclusively Belgian, heavily concentrated in a few financial trusts—and new capital, which entered on terms freely negotiated by the new order. Economic relations with respect to colonial capital required continuous struggle. To deal with new capital, the key was diversification of sources (Japanese, American, West German, French, Italian), which would assure a variety of partners—and, sotto voce, a number of countries with an interest in the well-being of the New Regime. Further, the Zairian state generally acquired a minority share of enterprise ownership in return for its grant of a concession.

The distinction between old and new capital sharpened in 1973–74 with the declaration of Zairianization and radicalization measures (see chapter 11). The gathering Zairian diplomatic offensive had encountered continuing suspicion in radical Third World quarters, a legacy of Mobutu's First Republic role and his American connections; suspicion was reinforced by the apparent stampede of Western capital into Zaire. For Mobutu to win acceptance as a major Third World statesman a more Third World image was needed. At the Algiers summit conference in September 1973 Mobutu gave private assurances to a number of leaders that decisive measures to consolidate economic independence were in the offing. On 30 November 1973 the audacious adventure of "Zairianization" was announced, followed a year later by "radicalization." These measures, soon to prove a recipe for disaster, in an immediate sense were a stunning accomplishment. At a blow, by sudden proclamation, the state had become either the parastatal manager or the patrimonial dispenser of nearly all of the economic structure built up before 1969, without seriously providing for compensation.[38] This sovereign gesture, the United Nations speech of 4 October 1973, the rupture with Israel, and verbal assaults on Belgium and the United States during 1974 did win momentary admission for Mobutu to the chapel of radicalism abroad.

The regime's ambitions for state expansion necessarily implied conflict with organized religion. The Protestant churches, claiming about 20 percent of the populace as communicants, did accommodate regime requests to regroup as a single entity, with the assorted individual churches bequeathed by the diversity of mission affiliations as autonomous units under its umbrella. The small Muslim community and the influential Kimbanguist church received more official recognition than they had ever known in the past. But the crucial adversary was the Catholic church, whose active following included 40 percent of the population.

The resources and scope of the Catholic church were great, and cannot be fully described by a mere recitation of their quantitative features. To begin with, the hierarchy and worldwide structure of the church provided an institutional infrastructure of resiliency and solidity. At the beginning of the regime's expansion phase, the Catholic church in Zaire counted 1 Zairian cardinal, 27 of 46 dioceses headed by Zairians, 587 Zairian priests, 394 Zairian brothers, 1,115 Zairian nuns, and 11,746 national catechists; these were supported by foreign priests, brothers, and sisters numbering 2,774, 286, and 3,078 respectively.[39] The impact of these numbers was enhanced by the high quality and moral abnegation of many of the personnel. Until the 1950s the church provided to Zairians the only avenue of social promotion where full equality with Europeans could be obtained, and the priesthood attracted some of the most gifted young men of the pre-independence generations. Among Europeans, church personnel were willing to accept the occasional insecurity and relative material deprivation of long-term service in the hinterland, which secular expatriates were much less willing to endure.

As a result of these conditions the church was much more than a com-

munity of believers; it was an organization of national scope, whose penetration of the interior was comparable in scale to that of the state, and
whose social service structures were generally far more effective. This was
especially true in the critical domains of education and health, the two most
important public services in the eyes of the rural population. In 1974 Catholic schools enrolled 61.7 percent of Zaire's primary pupils and 42.1 percent
of its secondary students, as compared to 13.8 percent and 35.4 percent in
the state schools.[40] Even more important than the raw figures were the
quality differentials; as measured by success ratios in the state examinations, virtually all of the top schools were in the Catholic network, with the
exception of some of the Protestant schools. The religious schools were
able to assure both regular payment of personnel and pedagogical supplies, in dreary contrast to the state school network, which was demoralized by overcrowding, chronic staff shortages, pay arrearages, lack of instructional materials, and venality in the administration. In the health
sphere, official estimates in 1972 conceded that 75 percent of the meager
health services available to rural populations came through the churches.[41]
In addition, church personnel performed many other hinterland services
which defy measurement—road repair, community development, and the
like. Often in rural zones only a church brother knew how to repair motor
vehicles. The role of the church was thus pervasive, and its moral credit
made it an uncomfortable competitor for the comprehensive allegiance
which the regime sought through ideological mobilization.

The Catholic church welcomed the New Regime, and generally supported the consolidation of its authority. Apprehensions within the hierarchy became discernable during the phase of ascendancy; the hegemonical
ambitions of the MPR aroused suspicion, and a conference of bishops in
August 1969 privately noted "dictatorial tendencies" in the regime.[42] Despite occasional friction, however, state-church conflict was subdued until
the expansion phase.

Cardinal Malula chose to give public voice to developing fears concerning the regime's intentions at a mass celebrating the tenth anniversary of
independence, and in the presence of both King Baudouin and Mobutu.
He regretted the inequities of resource distribution, and denounced political elites for "a fascination with the triumphant and the superficial, and a
hunger for the lavish."[43] To Mobutu this was an unforgiveable act of lèse-
majesté, though he did not respond immediately.

The Catholic church in turn viewed as an affront the sudden swallow-
ing of its educational monument, Lovanium University, into the secular
Université Nationale du Zaire in August 1971. More serious was the re-

gime's announcement in December 1971 that JMPR branches had to be established in the seminaries. After weeks of tension and closure of the seminaries, in April 1972 the bishops accepted JMPR cells on the condition that their party links pass through the church hierarchy.

Another battle took place over the concept of authenticity, which the hierarchy began to see as an implicit threat to Christianity. The regime's stress on "mental decolonization" and "cultural disalienation" could be read as a disguised attack on Christianity as an import from the West; so too could the appeal to the values of traditional African culture as a spiritual resource and as an alternative to indiscriminate Westernization. On 11 January 1972 the Catholic weekly *Afrique Chrétienne* decried a resurrection of a past which was "gone forever . . . Since our world is no longer that of our ancestors, their concept of life cannot be ours either . . . It is not by resuscitating a discredited philosophy that we will win the battle of the modern world."[44] The article was denounced by the regime as "subversive and counter-revolutionary," and the journal suspended for six months.

One symbolic accoutrement of the authenticity campaign, the 1972 elimination of Christian forenames, was treated by the Catholic church as a particular affront. Mobutu's renunciation of "Joseph-Désiré" was provoked by offensive articles in the Belgian Catholic daily *Libre Belgique*, which belittled the change of place-names and compared Mobutu to Caligula. The church hierarchy in Zaire expressed short-lived opposition to the name changes, but soon gave way before the regime's insistence that all were required to take on authentic names.[45]

Even if quickly abandoned, the church opposition to the name changes was seen as a direct challenge to the state, and led to a dramatic riposte. The chief Catholic prelate, Cardinal Malula, became the target of regime attacks as a "renegade of the revolution," was evicted from the handsome residence the regime had built for him, and was forced to leave the country for three months in February 1972.

In late 1972 the regime banned all religious broadcasts, and dissolved church-sponsored youth movements such as the scouts. Indoctrination of youth should be an exclusive preserve of the party, it was argued. The zenith of this campaign came at the end of 1974 when the religious school networks were nationalized, celebration of Christmas as a public holiday was ended, and the display of religious artifacts was tightly circumscribed to the interior of churches (the school networks were returned to the churches 18 months later when the state proved unable to operate them effectively).

Not only were the hegemonical claims of the presidential political core of the Mobutu regime extended over the religious sphere, but they were also applied to the formal institutions of the state itself after 1972. The device for accomplishing this end was the imposition of party dominance over the security forces and the administration. Following the 1972 MPR congress, it was announced that party cells were to be formed in military units. This was a radical change of direction: from colonial days through the initial years of the Second Republic, a militantly apolitical—even anti-political—orientation had been inculcated among the troops. Politics and politicians were a veritable cancer on the body politic; the army, highest custodian of the nation, was to remain far removed from this sordid fray. The new conception of the MPR as the nation politically organized implied an altered relationship between the military and the state, which was not easily accepted by a segment of the officer corps steeped in apoliticism.

The concept of the administrative role also changed significantly. The new doctrine of party hegemony implied a de facto fusion of party and state organs within regional administrations. From 1973 until a repeal in 1980 the hierarchical chiefs of the different administrative echelons (regions, subregions, zones) were explicitly designated as "political-administrative cadres." At the lowest level—the collectivity and the locality units of governance headed by locally recruited chiefs—the law of 5 January 1973 purported to fully incorporate the rural periphery into the state domain by (in effect) abolishing chieftaincy.[46] In only a few areas did chiefs constitute a potent rural force, and in none were they a real challenge to power at the national level; but the monolithic impulses of state expansion were running strong, and it was no longer tolerable that there remain localized cocoons of autonomy whose principles of solidarity were not those of the MPR and Mobutism.

The new law therefore provided that all chiefs were to be named by the interior minister, were to derive their authority purely from their place in the state hierarchy, and were to be freely transferrable. Customary criteria were no longer to be considered. This move was warmly supported by the bureaucrats of the state apparatus, who tended to consider the existing chiefs as incompetent, and not infrequently as obstacles; the conference of regional commissioners in 1973 "rejoiced at the abolition of traditional authority" and called for "rapid application of this decision."[47] We will explore in chapter 8 the way in which actual application fell far short of proclaimed objectives.

The 1974 constitution stands as the normative embodiment of the Mobutist state at its apogee. Drafted by the presidency, approved by the Political Bureau and National Legislative Council by acclamation, this document faithfully incorporates the presidential image of the new order. As noted by Mpinga, professor of administrative law and subsequently prime minister, the genius of the document lay in entirely setting aside external constitutional models. "Zairians," Mpinga told a distinguished audience in Brussels, "have no need to refer to Montesquieu to determine what form of government they need. In the revised constitution, the only factors considered have been the efficiency of the system, elimination of errors of the past, the Zairian concept of power and the chief, and certain modern realities."[48] There would, indeed, have been few if any models available for the consecration of centralized, untrammelled personal power provided by this remarkable constitution.

Article 28 of the 1974 constitution stipulated that in Zaire "there exists a single institution, the MPR, incarnated by its President." Article 30 provided that the "President of the MPR is *ex officio* President of the Republic, and holds the plenitude of power exercise. He presides over the Political Bureau, the Council of Ministers, the Legislature, and the Judicial Council." In effect, he named the members of all of these bodies, as well as all persons in command posts in the regional administration.[49] The creed of "Mobutism" was declared to be constitutional doctrine, and the Political Bureau was charged with examining cases of "deviationism" (Article 46). Though basic rights were guaranteed, all Zairians were declared to be members of the MPR (Article 8), and obligated to "support the revolution" (Article 27). The constitution did provide some restrictions on the presidency: an individual was limited to two five-year terms, could only change one-third of the Political Bureau membership during a given term, and could be tried by the Political Bureau for "deviationism." But Mobutu himself was exempted from these restrictions, and was given full authority to unilaterally alter any provision of the constitution.

In the perspective of subsequent events it is clear that the real power of the Mobutist state never approximated the leviathan vision embodied in the constitution. The bid for continental leadership was soon overtaken by events; the residual suspicions of Mobutu were quickly reconfirmed by the Angolan crisis in 1975. The permeation of the polity by the party, even at the pinnacle of MPR success, was always limited. The ordinary citizen learned to adapt behavior to the superficial requirements of the new order, and would turn out for the ceremonial events, such as support marches, if administrative pressure were sufficient. Even the MPR declined to respond to Mobutu's informally communicated invitation to acclaim him Life President at the 1972 congress. Yet at the time the image of force, power, and strength seemed real enough; the state at the high tide of its expansionist phase was an astonishing personal hegemony.

State crisis and decay

The fifth phase, which began in 1974, saw the state thrust on the defensive by a series of contradictions. At first the loss of elan seemed momentary and conjunctural; by 1976 it was becoming clear that a crisis was unfolding which would shake society to its foundations. As the crisis deepened and persisted and hopes for its end all but vanished, symptoms of state decay appeared and became general.

State expansion had been made possible by the exceptional availability of the resources needed to lubricate the exceedingly costly Mobutist system. For most of the period 1967–74 copper prices were very favorable— with one trough from late 1970 to early 1972—and in 1974 they surged to an all-time high. In addition, the state had substantially increased its fiscal pressure on the mining sector; tax revenues from copper increased sixfold from 1965 to 1974, though production was up only 50 percent. Until 1974 painful choices could be averted through the rapid expansion of state revenues, which rose from Z 186 million in 1968 to 539 million in 1974. The resource pool was further enlarged, from 1970 on, by the extraordinary availability of external credit. The external debt, fueled by a grandiose packet of costly investment schemes, soared from next to nothing to nearly $3 billion by late 1975, when the international financial community suddenly discovered that Zaire was virtually bankrupt. The sudden pulsating surge of resources through the state was largely devoted to patrimonial purposes; in this way the emergent politico-commercial class rapidly accumulated wealth.

The first omen of impending difficulties came in April–May 1974 with the acute drop of the copper price to less than half its peak level. The rise of oil prices was another blow, sharpened by the discovery that the Mobutu diplomatic blitzkrieg in the Arab world would not result in discounted prices. At the same time there came the shortages resulting from Zairianization measures. Above all, the swift monetary expansion produced by forced advances from the Banque du Zaire to cover government deficits generated new inflation; beginning in 1973, inflation rose to a 60–80 percent per annum rate, which continued into 1980. Endemic hyperinflation contributed to the state's growing legitimation crisis, eroding its credibility.

The Zairianization measures of 30 November 1973 proved to be a colossal miscalculation whose political and economic costs were very high. And though radicalization was intended to dissipate the gathering social malaise, these sweeping measures in turn proved a humiliating fiasco. By late 1975 the regime was in retreat from Zairianization and radicalization, and by early 1976 they had been all but abandoned. The limits of state capacity and competence were starkly revealed.

Externally, years of careful African diplomacy were undone by Zaire's costly intervention in the Angolan civil war on the side of a cast of losers that included the United States and South Africa. For much of Africa the exposure of South African and CIA involvement legitimated the larger Soviet–Cuban intervention on behalf of the triumphant Movimento Popular de Libertação de Angola (MPLA). Though a cluster of moderate African states stood by Mobutu, his credit plummeted with others, and diplomatic leadership was out of the question.

The Angola operation generated dissension within the security forces. According to Kamitatu, even within the army high command "a very large group opposed such an adventurous expedition."[50] The operation was even more unpopular with the rank and file, above all when it proved disastrous. With the public as well, the war in Angola was unpopular. Few felt any stake in the outcome; the growing ranks of the disaffected even observed with silent satisfaction the humiliating reverses inflicted on the regime. By 1976 the prevailing mood had totally altered; shattered was the relative acceptance, if not support, of the New Regime. Hounded by its creditors, isolated diplomatically, the new order was placed on the defensive for the first time. A sense of *fin-de-régime* was in the air. When Mobutu took his entire family to Switzerland in March 1976, where he sought rest and medical attention, rumors swept the country that the Guide of the Zairian Revolution had fled. Whether or not such a thought crossed his mind, he did return to confront a crisis whose massive proportions and long-term nature were becoming clear by late 1976.

The mood of profound demoralization which had settled on the country was given eloquent voice in a March 1976 pastoral letter by Archbishop Kabanga of Lubumbashi. Within hours the printed version of this moving document was sold out. Monsignor Kabanga denied that his devastating critique was aimed at an individual; it was aimed, he said, at an entire system:

> My brothers, let us have the courage to open our eyes and look not
> only around us, but within ourselves. The situation is grave . . .

It is hardly necessary to describe the general crisis—economic, social, and moral—which we now experience . . .

We bear daily witness to agonizing situations created by the intolerable behavior of many . . .

The thirst for money thus transforms men into assassins. Many poor unemployed are condemned to misery along with their families because they are unable to pay off the person who hires. How many children and adults die without medical care because they are unable to bribe the medical personnel who are supposed to care for them? Why are there no medical supplies in the hospitals, while they are found in the marketplace? How did they get there?

Why is it that in our courts justice can only be obtained by fat bribes to the judge? Why are prisoners forgotten in jail? They have no one to pay off the judge who sits on their dossier. Why do our government offices force people to come back day after day to obtain services to which they are entitled? If the clerks are not paid off, they will not be served. Why, at the opening of school, must parents go into debt to bribe the school principal? Children who are unable to pay will have no school . . .

Whoever holds a morsel of authority, or means of pressure, profits from it to impose on people and exploit them, especially in rural areas. All means are good to obtain money, or humiliate the human being . . .[51]

The decay of the state stood revealed by the sheer audacity of the publication of this explosive document, by its resonance among the public, and by the inability of the regime to respond with retaliatory measures against the Church comparable to those with which it had responded in its expansionist phase. Mobutu summoned the Zairian bishops to disavow the letter; they flatly refused.

Indeed, Mobutu sought on occasion to exorcise malaise by appropriating the letter's themes for self-criticism of the regime—though never for criticism of its leader. From time to time, from early days of the New Regime, Mobutu had used public occasions to attack unnamed high-placed persons for sabotaging the government. In July 1972 he told 100 thousand people that a purge of party cadres was necessary, as "the public . . . had recognized that it is especially in the entourage of the President, among those who claim to be confidantes of the ruler, that one encounters thieves, traitors, embezzlers, and malcontents who are asphyxiating the regime."[52] On 4 January 1975 Mobutu warned MPR cadres to "have their hands clean," and proclaimed that he had "declared war on the bourgeoisie."[53]

In the aftermath of an invasion of the Shaba mining region in March 1977, Mobutu declared in a major address that this crisis had revealed the betrayal of many high-placed cadres, "who expressed doubts, began to distance themselves, kept one foot in each camp, hesitated to wear their party buttons, and privately predicted the downfall of the regime" (on the invasion of Shaba, see chapter 9). On 25 November 1977, before an MPR party congress, Mobutu went much further, laying bare what he termed "the Zairian sickness" (*mal zairois*) in terms quite reminiscent of the pastoral letter. Systematic corruption had become a defining characteristic of the Zairian state, by presidential admission.

The candid analysis of present discontents by Mobutu evidently expressed sentiments widely—one might say unanimously—held in society at large. Left unanswered, however, was the question of why it was in a regime vesting total power in the president, that the untouchable caste could continue to enjoy immunity. Nor had it escaped public notice that the president himself was the largest single beneficiary of the Zairianization measures.

Symptoms of the profound social malaise began to surface in the form of wildcat strikes in Shaba and Kinshasa in 1976–77. Strikes were officially illegal, and the state-sponsored Union Nationale des Traveilleurs Zairois (UNTZA) preempted the field of organized labor; the strikes were thus largely spontaneous, sudden eruptions of discontent, specific to a given enterprise.

In February 1977 the normally docile legislature unanimously adopted reports flaying the regime for corruption, mismanagement, and the repressiveness of the territorial administration. As accomplices in these misdeeds Political Bureau members were invited to leave the session, and the assembly refused to approve the government budget, focusing particular criticism upon the scale of resources funneled into the presidency.[54]

By 1977 Mobutu was confiding to his intimates that survival of the regime would require a more repressive response to challengers. This was evident in the treason trial of Nguza Karl-i-Bond, then the number two figure in the regime.[55] Nguza received the death sentence (commuted) on charges which persuaded few; most observers felt his real crime was to have been designated as a likely successor to Mobutu by the Western press during the 1977 Shaba crisis. Further repressiveness was manifest in February 1978 in the grisly public execution of fourteen alleged leaders of a millenial sect in Bandundu, which had come into conflict with the state; hundreds of its followers also perished in a brutal military action against its adherents.[56] In the capital, in March 1978, a purported new plot was discovered by the regime, leading to execution of thirteen civilian and military figures.

To the external world, outside of the financial fraternity, the most visible manifestations of the Zairian crisis were the invasions of Shaba in March 1977 and May 1978 (widely known as Shaba I and Shaba II). Remnants of the Katanga gendarmes of the Tshombe secession and many more recent recruits, operating under the political label of Front pour la Libération Nationale du Congo (FLNC) from Angolan bases, struck in 1977 and 1978 in the richest copper regions of southwestern Shaba. On both occasions the FLNC scored spectacular initial successes against Zairian army detachments vastly superior in numbers and equipment. In Shaba II the FLNC even captured and held the major copper mining town Kolwezi for several days. In both instances foreign troops were summoned to oust the invaders—Moroccans in 1977, French and Belgians in 1978, each provided with United States logistical support. After Shaba II the copperbelt was garrisoned for a year by a mainly Moroccan African force.

While Mobutu derived some benefit from the astonishing array of external allies he was able to mobilize, especially in response to Shaba II, on balance these episodes were very costly. The demoralization and incapacity of the security forces were plainly evident to all. Further, it was evident that in both 1977 and 1978 the invaders had been warmly received by many.[57] The official explanation blaming the Soviets and Cubans for the invasions was not supported by persuasive evidence.[58] Rather, the crisis provoked a torrent of articles on Zaire in the Western press, almost uniformly unflattering, and some quite devastating.[59]

On the economic front, as hopes faded for short-term solutions Zaire drifted from one calamity to another. By the end of 1977 the external debt had reached $3.5 billion (including $900 million undisbursed) and the country was approximately $800 million in arrears on repayment, according to World Bank figures. Beginning in 1976 Zaire was compelled to appeal for debt rescheduling by its public and private creditors—first by a "London club" of banks in June 1976, then by a "Paris club" of governments in September (see chapter 12). In effect, temporizing solutions were found at each crisis point, providing neither real relief for Zaire nor the recovery of debts by creditors. Progressively stiffer conditions were imposed as both sets of creditors sought to tie rescheduling to compliance with International Monetary Fund (IMF) prescriptions. Zaire in extremis accepted these conditions, then proved unable to comply with them. By 1978 the regime was forced to accept an IMF-recruited team to supervise the Banque du Zaire, French personnel with a similar mission in the Ministry of Finance, and Belgian direction in the customs service and internal transportation systems. This was a long march back from the economic independence goals of the regime expansion phase.

There were, indeed, widespread doubts within and without Zaire about the capacity of the kleptocratic state to channel resources into public purposes in such a way that recovery was possible. So thoroughly had the "Zairian sickness" corroded the state apparatus that even in its hour of agony the system was unable or unwilling to prevent a massive diversion of resources into foreign holdings by the politico-mercantile class. Scandals in the coffee trade, in diamond and cobalt dealings, and in American rice aid (under Public Law 480) achieved international notoriety.

With the regime now wholly dependent on periodic salvage operations, whether political or military or economic, Mobutu faced continuous pressure for "reform." On the political side, the resourcefulness and ingenuity which had served Mobutu so well in the regime's earlier phases had not entirely vanished. In July 1977, to general surprise, he declared himself to be a preacher of democracy and the MPR to be a democratic party. Thus fully competitive elections were to be held for eighteen of the Political Bureau seats, for the entire membership of the legislature, and for newly created urban councils, all within the MPR framework. The electoral campaign provided several months of distraction, and attracted an enormous number of candidates. In 1978 and 1979 there was some leeway for the newly elected deputies to subject ministers to "interpellations." This practice was brought to an abrupt halt by Mobutu in February 1980. The short-lived era of "reform" remained largely cosmetic.

By 1980 Zaire was gripped by a profound pessimism. The decline of the state had reached a point where its capacity for recovery had become uncertain. Few could see any prospect of change under the existing regime, yet there was no visible alternative on the horizon. Still, the regime retained some of its earlier skill in dividing opponents and coopting potential rivals. Symptomatic of the surprising capacity of the regime to recuperate former individual opposition leaders was the case of Kamitatu. Once one of the regime's most prestigious opponents, Kamitatu in 1977 published in France a devastating critique of what he termed "the Zairian non-system" which "has degraded the national patrimony, is an object of ridicule"; the regime had exhibited "a policy of incoherence in all sectors of its activity, save one: the preservation of its own power."[60] Late in 1977 Kamitatu returned to Zaire to accept a modest post as research associate at the UNAZA Kinshasa campus; he became a minister in January 1980.

The life cycle of the Mobutu regime produced gradually changing images of the state itself. At its inception the New Regime could heap scorn on the First Republic as "mere anarchy unleashed upon the world," as *pagaille* incarnate. The state was weak and disorganized, but its Bula Matari potential was intact, awaiting only a strong leader to instill new discipline and purpose in its atrophied structures. During the phases of ascendancy and expansion, the state exuded an appearance of force and power. While not as effective as its colonial predecessor, the trends all pointed toward a restoration of its hegemony. This imagery was then exploded by the period of decay and crisis, in which the infirmities of the state again became conspicuous. Zairianization, radicalization, Angola, bankruptcy, the FLNC invasions—all exposed the limited competence of the state, while its legendary venality was described in chilling detail by the president himself. The state consumed the national wealth without producing justice, welfare, or security, to the helpless and demoralized bewilderment of its populace.

3

The State and Civil Society: Capital, Town, and Countryside

The changing character of the state, from Bula Matari to *pagaille*, from ascent to decline in the Mobutu years, interacted with remarkable transformations in civil society. The Bula Matari hegemon ruled over an essentially rural subject population, until its final years. Its central places were basically nodal points of European occupation. The chasm between European and African was fundamental and pervasive. Among Africans, while some differences of status and well-being existed, class differences were small; in relation to the dominant Europeans, Africans in many respects formed a single social and economic category. Until World War II ethnic differences were certainly noticed and ethnic classifications were established by Europeans, but ethnicity lacked social articulation, ideological expression, and instrumental purpose.

The postwar years brought tremendous changes to civil society, partly reflecting transformations of the state. Urbanization gained a formidable momentum, with both population and resources increasingly concentrated in the cities, above all in the capital. The rural sector experienced a prolonged deterioration in its terms of exchange with the urban economy and the state. The post-colonial state, in its various guises, profoundly affected class formation as access to state power opened the door to accumulation for a rapidly emerging politico-commercial class. Ethnicity became swiftly mobilized and politicized in the terminal colonial and *pagaille* years. Collective perceptions of the African populace as a relatively undifferentiated category (*indigènes* for Europeans, "African masses" in the nationalist ideological discourse) exploded in the face of new, far-reaching cleavages in civil society.

In this and the two following chapters we examine the social dynamics of contemporary Zairian civil society. We believe the interface with the political realm—the state—has been of particular importance in these transformations. They are, of course, reciprocal and interactive; we do not suggest that the state was a deus ex machina for all social change. But its impact has been substantial: urbanization has taken place around central points of state activity, where state resources circulate; power has been the constitutive field for emergent class relations; the political variable has played a determinative role in the activation and quiescence of ethnicity, and contributed to the definition of its categories.

We begin with an analysis of patterns of transformation in the urban and rural sectors of contemporary Zairian society. We then consider in turn civil society's cleavages along lines of class and ethnicity, in the Zairian case the two most salient forms of differentiation. In the final part of chapter 5 we explore the forces and processes through which state, class, and ethnicity are drawn together.

Five decades of change

When President Mobutu was born, in 1930, Kinshasa and Lubumbashi were cities of about 30,000 people each. No other community approached even 20,000. Victor Promontorio, a mulatto from Equateur, was about to begin his law studies in Brussels; for decades he would be the only Zairian university graduate. There were a handful of African priests, a Zairian station master in Kinshasa, a few Zairian senior clerks and skilled workers. The number of Zairians who had become permanently tied to the Bula Matari domain remained tiny. The great vehicular languages, Lingala and Swahili, were known only along the major lines of communication; their remarkable penetration of the countryside lay in the future. Kinshasa was not yet a predominantly Lingalaphone city, nor had Swahili established its hegemony in the Shaba copperbelt.

President Mobutu is a relatively young man; in his lifetime—and that of most of the political leadership—society has been transformed beyond recognition. By 1975 the capital had become a sprawling metropolis with well over 2 million inhabitants, and more than one-fifth of Zaire's population was urban. Alongside a slimmed European population, whose economic privilege remained intact, was a rapidly congealing politico-commercial Zairian bourgeoisie. A complex and fluid stratification pattern was emerging in the burgeoning central places, with a relatively static wage-labor force jostling with a poorly known but important informal sector and a large student population. Social and political competition, particularly sharp in the urban centers, had given rise to new mobilized and politicized ethnic identities, themselves multilayered and shifting. The vehicular languages were becoming mother tongues to new urban generations, and generalized multilingualism added an enigmatic dimension to the dynamics of identity formation. Civil society, as it hurtled through time and space, was continuously being redefined.

The urban explosion

The tremendous impact of the state stands out at once in the explosive growth of urban centers. This impact has occurred not only directly through the expansion of state services and employment, but also indirectly through siting of a host of service functions and consumer manufacturing around the initial state-fostered core. Larger enterprises have tended to concentrate in the capital, or to a lesser extent in the copperbelt, because of the available infrastructure and proximity to the decisional structures of the state. Of the cities listed in table 3.1, all but Likasi and Kikwit are regional capitals (and Kikwit used to be). The fantastic expansion of Mbuji—Mayi is attributable to the exodus of the Luba from Kananga and other areas in 1960 in the face of ethnic violence, and to the growth of illicit diamond production. The port and commercial functions of Matadi share with its elevation to regional capital status responsibility for its expansion. Lubumbashi is a particularly intriguing case; since the 1958 census the bulk of the copper production has shifted to Kolwezi, yet this slack has been more than compensated for by the growth of Lubumbashi's administrative and corollary service functions, as well as its informal sector.

Table 3.1 clearly demonstrates the sheer speed of urban growth. All cities except Kisangani have multiplied at least tenfold since 1940. The capital's population, which had been less than 2 percent of the national total in 1950, and 3 percent in 1958, was nearing 10 percent in the 1970 census. The overall population of the larger towns listed in table 3.1 had tripled between 1958 and 1970, whereas the total population in 1970 was 159 percent of the 1958 figure.[1]

The mushrooming of the urban sector has not been confined to the major centers. Similar patterns of population concentration are evident in smaller centers, where the predominance of administrative functions is even sharper than in major cities. While not many of the smaller centers owe their existence to mines, large plantation or forestry enterprises, or major mission stations, the great majority are subregion and zone seats, which together number nearly 200. One such town, Lisala, grew from a population of 1,757 in 1935 to 8,810 in 1958, and 27,689 in 1974; while Lisala is on the Zaire River, and thus is not as isolated as many administra-

Table 3.1   Urban Population Growth

City	1940	1950	1958	1970
Kinshasa	47,000	191,000	389,000	1,323,000
Lubumbashi	27,000	99,000	183,000	318,000
Likasi			75,000	146,000
Mbandaka	10,000	17,000	58,000	108,000
Kisangani	15,000	67,000	103,000	227,000
Bukavu	1,900	18,000	52,000	135,000
Kananga	4,900	15,000	109,000	429,000
Mbuji-Mayi			25,000	256,000
Matadi	9,000	18,000	63,000	110,000
Kikwit			13,000	112,000

Sources: Crawford Young, *Politics in the Congo* (Princeton: Princeton University Press, 1965), p. 207; "Les résultats du recensement de la population 1970 au Zaire," *Etudes Africaines du C.R.I.S.P.*, T. A., 140 (1972), pp. 9–10; Benoit Verhaegen et al., *Kisangani 1876–1976* (Kinshasa: Presses Universitaires du Zaire, 1975) 1:35; Henri Nicolai, *Le Kwilu* (Brussels: CEMUBAC, 1963), p. 393; Nzongola Ntalaja, "Urban Administration in Zaire: A Study of Kananga, 1971–73" (Ph.D. diss., University of Wisconsin–Madison, 1975).

tive centers, it has no significant productive economic base other than its role as subregion (and zone) headquarters.[2]

The human concentration has been accompanied by a resource flow into the major centers, above all into Kinshasa and, secondarily, the copperbelt towns. The capital has become an overwhelming suction pump, powered by the state, drawing up resources from below, and concentrating those originating in the external environment. Léon de St. Moulin, a distinguished demographer, has illuminated this process through a comparative study of per capita incomes in the 1958 and 1970 censuses; his findings are recapitulated in table 3.2. The censuses did not break down the figures below the provincial level. Former Kasai province has been split into the regions of Kasai Occidental and Kasai Oriental, and former Leopoldville province into the regions of Bas-Zaire, Bandundu, and Kinshasa; still, a simple extrapolation makes the significance of these figures quite clear.

In former Leopoldville province, the 72 percent increase in GNP between 1957 and 1970 was very heavily concentrated in Kinshasa. While Bas-Zaire has done better than any other rural area because of its proximity and ready access to the capital, Bandundu has suffered the same fate as the other hinterland regions. The Shaba increase has been likewise en-

Table 3.2   Per Capita Income Changes, 1957–1970

Region	(1) GNP per capita, 1970 ($)	(2) % of 1970 total	(3) % of 1970 population	(4) % increase in GNP, 1957–70	(5) % increase of population, 1957–70	(6) (4) − (5)
Kinshasa	280	17.4	6.1 ⎫		240.1 ⎫	
Bas-Zaire	114	8.3	7.0 ⎬	72	65.8 ⎬	+4.0
Bandundu	46	5.8	12.0 ⎭		34.5 ⎭	
Equateur	58	6.9	11.2	31	34.4	−3.3
Haut-Zaire	50	8.2	15.5	0	35.1	−35.1
Kivu	44	7.2	15.5	12	47.7	−35.7
Shaba	280	36.1	12.7	78	64.0	+14.0
Kasai Oriental	78	5.3	8.7 ⎫		103.9 ⎫	
Kasai Occidental	54	4.8	11.2 ⎭	53	94.5 ⎭	−45.4

Sources: Léon de St. Moulin, "La répartition par région du Produit intérieur brut zairois," Zaire-Afrique 73 (March 1973): 141–161. Columns 5 and 6 are our own calculation.

tirely situated in the copperbelt towns; the vast northern and western reaches of the region have experienced the characteristic pattern of rural decay. The apparent Kasai increase disappears when it is set against the very rapid population growth this area has experienced.

Many other indices confirm the same trend. More than 77 percent of the government-approved investment projects during the major period of capital inflow, 1967–72, were concentrated in Kinshasa and Shaba (table 3.3). In 1975, Bank of Zaire data showed that 89.7 percent of the electricity consumption was concentrated in Kinshasa and Shaba; table 3.4 gives similar figures for 1972. These two areas (with Shaba's consumption representing essentially the mineral industry) have accounted for 87 percent of the increase in power consumption since 1970. About 50 percent of the national health outlays in the early 1970s went to two Kinshasa facilities, especially the presidential showcase, Mama Yemo hospital. In 1972, 303 of 334 Zairian doctors and 40 percent of all physicians worked in Kinshasa. Meanwhile, an estimated 80 percent of the rural population was not provided with any formal health care services—and three-quarters of what was available in the countryside was provided by missions.[3]

The massive concentration of resources in Kinshasa became more conspicuous after 1973, when the country plunged into economic crisis. With imports severely restricted by the deepening foreign exchange impasse, the Kinshasa market was inevitably served first. Consumer goods remained

Table 3.3 Government-Approved Investment Projects, by Region, 1969–1972

Region	Percentage
Kinshasa	31.6
Bas-Zaire	10.38
Kivu	1.53
Shaba	46.83
Haut-Zaire	6.28
Bandundu	0.06
Equateur	1.42
Kasai Oriental	0
Kasai Occidental	0

Source: Ngoie Kapaji, "Projets d'investissement et croissance de l'économie zairoise de 1970 à 1972," *Zaire-Afrique* 70 (December 1972): 618, based in documentation of the Institut de Recherches Economiques et Sociales, Universite de Kinshasa.

Table 3.4 Power Consumption by Region, 1972

Region	Percentage of national consumption
Kinshasa	14.7
Bas-Zaire	4.1
Bandundu	0.1
Equateur	0.4
Haut-Zaire	1.9
Kivu	2.0
Shaba	75.2
Kasai Oriental	1.2
Kasai Occidental	0.4

Source: Ernest J. Wilson III, "The Political Economy of Public Corporations in the Energy Sectors of Nigeria and Zaire" (Ph.D. diss., University of California–Berkeley, 1978), p. 581, based on *Rapport annuel*, Department d'Energie, Zaire Government.

relatively available in the capital, while intense shortages developed in interior centers, where inflation was correspondingly more severe than in Kinshasa, on whose markets the national price indices were calculated. Petroleum products were a case in point; in 1977, oil company executives estimated that 14 million barrels were needed to clear the market, while only 8 million were being imported.[4] The Kinshasa market was nearly fully

Table 3.5   **Demand Bank Deposits by Region, 1971–1974 (in thousands of zaires)**

	1971		1974	
	Total	%	Total	%
Kinshasa	64,355	64.0	160,068	71.4
Shaba	20,335	21.7	34,200	15.2
Rest of country	14,183	14.3	30,050	13.4

Source: Banque du Zaire, *Rapport Annuel*, 1974, pp. 228–229.

supplied, with only infrequent moments of shortage; hinterland towns were without gasoline for weeks on end. World Bank data indicate that in 1977 some 86 percent of Kinshasa's petroleum requirements were met, while other regions received only from 45.3 percent (Kivu) to 74.7 percent (Shaba) of their needs. In that year Kinshasa consumed 53 percent of all oil products used in Zaire.[5] Black market prices for gasoline rose to $12 per gallon in the interior, nearly ten times the 1973 price.

Whereas in 1956 the capital had provided only 8.5 percent of Zairian wage employment, by 1969 20 percent of the regular jobs were in Kinshasa. About 30 percent of Zaire's total remunerations were paid in Kinshasa, and approximately 24 percent of the total government budget expenditures were effectuated in the capital.[6] By the early 1970s, more than 71 percent of the demand bank deposits were concentrated in Kinshasa (table 3.5). If data for Shaba—meaning essentially the copperbelt—are added, 90 percent of Zaire's wage employment and 77 percent of its remunerations are accounted for.[7] On a smaller scale, a similar pattern of resource flow to the lesser urban centers from the hinterlands can be observed, as Schatzberg has demonstrated.[8]

The process of resource concentration in Kinshasa and the Shaba copperbelt was further reinforced by the character of Zairian external economic linkages (see chapters 10, 12). While colonial investment had been widely distributed throughout the country, the new influx of foreign capital in 1970–74 was wholly concentrated on mineral development in Shaba, manufacturing enterprises in the capital area, and energy infrastructure to service these undertakings. Much of the investment was in fact supplied by the Zairian state, underwritten by loan capital profusely offered by Western banks, governments, and contractors. By 1975, when economic disaster had struck, the state found itself under intense and unrelenting pressure from its creditors, with no choice but to focus its meager resources upon

Table 3.6 Zairian Wage Employment, 1915–1970

Year	No. of wage earners[a]
1915	37,368
1920	125,120
1925	274,538
1926	421,953
1930	399,144
1935	377,531
1940	536,055
1945	701,101
1950	962,009
1955	1,183,000
1967	796,800
1970	934,600

Sources: Young, *Politics in the Congo*, p. 206; Banque du Zaire, *Rapport Annuel*, 1967, pp. 66–67; International Bank for Reconstruction and Development, "The Economy of Zaire," vol. 3 (1975), table 1.2.

a Excludes casual labor, part-time market traders, and rural villagers selling collected produce to plantation enterprises.

salvaging the projects to which it had become committed. This necessity all but foreclosed the possibility of significant deployment of resources to rural areas in general and to regions distant from the capital and unblessed by mineral endowment.

Remarkable changes in the structure of employment also offer valuable clues to the dynamics of urbanization and the impact of the state on that process. Total wage employment, which rose dramatically during the 1920s, then again in the postwar decade, has stagnated since that time (table 3.6). At the same time, the sectoral distribution of the wage labor force has altered radically. Since the Second World War mining has become more capital-intensive, with a consequent drop in numbers of workers employed, in spite of a considerable expansion in output (table 3.7). Consumer industries serving the urban markets have expanded, bringing some new employment. Plantations had a growing work force in the 1950s, but this wage sector has also declined since 1960. The slack has been partly taken up by a vast expansion in the number of state employees (table 3.8). In Kinshasa, the state wage bill increased by 36.8 percent from 1958 to 1966, while private sector wages shrank by 38.5 percent.[9]

Table 3.7   Sectoral Employment, 1958–1970

	1960	1967	1970
Agriculture	180,831	133,957	269,500
Mining	77,622	59,169	59,800
Industry	38,068	50,014	140,000
Construction	16,628	14,364	19,500
Transport and communication	60,172	56,697	70,000
Banks, finance, commerce	20,913	24,268	110,800
Private services			47,100
Government	167,900	290,500	274,000
Education	37,300	60,000	75,600
Military	23,100	53,000	63,000
Aggregate employment	562,134	628,969	997,600

Sources: Banque du Zaire, *Rapport Annuel*, 1967, pp. 66–69; International Bank for Reconstruction and Development, "Economy of Zaire," vol. 3 (1975), table 1.2.

Note: The figures for 1960 and 1967 were drawn from the 1967 Banque du Zaire annual report, while those for 1970 are from the World Bank report on the Zairian economy. The differences between the totals in the last row and the sums of the figures above them are largely artifacts resulting from the use of differing classification systems for agricultural and commercial sector employment, and from the absence of a private service category in the Banque du Zaire tables.

Table 3.8   Public Sector Employment of Zairians, 1960–1978

	1960	1967	1970	1975	1978
Civil service personnel (full status)	11,500	26,500	26,200	21,500	
Contract personnel	96,000	150,000	99,900	105,800	
Teachers	37,300	60,000	75,600	143,400	230,100
Military[a]	23,100	53,000	63,000	70,000	
Total	167,900	289,500	264,700	340,700	410,700[b]

Sources: Banque du Zaire, *Rapport Annuel*, 1967, p. 72; International Bank for Reconstruction and Development, *Zaire: Current Economic Situation and Constraints* (Washington, 1980), p. 79.

a The 1960 figure does not include the national police; the 1967, 1970, and 1975 data do include them. None of the figures include local police employed by collectivities and localities.

b Except for teachers, breakdown of total not available.

The most rapidly expanding segment of the public sector has been the school system: the number of teachers expanded from 37,300 to 143,400 between 1960 and 1975, then soared to 230,100 by 1978.[10] By the 1970s education was consuming nearly a quarter of the state budget. The expansion of the educational system was in large measure an urban phenomenon, especially at post-primary levels, and now constitutes an essential but little-noted vector in the urbanization process. A substantial fraction of city populations is comprised of school pupils. De St. Moulin discovered that in Kinshasa 49 percent of the 20-year-old age cohort was still enrolled in the educational establishment.[11] Schatzberg found that 36 percent of the Lisala populace in 1974 was attending schools, and has subsequently demonstrated that this figure is quite representative not only for Zaire, but for other African states.[12] The necessity of migrating to town to find post-primary study opportunities has been an exceedingly potent factor in the rural exodus; whether or not pupils are able to complete the junior or senior secondary cycles, few young persons return to the village community, at least not in the years of young adulthood.

The gap between the swelling population and the stagnant employment market in Zairian cities has been filled by the burgeoning informal sector.[13] The emergence of this sector was retarded by the colonial state, which till the late 1950s maintained relatively effective urban influx controls and a tentacular regulatory net around the towns, choking off both petty trade outside prescribed channels and "anarchic" housing construction. The sheer geographical expansion of large cities, such as Kinshasa since 1960, has spawned a host of new activities outside the formal employment sector: taxi and private bus services (using nondescript vehicles), housing construction, secondary neighborhood markets, bars, errand services, casual domestic services, petty artisanship and trading (tailoring, bicycle repair, shoe repair, for instance), petty retailing of beverages or charcoal. Beyond these more or less legitimate activities, many have subsisted on more devious activities involving stolen property or other illicit goods. Not only has the informal sector provided the sole means of livelihood for an indeterminate but substantial number of people but many who have held regular wage employment derive supplementary income from such pursuits. In cities near borders (Kinshasa, Lubumbashi, Bukavu, Kolwezi, for example), diverse smuggling occupations have become important revenue sources.

The wage structure suggests why this informal sector activity is necessary. In 1967 the legal minimum wage set the ceiling for the majority of wage earners. Some 56 percent of the wage earners earned no more than 110 percent of the legal minimum, and 77 percent received no more than 130 percent of this figure.[14] The average monthly household expenditure, Z 32.83, was more than twice the legal minimum monthly wage of Z 12, suggesting that most households had additional sources of revenue. Food represented two-thirds of expenditures, and 55.9 percent of the households went hungry at least five days per month. On the other hand, the level of beer consumption was quite remarkable; the two Kinshasa breweries sold 894,222 hectoliters per year, worth $17 million, which averaged $8 per household ($2 = 1Z, 1967–74). Schtazberg demonstrates that Zairian beer consumption rose from 1.70 liters per capita in 1946 to 10.07 in 1960 and to 20.60 in 1973.[15] Beer consumption has been much heavier in towns than in villages, both because of relative price and availability. Its magnitude in the urban sector is suggestive of the supplementary resources entering households beyond wages.

Another important indicator of urban change has been the dramatic change in sex ratios in cities. Despite the policy of urban labor stabilization undertaken in response to the labor crisis in the 1920s, throughout the colonial period males significantly outnumbered females in the towns. The pattern has shifted significantly since independence; the trend indicated for Kananga in table 3.9 has been general throughout the country.

This change has occurred in spite of the very large educational handicaps faced by women: in 1961–62 only 13.8 percent of the secondary school students were female, and the figure was still only 18.9 percent in 1967–68.[16] Women have found income opportunities in trade; a 1967 Kinshasa survey discovered that 35.2 percent of the wives in the households surveyed had regular earnings, primarily in the market.[17] However, it is apparent from the Kananga figures that many of the urban women are not married. Nzongola suggests an explanation:

> Whereas rural men see few opportunities in the "unexploding" urban economies of Zaire, rural women and those living in small towns perceive the immense possibilities of emancipation and economic independence offered by the big city. A Zairian woman can, simply by virtue of her looks, become relatively well-off overnight as a second wife or a mistress of an important man or, in a modest way, as a *femme libre*, with possibilities for travel and trading activities in the region or across the whole country.[18]

By assembling these different trends and processes we may suggest that a novel form of urban society has been crystallizing in Zaire, in which pro-

Table 3.9   Sex Ratios of Adult Zairians in Kananga, 1955–1972

	% males	% females	Sex ratio
1955	59.7	40.3	148.4
1957	52.5	47.5	110.4
1970	48.1	51.9	92.7
1972	46.8	53.2	87.9

Source: Nzongola, *Urban Administration in Zaire*, p. 94, citing Ministry of Interior census reports.
Note: Adults are persons 19 years or older.

ductive enterprises, at least in the classical sense, play only a minor role as an economic motor force. Perhaps the extreme case is the second-largest city, Kananga, which had only 10,000 wage earners in 1973 out of a population of 429,000.[19] The most decisive force fueling the growth of the urban activity has been the state itself, particularly if we include in this concept the fast-growing educational system, which not only accounts for the most rapidly enlarging pool of jobs, but whose pupil clientele constitute the biggest single category of urban residents. Around the state core a vast panoply of secondary redistributive activities has grown up, with the state serving directly or indirectly as financier. The largest single payroll has been that of the state. Even more important has been an indirect state impact through improper diversion of its resources or illicit exercise of its authority—unreceipted fines, petty payments to obtain state services, which then recycle into speculative commercial endeavors—taxis, housing construction, bars. The urban population has not only swollen but stabilized. Not only have the cohorts of urban-born children been swiftly expanding, but the average length of city residence has increased. In Kisangani, by 1973 the average city dweller had been in the town for more than ten years, and 30 percent of the city's population had arrived before independence—a figure all the more remarkable when one considers that the population had more than doubled since 1960.[20]

While the Zairian city has been dependent upon the state, the state has been in part hostage to the city. To limit its wage bill and dampen urban unrest, the government has held down the fixed prices paid to rural producers for food and for export crops. Faced with these disincentives, villagers have declined to expand food output to match the rhythm of urban growth. The government has been increasingly forced to turn to international markets to obtain food supplies for the cities. Whereas in 1959 Zaire had a small favorable trade balance on food products, by 1977 the food import bill was $300 million, consuming one-third of the foreign exchange.

The risk of major disorder, above all in the capital, has been an ever-looming menace. Very large detachments of security forces are permanently garrisoned in the Kinshasa region. The regime has long seen the pace of urban growth as malignant, and has devised a series of inefficacious therapies. The common theme has been the forced return of the "unemployed" to rural areas, where the ennobling task of cultivation awaits them. Needless to say, few have responded to the appeal; evasion of this kind of edict is one of the first survival skills the new urbanite develops.

Here we see illustrated the contradiction between the apparent power and scope of the state's regulatory claims and its empirical frailties. A yawning gap lies between its goals and its capacities, into which many of its more cherished policies have tumbled. Shipping out urban population deemed surplus—above all, adult males without wage employment—would have required an exceedingly fine-meshed administrative screen. Most individuals have been able to swim through the tattered net periodically thrown over the urban unemployed, if need be by placing a strategic *pot-de-vin* (bribe) that caused the strands to part. While the state has not shrunk from coercion, it has had neither the ability nor the will to approach the problem with Cambodian-style determination. Short of this, hortatory appeals for a return to the land have at once encountered the powerful currents of a perceived advantage in urban residence.

Rural exodus: poverty and deprivation

Immigration to the cities is of course only another way of saying emigration from the countryside, and in our search to understand the huge increase in the urban population we must explore "push" factors as well as the "pull" factors that have drawn Zairians to the cities. The flight from the countryside is not a new problem; it first became visible during World War II. Colonial circles generally recognized that the harsh, extractive measures imposed on the peasantry in the name of the war effort played a large part in that flight. These pressures slackened in the final colonial years, and the welfare apparatus of the state, joined with that of the missions, was extended into the countryside, without appreciably slowing the rhythm of urban migration.

After independence a number of factors diminished the relative attraction of rural life for those with a serious option of migration—essentially the young population. In the First Republic period villages had little protection against various armed bands—military, police, party youth groups, insurgents. Although most insurgents disappeared after the consolidation of the New Regime, there remained the problem of diverse security forces (MPR youth and disciplinary brigades, gendarmes, soldiers, local police) who believed that their inadequate supplies and irregular pay entitled— even compelled—them to live off the land. The deterioration of rural road networks made trading posts in the bush unprofitable, and greatly raised the effective price of commodities which could not be locally produced. Government-fixed prices lagged far behind inflation, and the state's proclivity for granting monopolies to buyers of major cash crops restricted benefits which cultivators might have derived from the growing shortage of food crops. The real value of the services supplied to the rural sector, particularly those of the highly valued health facilities, declined sharply; medical supplies for village dispensaries became exceedingly rare. Although their number was increased, rural schools faced insurmountable supply problems, and teachers were frequently demoralized by pay arrearages. Amenities supplied through the mission network fared much better than those of the state, but the church systems lacked the resources to expand. Finally, the growing venality of the rural capillaries of the state administration, reflecting problems whose origins lay in the nature of the state, made the state-village nexus primarily one of oppressive extraction rather than an exchange of fiscal contribution for valued service.

The motivations for migration are undoubtedly complex; the abundance of explanatory hypotheses bears witness to this. However, Bates offers convincing testimony that the bottom line contains a cost-benefit calculation of material advantage.[21] It is not difficult to understand why, for a young Zairian with some education, the risk of uncertain employment and urban insecurity is far outweighed by the manifold obstacles to wresting a life beyond the subsistence level in the rural sphere.

The deteriorating terms of trade between the urban centers and the rural periphery in Zaire deserve closer scrutiny, as the sociopolitical implications of the continuing rural exodus and (in effect) the refusal of the countryside to feed the towns are far-reaching. The evidence is somewhat scattered; there have been only a few careful field inquiries into rural change in recent years. However, the findings from different areas are completely concordant, and when combined with the evidence of less systematic interviews leave little doubt as to overall patterns.

We should first note that there are a few zones which have escaped the general trend of impoverishment, of which the most important is Bas-Zaire, especially the region between Kinshasa and Mbanza–Ngungu (Thysville). The explosive growth of Kinshasa, especially after independence, opened commercial opportunities far more favorable than those available in most interior areas. Ndongola documents the swift response: between 1959 and 1963 cultivated areas in Bas-Zaire increased from 77,495 hectares to 147,692; food shipments from this area to Kinshasa rose from 40,000 tons to 125,000 annually by road, and from 26,000 tons to 55,817 by rail.[22]

There have been a few other islands of relative rural prosperity. In the Bumba zone on the upper Zaire river, a modest center of rice production expanded output from around 11,000 tons annually in the 1950s to 23,000 tons in 1970, and to 28,000 tons in 1971; in that time the number of planters almost doubled.[23] In the diamond-mining areas of Kasai Oriental, a flourishing clandestine diamond production developed in the 1960s, which was commercialized through West African trading intermediaries; by 1967 exploitation had reached a level estimated by mining company executives to be equal to the official annual production of 12–14 million carats.[24] Kanyinda notes that Luba chiefs complained bitterly about the ease with which "young Luba adventurers acquired money, to become drunkards, headstrong and disobedient."[25] Small areas of high-value crop production—arabica coffee, tea, pyrethrum, quinine, as well as vegetables—could be found in eastern Kivu.

Much more characteristic is the situation chronicled by Ewert in an invaluable study conducted in 1973–75 in the Kwilu area of southwestern Zaire. From a carefully executed survey and patiently conducted group discussions carried out over a two-year period by a community development team there emerged a lucid village consciousness among the villagers of the situation in which they found themselves. Farmers' grievances centered around four points: lack of money, unreliable and venal marketing outlets for their main cash crop (palm oil), inflated prices for consumer goods and declining real values for their produce, and high taxation levels.[26] Similar grievances are encountered in most of rural Zaire.

Many factors have discouraged Zairian villagers from the dangerous and difficult work of scaling oil palms to harvest their fruits. Trucks from the palm oil companies pass by infrequently to purchase palm fruits and nuts; the former deteriorate rapidly in value once cut. For the companies, collection costs have been increased by the very poor condition of the roads, which has sharply raised maintenance costs on vehicles. And not only has the reliability of marketing arrangements diminished, but the incidence of dishonesty has increased; in the words of the palm cutters studied by Ewert,

> The people in Kinshasa [i.e., the owners of the palm oil company] send our money to Kikwit. The accountant in Kikwit first takes his share for himself and then sends the rest to the oil press. The manager of the oil press takes part of what is left for himself and gives the rest to the *capita* who is supposed to pay us. The *capita* takes his share so there is almost nothing left for us . . . If you cut 14 cases of nuts in a month, you will only be paid for three and the *capita* will tell you that the rest spoiled, but actually, they all stole the money.

When the Kwilu villagers considered using state courts to enforce their rights, their chances of success were deemed small. One middle-aged farmer offered the following analysis to a community meeting:

> What? We the people of the village accuse an accountant, a manager, or a *capita*? Yes we can. We can go to Kikwit and accuse the people who steal our money, but do you know what will happen? These people with the money will go to the court and pay off the judge and nothing will happen to them. But they will also have us who accused them thrown into jail for having accused them. First *they* steal our money and then if we say anything, they have *us* put in jail.[27]

The perception of declining returns for cash agriculture in the village is completely accurate not only for the Kwilu communities studied by Ewert, but for most Zairian villages. We may compare real prices for agricultural commodities, derived from the International Monetary Fund data by Gran (table 3.10), with Ewert's evidence on Kwilu prices for consumer goods of the type sold in the villages (table 3.11). Prices in table 3.11 apply to the regional center of Kikwit; retail prices in the villages studied by Ewert, several dozen kilometers distant, were from 33 to 50 percent higher. The much higher costs in the villages reflected the very high costs of transportation, a result in part of the deterioration of rural feeder roads. The Kikwit figures are representative of general patterns in smaller rural centers outside the immediate Kinshasa and Shaba copperbelt zones. The combination of steadily decreasing returns for peasant produce (table 3.10) and simultaneously increasing prices for the kinds of commodities peas-

Table 3.10   Index of Government-Fixed Agricultural Prices, 1960–1974
             (June 1967 = 100)

	1960	1970	1974
Maize, Shaba and Kasai	114.9	100.7	96.0
Manioc, Western zone	126.4	75.6	36.0
Rice	157.9	109.2	104.0
Beans	137.9	90.7	43.2
Cotton (first quality)	172.4	85.0	67.5
Palm oil, except in Bas-Zaire	241.4	79.3	64.8
Robusta coffee, Bandundu	195.4	90.7	64.8
Arabica coffee	202.0	93.9	52.4

Source: Guy Gran, ed., *The Political Economy of Underdevelopment* (New York: Praeger, 1979), p. 5, based on IMF data.

ants need to purchase (table 3.11) well illustrates the growing squeeze on the village.

The state has continued to enforce not only low prices, but production quotas. Ewert recounts a confrontation between the collectivity chief and the locality chief of the villages he surveyed; the former bitterly attacked the locality chief for the "laziness" of the villagers, and warned that, "unless the villagers began cutting palm nuts immediately, he would dispatch a group of policemen to the area and they would force the people to work." [28]

In their exchange these Zairian administrators reflected the deeply ingrained bureaucratic habits derived from the colonial legacy. Regier, who spent years doing community development work in Kasai Occidental, recalls his encounter in the 1955–57 period with the local Belgian agricultural agent, known as the "cotton man" for the vigor of his efforts to enforce acreage quotas and to induce the use of insecticides: "That the use of force was very much a part of his professional life was evidenced by the fear the local villagers had of him. They called him *Tambua* (The Lion) because of his fearsome tactics. Further evidence were the scars he proudly showed me on his knuckles. He said they came from 'pushing people's teeth down their throats.'" [29]

As in the colonial era, coercion has been applied not only through acreage quotas, but also through taxation. All adult household heads were required to pay a *contribution personnelle minimum* (successor to the colonial head tax), which in the early 1970s was Z 3.5 annually, and an additional "small tax" of Z 1 and party dues of 20 makuta.

Table 3.11   Consumer Goods Prices, Kikwit (Bandundu), 1968–1976
(prices in makuta, then valued at 50 makuta = $1)

	1968	1970	1972	1974	1976
Sardines, 125 gm can	11.8	10.0	13.0	15.0	29.0
Powdered milk, 454 gms	53.3	54.5	68.0	97.5	150.0
Kerosene, 75 cl.	5.6	4.5	6.0	7.0	10.0
Box of wooden matches	1.0	1.0	2.0	2.0	3.0
Wax cloth, 6 yds.	472.0	539.0	744.0	980.0	1,800.0

Source: David Merrill Ewert, "Freire's Concept of Critical Consciousness and Social Structure in Zaire" (Ph.D. diss., University of Wisconsin–Madison, 1977), p. 170.

In addition to relatively heavy direct local taxation, peasant incomes have been affected by other state fiscal and economic policies. Substantial export taxes are levied on all cash crops destined for foreign markets. Although villagers may not perceive the incidence of this taxation, in the final analysis it is paid by the peasant producer. The extent of this fiscal burden is illustrated by the palm oil case; palm oil is the major cash crop in the Kwilu area. In 1975 the World Bank listed five different taxes on this commodity: (1) export duty, from 2 to 15% of export value, depending on the price level; (2) a turnover tax of 6.75% of export value; (3) a research tax of 2%; (4) a statistical tax of 1%; (5) an inspection tax of 20 makuta per ton.[30] State pricing policy, designed to assure a low-cost supply of palm oil for cooking in urban centers, has created a de facto tax as well. The palm oil price, held stable from 1967 to 1975, applied to the domestic market only, but the government forced palm oil companies to sell at least half of their output on the domestic market at prices far below prevailing international levels. This policy not only drove a number of palm oil companies out of production, thus diminishing the number of buyers for village palm produce, but also drove down prices paid by companies to villagers.

Import duties have ranged from 12 to 68 percent; prices of some goods—clothes, household and farm implements—are affected by these duties. The state also levies a turnover tax at each stage of the distribution chain—a fiscal charge automatically incorporated into consumer prices.

School fees have been a quasi-fiscal charge, although they do purchase a direct service. Villagers have well understood the link between education and social mobility, and have seen that schooling represents their children's only hope of escape from the poverty trap—and, ideally, some old age security for the parents. In the Kwilu villages studied by Ewert, primary schooling was accessible, with a fee of only Z 1 per pupil per year, though there was likely to be informal payments to the principal and the teacher for enrollment and for passing to the next grade. Such payments often took the form of gifts in kind—firewood, building materials, or food—or forced, unpaid labor on school buildings or housing for teachers. Hopes of real mobility required going beyond a rural primary education to at least secondary schooling; and fees at secondary schools were Z 13–15 per year, while informal payments to school directors were often higher than tuition.

Beyond regular fiscal charges and levies for services, taxation through penal mechanisms has been a significant drain on Zairian village resources. Failure to plant acreage quotas or to participate in required unpaid labor on state projects, or contravention of sanitary regulations (a nonconforming latrine, for example) can bring fines of Z 5 or 10. Even more burdensome have been the illegal taxes levied by government agents: roads throughout the country are laced with roadblocks erected by army units, party youth groups, or local police, at which peasants may be asked to produce their identity cards, MPR cards, or even documents demonstrating ownership of animals being transported to market, and at which fines may be levied or produce confiscated for alleged contraventions.[31] Newbury reports an episode that took place in 1982 in eastern Kivu, where there had been a multiplication of local illicit taxes on women cultivators who were transporting their cassava to market on foot. In the ten kilometers to market, three different levies were imposed at stream crossings where barriers could not be evaded. These fiscal impositions were rendered intolerable by the perception that, in contrast to earlier times when taxes paid for road maintenance, "as far as the women could tell, the money collected from the tax was being used for no evident public good." When this grievance was joined to their recognition of a steadily declining exchange value for their cassava, they were driven to the unprecedented act of collective and militant female protest.[32]

Precise calculations of the fiscal pressure of the state on the peasantry are impossible to make, as the incidence of indirect taxes—export duties, or artificially low agricultural prices imposed by government decision, not to mention illicit taxation—is beyond the range of exact measurement. It does not seem an exaggeration to estimate that as much as 50 percent of real and potential village income is extracted by the state or its representatives.

To put this heavy fiscal impact in perspective, table 3.12 provides reliable figures on the actual income distribution in a representative set of vil-

Table 3.12   Income per Month by Sex, Rural Bandundu
             Sample, 1973–1975 (%)

Monthly income	Women (N = 51)	Men (N = 49)
None	11.8	16.3
Z 1–3	51.0	24.5
Z 4–6	29.4	32.7
Z 7–9	5.9	12.2
Z 10 or more	0	2.0

Source: Ewert, "Freire's Concept of Critical Consciousness,"
p. 120.

lages. One may note that more than half earned less than Z 3 (then worth $6 officially) per month; the mean annual income was Z 36.24 for women, and Z 54.48 for men.

This remarkably high level of extraction persists in part through inertial force; the sundry fiscal and regulatory habits and mentalities of the Bula Matari state live on. Indirect taxation benefits from its relative invisibility, for few villagers understand the operation of the export or turnover taxes. What is widely recognized is the decline of the value of services rendered and amenities provided by the state, at least in contrast to those made available by the welfare state of the 1950s, which serve as a reference point. Only unremitting pressure by the New Regime can sustain its impositions. Local representatives of the state apply the leverage of coercion partly because of pressures from those higher in the hierarchy, but partly also—perhaps primarily—because their own survival is at stake. Local administrations must collect enough in taxes and fines to provide their own salaries; the extent to which bureaucratic energies are consumed by this ceaseless battle has been demonstrated for rural settings by Schatzberg and for urban settings by Nzongola.

The degree of coercion necessary is illustrated by figures for prison sentences imposed from 1969 to 1974 in the Lisala zone. A large fraction of the offenses were directly related to enforcement of state authority, and about 25 percent dealt directly or indirectly with infractions of agricultural regulations. The total of 12,571 prison sentences is placed in perspective if we note that the zone's population is approximately 150,000; of these, about half are children. The great majority of the prison sentences were imposed on men, which means that the actual pool of potential regulation-breakers was roughly 37,500. We should also note that these figures take cognizance only of those infractions prosecuted through the local tribunals. In many instances agricultural officers, sanitary agents, or local officials will impose a fine on the spot, which will never appear in statistical records if they then choose not to turn the proceeds over to the local state treasury.

In the face of such pressures, the typical response of Zairian villagers has been to flee. In a curious inversion of the response to the impositions of the Congo Free State, they usually flee not away from the transportation routes, but toward the towns. This is the major "push factor" involved in rural-urban migration.

On occasion, of course, rural people have responded to oppression with neither passivity nor flight, but with resistance. In 1959–60 the slackening of coercive controls by the Bula Matari state led to the explosive externalization of accumulated rural grievances, which provided, in many regions, much of the motor force of Zairian nationalism.[33] In 1964–65, faced with a weak and disorganized state and already bitterly disappointed by the discovery that, for villagers, the gift of independence was an empty box, rural populations in many parts of the country responded to the call to insurrection.[34] No such response has been possible under the New Regime, and while the early Mobutu years offered some new hope, discouragement and resignation have set in during the years of decay.

Astride the changing relationship between city and countryside has stood the state. No theme has been more prominent in the ideological liturgy of the New Regime than a commitment to the rural sector. Soon after taking office President Mobutu proclaimed the slogan *retroussons les manches* (let's roll up our sleeves) and a concomitant return to work on the land. Nineteen sixty-eight was designated the "year of agriculture"; a few years later agriculture was labelled the "priority of priorities." In his "ten scourges" speech of 4 January 1975 the president stigmatized "the agricultural crisis which sacrificed the peasantry to industry," and pledged that agricultural production brigades would be formed to repair this neglect. The 1977 Mobutu Plan once again denounced the agrarian impasse, and called for a massive infusion of new resources in the countryside. The dangers of hypertrophic urban development, and the attendant evils of unemployment and crime, were excoriated with equal regularity.

Yet the impact of the state on rural-urban relationships has been quite contrary to the expressed intent. The concentration of state resources and services in the urban sector—above all in the capital—on the one hand, and the high extraction from and low return of services and amenities to the rural hinterland on the other, have continuously reproduced the twin crises of rural decline and urban explosion. The state repeatedly proclaims its will to halt the rural exodus, yet seems quite helpless to arrest trends fostered by its own acts, conscious and unconscious.

In sum, the unequal dialectic of the urban-rural relationship, with its enormous implications for the future of society and polity, finds its motor force in the inequality of resource distribution between these two sectors. Inequality is the bedrock of any complex society; what has analytical importance is the set of social groupings founded upon the unequal command of resources and the relationship of the set to the structures of state power. These factors constitute the bridge that leads us from the urban-rural relationship to the dynamics of Zairian class formation.

4

The Dynamics of Inequality: Class Formation

Once upon a time God, who created the world, decided to reward his sons living on this earth. He warned them in advance that he would throw down from heaven two packages containing the different rewards.

On the day agreed upon the packages were thrown down from heaven. The elder son rushed forward to the bigger package, leaving the smaller one to the younger son.

The two packages were opened in front of the assembly, [which was] filled with wonder. The bigger package contained French, a very good French. The smaller package contained money, a lot of money and the necessary skills to increase its amount.

The elder son is the ancestor of the intellectuals. These master French and speak a refined French, indeed. But they eat cow skin. The younger son is the ancestor of the traders. They speak little French, if any. But they were rewarded with the money and with the skills to increase its amount.

The history of Butembo is the history of a battle between these two packages.

Popular parable, Butembo, Kivu, 1980[1]

The Butembo parable projects as a genesis fable a contemporary folk perception of social cleavage. To the Zairian anthropologist who encountered it on returning to his home area after a five-year absence, the parable was new. Indeed, it rested upon a novel configuration of locally dominant classes. In Butembo a new group of locally recruited, successful merchants (the money package), based in the burgeoning informal economy, had become the most wealthy and powerful group; the local representatives of the state (the French package) faced eroding standing and influence as a consequence of the decline of the state. In the folk sociology of Butembo, class formation is rooted in possession of French or money, an intuition which compares honorably with the insights reflected in more academic categories, such as mode of production or occupational rank.

In Zaire the two most salient and persistent cleavages within civil society are class and ethnicity. Both are related—class most directly—to patterns of inequality, actual or perceived, and to the struggle for resources within the arena primarily bounded by the state. The character of class and ethnic relationships is reflected in the state itself; in turn, the state partly determines the outcomes of class and ethnic competition, and even the categories in which class and ethnic cleavages are expressed.[2]

On the concept of class

We conceive of a "class" as a social aggregate within the polity, defined by its common role, function, and status within a socioeconomic setting primarily bounded by the nation-state, but influenced by the external arena. Unlike ethnicity, class is above all an analytic construct, although it may become a subjective collectivity as well, as classes are to a degree in industrial societies.[3] Like ethnicity, class is relational; both objectively and subjectively it is a device for ordering a social universe. The international political economy, the domestic economic structure, and the state are motor forces of class formation, not necessarily in that order.[4] Economic differentiation is the most salient aspect, but not the only one. Class differentiation may originate in divergent access to status or power or in unequal command of societal resources. The several dimensions of class formation are interactive; unequal political power may be transformed into high levels of economic differentiation, or vice versa. Finally, class is a dynamic phenomenon, not a static one, and is in a continuous flux shaped by context and situation. These definitional reflections are not intended as a lexical innovation, but only as a means of clarifying our own usage, drawn from a small fraction of the vast literature.

There is a marked tension between the specificity of a particular national society in space and time and the universality of the categories of class analysis. We feel that appropriate classifications of social groups must derive inductively from the political universe under consideration (although the boundaries of that universe need not coincide with those of the state). At the same time, such classifications are necessarily influenced both ideologically and analytically by the dominant categories of class analysis applied elsewhere (as well as by the effects of the international arena upon the given polity); so deeply embedded are these conventional labels (despite the variety of definitions) that they serve as inescapable orienting metaphors. Whatever the methodological premises of the investigator, such terms as "bourgeoisie" (ruling class, elite, middle class), "proletariat" (workers, wage earners), and "peasants" (villagers, smallholders) are an inevitable part of the subconscious cognitive structure. Through the ideologies of the contemporary world, and the powerful impact of various Marxist schools, as theory and praxis these mental constructs of society have gained wide diffusion among the politicized sectors of the population, as well as among observers. Ossowski has cogently observed that "facts are powerless against stereotypes supported by emotional activations. An intellectual scheme that is rooted in the social consciousness may within certain limits successfully withstand the test of reality."[5]

In Zaire, we are struck by tremendous alterations in stratification patterns since the 1950s, the swift changes of fortune experienced by particular social categories, and the changing meaning over time of particular class labels. In treating class as a dynamic concept, we have found the contextual framework developed by Schatzberg especially suggestive. He argues that whereas social classes change as the sociopolitical context changes, the class characteristics of the individual are even more contradictory and changeable: "The individual actor can, and does, belong to different class alliances at the same time . . . The degree of class identity will vary depending upon the geographical, social, political, and economic junctures of the moment in question."[6] We share with Schatzberg the desire to capture the process of flux and change in class formation and interaction. With this goal in mind, we will consider the social categories of particular importance in the Zairian political process, the relationships among them, and the degree of class consciousness each possesses.

Categorizing Zairian classes

We believe that the technique of interrogating the social consciousness to identify the operative categories of social class has fruitful possibilities. In a seminal article Nzongola brings together the folk perceptions of Zairian stratification and the more conventional categories of class terminology. "Five words," he writes, "are ordinarily used in the press and in conversations as categories of social stratification . . . chômeurs, intellectuels, commercants, villageois, and travailleurs."[7] These translate into a lumpenproletariat, national bougeoisie, petty bourgeoisie, peasantry, and proletariat. The two top categories in the Nzongola list, *intellectuels* and *commercants*, coincide with the two "packages" of the folk parable in Butembo.

Other authors have suggested classifications of Zairian social groups in the post-independent context. Coméliau offers a taxonomy very similar to

Table 4.1 Stratification and Class in Zaire

Nzongola's "Zairian social vocabulary"		Coméliau	Lacroix
		Foreign minority	Foreign corporate managers Foreign settlers Foreign salaried employees
National bourgeoisie (politicians, bureaucrats, wealthy traders)	(*Intellectuels*)	Bourgeoisie	Public officials (politicians, administrators, military personnel)
Petty bourgeoisie (clerks, teachers, soldiers)	(*Commercants*)	Sub-bourgeoisie Traders	Intermediaries Local producers (truck farmers, artisans, transporters)
Workers	(*Travailleurs*)	Urban workers Rural wage earners	Export industry workers (miners) Domestic industry workers
Lumpenproletariat	(*Chômeurs*)	Unemployed	
Peasants	(*Villageois*)	Peasants	Cash farmers

Sources: Georges N. Nzongala, "The Bourgeoisie and Revolution in the Congo," *Journal of Modern African Studies* 8, no. 4 (December 1970): 520; Christian Coméliau, *Fonctions économiques et pouvoir politique* (Kinshasa: Institut de Recherches Economiques et Sociales, 1965), p. 74; Jean Lacroix, *L'industrialisation au Congo* (Paris: Mouton, 1966), p. 200.

that of Nzongola, except for the addition of the foreign minority as a distinct group, and a distinction between urban and rural workers.[8] Lacroix, an economist informed by the sociological literature, produces a longer list based more upon economic function, and less influenced by the classical categories of class analysis.[9] (For a juxtaposition of these classifications, see table 4.1.)

The classifications of Nzongola, Coméliau, and Lacroix may be compared with the categories developed by revolutionary analysis during the Mulele uprising of 1963–64—the most ideological of rebellions. In the partisan camps Mulele, influenced by his contact with Marxist–Leninist thought, created a social catechism which distinguished between the poles of wealthy oppressors and exploited masses, a fourfold division: (1) foreign imperialists who extracted the wealth of the country; (2) *reaction-*

naires or the politicians and their bureaucratic collaborators who facilitated the pillage; (3) *retardataires*, or persons in intermediate positions, such as teachers and clerks, who failed to perceive their exploitation; and (4) the *masses populaires*, above all the peasants or villagers.[10] Evident once again is the impact of ideologies on class analysis, in this instance filtered through the rural perceptual screen. While visibly inspired by world revolutionary thought, Mulele faced the practical necessity of using a social vocabulary readily understandable to his village partisans.

The differences as well as the similarities among the categories of the four men are instructive. While Nzongola is in the Marxist tradition of scholarship, Lacroix developed his list more inductively, basing it upon economic functions. Mulele's concept was intended as a moral charter for revolutionary action; in this sense it is a lineal descendant of the portrayal of class in *The Communist Manifesto*.

More recently, as new patterns of dependent economic linkages with the West came to partly eclipse those bequeathed by the colonial legacy, and as the spectacular enrichment of Zaire's dominant politico-commercial class contrasted ever more sharply with the pauperization of the populace, analytical attention focussed increasingly on the politically ascendant group. Verhaegen, in developing a theory of "technological imperialism," lays particular stress on the university-trained generation that has come to dominate the upper strata of the state apparatus in the New Regime era. As presumed porters of technocratic skills, the degree-holding stratum was to displace the "incompetent" and "corrupt" office-holding class of the First Republic, whose dereliction led to the *pagaille* state. These custodians of technocracy, Verhaegen argues, became the intermediaries for "technological imperialism," a veritable faustian pact in which foreign capital foisted upon the Zairian state exotic, costly, and above all unprofitable technologies. The profit, shared by international capital and the technocratic class with its political overlayer, came entirely on the transaction; the long-term loss was inflicted upon the Zairian state in the form of debts, and ultimately upon the mass of the populace whose standard of living was lowered.[11]

Gould argues that corruption in Zaire is the transmission belt linking external and internal processes of class formation. The cockpit of venality is the state, whose bureaucracy (broadly defined) becomes an internal hegemonic class and the faithful ally of the "international bourgeoisie." This overly schematic conceptualization, while sparkling in its morphology of corruption, does not offer a very discriminating framework for detailed class analysis.[12]

More useful, and particularly influential in recent class-centered analysis, is Rymenam's presentation of the Zairian state bourgeoisie as a three-layered class:

> (1) The presidential clique: This is composed of members of the presidential family, and some docile auxiliaries, generally foreign Africans. It includes some dozens of persons who head the most important economic enterprises, or control the most delicate slots in the political and military structures.
>
> Their opportunities for corruption are virtually unlimited, and their impunity is total and guaranteed. Incompetence is general.
>
> The only visible sign of presidential authority over them is their periodic reshuffle, so that even in the presidential family there are no solid fiefdoms. The fate of this clique is completely linked to that of the president.
>
> (2) The reigning fraternity: It is recruited especially from the ethnic group . . . and region of the president . . . The fraternity also includes personalities from other regions, chosen for their representivity , , , or their competence . . .
>
> The members of the fraternity, who number several hundred, occupy almost all the important political, economic, and administrative posts, but no position is guaranteed. Periodic rotation is the rule.
>
> Entry to the fraternity is marked by the grant of spectacular presidential gifts (Mercedes cars, sumptuous houses . . .) . . . each new incumbent, as soon as installed, may carry out with impunity massive embezzlements . . . No doubt these are part of the system of presidential control of political personnel.
>
> Impunity is not complete, but even the slightest sanctions are taken only for political faults . . .
>
> After his nomination, the new "brother" reproduces at his level of the hierarchy the same clique system. He surrounds himself with persons of his ethnic group, binding them by ties of corruption . . .
>
> (3) The potential grande bourgeoisie: This layer includes all those who, by their competence, their popularity, or their functions are possible candidates for entry to the brotherhood—university professors, functionaries, deputies, experts . . . [and,] to a diminishing extent, politicians of the first republic.
>
> Access to the resources of corruption is real but limited . . . members do not enjoy guaranteed impunity.[13]

While Rymenam considers members of the top two levels to be a *compradore bourgeoisie* dependent on imperialist powers, they are at the same time nationalist, and strongly support measures to enlarge their share in the economy. Yet the foreign minority remains a crucial reference point; Mukenge observes that all Zairian elites measure success in relation to Europeans working in the same field. European clients, employees, and counselors are potent prestige-builders.[14]

Any given list of class categories is open to debate, as are the criteria for its establishment. Conceding the Marxists' point that one motor force of class formation is control of the productive facilities, we maintain that other forces intervene to shape the boundaries of each class and the extent to which each possesses the corporate solidarity implied in the notion of "class consciousness." We see class in Zaire defined by political power, command of economic resources (including control of productive facilities, trading capital, public funds, and urban property), education, occupational status, and (in some instances) rank in a residual political stratification attached to much-modified pre-colonial social structures. While these constitutive principles tend to overlap, they do not always do so, and somewhat different social categories could be derived from each criterion.

For convenience in exposition, we will make use of the Nzongola and Rymenam categories, somewhat amended and adjusted to our perspective. We add to them the expatriate minority. While parsimonious analysis requires using some small set of categories, it should be borne in mind that an element of reification creeps unbidden into the discussion.

The external estate

The expatriate minority, which numbered 110,000 at its peak just before independence, has diminished in numbers and changed in composition, but remains economically crucial. In the colonial period its social hegemony was complete, through the Bula Matari state, the protective infrastructure of colonial capitalism, and the Catholic church. About 10,000 Belgians manned the state apparatus, a roughly equivalent number served as missionaries, and about 22,000 were private-sector executives and self-employed settlers (planters or businessmen). There were about 10,000 non-Belgian expatriates, mainly Portuguese and Greek, in trade and small industry.[15]

The 1960 crisis brought on the flight of the majority of the expatriate population, resulting in Africanization of the command structures of the bureaucracy and the security forces at a far more rapid pace than had been anticipated in the decolonization formula. Symbolic of the transformation of the expatriate sector was the influx of several thousand United Nations employees in 1960. While this group was highly privileged as regards remuneration, it had no roots in the production system. In particular sectors of government the UN group had important influence, which until 1964 was reinforced by the presence of a UN security force, as well as by the near-total dependency of the Zairian state. The UN technical assistance program had ended by 1970, but similar functions were fulfilled by several thousand foreign personnel of various nationalities who served in the educational system, in some public sector agencies, and with foreign aid missions. To an important degree this group, with its cosmopolitan life style, frequent travel, ownership of automobiles and high-cost household consumer goods, and housing standards, served as a pole of social reference for the Zairian politico-commercial class.[16] One technical assistance agency, the Rockefeller Foundation, estimated in 1975 that the average cost (remuneration and other charges) of maintaining one person and dependents was $50,000 a year.

The private sector changed much more slowly. Unlike Belgian functionaries, who left in 1960 under the impression that they enjoyed career guarantees in the metropolitan civil service, corporate personnel had to seek other jobs if they left Zaire for more than a brief time. While some Zairians were promoted to managerial rank by corporate enterprises, corporate direction remained firmly European well into the Second Republic. Within UMHK, the number of Zairian cadres (management-level personnel) rose from virtually none in 1959 to 229 (out of a total of 2,247) in 1965. By 1974 Zairian cadres of Gécamines, successor to UMHK, numbered 1,135 out of 2,497; by 1980, 2,261 out of 3,260. Zairian cadres, however, were concentrated in the public relations, personnel, and administrative branches of the company, while expatriates remained decisive and preponderant in the productive end of corporate activity.[17] Some 70 percent of the total wage bill for the 31,597 persons employed by Gécamines in 1974 went to managerial personnel. Expatriate employees, engaged indirectly by the Belgian firm providing management services, Société Générale des Minerais (a subsidiary of the giant holding company Société Générale), received substantially higher salaries and perquisites than Zairian staff employed by Gécamines directly, as well as the inestimable advantage (from 1973 on) of having their salaries indexes to the inflation rate. These figures continue to be quite representative for the corporate sector, even after enterprises such as Gécamines have passed under formal state control. Some corporations, such as the diamond-mining firm Minière de Bakwanga (MIBA), were much slower than Gécamines to accept dilution of expatriate managerial control.

After independence, the expatriate settler group tended to fuse with

the largely non-Belgian "intermediaries." The Belgian planters had become significant only in the post–World War II era, and were artificially
nurtured by various subsidies—nearly free land, state credit, protected
marketing facilities, privileged access to the administration; they tended to
give way after independence to entrepreneurs from the Mediterranean
mercantile complex (Greeks, Cypriots, a few Levantines, Italians, Jews,
Portuguese). The latter diversified their activities from their initial trading
base, absorbing farms, mills, or small factories into essentially family-
structured mercantile networks. Peripherally joined to this group were
West African and Indo–Pakistani traders. The entrepreneurial group was
especially well constituted to benefit from certain characteristics of the
post-colonial state: limited regulatory capacity, permeability to corruption, opportunities for fiscal evasion and for windfall profits on speculative
trade during periods of inflation (1960–66, 1973 into the 1980s).

The kinship mercantile circuits traversed national boundaries and facilitated trade manipulations which neither Zairian traders (at least initially)
nor larger companies could risk. The former lacked an international network, and the latter, as Coméliau observes, were constrained by "the importance of their facade" and their overall desire for "a minimum of stability."[18] Smuggling, rigged invoices, and illicit currency transactions were
risky, but extremely profitable. The potential scale of these operations is
demonstrated by the rapid development, beginning in about 1962, of the
West African clandestine diamond-trading network which at its peak was
handling roughly $50 million worth of export trade; it had the evident
advantage of escaping taxation (MIBA paid about $18 million in taxes in
the late 1960s), but lacked the benefits of legal property protection, the
facilities of the banking system, and regular transportation. (This clandestine trade, described briefly in chapter 3, still continues.) No doubt
there were significant costs in the form of irregular payments to state
agents to permit the operation of the network.[19]

This mercantile segment experienced momentary eclipse in the 1970s
with the expulsion of West African traders in 1971, and the expropriation
of Mediterranean and Asian businessmen in 1973 and 1974 through
Zairianization and radicalization measures. While no restitution has been
made to the West Africans, a "retrocession" of many expropriated enterprises in 1976 permitted a substantial return of the Mediterranean and
Asian elements. A study of locally-owned business enterprises in Kisangani
in 1980 revealed that nearly half were in the hands of resident Greeks and
Asians.[20]

The missionaries constitute a special subcategory of the expatriate elite.

Their numbers have declined somewhat from the pre-independence peak, and their functions have changed. Both Catholic and Protestant missions in late colonial times sought institutionalization of an African church—the Protestants, a self-governing church; the Catholics, a church within the universal hierarchy. While the pace of Africanization of local churches was evidently slowed by a preoccupation with "standards" of Christian practice, the missions attached a very different value to localization than did the state or corporations. It is no accident that the Christian churches were far better equipped for the trauma of decolonization than the state.

At the time of independence the expatriate missionaries still played a dominant role in the churches. In 1959, Zairian priests constituted not quite 10 percent of all ordained Catholic personnel, and 4 of 49 bishops were African. By 1975, the majority of Catholic priests were Zairian, as were 39 of the 53 bishops.[21] Protestant missionaries, after 1960, withdrew first upward through the church hierarchy, then outward, leaving the church per se a Zairian community but continuing to offer support, especially in the social realm. Considerable friction attended this transition.

Thus the number of expatriate missionaries slowly declined, and their influence diminished. There was no discontinuity in their function in 1960; they either stayed, or withdrew briefly during the crisis of independence. They were far more ready than most post independence expatriates to work in the rural hinterland. Particularly in the educational field, they have played a crucial role in the post-primary educational network; nearly all the best schools have been operated by the mission systems. At the same time, while they have lived comfortably, their consumption standards have been far more modest than those of the expatriate business, technical assistance, and diplomatic communities. Their status has remained high because of their ties to the prime mechanism for social mobility—the schools— and the quality of the health services they provide, which contrasts sharply with the defective services of the state. A high proportion of the population has been at least nominally Christian; the Christian population was estimated at 68 percent in 1975, of which two-thirds were Catholic and one-third Protestant or Kimbanguist.[22]

After a sharp drop to perhaps 30,000 in the immediate aftermath of independence, Zaire's expatriate population has fluctuated between 40,000 and 60,000 since that time. The economic returns to the foreign minority have remained remarkably high—about one-third of total wage payments in 1964. In 1968, expatriates accounted for nearly 50 percent of the private sector wage fund.[23] At least two-thirds of the expatriates lived in the capital or the copperbelt cities.

While members of the contemporary external estate have shared a certain number of interests and concerns, it has been a less coherent social category than its colonial predecessor. Most expatriates have enjoyed high consumption standards, and had a basic interest in the perpetuation of the existing order. Not far below the surface has lurked a preoccupation with physical vulnerability, should the fabric of state authority unravel. Those with business interests, while sharing the general cynicism concerning the Mobutu regime, nonetheless have seen little reason to believe that their situation would improve under alternative arrangements. In the eyes of the populace, the expatriates' visible opulence, racial distinctiveness (and for some, exclusiveness), and perceived role as crucial supports for the existing order have tended to identify them as a single group. Nonetheless, there are sharp divisions within the external estate, defined by nationality and function. Belgians, French, Americans, and Japanese constitute distinct social universes. The more political preoccupations of the diplomatic establishments only partly overlap the profit-oriented perspectives of the multinational corporation executives.

The politico-commercial class

In political terms, the most crucial social category in contemporary Zaire is what Nzongola calls the "national bourgeoisie," and what we would prefer to call the "politico-commercial class." Whatever the name, it has constituted the ruling class since independence. As there have been significant changes in its definition and its base since 1960, it requires careful scrutiny.

Dumont first drew attention to the existence of such a class in black Africa, writing in 1962 of "a 'bourgeoisie' of a new type, that Karl Marx could hardly have foreseen: a bourgeoisie of the public service."[24] Since then a number of writers have noted the rise to power of what has often been termed an "administrative" or "bureaucratic" bourgeoisie.[25] Samoff usefully summarizes the argument:

> "Bureaucratic bourgeoisie" certainly seems to capture the essential situation of a leadership that operates the machinery of state but has little independence base in the national economy. It is a leadership drawn from the militants of the anti-colonial movement and from the ranks of the technical and administrative staffs of the . . . post-colonial governments. Having secured power through the imported institutions of the Europeans . . . this leadership used its access to power to consolidate its position . . . [and] to build for itself an economic base.[26]

The critical features of this group lie in its dependency upon the state as the source of its social standing, and its use of political power as the lever for expanding its role into the economic sphere. Its origins are traceable in part to a particular social conjuncture: the expansion of post-primary educational opportunity to significant numbers of a generation born between 1925 and 1935, which in turn opened access to the clerical ranks of private and public bureaucracies. This generation was strategically positioned to be catapulted by a political conjuncture—the anti-colonial revolution—to levels in the state apparatus previously foreclosed, and above all to control over the state machinery.

To pursue the origins of the politico-commercial bourgeoisie further, we may see it in germ in the emergence of what became known as the *évolué* class during World War II. Until the 1920s the only elites that interested the colonial state were the chiefs, whose mission of order maintenance and fulfillment of state norms could be accomplished with little education.[27] The church missions from the beginning had sought to create a Zairian clergy and a complement of catechists through education, but till the 1920s their modest school infrastructure was entirely devoted to biblical instruction and religious training. Grévisse notes that "Belgian colonial policy had always been to elevate the indigenous masses before forming a local elite . . . in the meanwhile, it could only be a matter of preparing accessory elite, neither too many nor too few, but sufficiently diverse to meet always rising needs [for skilled personnel]."[28]

In 1926 provision was made by the state for an educational system extending beyond evangelical needs, a step which paralleled the commitment to a stabilized urban work force. There was some sporadic discussion of defining a special legal status for Zairians who had fully adopted "European civilization." In the 1930s this group was considered to include a few priests and the paramount chiefs of Rwanda and Burundi.[29]

By the end of World War II, in the larger centers, there had appeared in the shadow of the Bula Matari state small clusters of young men possessing a post-primary education, the capacity to express themselves well in French, and dexterity in using a European model for their external behavior and life style (as far as their meager finances would permit)—the French package of the Butembo fable. This petty bourgeoisie in embryo, employed in the clerical ranks of public and private hierarchies, laid claim to a status and treatment different from that applied to the mass. It was at this point that the term *évolué* came into general circulation.[30]

The term is rich in connotations. It referred above all to a status group, and not to an economic category. Though the group's members had similar occupational roles as clerks, teachers, and nurses, the struggle that imbued the group with a collective consciousness was about honor, in the Weberian sense. Europeans not only totally dominated the economic and political structures, but also had absolute power over the definition of status. To some extent the field of honor may be viewed as a tactical choice, as the colonial system per se was still deemed too impregnable a fortress; the issue of elite status was an acceptable terrain of debate for Bula Matari, while decolonization was not. Yet a careful reading of the evidence leads to the conclusion that the primary concern of the *évolués* was to demand treatment as a set of persons who had adopted European behavioral norms.

Implicitly accepted was the premise that rights belong to "civilized" persons; patterns of behavior and culture associated with Europeans were, axiomatically, the yardstick of civilization. *Évolué* status required not only being *pene-pene na mundele* (near-Europeans), or "black whites," but also exhibiting social distance from humbler strata of Zairians. This did not mean, of course, severance of kinship and communal ties, but it did mean that even intimate social bonds included affirmation of status differentials.

In subtle and important ways *évolué* status was conferred, not merely gained through white-collar employment and a certain educational level.[31] Beyond external behavior, there was a moral judgement involved, informally rendered by an appropriate European sponsor. It was the missionaries, especially the Catholics, who through the school, their multiplex social connections with Zairians, and their function as moral custodians of "civilization," who often played the decisive role in conferring status. Thus it was that neither Lumumba nor Mobutu were considered proper *évolués* by many Europeans. Both were expelled from schools; Mobutu was conscripted into the army as a disciplinary measure, while Lumumba was subjected to criminal prosecution on a morals charge (embezzlement), turned down in his application for an "immatriculation card" (possession of which was a juridical form of *évolué* recognition), and—to his bitter disappointment—refused admission to the new Lovanium University in 1954 (for which he lacked the requisite qualifications).

Priests and pastors, it may be noted, were not really *évolués*. They occupied roles which carried automatic status; theirs were the sole functions accessible to Zairians in colonial society that placed Zairians on a footing close to social equality with whites. *Évolués* were clerks, generally speaking, but not all clerks were *évolués*. *Évolués* were intermediaries between the whites and the mass of blacks, but many of the intermediaries—clergymen, NCOs, chiefs—were not part of the *évolué* group and did not have *évolué* status.

The counterpart of *évolué* identification with the colonial enterprise and the demand for honor was a sense of differentiation from the African masses. A famous early expression of this sense was the statement of a number of Kananga *évolués* following a mutiny of the Force Publique (colonial army) in 1944:

> There has taken shape, beside the native mass, backward and little educated, a new social class, which is becoming a kind of native bourgeoisie. The members of this native intellectual elite do everything possible to educate themselves and to live decently, as do respectable Europeans. These *évolués* understand that they have special duties and obligations. But they are persuaded that they deserve, if not a special status, at least a particular protection from the government, which would shelter them from certain measures or treatments which may be appropriate for an ignorant and backward mass.[32]

While there was a revenue disparity between the *évolué* group and the mass of the population, the more salient fact was that *évolué* income was very modest. Top clerks might earn more than $100 per month, but these were a handful; a 1956 survey in Mbandaka found that fewer than 10 percent of the clerks earned as much as $80 monthly, while 55 percent received less than $60. Workers, at that time, might earn in the vicinity of $25 monthly.[33]

The opening up of the political process after 1957 offered *évolués* a new pathway to fulfillment of their status aspirations and a redefinition of their self-concept. It was in these years that the silent process of displacement of the term *évolué* by *intellectuel* began. Initially, election to the newly created urban council seats and to political party leadership offered only status, not material rewards. But for the first time status allocation lay in an African political process rather than in European hands.

The repudiation of the *évolué* label was a logical concomitant of nationalism. *Intellectuel*, as substitute term, is equally interesting in its connotations. It was a status, and not a class, self-concept. While it implicitly rejected the European standard of reference embedded in *évolué*, it reaffirmed a significant part of its content: elite recognition was conditioned upon Western education. A specialist in African medicine was not an *intellectuel*, but a medical assistant was. Thus conceived, the Zairian *intellectuel* group was very different from the European social group known as "intellectual," understood to be those devoted to pursuits of the mind (scholars, writers, artists) who are a somewhat free-floating element in the social structure. The Zairian *intellectuel* was defined by at least partial secondary education and white-collar employment. We may note that by the end of the colonial period Europeans (especially missionaries) had lost their capacity to determine this status.

While some status, but little wealth, was open to the *évolué*, it was virtually impossible for Zairians to accumulate either status or wealth in trade. In 1953 African traders in Kinshasa owned only 463 vehicles; in Lubumbashi in 1955, of 1,309 Zairian traders only 2 had incomes of more than $2,000.[34] Merlier arrived at a total of 30,000 Zairian artisans and traders in the 1950s, which he dismissed as a *couche sociale squélettique, sans grand avenir* (skeletal social class, without much future).[35]

Those who achieved real success in trade were rare; the best known, Kapend Joseph, was the exception that proves the rule. A slave until 1924, he was able to get a start because the Lunda zone of his birth was so marginal economically that the web of European business blocking African advance elsewhere was largely absent. He began by selling cassava (from whence came the family name "Tshombe," a local Shaba word for cassava), which he transported by foot or bicycle. A Methodist missionary helped him obtain a car in 1930—he was probably the first Zairian to possess a motor vehicle—and to parlay the cassava trade into a more diversified business empire that included a string of stores, hotels, and transport firms. His empire made him a millionaire—in Belgian francs—before independence. The commercial empire segmented at its periphery, with portions hiving off under the direction of family members and eventually other Lunda clients, in the "spiralist" strategy of mobility well analyzed by Vincent in Uganda.[36] Kapend Tshombe made his status multidimensional by marrying an impoverished princess who was descended from a nineteenth-century Mwaant Yav (king). Three of his sons succeeded to kingship in the Lunda system, and a fourth, Moise Tshombe, became leader of the secessionist Katanga state, then prime minister of Zaire in 1964–65.[37]

For the most part, however, Zairian traders and artisans were what Mukenge terms "subsistence merchants," earning only enough to survive at a very modest level.[38] Not only were prospects for real economic success poor before 1960, but the status accorded this group was low. Thus it attracted only those excluded from the white-collar sectors by the highly selective mechanisms of the educational pyramid. Of Mukenge's sample of Kinshasa traders in the mid-1960s, 23.9 percent had never been to school, 29.6 percent had incomplete primary schooling, and 24.1 percent had completed the primary cycle. Only a handful, 4.1 percent, had made use of vocational schooling, believed to be of low quality and lower prestige.[39]

After independence the dynamics of class formation altered radically, with politics playing the central role, and the social group then known as *intellectuel* positioned to take advantage of the changing social structure. The first beachhead on a wholly new revenue level came through the electoral process in 1960. For the first time several hundred well-remunerated offices opened up, in which power was joined to salary levels impossible for Zairians to attain under the colonial system. In turn, the new ministerial offices at national and provincial levels permitted the constitution of an immediate clientele of cabinet employees, bringing the total number of personnel derived through the political process to two to three thousand in the First Republic.

An even larger breach in the colonial barriers to mobility occurred through the flight of European functionaries and army officers. These positions were immediately filled, primarily on a basis of seniority, by the Zairian clerks and NCOs poised below. While there were salary increases at all levels of the administration, these were rapidly consumed by inflation. The dramatic material gains were incurred by those who catapulted from the clerical to the senior executive ranks of the civil service. Clerks did not enjoy the same breakthrough in the private sector, where most foreign managerial personnel stayed in place.

There appeared at once, in the shadow of the state, a new politico-commercial sector. The politicians took the lead, with their clientele, but many top bureaucrats also sought to convert their new levels of remuneration into capital accumulation through investment in commerce. The competitive advantage, for the politico-bureaucratic sector, occurred in economic activities where entry was not limited by technological factors, and where state regulatory functions permitted the conversion of political influence into economic leverage. Such activities included the acquisition of urban land titles, construction of rental housing, supplying the state, and, after 1961, the import-export trade.

The inflation which gathered momentum from 1961 on offered particularly lucrative opportunities in the import trade. Licensing of imports was introduced in 1961, and tightened in 1963; very quickly these measures fostered the emergence of Zairian importers whose primary market advantage was access to political influence. This new mercantile class, largely recruited from the political stratum or from entrepreneurs with close political connections, in the early years often developed arrangements with firms owned by foreign minorities to overcome the major handicap of limited Zairian access to credit. In these commercial coalitions (reminiscent of the "Ali-Baba" combines in Indonesia, in which a politically influential Indonesian had a silent Chinese partner), the Zairian merchant obtained the import quota, which was then in effect sold to a European distributor for a high commission. With the swift depreciation of Zairian currency, the acquisition of foreign exchange at the official rate, which was several times that on the parallel markets, provided a windfall-profit margin so high when converted into goods that there was ample room for a generous return to both Ali and Baba.[40]

Recruitment of the political class in 1960 was heavily from the clerical ranks where the *intellectuels* found employment. Of the twenty-three persons of ministerial rank in the Lumumba government in 1960, all but four were former clerks. Only four had been private-sector employees, the remainder having been government servants. Of the exceptions, one was a university graduate (Kanza Nsenga) who had been denied government administrative employment on completion of his degree in 1957, two had been medical assistants, and the fourth had been a teacher.

The 1960 recruitment pattern proved to be exceptional. The parliamentary elections of 1965 did provide entry for 138 new deputies (299 seats were at stake), but otherwise access to political roles came through cooptation and patronage rather than open competition. This trend, visible in the first republic, became institutionalized under the patrimonial authoritarianism of the New Regime.

Corruption soon was to become an important source of mercantile capital for the politico-commercial class. Mukenge found that by 1967 corruption had already reached a "spectacular scale"; through an analysis of newspaper accounts of reported instances, he found references to hundreds of cases, in many of which embezzled funds were never recovered.[41] One estimate placed the scale of misappropriation of state resources in 1971 at 60 percent of the national budget.[42]

An exceptional opportunity for enlarging the wealth of the politico-commercial class was provided by the Zairianization measures announced on 30 November 1973, whereby much of the commercial sector and all foreign-owned plantations were to be placed in the hands of Zairians. Chapter 11 examines these important measures in detail; at this juncture we note only that an enormous array of private enterprises was converted into public goods, and that the most lucrative businesses were attributed to the political leadership. In an astonishing frenzy of predatory expropriation of resources, the economic base of the politico-commercial class dilated, and a new label entered the social vocabulary: *acquéreur* (acquirer)—one who gained possession of a foreign business.

Like *évolué* and *intellectuel, acquéreur* is rich in social meanings. It be-gan as a technical and administrative term designating the beneficiaries of the November 30 measures. As almost all top political cadres were bene-ficiaries, the term rapidly became transformed in the social consciousness into an alternative word for regime's cadre. At the same time, it became pejorative, an epithet yelled by children at the Mercedes speeding down the street. *Évolué* and *intellectuel* were status terms, conveying a sense of honor; *acquéreur* was an economic label which precisely described the pro-cess through which the political class was penetrating the economic struc-ture. In the metamorphosis from *évolué* to *acquéreur*, social respect was transformed into class conflict.[43]

The crystallization of a ruling politico-commercial class is accompanied by externally visible symbols. In Zaire the French terms of formal address, *Monsieur* and *Madame*, were dropped in 1971, in the name of authenticity, in favor of the ostensibly egalitarian titles of *Citoyen* and *Citoyenne*, resur-rected from the lexicon of the French Revolution. However, the populist intent often disappeared from everyday usages. For example, foreigners are at times taken aback to be addressed by ordinary Zairians as *Citoyen*. In this usage, *citoyen* becomes a class concept, a label reserved for the privi-leged; thus a member of the foreign minority, who like the political cadre is viewed by the poor as wealthy, is a *citoyen*, while a worker is not.[44]

At the same time, and also pursuant to the ideology of authenticity ar-ticulated by the regime, European suits for men were replaced by edict with a collarless suit, worn without shirt or tie—the *abacost* (*à bas le cos-tume*). The poor could not afford to equip their wardrobes with this garb, which soon became a sartorial symbol of class rather than an articulation of national identity.

The ruling class remains fluid, dependent, ambivalent, and insecure. Few have command over productive resources that are not tied, indirectly or directly, to either exercise of a political role or immediate access to po-litical influence and protection. There is a considerable turnover in the political roles (see table 4.2), and with them a rise and fall of economic standing. Because economic holdings within the country have been uncer-tain, there has been a strong preference for activities which hold hope of high and immediate returns—urban property, taxis and trucking, the import-export trade. Longer-term security has been best assured by secret-ing assets abroad. Across generations, status could best be bequeathed by investing large sums in educating children in Europe. When Mobutu de-creed as part of the ill-fated radicalization measures of 1975 (which he

Table 4.2   **Length of Service as Minister and/or Political Bureau Member, 1965–1975**

Number of years in office	Percentage of all ministers and/or Political Bureau members ($N = 172$)
10	1.2
8–9	2.3
5–7	20.3
3–4	18.0
1–2	41.3
less than 1	16.9

briefly described as a "war on the bourgeoisie") that all children were to be brought back to the country to be educated locally, it developed that several thousand youngsters were affected; the measures were never applied.

Within the politico-commercial class a constant tension exists between status aspirations and economic security needs. The insecurity of elite rank, and the ever-present risk of political ruin for all but the members of the presidential family, dictate accumulation of as much property as possible, and above all the placement of assets abroad beyond the reach of changing whims at the political summit. Yet at the same time vast sums are allocated to costly prestige items, such as the famed Mercedes-Benz. Mobutu noted indignantly at the end of 1974 that, following the massive distribution of foreign property to the politico-commercial class, Zaire became the leading African importer of Mercedes cars.

While political power or influence has usually been the key to economic enrichment in Zaire, as the Second Republic became institutionalized wealth was also a prime factor in filling political office. Thus mercantile success began to interpenetrate with political standing in shaping the politico-commercial class. This first became apparent in the wealth criterion often applied in screening the 1970 legislative candidates.[45] Even more spectacular evidence emerged in the 1977 elections for the highly coveted seats on the MPR's Political Bureau, in which half of the seats were allocated by competitive balloting for the first time. Some 167 candidates entered the contest for the 18 seats, expending very large sums of money in pursuit of this office. While Political Bureau salaries are very high—they were $6,000 per month in 1974—it would appear that status recognition must have been a central motivation.

The 1977 campaign themes, especially for the Political Bureau, provide revealing insights into the class content of Zairian concepts of leadership and status. Many candidates stressed their commercial success as validation of their qualifications for election. The top vote-getter in Kinshasa, Kisombe Kiaku Muisi, a highly successful businessman and a notable in the Kimbanguist church, ran a full-page advertisement in the Kinshasa daily *Elima* for several days to extol his business virtues. These included ownership of a furniture factory, a luxury department store, and a national network of shops. He operated several large farms (cattle and poultry), and employed more than fifteen hundred persons, including thirty expatriates and twenty university graduates. His business empire had permitted him to construct schools, dispensaries, temples, roads, and bridges. The successful candidates in this balloting were nearly all well-known commercial figures; only half had previously held high political office. These men who were highly successful at business and then entered politics reversed the earlier pattern.

The politico-commercial class has ambivalent relations to the external estate. Hostility and conflict has been most marked in relations with the colonial and Mediterranean segments of the foreign minority; this conflict reached its zenith in 1973–75 when an effort was made to entirely displace these groups. More cooperative relationships have been characteristic of linkages with the new group of multinational corporate representatives, and partnerships have occurred.[46]

A somewhat separate issue is the connection between the Zairian ruling class and the diverse Western agencies (states, international institutions, multinationals, banks) collectively labelled the "international capitalist system" by some analysts. This question has been confused by indiscriminate application of the term "metropolitan bourgeoisie" to both the resident foreign minority in Zaire and external political and economic forces. We examine this issue in detail in chapter 12; suffice it to note here that for most Second Republic years alliance with important segments of the Western external world has been a significant support for the politico-commercial class. As the Zairian state entered its phase of decline in 1974, Western backing became at once crucial to the survival of both the state—in its existing form—and its hegemonic internal group. While even within the politico-commercial class there was sharp resentment of the exorbitant perquisites and regional exclusiveness of the inner core (the presidential clique), there was also widespread fear of the social tumult which might accompany the collapse of the system. With its basic security at stake, the politico-commercial class found no real alternative to the alliance with

Western political and economic interests, with the partial subordination of Zairian interests which was the logical corollary of junior partner status.[47]

The new commercial class

On the margins of the politico-commercial class there emerged in the late 1970s a more strictly mercantile group of Zairians who steered well clear of the treacherous shoals of political involvement, but who took advantage of the opportunities offered by the character of the state and the growing black-market economy induced by its frailties. The penetration of this new social category into the social consciousness is eloquently signalled by the Butembo parable; these are the descendants of the younger son who seized the smaller package tossed down by divine providence: money, and the necessary skills to increase its amount. Indeed, folk perceptions were swifter to incorporate the novel group into collective cognitions than many academic analysts; as late as 1978, this social category was dismissed as inconsequential by such influential students of class formation as Verhaegen ("there is thus no economic bourgeoisie currently in the process of formation in Zaire") and Gould ("the national bourgeois elite . . . have in effect absorbed the commercial bourgeoisie").[48]

The new mercantile class is particularly visible in regional and secondary centers, where the presence of the political and bureaucratic armature of the state is less overpowering than in the capital, and where its incapacities are more manifest. Vwakyanakazi documents the crucial importance of the merchant group in Butembo, where they have come to eclipse the state. For most of the Butembo group accumulation has occurred during the Second Republic years. They began with virtually no capital in trade and transport, and they were not *acquéreurs*; they owe their success to commercial acumen. Most have had relatively little education; they are quite distinct from the bureaucrats and teachers who inherited the French package. In a relatively brief period they had accumulated sufficient capital to supplant the state in supplying public infrastructure useful in their mercantile activities (an air strip, an electricity supply).[49]

MacGaffey provides important supporting evidence from the regional capital of Kisangani. Of the substantial commercial businesses she inventoried in 1980, 23 were owned by politicians and military officers; just over 50 by Mediterranean or Asian aliens; 28 were outlets of large international or national wholesale houses; 32 belonged to members of the new mercantile class (9 of whom were women); and several others were essentially depots for a Nande (northeastern Kivu) vegetable marketing combine.[50]

Other high-status groups

Priests and pastors, the Zairians having highest status before independence, were eclipsed in the early independence years. A handful of priests left the church for politics—a provincial president in Uele and a Sankuru vice-president were former priests. This leakage ceased, and by the 1970s the prestige of the churches and their personnel had begun to rise again. Social services offered through church channels, in the education and health fields, have retained their quality, in contrast to those of the state. Kimbanguist, Protestant, and Catholic churches have remained free of the taint of corruption which affected the state. While the churches have not been channels to power and influence, they have offered status and security.

Ranking military officers share many attributes with the politico-commercial elite. General officers, and officers a rank or two below them, have had ample opportunities for ancillary business activities, and can count on patrimonial rewards from the president in return for fidelity. With repeated purges at the top, there is no security of tenure; the uncertainties and risks of high military rank impel a search for economic bases outside the service. In 1975 alone, twelve of twenty-three general officers were removed by purge or death; high turnover at the top continued in the late 1970s.

Zairian university staff became numerous only in the 1970s, and have become a remarkably significant segment of the top politico-commercial elite. In the 1974–78 period, six served in the Political Bureau and two others in the Council of Ministers. Those on the Kinshasa campus, particularly in the fields of economics, commerce, and law, have abundant opportunities for consultancies in the public, parastatal, and private sectors, and tend to become an extension of the politico-commercial elite. Higher education is a more enclaved function in the other university seats, with relatively high status but a more marginal economic situation. Ancillary professional or commercial activities are of limited scope, and occult revenues such as those widely available to the politico-commercial class are unusual. The remarkable prestige of a professorial title is reflected in the number of wealthy members of the politico-commercial class who seek appointments to offer courses at a university campus, even though remuneration is trifling.

Zairian career personnel in the larger private enterprises are a distinct group, resembling the transnational class that Sklar suggests is found in the mining parastatals in Zambia. He argues that "the managerial bourgeoisie consists of a local wing, which is normally nationalistic, and a corporate international wing that tolerates and patronizes local nationalism."[51] Enterprises such as Gécamines offer a far more disciplined work structure, a professional environment freer of political risks, and much more secure salaries and perquisites than government service. By the early 1970s employment with firms such as Gécamines, MIBA, or SNCZ (the national railway) was far preferred by graduating university students to entry into the public bureaucracy. Though Zairian cadres are paid much less than their expatriate counterparts, Mukenge's data show that their remunerations are from five to six times as high as the salaries of those holding comparable ranks in the government structures.[52] Such enterprises are far less tolerant of parallel commercial activities than is the state; managerial cadres in Gécamines and similar enterprises, for example, did not become *acquéreurs* during the 30 November distribution.

The sub-bourgeoisie

Below the politico-commercial class and other social elite groups we encounter a large category of increasingly marginalized and frustrated persons, whom Nzongola terms the "petite bourgeoisie" and Coméliau labels the "sub-bourgeoisie": clerks, teachers, junior officers and noncoms in the armed forces, collectivity and locality chiefs.[53] We will term this group the sub-bourgeoisie.

Classical Marxist analysts define the petty bourgeoisie as persons who fall between the bourgeois and proletarian poles; they are not laborers in the production process from whom surplus value is extracted, nor do they employ or control the labor of others. Originally this concept referred especially to artisans and shopkeepers; more recently, salaried employees at subaltern levels of private and public bureaucracies have been included.[54] We would suggest that the distinguishing attributes of the salaried sub-bourgeoisie are life-style aspirations very similar to those of the politico-commercial class coupled with an ever-growing gap between hopes and reality, and their demarcation from the elite groups by a sharpening social closure. Socially expendable and politically powerless, they are at once frustrated and impotent.

The growing influx of university graduates after 1965 increasingly foreclosed real mobility prospects for this group, whose predecessors in the 1950s had been the heirs to the political kingdom of the First Republic. No fewer than 53.1% of the ministers and party leaders in the 1965–75 period were university graduates. Secondary school diploma-holders, who topped the social pyramid in the late 1950s, could expect monthly salaries of only Z 30–50 by the middle 1970s. Pathways to political promotion had likewise been closed; by 1970 cooptation to higher ranks was virtually restricted to university degree-holders. We see the process of social closure suggested by Weber and elaborated by Parkin and Schatzberg:

> By social closure Weber means the process by which social collectivities seek to maximize rewards by restricting access to rewards and opportunities to a limited cycle of eligibles. This entails the singling out of certain identifiable social or physical attributes as the justificatory basis of exclusion.[55]

During the First Republic the sub-bourgeoisie enjoyed very large increases in nominal salary rates, although these were subject to constant erosion by inflation. Further, outside Kinshasa pay arrearages in the public sector were frequent and often prolonged; subaltern employees were the hardest hit. Some had made modest gains, but by 1965 there was a general conviction that social well-being had eroded (see table 4.3).

Under the New Regime, while there have been public-sector wage boosts (particularly in the early years), these have fallen far behind inflation. Lower-level state employees received increases of 30 percent in 1966, 25 percent in 1967, 15 percent in 1968, 10 percent in 1969, 20 percent in 1970, 33 percent in 1975, and 20 percent in 1976. During the same period there was a 300 percent devaluation in 1967 and a 42 percent devaluation in 1976. A 1967 stabilization plan did stop inflation until 1973; there was thus a brief period of relative improvement between 1968 and 1971, with accelerating erosion beginning in 1973, when inflation reached 25 percent. Inflation rose to 45 percent in 1974, then ranged between 60 and 80 percent during the 1975–80 period.

Subaltern employees have had little opportunity to augment their declining real salaries with ancillary commerce or occult revenues. They have

Table 4.3   Changes in Remuneration Level within the Sub-Bourgeoisie, 1960–1965
(index levels of 31 Dec. 1965, based on 30 June 1960 = 100)

	Nominal	Real
Government clerks	678–1,073	139–129
Government messengers	498	102
Sergeants	571	117
Privates	414	85
Secondary school teachers	333	68
Primary school teachers, without diploma	566	116

Source: Lacroix, *L'industrialisation au Congo*, p. 203, based on documentation assembled by the Institut de Recherches Economiques et Sociales, Université de Kinshasa.

lacked the capital for the former, and have been too low in the decisional structures for the latter, except for very petty levels of *matabiche* (graft). Paradoxically, in many offices they have been subject to higher work discipline than higher echelons: they are more likely to be present during working hours, whereas higher officials are frequently absent from their offices for long stretches of time.

Teachers are the most rapidly expanding occupational group, increasing from 37,300 in 1960 to more than 200,000 by 1980 (it is impossible to be precise, given the large number of phantom teachers); they now constitute the largest single occupational category in the wage sector. A sharp status distinction exists between primary and secondary school teachers. The former earn little more than ordinary workers, and generally have less than a secondary school education. Primary schools are distributed throughout the hinterland, and thus many teachers labor in small communities and rural areas. Many have only a limited command of French; within a rural stratification framework, their status and more or less regular salary demarcates them from the ordinary villagers. Within an urban social pyramid, they fall in the lower reaches.

Secondary school teachers are much closer to the politico-commercial class, but are distinct from it in their more modest remuneration and their lack of power. Yet even those without university-level degrees earn more than twice the salary of primary school teachers (about Z 100 monthly in the early 1970s), and those qualifying for the 100-Z university diploma bonus are four times as well paid. Secondary school teachers are far more likely to be posted outside their home area than their primary school colleagues; their income levels bring them closer to the life style of the dominant elite.

A clear indication of the relatively low status of the secondary school teaching profession lies in the aversion of university graduates to such employment. One of the more pathetic pieces of bureaucratic fiction in the mid-1970s was the annual "conscription" of new graduates, particularly in nontechnical fields with numerous cohorts, such as letters and social sciences. The "assignments" were published in the press; though we do not have precise figures on how many actually reported for duty, it was beyond doubt only a minority. The postings were generally to the smaller centers with poor amenities, long-delayed entry into the payroll system, and limited prospects for mobility. A 1975 survey of graduating university students in Kisangani offers interesting evidence on this point. Though the largest faculty on the Kisangani university campus is pedagogy, and 84 percent of those sampled were registered in this faculty, only 9.8 percent wanted a career in secondary teaching. The reasons given for rejecting the secondary school as employer were the insufficiency of remuneration and the difficulty of the work.[56] The students sampled, who were mainly in education, were quite accurate in their perceptions of the prospects for mobility in their field of specialization. In the nationalist period and early First Republic days there was some recruitment of political personnel from the secondary school teaching corps; this all but ceased during the Second Republic. Of the 212 ministers and MPR ruling organ members during 1965–75, only 15.6 percent came from a teaching background, and most of these were from the 1960 generation of politicians.[57]

While secondary school teachers have had an important role, through the grading process, in determining a student's future, the key examinations are administered by the state. The principal opportunity for conversion of the school gatekeeping function into material resources lies in graft in the registration process and in issuing school certificates; this power rests with the principal and other administrators, not the teachers. The school networks of the churches generally have retained enough supervision and discipline to restrict these practices; however, they have been widespread in the state school network, as President Mobutu noted in his 25 November 1977 speech on the *mal zairois*. Rural primary school teachers are able to require some goods in kind—firewood, building materials for their houses, even food—but the value of these items is quite limited.

Military personnel below the rank of field grade officers also have very modest levels of remuneration. Ordinary soldiers earn no more than unskilled workers, and differ only in their possession of uniform and gun. Junior officers and noncommissioned officers have salaries equivalent to those in the middle levels of the civil service; but living conditions in many garrisons are very poor, as the camps were constructed to house an army of 24,000 (far less than half its size in the 1970s) and very little new building has been done. There are irregularities in military wage payments—particularly at interior garrisons—which fosters extortionate practices by military personnel, who extract directly from the civil population what they feel to be their due. This is achieved through the forcible requisition of foodstuffs, the demand of ransom (in effect) at roadblocks, the seizure of goods at the marketplace without payment, and the like.

The microbureaucracies at the local level, especially the approximately one thousand collectivities, provide returns for the chiefs and a handful of their top associates which make them—on a rural scale—a petty gentry. As with other elements of the sub-bourgeoisie, the gap between this group and the politico-commercial class is wide and growing. Chiefs in particular received in 1975 a Z 50 monthly salary from Kinshasa, to which is added diverse *avantages dans la caisse* and related occult revenues funded by the local taxes levied on villagers. A careful analysis by Schatzberg of collectivity budgets in the Mongala subregion shows that 80 percent of the revenues went for salaries, though this was partly obscured by vague rubrics such as "diverse" payments, or fictitious budget entries (such as Z 1,500 in one collectivity for nonexistent magazine subscriptions for an imaginary JMPR center). Subaltern collectivity personnel actually received only a portion of the very modest wages nominally due; over the period 1968–75 it was found that in the Mongala collectivities lower-level employees were paid approximately two-thirds of their official salaries.[58] If we may assume that these collectivities were representative, the national total of collectivity personnel in 1975 was approximately 66,000, of whom 44 percent were police.[59]

The sub-bourgeoisie is at once totally dependent upon the state for its livelihood, yet quite disgruntled with its status and economic situation. The scale of disaffection was well illustrated, within the military sector, by the shabby performance of the Forces Armées Zairoises (FAZ) when confronted with the incursion of relatively small numbers of Katanga gendarmes from neighboring Angola in 1977 and 1978. Despite their discontent, they function as the indispensable capillaries of the power system, articulating the action of the state as a control mechanism. In many areas affected by the 1964–65 rebellions the sub-bourgeoisie was decimated; top personnel could more easily flee, and the violent social frustrations at the mass level were decanted upon those representatives of the state who were within reach. The fear of unleashed mass anger, joined to the mentalities and habits of role requirements, exerts powerful pressure upon the subaltern agents to remain within the established framework of state action.

We should stress that the term "sub-bourgeoisie" (or its analytical analogues such as "lower middle class") is an analytical abstraction, and does not refer to a self-conscious group. Similarities of social circumstances, and a common niche on the stratification scale, make the category convenient to apply. Consciousness, however, would apply only at the occupational level.

The informal sector

Personnel of the informal sector constitute a large, rapidly growing, and singularly elusive category; there is little solid documentation concerning the group as a whole, though several important studies capture some of its aspects: Mukenge on small businessmen, Houyoux on Kinshasa household budgets, Raymaekers and Mpinga on the burgeoning "squatting" zones where many of the group dwell.[60] The tremendous growth of Kinshasa in the face of a stagnant wage employment market is one measure of the informal sector's size; another is the extraordinary explosion of cities such as Kananga, with only 10,000 wage earners in a 1970 population of 429,000, or Mbuji–Mayi, whose population multiplied tenfold from 1957 to 1970 despite the fact that the major private sector employer, MIBA, had a labor force of only 4,000.

The informal sector concept overlaps that of unemployment. Many of those in the informal sector—especially those with some educational qualification (the school-leavers)—continue to seek regular wage employment. Kinsmen may support them for a time while the job search continues, but generally some subsistence-generating activity must be found, even though the earnings for most are meager, irregular, and insecure. Women are much more likely than men to be forced into exclusively informal sector activities; they are rarely hired for unskilled manual labor jobs, and are much less likely to have sufficient schooling to compete for a post with educational prerequisites.[61]

The relative rigor of colonial influx controls kept this sector to modest proportions until the final years of Belgian rule, when the authority of Bula Matari was eroding. The various forces producing rural exodus, analyzed in the preceding chapter, brought about a remarkable enlargement of the informal sector after independence. Many of its members dwelled in the new squatter quarters that sprang up everywhere on the urban periphery. Raymaekers' study of Kinshasa squatters in the early 1960s suggests that initially there was greater social cohesion—even satisfaction—in the group than the conventional image of anomie would allow. A remarkably high percentage of squatting-zone denizens—73 percent—were satisfied with their residential living conditions; only 5 percent blamed their economic difficulties on the politico-commercial class that dominated the state structures. In the Matete zone, a squatter area, of the petty traders and artisans some 60.8 percent felt that their future prospects were good; only 39.8 percent shared this view in Kintambo, the other commune sampled.[62]

A more hostile and frustrated social awareness was concentrated in what is termed the *jeunesse désoeuvrée*, or young men without either education or regular employment. The immediate object of their social antagonisms was their peers in school. The young pupils reciprocated with disdain, tinged with fear and hostility, for the *chômeurs*. "'If you speak French like a schoolboy, then you will be beaten,'" exclaimed a *chômeur*; "'it is especially the *chômeurs* who provoke riots,'" responded the schoolboy.[63] Well structured in small gangs, the *jeunesse désoeuvrée* invested their social energies in drugs, sensuality, sports, music, and subsistence crime. (Nzongola, following Marx, concludes that the lumpenproletariat of the informal sector is "'a recruiting ground for thieves and criminals of all kinds,' a factor that reduces its revolutionary potential.")[64]

The informal sector is a more diverse social universe than is apparent from the modesty of its characteristic residential zones, the "squattings." While most denizens live at the margin of survival and few are well-off, the more successful marketwomen, masons, tailors, repairmen, or for that matter criminals, do fairly well and some move up into the mercantile class. In the early 1960s the queen of the Kisangani marketplace, Madame Bangala, stitched together a short-lived but substantial commercial empire. Indirect evidence—such as extraordinary levels of beer consumption—suggest that more money circuits through this sector than is readily apparent. Yet poverty grips most in the informal sector, and the broad social and economic crises of the 1970s had devastating effects. But the informal sector remains socially and politically passive, partly because of the presence of massive security forces in urban areas, above all in the capital. Probably such stoicism in the face of overwhelming adversity also reflects the underestimated extent of social cohesion and redistributive mechanisms within these communities. Social leadership, partly self-constituted, appears in the form of neighborhood chiefs.[65] A marked tendency toward ethnic regrouping provides micro-integration, and dilutes any tendency to class-consciousness among this group.

For these reasons, we feel the term "informal sector" better conveys the contours of this group than "lumpenproletariat." Within the informal sector there are important cleavages between youth and adult, schooled (or school attenders) and unschooled, established traders and artisans and those surviving by irregular and ephemeral tasks, delinquent bands and those making a legitimate livelihood. The ingenuity of the informal sector for survival is more striking than its potential for revolutionary mobilization.

The working class

The important category of laborers has more precise boundaries than the informal sector, both analytically as a "class-in-itself" and subjectively as a "class-for-itself." At first glance, the regularly employed urban worker appears to enjoy a relatively secure revenue and a margin of assured subsistence over the survival level, which have led some analysts to categorize this class as a "labor aristocracy."[66] Their argument holds that the workers are "parasitical on other segments of the society and instrumental in serving the ends of neoimperialism either as direct employees of the state or as auxiliaries of the external estate," "trained in metropolitan institutions imbued with Western tastes and prejudices, or in local institutions heavily penetrated by the influences of the external estate."[67] To some extent, policies designed to guarantee workers cheap food prices by holding down returns to peasants have had the effect of pitting villager and laborer against one another, to the common benefit of the politico-commercial class and the foreign minority.

We discern four significant subdivisions of the Zairian working class: employees of public and parastatal bodies; employees of large private enterprises (or ostensibly public ones managed like private sector corporations, such as Gécamines); workers employed by small enterprises; and those who work for rural employers, especially plantations and forestry firms. If there is a labor aristocracy it exists only in the Shaba copperbelt firms, and particularly in Gécamines; the ablest student of the Lubumbashi proletariat, Mwabila, does employ the term.[68] There is a very high degree of stability in the work force of the large copperbelt firms; indeed, Gécamines gives hiring preference to children of employees, who constitute an important fraction of new recruits. In a sample of 400 workers in five Lubumbashi enterprises, Mwabila found that 70 percent had been with their employer for more than five years, while 38 percent had more than ten years of continuous service.[69] In addition to employment security, Gécamines workers are provided company housing, albeit in rather paternalistic compounds. Far more valuable during the deteriorating conditions of the 1970s were assured supplies of food and other basic consumer goods, available in company canteens, and an excellent medical service.

The most disaffected segment of the working class is that employed by the public sector; especially alienated are those in the *sous contrat* group, whose numbers have fluctuated from 100,000 to 150,000. These laborers, who are not covered by the civil service statutes, have been particularly subject to sudden layoffs, pay arrearages, and uncertain work conditions. The labor force of the smaller enterprises generally lacks the paternalistic perquisites offered by Gécamines and a few other giants. Employees of rural enterprises have in common their remoteness and isolation, and overwhelmingly localized recruitment patterns. While they have close links with surrounding rural populations, they have virtually no contact, through syndical or any other channels, with workers elsewhere. Lux, in a study of a forestry enterprise in Mayombe (Bas-Zaire) in the late 1950s, found high work-force stability rates akin to those documented in urban Shaba by Mwabila.[70]

Labor history in Zaire has been marked by episodic but generally ephemeral instances of class-conscious proletarian uprisings. The first of these occurred in Lubumbashi in 1941. At least sixty persons were killed, and memories of this event, which achieved epic proportions in the social consciousness, retain much higher figures. The uprising by Matadi dock workers in 1945 also clearly ranks as a proletarian episode in the collective awareness and in the worker-centered social idioms through which the awareness was expressed. The strike and related actions were specific to workers; peasants abstained, as did the *évolués* in most instances, although on occasion they served as spokesmen for the strikers.[71] During the cornucopia of the 1950s working-class consciousness seemed to fade, coincident with the rising significance of ethnic social mobilization.

In the confusion of the First Republic years there was sporadic labor unrest, provoked by the disconcerting new phenomenon of inflation and other economic dislocations. There was even a short-lived general strike in Kinshasa in March 1962. The feebleness of labor organizations, and above all the fundamentally weak position of employed workers when a reserve army of new urban migrants lurked outside the factory gates, circumscribed these inchoate manifestations. Another moment of visible proletarian consciousness occurred in 1967, when the 300-percent devaluation which was the centerpiece of the stabilization program struck hard at real earnings. However, the *New Regime*, at the peak of its strength, easily mastered the syndical reflex, which was then dissipated by a period of stable prices, briefly improved real wages, and more orderly urban markets. A dramatic deterioration in the well-being of workers began in 1974, giving rise to a wave of wildcat strikes in Shaba and Kinshasa from 1976 on. These were spontaneous moments of class solidarity; they were usually limited, however, to particular enterprises. On each occasion the regime moved swiftly to offer some concessions and to dissipate the immediate discontents, while threatening reprisals against those identified as leaders. In the 1976 strike of SNCZ personnel in Likasi, palliative regime gestures were linked to allegations that Kasaian elements were the instigators of unrest. In Kinshasa in December 1976, when Air Zaire workers threatened to blow up aircraft unless the tradition of a year-end bonus was maintained, the incident ended when the demand was met.

These episodic outbursts do suggest a nascent proletarian consciousness. A number of factors intervene to constrain its development within situational contexts. The saliency of ethnic mobilization, particularly during the First Republic years, has been one evident factor. Even though cultural politicization has been much lower in the Second Republic years, social intimacy and trust repose primarily upon ethnic affinity. Mwabila found that workers generally entrusted their professional problems to the most senior employee from their cultural community rather than using the institutional channels of the official union to reach management.[72]

Orientations toward work also play a part. Professional identity is shaped by the enterprise rather than by consciousness of belonging to a class of "workers." In 1970–71—a time of relatively favorable wage conjuncture—Mwabila found that 81.5 percent of his sample believed the profits of their firms to be very high, but only 28.5 percent believed their salaries to be too low. To compound the irony, the great majority believed they had been better off during the colonial period (in real wage terms, a fully accurate perception). A connecting thread resolving these apparent contradictions was the pervasive fear of loss of employment: social adventures were ruled out, because of external family obligations; changes of job were excluded because of the risks.

Class, we have argued, is above all a relational concept. Zairian workers, and the urban and rural poor in general, have a clearly articulated consciousness of social polarization and inequality. "We" may not be a clearly bounded concept, and is fragmented by workplace, city, and ethnicity.

Table 4.4   Indices of Wages, Prices, and Real Wages, Kinshasa, at Official Minimum
Wage (UNTZA data) (1960 = 100)

	Wage index	Price index	Real wage index
1 June 1960	100	100	100
1 May 1964	383	575.9	67
1 October 1971	960	1486.2	64
5 September 1975	1274	3099.5	41
27 March 1976	1530	5888.1	25

Source: Union Nationale des Travailleurs Zairois, "Position concernant la politique des salaires" (Kinshasa, 1977), mimeograph.

"They" is a more clearly focussed social category: *acquéreurs*, politicians,
top cadres, *abacost*-wearers, *citoyens* of the regime estate, owners of Mercedes cars. What makes inequality intolerable is the relentless erosion of
the margin of economic survival of wage earners, as well as of the poor as
a whole.

In the First Republic years independence was accompanied by a wage
surge, in evident response to the explosive social expectations unleashed by
the independence movement; by 1961 wages stood at a historic high. The
gathering forces of inflation then eroded these gains, with a particularly
sharp drop coincident with the shock of the 1967 stabilization plan. Lacroix
has shown that in periods of inflation (1961–67, 1973 on) goods disappear from the rural hinterland as traders can exploit the shortages and soaring prices at lower marketing costs by confining their operations to the
urban centers.[73] After 1967 inflation was halted for several years. Real
wages began to creep upward again, and goods started to flow back into
the countryside. The renewed inflation from 1973 on again forced down
real wages, at a much faster pace. Paradoxically, the greater concentration
of power in the hands of the regime during this second inflationary period
has made it possible to combat inflation by holding down wages, although
even the bare figures in table 4.4 make clear that the wage push has had
nothing whatsoever to do with erosion of the currency.

The dramatic impoverishment which has occurred stands revealed in
tables 4.4 and 4.5. It should be noted that these grim statistics are based
upon official data: table 4.4 is drawn from material assembled by the government trade union (UNTZa), while table 4.5 is based upon World Bank
data collected in collaboration with the Bank of Zaire. In figure 4.1 wage
movements are graphed over a longer time frame. While small upward

Table 4.5   Indices of Nominal and Real Wages and Salaries, 1974–1977
           (IRBD data) (1970 = 100)

	1974	1975	1976	1977
Retail price index	174.2	249.0	400.4	626.7
Real wages and salaries				
Private sector	83.3	68.0	54.0	37.0
Public sector	91.8	72.6	56.3	38.6

Source: International Bank for Reconstruction and Development, "Economy of Zaire" 1 : 20.

wage adjustments were made in 1976 and 1977 (about 30 percent), in 1978 (about 15 percent), and 1979 (about 30 percent), these were only a fraction of the inflation rate, which raged at a 60–80 percent rate throughout the post-independence period. By the beginning of 1978 the real wage level was approximately from 10 to 15 percent of the 1960 level.

In the public economy colossal pauperization has afflicted the lower classes. The social consciousness which attends this process is, for the moment, expressed in terms of distrust, cynicism, and despair. The angry glances at the passing Mercedes, whether its occupant is a member of the foreign minority or the politico-commercial class, become readily comprehensible. We can also better understand the disconcerting remark, frequently made by ordinary Zairians, that in material terms life was more abundant in *le temps des belges*.

The nature and situation of the peasantry have been discussed in chapter 3; we will not retrace that ground. Suffice it to say that the description of the pattern of deterioration among the lower social classes of the urban sector applies with perhaps greater force to rural society.

Social mobility and closure

Mechanisms of social mobility and closure have altered over time. The first colonial decades offered little opportunity for socioeconomic mobility. The long boom from World War II until 1957, and the belated effort to create an auxiliary Zairian middle class to join in the vaguely adumbrated Eurafrican designs of Bula Matari, did begin to provide significant openings to the postwar generation that emerged from the now-swiftly expanding school system. Mobility channels were wide open in the 1960s, as the educational infrastructure was radically enlarged.

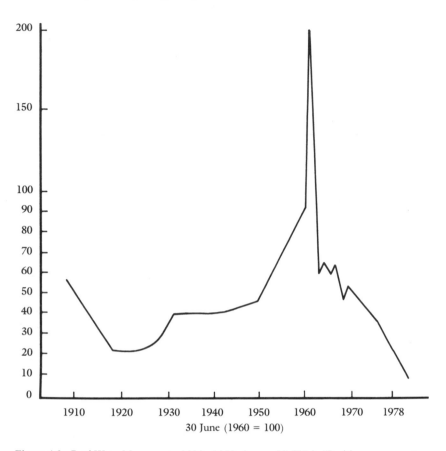

Figure 4.1. Real Wage Movements, 1910–1978. *Sources*: UNTZA, "Position concernant les salaires"; J. Ph. Peeman, "Le rôle de l'état dans la formation du capital au Congo pendant la période coloniale," *Etudes et Documents* (Louvain, Belgium: Institut pour l'Etude des Pays en Développement, Université de Louvain, 1973), pp. 52, 68, 167; Joseph Houyoux, *Budgets ménagers, nutrition et mode de vie à Kinshasa* (Kinshasa: Presses Universitaires du Zaire, 1973), p. 28.

By the 1970s social closure mechanisms began to appear. The state apparatus had expanded to its possible outer limits as a result of its fiscal crisis. Stagnation of formal employment and the economy meant that a static number of desirable, mobility-linked jobs were available to a swelling number of aspiring, ambitious young people emerging from all levels of the educational system. Schools became much more uneven in quality as they grew in number; opportunities for the child increasingly depended on access to the best schools, generally urban and church-operated. The top segment of the politico-commercial class began sending its offspring to Europe for education, guaranteeing that their technical qualifications would be far superior to the sons and daughters of humble strata, who were—and are—most likely to be thrown back upon the low-quality, overcrowded state network. The cultural gatekeeping functions performed by missionaries in *le temps des belges* have disappeared, but in place have emerged quite powerful social selectivity processes linked to the stratification of school quality.

As the social closure barriers swing into place, channels of political clientage become all the more important. The fence can still be climbed, but more and more the helping hand of a sponsor well-placed in the social hierarchy becomes critical. Clientage requires establishing affinities with a potential patron: fidelity and reciprocal service, to be sure, but also proximities of kinship, ethnicity, and region.

But the reality of social closure has by no means effaced the powerful myth of mobility associated with the educational system; an understanding of the myth's power is central to grasping the relative passivity of lower classes in the face of congealing structures of inequality and deteriorating material conditions. The tremendous expansion of the educational system seemingly opened the school to all. In practice, survival in the educational system until a diploma of some market value—from a secondary school or beyond—can be obtained has depended on access at the secondary level to that small fraction of the school network where instructional quality offers the pupil a real chance of passing the state examination. Verhaegen aptly summarizes the social impact of mobility myths linked to the schools:

> The idea remains intact that success in school can assure the greatest professional and social advantages and lead to the summit of the social pyramid. The school in Zaire is, in principle, and for some time will be, open to all. For this reason, in a society which has become profoundly unequal and unjust, the school acts as a powerful equalizing myth. All or almost all accept their disastrous situation and present inequality because there subsists for each individual the hope of change and promotion through the school. Education thus procures for the regime the greatest part of its legitimacy.[74]

Toward social explosion?

In three short decades the class structure of Zaire has undergone astonishing transformations. In 1950, the European ruling class was still unchallenged in its state, corporate, and mission branches. In 1960, the transfer of political power provided the opening for the *évolué* class of the late colonial period to transform itself into a politico-commercial class. By 1965, a university diploma was necessary (but not sufficient) for admission to this group. The resurrection and expansion of the state provided the resource base for rapid accumulation by a segment of this class. This process was accompanied by an intense mercantilization of the state, in relentless pursuit of maximal private rents through the exercise of public authority. In the telling phrase of Ilunga, "economic man [was] king in the political arena and political man [was] king in the economic arena."[75]

The external estate, while removed from formal political authority within the state, has remained important. The state itself, however derelict, is still important as a protector of the economic activities and opulent enclaves of external-estate members. Their apprehensiveness over the uncertainties involved in any change of incumbents has made them at least tacit supporters of political continuity. The state in turn depends heavily upon the external estate for operation of the extractive infrastructure of the mining sector that provided most of its revenues. Intimately linked to the external estate is the set of Western states which ultimately stood behind it. External military interventions, justified by protection of the external estate or of critical productive installations occurred in 1960, 1964, 1977, and 1978. These events served to instill among lower classes the conviction that their rulers, if challenged, could again rely upon outside force—a second crucial explanation, along with the myth of mobility through education, for mass passivity in the face of pauperization.

Both the politico-commercial class and the external estate have overconsumed the diminishing resources of the state, particularly during its phase of decline. Payments accruing to the external estate and to the multinational corporations, banks, and contractors they represented have had to continue, even though many of the projects they implemented have been costly drains on the economy (see chapter 10). The politico-commercial class has been unwilling or unable to curb the scale of its revenue extraction through the state, even when the revenue base has been shrinking. The cumulative logic of its action has created a veritable "tragedy of the commons," whereby the means of its sustenance has been progressively destroyed.

Meanwhile, the decline of the state and the corollary swift growth of an underground or parallel economy have induced the appearance of a new mercantile class wholly separate from the external estate and the politico-commercial class. Its future scope for growth and consolidation, and an eventual political role, remains unclear. It is too recent for its social implications to be clear.

The lower classes—sub-bourgeoisie, workers, members of the informal sector, and peasants—have experienced a sharp loss of status and well-being in the public economy. Indeed, if one confined estimates of their loss to measurable income flow, pauperization would appear to be total. Yet somehow survival has been possible; mass starvation has yet to appear. The vitality of the parallel economy is the explanation. As Oberschall has observed, "Despite the inefficiency, corruption, and poor performance of the formal sector, the total economy and society of Zaire have not broken down because the African informal sector has been vigorous and has enabled Zairians to survive."[76] The very decline in the capacity of the state to regulate and restrain these parallel markets helps explain the dynamism of these spheres of survival.

The dramatic inequalities of the class structure in the New Regime era seem to presage a social explosion of terrible proportions. With the right conjuncture of circumstances, this could well occur. Three primary constraining factors have at least delayed its advent: the educational mobility myth, the perception that external forces guarantee the state, and the survival alternative through informal-sector activities.

Ilunga provides an illuminating recapitulation of the paradoxes of the state-civil society nexus by suggesting that the latter is partitioned into zones of "existence" (the politico-commercial class and the external estate) and "non-existence" (the lower classes):

> The system is far more sophisticated than anticipated . . . it looks very much like a spider web from whose nodal and secondary centers one moves progressively from a zone of existence to one of non-existence. The zone of existence is one in which people can, socially speaking, have more or less acceptable standards of living in modern terms and in accordance with the canons of the existing ideology . . . Politically, this sector of the population makes up the real nation to which the ruling group feels more or less responsible. It is to this sector that the government addresses itself and in terms of which it governs. As one moves . . . into the zone of non-existence . . . there is no social life dominated by money and its corollaries nor specific political power vis-a-vis the ruling group. In this sense, transfer from the zone of existence to that of non-existence practically means civic and political death.

Though many Zairian and foreign observers have predicted calamity, Ilunga concludes that "the dynamite seems to be wet and the detonators too small to blow up the mountain."[77]

5

The Ethnic Dimension of Civil Society

"Between a brother and a friend . . ."

We have argued, in other works, that ethnicity in Zaire needs to be conceptualized within a dynamic framework. It can be easily demonstrated that many of the cultural labels in common use today did not exist a century ago, or that some collective designations are applied to social aggregates whose boundaries are very difficult from what they once were. Early colonial administrators went astray by assuming that a single-dimensional cultural map existed, with discrete boundaries demarcating "tribes." In reality, no such chart has ever been plausible, either today or fifty years ago. Empirical cultural identities are multiple, shifting in response to context and situation. Not wishing to recapitulate what we have previously published on this subject, we will focus first on political aspects of ethnic change, then explore the interaction of class and ethnicity.[1]

"Between a brother and a friend," declared President Mobutu before the United Nations on 4 October 1973, "the choice is clear."[2] This poignant phrase was offered as justification for the surprise decision to rupture relations with Israel, a break which lasted until 1982. The fraternal imperatives of Afro–Arab solidarity had to eclipse the history of amicable relations with Israel, once the issue was sharply posed. In the months that followed the phrase recurred in countless conversations, in jesting reference to the pervasive yet elusive role of ethnicity in shaping and flavoring social and political interactions.

What made the quotation so toothsome, extracted from its context, was its apparent contradiction of the official ideology of the New Regime. Denunciations of "tribalism" are de rigueur on formal occasions of presidential or party moral exhortation; regime spokesmen claim reduced levels of ethnic behavior in politics. Constant vigilance is required to detect tribalism, a sin invariably committed by others. While it has been officially exorcised, in many subtle, complex ways its continued presence is evident, flavoring social transactions and political perceptions. Pervasive, yet elusive: the higher obligation to brother than friend may be clear, but the questions of who is brother in what circumstances, and what choice must be made in his favor, are far less self-evident.

The nature of ethnicity

Ethnicity, in contrast to class, is defined by consciousness. It is rooted in a collective recognition of affinity, to which social and emotional meanings are attached. Its imputation of intimacy finds reflection in the frequency with which kinship metaphors are used to express it; a co-ethnic is a brother, not a mere friend.

A given category of ethnic consciousness is founded upon a set of cultural traits, integrated into a collective representation of the group. A shared speech code is a widespread (though not universal) marker of ethnos. So are shared rituals of daily life, shrines, and belief systems. Ethnos links itself to the past through legends of common ancestry, and to the future through a conviction of shared interests. These elements are woven together, in variant forms, in symbolic systems whereby a group comes to recognize its commonalities, and its sense of affinity is reproduced across generations.

Like class, ethnicity is a relational concept. "We" assumes meaning in relationship to "they." The function of a symbolic structure attached to ethnos is not merely to delineate the self, but to demarcate the collective "we" from relevant others within the social field.[3] "We" and "they" are not simple equivalents, however; as Epstein argues, "the powerful emotional charge that appears to surround or to underlie so much of ethnic behavior" lies in the particular affective force associated with "weness."[4] "We" normally attaches positive connotations to the cultural properties believed to define its identity; the sundry "they" groups found in its cognitive map frequently have vaguely or even intensely negative characteristics and evoke condescending feelings or fear.

Cultural maps within a given social field are not necessarily symmetrical. Particularly in the African urban context, "we" is likely to simplify its mapping by reducing "they" to a finite, easily comprehensible number of others, grouping those who appear similar from the "we" perspective because of broadly similar languages, cultural practices, or regions of origin.[5]

Ethnicity has both instrumental and primordial aspects.[6] Instrumentally, ethnicity is asserted in the competitive pursuit of scarce social goods and values. It becomes manifest when it is useful to a group in securing advantage or resisting deprivation. Its activation may also reflect the interest of an ethnic elite in buttressing its claims to political leadership. It is the instrumental dimension of ethnicity which explains its situational impact upon politics. Ethnicity is activated when circumstances dictate its political use, in contexts in which actors perceive competition, conflict, or threat as ethnically textured.

The potency of ethnic mobilization would be incomprehensible without recognition of its primordial dimension. Ethnic consciousness rests upon shared symbolic meanings, emotionally laden and deeply rooted, which can trigger fears, anxieties, and animosities. The capacity of these affective symbols to supply "we" and "they" demarcations lies in their ability to project themselves as primordial attachments—however novel or ill-defined a given unit of identity may be.

Constitutive elements of ethnicity

While ethnicity has a primordial facet, it cannot be conceived of as immanent essences of identity, transmitted unaltered through generations. On the contrary, like class, ethnicity in Zaire has changed its visage with disconcerting rapidity in recent decades. To grasp its dynamics, we must glance at its most important constitutive vectors, particularly the colonial state, and the political context during the demise of the Bula Matari state and the *pagaille* years.

Formally, the colonial state created two racial estates: the European ruling class, and the African subjects, categorized in the legal ideology of Bula Matari as a subordinate "native" class. But within the overarching white-over-black framework the colonial state was playing a critical role in the shaping of cultural identities, in ways that few understood at the time. Contributing to this process were the spread of educational facilities and the emergence of urban nodal points, new routes of population movement by rail and road, and new labor recruitment patterns. Probably more important were the ethnic categories developed by the state for administrative convenience, the stereotypes attached to particular groups, and the standardization and diffusion of selected languages through school and catechism. The drafting of ethnic maps became a favorite pastime of the administration—a pastime which had the same impact in Zaire as that found by Raymond Apthorpe in Anglophone Africa: "The colonial regimes administratively *created* tribes as we think of them today."[7] The ethnic labels utilized in classification on identity cards, in language standardization, and

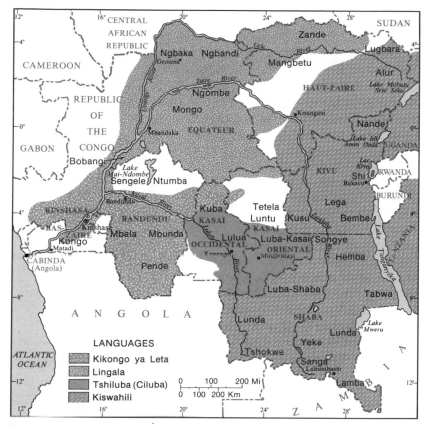

Map 3. Language Distribution and Ethnic Groups

in census categories acquired a momentum of their own and fed back into the shaping of social identities.

A curious form of ethnic imperialism may be found in the monographs of some European writers of the colonial era. The political concept of Mongohood originated in the massive two-volume study by former provincial governor Georges Vanderkerken, published in 1944.[8] A cluster of missionary-scholars—A. de Rop, G. Hulstaert, and E. Boelaert—based at the main Sacred Heart station at Mbandaka assiduously promoted the Mongo language and culture, and defended the latitudinarian theories of

Vanderkerken as to the outer boundaries of the Mongo community. The scope of the Luba zone was likewise given extraordinarily broad definition in the classic study by Edmond Verhulpen; it is remarkable how frequently Zairian scholars today reiterate the classification of groups such as the Hemba, Kanyok, or Luntu as "Luba," using this work as their authority.[9]

The colonial impact at times inhibited the coalescence of potentially incorporative identities. For example, in Sankaru the development by both Catholic and Protestant congregations of Otetela versions as a distinctive speech code, separate from the Lomongo grammars promoted from Mbandaka, was quite important in creating a Tetela solidarity apart from the broader Mongo category. In Bas-Zaire, the institutionalization of several regional versions of Kikongo by different mission congregations played a significant role in the subsequent politics of Kongo identity. (Among the versions were Kiyombe, promoted by Walloon Scheutists; Kindibu, by Redemporists; Kitandu by Flemish Jesuits; and Kikongo ya Leta, by Walloon Jesuits; American, British, and Swedish Protestants also contributed their part to dialectical differentiation.)

These illustrations by no means exhaust the impact of the colonial system on the shaping of ethnic definitions and boundaries. But it is important to note that a complex process of ethnic change was triggered, whose significance was concealed by the European–African fault line in social geography.

The sequences and structure of politics in the terminal colonial period and the First Republic years likewise had an important impact on the constitution of ethnic fields of competition and mobilization. Dramatically shifting contexts of political struggle evoked differeing ethnic perceptions and demarcations. Open political competition among Zairians occurred first in 1957 and 1958 in seven major cities. The colonial state, still in control of the blueprint for change at this juncture, sought to permit circumscribed African political participation in municipal institutions. To avoid direct European–African competition, cities were divided into a numberr of "communes," each to elect its own council and mayor (burgomaster). Thus the arena of competition was the commune rather than the entire city. Europeans, dwelling in residentially segregated areas, formed their own commune, while the Zairian populace was able to compete electorally only for limited authority within the African quarters.

Further, since political parties were not permitted, candidates were thrown back on the organizational resources of the assorted voluntary associations that were tolerated; of these, only the ethnic organizations provided politically communications capable of linking the numerically small elites, who provided the candidate pool, and the mass, whose adult male component was to be permitted to vote. Ethnic organizations varied enormously in scope and effectiveness, and by no means all potential groups possessed such vehicles. But the best known of these, such as the Alliance des Bakongo or Lulua Frères, played a highly visible role, and indeed were credited with a more powerful impact than they actually had.[10] Above and beyond the role of ethnic associations per se, individual candidates quickly discovered that the most efficacious means of identifying a vote bank was through cultivation of those who recognized cultural affinities.

Thus the structure of politics at this first moment of competition mobilized latent social conflict within the African urban social fields. Conflict polarized around a largely novel set of urban ethnic self-identifications, which had gradually taken form in the postwar years; before World War II, no town was large enough for conflict within it to have much valence. Each city was a distinctive social field, with its own patterns of competition or even categories of self-awareness; the same individual might be Ngala in Kinshasa and Ngombe in Mbandaka, or Luba in Kananga and Kasaian in Lubumbashi. The central issues of conflict related to security, status, and mobility. Everyday social discourse began to take note of disparities among levels of prosperity of urban ethnic collectivities. Although most resources remained firmly under European control and allocation, Africans were beginning to staff personnel offices and primary schools, and thus to influence access to employment and education. Many Europeans as well applied ethnic stereotyping in making rules affecting hiring or the attribution of favor; particular groups were "industrious," "open to civilization," "intelligent," "faithful collaborators," or otherwise deserving of special consideration. And now the new municipal representative organs were to gain command over some significant resources, such as the allocation of urban land plots. Although the elections had no issue content, there was reason to believe their results would be meaningful.[11]

Thus ethnic politics in 1957 meant "Kongo" versus "Ngala" in Kinshasa, "Lulua" versus "Luba" in Kananga, "Mongo" versus "Ngombe" in Mbandaka, "Kasaian" versus "authentic Katangan" in Lubumbashi. The cognitive process tended to shape conflict in polarities around the largest and most salient urban ethnic categories. In all but Kisangani the social reductionism of urban ethnicity had prepared the way for this polarization, as common discourse was based on a highly simplified cultural typology, with only a few major labels. The electoral process itself tended to further mold the underlying diversity into a dichotomized pattern. The results suggested that organization, discipline, and solidarity were more important than numbers: in Kananga, Lulua candidates, with a support base of 25 percent of the population, stunned the Luba–Kasai competitors, whose base was 56 percent; in Mbandaka, the Ngombe (19 percent) won over the Mongo (41 percent). In the Kananga instance, the Luba defeat came not from any tendency to vote for Lulua candidates, but rather from the fact that Luba instrumental solidarity operated at a different level—that of the *tshisamba*, or politico-kinship unit, which remained the real basis for rural organization. A single slate of Lulua candidates thus triumphed over multiple lists of Luba aspirants.[12] The lesson was clear; communal safety lay in utilizing the most incorporative level of cultural solidarity available. Ethnic mobilization was an imperative for reasons of self-defense, if no other. What generally escaped notice, however, was that the cultural map of the larger towns was very special; redefinition of the political arena would produce quite different results.

Redefinition was to occur far more suddenly than anyone anticipated. The new urban institutions had barely begun to function when nationwide elections were held in May 1960 to choose members of national and provincial assemblies, which in turn would designate the Zairian central and regional governments. Now the stakes were tremendous; it was no longer simply a matter of city land parcels, but of the whole political system. A monumental redefinition of power relationships was to occur, through a game whose rules derived from the dramaturgy of competitive elections. Uncertainty was total concerning the conduct of the game, and the meaning of its outcome. Equally plausible were dreams of unimaginable gains and fears of disastrous insecurity. The political context activating and defining ethnicity was very different from that in 1957. The urban social fields, although they were the points of departure for political organization, were numerically eclipsed by the 80 percent of the electorate that dwelt in the countryside. Although some ethnic categories mobilized by the urban elections were easily translatable to a rural hinterland (Kongo or Lulua), others had no clear-cut rural counterpart. Numerically very large ethnic clusters (in Bandundu, southern Kasai, northern Shaba, Haut-Zaire, for example), too weakly represented in the major towns to count in the ethnic dichotomization of urban elections, now would carry great weight in the national and provincial assemblies.

The extremely telescoped time dimension of the 1960 election, the absence of an institutionalized national arena of African political participation, and simultaneous power contests at central and provincial levels all militated against organization of competition on a Zaire-wide basis. With only three months to organize, contending political organizations and leaders found that the imperatives of rapid constituency-building made cultivation of ethnic and regional clienteles obligatory. Many employed aggressive nationalist vocabularies, but a more private idiom of affinity was informally utilized. Only two movements made a real effort to organize on a national basis. One of these, the Parti National du Progrès (PNP), was a creature of the colonial administration, and benefitted from its national organization; more closely inspected, however, it turned out to be a loosely knit confederation of local movements. The closest to a genuine national movement was the Lumumba wing of the MNC (MNC/L); national unity was the central plank in its political platform, and a passionate commitment on the part of its leadership. Although its nationalist ideology earned it nuclei of intellectual support in all towns, and though it was the most successful party, its real electoral base had two principal components: (1) nearly unanimous support in Kisangani, where ethnic polarization had not occurred in the urban elections and where Lumumba was viewed as a native son, which brought with it backing in the large rural hinterland linked to Kisangani by demography and political communication channels; (2) the Tetela–Kusu ethnic homeland of Lumumba, and some of its Mongo extension.[13]

Strategies and calculations more complex than simple appeals to ethnic unity were required. For much of rural Zaire, familiar reference groups were very small. The crux of the game was to stitch together numbers of voters sufficient to control a bloc of seats in the prospective assemblies. This meant claiming expanded boundaries of ethnicity, stretching concepts such as "Kongo" or "Mongo" to their outermost conceivable limits;[14] defining region rather than ethnic group as the political building block (as did the Parti Solidaire Africain, or PSA, in Kwilu);[15] or postulating a confederation of ethnic groups presumed to have common interests (the Confédération des Associations Tribales du Katanga of Tshombe).[16] These schemes were by no means universally successful; the ABAKO, for example, was profoundly disappointed to find itself in a minority in the former Leopoldville provincial assembly, which its leaders had believed they were certain to dominate demographically, or by winning over culturally similar groups. The Mongo vehicle, Unimo, mobilized only a fraction of the area to which its organizers laid cultural claim.

The fears and insecurities engendered by the tumultuous electoral campaign, confirmed by the disorders which emerged immediately following independence, created a political environment saturated by ethnicity. Attention soon shifted to maneuvering for place and perquisite within the assemblies themselves; there ethnicity became interwoven with personal advantage, and the parties quickly dissolved into intricate factions. Mass perceptions, however, traumatized by the guerrilla theatre of the elections, continued to find the ethnic meanings politicized by the parties to be the surest guide to political understanding.

The dialectics of fragmentation and faction at the central and provincial levels, and its paralyzing impact, gave rise to the notion that stable governance required smaller, more homogeneous provincial units. It was to implement this postulate that the six original provinces were reconstituted into twenty-one during 1962 and 1963—again redefining the political field within which ethnicity was defined.

The provincial reorganization law of 27 April 1962 set forth three criteria for the creation of new provinces: a population of 700,000, economic viability, and a petition signed by two-thirds of the provincial and national deputies from the region in question. The first two proved totally inoperative: population movements since independence, and demographic uncertainties, permitted almost any morsel of territory to lay claim to the requisite population, and economic viability was impossible to determine administratively, much less politically or juridically. In practice only the third criterion was used, which meant that self-determination by politicians was the rule.

While in reality individual ambitions and ministerial sugarplums played a large role in petition-signing, the popular perception of the process hinged mainly upon ethnoregional factors. What people, by some sort of natural law of cultural affinity, belonged together? In a few cases this was relatively clear, as in the Kongo province or the Luba homeland in Kasai; for most, however, it was not. Only superficially is the proposition of ethnic self-determination appealing; for the proposition begs the critical question of precisely what cultural units may exercise this choice. In general the new provincial lines closely followed the contours of the colonial districts, which constituted the administrative echelon directly below the provinces.[17]

Once again the focus of ethnic definition had shifted. Left far behind were the urban-centered cognitions of the urban elections and the experiments with incorporative ethnic mobilization of the national campaign. The critical issue now was boundaries: where did one natural community begin and another end? The most bitter disputes of this period involved the disposition of groups such as the Kanyok, the Rega, or the Bobangi, who had figured not at all in the lexicon of earlier ethnic conflict. Substantial zones were categorized as "disputed territories," whose fate was to be determined by referendum. A wholly new arena of polarization thus emerged as rural communities were forced to take sides among competing definitions of their identity.

At the same time, a second new arena was forming at the centers of the new provincial entities. Even in provinces widely believed to be homogeneous, power struggles revolved around previously almost unknown identity labels. In the Luba province of South Kasai, factions were identified as Bena Tshibanda (downriver) and Bena Mutu wa Mukuna (upriver); in Sankuru, Eswe (savanna Tetela) were at bitter odds with Ekonda (Tetela and other forest dwellers). The central government provided substantial, and at that time only loosely controlled, budgetary resources to the provinces; the game was worth the candle for the politicians who organized the combat. In so doing, they catalyzed one more layer of cultural cleavages.

These kaleidoscopic patterns of ethnic politics in the 1957–65 period illuminated crucial aspects of ethnicity in Zaire. The political variable played a commanding role in the mobilization of instrumental ethnicity. Swift changes in political context altered the structure of choice, and the arena of conflict and competition. Not only were different levels of personal identity involved, but a calculus of possible combinations; leader and follower needed to make choices concerning coalitions of interest and affinity, often defined in opposition to a relevant other perceived as aggressive or threatening. Faced with the complexities of these processes, we recognize the cogency of Southall's observation that the essence of ethnicity in contemporary Africa is "interlocking, overlapping, multiple collective identities."[18]

Ethnicity, used as a guide to political behavior, appeared to serve the instrumental needs of both leader and follower. Politicians required an electorally demonstrable following to accede to the power and status (and ultimately the class position) attached to high office; no comparably effective avenue to clientele-building was open. For the mass, torn between momentary hopes of unimaginable abundance and fears of calamities which might lurk in a suddenly unpredictable future, security seemed to lie in vesting trust in affinity.

The central issues, in this context, were resource distribution and domination. In the richly evocative Nigerian phrase, politics was "cutting the national cake." The output of the state was perceived as divisible into slices of possibly unequal size, sweet to the taste, and intended to be eaten. A "they" category, in control of political institutions, would exploit its power to impose its dominion upon "we," and to reserve for itself the lion's share of state resources.

Uneven development during the colonial era supplied a reservoir of accumulated grievance that shaped perceptions of these issues. Some groups enjoyed advantages deriving from favorable locations along communication routes or proximity to centers of employment, from favorable stereotypes perceived by the European ruling class, or from relatively early access to the school system. These groups, such as the Kongo or the Kasai Luba, were particularly conspicuous in the *évolué* class by the 1950s, at which time many other groups had begun to grow conscious of their relative disadvantage. Electoral competition translated these perceptions of comparative advantage or disadvantage into political issues.

To grasp the fluidity and circumstantial malleability of ethnicity, we should take note of the relative weakness of its primordial dimension. While ethnic consciousness is not solely instrumental, most cultural groups have lacked the richly embroidered *mythomoteur* of such people as Bengalis, Tamils, or Armenians.[19] Full realization of the primordial potentialities of identity requires weaving the symbolic structures of identity into an elaborate ideology, which makes explicit cultural content and builds an historical mythology of epic proportions. Constructed from such elements as a standardized written language, a diversified literary tradition, a codification of the common cultural "givens" of the group, an ostensibly scientific reconstruction of its history, and a specification of its icons, a fully developed ideology provides an enduring charter of identity, and a clearcut delineation of its boundaries.[20]

In the Zairian context such ideologies are not wholly absent, particularly among groups such as the Kongo, Luba, or Lunda whose oral legends relate their origins to substantial political kingdoms.[21] Full development of cultural ideologies requires an intellectual class, with the resources of literacy. In the Zairian case, this function was initially fulfilled by European missionaries, administrators, and—later—anthropologists, whose impact on ethnogenesis we have already noted. Ethnic associations played some part in the construction of cultural ideology in the 1950s, most notably that of the ABAKO, whose initial major purpose was promotion of a standard form of the Kikongo language; that language had been crippled in its rivalry with Lingala by competing written versions, created from differing regional dialects by various mission orders. Subsequently, important ideological contributions came from the Zairian intelligentsia, but since 1965 the overt construction of cultural ideologies has been declared illegitimate by the official doctrine of "authentic Zairian nationalism."[22] Thus instrumental articulation of ethnic consciousness in the political arena is relatively unconstrained by rigid primordial categories, and is subject to wide situational fluctuation.

Ethnicity under the New Regime

The centralized, unitary, patrimonial, authoritarian nation-state fashioned by the New Regime totally altered the arena of social identity. Pursuing his vision, Mobutu had two critical advantages over his predecessors: a security in office and relative control of events which no other ruler had enjoyed; and the empirical data on ethnicity in politics provided by the First Republic.

Mobutu thus had both a well-calculated strategy for confronting political ethnicity and the means to execute it. He also had the priceless asset of easily conceded approval for the goal of eliminating ethnicity from politics. Almost everyone was against tribalism, even though nearly everyone had of necessity to use it as a social and political resource. The authoritarian edicts proclaiming national integration came unilaterally from the summit, but encountered little resistance at the base, and indeed met with general assent in the early years.

The program for the de-ethnicization of Zairian politics can be summarized in three points: (1) suppression of institutional arenas which ethnicity could be mobilized; (2) apparent exclusion of overt ethnic patronage within the state; (3) prohibition of articulation of cultural ideologies.[23] The first plank was implemented by dismantling electoral assemblies and political parties, which was accomplished during the regime's first year. The bewildering assortment of First Republic parties—250 parties had participated in the 1960 national elections, and 233 in the 1965 balloting—was swept away by the stroke of a pen. In their place, in 1967, was created the MPR, constitutionally defined in 1974 as "the nation politically organized": one nation, one party. The twenty-one provinces were recombined into nine regions, which became mere administrative subdivisions of the recentralized state. Urban councils lingered on for a time, but without function or meaning.[24]

First Republic politicians had sustained their clientele through the quite open use of the armature of the state as patronage resource. Particular ministries had become ethnic fiefdoms, both at the central and provincial levels. Local administrators were named at the provincial level, with ethnic criteria frequently paramount. Most of these practices were swept away by the New Regime's total centralization of state power and the concentration of authority in the presidency. The state remained a vast patrimonial domain, but the distribution of prebends and benefices was above all a presidential prerogative.[25] Functionaries in the command hierarchy of the regional administration were posted outside of their ethnic zones as a matter of principle. Control of particular ministries was frequently rotated, inhibiting the concentration of particular groups in given departments of government. The de facto fusion of party and state hierarchies in late 1967 meant that the same new practices prevailed within the MPR.

Open appeals to cultural solidarity were stigmatized as subversive, and were a mortal danger to any visible leader advancing them; sackings were frequently justified as a punishment for tribalism. *Tribu oui, tribalisme non* was a regime slogan; it was legitimate to acknowledge the existence of ethnicity, but not to ground official behavior or solidarity appeals upon it. The organizational expression of ethnicity, the ethnic association, was proscribed in 1967. In truth, groups such as Lulua Frères or Liboke lya Bangala had already lost much of the élan they had possessed on the 1950s. Yet Kajika, in a 1969 study of Lubumbashi, found that despite the dissolution thirty-four ethnic associations still maintained an informal existence, while quasi-ethnic groupings subsisted through the medium of religious movements and dance groups such as the Kalela. The official suppression of ethnic organizations, Kajika discovered, was much regretted.[26]

To give symbolic content to the nationally integrated character of his regime, Mobutu has relied from the outset upon a carefully distributed ethnic representation in top political offices. In the very first New Regime Council of Ministers there was one minister chosen from each of the then twenty-one provinces. The first two prime ministers of the Mobutu era, Mulamba Nyunyi wa Kadima (1965–66) and Mpinga Kasenda (1977–79) were Lulua and Luba respectively, and were both from Kasai. An analysis of the regional origins of the 212 regime ministers and MPR ruling organ members who served between 1965 and 1975 confirms the apparently representative distribution (see table 5.1).

While the overall pattern revealed by table 5.1 demonstrates a relatively balanced ethnic representation in quantitative terms, there are some modest deviations from a random distribution. The two most self-conscious groups, the Kongo and Luba–Kasai, who are strongly represented in the educated elite and are often believed to be suspect in the eyes of the New Regime, are not markedly under-represented in terms of the total population (though they may be in relation to the size of their elites). The most under-represented area is Kivu, no doubt partly because of its remoteness from the capital and the small number of Kivu people in Kinshasa society. One may note in passing that the relatively favorable representation of the Tetela–Kusu contrasts sharply with their perceptions of reality. This group, like the Kongo and Luba, has tended to believe itself out of favor with the Mobutu regime because of its political heritage as the ethnic homeland of

Table 5.1 Regional Origins of Second Republic Political Elite, 1965–1975

Ethnic/regional group	Number	%	Approximate % of 1970 population
Kongo	27	12.7	10.3
Bandundu (less Maindombe)	23	10.8	11.2
Equateur (plus Maindombe)	43	20.3	14.0
Haut-Zaire	25	11.8	15.4
Kivu (less Kusu)	13	6.1	15.0
Tetela-Kusu	15	7.1	3.3
Luba-Kasai	15	7.1	6.1
Other Kasai (less Luba and Tetela)	20	9.4	12.6
North Shaba	17	8.0	6.5
South Shaba	10	4.7	5.6
Missing	4	1.9	
	212	100.0	100.0

Source: Survey by the authors. We have used ethnoregional categories of special relevance to the Mobutu era.

Lumumba. The ambiguous stand of the regime toward Lumumbism—appropriating its symbols while generally eschewing its radical impulses—has contributed to the sense of unease, which was reinforced in 1975 by the fingering of several Tetela officers as conspirators in an obscure *coup monté et manqué*. But the Tetela–Kusu representation in 1965–75 overstates their real influence; most Tetela–Kusu in the cabinet or Political Bureau held relatively unimportant slots, and tended to be rotated out of office quickly.

The impact of ethnic representation has been qualified by the public's discovery that those from their group selected by the president for high office are intended to function only as symbolic delegates, and not as active spokespersons for their groups. The prime qualification for office is *fidelité au Guide*. Active promotion of regional claims has been a passport for speedy exit from high office.

The regional administration of the state has also been de-ethnicized through the principle of posting administrators outside the area of their origin. In addition, regional administrators are subject to frequent transfer, making it difficult to construct personal fiefdoms from the institutional base of state authority. As top state officials are invariably the most powerful and often the wealthiest Zairians in administrative seats—especially in

the smaller seats without major enterprise—the social hierarchy constitutes a distinction between the local population and "strangers" (which
may well be a source of local resentment). The politico-commercial class,
tied to the state, is in this sense a national class, subject to posting to any
corner of the republic (though most of its members are concentrated in the
capital). The local linkages that top state cadres create in a given post are
commercial, not political.[27]

The ethnic inner core

While the strategy of demobilizing ethnicity and depriving it of institutional channels for political articulation has been successful in reducing the
saliency of cultural pluralism in the formal realm, it has failed to remove
ethnic connotations from mass perceptions of the exercise of power. The
conviction is well-nigh universal that when the outer husk of Zairian national ideology is broken away, the inner core is Equateurian and Lingalaphone. We may adduce three major reasons for this: (1) the regional character of the inner security coalition that is the heart of power maintenance;
(2) the inevitable regional-ethnic connotations corollary to the personalization of political power; (3) the linguistic policies and ambitions of the
regime. Before examining each of these, we should explore the absence of
one factor: the regime exhibits almost no trace of open ethnic chauvinism.
As powerful cultural ideologies have so frequently undergirded communal
conflict elsewhere in the world, the relative absence of this factor requires
some explanation.

Mobutu himself is an Ngbandi, a group of modest dimensions whose
domain, as fixed by colonial occupation, stretches southward for about
100 kilometers from the vicinity of Mobayi-Mbongo (Banzyville) to
Yakoma; along the Ubangi River it forms the frontier with part of the
present Central African Republic. Historically, the Ngbandi were in close
symbiosis with the Zande state formation process to the east in Uele. Orthodox colonial criteria placed them in the "Sudanic" linguistic group,
which stressed the discontinuities with the Bantu languages to their south.
More contemporary and linguistically sound classifications (in particular
that of Greenberg) situate them in the Adamawa-eastern subgroup of the
broader Niger-Congo family, which also includes the Bantu languages.[28]
The Ngbandi region was one of the most isolated during the colonial era:
it had neither significant economic resources nor communications routes;
nor did it have mission infrastructure. As a result, relatively few Ngbandi

migrated to towns; in the Equateur provincial capital they were only 2 percent of the population in the 1950s.

There was some evidence, little noted at the time, of Ngbandi cultural self-assertion in Kinshasa in the 1950s. In the context of emerging cultural-political regroupings in the capital, some Lingalaphone elites sought to counterbalance the increasingly dynamic Kongo movement (ABAKO) with an "Ngala" umbrella organization that would bind together the diverse migrants from the upper river. Their most important ties were social competition with the Kongo, and common urban use of Lingala. This movement, the Liboke Iya Bangala, was particularly associated with Bolikango Akpolobako (Jean), and was given discreet encouragement by the powerful Scheutist order, whose main bases were upriver. The Ngbandi—as well as some other north Equateur groups—were very reluctant to participate in this ethnolinguistic alliance. Burssens has noted that the Ngbandi were "the most proud, the most self-aware" of the ethnic groups north of the Zaire River in Equateur, adding that "their authority was rather easily accepted by other groups."[29] Verhaegen describes Ngbandi resistance at this time to submersion in the "grande ethnie Bangala," then being politically promoted by Bolikango and the Liboke:

> The memory of their warrior superiority seemed to retain its vitality among some Ngbandi leaders. The hypothesis is thus plausible that such memories favored among them a consciousness of ethnic superiority and the emergence of a certain micronationalism, whose development was then encouraged by a rather strong cultural homogeneity. This explains why the Ngbandi offered—at a time when political life, in the framework of the colonial system, could only induce motivations and alignments of an ethnic nature—a resistance to the centripetal movement which the Liboke tried to imprint upon all the populations of the inter-Zaire-Ubangi area.[30]

Traces of the "warrior" tradition may be found in the praise-name Mobutu took for himself when, under the banner of authenticity, all Zairians were required to drop European forenames for Zairian postnames: "Sese Seko Kuku Ngbendu wa za Banga" means approximately "the all-conquering warrior who triumphs over all obstacles."[31] However, Mobutu has never openly celebrated the ethnic virtues of the Ngbandi, nor has he made use of the Ngala category. His cultural image is related to Equateur regionally, and to Lingala linguistically. Although the small community of Gbadolite is celebrated as his ancestral village, he was actually born in Lisala—an Ngombe town—and grew up in Mbandaka and Kinshasa.

His mother, given extraordinary prominence in regime hagiography, lived her final years in Gemena (where a large tomb was erected in her honor); this is located in Ngbaka territory, and is not an Ngbandi community. Ngbandi warrior tradition aside, there is no comparison between the ideological affirmation of cultural identity among groups in the north Equateur area and the affirmations of groups such as the Kongo, Luba–Kasai, or Lunda.

Thus the ethno-regional coloration of the regime has little to do with Ngbandihood. Nor is it a consequence of intense regional pride of Equateurians, projected upon the public realm. Rather, the perception of Equateur/Lingalaphone domination, widespread amongst the citizenry, originates in the nature of the regime and its exercise of power. We now return to the reasons for this perception, sketched out above.

In the early years of the regime, when power was less completely concentrated in presidential hands, this orientation was less evident. As time went on, an inner core of Equateurians became increasingly visible, above all in the security apparatus. The Forces Armées Zairoises have always been commanded by officers either from Equateur or from adjoining areas of Haut-Zaire. Until 1972 the army was commanded by a relative of the president, Bobozo Salelo; he was replaced by General Bumba Moaso, a Budja. After the retirement in 1972 of General Bobozo and a number of other old Force Publique noncoms, the senior officer was Massiala Kinkela, a Kongo, who was always excluded from top command functions and who perished in a mysterious helicopter crash in September 1975. The predominance of the Equateur inner core, dubbed by Rymenam as the "presidential family," also extended to the most sensitive levers of financial control.

The growing personalization of the regime after 1970 had as its inevitable concomitant a heightened consciousness of its regional center of gravity. In a political environment highly sensitized to cultural distinctions, no one can shed his ethnicity. Thus the personality cult which gathered momentum in the 1970s, and culminated in the constitutional imposition of "Mobutism" as regime doctrine, escalated the saliency of ethnoregional cues in mass cognitions of regime action.

Further, the central role accorded to Lingala by the regime entrenched regionalized perceptions of power. Lingala has been invariably used by Mobutu in mass gatherings; in contrast to Lumumba, who had a fluent mastery of Swahili and Tshiluba as well as Lingala, it is the only vehicular language Mobutu knows well. Lingala is also the language of the military, which initially installed the New Regime. There have been clear indications that the regime would like to have Lingala recognized as the national language; a congress of Zairian linguists held in Lubumbashi in 1974 was intended to provide scientific cover for this aspiration, but the Kinshasa contingent had to retreat in the face of very strong opposition from Shaba and Kasai delegates.[32]

The "affirmative action" policies of the regime, aimed at geographic balance through equitable region access to higher education, have tended to foster a suspicion that there are culturally-inspired social closure mechanisms operating to the disadvantage of groups strongly represented in the university populations, such as the Kongo and Luba-Kasai. After the university reform of 1971, regional quotas were instituted for access to higher education, with each of the nine regions purportedly having a roughly equivalent number of students. The regime's choice of a regional rather than an ethnic basis for a quota system reflected a broader strategy, in which pluralism was officially grounded in administrative entities rather than in ethnic groups per se. The quota system also had quite anomalous results: the Kasai Oriental region, which contained the Luba-Kasai, also was populated by groups like the Kanyok and the forest Tetela, who had been strongly disadvantaged; being merged with the Luba quota was a crushing handicap.

The quota system was intensely unpopular even among its presumed beneficiaries, the students from Equateur and Haut-Zaire.[33] In fact, the university registration procedure was far too porous for such a system to be applicable; of the first-year class at Lubumbashi in 1973–74, some 30 percent were from Kasai Oriental (whose hypothetical quota was 11 percent), while Equateur and Haut-Zaire enrolled only 2 percent each (a reflection of their geographical distance).[34] The historic patterns of regional inequalities in the educational infrastructure were very difficult to reverse, as table 5.2 demonstrates.

The ratio between the two totals in table 5.2 offers a rough measure of the dynamic of educational expansion. What stands out, in the face of regional balance policies, is the formidable energy of expansion visible in Kasai Oriental and (to a lesser extent) Bandundu, which have enjoyed no government priority, while Equateur, unlikely to have been neglected, ranks near the bottom.[35] Even sharper is the lag in Kivu, for reasons which are not immediately apparent.

In sum, the new context of the Second Republic gave yet another shape to ethnic definitions. Politics became centralized and nation-centered; there was only one arena, at Kinshasa. The political vocabulary of ethnicity now

Table 5.2   Comparison of Secondary School Populations, 1962 and 1978

Region	(1) Secondary school enrollment, 1962–63[a]	(2) Final year students, secondary school, 1976–77	Ratio, 2:1[b]
Kinshasa	9,499	4,364	.46
Bas-Zaire	5,012	3,611	.72
Bandundu	4,432	5,079	1.15
Equateur	2,481	1,371	.55
Haut-Zaire	4,127	3,911	.95
Kivu	5,381	1,988	.37
Shaba	(secession)	3,437	
Kasai Oriental	2,992	8,420	2.81
Kasai Occidental	3,027	1,641	.54
	36,951	33,822	.94

Sources: J. Dehasse and B. Maiter, "Données complémentaires sur l'enseignement supérieur dans la République du Congo," *Etudes Congolaises* 5, no. 10 (December 1953): 2; *Elima*, 21 June 1977.
a Includes the last five years of the secondary cycle; final year enrollment was only 739.
b Calculated by adding a notional figure for Shaba by averaging other totals.

centered on four orienting foci: the nine administrative regions; a small number of very large and visible ethnic units, such as the Kongo or Luba; the zones demarcated by the four major vehicular languages—Lingala, Swahili, Tshiluba, and Kikongo—which were not coterminous with either the regions or the ethnic groups; and the major cities, which were poles of social fields. An ordinary citizen in Lubumbashi might refer to the same luminary from Kinshasa as Equateurian, as Mukongo (whether he was or not, as this might be the only ethnic designation that was known so far away), as Lingalaphone, or as a "person" from Kinshasa. Ethnic reality is of indefinite potential complexity, yet public cognitions can deal easily with only a few salient categories; thus in social perceptions the national scene must be resolved into a manageable and parsimonious typology.

Within this framework, the national integration policies of the New Regime have had a mixed impact. On the one hand, they have succeeded in preventing open ethnic mobilization and confrontation, and have had some effect on the strenuous efforts to build affective attachments to Zaire as a nation-state (though not necessarily on attachments to the regime). On the other hand, the growing public perception of the hegemonic inner group, regionally recruited, has focused growing resentment on Equateurians. The nature of these cognitions was expressed by student political slang on the Lubumbashi campus of UNAZA; the terms used to denote Equateur and its towns were "Nazareth," "Bethlehem," "promised land," and the like.[36]

However eclipsed open affirmation of ethnicity may be, it remains likely that a return to full-scale political competition would remobilize ethnicity, though not necessarily as the sole determinant of alignments. Until 1977, the only arena in which any open electoral competition had been permitted was within the universities and in some secondary schools. The regime calculated—correctly—that if the party youth organization to which students were required to belong was to have any utility at all, participation by members in the selection of their leaders was imperative. Campaigns were quite heated, but ideological competition outside the amorphous framework of official party doctrine was proscribed. The electoral slates were based upon ethnoregional blocs of the sort noted above.

For the 1977 elections for the Political Bureau, national legislature, and urban councils, the regime devised an astute strategy for restraining ethnicity. An unlimited number of candidates was permitted for each seat, and there was only a small degree of political screening; thus the 18 Political Bureau seats attracted 167 candidates, while there were 2,090 contestants for the 270 legislative seats. With an average of 10 candidates per seat, and the voter permitted one choice, ethnicity was diluted by the inevitable multiple candidacies among larger groups. Yet the ethnicity issue could quickly emerge; in the final days of the Shaba campaign strong attacks on Kasaians rekindled tensions reminiscent of the earlier elections.

Class and ethnicity and clientelism

By way of conclusion, we will examine the interconnections between class formation and ethnocultural transformation. These processes are almost invariably considered separately; class and cultural pluralism, in particular, belong to different analytical and even philosophical traditions, which have too often treated one as a concealed manifestation of the other. Yet the heart of the matter surely is not that these processes occur simply in parallel social causeways, but rather that each spills over into the other. The task of the analyst is to trace their intricate commingling.

One set of intercept channels, linking the streams, consists of patron-client networks, which ramify through all levels of Zairian society. This complex of relationships, founded upon asymmetries of power, status, and wealth, relates the weaker to the stronger through ties of dependency. The client accepts a submissive, subordinate relationship to his patron, and the obligation to provide his patron with services; in return, the patron provides favors to the client which he would not otherwise be able to obtain. As either party may at least theoretically withdraw from the relationship, particularly in urban settings, its persistence ultimately depends upon a perception of mutual advantage. Each party is likely to seek benefits from the linkage. At the same time, the operation of patron-client nets are constrained by social ideologies. A well-placed patron cannot easily evade the claims of a kinsman in acute distress; a client cannot readily reject demands of a patron for social support, because obligation is not only prescribed by the contingent requirements of the patron-client dyad, but also underwritten by the social values of reciprocal duties.

Formation of a patron-client relationship is based not only on reciprocal advantage, but on some principle of affinity which supplies a social logic to the network. Kinship and ethnic affinity are the most frequent bases for network formation, although other bases are possible; formal roles of unequal relationship may be complemented by informal patron-client ties, as in the cases of teacher and student, priest and communicant, employer and employee. The network may be merely episodic, formed for short-term purposes, or it may be enduring. The comprehensiveness of social exchanges covered by a patron-client tie may also vary considerably.[37]

The nature of the Zairian state and the ongoing crisis in Zairian society are potent generators of client ties. There are, to begin with, innumerable everyday problems which beset those lacking leverage over state decisional structures: obtaining a permit, averting a sanction, gaining access to a state facility, for example. Such a problem, which may be totally insoluble through routine channels or because of the limited financial means of a poor person when some payment is required, may be rapidly settled if the right intermediary is found. While the relationship between a client and the patron whose intercession can turn the key may be very short-term if the difficulty is nonrecurrent, some problems require ongoing attention and thus can generate sustained relationships.

Mobility-related transactions constitute another field of patron-client relations. These include transactions to obtain employment, to gain entry into schools, and to meet educational costs. Survival favors are a third important source of clientage. Health is a constant preoccupation, and sickness in the family a frequent crisis. Though the best employers, such as Gécamines, provide good medical service to their employees and dependents, most Zairians are not so fortunate. Medical supplies are scarce, and often beyond the means of the poor.

The activation of patron-client ties is a game with indeterminant rules. The prospective client must lay claim to some relationship to the patron which will legitimate the appeal for assistance. Several factors govern patron response: value attached to the ties invoked, possible reciprocal benefits, the credibility of any negative sanctions threatened by a petitioner (kin group retaliation, for example). These values must be discounted by the material or professional costs or risks entailed in providing the favor.[38] No two individual patrons respond in precisely the same way, though very few reject out of hand all such approaches. Equally rare are those who believe that governmental decisions are made according to formal criteria alone.

The political context of the New Regime enhances the social importance of such networks. Collective demands, be they ethnic or in the name of some other social principle, are not legitimate. The ancillary organizations of the party, designed to incorporate particular sectors such as labor, youth, and merchants, are not effective channels for seeking either collective or particularistic goods from the state. The individual is atomized when faced with the state. Access strategies depend upon finding vulnerable or soft entry points. Without mediation, the state, enmeshed in myriad regulations, hardened by its inertia and inefficiency, is difficult to penetrate.

The flavor of these transactions is conveyed by responses to a Zairian researcher, who asked a sample of civil servants in one Lubumbashi regional service whether they would reply favorably to a request for special service from a co-ethnic whom they did not know personally, if the favor required laborious or annoying efforts to pursue the issue through several offices. Two-thirds of the twenty-seven respondents indicated that they would, though with reservations;[40] of the twenty-seven, six said they would be influenced by ethnic solidarity, and three justified their response in defensive terms, observing that "everyone does it" (this response followed the van den Berghe precept which states in the context of a universal expectation others will act on the basis of ethnicity, and that self-defense justifies similar behavior).[41] Two others argued that the client would have to *bouger* (offer payment) like anyone else.[42] A number indicated that ethnicity alone was not enough; one would need to know the individual. Several categorically denied they would be influenced.

There is a crucial asymmetry in patron-client transactions. The more important the service, the more immediate must be the relationship; usually involved is some far more precise social connection than common membership in an ethnic community which may number several hundred thousand. Yet others observing the transaction will cognitively transform it into an ethnic exchange; the common ethnic origin will be readily visible, while more intimate kinship ties would not be. Thus the state, while constantly proclaiming formal anti-ethnic rules, equally consistently resensitizes the cultural environment through the personalistic informal codes which govern its actual behavior.

The clientage phenomenon also operates to provide important trans-class linkages. Kilson notes what he terms the "asymmetrical" nature of the new elite, who "are impelled, by force of traditional obligations, to assist their poorer kin, and usually in ways that mitigate a great widening of the social distance between the upper and middle categories and the poorer sections."[43] The most important favors that may be solicited from a wealthier kinsman lie in the fields of mobility and survival: temporary lodging when newly arrived in a city, help with school fees, assistance with employment, aid during a family crisis, illness, or death. This kind of exchange is essentially limited to the kinship sphere; common ethnicity does not normally constitute a convincing claim to such transactions.

There is an evident concern to avoid redistributing all the household wealth to kinsmen. Kajika observes that in Lubumbashi house owners were reluctant to rent to relatives, preferring to give them temporary free lodging; it was too hard to collect rent from them.[44] Mukenge has found that while all businessmen supported some not very useful relatives, this in itself was not an insuperable block to wealth accumulation; one of the skills of entrepreneurship is the effective use of kin clients. Some 30 percent of the small business employers hired relatives exclusively, though 36 percent employed no relatives. Unskilled but nonservile functions often went to relatives, as did positions of special trust, such as bookkeeping and tending the cash register.[45]

The essential function of kinship clientage in the social sphere is not to impede the crystallization of the politico-commercial class, but rather to sustain some hopes of mobility for lower-class members. The clientage channel provides an alternative to mobilization of the poor as a class, especially when political action seems impossible or hopeless. Many nurture at least the hope that individual survival mechanisms can be found through clientelist links. Given the disparity in numbers between the prosperous minority and their many poor relatives, the "hope" often is no more than that.

We may return from clientelism to the broader issues of class and ethnicity by way of Bertrand, who develops an intriguing connection, from a Marxist perspective, in a study of Congo–Brazzaville. The pervasive clientage networks, within the state sector, bring about transactions which articulate between what he terms the "lineage mode of production" (based on Meillassoux and Terray) and the capitalist mode.[46] In the capitalist sector (a handful of mines and forestry enterprises) workers really sell their labor, but in the "bureaucratic-tribal sector" (the state) patron-client nets determine employment and advancement. What Bertrand sees as an emergent peasant class, harboring a very palpable anger at the state bureaucracy, is driven back to the lineage elders, who in alliance with the bureaucratic caste convert these resentments into ethnic antagonisms. "The state apparatus," he writes, "is thus the essential political superstructure for articulation between the dominated lineage mode of production and the dominant capitalist mode of production. Direct heir to the colonial administration, the state secretes a social stratum which [is] primarily in the service of capitalist interests because it lives on them and capital is dominant, [but which] must nonetheless support itself . . . on the lineage hierarchies . . . through their major political expression, tribal 'solidarity.'"[47]

The political sociology of Congo–Brazzaville, as analyzed by Bertrand, is remarkably similar to that of Zaire, despite the commitment to Marxist–Leninist ideology in Brazzaville since 1969. We would differ from Bertrand in the formulation of the interaction of class and ethnicity, while noting a similar tendency for social tensions deriving from stratification to become articulated as ethnicity. However, the "lineage mode of production" is a defective concept for capturing the dynamics of ethnicity; contemporary ethnicity in the urban and national arenas has little to do with the localized structures which serve as the basis for the "lineage mode" theory, nor are the artisans of ethnic solidarity movements in any sense the "lineage elders" purported to be the dominant class in the lineage mode.

The clientage nexus between class and ethnicity is stated with particular cogency by Mwabila, whose formulation we find persuasive. In explaining the failure of current misery to serve as a crucible of class consciousness for the impoverished, he points to

> the accelerated development of ethnic consciousness in recent years and the individualization of the response to misery.
>
> Ethnic consciousness became accentuated by the policy labelled Zairianization, inaugurated in 1973 . . . As a result of this policy . . . a middle class appeared, essentially composed of "Zairian businessmen," while at the same time a "national bourgeoisie" became reinforced; to a growing de-

gree, the latter based itself upon the group consciousness of the various
ethnic communities to which its members belonged.

A new type of class alliance founded on ethnic solidarity thus took the
place of worker solidarity and consciousness of material conditions . . . It
was, in fact, an alliance within which there occurred a kind of chain of cli-
entalization, internal to the ethnic group, whose final object was to hoist
the wealthy members of the ethnic group into the proximity of political
power, so that the "interests" of the ethnic group and geographic region
might be protected.[48]

Complementing the Mwabila formulation is a closely reasoned statement by Jewsiewicki, which weaves together state, class, ethnicity, and clientelism. Ethnicity, paradoxically, is an "initial instrument" linking an urban and industrial society to the rural world through the ideology of
commonality which it provides. At the same time, the social categoriza-
tions imposed by ethnic consciousness serve to negate incipient class solidarities. Ethnicity, in daily existence, is often experienced through political
clientelism, and tends to become "a structure of exploitation for the profit
of the bourgeoisie and the bureaucracy." Through its fragmentation of
emergent classes, "ethnicity spares the state the need to repress a number
of social conflicts, thanks to the vertical integration and clientelistic mechanisms it provides."[49]

Finally, we return to our argument that the state itself is the most decisive single factor in the complex pattern of mutations and reformulations
of social consciousness within civil society. The nation-state, as political
arena and as overarching institutional superstructure, provides the framework, context, and situation which shape the particular class and ethnic
configurations at any given moment. Social consciousness is not—or not
yet—congealed into permanent, structured categories. The multidimen-
sionality of both class and ethnicity make hazardous the assumption that
the forms of collective identity and action can be inferred from those
which have prevailed at other times and places.

In our view, neither class nor ethnicity can serve as the sole explanatory
framework for capturing the essence of sociopolitical change. Not only
must both be utilized, but the indeterminacy of the two taken both separately and cumulatively must also be conceded. We would subscribe to the
cogent conclusions of Schatzberg:

> Failure to appreciate contextual subtleties has led, more often than not,
> to a denial of the existence of class and class consciousness. But I believe
> the reason class has not usually appeared in its analytically identifiable

Marxian trappings is that it is a contextual consciousness which often crosscuts itself. Africans, like others, can and do maintain more than one ethnic identity. Which one becomes salient in a given situation is very likely to depend upon the socio-political context of the moment. So, too, social class. As the context changes, the same individual may well display more than one class identity . . . These shifts in consciousness depend upon the context and have little to do with any changes in the "objective" material conditions of the people involved . . . like Walt Whitman, we are all large and contain multitudes.[50]

6

The Patrimonial State and Personal Rule

*Only one man, previously noted for his outstanding services to his coun-
try, can assure the well-being of each one of us and create the conditions
propitious of the people's moral and spiritual growth, and offer them a
common ideal, the feelings of a joint destiny and the knowledge of belonging to one country.*

1970 MPR Congress[1]

In our initial chapter we suggested that patrimonial patterns of rule have
characterized many post-colonial African states. Since the days of Leopold,
Zaire has regularly illustrated these general patterns in exaggerated, even
caricatural form; they have found new confirmation in the exceptional
patrimonialization and personalization of the state in the Second Republic
years. We begin our consideration of institutional and ideological dimensions of the state by examining its patrimonial nature and the background
of its ruler.

Even though the colonial state, in its origins, was a personal fiefdom,
over the years its rule became increasingly bureaucratized. The hegemony
of the state was upheld by a socially distant European bureaucracy, paternalistic yet impersonal. Belgian doctrine, which shaped the internal functioning of the colonial state apparatus, reflected the legalistic orientations
characteristic of the continental state. Administrative agents were equipped
with ample discretionary authority for the enforcement of state edicts directed at the subject populace. But colonial rule was highly institutionalized, operating through a dense matrix of laws and regulations.

The structural model of the colonial state was important to the New
Regime's initial designs for restoring the full hegemony of the state over
civil society. The *pagaille* years, many believed, had demonstrated the validity of one of the premises of colonial state ideology: civil society, whose
cleavages were inevitably productive of endemic disorder, was inherently
unruly unless controlled by a comprehensive state hegemony. The initial
state resurrection measures of the New Regime—centralization, hierarchy,
unity of command—seemed to reflect a restoration of the colonial ide-

ology. "Politics," productive of faction and fratricide, was to be eliminated through dissolution of the political parties.

But a new vocabulary of monistic state structure which had no colonial antecedent soon began to appear. The unity of the state was to be embodied in its leader. "A village has only one chief," "our ancestors were ruled by an unchallenged and unchallengeable chief"; "an organism with two heads is a monster': such slogans were emblematic of the gradual patrimonialization of power.[2]

Patrimonialism

Patrimonialism, advanced as a regime type by Max Weber, describes a system in which high office is bestowed in return for personal service to the ruler.[3] The political elite are tied to the ruler by links of individual clientage. The reservoir of state offices forms a pool of prebends, whose attractiveness is a potent incentive to personal loyalty and service. In return, the client has the right not only to hold the office, but to exploit it for his own benefit. All significant posts are held at the pleasure of the ruler; above all, constantly reaffirmed personal fidelity and services are indispensable. Any suspicion of a slackening of loyalty is grounds for instant removal.

Faithful service alone is not enough; the client must demonstrate his utility through effective service. The ruler depends upon the office-holder to demonstrate an ability to secure compliance with presidential orders, and to cope with the management of his particular sphere of authority—with the first priority being the maintenance of political control. The patrimonial fief-holder must not only exercise control over his (or occasionally her) domain, but remain dependent. In analyzing Zaire's ascendancy phase we have described the progressive elimination of the baronial figures of the First Republic, who retained significant political resources of their own. Politicos of the old Binza group were a danger; they brought to the political arena their own clienteles, and—worse yet—had independent access to external forces, and particularly to Belgian or American influence. By the time patrimonial ascendancy has been established in 1970, there was literally no one in the state domain who held a position other than through presidential grace.

Client office-holders have been constantly reminded of the precariousness of tenure by the frequent of office rotation, which simultaneously fuels the hopes of those Zairians anxiously awaiting just outside the portals of power. The MPR Political Bureau, for example, was revamped a dozen times in the first decade of party life. No one (except, of course, Mobutu) has been continuously a member, and only six persons have figured on as many as half of the membership lists. Only 41 of the 212 top figures held high office for as long as five years in the 1965–75 period.

Insecurity has been sustained among top state and party personnel by the frequent application of sanctions. During the first decade of the Mobutu regime, 29 of the 212 leaders went directly from their posts to prison, on either political or corruption charges. An additional 26 were removed on grounds of disloyalty or dishonesty, with penal sanctions. The president or the ubiquitous Centre National de Documentation receives a continuous flow of denunciations of high office-holders, which is used as leverage over them. Virtually all have subsidiary business activities, and most are vulnerable to allegations of corruption or nepotism. The Pentecost Plot hangings vividly demonstrated the dangers of forming combines, and the possible role of *agents-provocateurs*. Frequently in presidential speeches reference is made to unnamed disloyal or corrupt persons in the leadership ranks, another reminder of the insecurity of high office. Cumulatively, these devices constitute a powerful mechanism of informal intimidation, and suggest why systematic opposition has never arisen within the top organs of the state.

The rewards for loyal service, however, have been commensurate with the risks. In 1974 the salary of a Political Bureau member was Z 2,600 per month, and additional allowances were made for housing, transportation, domestic servants, and entertainment. For most, this was only the beginning. Occult revenues were likely to surpass the official salary.

Though sanctions could be severe, a fall from grace was not necessarily permanent. Those jailed seldom remained in prison for very long. Repentance and renewed cultivation of the favor of the sovereign could make possible a return to full grace. At the least, the disgraced client might be permitted to retire to management of the mercantile domain which had usually been carved out while in high office. The remarkable career of Nguza Karl-i-Bond furnishes an intriguing example. Despite his ties to Tshombe he rose rapidly to become foreign minister from 1972 to 1974 and 1976 to 1977; from 1974 to 1976 he was Political Director of the MPR. In 1977 he was accused of high treason, sentenced to death, and subjected to unspeakable tortures. A year later not only was the death sentence commuted, but he was released; he became prime minister in 1979. In 1981 he fled into exile to join the opposition groups, yet in his embittered autobiographical analysis of the Mobutu regime he exhibits paradoxical nostalgia for his patrimonial service: "It was Mobutu who named me

Ambassador at Geneva, Minister of Foreign Affairs, Political Director of the Party . . . Nobody imposed these decisions upon him. He, therefore, chose the person whom he judged could render the best service in a specific domain of national life. The fact that this person had spent six years at his side, in filling ever more important positions of confidence, demonstrates that he merited this confidence."[4]

The Zairian presidency itself, in keeping with the monist nature of the patrimonial system, became the most powerful institution of the state. Composed of courtier-technocrats, after consolidation was completed, the secretariat was above all the instrument for transmission of the presidential will. Policy organs whose missions enjoyed momentary priority were likely to come under the direct tutelage of the presidency, as were those of key economic importance (such as Gécamines). Security affairs and key transactions with external political or financial milieux were located in the presidency.

In addition to the trusted functionaries of the presidency, there was a shadowy entourage of more occult figures, Zairian and foreign. Some, like Litho Maboti, had close family ties. Others were available for personal services; one of these was Dr. William Close, an American physician once linked with Moral Rearmament, a movement in which Mobutu had earlier shown some interest. (Close, who once enjoyed intimate ties with the president, became disillusioned and had fallen from favor by the mid-1970s.) Of uncertain status was a Senegalese diviner who apparently also attended to the personal well-being of the president.

The paradigm-setting example of the successful client was Bisengimana Rema, who for a decade remained as head of the presidential secretariat. An engineering graduate, he became a master at translating the general policy initiatives of the president into concrete measures. Hard-working, self-effacing, discreet, he held himself on call day and night for the president, and avoided the Kinshasa diplomatic and social circuits. Of Rwandan Tutsi origin, he had neither a political constituency nor any prospect of creating one. Indeed, many Zairian elites saw him as a foreign intruder, and he was cordially disliked by many. This made him all the more useful to the president, as his dependency was total, and his technocratic skills made him an invaluable alter ego. The combination of dependency and competency made him an ideal courtier.

The patrimonial system could draw upon a continuous supply of the ablest talent in Zaire. For the upward mobile and the ambitious, career advancement at some point required accommodation to the conventions of patrimonialism. The top jobs in a very broad institutional spectrum, from the university to Gécamines, depended in the final analysis on presidential favor. Once in office, the incumbent had little choice but to conform to the patron-client role prescribed by the basic framework of the system.

Not only public office, but state resources were utilized to sustain the patrimonial presidency. By the 1970s, official figures showed that expenditures made directly by the presidency were approximately 20 percent of the operating budget, and usually a larger fraction of the small capital budgets. The extraordinary scale of this presidential financial intervention, outside the normal framework of budgetary control, was a constant target of external criticism of Zairian state finances; yet Mobutu clung tenaciously to the practice, an essential ingredient of Mobutist politics. A significant portion of these funds went to ad hoc outlays, through which pressing needs were filled by direct presidential benefaction. This bounty is well described by an admiring journalist who followed Mobutu on one of his swings through the interior: "Mobutu always tries to resolve on the spot as many problems as possible. If a given community lacks an indispensable vehicle, if the budget of a school or a dispensary has been forgotten, the credits are at once accorded."[5] Such largesse was portrayed as a personal gift from the president. Patrimonialism and its command of resources help us to understand the adventure of the 30 November measures; while Zairianization had multiple objectives, it is hard to overlook the fact that the expropriation of commerce and plantations provided a huge new pool of resources for patrimonial distribution.

The sharpening economic crisis from 1974 on greatly weakened the regime because of the severe shrinkage of resources under presidential control. Patrimonialism is a process, not a permanent relationship founded upon a single transaction. When the flow of public goods decreases, there is necessarily an erosion of the solidity of client ties; patrimonialism in Zaire, like the currency itself, experienced successive devaluations.

Personalism

The personalization of power in the New Regime reached its peak in 1974, when public ideology was renamed "Mobutuism." The president had acquired an array of praise-names daily reiterated in the regime media: Guide of the Zairian revolution, the Helmsman, Father of the Nation, Founding President. The press carried a front-page photograph Mobutu nearly every day; pictures of the president were de rigueur not only in all public places, but also in the homes of the politically ambitious. The extravagance of the personality cult at its 1974–75 peak is exemplified by a declaration by Interior Minister Engulu:

> In our religion, we have our own theologians. In all religions, and at all times, there are prophets. Why not today? God has sent a great prophet, our prestigious Guide Mobutu—this prophet is our liberator, our Messiah. Our Church is the MPR. Its chief is Mobutu, we respect him like one respects a Pope. Our gospel is Mobutism. This is why the crucifixes must be replaced by the image of our Messiah. And party militants will want to place at its side his glorious mother, Mama Yemo, who gave birth to such a son.[6]

For one period of several weeks in early 1975 official media were forbidden to mention by name any other figure but Mobutu; other persons were referred to only by the title they held. Power at the summit was totally personalized; all other office-holders disappeared into anonymity.

The justification invoked privately—and at times publicly, when regime spokesmen felt constrained to deny that a personality cult was being erected—was that the populace could not understand power in abstract terms. The state, to win full legitimacy, required personalization. The analogy of the little community of the ancestral village was invoked: the people recognized their own embodiment in a chief, incarnation of the community, and as such accorded an automatic and unquestioning obedience. Mobutism thus could be seen as the marriage of Mobutu and his people, who offered, Nguza has argued, "an homage to Mobutu for his genius, his thought, and the courage of his action."[7]

Personalization was not at first a central characteristic of the regime. Initially, Mobutu tried to harness the residual charisma of Lumumba, and to create the impression that he was a servant of the nationalist vision of the martyred prime minister. Lumumba was declared a "National Hero," and construction began on a towering spire in Kinshasa in his honor (it was never completed). As the ascendancy of Mobutu consolidated, the Lumumba legend was allowed to slip slowly into the shadows. The monument quietly became a party memorial; the farmhouse near Lubumbashi where Lumumba was murdered, designated as a national shrine in the early Mobutu years, was allowed to fall into disrepair, overgrown with weeds and seldom visited. In 1974, on the eve of the unveiling of Mobutism, for the first time the anniversary of Lumumba's death was allowed to pass without public commemoration. The national pantheon had room for only one hero.

The transfer of official charisma to Mobutu involved the imputation of extraordinary qualities of strength, courage, and heroism. Moments of exceptional martial accomplishment were recalled and extolled. The most frequently related was Mobutu's encounter in June 1964 with insurgents at Kamanyola, south of Bukavu, where he had rallied his fleeing troops and personally led the capture of a strategic bridge, advancing on foot alone well in front of his soldiers. In 1975, the miracle of Kamanyola was commemorated by formation of a new, elite Kamanyola Division, initially trained by North Koreans. On a more banal level, the finely sculpted cane which Mobutu inevitably carried was said to be so heavy that twenty men could not carry it—yet the president easily raised it aloft to acknowledge the applause of a welcoming crowd.

As leader, Mobutu was credited with remarkable accomplishments. The restoration of order, the rehabilitation of the state, renaming of the country and its currency, the gigantic development projects of Inga and the Maluku steel mill—all of these *hauts faits* were the personal realizations of a man whose powers bordered on the supernatural. At the apogee of adulation, as Engulu suggests, a clear hint of divinity intruded.

These accomplishments were recited in countless political songs, of which the most important was "Djalelo," recognized as a presidential hymn and played as a greeting to the chief. Its words convey the flavor of official praise:

> *Today we are going to admire the Guide Mobutu*
> *If you see him, admire him,*
> *If everyone sees him, let them admire him,*
> *The country is called Zaire,*
> *The money is also called Zaire,*
> *Kinshasa is the creation of Sese Seko,*
> *Shaba is nothing more than the work of Kuku Ngendu [Mobutu],*
> *The MPR is the party of Zaire,*
> *The country is the heritage of our ancestors.*[8]

The Bonapartist technique of direct communion with the mass was a favored Mobutu technique, before state decay made it unfeasible. Especially from 1969 to 1975, presidential travels through the country were frequent; his visits took him to communities large and small. He delighted in the *bain de foules*, in immersing himself in the crowds attracted by his visit, in savoring their applause. A meeting was inevitably organized, where the president harangued the crowd, often responding to questions,

using many homilies and proverbs, disarming his audience with an element of self-criticism (of the regime, never of himself) while claiming full
credit for order and the *hauts faits* of the regime. In these settings, Mobutu
was remarkably effective, and elements of charisma were present in the
communion with the assembled crowd; the president invariably dominated these events with the force of his personality, the charm of his direct
and seemingly candid oratorical style, and the sheer aura of majesty which
surrounds political power.

The growing personalization of rule, the marriage of Mobutu and the
populace consummated on the altar of the state, had important consequences for the nature of policy formulation. By the close of the ascendancy phase, major regime choices were being made by the president
alone. Such momentous measures as Zairianization and radicalization
were decided upon with little if any consultation, and no consideration at
all given to possible difficulties of implementation. The state was thus exposed to truly colossal policy miscalculations, of which these two measures
are outstanding examples.

Yet by enshrouding the state in the political personality of Mobutu
criticism was made extremely difficult; anyone identifying policy flaws ran
the risk of lèse majesté. In the phase of power consolidation, Mobutu had
sought—and listened attentively to—a wide range of policy counsel. The
young nationalist technocrats in the presidency, the old politicians, international advisors, some diplomats such as the American ambassador, overseas financiers such as Maurice Tempelsman, all had frequent access. Those
who worked with Mobutu at the time attest that policy advice could be
candidly and forthrightly expressed; Mobutu listened with noncommittal
interest. While not all early policies were successful, a number, such as the
1967 currency reform, were well-crafted and effective. The large component of whimsy and caprice which characterized later policy choices was
not yet visible.

By 1970 technocrats on the presidential staff had become courtiers, and
policy advice had to be coated with a thick layer of fawning sycophancy.
Those wishing to draw presidential attention to policy difficulties had to
preface their carefully formulated observations with ritual flattery about
the inspired genius reflected in the policies, then suggest through subtle
indirection that some minor difficulties might be removed at the working
level. By the early 1970s, there was almost no one who could speak openly
to the president.

The isolation of power and the insistent flattery by courtiers takes its
toll on most, and Mobutu was no exception. The intense pride Mobutu

felt for Zaire as a virtual projection of his personality led to his increasing susceptibility to real or imagined affronts. The most outstanding instance resulted in a diplomatic crisis with Belgium over the publication in early 1974 of an anti-Mobutu book by Jules Chomé, a left-wing Belgian lawyer.[9] The Chomé book contained no really new revelations, and focused upon allegations concerning Mobutu's connection with the CIA and his complicity in the Lumumba assassination, which were well known to all observers of the Zairian scene; Mobutu nonetheless chose to make its appearance in Belgium an affair of state. In France, where it was originally published, he demanded—and obtained—application of a 1939 French law permitting seizure of publications defamatory to a foreign head of state. Belgium, he insisted, should find a means to do the same. Belgium explained that however deplorable the contents of the book might be, neither law nor constitution gave the authorities the right to confiscate it; the explanation was summarily rejected by Mobutu, who tore up a treaty of friendship and cooperation in retaliation.

There were a number of other significant, if less spectacular, examples of the easily wounded sensitivities of the president. The regime angrily denounced *Le Monde* in February 1974 for publication of a series on Zaire which accurately read some of the early symptoms of the impending crisis, though it was by no means wholly unfavorable. The Belgian and American ambassadors were targets of public denunciation for slights to the regime—the former for belittling, in private conversations, Mobutu's accomplishments, the latter for responding to a summons from the Foreign Ministry in tennis attire. In December 1973, in an unexpected and apparently unplanned move, the five oil companies that distributed petroleum products in Zaire were suddenly expropriated; they had first been attacked in the media for sabotaging the economy by diverting petroleum shipments bound for Zaire to Western markets at the height of the Arab oil embargo. An audience accorded to a delegation from the companies to explain their position went badly; the spokesman, a Belgian representing Petrofina, gave Mobutu a hectoring, paternalistic lecture on the principles of the oil trade. Nationalization followed immediately.[10]

Mobutu: the early years

It is tempting to seek in the psychobiographical realm for an understanding of the tremendous drive for power, the compulsion for its personalization, and the hunger for adulation that mark the complex political personality of Mobutu. While we leave to other hands a full Eriksonian inquest, some unusual features of Mobutu's formative experiences are striking and deserve mention. The childhood years were scarred by a number of trauma; the president has frequently referred to his humble background as the son of a cook, and to being a victim of a difficult childhood.[11]

Mobutu was born in Lisala on 14 October 1930. His father, Albéric Bemany, came from the area on the frontier of the Central African Republic, in what was then the territory of Mobayi–Mbongo. A catechist and a domestic servant for the Capuchin missionaries, Bemany was the nephew of a well-known warrior-diviner from the village of Gbadolite, which the president considers to be his ancestral village. Transformed by Mobutu into a costly model community, the village has a well-appointed presidential palace often used as a rural retreat.[12] Mobutu was given the name of his uncle, Mobutu Sese Seko Nkuku wa za Banga (all-conquering warrior, who goes from triumph to triumph).

Little is known of Mobutu's childhood beyond information later published in his campaign biography of 1961, which was supplied by Mobutu himself. In that biography Mobutu related an incident which he explains as the genesis of his fearlessness:

> One day, [Mobutu, his grandfather, and his great-uncle] found themselves nose to nose with a leopard perched in the lower branch of a tree. Joseph-Désiré [Mobutu] had never been so near such a large beast, and threw himself into his grandfather's arms.
>
> "You're not a man," the old one hissed. Joseph-Désiré, wounded to the quick, regained his composure. Swift as lightning, his spear struck the head of the leopard. The beast was not dead, and fled into the bush. The grandfather forced his grandson to pursue it, and to recover his weapon.
>
> "Since that day," Mobutu explains, "I have feared nothing."[13]

Bemany had married Marie-Madeleine Yemo, who previously had borne four children as one of many spouses of a prominent chief in the Mobayi–Mbongo area. She followed Bemany to Lisala, on the Zaire River, where he was in domestic service to a colonial magistrate. His talents as a cook took the family to Mbandaka, then to Kinshasa, where he died in 1938. The widowed Yemo had no means to maintain the family in Kinshasa, and in 1940 followed the migration pathway backward, first to Mbandaka for several months, then to the Mobutu ancestral village of Gbadolite. There she came into conflict with the paternal family over the levirate rights of one of Bemany's brothers; by 1941 the family had left Gbadolite, and the young Joseph-Désiré sought to resume his schooling, first near Gemena, then at Libenge, and finally in Mbandaka.

Mama Yemo, who died in 1971, evidently had a powerful influence over the young Mobutu, even though after 1940 he spent much of his adolescence away from home. The death of his father at an early age, and the subsequent rupture between Mama Yemo and the father's family, are reflected in the vast hagiography devoted to Yemo in the presidential years, and the rarity of the president's allusions to his father. Many believe that Mama Yemo did exercise some influence over her son, even after he reached the presidency; indeed, some analysts suggest that the more extravagant features of the personality cult appeared only after the restraining maternal influence was removed by her death. A monument was erected in her honor in Gemena, where she died, and the country's most important medical center, the Mama Yemo hospital in Kinshasa, was named after her. One of the reasons for the furious presidential reaction to the student demonstrations of June 1971 was the circulation of tracts implying that his late mother had been a *femme libre*.[14]

Mobutu, who had finished fourth grade in Kinshasa, spent the next decade in and out of school; it was not until about 1948 that he was able to advance to junior high school at Mbandaka. He had frequent disciplinary encounters with the various Catholic missionaries whose schools he attended (Capuchins, Scheutists, Frères des Ecoles Chrétiennes), and in 1950 he was definitively expelled, at the age of nineteen. According to Monheim, the expulsion resulted from an unauthorized vacation junket to Kinshasa.[15] Monguya suggests a more discreditable explanation: the missionaries, he claims, attest to Mobutu's "adventurous character, his proclivity for delinquency, and his burglary of the mission library," which led to a six-month prison sentence and a seven-year disciplinary conscription into the colonial army.[16]

The period of military service, which was to prove such a decisive asset later, was an opportunity for Mobutu to demonstrate his abilities. Unlike many army recruits, he had an excellent command of French, which quickly won him a desk job. In November 1950 he was sent to the Kananga military school, where Zairian noncommissioned cadres were trained. There he came into contact with many of the military generation who were to assume control of the army after the flight of the Belgian officers in 1960, including his distant relative Bobozo, then serving as an instructor at the school. In 1953 Mobutu was transferred to army headquartes in Kinshasa; by the time of his discharge in 1956 he had risen to sergeant-major, the highest rank open to Zairians, in the accounting section. He also had come to the notice of some senior Belgian officers, one of whom, Colonel Marlière, served as godfather to Mobutu's first child, born in 1955.[17]

In 1956 Mobutu had begun to write newspaper articles under a pseudonym (de Banzy), which brought him into contact with Pierre Davister, a Belgian liberal and editor of the Kinshasa journal *L'Avenir*. At that time, a European patron and protector was of enormous benefit to the ambitious young Zairian; under Davister's tutelage Mobutu, upon his discharge, became an editorialist for the new African weekly *Actualités Africaines*. Davister subsequently was to provide valuable services by giving favorable coverage to the Mobutu regime as editor of his own Belgian weekly, *Spécial*, before breaking with the regime in the 1980s.

Mobutu thus acquired visibility among the new African elite in Kinshasa. Through his military and journalistic careers, he found powerful European patrons. Yet one portal to status in colonial society remained closed: the church. We have discussed earlier the crucial role played by missionaries in placing a moral cachet upon young Zairians; full recognition as an *évolué* hinged upon this conferral of grace. Mobutu, to the Catholic missionaries, was an intelligent but dissolute young man, lacking the moral qualities expected of those to whom full blessing was given. Mobutu returned this animosity in kind; he refused to perform a Catholic marriage with his wife, boycotted the Catholic-sponsored *Courrier d'Afrique*, and aligned with anticlerical milieux. The prolonged childhood struggle with his moral censors, and the denial of esteem, clearly left their mark.[18]

Mobutu went to Brussels in 1958 as a member of the large contingent of Zairians to be exhibited at the Brussels World Exposition as specimens of Belgian colonial achievement. In February 1959 he had another opportunity to visit Brussels, and managed to secure a nomination for an apprenticeship in the colonial propaganda agency, Inforcongo. There he had the opportunity for advanced study, in addition to his labors as *stagiaire* (intern).

It was during the crucial period of 1959–60 that politically ambitious young Zairians were busy constructing political networks for themselves. Residence in Brussels in these frenetic months prevented Mobutu from following the pathway of many of his contemporaries at home, who were building ethnoregional clienteles. Probably this avenue to political ascendance was closed anyway; Mobutu came from a relatively small and peripheral ethnic community, and within the Ngala network in Kinshasa (Lingala-speaking migrants from the upper river) he stood no chance of competing with such entrenched notables as Bolikango. In Brussels the young journalist developed a different sort of contact, which was to play a vital role in his subsequent rise. Diplomatic, intelligence, and financial milieux, faced with the prospect of an early independence for the colony, eagerly sought out Zairian students and *stagiaires* in Belgium. Among those entering these ramifying circuits was Mobutu; it was in 1959 that he formed a profitable friendship with financier Maurice Tempelsman, and a close connection with Lawrence Devlin, the CIA operative, who was then posted in Brussels to develop Zairian contacts.[19] Mobutu was believed by well-informed Belgians to have been recruited as an informer by Belgian security services.[20] He also established contacts with the small cohort of Zairian university students in Belgium, many of whom were to serve him later. He had developed a friendship with Lumumba dating from the latter's arrival in Kinshasa in 1957; by early 1960 Mobutu had been designated as head of the MNC/L office in Brussels. He attended the Belgo-Zairian political and economic round table conferences on independence preparations in the first quarter of 1960, returning to Zaire only three weeks before independence.

Mobutu thus brought to the new world that opened up with independence an unusual combination of psychic energy and personal resources. As a child he had developed a close attachment to his mother, yet he was precociously thrust upon the world to fend for himself. He had endured repeated thwarting of his status aspirations within the mission-dominated school system; but the final punitive blow of the mission fathers—provoking his conscription into the army—was turned into his first real success. His career as a Kinshasa journalist and Brussels *stagiaire* had opened to Mobutu a wide array of contacts—the new Zairian political generation, the embryonic technocratic intelligentsia in the universities, financiers, intelligence operatives, senior Belgian colonial military officers, the crucial generation of Zairian noncoms waiting impatiently for promotion. The center of gravity of Mobutu's multilayered network of Zairian contacts was grounded in the Equateur region, natal province of a large fraction of the emergent Zairian elites in the capital.[21] Ambitious, charming, keenly intelligent, diversely if not deeply educated: the future president was an extraordinary young man. The diversity of his background was of great value to Mobutu after 1960, and surely helped bring him to power.

The crises of July through September 1960 provided Mobutu the opportunity to emerge as an effective commander of the army and as a political arbiter. On the basis of Mobutu's MNC/L activity in Belgium, earlier personal friendship, and military experience, Lumumba named Mobutu secretary of state for defense, while retaining himself the ministerial portfolio. Mobutu was thus thrust into the center of the events triggered by the army mutiny 5 July 1960, and the panic flight by Europeans which followed. On several occasions he confronted bands of mutineers, and succeeded in at least momentarily calming them; most notably, he and two other young political figures persuaded an angry column of mutineers marching from the Mbanza-Ngungu garrison toward Kinshasa to return to their base on 6 July. When Lumumba endeavored to deflect the anger of the troops by immediate promotions and the removal of European officers, Mobutu was a logical candidate for a key command post; he had demonstrated some influence with the troops, had seven years military experience, and standing as a senior noncommissioned officer. Lumumba named as commander-in-chief Victor Lundula, a well-respected medical aid in Likasi, who had had thirty months of army service during World War II; Mobutu became chief of staff. Lundula, who had ethnic ties with Lumumba, was faithful to the prime minister; but in the struggle for control of the disorganized army which ensued, he was poor competition for Mobutu. He lacked the network of personal ties with the newly promoted officers, the political base in Kinshasa, and the external connections that Mobutu was able to deploy. Perhaps above all he lacked the will to power. Mobutu was able to oversee army promotions in critical garrisons in Kananga, Equateur, Kinshasa, and Bas-Zaire. By the time of the fatal rupture between Mobutu and Lumumba in late August, Mobutu had relative control over, or at least predominant influence in, the centrally located army garrisons. After Kasavubu announced Lumumba's revocation as prime minister on 5 September 1960, and Lumumba sought to block this action through Parliament, Mobutu staged his first coup on 14 September. He declared that both Kasavubu and Lumumba were neutralized, and on his own authority installed an interim regime (the "College of Commissioners") composed primarily of university students and graduates.

The relationship with Lumumba, from the early friendship to the eventual downfall and death of the prime minister, left a deep mark on Mobutu's career. He rose to political prominence in the MNC/L entourage. By August 1960 the tensions between the two had increased rapidly. Mobutu blamed Lumumba for the Luba massacre that month at Bakwanga, when an army offensive to recover the seceded regions of South Kasai and Katanga ran amok. At the beginning of September, Mobutu reportedly believed that Lumumba intended his assassination.[22] After the eviction of Lumumba from office, Mobutu had good reason to fear his return to power. Kamitatu recites the scene when Lumumba, after his nearly successful attempt to escape to Kisangani, was brought back to Mobutu's residence in the Binza paracommando camp in late November: Mobutu, Kamitatu writes, "scrutinized Lumumba with a malicious air, spat in his face, then said to him, 'Well! you swore to have my skin, now it is I who have yours.'"[23] In early January 1961, when soldiers at the Mbanza-Ngungu garrison momentarily released Lumumba from his solitary confinement, the decision was taken by the Kinshasa authorities to transfer him to Katanga, where he was killed.[24] The removal of Lumumba did not eliminate his martyred memory, or dispell the shadow it was to cast over subsequent events. Once in power, Mobutu sought to remove this pall by first elevating Lumumba to the status of national hero, then gradually effacing Lumumbist symbols and promoting in their place the legend of Mobutu himself as savior-hero.

Throughout the First Republic Mobutu was both soldier and political figure. The army became his prime base, but at the same time he sustained his intimate set of networks among political milieux, Zairian and foreign, and was an active participant in all major decisions as a central figure in the Binza group. Thus there is no surprise in the fact that Mobutu, a fundamentally political figure whom the accidents of circumstances had cast in uniform, from the outset constructed an essentially political regime—first through depoliticization, then by reconstructing his own personalist political domain. The military side of his personality reemerged in 1983 when he promoted himself to the rank of field marshall.

The presidential fortune

The final aspect of the complex presidential personality which deserves consideration is the thrust for wealth. Mobutu never forgot his humble origins as the son of a cook. Salaries of Force Publique noncoms were very low; when Mobutu in 1957 was able to earn as much as $100 per month as a journalist, he considered himself fortunate. At the end of 1959 in Brussels, with his third child about to arrive, Mobutu had no more than $6 to his name.[25] There is no evidence that he amassed significant personal holdings during the First Republic; the funds that passed through his hands had to be utilized largely to sustain the fidelity of his army, and he had not become conspicuously active in the mercantile realm.

This situation changed dramatically once Mobutu achieved supreme power. The patrimonial exercise of power required large sums, some of which could be diverted into personal holdings. By the time of the expansion phase, word began to spread that Mobutu had become one of the world's wealthiest men, with extensive property interests in Belgium, Switzerland, France, and Ivory Coast. In 1975 an opposition journal in Brussels printed an imposing list of presidential holdings abroad:[27]

Residence and estate in Switzerland, near Lausanne	$ 3,750,000
Chateau at Namur	$ 1,625,000
Villa at Rhode-St.-Genese	$ 875,000
Estate, and football field of S. A. Royale Belge	$ 1,500,000
Ten-story building, Boulevard Reyers, Brussels	$ 2,000,000
Building on Boulevard Lambermont, Brussels	$ 1,000,000
Other properties in Belgium	$ 12,500,000
Residence in Paris, Avenue Foch	$ 750,000
Residence at Nice	$ 1,250,000
Residence at Venice	$ 625,000
Chateau in Spain	$ 1,250,000
Building at Bangui, Central African Republic	$ 250,000
Villa at Abidjan, Ivory Coast	$ 500,000
Funds on deposit in Swiss banks	$125,000,000

Since coming to power the president has also acquired a vast agricultural empire within the country, primarily as a result of the 30 November measures, of which Mobutu was a major beneficiary. The fourteen major enterprises distributed to the president or his wife by these measures were grouped into a conglomerate entitled Cultures et Elevages du Zaire (CELZA), incorporated on 1 July 1974.[27] CELZA listed its capital as Z 750,000, of which Z 500,000 was constituted by the assets of the expropriated enterprises (valued at far less than their true worth), and Z 250,000 was capital underwritten by the president and his wife, who were sole shareholders. In 1977 the fourteen plantations of CELZA employed 25,000 persons, including 140 Europeans, making it the third-largest employer in the country after the state and Gécamines. Tables 6.1, 6.2, and 6.3 provide data on the scope of the CELZA agricultural empire and related holdings of the Mobutu family.

In addition, Mobutu has become the largest shareholder in the Banque du Kinshasa, where the parastatals are required to bank, and has acquired indirect interests in the Zairian operations of ITT-Bell, Fiat, Gulf, Pan Am, Renault, Peugeot, Volkswagen, and Unilever. Through his intimate ties of friendship and his business partnership with Maurice Tempelsman, he has also become involved in diamond marketing (see chapter 10). The Binga plantation alone (flagship enterprise of the CELZA group) was said

Table 6.1   The CELZA Plantation Empire

1. Société des plantations d'Irabata Niendje, Walungu Zone, Kivu
2. Plantations de Gombo-Reco, Walungu Zone, Kivu
3. Domaine de Katala (Plantation Vanden Vyre and Van Overberghe), Rutshuru Zone, Kivu
4. Société d'Elevages au Zaire, Kambaye Zone, Kasai Oriental
5. Agriuélé (*Société agricole et industrielle du l'Uélé*), Rungu Zone, Haut-Zaire
6. Elubani (*Société des Elevages de l'Ubangi*), Libenge Zone, Equateur
7. Société des grands élevages du Bas-Zaire, Boma Zone, Bas-Zaire
8. Société J. Van Gysel pour l'élevage et culture au Marungu, Moba Zone, Shaba
9. Socituri, Rungu Zone, Haut-Zaire
10. Socodia, Rungu Zone, Haut-Zaire
11. Aramvoglou, Rungu Zone, Haut-Zaire
12. Vanos et Cie., Rungu Zone, Haut-Zaire
13. Plantations Binga-Bosondjo-Bokonge, Lisala Zone, Equateur
14. Compagnie de Lukolela, Boende Zone, Equateur
15. Plantations Bangala, Lisala Zone, Equateur
16. Plantations Bamboli, Isangi Zone, Haut-Zaire
17. Mopila, Isangi Zone, Haut-Zaire
18. Lipton-Zaire, Goma Zone, Kivu
19. Sozagal, Gombe Zone, Kinshasa
20. J. V. L. Mushie, Mushie Zone, Bandundu
21. Torrefaction V. D. W., Gombe Zone, Kinshasa
22. Plantations Kilometre 206, Bafwasende Zone, Haut-Zaire

Source: Foreign Agricultural Service, U.S. Department of Agriculture, Kinshasa, ZR 8013, 17 May 1978.

Table 6.2   CELZA Share of Total Zairian Production, Agricultural Commodities, 1976 (in metric tons)

	CELZA	Zaire	CELZA % of production
Palm oil	20,898	155,000	13
Palm kernel	4,298	59,000	7
Coffee	5,547	86,000	6
Cocoa beans	1,161	5,000	23
Rubber	7,053	27,000	26
Tea	921	6,000	15
Conchona	272	2,873	9

Source: Foreign Agricultural Service, U.S. Department of Agriculture, Kinshasa, ZR 8013, 17 May 1978.

Table 6.3 Cattle Holdings in Zaire, 1975 Estimates

Cattle ownership	Estimated number of head
Small peasant herds	600,000
Office National pour le Développement de l'Elevage (parastatal)	100,000
CELZA	132,000
Domaine de la N'Sélé (presidential parastatal)	45,000
Société Générale d'Alimentation (Litho)	33,000
Other ranches and mission holdings	90,000

Source: International Bank for Reconstruction and Development, "Zaire: Ituri Livestock Development Project Appraisal," report 1305-ZR, 23 February 1977, annex 1, pp. 2–3.

by a Belgian visitor to have made a $1-million transfer to Mobutu's private Swiss bank account in 1976.[28]

Through the various companies he or his immediate family controls, Mobutu has succeeded in funneling very large sums into foreign sanctuaries, in addition to his foreign real estate holdings. The Bank of Zaire has estimated that in 1978 alone fifty Zairian companies controlled by regime barons had illegally secreted abroad some $300 million in export proceeds; of these firms, eight of the largest were owned by Mobutu or his immediate family.[29] The two parastatal corporations with the largest cash flow, Gécamines and Société Zairoise pour la Commercialisation des Minerais (SOZACOM, created in 1974 to manage export sales of copper and other minerals), have been under the direct tutelage of the presidency, permitting diversion of some of their proceeds. A parliamentary commission of inquiry in 1979 had the audacity to finger the president for illegal withdrawals of $150 million in foreign exchange from the Bank of Zaire for his private use from 1977 to 1979.[30] Former Prime Minister Nguza told a U.S. congressional committee in September 1981 that in April of that year, at the time of his defection, Mobutu had just ordered the Bank of Zaire to transfer an additional $30 million to his personal account abroad; and that at about the same time 20,000 tons of copper (roughly 5 percent of Zaire's annual production, then worth roughly $35 million) was privately sold for Mobutu's benefit. Nguza also testified that "an unknown quantity of cobalt and diamonds were exported by chartered aircraft to European countries with the proceeds of these sales deposited directly into Mr. Mobutu's personal accounts abroad."[31]

The scale of the personal presidential impact on the economy would appear even larger if other persons with close family ties, such as Litho

Maboti, were included. A recent livestock survey, for example, showed that three-fourths of the ranch cattle in the country (excluding peasant holdings) were in the hands of CELZA, the Presidential Domain of N'Sele (a quasi-public entity under Mobutu's control), and the Société Générale d'Alimentation (SGA), headed by Litho. A correspondent for *Le Monde Diplomatique* affirmed that one-third of the total national revenue was in one way or the other at the disposition of the president.[32]

Not all diverted funds have been available for personal use, by any means. To sustain the system, large patrimonial investments have been necessary to ensure the continuing loyalty of the presidential fraternity of close collaborators who staff the key agencies of the state and, above all, the security forces. To some extent the faithful have been permitted, or even encouraged, to remunerate themselves by participating in similar schemes to intercept public resource flows. However, direct presidential payments have often been required. As well, the president has drawn upon his ample privy purse for presents to communities he has visited, or for the resolution of some particularly urgent problem, as we have seen. The regime justified one controversial cobalt sale outside regular channels by the claim that the foreign exchange thus raised went for the immediate purchase of French buses for Kinshasa. New buses did indeed appear on the streets of Kinshasa, and much, or even all, of the yield from that particular transaction may thus be accounted for. Yet even after patrimonial costs have been deducted from revenues, colossal sums have remained available to swell the individual retirement account of the president, and to momentarily slake his singularly insatiable thirst for the accumulation of wealth.

In the personalist patrimonial state fashioned by Mobutu, we may discern much that resembles what Linz, borrowing a Weberian term, has labelled "sultanism":

> The personalistic and particularistic use of power for essentially private ends of the ruler and his collaborators makes the country essentially like a huge domain. Support is based not on a coincidence of interest between preexisting privileged social groups and the ruler but on the interests created by his rule, the rewards he offers for loyalty, and the fear of his vengeance. The boundaries between the public treasury and the private wealth of the ruler become blurred. He and his collaborators, with his consent, appropriate public funds freely, establish profit-oriented monopolies, and demand gifts and payoffs from business for which no public accounting is given; the enterprises of the ruler contract with the state, and the ruler often shows his generosity to his followers and to his subjects in a particularistic way. The family of the ruler often plays a prominent political role,

appropriates public offices, and shares in the spoils. It is this fusion of the public and the private and the lack of commitment to impersonal purposes that distinguishes essentially such regimes from totalitarianism.[33]

The legitimacy crisis of the patrimonial state

As time has gone by, the patrimonial state has increasingly appeared to its civil society as "sultanism" incarnate, and there has been a corresponding deepening of a crisis of legitimacy for the state itself. Initially, regime efforts to institutionalize patrimonial rule through a single party reflecting the presidential will and through exaltation of the president had some success. But over time the corrupt exchanges which were the essential lubricant of patrimonial power became increasingly pervasive and visible. In 1972, Willame analyzed the patrimonial character of the Zairian state with little mention of corruption.[34] By 1977 Mobutu himself had denounced the state as "one vast marketplace" in terms that echoed Andreski's definition of the graft-based kleptocratic state: "The essence of kleptocracy is that the functioning of the organs of authority is determined by the mechanisms of supply and demand rather than laws and regulations."[35]

The authority of the colonial state rested not only upon its force, however important that was, but on a grudging respect for its effectiveness and probity. While its exploitative and oppressive character was recognized, its honesty was not in question. The progressive permeation of the patrimonial Mobutist state by venality to the point where corruption itself became the system (as Gould has argued) eroded its credibility, and in turn its legitimacy.[36] As in Cuba in the 1950s and Nicaragua and Iran in the 1970s, corruption has become the most visible defining property of the Zairian state.[37]

The state has thus lost the capacity to incorporate a public-regarding ethos into its daily behavior. The moral vacuum which has enveloped the public realm has given a strangely prophetic ring to words attributed to Patrice Lumumba: "If I had been a soldier for religion, they would have considered me a martyr. If I had been born in Asia, they would have made of me a prophet. But I was born in a country without faith or religion."[38] Civil society lacks the capacity to impose a new moral order upon the kleptocratic state, to which it has access only through the patrimonial circuits of clientelism. In the words of one leading Zairian intellectual, Ilunga Kabongo, it oscillates between a hopeless moral revolt and the daily necessity to survive by accepting the rules of the amoral public realm. What he has said of Africa might be said particularly of Zaire:

> Africa moves between religiosity and cheating, between praying and stealing—praying at night and stealing during the day. Praying Africa awaits the miracle and urges it as a solution to illness, poverty and wretchedness. That is the Africa of the night, of Saturdays and Sundays. The Africa of the week and the day manages to get along, the corrupters and the corrupted dying between two worlds in search of survival.[39]

7

In Pursuit of Legitimacy: Party and Ideology

In our opening chapter we suggested that the pursuit of legitimacy is a prime imperative conditioning the action of the state. A certain prescriptive legitimacy may reside in the simple prolonged exercise of state power by rulers whose authority appears beyond challenge. The elements of tacit legitimacy enjoyed by the Bula Matari state rested essentially upon the effective and sustained monopoly of coercion, given ideological articulation in the doctrines of trusteeship, the "civilizing mission," and parsimonious dispensation of welfare for its subjects. This basis for state legitimacy was largely dissipated in the *pagaille* years by the spectacular deflation of state authority.

The New Regime, in pursuit of an elusive legitimacy for the state it sought to build, initially projected itself as a caretaker authority whose mission was the restoration of a strong state. With civil society risking dissolution through the intensity of its unrestrained struggles, salvation, for most, seemed to reside in a program of state resurrection. A short-lived legitimacy was available for the Mobutu regime through this transitional mission. But the New Regime had more extended ambitions; it sought a formula for indefinite perpetuation of its rule, and a fusion of the fortunes of the regime and the state. The institutional device for fulfilling the legitimation imperative, unveiled in 1967, was the MPR—"the nation politically organized." In the ideological realm, a legitimating myth was sought in the successive doctrines of "authentic Zairian nationalism," "authenticity," and "Mobutism."

In our efforts to identify the nature of the MPR and its ideology and to examine its effectiveness in legitimating the state, we shall begin by presenting the party as it presents itself, setting forth a chronology which can be linked to the periodization of regime development described in chapter 2. Then we shall examine the functioning of the party, both in terms of the functions assigned to it in official literature and those usually ascribed to parties in treatises on comparative politics.

Prelude to the MPR

Initially, the orientation of the Mobutu regime was anti-political and very much anti-party. The Proclamation of the High Command of the Congolese National Army, by which the 1965 coup was announced, began by arguing that there was a contrast between the military situation, alleged to be "satisfactory," and the "complete failure" of the political leaders, who had "shut themselves up in a sterile struggle to gain power without any consideration for the well-being of the citizens of this country."[1]

While the proclamation of the high command made no explicit mention of the political parties, there were signs of danger for the existing parties in the message President Mobutu sent to the joint session of the legislature on the afternoon after the coup. The message reiterated that the new government (whose ministers represented provinces, not parties) would serve for five years, and that a *régime d'exception* (analogous to a state of emergency) was to be imposed throughout the country.[2] Political activities by parties were suspended. The parties themselves, however, were not at once dissolved, and in fact continued to function. Several issued communiques in support of the coup.

One evident reason for taking no action against the political parties during the early weeks of the regime was that Mobutu needed the support of at least some of the politicians and parties. In particular, Mobutu seemed to be seeking the backing of the FDC of Nendaka and Kamitatu, the principal organized force opposed to the CONACO of Tshombe. In fact, the Mulamba government relied to a considerable extent upon the old politicians of 1960–65, and especially upon those associated with the FDC. That reliance was nowhere acknowledged in the public pronouncements of Mobutu. To the contrary, his continuing verbal assaults on the "politicians" presaged both his attempts to reduce their participation in his government and to create a personal political instrument.

Unlike sweeping measures of later years, instituted almost overnight on the basis of little apparent preparation, creation of the MPR was an incremental process, occurring over a period of about sixteen months. The first step was the creation of the Corps des Volontaires de la République (CVR).[3]

The Mobutu coup had taken place in the context of intense activity on the part of political "youth movements" in the capitol. Two days earlier, the Ligue des Jeunes Vigilants (League of Young Vigilantes) had organized a militant demonstration of 200 people at the Belgian Embassy in Kinshasa. According to its statutes, the purpose of the Ligue was "to fight resolutely and firmly against the forces which destroy national consciousness and the sense of responsibility, to assure the education and the *encadrement* of the people in order to build a truly free Congo, rid of the fear of imperialism, of the exploitation of man by man, [and] of obscurantism, [and] oriented toward the route of progress of the popular masses."[4] The CVR, and later the MPR, would echo the diffuse radicalism of this pronouncement. Mobutu seems to have viewed such groups both as a threat to be harnessed and as potentially valuable allies in the struggle against the old politicians.

During December of 1965 Mobutu met with a number of young political figures, including N'Kanza Dolomingu, president of the Union Générale des Etudiants du Congolais (UGEC) and well known for his leftist views, and N'Sengi Biembe (Gaston), editor of Mobutu's mouthpiece, the newspaper *Actualités Africaines*. The object of these conversations was the creation of a movement to support the new regime.

Formation of the CVR was announced to the public of 9 January 1966. The leaders set forth their objectives of defending the New Regime and promoting national consciousness:

> Following the diabolical maneuvers being deployed by the enemies of the Congo, within and outside the country, to sabotage the salutary measures taken by Lieutenant-General J. D. Mobutu, President of the Republic, there has just been created at Leopoldville, on January 9, 1966, an organization named the "Corps of Volunteers of the Republic."
>
> This organization, whose principal objectives are to promote national consciousness and to interest the Congolese population in the reconstruction of the country, addresses itself to all the citizens, without distinction of religion, situation, tribe, or philosophy.[5]

Rapidly the CVR produced an organizational chart, a membership card, and a program of action. Full-page advertisements began appearing in the newspapers, indicating the symbolism of the CVR initials:

C = *Conscience nationale* (national consciousness)
V = *Vigilance*
R = *Reconstruction*

A serious attempt followed to co-opt the leadership of the UGEC, the most articulate and radical of the youth organizations. The initial list of CVR leaders included, in addition to a number of lesser-known young men from the public and private sectors, both UGEC President N'Kanza Dolumingu and Kamanda, former UGEC secretary for international affairs (then a lawyer at the Kinshasa Appeals Court). Both declined to participate, and their names were not included in later lists. Subsequent events suggest either that the gap between Mobutu and the most radical opposition elements was too wide to be bridged (N'Kanza Dolumingu was soon sentenced to a prison term), or that such elements had to be co-opted at the highest level (Kamanda was named secretary-general of the presidency in December 1966, at the time when the prime ministership was abolished and Mobutu became head of government).

It is possible that there was an initial hesitation to join the CVR because its relationship with the New Regime remained ambiguous. At the beginning of February 1966 this point was clarified when Mobutu and his relative, Litho Maboti, then Minister of Finance, signed up as CVR members and received cards no. 0/0001 and 0/0002, respectively.[6]

The CVR established branches throughout the capital and in at least some of the provinces, and began activities suggested by the symbols *conscience nationale*, *vigilance*, and *reconstruction*. It organized a public meeting in Kinshasa to protest the sheltering of pro-Tshombe mercenaries by the Portuguese in Angola. The CVR branch at Kananga practiced *vigilance* by denouncing Belgians who kept firearms and West Africans who participated in diamond smuggling. And the Bas-Zaire branch, among others, called on the national office to supply it with such items as cloth and needles, picks and shovels for voluntary labor and training programs.[7]

The ideology of the CVR was spelled out in greater detail during its first national seminar, held in Kinshasa in December 1966. In many respects this ideology prefigured the ideas of the MPR, which would be created soon thereafter. The CVR ideology was declared to be "nationalism"; "economic independence" was made a major objective (with somewhat contradictory references to "socialization" and a "mixed economy"), along with "nationalization of the educational system." Mobutu was proclaimed "Second National Hero," after Lumumba.

The CVR referred to itself as a vanguard movement rather than a party, and its contradictory statements regarding parties doubtless reflected the fact that Mobutu's own opinion on the subject was evolving:

> The Corps of Volunteers of the Republic believes that a single strong organization of the masses must be begun, in order to inculcate a consciousness of their national and international responsibilities. More specifically, the birth of one or two political parties must be favored, unburdened by tribalist ideologies [that are] contrary to the interests of the Congolese people.[8]

Mobutu faced a dilemma. The public was highly ambivalent regarding politicians and parties. The term "politician" had become virtually synonymous with "thief" or "traitor," as was attested by the violence directed against members of the 1960 political generation during the 1964–65 rebellions. At the same time, particular parties and politicians retained substantial credit with their respective constituencies. The ability of politicians of the MNC/L to influence the rebels in 1964 and to save prospective victims testified to the audience these politicians retained.[9] Similarly, the very low vote in Bas-Zaire for Mobutu's new constitution in the 1967 referendum demonstrated the continuing attachment of the Kongo people to the ABAKO party. Mobutu's problems were, therefore, how to break the hold of these parties on their respective constituencies, and how to work with the politicians without granting them access to their clienteles.

The MPR: from "movement" to "sole institution"

Agitation for a return to party politics remained dormant during 1966, only to reawaken early in 1967, partly stimulated by the CVR reference to the need for one or two parties. Seeming to respond to such agitation, Mobutu dissolved Parliament on 23 March 1967, after criticizing that body for its failure to draft a new constitution and for the fact that many members were under the influence of "foreign ideas." In the same speech he outlined the new constitution which would be submitted to the electorate in a referendum in June (and which specified, notably, that there would be no more than two parties). In the same speech he revealed his intention to create a political organization, "a movement and not a single party, a movement which will be animated by the Chief of State himself, a movement of which the CVR is not at all the embryo."[10]

This announcement, and a subsequent leak of plans for the new movement by the newspaper *Le Progrès*, had the immediate effect of setting off a race among the old politicians to volunteer as organizers of the second party, which appeared to be promised. On 18 April, Mobutu refused to allow a revival of the MNC/L, which had been proposed by Antoine Kiwewa, leader of one of its factions. On 19 April a spokesman for the ABAKO asked official recognition of a "Union of Nationalists of Revolutionary Africa" (UNARCO), which would group his party and nine others. This effort, and a parallel one for a regrouping of Lumumbist parties, received a cold shower from Mobutu:

> All those who espouse the politico-economic program, or the policy of the government, of the new regime, should align themselves behind the president, in the MPR . . . In contrast, those who do not approve of this policy . . . and those who think it opportune to clandestinely incite confusion and doubt in the country so as to embarrass the action of the government of the Second Republic, must make themselves known, regroup themselves in a political organization, and this in a methodical way. Such a party can only exist when, regrouped in the political organization, its members will have found a leader, and will have deposited their statutes at the Ministries of the Interior and of Justice. After publication of the statutes and of the composition of [its executive] committee, the second party will exist, insofar as it obeys the law against tribalism, racism, regionalism . . . That is to say that it will not in any case be able to regroup the former political organizations put on the shelf by the new regime.[11]

Despite this warning, UNARCO did attempt to organize and to deposit its statutes at the ministries, but recognition was denied.

The reaction of the CVR to creation of the new party was ambivalent. What was the CVR to do, since it had been the mouthpiece of the man who now headed the MPR? In particular, what was the CVR to say, having denounced the former politicians, when Mobutu unveiled an MPR executive committee composed almost exclusively of these politicians? In the event, the CVR meekly accepted incorporation into the MPR; President N'Sengi Biembe asked for an interview with Mobutu, following which he announced that the CVR and its "millions of militants" were joining the MPR. In recompense, Mobutu incorporated N'Sengi Biembe and CVR secretary-general Kabayidi into the national committee of the MPR.

The following month Mobutu took steps to complete the organization of the de facto single party and to define its ideology. After a three-day cruise on the president's boat, the congress of the new party, comprised of national and provincial leaders, approved an organizational schema according to which there were three organs at the national level, plus committees at the provincial, district, territorial, section, and cell levels. The national organs were, in order of importance, (1) the Congress, presided over by Mobutu, as Founder-President; (2) the Political Bureau, with nine ex-officio members and six others named by the president; (3) the National Executive Committee (eliminated in 1972).

That the MPR was to be "animated by the Chief of State himself" was underscored by the fact that the only publicly announced conclusions of the first congress dealt with matters of organization. Two weeks later, in May 1967, the N'Sele Manifesto appeared over the signature of General

Mobutu, setting forth the ideology of the new movement (see the section Ideology as Response to the Legitimation Imperative, below); there was no indication that the manifesto had been approved or even discussed at the congress.

In October 1967, in what was to become a regular pattern, Mobutu ordered a reorganization of the party to remedy perceived shortcomings. The Political Bureau's function of "guidance" was defined to include the power to control, coordinate, and direct the provincial committees of the MPR, and to see that these carried out their duties faithfully. This was a clear gain for the Political Bureau, at the expense of the National Executive Committee; the latter saw its membership cut from ten to five to reflect its more limited role. Further, the Political Bureau now was clearly superior to the Council of Ministers, the party having been defined as the "organ of conception" while the government was merely the "organ of execution."

Curiously, the subordination of the state to the party took the opposite form at the provincial level. In the provinces (and to a lesser extent in the districts and territories) the problem was "dualism," stated in the following terms in the official party history:

> In certain cases, the Governor did not want to leave any freedom of action to the [provincial] MPR President, feeling that any act taken by the latter could only diminish his own authority and hinder the proper functioning of the province. In other cases, the [Provincial] MPR President wanted to take over all the prerogatives of the Governor of the province.[12]

In Equateur Province the dispute between Governor Jonas Mukamba and Provincial President Louis Drama was especially acute. Scenes occurred at receptions over which should be introduced first. Drama insisted that his official car, like that of Mukamba, should fly the pennant of the republic, since he too was a representative of President Mobutu. Conversely, Mukamba cited his legal responsibility for administering the budget in the province as grounds for taking over MPR funds, since these were in the province. When Mukamba decided that each functionary should bring a brick for the construction of a school, Drama reversed the order; his grounds for doing so apparently were that since he "represented politics in the province, . . . he could do anything because politics was everywhere in the province."[13]

The problem of dualism at the provincial level throughout Zaire was resolved simply by making the governor head of the MPR. His deputy, the provincial commissioner, was made first vice-president of the MPR, while the erstwhile party provincial president became second vice-president and was made a state functionary. In other words, while the party organ was placed above the state institution on the national level, the reverse occurred in the provinces.

Dualism between state and party continued to pose a problem, however; between 1970 and 1974 further steps were taken to eliminate it through a progressive fusion of party and state, with the party theoretically supreme. In 1970, the First Extraordinary Congress of the MPR approved a constitutional amendment declaring the party to be the "supreme institution of the Republic, represented by its President. All the institutions are subordinated to it and function under its control." In 1974, the party was declared to have absorbed the state. According to the Revolutionary Constitution of 1974, the MPR was the sole institution of the country, "the Zairian nation politically organized." Any other body, such as the National University or the National Association of Business (ANEZA), was only a branch of the MPR, a formality primarily reflected on letterheads.

In reality, however, the state had absorbed the party. As the executive secretary of the MPR, Kithima bin Ramazani, explained, "The most recent restructuring, that which fused the state structures and those of the party into a homogeneous whole, had as an unfortunate consequence the progressive extinction of the activities of the party, to the profit of those of the state. And the pre-eminence of the MPR, clearly affirmed with force in our constitution, thus became more and more a dead letter in the political and social practice of our country." In turn, the fact that the MPR's preeminence was "becoming a dead letter" allegedly led to "the appearance . . . of ideological theories and practices contrary to the spirit and principles of Mobutism, the crumbling of the militantism of the *cadres*, their cynical opportunism, and the demobilization of the popular masses."[14]

Whether opportunism, apathy, and cynicism were attributable to the formal relations between party and state is debatable, but Mobutu chose to follow this diagnosis, creating an Executive Secretariat of the MPR in February, 1978. Kithima was named Executive Secretary; his principal tasks were "to animate from the interior, to guide, and to oversee politically and ideologically all the organs of the Republic of Zaire," and to breathe life back into the moribund party.

The Political Bureau, principal organ of the MPR other than the office of Founder-President, also has undergone frequent changes. There were ten major reshuffles from 1967 to 1979, in which the number of members ranged from 15 to 35. In 1974 the Political Bureau was given a "College of Councillors"—i.e., its own staff of presumed experts. The following year a "Permanent Committee" was created within the Political Bureau, and became for a time the effective organ of conception. In December 1977, the entirely appointive Political Bureau gave way to one in which 2 members were elected for each region (including Kinshasa), and only a minority of 11 members were nominated by the president. (Soon thereafter, 7 additional members were appointed, to end the brief majority of elected members.) And in 1980, a new, 120-member central committee was announced, to become "the organ of conception, of guidance and of decision, and to absorb all the constitutional attributes hitherto devolved upon the Political Bureau."

The regional background, political orientation, educational level, and sex of those Mobutu chose as members of the party's ruling organs were so many signals sent to various groups that their concerns were being taken into account. For example, any rise in the number of university graduates was a sign to university graduates and students that the regime was open to new talent, and the inclusion of a greater number of women was a symbol of a progressive "regime orientation" (thought the female members, to date, have not been persons of forceful disposition or political standing of their own except for Lusibu Zala N'kanza [Sophie Kanza]). Over time, there was a reasonable regional balance, though not necessarily equality of influence.

Other purposes were served by the constant rotation of membership. Appointment to the Political Bureau not only carried with it the highest political prestige and status; it also brought rich material benefits. While the salary of members varied over the years, it has been as high as $6,000 per month—not to mention free housing, servants, and vehicles, representational allowances, and invaluable openings for mercantile activity. But only a bare handful of members remained for more than a couple of reshuffles. The rotational practice not only provided powerful incentives for those seeking a moment in the sun of high office to curry presidential favor, but it also placed a curb on any disposition to assertiveness. Those who irritated the president were certain targets for replacement at the next reshuffle, which was never more than a year away. Thus the shifting patterns of membership had some policy and symbolic significance; they also constituted the very essence of patrimonial politics.

Corporatist role of the MPR: JMPR

In the performance of its central mission of societal *encadrement* ("the nation politically organized"), the party needed to impose its grid upon those recognizable groupings which were actually or potentially corporate entities. This was done by forcing all such groups to organize into single national bodies, which could then be incorporated within the party structure as ancillary organizations; no competing bodies outside the party framework would be tolerated. A whole panoply of ancillary organs thus came into being, representing such groups as women and merchants. For the regime, the two most strategic groups were youth and workers; we will focus upon these sectors to illustrate the process by which party hegemony was imposed upon societal groupings.

The challenge of incorporating young people into the MPR was from the outset a pressing concern. It was not merely accidental that the New Regime's first experiment in political organization, the CVR, was aimed specifically at the young. Youth has a potent demographic weight in Zaire, as elsewhere in Africa, reflecting the age structure of a population, in which more than half are less than eighteen years old. The flight of the young from the countryside has made the youth phenomenon particularly critical in the large urban centers, where the most serious security threats to the regime are likely to arise. Increasing numbers of the young have survived in school beyond the primary level, and have thus been more easily susceptible to political mobilization appeals. This same group has encountered growing difficulty in finding satisfying (or indeed any) employment outlets. The ease with which the 1960 political parties organized volatile and at times violent youth wings was evidence of the availability of the young, especially in the towns, for social and political action. So also were the 1964–65 rebellions, in large measure youth phenomena. The dreams of the young were most stirred by the political promises of 1960; the disappointment experienced by all but the most highly educated was correspondingly intense. For the New Regime, the question was how to at least neutralize the volatility of youth, while capture of the energies of the young for actual support of the regime would have gone a long ways toward securing the regime's power. But in practice the quest for a viable formula for their *encadrement* has been unending; the young are still a singularly elusive quarry.

"Youth," as the term is employed in Zairian politics, is a heterogeneous category. By and large it includes boys and young men in their teens and twenties; girls and young women are included only as an afterthought. "Youth" range from the uneducated and unemployed young men of the countryside, who enlisted massively in the insurgent ranks in 1964, to the would-be elites studying in the universities, other post-secondary institutes, and secondary schools. Somewhere between the two extremes falls "organized youth," members of the political and apolitical youth organizations; in addition to the youth wings of the old parties, these have included Young Christian Workers, Scouts, and a variety of other bodies affiliated mainly with one or another religious denomination.

The initial structure of the MPR, in May 1967, left youth in an ambiguous position. The first National Executive Committee included a secretary for youth affairs, André Shabani. There was also a youth department under a different leader, Kibassa-Maliba. The division of responsibility was unclear, as the MPR leadership soon came to realize:

> Youth, practically left on its own, was represented in the various organs of the Party by a member of the MPR who had no relation with (youth), due to the lack of adequate organization. Youth remained badly informed on the realities of the country. It was divided into diverse political or confessional tendencies. This youth was, however, like all youth, full of ardor and good will and could constitute a vital force for the revolution which was beginning. But for that, it was necessary to furnish it with a *cadre* which could ensure its realization, its full blooming.[15]

In order to provide for the *encadrement* of these young people, the Political Bureau decided in July 1967 to "complete the structure of the MPR" by the creation of the Jeunesse du Mouvement Populaire de la Révolution (JMPR). JMPR committees were to be established at the different party levels—the region, subregion, section, subsection, cell, and subcell (which corresponded in territorial terms to the province, district, territory, circumscription or collectivity, *groupement* or *quartier*, and village).

Thus a distinct youth wing of the party was created, and with it a new set of problems. Given the overlapping responsibilities for youth affairs at the national level, it is not surprising that conflict over the establishment of JMPR branches quickly surfaced. The newspaper *La Dépêche* reported in September that "confusion reigns in the installation of committees."[16]

The establishment of the JMPR in Shaba provides a good example of the kinds of difficulties encountered. Kithima, the Permanent Director of the Political Bureau, sent Kanyiki to Lubumbashi with a list of half of the membership of the provincial JMPR committee, which was to be completed there. At the same time Shabani, national youth affairs secretary, asked Baudouin Kambimbi to set up a provincial JMPR committee for Shaba. Young men were soon circulating in the streets of Lubumbashi wearing JMPR uniforms, yet no one knew who had enrolled them and which committee was in charge of them. The provincial president then called in all JMPR uniforms. On 5 October 1967 an extraordinary assembly of the JMPR in Kinshasa placed the blame on Shabani for the confusion created by launching competing JMPR committees in Shaba.[17]

The problems of the JMPR between July and October 1967 involved both the structure of the youth wing and its place in the MPR structure, as well as the type of young people the youth wing enrolled. As the official history of the party explains, "The first national committee of the JMPR was directed by Citizen Boyoko. The composition of the Boyoko committee shows that the JMPR in the beginning occupied itself principally with the idle youth, the youth without work, those for whom the diverse youth movements of the era took no responsibility. The situation contributed, for a while, to discrediting the activities of the JMPR, which was identified too easily as a band of delinquents."[18] The youth wing was therefore tied more closely to the party, and reoriented to take into account other categories of young people—notably the students.

In November 1967 Kibassa-Maliba was promoted from head of the youth affairs department to the three posts of JMPR head, Political Bureau member, and Minister of Youth and Sports; this was seen as giving greater prestige to the youth wing. A secretariat for students was created within the national JMPR structure, and the first efforts were made to organize JMPR units within the institutions of higher education.

The November 1967 measures did not resolve the JMPR difficulties. The "juvenile delinquent" image persisted, which led the Political Bureau to create a disciplinary brigade within the JMPR—an elite corps with the responsibility for maintenance of order and discipline.

By 1970 the national leadership of the MPR was relatively satisfied with the internal organization and functioning of the JMPR, but felt that the relationship between the youth wing and the parent group needed changing. Various experiments were attempted before the customary final solution to dilemmas of formal hierarchy was adopted: attaching the JMPR directly to the presidency.

The JMPR struggled for a number of years to outbid the existing religious youth groups for the support of young Zairians, with mixed results. Eventually the issue was settled by the banning of the competing groups. In 1970 the Political Bureau decided to place all "organized youth," of whatever tendency, under the JMPR, though their organizations continued to exist. This compromise proved unsatisfactory to the MPR leadership, and in 1972 (as radicalization gathered force) the organized youth groups were suppressed on the ground that "religion, being a private affair, could not constitute a factor of division among the young people of the big MPR family."[19] Thus the suppression of religious youth groups can be seen not only as a move to strengthen the JMPR, but as part of the more basic struggle between the party-state and the Catholic church.

The struggle to win over students to the JMPR was the most difficult of the problems faced in implanting the youth wing. Student organizations supported Mobutu for approximately a year—until December 1966—on the basis of his promises to work for real independence and development. However, they came to constitute one of the "islets of resistance," in the words of the official party history, and in particular they were strongly critical of Mobutu's failure to pursue the campaign against the mining company UMHK to what they saw as its logical conclusion.[20]

In 1967, as relations between the student organizations and the regime deteriorated, there was made what the party termed "a timid beginning" to the "installation of JMPR committees in the three universities and the higher institutes of the country. In most cases, unhappily, bad students, enjoying no prestige in their communities, were made leaders of the JMPR. Thus it was that, in the beginning, the student JMPR was strongly combatted by the student associations, which remained very strong and very influential in student circles."[21]

In January 1968 demonstrations against the arrival of American vice-president Hubert Humphrey led to the arrest of UGEC president N'Kanza Dolumingu. On 19 January, the national secretary of the JMPR called for the support of the government in its efforts to penetrate the universities, and in particular for the banning of UGEC. Two days later he urged that UGEC be forced to incorporate into the MPR.[22]

After those threats Mobutu made another effort to recover the student movement. On Independence Day in 1968 he announced that scholarship would henceforth be allocated rationally according to development needs (thus meeting, at least rhetorically, the student demand for planning), and that he would undertake a "great national dialogue with all the vital forces of the country." He specifically mentioned the army, the chiefs, labor, management, the churches, the civil servants, academia, and the students. The president did meet with delegations from these sectors, including the students, but he was unable to gain student support for his program.

In February 1969, Education minister Kithima carried the dialogue a step further, meeting with administrators, professors, and students to discuss the restructuring of higher education. This Goma Colloquium appeared to be successful in that agreement was reached on the principle of "co-responsibility" (a concept introduced by Kithima), which was to govern the participation of each group in the management of the universities. But shortly after the meeting Kithima was fired because he had released the text of the Goma agreement "prematurely." The Council of Ministers then rejected the Goma agreement on the grounds that "co-responsibility" was incompatible with the hierarchical organization of Zairian society. Demunter suggests that the rejection of the agreement had less to do with the merits of the arguments than with the fact that the debates at Goma revealed to the government important differences of opinion among the students; UGEC was pitted against the various university campus associations. These divisions made it less necessary to accommodate the student organizations, and especially UGEC.[23] However, government rejection of an accord which students believed had been accepted hastened the deterioration of government-student relationships.

The explosion came in June 1969, when a street demonstration in Kinshasa by Lovanium students (and some others) was violently dispersed by the army, with several dozen fatalities. In response to the incident the MPR Political Bureau "decided to reinforce the activity of the JMPR in student circles, and to start on the civil and political education of the students. Thus it took the decision to suppress all the student syndical associations, which were replaced by sections of the JMPR. It was decided also that the N'Sele Manifesto was going to constitute, from that point onward, the basis of the obligatory instruction in civics in all the schools of the country."[24]

In 1971 further student unrest provoked another conclave, from which emerged the National University of Zaire. The National University replaced the former Catholic, Protestant, and state universities, and incorporated also the other post-secondary institutes. Elimination of foreign control over the former Free University of the Congo (Protestant) and Lovanium University (Catholic) of course met one of the student demands.

Once the JMPR framework had been imposed on the students, it was possible for the party to compromise with the students without losing face. By the early 1970s JMPR sections in the universities seemed to be relatively free to choose their own leaders and to defend the interests of the students, as long as the fundamental orientation of the regime was not called into question. Indeed, the JMPR university sections were given extensive statutory rights of co-responsibility. JMPR representatives had the right to participate in all department and faculty meetings. On such mundane (but important) issues as scheduling examinations, academic authorities found close consultation with JMPR representatives to be indispensable.

In sum, the role of the JMPR was quite analogous within its milieu to that of its parent body in relation to society as a whole. It was quite effective in eliminating all competitors and in exercising an organizational monopoly in the student and youth spheres. The rewards that filtered down to those exercising leadership positions were sufficient to produce a pool of candidates for its posts of responsibility, as well as for such agencies as the Brigade Disciplinaire. The JMPR thus preempted organizational expression of youthful discontents, and co-opted a number of ambitious youths; as Schatzberg argues, it wholly failed to mobilize real support outside the realm of ritual and ceremony.[25]

Corporatist Role of the MPR: UNTZA

Worker organizations also were an immediate target for the co-optative strategy of the party. Unions had been permitted to emerge in the 1950s under the tutelage of Belgian syndical representatives. In the First Republic years the legacy of Belgian labor divisions on the one hand, and the competitive solicitations of international labor movements on the other, fostered a diversity of unions. The most important were the Union des Travailleurs Congolais (UTC, of Catholic inspiration), the Fédération Générale des Travailleurs Kongolais (FGTK, representing the socialist tradition), and the Confédération des Syndicats Libres du Congo (CSLC, representing mainly civil servants and teachers—an effort at regroupment, partly stimulated by the International Confederation of Free Trade Unions). While the unions were too weak and divided to carry out collective bargaining, they did serve to some extent as forums for the articulation of worker discontent.

Sporadic gestures toward cooperation among unions occurred during the First Republic, and the desirability of syndical unity was a commonplace observation. It took on new meaning in December 1966 when the national seminar of the CVR denounced the existing national union organizations for being as defective as the political parties, and called for their elimination in favor of a new national union. The three major unions reacted indignantly, rejecting "phalangist" formulas imposed from above. They instead formed a coordinating body to work toward fusion over an eighteen-month period. Mobutu in turn imposed a three-month deadline for unity, which was met despite sharp opposition from the unions. In June the Union National des Travailleurs Congolais (later Zairois) (UNTZA) was launched.

By the time this transpired, the MPR had also been established; its charter, the N'Sele Manifesto, set forth a radically new concept of the function of a labor movement. "The union," read the document, "must no longer be merely a force of confrontation, but an organ of support for government policy. It must be a communication link between the working class and the state. It expresses the desires and wishes of the workers, and in return informs them of the decisions taken for their well-being and the improvement of their living conditions."[26] Thus, as Ngoie observes, "the union committed itself to support the wage policies of the government . . . leaving the workers with the impression of being abandoned to themselves in the struggle pitting them against employers." One UNTZA leader noted that "we have been obliged to stray from our syndical role, that is to align ourselves with the authorities to prevent or stop certain movements of social agitation."[27]

Symbolic of the co-optation of the syndical forces was the appointment of the three most prominent unionists, Bo-boliko, Kithima, and Bintu, to key party roles. The first was continuously a member of the Political Bureau from 1968 to 1980, the second was first general secretary of the party, while the third was labor minister from 1970 to 1975. All now are very wealthy members of the politico-commercial class.

While the UNTZA was fundamentally a regime organ for channelling and controlling the potential social force of the workers, its leadership did at moments reflect the discontents that boiled up within worker milieux. Mwabila found that while workers did not strongly identify with the UNTZA, 58 percent described it as useful in resolving working-condition issues.[28] In December 1973, UNTZA leader Kikonge scandalized national assembly deputies by a forthright denunciation of the evident greed with which they queued up for businesses Zairianized by the measures of 30 November 1973. When Kikonge was finally ousted for his occasional critical outbursts, the regime felt it expedient to permit elections within the organization to replace him, a favor granted to only one other group— university students—in a setting where organizational leadership was generally conferred by presidential appointment.

Elected in Kikonge's place was Siwa dio Banza, who had achieved notoriety by vocally supporting a critic of the Mobutu regime, and who had been momentarily disgraced. His designation as UNTZA head marked his rehabilitation. Regime misgivings about the docility of the UNTZA continued, however, and were reflected in an abortive campaign in 1975 to replace the union with JMPR sections in businesses.

Other sectors which were strategic targets for party penetration were the Catholic church and the armed forces (MPR action in these spheres is discussed in chapters 2 and 8). The administration itself was likewise an object of party organizational efforts, both through the designation of bureaucratic command functions as "politico-administrative," and through the introduction of party cells into the state apparatus (see chapter 9).

MPR functions: regime legitimacy via elections

The MPR makes the claim basic to all political parties, and by which parties can be distinguished from other groups: it brings together people "who seek, in the name of that organization, electoral authorization from the public for specified members of that organization to exercise the political power of particular government offices."[29] Historically, of course, the origin of parties was closely linked to the emergence of elections as a device for selecting representatives to national deliberative bodies. Parties became vehicles for structuring political competition; in the performance of this role, they became mechanisms for recruitment of political leadership, for aggregation of interests, and for political education. In Zaire as well, the first flowering of political parties was stimulated by the introduction of competitive elections, initially at the urban level in 1957.

The irony of the MPR's claim to seek electoral authorization for the exercise of power is double. The party was imposed upon the people, and it came into being to prevent political competition rather than to organize it. Nonetheless, elections in the contemporary world play a powerful role in providing at least a formal legitimacy to power-holders; thus we find in most authoritarian regimes periodic rituals by which electoral benediction is placed upon power really held by force. Zaire under the New Regime has offered no exception to this pattern; in the Mobutu era, national elections were organized in 1970, 1975, 1977, and 1982. Insight into the MPR's function of legitimating the Mobutu state can be obtained by examining these elections, however circumscribed they might have been.

In 1970, both the president and members of Parliament were submitted to the electorate, on a single slate. In 1975, only the legislature was to be elected. And in 1977, eighteen Political Bureau seats, the legislature, and urban councils were selected competitively, while Mobutu once again was sole presidential candidate. Additional elections were held in 1982, based on a formula similar to that used in 1977; Political Bureau seats were not on the ballot, but new rural council seats were. In 1984 presidential elections were held, with Mobutu energetically carrying his unopposed campaign to the farthest reaches of the country. One university professor, Ngoma Ngambu, had the temerity to put forward his dossier to the party as an alternative candidate; he was arrested for his impudence.

The first national elections of the Second Republic were held in November 1970, five years after the coup, in fulfillment of a promise Mobutu had made upon taking power. On two successive weekends the population voted, first for president, then for members of the single-chamber National Assembly. Would-be deputies submitted their dossiers, including a certificate of good conduct from the judicial authorities, at the zone level, and a Z 100 deposit. The MPR zone committee then scrutinized the candidacies, offered its observations on their "militancy" and political merit, then passed them on to the subregional committee. A similar review occurred there, then again at the regional level; the dossiers were finally transmitted to Kinshasa for screening by the Political Bureau and the president. Out of this process came a single slate of official candidates, which the populace was invited to endorse by plebiscite.

Schatzberg provides important insight into the candidate selection process in the Mongala subregion, where he had access to the relevant official records. There were 64 candidates for the 15 available seats. The zone and subregion committees ranked them on a scale ranging from elite to zero (the same scale used by the Belgian colonial service). Several criteria emerge from analysis of the committee appraisals. Wealth was quite important, not only because of the substantial deposit required, but also because a number of the well-rated applicants had performed free services or otherwise offered material support to party activities. Regular participation in organized party activities (meetings, support marches, and the like) was indispensable. Well-known politicians with strong Kinshasa connections generally received very positive evaluations; it would have been dangerous to find otherwise. Contributions to *vigilance* also helped; the evaluation of one contending deputy read: "Convinced militant propagandist. Rating: elite. His devotion has gone so far as denouncing party reactionaries at Abumobazi. Independent plantation owner, transporter, and bar owner."[30]

How influential the local screening process was in Mongala is uncertain; it certainly removed from the fray a number of contenders (through poor ratings), who in any case would not have been selected in Kinshasa. Candidates with strong Kinshasa political connections had a potent advantage; 3 of the 15 chosen were at the time either ministers or Political Bureau members (see table 7.1).

Since the Political Bureau (and Mobutu) made the final choice of candidates in the 1970 election, particular Political Bureau members might

Table 7.1   Occupational Distribution of Legislative Candidates,
Mongala Subregion, 1970

	Total no. candidates	% of total	Successful candidates	% of total
Merchants, bar owners, plantation owners	25	39	2	13
Company employees	7	9	1	7
First Republic politicians	15	23	8	53
Bureaucrats	10	16	3	20
Chiefs	1	2	0	0
Teachers	2	3	0	0
Trade unionists	2	3	0	0
University administrators	1	2	1	7
Unknown	1	2	0	0

Source; Michael G. Schatzberg, *Politics and Class in Zaire* (New York: Africana Publishing Co., 1980), p. 108. Reprinted by permission of Holmes and Meier Publishers, New York. Copyright 1979 by Holmes and Meier Publishers, Inc.

have a crucial influence on candidacies from their region. For example, Eugène Lutula, a savanna Tetela of PNP (moderate) political background, was the unofficial representative of the Sankuru subregion in the Political Bureau from 1968 to 1970. Under his influence, a very unrepresentative slate of 9 candidates was chosen: 8 of the 9 were Tetela, although the Tetela constituted a bare majority of the population; 6 of the 8 Tetela were savanna Tetela, like Lutula, although forest Tetela were more numerous; 3 of the 6 represented the tiny Sambala minority (Tetela who had arrived in Sankuru from Maniema at the beginning of the colonial era, and had helped the Congo Free State to pacify the local people). Two of the savanna Tetela were PNP of 1960, again like Lutula himself, even though Sankuru had voted overwhelmingly for the MNC/L.

The voters of each electoral circumscription (the subregion) were presented with a slate of candidates to ratify. The first candidate on the list was a Political Bureau member, necessarily standing outside his area of origin; the remaining candidates were local persons chosen by the Political Bureau. For the presidential election, the voters were presented with the single MPR candidate, Mobutu. In theory, the voter could either ratify the party's choice, by casting a green ballot, or reject it by casting a red one. In reality, under pressure to demonstrate favorable results in their jurisdictions, administrators actively promoted the green ballot. It is impossible to say how many red ballots were in fact cast.[32] Regional commissioners vied with each other to approximate (or even exceed) a 100 percent affirmative vote for Mobutu.

Essentially the same system was followed in 1975, when a new National Legislative Council was elected. One notable change was the reduction of the number of seats from 420 (elected in 1970) to 270. This reduction, together with the fact that many of the deputies of 1970 sought reelection, meant that relatively few new deputies (or people's commissioners, as they now were known) could stand for election—although only 63 of those elected had served in more than one previous legislature. For example, the 17 candidates from the City of Kinshasa included 15 incumbents and only 2 new candidates; however, all 17 alternates were new. The 31 candidates from the Bandundu region included 23 incumbents and 8 new candidates.[33]

In 1975, in many areas electors were spared the inconvenience of spending long hours at polling booths to perform the ritual act of voting for the single list. Meetings were organized at which the list of candidates was read; the applause of the assemblage was taken to be approval by acclamation of the party nominees.

In 1977 elections took place in a radically different context. Mobutu's seven-year presidential term was to expire, and the occasional hints of a "life presidency" for the founder of the MPR had not been pursued. The profound economic crisis had shaken the confidence of the regime, and the ineffectualness of the national army during the Shaba I episode in March and April of 1977 had exposed the weaknesses of the regime's foundations.

Western powers had been called upon to bail out the Mobutu regime, both economically and militarily; in return they demanded a program of reform, loosely defined, which was intended to permit the regime to overcome its past infirmities. Conventional diagnoses identified the excessive centralization of power in the presidency as a major flaw. In a political masterstroke, Mobutu seized the occasion to adapt to his own purposes key elements of the program pressed upon him by his external "partners": he announced sweeping alterations in the electoral process in the name of "democratization."

In its style, the democratization initiative was vintage presidentialism. Recurring throughout the speech were statements which declared that as a result of manifest shortcomings "I have decided" upon a given electoral reform, which "I will bring into application." In fact, several of the democratization moves required major changes in the 1974 constitution. The 1977 elections were carried out through simple presidential directives, and the drafting of new constitutional provisions to retrospectively ratify the alterations already put into practice was a task entrusted to jurists in early 1978.

Mobutu, declaring that he had always been "a preacher of democracy," came up with a quite ingenious and original formula for single-party elections. The issue of single-party democracy was not new in Africa. It was first squarely faced in 1965 by Tanzania, where a presidential commission devised the procedure of permitting two candidacies in each constituency—a distant analogy to the American primary election system. Similar schemes had been advanced in Zambia and Kenya. However, the Mobutu formula went much further, in two respects: first, the direct election mechanism was extended to the supreme party organ, the Political Bureau—something which had never been tried in any single-party system in Africa or elsewhere; second, rather than two or three candidates per constituency, screened by the party, there was no limit placed upon the number of contenders, and no formalized process of filtering candidacies.

Four sets of elections were prescribed. There were to be two elected Political Bureau seats per region (half of the seats remained appointive). The 270 seats in the National Legislative Council, which were not scheduled for election until 1980, were also to be placed into competition. In addition, urban councils, which had been abolished at the end of the 1960s as part of the centralizing trend, were to be recreated, and their members elected. Finally, a special MPR congress would be summoned in November 1977 to nominate a single candidate for the presidency, the only office for which an election had originally been scheduled.[34] Only the presidential election was exempted from the new democratization; to no one's surprise, the MPR Congress duly renominated Mobutu, who again secured plebiscitary endorsement from the electorate.

All of the other elections were hotly contested, and indeed the energies of the politico-commercial class were fully occupied for several months by the campaign. The excitement of the electoral process momentarily placed the regime on the political offensive for the first time since 1974. While the contest, within the formless ideological space defined by MPR doctrine, offered no discernible programmatic alternatives to the populace, the sheer dramaturgy of this unexpected event provided an interlude of distraction from the unending crisis.

The rationale offered by the president for this sudden exercise in democracy merits brief attention. His reflections upon the Shaba crisis, Mobutu indicated, led him to believe that "our system ran the risk of asphyxiation." The voice of the people was often "stifled," a defect which had to be remedied by a process for "offering constructive criticism." As the MPR "is a national, democratic movement, representing the entire Zairian population, it is the role of the people to choose their representatives, without intermediaries." The Political Bureau, whose members had been chosen "for competence, or by reason of the functions they exercised," was becoming too corporate, a simple aggregate representing such institutions as the Council of Ministers, the legislature, the judiciary, the army, and the unions. The proposed elected members of the Political Bureau would have to be permanent residents of the regions they represented, coming only periodically to Kinshasa for meetings. Thus would be avoided a situation where a region was represented by persons "who practically never set foot in the area, and did not understand its daily problems."[35]

As little effort was made to restrict the entry of candidates, 167 filed to contest the 18 Political Bureau seats, and more than 2,000 filed for the 270 parliamentary seats. But the impossibility of openly attacking the regime and the necessity of conforming to MPR doctrine (however vague) had the effect of circumscribing campaign discourse, which tended to focus upon the personal achievements of the candidates and their commitment to obtain such amenities as schools or to support popular football teams. Candidates could not form combines, and their sheer multiplicity limited, though it did not eliminate, the coalescence of de facto ethnic blocs (large groups tended to field numerous contestants). Spending was especially lavish at the Political Bureau level, where serious candidates were likely to be either established political barons like Bomboko, Nendaka, and Litho, or wealthy merchants such as Mwana Ntabe-te-Musingo of Kivu.

While the campaigning was generally uninhibited, there were widespread charges that the results had been manipulated, particularly for Political Bureau seats. It was widely believed that results were doctored to prevent the election of certain prominent figures, including Kalonji Mutambayi (Isaac), a leading Luba-Kasai and Protestant personality; "nationalist" politico Mungul-Diaka of Bandundu; and Kambere Mubumba of Kivu, who had a very large Nande ethnic constituency. While there was never an opportunity for the allegations to be publicly documented, informed observers of the elections generally believed that there was some substance to charges. There were many fewer such claims made against the legislative elections, and virtually none against the urban council balloting.

While there was little discernible change in the operation of the partially-elected Political Bureau, the new National Legislative Council was much more assertive. (It may be recalled that more vigorous criticism of the regime had begun in early 1977, when the former legislature had actually rejected the presidential budget and denounced excessive presidential account outlays). The weapon of "interpellation" of ministers was extensively used as a mechanism for raising policy issues, although the ultimate seat of all important decisions, the presidency, was exempted from this process. In 1979 a group of Kasai Oriental deputies defied presidential pressure and affixed their signatures to a report charging that the national army had been responsible for the deaths of approximately 300 young persons who had been surprised at a site where clandestine diamond exploitation was going on, near Mbuji-Mayi (this was a crucial survival activity in that relatively isolated area). In February 1980, Mobutu appeared to put an end to the democratization experiment, indicating that the electoral process would not be repeated at the Political Bureau level, that party pluralism would never be tolerated, and that the interpellation mechanism was going to be circumscribed. Nonetheless, some deputies audaciously pursued inquiries into public expenditures, and documented huge diversions of state funds by the president (see chapter 6).[36]

The episode of the thirteen deputies was revelatory of the obsessive insistence of the party and the regime on political monopoly. The quest for legitimacy could accommodate individual competition for political positions, but not any form of organized opposition. The thirteen organized their challenge with meticulous respect for the formal legality and constitutional requirements of the regime. In addition to their denunciation of venality and waste, they published in November 1980 an open letter to President Mobutu, which was carefully drafted in the style of a legal brief but provided a comprehensive critique of the regime and its works. The thirteen were careful to include in their number parliamentarians from various regions, to forestall the charge of "tribalism." They also disassociated themselves from any advocacy of violence, invoking the constitution itself as protection for the expression of their views. They made no effort to organize for themselves a mass base. The regime found their action an intolerable affront, and responded with a blend of coercive pressures and cooptive seductions. Particularly irritating to Mobutu was their invocation of the defunct second-party clause of the 1967 constitution, under which, they announced in 1982, they intended to create a party titled Union pour la Démocratie et le Progrès Social (UDPS). The thirteen were arrested, amnestied, and rearrested during the 1981–84 period, before Mobutu finally succeeded in 1984 in inducing several from the group to return to the regime fold.[37]

Ideology as a response to the legitimation imperative

In tandem with the promotion of the MPR as an institutional vehicle for legitimation, the regime sought to erect an ideological foundation for its authority. The Mobutist state required a legitimating myth which was distinctive, demarcating Zaire from other African states as well as from its own past, and yet which drew upon certain common themes in African nationalist thought. From 1966 until about 1970, "authentic Congolese [Zairian] nationalism" was the regime motif. In 1971 this was eclipsed by an ambitious promotion of "authenticity" as a philosophic innovation of the new order. In 1974, this in turn was supplanted by "Mobutism."

The new regime posited its initial legitimacy upon the rejection of the First Republic and all its works, and did not begin to exhibit ideological pretensions until the end of its consolidation phase. The parameters were initially set by the political vocabulary of the First Republic. The great issue of 1960 had been "unitarism" vs. "federalism," slogans above all associated with the political personalities of Lumumba and Kasavubu. Though each in his own way was a determined adversary of colonialism, their contrasting political styles (Kasavubu's enigmatic reserve vs. Lumumba's passionate aggressiveness), their differing constituencies (Kasavubu's Kongo ethnic community, Lumumba's Congolese/Zairian "nation"), and their separate external alliances during the 1960 crisis (Kasavubu's Western powers and moderate African states, Lumumba's radical African states and Soviet bloc) superimposed on their rivalry the appearance of a right vs. left dichotomy. Especially in parliamentary politics in 1962–63, the political lexicon came to identify the Kasavubu–Adoula–Binza group forces as "moderate" and the opposition coalition as "Lumumbist" or "nationalist" (the latter two terms becoming virtually coextensive).[38] The challenge to Mobutu, as he gradually moved beyond rejecting the past and extolling the virtues of unity and hard work, was to dissociate himself from the moderate bloc to which he had been linked while at the same time maintaining the distinctiveness of the New Regime. The new ideology was also to conflate regime and state; through the identification of the central purposes of the regime with an enduring legitimating myth of the state, the unfolding design of indefinite perpetuation of the New Regime began to come into view.

"Nationalism" began to emerge as a theme in 1966, when Mobutu declared Lumumba a National Hero. The campaign against Tshombe provided the occasion for the regime to repudiate neocolonialism and to assert

its goal of economic independence. The dispute with Belgium over the colonial chartered companies (the so-called *contentieux*), the Bakajika Law
asserting Zairian land and mineral rights, and, late in 1966, the sharpening
struggle with the UMHK offered contexts within which the New Regime's version of nationalism took shape.

While drawing upon the emotion associated with the symbols of Lumumba and nationalism, Mobutu wished to maintain a sharp distinction
between official nationalism and the Marxist doctrines which were becoming dominant in student leadership circles. In its 1966 congress the UGEC
declared its commitment to "scientific socialism," but did not sever all ties
to the regime. There was at least some general student support for the
leadership stance; a UNESCO-sponsored survey of university student attitudes carried out in five African states at that time found that radical nationalism was strongest in Zaire.[39]

It was difficult to make such distinctions without a formal statement of
regime doctrine against which deviation could be measured. Creation of
the regime party, the MPR, made such a doctrinal statement doubly necessary. It was unveiled in the N'Sele Manifesto, published on 19 May 1967.

The N'Sele Manifesto declared nationalism to be the doctrinal touch-
stone of the MPR. This nationalism revolved around affirmation of the independence of the country, for which restoration of the authority of the
state and of its international prestige were absolute prerequisites. Nominal
political independence had to be completed by the conquest of economic
independence, "the essential objective to which all efforts of the nation
must be directed." Because economic independence was "the sole means to
achieve a real amelioration in the standard of living of the populace," the
MPR would have to "engage in a pitiless struggle so that our country will
no longer be an economic colony of international high finance."

A foretaste of a lexical trend which was to become more pronounced in
subsequent years appeared with the introduction of the term "revolutionary" to characterize the regime, its party, and their doctrine. In what sense
these were revolutionary was never clearly specified. The term, however,
betokened a more ambitious claim for the mission of the New Regime;
beyond simply restoring the country to order and stability, the regime
would carry out a societal transformation, albeit without a blueprint.

By its commitment to "revolution" and to the struggle against "international high finance" the new party gave considerable rhetorical satisfaction to would-be critics in the universities and elsewhere. But the manifesto made it clear that the Zairian pathway to modernity was to be unique,

conceived within a national perspective, "without reference to foreign thinkers." The manifesto underlined particularly its distance from scientific socialism:

> The Congolese revolution has nothing to do with that of Peking, of Moscow, or of Cuba. It is not based upon prefabricated theories, or borrowed doctrines. It is revolutionary in its will to base itself upon the population, and [in] its goal, which is to change the former state of affairs. But it is a truly national revolution, essentially pragmatic . . . It repudiates both capitalism and communism, for both these systems which dispute the hegemony of the world have divided countries and peoples into opposed camps.

From this passage came the oft-repeated phrase "neither left nor right" (later, "nor even in the center" was added); the specificity of the Zairian revolution could not be situated on a spectrum derived from alien ideologies.

The concept of *grandeur* also ran through the document. "Great projects," appropriate to the vast scale of the country, were promised; "the union of all . . . for the force and the grandeur of the Republic" was pledged. Zaire would adopt a foreign policy aimed at making its presence felt around the world. According to an officially inspired commentary on his ideology, Mobutu was driven by "the inflexible will to transform the equatorial forest into [a] terrestrial paradise."[40]

"Authentic Zairian nationalism," then, moved the regime beyond the antipolitical rhetoric of the early months. The major themes of Lumumbism and of radical African nationalism had been converted into new state doctrine. At the same time, the claim had been staked for the specificity of this doctrine: it was to be both unique to Zaire and distinctive to the Second Republic.

In 1971, as part of the multifrontal political offensive of the expansion phase, the adjective "authentic" was transformed into the full-fledged doctrine of "authenticity." The president wished recognition not only as a leading political figure, but also as a major thinker; this explains the decision to unveil "authenticity" at a congress of Senghor's Union Progressiste Senegalaise in Dakar rather than before a home audience.

The new Zairian doctrine, as presented by Mobutu, did in fact bear a family resemblance to the Senegalese poet-president's *négritude*. Zaire had been, Mobutu declared, "in search of a method. And, at this hour, I believe that we have found it . . . We are seeking our own authenticity, and we will find it because we wish, in the innermost fibers of our being, to discover it. In a word, we Congolese wish to be authentic Congolese."[41]

The essence of authenticity was a return to the ancestral heritage as a spiritual resource. The goal of modernity was to be relentlessly pursued, but the alienating materialism of the Western world was to be averted through situating this quest within the moral framework bequeathed by the ancestors. The past thus unlocked the door to the future, and made possible an indispensable mental decolonization.

Among the useful concepts Mobutu believed he discerned in Zaire's cultural heritage was monistic leadership:

> In our African tradition, there are never two chiefs; there is sometimes a natural heir of the chief, but can anyone tell me that he has ever known a village which has two chiefs?
>
> That is why we Congolese, in the desire to conform to the traditions of our continent, have resolved to group all the energies of the citizens of our country under the banner of a single national party.
>
> It is the same concern for authenticity which has always led us to avoid founding our policy upon external advice, from whatever quarter. Among us, in the Congo, a chief must . . . seek counsel among the elders. He must inform himself; but after having taken counsel and informed himself, he must decide and resolve the issue alone, in full cognizance of the problem. For it belongs to the chief to live with his own decision, to evaluate it, and to accept its consequences . . . It is on this sole condition—because he will have weighed in advance the consequences and accepted alone all the risks of his option—that his decision will be honest, and therefore good for the People and, finally, authentically democratic."[42]

It should be stressed that this mining of Zairian tradition was carried out in a very selective fashion. The notion of checks on the authority of the chief was slighted; the possibility of removing an unsatisfactory chief went unmentioned. It is widely believed that Mobutu's attempt to have himself named Life President in 1972 foundered when former Political Bureau member Kasongo Nyembo, a major chief of the Shaba Luba, remarked that "not even the Emperor of the Luba serves for life." As for the situation of a village having two chiefs, that arose frequently, and continues to arise; often the solution has been the secession of a portion of the village, under the leadership of the unsuccessful claimant.

The imposing media resources of the regime were mobilized to promote the new doctrine at home and abroad. As a concept, authenticity encountered a number of critics, whose objections fell into two categories: the undue glorification of the past, and the vagueness of the creed. The first criticism was most forcefully made by the Catholic hierarchy, which detected a subtle antichurch position in the celebration of the wisdom of the ancestors. The second failing was widely, if discreetly, noted among intellectuals. Mulumba Lukoji gently raised the issue of vagueness publicly in reviewing the 1972 MPR congress, which to his disappointment had neglected to define and deepen the authenticity concept.[43]

Mobutu did somewhat amend the doctrine in response to the first objection. The goal, he said, was not *retour à l'authenticité*, but *recours à l'authenticité*. No one urged a journey back in time, or rejection of modernity; "recourse to authenticity" was a method by which contemporary problems could be addressed.

The flaw of vagueness was not so easily repaired. In 1973 a major international colloquium was announced, which was to assemble renowned intellectuals from the entire globe to acclaim and to elaborate authenticity. The kind of distinguished assemblage required to lend both continental status and philosophic depth to the new creed could not be put together; the colloquium was twice postponed, and finally abandoned.

Symptomatic of the diffuseness of authenticity was the difficulty of identifying measures attributable to it. The renaming of localities and streets, the replacement of Christian forenames with African postnames, and the renaming of the country were all appropriate gestures of national dignity, yet no less superficial because of that. Indeed, regime critics delighted in pointing out that the term "Zaire" was in reality a Portuguese deformation of a Kikongo word (*nzadi*) meaning vast river.[44] The sartorial adaptations, supplanting conventional Western business attire with the graceful, multicolored long cloth for women and the collarless *abacost* for men, were perhaps more meaningful; but elegant and costly imported versions of the African clothes soon came to enjoy prestige. The uniformed, mostly female, party dance troups (*animation*) that were organized everywhere in 1973 incorporated elements of the national heritage in their routines. While their entertainment value was clear, *animation* as a form of authenticity in action lacked conviction.

Another troubling intellectual problem lay in defining what cultural heritage served as a point of reference for authenticity. Senghor had resolved this issue by postulating a general "Negro–African" culture common to all of black Africa; *négritude* was not particular to Senegal. This solution was not acceptable to Mobutu, who sought validation of the concept of Zaire as a nation (and who wanted to make an ideological contribution distinct from that of Senghor). At the same time, authenticity could not subvert the unity-building, nation-exalting imperatives of new order doctrine; it could not be allowed to shatter into a large number of particular ethnolinguistic cultural components, or to foster a mere aggregation of entities. The recourse to authenticity as a legitimating myth required a vision of an organic Zaire, even if it was a Zaire undiscovered by the ancestors. This dilemma was all the more poignant because the best-known and most prestigious historic cultures of Zaire, such as the Kongo, Kuba, Lunda, and Luba, lay outside the core areas of support for the regime.

The architects of authenticity had the work of two Belgian scholars, Placide Tempels and Jan Vansina, to build upon. By radically different methodological pathways, each offered powerful support for the concept of a common Zairian heritage. Fr. Tempels, on the basis of his missionary immersion in the culture of the Shaba Luba, proceeded by deduction to reconstruct a coherent and logical African cosmology that centered about the concept of "life force" and an ultimate supreme being. Tempels entitled his influential 1948 study *Bantu Philosophy*, suggesting the applicability of his epistemological discovery to an area that extended far beyond the actual delimited area within which his own observations had been made.[45] While Tempels was seeking an evangelical biochemistry that would permit an efficacious grafting of Christianity onto African cosmology, he provided a subtle and potent ideological weapon, which was borrowed by those seeking to valorize the unity and worth of African philosophy. Mabika Kalanda, in the most important Zairian essay on political thought, pays an interesting tribute to Tempels:

> To this day, we have not read any criticism demonstrating that the author of "Bantu Philosophy" has exaggerated the generality of his study undertaken in Katanga Luba milieux.
>
> Educated Africans who . . . have read this book recognize in it their own philosophy. For some, [the book's message] provided the dreamed-for occasion to exalt their "négritude," the possibility of transcending . . . inferiority inflicted, of denying the state of "savagery" [alleged by the European colonizer] . . .
>
> The book of Father Tempels . . . sufficiently proves that the apparently "naive" behavior of the Muntu is based upon a philosophic conception of the world. Secondly, and this is crucial, this conception does not differ in its essence from other conceptions, for it is based upon a human aspiration to explain the problem of life and death, the problem of being and values: fundamental problems which preoccupy mankind everywhere and always.[46]

Vansina, after an exhaustive survey of Zairian ethnography, concluded inductively in a 1966 work that "the cultures of the Congo resemble each other strongly when one compares them to other African cultures, and even more if they are compared to other cultures in the world . . . The thoroughgoing unity of Congolese cultures is the most important conclusion of our study: it will permit, we hope, the achievement of a general Congolese culture."[47]

While it is doubtful that Mobutu ever read either Tempels or Vansina, their ideas were widely held among Zairian university graduates, including, presumably, some of those who were among the president's closest advisors. By 1970, public references to the cultural heritage were typically general, as when journalists referred to "Bantu wisdom" rather than to the wisdom of specific groups. The influence of Tempels is clear in one official definition of authenticity:

> The term authenticity takes the sense of a movement tending to revive the moral, cultural, philosophic, social and economic values distinct to the Zairian nation. Such a movement repudiates contradictory foreign ideas. It proceeds from a crystallization of consciousness of the particularity of Zairians, and the conviction that their cultural patrimony is not, as the colonialists had maintained, the product of an infantile imagination, but the expression of the soul of a mature people, who have no reason to abase themselves before European culture.[48]

In the enthusiastic analyses of some regime spokesmen, a prime deduction from authenticity doctrine was a grounding of claims of untrammelled personal power for the ruler in the African cultural heritage:

> If not an actual hero or extraordinary being, the leader is in the eyes of the African a person endowed with an inexhaustible will to action, a power of command out of the ordinary. He is, in a way, a sorcerer, that is, a man inspired, endowed with a power which one cannot resist without being overpowered with his supernatural force . . .
>
> When the orders given by a chief are obeyed, there is an increase in the vital force of the group. At bottom, there is the conviction that the chief, as intermediary between the living and the ancestor spirits, translates, through the orders he gives, the spiritual sources which bring life to the community. If these orders are not respected, the life-force or the collectivity is weakened, by death, by illness, by sterility, by poor harvests or other natural calamity . . .
>
> . . . The strong authority of the chief, and the spontaneous obedience of Africans . . . are based on the Bantu philosophy of life-force.[49]

The traces of Tempels' argument are very clear in these passages. But the author, going beyond Tempels, suggests that supernatural powers derived from African culture must be combined with the new magic of European technology:

> There is no doubt that the majority of Africans believe in the influence of supernatural forces and sorcerers who communicate with the ancestral spirits. It is no less true that they are impressed by European science and technology. Thus . . . they believe that those who possess science and technology are also magicians. He who brings together the two magics is the greatest magician of all . . .
> It would not be astonishing if General Mobutu Sese Seko was considered today the greatest magician of all, the greatest sorcerer ever by those who are older than he.[50]

Beyond those who pointed to conceptual flaws in the idea of authenticity were radical critics of the regime (Tutashinda and Nzongola among them) who raised more fundamental objections to the doctrine. Authenticity, in their eyes, was simply irrelevant; worse, it masked the subordination of the country to external imperialist interests and to the hegemony of the politico-commercial class. In an argument which has some cogency, they maintained that the portrayal of Zaire's problems as primarily cultural deflected attention from the more basic issues of class and dependency.[51]

At the level of visceral sentiment, however, the idea of "cultural disalienation," of being modern and yet being oneself, did strike a responsive chord among those who were products of the still Western-modeled formal educational system. Like its distant relative *négritude*, authenticity addressed the concerns—the "ambiguous adventures" of status definition and personal mobility—of the intellectuals, as socially defined in Zaire. However problematic its philosophic content, the notion of authenticity filled some expressive needs. The same could not be said about the ultimate metamorphosis of regime ideology into the personal cult of "Mobutism."

The presidential doctrine of Mobutism was ostensibly approved by the Political Bureau on 11–13 July 1974, and was publicly unveiled shortly thereafter as part of the new constitution. Mobutu, the quintessential man of action, evidently had neither the time nor the amanuensis to convert his political reflections into an integrated holy book. Thus the doctrine was to be discovered cumulatively in the teachings, the speeches, the thoughts, and the actions of the president. Maoism, after all, was best known to the world through the little red book, a compilation of brief homilies and aphorisms, and not through any integrated presentation of his embellishments of the Marxist–Leninist philosophical legacy. (Taken cumulatively, Mao's writings did offer a well-conceived adaptation of Marxism–Leninism to China's special circumstances.)

Mobutu himself gave an extended exposition and defense of his creed in a lecture to the first session of the MPR's ideological institute, the Institut Makanda Kabobi, on 15 August 1974. The institute itself, Mobutu argued, had a crucial role to play in diffusing "the teachings of the Founder-President . . . , which must be given and interpreted in the same fashion throughout the country." Political Bureau members were accorded new and decisive responsibilities as "repositories and guarantors of . . . Mobutism, [and had to be] vigilant concerning any heresy or deviationism in the movement."[52]

Mobutism was not designed to replace the previous versions of official ideology, but was their logical culmination. Thus it incorporated the concepts of authenticity and nationalism as "Mobutian pragmatism," by which was meant the rejection of preconceived foreign theories and the search for guidance through the renewed sense of self.

Through pragmatism, the intriguing concept of "deviationism"—considered sufficiently important to be included in the constitution—was circumscribed. Mobutu declared that he "had never ceased preaching pragmatism . . . We must keep our feet on the ground." For this reason, the Political Bureau would have to study very carefully the instances of deviationism, "as I do not wish, after me, the Political Bureau to become an inquisitor, or that there be Joans of Arc burned at the stake."[53]

Whatever the practical limits of deviationism, Mobutism, in the vision of its creator, was no modest doctrine. Mobutism translated the marriage between the chief and his people; "the People and the Chief constitute one same and sole person." The new presidential philosophy was comparable to Christianity:

> When one speaks of Christianity, one understands by it the teachings, the thought and the action of its founder, Jesus of Nazareth . . .
>
> Such an idea could not long subsist if it was not conceived and expressed through a solid organization and structure. This structure, for Christianity, is the Church, and for "mobutism," is the *Mouvement Populaire de la Revolution* . . .
>
> In the Church, priests are the transmission chain of the message of Christ to all the faithful. In some way, the cadres of the *Mouvement Populaire de la Revolution* transmit the thought of the Founder-President to the popular masses.[54]

It is difficult to know how seriously to take Mobutism, or how seriously the Zairian population might have taken it under more auspicious circumstances. In the event, Mobutism was soon swallowed up in the deepening crisis confronting Zaire, and by 1976 the term had receded from the official vocabulary. The Helmsman, now captain of a ship engulfed in a sea of disaster, drifting from one expedient to another, was too busy seeking any safe port to exalt his clairvoyance.

Party, ideology, and regime legitimacy

Party and ideology, then, were the two crucial realms for the pursuit of legitimacy. Enormous efforts were deployed in both spheres, which could hardly have been wholly without effect. During the phase of ascendancy these legitimating forces appeared to have some real power, though far less than was claimed. But in the crisis years the regime party and ideology became increasingly irrelevant as responses to the imperative of legitimation.

The MPR had drawn its legitimacy-building model from the mass single parties of the early 1960s, even though this formula had already become somewhat tarnished by its disappointing primary exemplars in Ghana, Mali, and Guinea. Those parties had also been the organizational inspiration for the MNC/L, whose heritage Mobutu sought to co-opt. However, Mobutu was creating his political movement in a context quite different from that of the anticolonial political mobilization which had given rise to the Convention People's Party (CPP) of Ghana or the Parti Démocratique de Guinée (PDG) of Guinea. The Zairian party was not to be a vehicle for mass mobilization to confront colonialism and seize power; rather, it had to be an instrument for the legitimation and consolidation of an existing regime. The army had permitted seizure of the state; the state was the bastion from which the party was launched and expanded. Thus such concepts as "mass mobilization" took on very different connotations in Zaire. The party had as an essential mission a didactic task: explaining to the populace the program of the regime and its goals. Once properly understood, ran the inarticulate major premise, these high purposes would necessarily win the enthusiastic support of the citizenry.

The establishment of a political instrument that appeared to resemble the single parties in many other African states certainly helped to win external legitimacy for the regime. Within the country, the apparent similarities between the MPR—voice of a united nation and "authentic Zairian nationalism"—and the earlier party concepts and ideals associated with Lumumbism were important in gaining the initial support of a number of intellectuals and politicians who stood to Mobutu's left, for whom the one-party state with its characteristic ideology was a potent symbol.

Another model which played some modest role during the era of regime expansion was that of China and North Korea. Mobutu paid state visits to these countries in 1973 and 1974. Both countries had party systems which appeared to have achieved many of the most fondly cherished goals of the New Regime. Ancient cultural traditions had been transformed by a new political consciousness built by the ruling parties. Millennial poverty was being conquered through the disciplined efforts of peoples united as one behind their parties and leaders. An exemplary adulation of the populace for their leader was everywhere visible. Or so it appeared, as perceived through the pomp and pageantry of an official visit, or through the conversations held by the very large presidential retinue with Chinese or North Korean officials.[55]

To serve effectively as a legitimating institution, it was indispensable that the MPR establish an operative linkage with the populace. With respect to the political elites, the MPR accomplished this in two ways: preemption and co-optation. Since the MPR filled the "political space" of Zaire, its omnipresence precluded alternative political organizations to which citizens might have affective ties, while its legal supremacy provided justification for prohibiting other movements. In this respect, the MPR resembled single parties in Africa and elsewhere (e.g., the Soviet Union or China).

The MPR provided the regime with a useful vehicle for the participation of some politically active Zairians. At the upper levels, it served to co-opt a reasonable cross-section of the First Republic politicians, many of whom still had considerable followings. Here we may note that whereas politicians as an abstract category were totally discredited, individual figures maintained a continuing reservoir of support among local and ethnic clienteles. This distinction is reminiscent of Strickton's observation, made in the Argentine context, that rural tenants generally felt strong animosity toward "landlords" as a social category, but might well have cordial clientage ties with the individual "patron."[56]

The party monopoly on selection for the leading political posts in the country compelled the ambitious to channel their energies through its activities. Some did so with ostensible enthusiasm—especially persons from the Equateur region, who had reason to believe that they stood an excellent chance of seeing faithful service well rewarded. Others did so with ambivalence, playing an active part in the ritual, and yet—in intimate circles—remaining very critical of both party and regime. Those who made their reservations known placed their promotion prospects in jeopardy. There were few known cases where persons refused an invitation to assume an important party function, whatever their private views may have been.

The use of the concept of "militancy" as a criterion in personnel evaluation within state agencies was a further incentive to public affirmations of fidelity on such occasions as support marches or public meetings. Indeed, in the mid-1970s it was stated that "militancy" would be a factor in university promotions. In practice, the only operational measure appears to have been participation in formal activities—or, in the case of merchants, the provision of critical services and supplies (such as vehicles and beer) to the party, as Schatzberg shows.[57]

The MPR functions of co-optation and recruitment existed not only at the top of the social scale, where they focused on membership in the Political Bureau (and, after 1980, the Central Committee), but also at the bottom, where the JMPR was of some importance. Herbert Weiss, an experienced observer of the Zairian political scene, stresses the impact of the youth wing, "especially in formerly rebel areas. In some places the legitimization of 'youth bullying' had the effect of coopting potential troublemakers or rebels." Schatzberg goes so far as to say that, of the party organs we have been discussing, only the Political Bureau and the JMPR had lives of their own.[58]

In its drive to establish effective linkage, the MPR was generative of a large body of political ritual. The organization of these activities was a considerable drain on the time of ranking officials. If, for example, a support march was ordered, persons in positions of responsibility could not afford to permit it to fail. As one measure of the volume of such activity, we may note that in 1973–75 approximately 10 percent of the class days during the academic year were cancelled to make way for party ceremonials. Through its *animation*, its rallies, and its marches, the party maintained a high visibility.

For a time, immense energies were devoted to the didactic resources of the MPR, on which such high hopes were placed: the media, the obligatory courses at all levels of the school system, the songs and rallies. Yet as time went on and the novelty of the MPR wore off—even before the crisis—the functions of the party were steadily reduced to occupying political space and providing patrimonial links to members of the politico-commercial class. In the process, much of the MPR's legitimation role vanished.

As a legitimating instrument, ideology followed a similar pattern. Its effectiveness diminished in direct proportion to its increasing personalization. Authentic Zairian nationalism appropriated the symbols of Lumumbism and asserted quite similar doctrines of national unity, which was to be preserved by a strong and centralized state that jealously guarded political sovereignty and struggled to extend it to the economic sphere. Even though the Marxist preferences of the radical cutting edge of the university generations of the mid-1960s were eschewed, Mobutu succeeded in legitimating the program of his regime among many intellectuals as well as members of the general population. Mobutist nationalism perhaps reflected the interests of the emergent politico-commercial class, but it appealed strongly to other social categories as well.

Authenticity, which extended the logic of nationalism to the cultural sphere, initially had genuine resonance. The argument that one ought not lose one's culture in becoming modern is a powerful one, whose appeal can be seen in other areas of the Third World. As time went on, the inability of the regime to define authenticity except through superficial gestures, and the identification of authenticity with the political personality of the president, diluted its impact. The novelty of changing names, *animation*, and the like wore thin, and it became apparent that authenticity simply justified the power and privilege of the ruling group. When ideology degenerated into a simple personality cult, its credibility neared the vanishing point.

Running parallel to the downward spiral of the MPR and regime ideology, and of course closely linked to it, was a steady rise in public cynicism, a negative index of legitimacy. In the early years there had been some real enthusiasm, and a much broader willingness to give Mobutu a chance. In recent years, a few conversations would suffice to capture for visitors the mood of profound demoralization in contemporary Zaire—a frame of mind in which there is little place for the moral homilies and political exhortation through which the party sustains an episodic quest for relegitimation.

8

Regional Administration

Importance of the territorial administration

If there is a striking resemblance between the Mobutist state and its *Bula Matari* predecessor it is to be found in the regional administration. The territorial administration of the Second Republic has as its major function the control of the population. It counts the people, regulates their movements, issues identity cards, reports on their "state of mind," and taxes them to pay for the operations of the local administrative units which carry out these tasks—in short, it enforces state hegemony. Although the labels attached to the administrative units and to the administrators who head them have changed since the colonial era, the structures themselves are similar. In many ways, the texture of the relationship between the citizen and the state apparatus resembles that of *le temps des belges*.

Probably the greatest differences between the present administration and its colonial predecessor lie in the related areas of probity and competence. Few would dispute the effectiveness or probity of the colonial administration, within its own terms of reference; but the present administration has been repeatedly criticized by Mobutu himself as corrupt and inefficient.

From the days of Leopold the regional administration was the crucial armature of the colonial state. In the early phases, the regional administration had the task of assuring the "effective occupation" of the vast territories claimed by Leopold in order to make internationally secure the title to these domains. There followed the challenge of appropriating the labor of a sufficient portion of the populace to lay the foundations for colonial capitalism and ensure a fiscal flow that would cover the consumption needs of the state itself. A thorough penetration and control of the subject society was basic to the colonial project throughout the Belgian era; the loss of territorial mastery in some zones in 1959 was a mortal blow to colonial self-confidence.

Territorial control was no less central to the policy calculus of the New Regime. The loss of effective regional administration, and the fragmentation of administrative authority through a multiplicity of factionalized provincial jurisdictions, were defining characteristics of the First Republic *pagaille*; during the 1964–65 rebellions the liquidation of vestiges of state power even remotely responsive to Kinshasa in large areas of the republic was fatal. Reestablishment of the authority of the state, by restoration of the ascendancy of its regional administration, was a central priority for the Mobutu regime.

Initially, it appeared that this goal was being met. The unified hierarchical grid of the centralized state was restored, at least in form. The acute shortage of Zairian personnel possessing the formal educational qualifications deemed requisite for command functions within the state apparatus was overcome. But new pathologies became apparent by the 1970s; the credibility of the state was at issue as its inability to perform basic services became manifest and corruption pervaded its apparatus.

To illuminate the nature of the state, we explore in this chapter the operation of its regional administration; its hierarchical structure, its personnel, and its practical functioning are studied through two policy cases—the reform of chieftaincy and the regrouping of villages. We then turn to the mechanisms of venality which have been so destructive to state credibility and legitimacy.

It should be noted that our focus here is not on the central bureaucracy of the state. This is not to suggest that the capital apparatus is not important; in such a centralized system of governance as New Regime Zaire, the reverse is the case.[1] But we feel that the state-society interaction is best viewed at the point where public authority rests directly upon the citizenry, and where hegemony is extended to all parts of the territory.

Territorial administration: the Belgian model

The Belgian regional administration had a number of distinctive characteristics; immediately striking was its symmetry. Territorial control was assured by a neat system of nesting territorial subdivisions, such that the entire colony was divided into provinces, each province into districts, and each district into territories. All units on a given level were juridically equivalent. In this respect, the Belgians were very much the heirs of Bonaparte, the Mpinga has pointed out.[2] There were about 125 territories and 25 districts (precise numbers fluctuated); a territory was, on average, nearly as large as Belgium, or [roughly equivalent to the state of New Jersey. The territory was the most crucial echelon of administration, as it represented the point at which the European administration exercised its control upon African intermediaries (chiefs).

The province, the district, and the territory (renamed by Mobutu region, subregion, and zone) all were headed by Belgians. A given territory generally included several *postes détachés*, or simply "posts," each headed by a Belgian. Below the territories and posts, and supervised by them, were the "native circumscriptions," or units of local administration, headed by African chiefs.

Also characteristic of the Belgian administration was its size in relation to the population being administered. It has been observed that "as early as the 1920s the density of administration in the Congo was unequalled in Africa, with the insignificant exceptions of Mauretania and Dahomey. By the time of independence, there were 10,000 Belgian civil servants and officers in the administration, magistrature, and army. No Congolese, rural or urban, could have failed to perceive that he was being administered." By way of contrast, the British Indian Civil Service had only 760 British officials in 1939.[3]

The colonial administration also functioned without substantial oversight or control from outside bodies. There were consultative provincial councils appointed by the government, but until the last few years of the colonial period they represented only European interests. At the very end of the period urban and territorial councils were authorized. The former were created in 1957, and continued to function in the major cities until the end of the 1960s (the last elected organs from the First Republic to survive). Territorial councils never really took shape. In the First Republic the province was a political echelon of governance, with an elected assembly and ministers theoretically responsible to the assembly. However, such elected bodies were never created at the basic working level where the central state territorial apparatus had its interface with the local intermediaries (chiefs) whom it had created.

The symmetry and formalism of the Belgian system, its density, and its relative freedom from control by legislative councils have been powerful influences on contemporary Zaire, as has the Franco-Belgian administrative tradition which the Belgian colonial system reflected. The New Regime has attempted not only to reconstitute this system, but to extend its application to the cities and to the local level in the countryside. In the process, the degree of regional variation which did exist within the cartesian frame of the colonial state has vanished.

Recentralization under the New Regime

Mobutu did not simply inherit the colonial administrative hierarchy; as we have suggested, he had to recreate it from the decentralized and politicized administrative structures of the First Republic. Under the provisional constitution of 1960 the territorial administration, previously under the governor-general, was placed under the newly created Ministry of the Interior and Customary Affairs. Each province now was headed by a president; unlike the pre-independence Belgian governors, these were not appointed civil servants, but politicians elected by the majority in the provincial assembly. As well, each province had a council of ministers; the provincial governments controlled the territorial administration. The six original provinces, now fragmented into twenty-one, were assured a large autonomy by the weakness of the center.

In February 1966, only about two months after he had seized power, Mobutu signalled his intention to bring the provinces to heel by reunification and depoliticization. During the course of 1966 his design was executed through the reduction of the number of provinces from twenty-one to eight, and the creation of the capital district of Kinshasa. The provinces became, as in colonial times, purely administrative subdivisions; their chief officers, named by the president were responsible only to Kinshasa, were rotated frequently, and were usually assigned outside their home areas. Political organs—parties and provincial assemblies—were swept away, and lower-echelon administrative personnel were once again appointed by the central government. The provincial governor—retitled "regional commissioner" by Mobutu in 1972—served at the pleasure of the president; he (or occasionally she) was the embodiment of the national state within his jurisdiction. Indeed, as Nzongola points out, Zaire's regional administration conformed almost perfectly to the defining characteristics of a prefectorial system.[4]

The prefectorization of the governorships occurred in three stages. When the New Regime seized power, the elected provincial governors were initially left in office. When the provinces were consolidated, their governors—later regional commissioners, as we shall refer to them hereafter—were first appointed from the extant pool of governors, although they were rotated away from their region of origin as of January 1967. Subsequently, this initial group was gradually replaced by a new set of appointees, who generally had not held high electoral office in the First Republic.

While by this time the regional commissioners were clearly dependent upon the president, problems of control did not entirely disappear. At first the commissioners were kept on a short leash by the simple expedient of shifting them very often. Following the initial set of assignments in January 1967, there was a reshuffle in August of the same year (in which five of eight commissioners were changed), another in August 1968, and then additional rotations at least annually. Despite the frequent changes some commissioners briefly succeeded in building up personal political machines (notably Manzikala in Shaba in 1967). To prevent this from happening, and to keep an eye on the regional administration, Mobutu briefly added a parallel control organ of state inspectors. The state inspectorate seems not to have served its purpose; it was abolished in 1971. By the 1970s Mobutu had also abandoned the practice of frequent reshuffling of the regional commissioners; instead, they were named to three-year terms.

Although in theory the Mobutist state has been highly centralized, in practice the prefects have enjoyed a degree of autonomy. Presidential decisions have often been rather loosely defined. The 1967 constitution stipulated that "the ministers are the chiefs of their departments, they apply in their departments the program fixed and the decisions taken by the President of the Republic." (By analogy, the same stipulation applied to regional administrators.) In a memorandum it was added that "the word 'decisions' which appears in article 31 (line 1) must be understood in a very broad sense. It can be a question of decisions taken in other forms than that of the ordinance: declarations over the radio, at the Council of Ministers, etc."[5] Such decisions were made frequently. Regional administrators would often have nothing more to go on than a radio broadcast, telephonic instructions, or a vaguely worded telegram; thus they had considerable discretion as to how decisions should be implemented. There were, at the same time, risks; if their interpretations were subsequently to incur presidential displeasure, their posts could be at stake.

In his public criticism of the structural defects of the regime in July 1977, Mobutu confirmed this point:

> One admits that we make good decisions, certainly, but we are reproached because these decisions are not well executed. . . . In fact, I have

noted myself, on a number of occasions, this deficiency. Most of my decisions are taken through major speeches, like the one today. My collaborators listen to me, they applaud me, and that is the end of the matter.

Beginning today, I am requiring that they have with them, at every moment, the texts of my speeches *where they may find the directives for their work* [our stress].

As regards the territorial administration per se, Mobutu announced that there would be "for the regions, a greater management autonomy and a corresponding reinforcement of the power of the Regional Authority." The region, he added, "must be considered an independent entity, which must be self-sufficient."[6]

The regional commissioner was declared to have full command and authority over all state services in his jurisdiction; the same was to hold true for the subregion and zone commissioners. Regional commissioners were also given authority over army and gendarme units posted in their areas.

During the 1977 liberalization reform, undertaken as a result of external pressure, "decentralization" of the regional administration was declared to be a major goal. For a brief period this objective enjoyed considerable verbal vogue, and some modest changes did occur. For example, in 1978 a number of subregional commissioners were assigned to their own ethnic areas, on a trial basis, on the ground that they would better understand local problems. Had decentralization been genuinely applied, through this and other measures, the character of the contemporary state would have undergone important changes.

By 1980 the rhetorical stress on decentralization and the other reforms of 1977–1978 had faded. In any event, the issue of decentralization has not affected the basic "command" style of the regional administration. Within the administration, this style has been embodied in the oft-cited slogan "unity of command structure." A similar command relationship exists between the administration and the citizenry. In a frank assessment of the intimidating character of prefectorial linkage with the populace, then-Interior Minister Engulu told a session of top party cadres at the Institut Makanda in 1974:

> By [its] reflex of fear, the population conveys a profound trauma and a lack of confidence in its leaders. Where do this trauma and lack of confidence come from? No doubt from the brutal treatment suffered by the people in the interior. Let's look at some of the common charges aimed at territorial cadres. Most of them act in their jurisdictions as if they were in a conquered land. For the purported purpose of preserving their authority, they

treat the population with arrogance and condescension. Distant, they approach the people only on the occasion of mass meetings. The welcome reserved for citizens in administrative offices is as indecent as the one reserved by the colonialists for the natives. Territorial agents love to threaten the population with arrest, they like to surround themselves with uniformed bodyguards conspicuously armed with revolvers and rifles. Abuses abound.[7]

The politico-administrative cadres

An important change from the colonial concept of prefectorial delegates of the state has been their designation as "politico-administrative cadres." The first regional commissioners, who were simply former politicians, continued to be considered "political" even after the initial pool of former provincial governors had been phased out. Subregion and zone commissioners had not (for the most part) been former politicians, and even under the First Republic they were always considered prefectorial representatives of the provincial political authorities. The institutionalization of the MPR as the supreme political organ, and its theoretical absorption of the state, axiomatically transformed those holding command posts into political as well as administrative personnel. In the didactic style of regime ideology, this new doctrine was explained to a conference of regional commissioners in January 1973:

> [During the first republic] the numerous political parties were, as the N'sele Manifesto pointed out, "groups with neither cohesion nor program, without a general vision, or national consciousness, solely organized on a tribal basis and motivated by often sordid personal ambitions."
>
> Thus the state functionary was forbidden to take part in politics. . . . However, within a broad movement of national unity which rejects even the label of political party [the MPR] and thus renounces any division in the national community . . . the state agent plays an integral role.
>
> It is therefore logical to conceive [the regional officer] as a politico-administrative agent, who henceforward impregnates the administration with the rhythm and mood of the Revolution.[8]

The point was further elaborated by Interior Minister Engulu Baanga when he addressed the party institute in September 1974:

> The renovation of field administration results from the integration of MPR structures into the state apparatus. . . . The territorial service thus

becomes the central structure of the MPR. . . . The new [1974] constitution enshrines in place of the principle of separation of powers, of foreign
inspiration, the traditional and authentic doctrine of the unity of authority,
to the benefit of the MPR, which is embodied by the President. . . .

One of the objectives of the radicalization of the MPR . . . is the political motivation of the citizen. This mission is devolved upon the territorial
service, implying a dual action of education and ideological tutelage.[9]

The stress on the political function has not been merely theoretical. It
has been reflected in the increased obligation of prefectorial representatives
of the state to see that party ceremonial functions are maintained. On frequent occasions orders are received to organize support marches, or to
conduct a series of political meetings to expound some new direction in
regime policy, or to organize a dignified (and expensive) reception for a
regime official on itinerance. These tasks consume the energies of the zone
and subregion commissioners, are a major drain on the frequently meager
resources available to them, and often make necessary the generation of
illicit revenues.

None of these administrative echelons, from the region to the zone,
have fiscal autonomy; they are dependent on funds periodically sent from
Kinshasa. In recent years, in the context of the overall economic crisis, it
has been rare for local administrators to receive all the *frais de fonctionnement* to which they are entitled. The order of the day at the local level is
what is popularly known in Zaire as "Article 15," after a fictitious clause in
the 1960 Sud-Kasai constitution which simply instructed state authorities
to *débrouillez-vous* (improvise). It would be virtually impossible for regional representatives of the state to fulfill the obligations laid upon them,
even if they combined the highest order of proficiency and probity. In fact,
few meet these standards. In the more remote areas gasoline is only infrequently available, spare parts for machinery can be found only in larger
cities, and vehicles or even typewriters are difficult to repair. Like that of
the constable in Gilbert and Sullivan, a prefect's "life is not a happy one."
Yet, for most, their positions are relatively well remunerated, and far more
attractive than any available alternative. They must make do as best they can.

The initial regional commissioners and their assistants (and the provincial presidents of the First Republic) were distinct in background from
their subordinates who headed the districts and territories. The former
were elected politicians, while the latter were mainly clerks of the colonial
era who had been hastily promoted in 1960 to fill the places vacated by
Belgians. Little by little, the disparity in background has been effaced as

elder administrators retired and younger people with more advanced training entered government service. The National School of Administration (ENA) supplied many of the graduates who closed the gap, until it was abolished in 1971 and absorbed by the social science faculty at the Université Nationale du Zaire in Lubumbashi. Graduates from Lovanium and overseas universities who entered government service usually did so at the central level, in Kinshasa, for assignments in the hinterland were much less attractive for a number of reasons. Regional schools were generally of lower quality.[10] Once assigned to the regional service, transfer to Kinshasa was difficult to obtain, and the prospect loomed of an entire career posted to dreary stations wholly lacking in attractive amenities. As the size of graduating classes in the social sciences has sharply increased at UNAZA, however, many of those who have specialized in such fields as political science and public administration have had no choice but to accept territorial service (which is still preferable to the alternative of secondary-school teaching).

While the ranks of the territorial service now include numerous ENA graduates and a sprinkling of UNAZA graduates, a number of command posts are still held by those without university diplomas. Indeed, many hold only a temporary commission in their present post, and have a permanent administrative rank in the civil service that is much lower than the rank called for by the functions they currently perform. The loss of the present post would entail a substantial salary loss—and, for some, loss of any claim to state employment. This point is illustrated by table 8.1.

Table 8.1 Position, Rank, and Salary of Regional Administrators, Lisala, 1974

Current position	Current Salary	Permanent rank	Salary if current mandate was revoked
Subregional commissioner	Z 270	Division chief	Z 143
Assistant commissioner	Z 225	First-class office attache	Z 86
Assistant commissioner	Z 225	None	0
Assistant commissioner	Z 225	None	0
Zone commissioner	Z 180	Bureau chief	Z 115
Assistant zone commissioner	Z 135	Bureau chief	Z 115
Assistant zone commissioner	Z 135	None	0
Assistant zone commissioner	Z 135	First-class auxiliary agent	Z 26

Source: Schatzberg, "Bureaucracy, Business, Beer: The Political Dynamics of Class Formation in Lisala, Zaire," Ph.D. diss., University of Wisconsin-Madison, 1977, p. 152.

Urban administration

The vast territorial administrative structure we have just described does not interact with the ordinary Zairian on a daily basis, although it has many indirect effects on his or her daily life. Direct contact occurs mainly through the critical local units of administration, the cities and rural collectivities, to which we turn next.

The extremely rapid growth of the towns has posed particularly serious problems. Before the introduction of elected local self-government in 1957, the cities had been divided into two sections: the *district urbain*, or urban district, restricted to whites; and the *centres extra-coutumiers*, or African townships, restricted to Africans. This distinction was abolished in a major reform in 1957 as the Belgians belatedly began to democratize the colony. In the cities to which the reform was applied (the six provincial capitals plus Matadi and Likasi), both sections of town were divided into communes and councils were elected for each commune. Each council proposed a burgomaster, who was confirmed (not automatically) by the higher authorities. Most routine tasks of urban administration were performed at the commune level. For the city as a whole, there was a council whose membership included representatives of the communal councils and of interest groups. At the apex was a European "first burgomaster," directly appointed by the provincial governor and responsible only to him. In other words, the reform did away with formal distinctions between black and white in the cities, but left a prefectorial administration at the top in the form of the first burgomaster.

The cities and the communes which composed them scarcely had an opportunity to operate under the legislative framework set down by the departing Belgians. Independence totally altered the context in which they functioned, effectively removing European participation and stripping the new communes of many of their ablest leaders, who sought provincial or national office. The case of Kisangani is instructive in illustrating the fate of the urban institutions. Communal elections held in December 1959 had led to the selection of three African burgomasters for the three African communes, and of a Belgian for the former *district urbain*. By the time of independence, six months later, the three African burgomasters had resigned—two to become national deputies (one of whom became a national minister) and the third to become a provincial deputy. In one case, a replacement was elected by the communal council, according to the law; in another, the provincial president intervened to appoint a successor of his choosing; and in the third the *echevin* (assistant burgomaster) continued to act as burgomaster despite the election of a new burgomaster. Further changes followed, reflecting changes in the provincial government. As Mayo observes in summarizing the confusing situation, the term of the burgomasters was three years, but none of them served that long; length of service apparently varied from one to twelve months. Under these circumstances, it is not surprising that the institutions of Kisangani functioned poorly.[11]

The tendency of the provincial governments to subvert the autonomy of their capital cities seems quite general. Kinshasa was a partial exception. In 1962, when the new provinces were created, the city was placed under the tutelage of the central government. Administered by a first burgomaster who was a career civil servant, Kinshasa enjoyed a certain autonomy because "the central government was too preoccupied with its fragile hold on the rest of the country to afford too much involvement in the administration of the capital."[12]

When the 1967 constitution was drafted, it was decided that Kinshasa would not become a region itself, but would have equivalent status. All cities other than Kinshasa were to be included in a region; within the region, however, each became a separate subregion. For example, the region of Shaba included six subregions as of 1975; these were the four districts inherited from the colonial regime, plus the two cities of Lubumbashi and Likasi (with Kolwezi in the process of becoming an urban subregion as well).

The urban subregions were divided into zones (equivalent to former communes), and these in turn into collectivities and localities. Like their rural counterparts, the urban subdivisions were headed by officials known as chiefs. But there was little resemblance, except in title, between the urban chiefs and the chiefs of the rural jurisdictions. The urban chiefs obviously had no customary warrant for their office; nor did they have the administrative infrastructure and order maintenance functions which characterized rural chieftaincies.

Although the framework of urban administration was prefectorial from the first months of the Mobutu regime, city administrations continued to enjoy financial autonomy until the end of 1973. Nzongola describes the practical side of this autonomy:

> Apart from a small subsidy granted by the central government and the payment of the salaries of national career civil servants or agents *sous-statut* who made up a minority of city employees, cities had to mobilize on their own the revenue necessary to meet their administrative costs and the chal-

lenge of urban development. This revenue was to be gathered from licenses, permits, fees for various administrative services, court fees and
fines, and above all, from numerous sales taxes established by the City
Council. Although the 1968 statute gave the council extensive powers in
the area of local development, the councillors' contribution to the running
of the city was for the most part limited to the ratification of annual budgets and local tax rates proposed by the executive authorities. Less than
adequate funds in the city's treasury meant that much of the revenue collected had to be spent on administrative costs, leaving very little for development purposes.[13]

From the end of 1973 until 1978 the cities and their constituent zones
enjoyed no autonomy. They became simply "deconcentrated" units of territorial administration like any other subregions, zones, or collectivities.
Funds collected in the cities were transferred to Kinshasa, and funds to run
the services of the cities were transferred to the various cities from Kinshasa. The subregional and zone commissioners who headed these units
were interchangeable with those of the rural areas, and like them could be
transferred to posts in any other subregion or zone. Commissioners of urban zones, unlike their rural counterparts, were permitted to be residents
of the units they administered.

In 1977, when Mobutu announced the liberalization of the political
system, the policy of treating urban and rural Zaire alike was tacitly abandoned. Elections were to be held for urban zone councils; each council
would elect a zone commissioner from among its members. It was not until 1978, however, that the policy of dealing differently with town and
countryside was given a legal underpinning. Under the terms of Law 78/
008 of January 20, 1978, the fiction oif administrative uniformity was
scrapped; the artificial collectivities of the cities were abolished, and in
Kinshasa supernumerary administrative level of the subregion was abolished as well.

Background to chieftaincy reform: the rural collectivities

The operating level of administration for the rural majority is found in the
units of rural government headed by chiefs. As in the cities, the regime has
attempted to more fully integrate these into the prefectorial system of territorial administration. We now turn to an exploration of the landmark reform of the chieftaincies in 1973, and unravel the reasons for its failure.

Even after independence, the chiefs who headed the rural collectivities were typically referred to as "customary" or "traditional"; yet most of them were not successors to pre-colonial rulers in any meaningful sense. The pre-colonial situations themselves had varied widely. They ranged from societies lacking the institution of chieftaincy (the Ngbaka of the present Nord-Ubangi subregion) to societies in which hundreds of thousands of people accepted a single ruler (as in the Lunda and Luba empires of the southern savanna). The typical case approximated neither of these extremes, as Vansina observes: "One found above all the small chieftaincy with a chief-of-the-land, who commanded several villages, and sometimes a political chief who commanded several chiefs-of-the-land and who had a court of central officers or of judges."[14] It should be clear that no simple administrative formula could have identified local chiefs in such diverse situations, or granted equal status to each.

Colonial overrule added another range of variation. The Belgians recognized three types of "native circumscription":

1. The chieftaincy, defined as a traditional unit whose chief was chosen according to customary law and was recognized by the state
2. The sector, an artificial circumscription formed by fusing several small traditional units
3. The *centre extra-coutumier*, or extra-customary center, composed of Africans living outside traditional units (for example, alongside a mine, a transportation facility, or a government post)

These were legal distinctions rather than sociological descriptions. The manner in which they were applied depended both on the Belgian perception of the nature of the pre-colonial polity and on the distinctive provincial administrative traditions. Thus a whole gamut of the situations could have been encountered: in former Leopoldville province, where the sector formula was favored, a quite centralized kingdom such as the Yaka state was placed within a sector; in provinces such as Kivu and Katanga the chieftaincy formula found more favor, and there were instances of artificial chieftaincies formed by the fusion of a number of small traditional units (the Kusu chieftaincies of the Kindu and Kibombo zones in Kivu, for example); in other instances, autonomy was granted to fragments of a traditional state too large to fit into the Belgian framework (the most notable example being that of the former Lunda state). Particularly ingenious was the compromise reached in Kasai, where the Kuba state was recognized as a chieftaincy coinciding with the zone, but was divided into a number of sectors, each formed by the fusion of a number of small subchieftaincies.

As a result of both the irregular distribution of the various types of pre-colonial polity and the differential impact of the colonial state upon them, the former chieftaincies, sectors, and centers are very unevenly distributed across the present-day regions. The three eastern regions of Shaba, Kivu, and Haut-Zaire account for almost all of the chieftaincies (see table 8.2).

The last major colonial overhaul of the native circumscriptions was undertaken in 1933, when the entire system was rationalized within a thoroughly elaborated juridical statute.[15] Everywhere the headquarters of the native circumscriptions had become recognizable outposts, with buildings, clerks, tax rosters, and small auxiliary police forces. They were kept under firm and constant tutelage by the Belgian territorial administration, which designated the chiefs, even where ostensibly customary criteria were used.

In 1957, as part of the package of reforms designed by the Belgians to gradually open the way to public participation, partly-elected councils for the native circumscriptions were authorized. This reform was soon wholly overtaken by the surge of nationalism, and actual application was quite uneven. Further, in 1959, when nationalist voices grew loud, the administration imagined for a time that universal suffrage could be turned to its advantage by utilizing the chiefs—long habituated to receiving their marching orders from the administration, and often suspicious of the urban *évolué* politicians—to mobilize a rural majority behind political parties under the influence of the Belgians (especially the ill-fated PNP). This move reinforced a widespread mood of animosity toward the chiefs—especially sector chiefs, who usually lacked customary legitimacy—who had too long served as faithful executants for the Buli Matari state.

In a number of areas, particularly where sectors predominated, chiefs were chased from office in the immediate post-independence period. In areas of MNC/L strength chiefs were often replaced by party militants. In Bas-Zaire the ABAKO abolished sectors, and communes headed by burgomasters were put in their place; in Kwilu province a similar process occurred.

In other areas politicians needed the support of the chiefs; this was notably the case in the secessionist regimes of Kalonji in Sud-Kasai and Tshombe in Katanga. And in areas where moderate politicians took power from nationalists, as in Sankuru, they typically reinstalled those who had been deposed. Because of their alignment with the Belgians in 1959–60 and with moderate politicians thereafter, chiefs—especially sector chiefs—

Table 8.2 Rural Collectivities by Type and by Region, 1972

Region	Chieftaincy	Sector	Center	Total
Bandundu	4	84	12	100
Bas-Zaire	0	55	3	58
Equateur	1	80	8	89
Haut-Zaire	141	57	11	209
Kasai Occidental	3	54	1	58
Kasai Oriental	6	60	2	68
Kivu	38	32	4	74
Shaba	53	36	9	98
Total	246	458	50	754

Source: Vundowe T'Angambe Pemako, "Le processus de l'intégration des autorités tradition-nelles dans l'administration moderne de la République du Zaire (de 1885 à 1972)" (Doctoral diss., Université Catholique de Louvain, 1973), p. 260.

were often targets of revolutionary violence during the rebellions of 1964–65 particularly in Kwilu, Maniema, and Sankuru.

After the first wave of antichief measures in 1960–61 chiefs tended to regain some of their status. In good measure, this was simply by default. The former clerks who succeeded to office as zone commissioners in 1960 had less authority over the populace than either the more effective politicians or the chiefs. And it was precisely these lonely bush administrations, overwhelmed by their tasks, who were supposed to exercise the tutelage of the state over the chiefs, appraise their performance, supervise the operation of their tribunals, and transmit state directives to them. A leading Zairian jurist concludes that "the chiefs did not at all lose their prestige or authority following independence. On the contrary, during the dark hours of the first five years . . . the customary chiefs enjoyed in practice a practically total freedom of action, which, unfortunately, encouraged certain among them to an unhappy inclination to abuse the power."[16]

At first, Mobutu adopted a legalistic position regarding the chiefs. As part of his campaign to depoliticize the country following the coup, he returned to office all chiefs who had been deposed for political reasons. Similarly, almost all administrative boundaries reverted to their 1960 positions, which had the effect of restoring the unity of a number of chiefdoms and sectors that had been divided after independence in response to popular pressure. These actions particularly affected areas where such populist parties as the MNC/L, ABAKO, and PSA had implemented antichief measures. During the early New Regime years Mobutu continued to court the chiefs. In a 1967 speech he declared that the chiefs were the "veritable cornerstones of our society, unanimously known and esteemed for their wisdom, their moderation, and their uncontestable authority." [17]

The first suggestion that a new orientation toward the chiefs was germinating appeared on 10 July 1968, in a decree concerned with reorganizing local judicial institutions. This law proclaimed the objective of entirely suppressing the customary tribunals, which were to be replaced by *tribunaux de paix*, organized by the zones, and thus within the centralized prefectorial domain. In theory this reform was of profound significance, as the local courts were a crucial component of the social control mechanisms in the hands of the chiefs. Further, they constituted, in effect, the only system of justice available to rural citizens trying to cope with everyday local litigation over family issues, petty grievances, and minor infractions. The *tribunaux de paix* were to be established within three years in the cities and over a ten-year period in the countryside. They were to be presided over by career magistrates, although they could co-opt, for cases involving customary law, two local assessors from a list of notables compiled by the Ministry of Justice. Chiefs were to be deprived of all right to apply sanctions; they could resolve local conflicts by mediation, but without the force of the state behind them.

In reality, there was little possibility of putting such a far-reaching transformation into practice. The volume of local cases was and is enormous; by one count, in Kinshasa alone some 360,000 cases were handled outside the national judicial apparatus. By the end of 1972 not a single *tribunal de paix* had been established. [18]

Reforming chieftaincy

In 1969 legislation was promulgated which seemed to betoken a favorable orientation toward the chiefs. The law of 12 March 1969 (Law 69/012) provided for elections for the chiefs of sectors and centers. Elections were held and the results reviewed by the interior minister, following which all or almost all of those elected were confirmed for a five-year term. Chiefs of chieftaincies continued to be chosen according to custom.

During the period 1970–72 Mobutu's public stance on chieftancy began to shift. Law 73/015 (5 January 1973) repudiated Law 69/012 on almost every point. Collectivities lost all autonomy and became simple territorial subdivisions. The distinctions among chieftaincies, sectors, and centers was abolished. Collectivity chiefs were integrated into the regional administration. A week later, the interior minister explained that the new law eliminated "the procedure of hereditary investiture that made of some citizens, born into families called royal or dominant, men superior to others by virtue of their ancestry . . . in flagrant contempt of democratic principles and our revolutionary constitution."[19] In other words, hereditary chiefs were the main targets of the reform.

Later that same year, Law 73/250 set down criteria for eligibility for the posts of collectivity chief and deputy chief (a new post), thus implementing their integration into the territorial administration. Chiefs of both categories were to have completed two years of post-primary school, to be physically and mentally competent, and to be militant in party terms. Strict application of these criteria would have eliminated many incumbent chiefs who were too old or had too little schooling; party militancy, existing largely in the eye of the beholder, could have been used to eliminate anyone unacceptable to the higher authorities.

The minister then ruled that all incumbent chiefs were considered to have resigned and would have to file candidacy papers like anyone else. The regional commissioners initiated the process of candidate selection at the zone level. In the course of screening by zonal, subregional, and regional officials, a number of incumbent chiefs in fact were excluded on grounds of unsatisfactory health, education, or militancy. The process of screening was meant to be confidential, but in practice was not; in several areas it reportedly led to "effervescence" on the part of the population—conflict between supporters of rival candidates.

The screening process was suspended by a telegram from the minister, and never completed. Presumably complaints from candidates screened out, and perhaps also reports of trouble stirred up, led the central authorities to change the method of applying Law 73/015. In August 1974, two months after the suspension, the minister telegraphed an order to regional authorities to transfer chiefs from one collectivity to another. This measure was to apply to all chiefs, with the possible exception of certain paramount chiefs; no mention was made of other criteria such as age, health, or education.[20]

In turn, this method of implementing the reform seems to have stirred up its own storm of protests. Even before the first of the transferred chiefs had left for his new post, the first protest reached Kinshasa. Chiefs from Kivu, Equateur, and probably other regions as well, flew to the capital or contacted relatives in the central government to seek exemption from the transfer orders. In response, the minister backpedalled; in a telegram of 18 October 1974, he informed the regional commissioners that the trans-

fer of chiefs applied not to "customary chiefs" (those of the former chieftaincies), but only to "administrative chiefs" (those of the former sectors
and centers); the chiefs of the former chieftaincies might be transferred at
some unspecified later date.

With the October message, January's objective of striking at hereditary
privilege had been totally abandoned. To resurrect it in part, the minister
sent yet another telegram in March 1975, ordering the replacement of
chiefs who were "broken by age" or "amortized"; chiefs of former sectors
and centers could be replaced by members of the territorial administration,
but in the case of the ex-chieftaincies, research would have to be carried
out to find an heir who was eligible under both customary law and Law
73/250.[21]

One can well imagine the frustration of the bureaucrats of the territorial administration. In a year and a half they had received four contradictory sets of instructions regarding the implementation of laws 73/015
and 73/250. Moreover, as was typical in such matters, instructions had
been sent by telegram, with no detailed follow-up. Inaction would have
been inexcusable in the eyes of Kinshasa, so each region had to work out a
means of applying the brief and vague telegraphic instructions.

Since the ministerial telegram of August 1974 had provided no guidance as to how chiefs were to be transferred, each regional commissioner
established his own system, as well as his own criteria as to which chiefs to
move, and where. There was an extensive transfer of chiefs in the 1974–75
period; in some regions there were even two waves of transfers. Not all
chiefs were transferred; in particular many of those in the chieftaincies
were left alone. In Shaba, for example, in the first round of transfers some
43 of 95 incumbent chiefs in rural collectivities were not transferred.[22] In
some areas the transfers initially worked fairly smoothly, as in Sankuru,
where the chiefs had little legitimacy;[23] in other areas the scheme engendered conflict and dislocation.

Many chiefs were not enthusiastic about the reforms. In Shaba, several
refused to be switched: one, from Dilolo, justified his refusal by saying,
"My wife has just had an operation and my child is sick, which obliges me
to remain here to see to their state of health." Thus he preferred to give up
his post to his replacement. But his continued presence in the collectivity
caused problems: villagers who were used to their former chief continued
to submit their problems to him; the new chief was isolated. In several
other cases, chiefs who had been transferred out of Dilolo zone and then
allowed to return took their revenge against people who had collaborated
with the ephemeral replacement.[24]

The experiment with switching chiefs lasted only about two years. In 1976 transferred chiefs were allowed to return to their original collectivities, although some who had been sacked for refusing the new post were not able to regain their posts. In terms of its initial goal of incorporating all collectivities into the prefectorial domain of the central state, the reform certainly failed.

Perhaps the most basic obstacle to success was the attempt to apply a uniform policy to widely differing situations. In some areas, the chieftaincy's long subservience to the Bula Matari state had emptied custom of its substance. This is illustrated in an intriguing transcript of an administrative inquest into a chiefly succession in northern Shaba:

> Administrator: What do you think of the succession in Kabondo circumscription?
> Notable 1: We have already stated many times that this affair is the decision of the District Commissioner, let him name us a candidate and we will accept. . . .
> Notable 2: When the whites arrived, they invested Kabondo Kimputu, we brought him tribute.
> Now that you are the whites, . . . give us another chief Kabondo. . . .
> Notable 3: When the whites arrived, they named chief Kabondo Dianda, when he died, they named Kabondo Kimputu, we brought them both tribute. Now you are the whites, give us therefore another chief Kabondo.[25]

In contrast, a few of the powerful chiefs completely eclipsed the territorial administration, and still do. This has been true of the Nyim of the Kuba, the Mwaant Yav of the Lunda, and the Shi rulers near Bukavu. The regime at some periods has simply designated these paramount rulers as zone commissioners as well as chiefs. Vundowe, a Zairian legal scholar who hails from an area of decentralized traditional structures, records his astonishment at visiting the Kuba area for research on local administrative reform: the power of the Nyim, Vundowe observes, was overwhelming; his authority was such that no directive from the state would be obeyed unless he gave his consent.[26]

Between these two extremes there still lie a great many other chiefs, whose historical legitimacy is questionable, but who nonetheless do possess a certain prescriptive force which comes from long familiarity with this form of leadership. Furthermore, the chief stays, while the state personnel at the zone level are frequently rotated; and the zone commissioner is a prefect of the distant and impersonal state, while the chief, whatever his flaws, is a local person. Such chiefs may be inept, abusive, and unpopular. They are nonetheless difficult to replace by extending the central apparatus downward one echelon.

Village regrouping

A second major policy venture through which the operation of the regional administration may be viewed was the regrouping of villages. Like the switching of chiefs, the measure lacked careful preparation, was imposed across-the-board without regard for local realities, and was dropped when difficulties were encountered. This reform was not wholly novel; the Belgians had required Africans in many parts of the colony to move their villages to a main road or to merge one village with another village in order to facilitate tax collection, labor recruitment, census taking, and other administrative activity.

The New Regime policy of regrouping villages dates from 1971. The rationale for the measure was the same as one of the arguments advanced by Nyerere for the *ujamaa* village scheme in neighboring Tanzania, which had been launched in 1967: the state could not afford to bring the basic social services to dispersed small communities situated off communications routes; for the minimum of social infrastructure—schools, a dispensary, a local road, safe water—to be provided economically, the state had to bring about a regrouping of the rural populace into units of optimum size, and within reach.[27] The flaw in the reasoning was that in Zaire little prospect of any of these facilities existed, except for the primary school.

When local administrators set about applying the instruction to consolidate villages, they found themselves creating new problems at least as numerous and serious as those they were solving. An example from Sankuru is indicative of what might transpire. In Lubefu zone, the administration drew up a plan to regroup the 18,800 people of Mondja-Ngandu Collectivity into eight localities, ranging in population between 1,200 and 6,800. The reaction of the Mondja-Ngandu population was mixed; the villagers applauded the promise that schools and dispensaries would be built in the enlarged villages, but were unenthusiastic about moving far from their fields or from sources of water. Those chiefs whose villages would have to move to new locations along the road were strenuously opposed to the plan, as were those village chiefs who feared domination by another chief if they lived side by side. Chiefs whose villages would form the nucleus of an enlarged village generally were supportive.

Regrouping did not go as planned. The local administration apparently had announced that each household was free to live in any locality, thus permitting people who so desired to escape the authority of their chiefs. Villages split into two or three new hamlets, in various locations. People from neighboring collectivities began to move into Mondja-Ngandu Collectivity, thereby creating still more tiny hamlets of a few households each.

On the other hand, some regrouping did take place. The locality of Tshumbe (a mission town and commercial center) grew dramatically during the regrouping period. The presence of a school was an attraction for many; others seem to have wanted to escape their chiefs.

A comparison of the results of regrouping in Mondja-Ngandu Collectivity to those in other areas suggests that the Mondja-Ngandu situation was far from unique. Regrouping proceeded rather uneventfully in Olemba Collectivity in northern Sankuru, where the population acknowledged descent from a common ancestor, and where each *groupement* occupied contiguous territory.[28] In contrast, in nearby Watambulu Collectivity where groups that did not acknowledge close kinship lived interspersed, difficulties similar to those of Mondja-Ngandu Collectivity were encountered. The Newburys report that villagers on Ijwi Island, Kivu, built new villages to comply with the order to regroup, but declined to live in them except when under administrative scrutiny. Identical responses in the Uvira and Bukavu regions have been reported by Bianga.[29]

By the middle 1970s the village regroupment campaign had been tacitly abandoned. It may be noted that the territorial administration did make significant efforts to carry out the Kinshasa directives; administrators cannot afford to ignore orders on a policy matter which momentarily, at least, commands priority with the central government. Sooner or later, an official from the subregion or region—or possibly even the president himself—might come and ask to see the resettled villages. The villagers in turn are forced to respond in some way to the orders from the state. They cannot openly defy them; to do so might bring a costly visitation from the local gendarmes. The resourcefulness and ingenuity of the villager in coping with the often incomprehensible demands of the state should never be underestimated. Creative dissimulation (the construction of exhibition villages to show visiting officials) appears to have been a successful response to village regroupment. Ostensible compliance for purposes unintended by the state (shifting residence to escape the clutches of the despotic chief) was another. From long experience, villagers can expect that major reform campaigns of this nature are like a passing storm. While the storm rages, one bows before the wind; when the tempest has moved on, life can resume as before.

As the Tanzanian experience with a much more systematically enforced village resettlement program demonstrates, there is a great gap between the conceptualization of such a measure at the center and its application on the periphery. Further, the interests of the state and the villagers are far from identical. The state, while wishing to extend its social services in an economical fashion to consolidated communities, also desires to ensure access for its officials to the local population, the ready collection of revenue and imposition of regulations, and the capture of peasant agricultural output for the national marketing system. The villagers share the desire for the amenities, but not for the other aspects of the state presence. In the Zairian case, they have good reason to be skeptical as to whether the promised social services will in fact be delivered. In addition, the villagers' choice of habitat has been influenced by various factors which state agents may fail to recognize when they propose new sites: reliable access to water, proximity to good land, the availability of food supplements (game, fish), or even the ritual significance of particular areas. Thus proposed resettlement sites which seem ideal to the administrative agent on a brief visit may have severe disadvantages from the village perspective.

One characteristic of administration in New Regime Zaire that is visible in both the reform of chieftaincies and the regrouping of villages is the short span of attention to policy. New measures are announced, and often have radical implications. The prefects receive their orders, which are frequently imprecise, and which fail to anticipate many of the practical difficulties of implementation. The local prefects—the zone commissioners and their immediate superiors—improvise some form of application, even if they are well aware of the impracticality of the proposals. Over time—perhaps a few months, perhaps two or three years—the campaign will have lost its momentum and ceased to command attention in Kinshasa. By this time, the reforms will have been overtaken by some other bold new initiatives that supersede the earlier priorities. At this juncture, even if no formal instruction is ever received to annul the earlier measures, local administrators may safely abandon them.

Failure of administrative reform

Whether one delves into the Zairian archives, conducts lengthy interviews, or merely scans the Zairian press, it is not difficult to compile a list of deficiencies of the Zairian administration. Thus we find Mobutu declaring in December 1965, in his first major speech following the coup, "Before such examples [of politicians stuffing their pockets], the public administration, national as well as provincial, has given in to inertia, ineffectiveness, and still more serious, to corruption. At every level, many of those who in our country had a bit of public power let themselves be corrupted, showing partiality to people or companies who paid them bribes, and neglecting the others. Their professional activity no longer was inspired by national or provincial interest, but uniquely by their own interest."[30]

There is no reason to challenge this presidential diagnosis of venality and ineffectiveness.[31] The most commonly suggested therapy does not match the cogency of the diagnosis. Again and again we encounter proposals for structural improvements (or simply changes in nomenclature) as remedies for flaws deeply entrenched in the character of the state and in the nature of its relationship with society.

This reflex seems to derive both from the Belgian colonial administrative tradition and from French public administration theory, with their cartesian notion of symmetrical administrative units arranged in a rational hierarchy. In such a system instructions flow downward through specified channels, and administrators at each level check to see that those on lower levels carry out the instructions. Elaborate formal regulatory controls are prescribed to ensure compliance and to verify the uses of public money. Theoretically there is little room for inefficiency, let alone misuse of state funds.

Since no administration anywhere in the world functions entirely according to a rational division of tasks or its own organizational charts, the mere fact that there are divergences from the model in Zaire is not surprising. To be sure, these may affect the delivery of services in some instances; for example, Nzongola has found that the specialized services provided in the city of Kananga correspond very imperfectly with those prescribed in the official organization charts.[32] Such seeming irrationality may well handicap the urban agencies in the performance of their intended functions. However, the same study amply demonstrates that the Kananga administration devotes most of its energies to generating a revenue flow to pay for its own operation, and that despite the good will and earnest endeavors of some of its agents, it lacks the resources and the capacity to deliver most of its prescribed services. Identical conclusions emerge from Margaret Turner's study of public housing agencies in Lubumbashi in the mid-1970s.[33] No amount of structural tinkering will alter these basic facts.

And yet the attempt to perfect the theoretical rationality of the administrative organization has been the most frequent response to those shortcomings which have been recognized in many presidential declarations. The administrative history of the agricultural service furnishes an exemplary case. Repeated structural changes have occurred in the distribution of rural development responsibilities within the state apparatus. None has made the slightest dent in the shortfalls of agricultural production; but the proclivity for bureaucratic formalism in the identification of remedies continues.

Nor are the problems of the administration simply a matter of formally trained personnel. There is a larger pool of university graduates available to the contemporary administration than was ever employed in the Belgian colonial service. While in the First Republic years part of the administrative difficulties could be attributed to the catapulting of low-ranking clerical employees of slender educational qualifications into top positions in both the central and regional administrations, this is no longer the root of the problem. Many of today's state personnel have not only the requisite formal educational attainments, but commendable bureaucratic talent and skill as well. The paradox of declining administrative performance in the face of increasing availability of skilled personnel is well stated by a Zairian scholar, Diombamba: "There appears to be a negative correlation between advances in education and training and the evaluation of the administrative performance: it appears that the higher the number of trained cadres coming out of the formal training institutes, the higher the level of deterioration in the performance of the public service."[34]

The issue lies rather in the nature of the state apparatus, particularly at its regional periphery. The disparity between the resources available to the state agencies and the tasks they are charged with performing is very great; the agencies lack means of transport and communication, operating funds for carrying out programs, and basic supplies. The state itself sees first to its own preservation and nurture. Studies by Nzongola of the urban administration in Kananga and by Schatzberg of the subregion, zone, and collectivity administrations at Lisala demonstrate in rich detail how the essential energies of these units of the state are committed to securing from their subjects a subsistence living for the state itself.[35] Simultaneously, the state is the primary vehicle for perpetuating social inequality and for class formation: while nurturing the state, the functionaries are at the same time nourishing themselves. The habits of force and coercion which characterized the Buli Matari state have lost none of their vitality; indeed, it is at once obvious that the ever-present threat of repressive action is indispensable to sustain not just the state's hegemony, but its survival. From these factors may be deduced the limited competence of the state to deliver promised services effectively, or to achieve its programmatic goal of promoting development.

Systematic corruption

Compounding these problems is pervasive corruption. Venality within the state is, of course, a universal phenomenon; American history offers many spectacular examples. A decade ago many students of political development took a quite indulgent view of the issue, stressing that robust economic growth and healthy polity operations had frequently been observed in tandem with corruption in the past, that the scope of the problem was easily inflated, and that the market for state services could only overcome its inherent rigidities if side payments were permitted.[36] While these arguments may have validity where the level of corruption remains moderate, when venality totally permeates the state, as had become the case in Zaire by the 1970s, the social and political costs are great.

Gould, a patient observer of corruption in Zaire, has established a taxonomy of ten major types of "corrupt behavior in the routine course of government business." One can pay public employees to have documents removed from government files, to misuse official stationery and seals, to provide a letter of recommendation, or even a job. Once employed, one may have to pay in order to get a salary, housing, or other benefits to which one is entitled.[37] From the point of view of a public official at a given level, one can obtain money from one's subordinates and from members of the public in a variety of illegal ways. Everything, as Mobutu declared in his "mal zairois" speech, is for sale; government services are subject to an "invisible tax." Such services may not be distributed to the first comer with sufficient funds; nepotism is an interactive factor. Affinities of family, ethnicity, or region may supplement or replace monetary payments to induce the grant of a government favor.

As Gould points out, the Zaire case offers no support for the notions that corruption is a lubricant for the state or that it makes the system work. Rather, in Zaire corruption has become the system; it is a system by which the powerful exploit the less powerful, who in turn exploit the powerless.[38]

The most trivial transactions with the Zairian state are costly not only for the average citizen; for such people, the sums involved in a given exchange may not be very large (though for a poor individual they may still be considerable). But as one progresses further up in the state apparatus, the amounts involved become much more important. Shaba's regional commissioner was receiving $100,000 a month in kickbacks in 1974, when his monthly salary was only $2,000.[39] The huge contracts with foreign firms for projects such as Inga-Shaba have provided other occasions for illicit payments.

Venality on this scale has serious repercussions for the resources available to the state. In 1976, for example, the revenues lost to the state through the illicit export of coffee, then selling for record prices, amounted to at least $300 million. Those involved included a number of the top state personnel and the presidential conglomerate CELZA.[40] Comparable irregularities are known to have occurred in the export of cobalt, diamonds, gold, and even copper.

The state payroll system is another engine of diversion of public funds. The 300,000-odd state employees are paid by a central computerized system; opportunities for corruption exist at various stages in this complex machinery. The new employee unwilling to make appropriate payments is likely to wait many months before his name is introduced into the computer; until then he receives no pay (though he may subsist through cash advances from his agency). If properly programmed, the computer will authorize the payment of back salary, whether or not this is due. Agency heads are often able to introduce fictitious names to the payroll, or to leave on the payroll the names of employees who have resigned, retired, or perished. Mobutu himself declared in a speech to French business leaders in mid-1979 that there were many thousand such names padding the education payroll; a similar situation exists in the armed forces.[41]

In addition to the corrupt siphoning of public funds, the state regional apparatus tends to accord priority to its own consumption needs, bringing about a wholesale transformation of development policies whereby the interests of the administration and the administrators become paramount. In 1973–74, for example, the central government decided to apply revenues from taxes on beer consumption to problems of rural development. As Schatzberg relates, "Local administrators were asked to establish lists of priority development projects which would benefit the rural areas. Most of the development projects submitted, however, called for the construction of new houses for the local administrators, new office buildings, and the electrification of rest houses used exclusively by the local bureaucratic elite." A comprehensive examination of public resource flows in the Mongala subregion and the Lisala zone leads Schatzberg to the conclusion that, "at least in Zaire, money does not trickle down."[42]

On the contrary, the corruption which had become systemic within the structure of the state by the 1970s has ensured that societal resources flow upward. Formal schemas of centralization or "unity of command" have become devices for ensuring that the control of state resource flows is concentrated at the upper echelons of the apparatus, where privatization of public funds occurs on the largest scale. With the state transformed into a machine of accumulation by the politico-commercial class, precious little remains for fulfilling the ostensible public-regarding functions of the state. A presumption of corruption flavors the daily encounters between the state's agents and its subjects. So pervasive has been the venality that functionaries cannot easily escape its clutches, even if they wish to. We believe that a number of state agents have been sickened and demoralized by the system in which they find themselves ensnared, yet the individual of high moral intent cannot easily elude complicity, if not full participation. While Gould perhaps goes too far in making corruption the central explanatory factor for Zairian underdevelopment, there is some cogency to his argument that, on the scale practiced recently, corruption serves as a major vehicle for class formation and the hegemony of the politico-commercial class, and for the perpetuation of external dependence.[43]

Through the prism of the regional administration, we may discern the ultimate paradox of the Zairian state. The dissolution of the state is both impossible and undesirable. Collective societal action, through the instrumentality of a state, provides the only hope for a better life for the mass of the Zairian populace. Yet the state apparatus in its present form is an exceedingly heavy burden upon society, and a major impediment to mass well-being.

9

The Seventh Scourge: The Security Forces

The paradox of force

In 1977, following the invasion of Shaba by Katangans from Angola, President Mobutu declared that the Forces Armées Zairoises had suffered a "moral defeat" because of the discouragement of the soldiers, caused in turn by the "negligence of certain of their leaders, irresponsible and greedy, not always devoted to the national cause."[1] Even earlier Mobutu had expressed dismay over the persistent shortcomings of the army; in the 1974 enumeration of the "ten scourges" ravaging Zairian society, he identified the seventh as "a costly and unproductive army."[2] Indeed, as House has observed, the problem went back to the coup which brought Mobutu to power: "Since the *Armée Nationale Congolaise*, or ANC [now FAZ] came to power in 1965, it has served paradoxically as the source of security for the Mobutu regime and as the principal creator of havoc in the country."[3] In other words, neither constitutional legitimacy nor party support would suffice to maintain Mobutu's rule were it not underwritten with visible force. Yet the army's legendary indiscipline and repeated incapacity to defeat even small and poorly armed foes make it an object of scorn. It is, as Mobutu declared, relatively costly to maintain. In addition, the threat of renewed political intervention by the army is ever-present. The hegemony and power of the state rest upon the force it controls, but that force is unreliable in times of crisis, its depredations undermine the credibility of the state, and its capricious actions may threaten the state itself.

To explore this paradox, we will first review the actual combat record of the armed forces during the Mobutu years, then search for explanations for the character of the FAZ. The mechanisms for maintenance of political control of the army merit consideration, as do the various efforts to improve its performance. While we focus primarily upon the army, by far the most important branch of the security forces, we also consider other components.

248

From the advent of the New Regime until 1980, the FAZ engaged in a half-dozen major military engagements:

1. The campaign to eliminate insurgent pockets subsisting from the 1964–65 rebellions
2. The Katanga gendarme mutiny in Kisangani in July 1966
3. The much more serious mutiny of mercenary and Katanga gendarme units from July to November 1967
4. The invasion of Angola, in coordination with FLNA forces, from August to December 1975
5. The 80-day war against FLNC invaders from Shaba, March through June 1977 (Shaba I)
6. The brief war against FLNC fighters who seized Kolwezi in June 1978 (Shaba II)

Recapitulation of these episodes will set the stage for considering the performance issue.

The combat record

Vestiges of the rebellions

In November 1965, although the main forces of the insurrection had fallen apart and most external assistance had ceased, there were still important areas in Haut-Zaire, Kivu, and northern Shaba where insurgent bands continued to operate. Despite the several hundred white mercenaries serving with the Zairian security forces, reimposition of central government authority proved slow and difficult. Eventually, factional strife among the exiled rebel leaders, and a final end to foreign supply, weakened the remaining insurgents.

At the beginning of 1967, insurgents retained effective control only in two small regions of Kivu and in seven or more pockets in Haut-Zaire.[4] Little by little, the army put down the remaining pockets of rebellion, except in the Fizi area of southeastern Kivu, where the insurgent forces put down deep roots.

Survival of the rebel pocket in the Fizi area has been a result of two main factors: first, the opposition between rebels and government had been grafted onto factional conflict within the Bembe ethnic group; second, the rebels had established some sort of modus vivendi with the government forces. By 1973, the rebels had retreated from their earlier bases near Lake Tanganyika to new ones deep in the mountains; as they retreated, they were accompanied by one Bembe faction.

A Bembe who had served as porter for the army during search-and-destroy missions in the hills above Fizi has confirmed the complicity between the FAZ and the rebels. He claimed that "all the military authorities are delighted to be named to the Fizi operational zone, because . . . it is their chance to make a fortune." Numerous high-ranking officers were engaged in trade, some operating boats between Mboke and Baraka, Zaire, and Kigoma, Tanzania.[5]

Dramatic confirmation of the continued existence of the Fizi pocket came in 1975, when guerrillas crossed Lake Tanganyika to a camp occupied by primate research specialist Jane Goodall and her colleagues and kidnapped four of them. The guerrillas identified themselves as members of the Popular Revolutionary Party, and demanded 200,000 pounds sterling, as well as the release of two of their colleagues who were supposedly under arrest in Tanzania. The guerrillas were paid some ransom, and the hostages were released. This insurgent pocket continued to exist into the 1980s; while it has posed no evident threat, its very existence raises the question of why the national army has been unable to remove it.

The 1966 Kisangani mutiny

The 1966 mutiny at Kisangani involved the Baka Regiment, a unit of the FAZ composed essentially of 2,000 Katangan gendarmes with white mercenary officers, under the command of Colonel Ferdinand Tshipola. The colonel and his men had been called back from Angola in September 1964 by then-premier Tshombe to reinforce the flagging national army in its efforts to subdue the rebellions. The regiment was left ethnoregionally homogeneous, with its own officers and logistical systems. On the first day of the mutiny, the Katangans seized the airport and the center of the city, while troops faithful to Mobutu retained control of the portion of Kisangani on the opposite bank of the Zaire River.

Attempts to negotiate a solution to the impasse failed. After a two-month standoff, the regime paid a heavy bonus to white mercenary units under Bob Denard to take the lead in crushing the mutineers.[6] The Mobutu regime placed the blame for the 1966 mutiny on Tshombe and external financial milieux favorable to his resurrection. We think it fair to stress more mundane factors, including army pay arrearages and the fears of the Katangans that they would be disarmed or dispersed among other units.

Mercenary-led revolt, 1967

There can be no doubt that the 1967 mutiny, which also began in Kisangani, was part of a broader conspiracy to return Tshombe to power. The spectacular *coup de main* by which Tshombe was kidnapped and interned in Algeria aborted the overall scheme (see chapter 2), but the mutinies of white mercenary units went forward regardless.[7] Beyond the Tshombe plot, there were again specifically military factors behind the revolt. The 1967 mutinies took place in the context of regime efforts to reduce its dependence upon the highly controversial mercenaries. The mercenary ranks, which had totalled 650 in December 1966, had been thinned to 189 when the mutiny broke out. The 5th Commando, composed of South Africans and Rhodesians, already had been dissolved. The Frenchman Denard had managed to transform the dissolution of his unit into a reorganization which put him at the head of a mixed brigade of FAZ regulars, Katangans, and mercenaries.

During the month of June 1967, Denard warned his Belgian counterpart, Jean Schramme, that the FAZ high command was planning to dissolve his units, disperse his men, and put them under Zairian officers. To prevent this from happening, Schramme launched the insurrection at Kisangani on 5 July. The mutineers (11 whites and approximately 100 Katangese) suddenly opened fire on FAZ troops and their families, killing and wounding hundreds. About 30 mercenaries were massacred by FAZ men in retaliation, and all remaining mercenaries joined Schramme.

The FAZ regrouped and fought back for a week, forcing Schramme to evacuate Kisangani. During this week of stalemate, he had managed to build his force up to 150 mercenaries, 600 Katangans, and 400 Zairian auxiliaries (apparently men without military training). Schramme then led his disparate force southeast into Kivu, eventually capturing the regional capital of Bukavu on 8 August; by this time his force had been augmented by other Katangan and Zairian renegades and additional stray mercenaries. En route there were several important engagements with the FAZ; in one of these encounters, at Kindu, the FAZ units performed very well.

Greatly outnumbered, the mercenaries and Zairians under Schramme held on at Bukavu for seven weeks. During the first four weeks, they inflicted a series of defeats on the FAZ forces. A number of weaknesses were visible on the Zairian side. Soldiers of Shaba origin were suspect of sympathy with the Katangan mutineers, which sowed discord in the ranks. Communication between units was poor; several attacks failed because only one of several units actually took part. Coordination between ground units and air support was lacking; this was illustrated by a costly attack by Zairian T-28 jets on their own units. Supply was still another problem. Attacks were not preceded by artillery barrages because inadequate quantities of shells were distributed. Often, attacks petered out because the units engaged ran out of ammunition.

These problems were serious not only because they frustrated the plans of the FAZ to crush the mercenaries, but because they demoralized the Zairian units, and even brought on the danger of mutiny. Indeed, one battalion did mutiny, on 2 October. In late October the FAZ task force in Bukavu was at last reinforced by large shipments of munitions, communications equipment, and the elite 2d Paratroop Battalion. On 29 October, a final assault began on the mutineer redoubt, now reduced by casualties and supply shortages. But it was still seven days before the remaining mercenaries and Katangans fled across the border into Rwanda. The FAZ had won its most important post-independence victory.

The triumph at Bukavu was a powerful boost for the army and the regime. It was the first time since independence that the Zairian armed forces had apparently defeated a major armed challenge to public order without large-scale external support or reinforcement by a squalid assortment of white mercenary soldiers. The success of the final push at Bukavu—and also those engagements during the Schramme mutiny campaign in which FAZ units had fought well—created the appearance of an upward trajectory for the FAZ. The poor performance of some units could be ascribed to the fact that they had not yet undergone retraining programs. Some retrained units, and the elite 2d Paratroop Battalion, had fought effectively. A related incursion from Angola into southwestern Shaba by mercenaries and Katangans was turned back.

If we examine these events more closely, however, the picture is less reassuring. The Schramme column had moved freely over hundreds of miles of east-central Zaire despite the presence of FAZ detachments in these zones. Once the Schramme force was sealed off in Bukavu, it took seven weeks for FAZ forces, which numbered 15,000, to roust them out, although the mutineers had been cut off from all external aid and resupply (an accomplishment in which several Western intelligence agencies played no small part). Resupply of the FAZ units in Bukavu was in good part carried out by U.S. Air Force C-130s, an operation which drew heavy congressional criticism. As well, planning and logistics for the final assault drew upon staff assistance from Belgian and American military personnel. The Denard incursion from Angola into Shaba involved only 80 men on bicycles; while a Zairian battalion did block their advance, it was aerial attacks from T-28 fighters that drove them back into Angola. Finally, the propensity of the army to escape control and wreak havoc on the civilian population was again demonstrated in the wake of the recapture of Bukavu. As House puts it, "When the army entered the city the entire remaining population fled before them. Everything from mattresses to doors and even bricks from buildings were disassembled and sold to foreign petty merchants or loaded on [army] trucks and shipped out. A major reconstruction program had to be launched to relocate the 190,000 former residents of Bukavu—most of whom stayed away for months in fear of the army."[8]

For several years following the mercenary revolt life was rather quiet for the Zairian armed forces. They did perform effectively in helping to suppress a revolt by the Hutu majority against the Tutsi-dominated government of Micombero in neighboring Burundi, and in the restoration of order in a camp of Angolan Frente Nacional de Libertação de Angola (FNLA) guerrillas in Zaire.[9] In 1975, when Zaire became directly involved in the Angolan civil war, and its army was found wanting once more.

Intervention in Angola

Zaire's involvement with Angolan liberation movements dated from the early 1960s, but the coup by the Armed Forces Movement in Portugal in April 1974 suddenly made Angolan independence an immediate prospect. Zaire, from whose territory the FNLA of Holden Roberto was operating, leapt into the conflict over the choice of a successor regime. In September Mobutu met secretly with General Spinola, head of the Portuguese government. They agreed to form a coalition government for Angola, to be headed by Roberto, Jonas Savimbi of the União Nacional para a Indepencia Total de Angola (UNITA), and MPLA dissident Daniel Chipenda; excluded would have been the majority of the MPLA, under Agostino Neto.[10] The agreement broken down when Spinola himself was ousted by left-wing officers at the end of the month.

Thus failed the effort to promote, with Portuguese connivance, an Angolan successor regime with close ties to Zaire. The possibility then began to emerge that the fate of Angola might be determined by civil war among the contending nationalist groups (with external participation probable) as a weakening Portuguese government, preoccupied with internal survival, progressively lost all influence over the dynamic of events. An ephemeral accord among the MPLA, FNLA, and UNITA for a coalition regime offered short-lived hope in January 1975; the coalition remained the OAU formula for Angolan independence until November. A flow of foreign support to all parties, initially covert, began to gather force early in 1975 (American support started in January with the decision to make an initial $300,000 grant to FNLA through Zaire). It is not clear when Mobutu began to consider military intervention in Angola; by mid-1975 the possibility of intervention had already provoked serious tensions within the top ranks of the Zairian officer corps.[11]

The first Zairian units had entered Angola in July 1975, when the MPLA appeared to be in the ascendant.[12] In August two more paracommando companies crossed the border, while South African forces occupied the Cunene Dam site in the south. Just before the day set for Angolan independence, Zairian units invaded Cabinda, along with irregulars from the Frente do Libertação do Enclave de Cabinda (FLEC). Altogether, the equivalent of four or five battalions was committed.

In October, a Zairian-FNLA force edged toward Luanda, while in the south a South African spearhead, with UNITA and FNLA units attached, began striking northward. As independence day approached, the Zairian-FNLA column was less than 20 miles from Luanda.

The tide of battle quickly turned in November. MPLA forces stiffened at the gates of the capital; Katanga gendarme units, which had been brought into alliance with the MPLA in January 1975 and had been provided with equipment and some training by external supporters of the MPLA, helped blunt the Zairian offensive. When these were joined by Cubans, equipped with the famed "Stalin organ" (a mobile multiple rocket launcher whose sound and fury exceeded its accuracy), the Zairian-FNLA force disintegrated. As units broke apart, it was well-nigh impossible to regroup and strike again. By December, MPLA and Cuban forces had carried their own offensive into the FNLA heartland.

As the FAZ-FNLA units retreated, they dissolved into disorderly bands of looters. Carmona, principal town of northern Angola, reportedly was thoroughly sacked before being abandoned without a fight; in Maquela de Zombo, close to the Zairian border, Zairian troops reportedly staged a mock attack, pretending to be MPLA forces, in order to drive out the populace and steal their belongings.[13]

Shaba I

The humiliating defeat in Angola deflated the myth of a gradually improving Zairian army. Yet it could still be argued that in Angola the army came up against a potent, well-disciplined, and heavily equipped modern fighting force—the Cuban army—which it could not be expected to match. What remained of the illusions concerning the capabilities of the FAZ were utterly dissipated by the fiasco of its encounters with the small and meagerly equipped FLNC invaders in 1977 and 1978. In 1977 the FAZ faced the first invasion by the FLNC—Shaba I. Although the invading force was very modest (1,500 to 2,000 men, according to the best estimates), the Zairian army was completely unable to cope with the threat and had to be rescued by the West.

The FLNC can be traced back to the Katangan gendarmery that Tshombe had created in 1960. A number of the gendarmes had taken refuge in Angola when the Katanga secession collapsed in January 1963; others had vanished into the countryside. When Tshombe became prime minister in July 1964, he incorporated approximately 17,000 former Katanga gendarmes into the national army as separate units; these groups were involved in the 1966 and 1967 mutinies described above. With the collapse of the 1967 mutiny, the surviving Katangans (several hundred) who had taken refuge in neighboring Rwanda were repatriated under amnesty pledges. They subsequently disappeared, and it was widely believed that they had been killed.[14]

At the same time that the main body of former Katanga gendarmes were absorbed in the army, others were integrated into a Katangan provincial police force. During 1967 a fiercely repressive campaign was carried out by Katangan governor Manzikala; the police were purged, and many fled to Angola, where they were joined by a number of youths in flight from the Manzikala reign of terror. The Portuguese organized these fugitives into units, dubbed the "Black Arrows," which were used as diplomatic leverage against Zaire and on occasion in anti-guerrilla operations, mainly against FNLA strongholds. In June 1968 the Black Arrows took on the political label of Front pour la Libération Nationale du Congo.

When Portuguese rule collapsed, the FLNC, primarily a paramilitary formation, had found itself in a cruel dilemma. The overtures from Mobutu for repatriation were distrusted, as the FLNC believed it would be likely to meet the same apparently fatal end as the Katanga gendarmes of 1967. An FNLA triumph in Angola also posed grave dangers, both because of its intimate links with Mobutu, and because of the FLNC's past complicity in repressive action at the side of the Portuguese. The solution was an alliance of circumstance with the MPLA. The FLNC rendered signal service to the MPLA in late 1975 by helping to halt the FAZ-FNLA offensive; in the process, its members acquired new arms and additional training.

At the conclusion of the Angolan civil war the FLNC had returned to their base area near the Shaba frontier. It was from there that they launched the invasion on 8 March 1977, seizing the towns of Dilolo (railhead, administrative center), Kisenge (manganese mining), and Kapanga (zone headquarters, near the Lunda royal capital). It soon became clear that the FAZ was offering almost no resistance to the invaders. As the *Washington Post* put it,

> The army of the official communiques is a predictably valiant, cool-headed force, launching air attacks on the Katangan invaders and retaking captured villages.
>
> The Zaire army depicted by intelligence reports from sources sympathetic to Mobutu, however, bears more resemblance to the panic-stricken, undisciplined mobs that passed for Congolese army units in the early 1960s. They flee rather than fight.[15]

Eventually, in mid-April, as the FLNC forces edged closer to Kolwezi and the FAZ made little visible effort to repulse them, the French government announced that it had put a fleet of military transport planes at the disposal of Morocco to airlift men and materiel to Zaire. Within a week, the Moroccans moved out from their Kolwezi point of deployment and reoccupied the areas abandoned by the FAZ. There were few real skirmishes; the FLNC was evidently reluctant to engage the Moroccan army. The last FLNC pockets within Shaba were eliminated during the final week of May; for the most part the FNLC simply withdrew before a superior force.

The main significance of Shaba I was its revelation of the continuing severe limitations of the FAZ, despite substantial Western aid and repeated retraining programs over the years, as well as Chinese and North Korean aid in 1973–75. The problem had several facets: morale, leadership, and maintenance of equipment. Morale was low, eroded by delays in the payment of troops and in the forwarding of supplies. Readily saleable provisions that did arrive—especially gasoline—often found their way onto the black market, with the connivance of army officers.

The aftermath of the Shaba I episode added further evidence of the liabilities of the Zairian security forces. Once the Moroccans had driven the FLNC out of southwestern Shaba, FAZ units engaged in a punitive "pacification" campaign in the zones from which it had fled. In fact, local populations had exhibited an often wary and ambivalent reaction to the FLNC presence; while there was little, if any, support for the national government, there was uncertainty about FLNC intentions and behavior. People had also feared vengeance by the national army if too much enthusiasm were shown for the invaders and the FLNC presence then proved ephemeral. Their fears proved well justified; pacification led directly to the exodus of a significant fraction of the population into neighboring Angola. The number of refugees exceeded 200,000, by the estimate of an international agency. There was certainly no planned effort to provoke such an exodus; rather, the outflow reflected the brutal nature of a reoccupation campaign by ill-disciplined armed forces.

Shaba II

In May 1978 the FLNC attacked Shaba once again. They seized the mining center of Kolwezi on 13 May, and were driven out by French and Belgian paratroopers a week later, although mopping-up operations lasted into June. Though much shorter than the 80-day war of 1977, the 1978 conflict claimed a considerable number of victims. In addition to the white civilians, whose deaths inevitably received the greatest attention in the Western press, these included large numbers of black civilians and black troops, both of the FAZ and of the invading Katangans, as well as smaller numbers of European troops. Shaba II once more demonstrated the infirmities of the FAZ, which may well have been responsible for more civilian deaths than the insurgents.

The attack of 13 May was not a total surprise. Many African residents of Kolwezi knew about the invasion, as was made clear by the high rate of absenteeism among Gécamines workers on 12 May.[16] The FLNC had skillfully infiltrated men and materiel into Kolwezi itself. Their attacking units passed through Zambia and approached Kolwezi from an unanticipated direction rather than repeating the itinerary from Angola used in Shaba I. Thus the attackers suddenly appeared in Kolwezi itself.

While the FLNC units at first exhibited considerable discipline in their relations with the civilian population, the control of the leaders over their men diminished as the week of occupation wore on. The invaders were joined by youth elements from the ranks of the Kolwezi informal sector and the unemployed, whose social anger was difficult to keep within bounds. Although announcements were made concerning a provisional governing committee, it became clear that beyond the brilliant first stroke of capturing Kolwezi the leadership had no prepared plan for either consolidating administrative control or pursuing the initial FLNC advantage.[17]

The recapture of Kolwezi on 19 May was essentially the work of paratroops from the French Foreign Legion and from Belgium. The American role was limited to providing air transport and to strafing Kolwezi during the paratroop drop. Following the retaking of Kolwezi, large numbers of local Africans fled, apparently fearing the vengeance of the Zairian troops. Several hundred FLNC survivors, fleeing from pursuing French paratroopers, crossed the northwestern salient of Zambia into Angola on 23 May in a convoy of at least 70 miscellaneous vehicles laden with goods looted from Kolwezi.

Shaba II affected primarily Kolwezi itself; there was no repetition of the unhappy pacification campaign in rural areas, but there were once again difficulties in the city itself that were occasioned by the indiscipline of Zairian troops. Further, the manifest inability of the FAZ to provide security for the most important complex of productive installations in the country, and refusal of most expatriate staff to return unless protected by non-Zairian armed forces, made necessary a second appeal to the Moroccan army. Both Belgium and France were determined to quickly withdraw their forces. Under the cover of an "inter-African peacekeeping force," 1,500 Moroccans returned to Shaba, along with token detachments from five other African countries with close ties to France (and to Mobutu): Senegal, Ivory Coast, Togo, Gabon, and Central African Republic. At this juncture discipline was so low among some FAZ elements that the Zairian authorities had to disarm them.[18]

Failures of the army

In many respects, in the aftermath of Shaba II, the wheel seemed to have come full circle, back to the dark days of 1960. The armed forces, while indispensable to the survival of the regime and the state, were at the same time one of the greatest burdens. Their numbers had been expanded to more than double the 1960 figure, yet the FAZ had proved repeatedly unreliable in combat. The hopes fostered by its limited successes in the 1967 mercenary mutiny had been dashed by its three debacles in 1975, 1977, and 1978. The costly equipment which had been acquired—especially the

Mirage jets—had proved of little value. The defense budget was about 10 to 11 percent of the national budget in the 1970s, but the limited security return on this investment validated Mobutu's stigmatization of the FAZ as the "costly and unproductive" seventh scourge.[19]

It is doubtful whether the Zairian armed forces have ever enjoyed much popularity with the citizenry since their establishment by the Leopoldian state. Yet they once commanded respect, when their performance was less embarrassing. The very deterioration of the formal capacities of the FAZ makes them more dangerous for the unarmed civil population, as there is neither recourse from nor protection against the depredations of uniformed personnel. The poor morale and the resentments of the troops, provoked by pay irregularities, the often miserable living conditions of the enlisted ranks, supply shortages, and the transparent venality of a segment of the officer corps, is deflected upon the civil population. Pilferage and exactions visited by the troops are undertaken partly for subsistence. For the ordinary person the net result is harassment—or worse—from security force members. Travel on any road means the vexation of numerous security force roadblocks. As the Lubumbashi archbishop described the issue in his 1976 pastoral letter, "[As to] the roadblocks established on the roads in the hinterland, and the major highways. We do not wish to call into doubt their military necessity. But it is unfortunate that this necessity is the occasion for ransoming all the peaceful citizens who pass by."[20] Such a military force, earning its living by banditry, sapped the strength of the state.

Some recent evidence suggests that in regions remote from the capital the military has lost all credibility as a repressive force. One scholar, returning in 1979 to the far northeast of the country after an absence of five years, found the local soldiery in tattered uniforms, the victims of long pay arrearages. A number were reduced to begging for food; lacking ammunition, they could no longer commandeer supplies at the marketplace. In return for being fed they were asked to provide labor for local farmers, a remarkably ironical enserfment of the coercive apparatus of the state to its rural periphery.[21]

Legacies of the colonial era and the First Republic

What may account for the paradox that the armed forces in post-colonial Zaire are both the pillar of the state and the scourge of the society? A first step in finding the answer is to examine the legacies of two key periods, the Bula Matari era and the chaotic First Republic, itself ushered in by the mutiny of the Force Publique in July 1960.

The armature of the Leopoldian state had been largely military, and even after the *reprise* in 1908 the Force Publique remained a bulwark of the colonial state. The troops, generally African conscripts, usually found themselves posted far from home in ethnically integrated units. Soldiers were indoctrinated with the ethos that the Force Publique constituted a distinct social category: its members were servants of the colonial state. Military and police functions were not clearly distinguished. Local unrest resulted at once in a show of force sufficient to sustain the superstructure of intimidation. The exclusively European officer corps maintained a ruthless discipline over the troops.

Under the best of circumstances the Force Publique would have faced a difficult adaptation to the new context of independence. But the worst of circumstances immediately prevailed; within a week of the realization of Zairian sovereignty, the entire army dissolved in mutiny. During much of the First Republic era the security forces were broken into several fragments. The new Zairian officers—for the most part former noncommissioned officers—had only uncertain control over their men; much of their energy was absorbed in purchasing their continued service by seeing that the payroll was met, which in a number of instances meant recourse to clandestine external sources of finance. Mobutu succeeded in gradually achieving ascendancy over most of the army, but his control was always incomplete, and a number of units were notoriously unreliable. To neutralize the potential threat to the center of power which these units represented, they were generally posted far from the capital. These segments of the army bore the brunt of the 1964–65 rebellions; the remarkable success enjoyed by the insurgents in the early phases of the uprisings was in no small part a result of the disaffection and demoralization of the government forces they encountered.

Until early 1964, the potential threat to the state from poorly controlled armed groups was partly countered by the presence of a United Nations peacekeeping force, which had neither the desire, the mandate, nor the capacity to assert a tutelary supervision over the Zairian armed forces, although it did keep them in check. When the UN force withdrew a third of the country was quickly engulfed in insurrections which the Zairian forces appeared unable to contain, a fateful decision was made by the Tshombe premiership. An auxiliary force of white mercenaries was created, and several thousand former Katangan secessionists were incorporated into the national army. In the short run, this strategy was successful in helping to turn the military tide against the insurrections. But a potent new vector of turbulence was introduced, as the mercenary and Katanga units had a contingent and uncertain commitment to the New Regime.

The mercenary and Katanga gendarme units were carefully kept away from both the capital and Shaba. When the pattern of conspiracy orchestrated by Tshombe intensified in 1966, these units became an increasing liability, yet they were also hard to disperse and remove. The mutinies of 1966 and 1967 finally provided the opportunity—at great cost—to eliminate these unruly elements.[22]

The legacy of the security forces was thus the brutality of the colonial era wedded to the mutiny of the First Republic. The tenuous control of the independent state over its forces meant that brutality was less focussed—from the standpoint of the Bula Matari state, less instrumental. The use of violence was more capricious and random. While a sense of fear among the populace was sustained, the heightened unpredictability of coercion perhaps made its instrumentalities even more disliked. Further, the question of political control over the army assumed an entirely new importance. During colonial times, the European-officered Force Publique was always under the close and unquestioned tutelage of the state (except for a brief period in 1940, when the wartime role of the Belgian Congo was momentarily at issue after metropolitan Belgium fell to the Germans). Since the moment of the mutiny, control of the armed forces by the political institutions of the state has always been at issue.

As we have seen, Mobutu was catapulted into the top rank of the army by Lumumba immediately after independence. The prime minister mistakenly believed that he could rely on the political loyalty of Mobutu, who was one of the few members of the 1960 political class who had any military background. Another was Victor Lundula, linked to Lumumba by ethnic affinity, who was designated as commander-in-chief after the Belgian officers fled; Mobutu was initially Chief-of-Staff. During the critical period from July to September 1960, Mobutu was able to pry Lundula out of the top post and assume a limited but decisive control over the army units closest to Kinshasa.

Mobutu thus was able to exercise some influence over the tumultuous process of promoting Zairian noncoms to the roughly 550 officer's posts which suddenly opened in 1960, especially in the western regions of the country. The authority Mobutu held was by no means that of a commander over his subordinates in a tightly hierarchical military organization; it was more analogous to that of a patron over a network of clients, whose loyalty was open to frequent renegotiation as the situation evolved. House describes this situation particularly well:

> From 1960–1965, . . . Mobutu succeeded in gaining the allegiance of the more powerful officers, many of whom had their respective fiefdoms within the ranks. Mobutu used ties of personal loyalty and the politics of threats and rewards to overcome the absence of an organized command structure. With tactical advice and financial support from the United States, Mobutu established his authority to the point where he could threaten, pay, or influence in other ways the upper ranks. . . . His control was much like that of the center of a spoked wheel: the officers were often divided by personal hatreds and rivalries and linked to their commands only by Mobutu at the center. By rotating officers often and encouraging them to report every piece of news or rumor to him personally, Mobutu established his supremacy over the command structure.[23]

House adds that the solidification of relative control over the armed forces was the most basic factor in positioning Mobutu to seize supreme power in 1965. While the army was unable to defeat the insurgents in the eastern part of the country in 1964, and had to commission mercenaries to perform this task, it was still the strongest single organized group in the First Republic. House's conclusion that "the ability to control army politics has been Mobutu's basic political strength" remained valid into the 1980s.[24]

The military role in the New Regime

The 1965 coup d'état placed Mobutu and the FAZ at the center of Zairian politics. As president, as well as minister of defense, Mobutu held important new resources in his hands. The keys to the public treasury were his, and could be used to lubricate the clientage networks; he now possessed more extensive sanctions that could be applied to the recalcitrant. Access to external clandestine funds was no longer necessary in the game of ascendancy over the military structure. The only other military figure in the cabinet, the popular Mulamba, was removed in October 1966, and the post of prime minister was abolished.

From the beginning there was ambiguity as to whether Mobutu or the army had seized power. The original proclamation began,

> At the invitation of Lieutenant-General Mobutu, commander in chief of [the Zairian armed forces], the high authorities of the army met November 24, 1965, at his residence.[25]

Similarly, in his speech to the Parliament on the afternoon of 25 November, Mobutu referred to "fundamental dispositions" taken by the high command.[26] Twelve years later, however, instead of speaking of power being conferred upon him by the high command, Mobutu referred to having taken power.[27]

Creation of the MPR aroused the jealousy of army officers by providing an alternative base for the regime. This was heightened by the raising of the MPR to supremacy and the substitution of its banner for the previous national flag; some army officers reportedly fulminated at the loss of the flag "for which we fought and died." The threat posed by the party to traditional army self-conceptions redoubled in 1972 when it was announced that party cells were to be organized within army units. This move offended both the army's sense of its own special dignity and status as creator of the New Regime, and its traditional belief in its apoliticism. Politics and politicians had been excoriated as the source of all evil at the time of the seizure of power; back in colonial times the army had been indoctrinated against politicians, who were said to be agents of subversion, division, and disorder. When the MPR was declared the supreme organ of the republic in 1972, most of the top officers were still from the pre-1960 noncom generation that found such conceptions of political party dominance particularly indigestible.

On Army Day (17 November) in 1972 General Molongya Mayikusa, then chief of cabinet at the Defense Ministry (and a younger, better educated officer), went out of his way to declare, perhaps with more force than conviction, that "the politization of the army is an innovation. From our point of view, this position does not constitute IN ANY WAY a problem" [the general's stress].[28] The same general, in a speech on the role of the army delivered at the party institute in 1974, provided an interesting gloss on this argument:

> [The army] used to resemble an army of mercenaries, who lived removed from the population at large. This was reflected in the fact that the soldier considered himself an elite, while viewing civilians as nothing but "savages." . . .
>
> The soldier was harshly judged: a person without faith or soul, torturer of the civil population, and furthermore ignorant. This antagonism was exploited to a point where the military and civil populations, though united by blood, thoroughly and profoundly detested one another. . . .
>
> Now that Zaire is going through a far-reaching revolution, the soldier cannot remain outside of it; the army must be in the service of Mobutism, because service to Mobutism is service to the Nation.[29]

To add insult to injury, the army was initially excluded from the distribution of spoils during the period of Zairianization. Mobutu did offer some appeasement by making the booty available to a few of the top officers and (briefly) including four high-ranking officers in the August 1974 Political Bureau slate.

Since the 1965 coup, therefore, a major preoccupation of Mobutu has been management of the army leadership; this has entailed knowing when not to oppose the generals, as on the Zairianization question or perhaps the issue of Mulele's execution in 1968.[30] To control the security forces Mobutu has created an elaborate system of clientage and fostered rivalries. The heads of the various services are responsible directly to Mobutu. Factions of officers are defined in terms of institutional affiliation (regular army, paracommandos, CND), ethnic or regional identity, generations and levels of training, financial advantages, and probably other factors as well. The gauge of an officer's importance is favor with the president, who exploits the rivalries among factions and individuals and tolerates inept performance as the price of personal security.

The problem of replacing the commander in chief of the FAZ gives insight into army factions. General Bobozo, who became FAZ commander in November 1965, was totally loyal to Mobutu. Not only were they related, but Bobozo had been Mobutu's sergeant in the Force Publique. Bobozo was a member of the old generation of officers; he had entered the service in 1933, but was not trained as an officer.[31] When Bobozo suffered a stroke in 1970, the logical successor was General Massiala, senior FAZ officer. He was a younger, more vigorous, and much better educated man than Bobozo, and enjoyed considerable popularity among the new generation of professionally trained officers. However, Massiala was of inconvenient ethnic provenience (Kongo), was feared for his potential ambition, and would have been more difficult to keep under control than Bobozo had been.[32]

The president solved the problem temporarily by naming Lieutenant-General Bosango, Inspector-General of the Gendarmery, as Acting Commander of the FAZ. Bosango was a member of the old generation, like Bobozo, and had in fact been reinstated at Bobozo's urging after being fired for cowardice during the rebellion of 1964–65. As commander, he posed no threat to Mobutu; as House put it, "he commands little respect from other senior officers and is treated with pure contempt by the junior officers [who] want a commander who is technically proficient."[33] Clearly this was only an interim solution.

Eventually Mobutu's choice for an FAZ commander fell upon Brigadier-General Bumba Moaso, who had the double advantage of being from Equateur region (like Bobozo and Bosango) and of being head of the Airborne Division. He was illiterate, but a forceful personality.[34] Bumba quickly rose to become one of the most powerful men in the country. When the armed forces were integrated into the MPR in 1972, he was given the new title Captain-General of the Zairian Armed Forces. He was one of a number of military leaders who entered the Political Bureau in 1974, when the MPR was merged with the state, and in 1975 was chosen to be one of eight permanent members of the Political Bureau.

Bumba's downfall came in 1977, following Shaba I. According to diplomatic sources, his removal was a result not merely of the poor performance of the FAZ, but more specifically of his remarks at a press conference in which he made the unsubstantiated claim that his troops had found Russians, Cubans, and Portuguese among dead enemy soldiers.[35] Mobutu avoided any public announcement of Bumba's downgrading, apparently in deference to his popularity with the FAZ, but he was stripped of authority and faded away into business pursuits.

To replace Bumba, Mobutu turned to General Babia Zongbi Malebia, Director-General of the Defense Ministry, a young graduate of Belgium's national military academy, and a long-time rival of Bumba.[36] The nomination appeared to be a victory for the young, professionally trained officers over the survivors of the Force Publique. But Babia had mainly occupied staff positions, was not forceful or ambitious, and was reliably loyal to Mobutu.

In the aftermath of Shaba I, Mobutu also announced a major restructuring of the military. A General Staff of the FAZ was created to function under the direction of Mobutu, with the assistance of Babia as coordinator. The president's Personal General Staff would be integrated into the General Staff of the FAZ in the form of a special brigade in charge of honor guards and presidential security. Mobutu, arguing that new blood and transformed mentalities were needed, retired twenty-eight generals and other high-ranking officers.

The apparent ascendance of the young, highly trained officers has to be balanced against the frequent purges of which they are the object. In 1975 those condemned to death for the so-called *coup monté et manqué* included three generals, a colonel, and two majors, all but one less than 40 years old.[37] And in 1978, eight officers, including the director-general of the Defense Ministry and the second in command at the Gendarmery, were executed (along with five civilians) for what Mobutu called a plot to sabotage the economy and drive him from office; again, these officers were mainly, if not exclusively, from the younger and better-educated group.[38] During the same purge, more than two hundred officers were dismissed; close observers of the FAZ were unanimous in the belief that those eliminated included many of the ablest officers.

These alleged coup attempts led to, or justified, a drastic narrowing of the ethnoregional base of the officer corps. Those sentenced in 1975 were mainly Tetela-Kusu from Kasai Oriental and Kivu. Many—perhaps most—of those eliminated in 1978 were Kasaians; this regionally selective purge was followed by an ordinance, after Shaba II, which prohibited recruitment from the two Kasais, Bandundu, and Shaba.[39]

One important dimension of Mobutu's political control strategy is structural manipulation. Mobutu has carefully avoided the emergence of a unified security force with a single command structure. The House metaphor cited earlier is quite appropriate: rather than the pyramid characteristic of most military organigrams, the Zairian structure is better depicted as a wheel, with the president standing in the center. The basic infrastructure pattern developed during the colonial period persists. Garrison troops are dispersed about the country; in Belgian times there were three *groupements* (very roughly analogous to regiments) based at Kinshasa, Kinsangani, and Lubumbashi. The number of *groupements* was gradually increased, reaching a total of nine by the 1970s (one per administrative region). Under a separate command structure are the gendarmes, attached in small units to the lower-level administrative divisions; they have a police mission. Elite units which have been successively created since 1960 (paracommando battalions, the Kamanyola Division, the Belgian-supported 21st and French-officered 31st brigades formed after Shaba II) are not part of either the *groupement* or the gendarmery structure; their commanders report directly to the president. At the inner core of power, there is a special presidential security force, again under Mobutu's direct command. General staff, logistical, and headquarters functions are carried out both by the Ministry of Defense, and—during much of the 1965–80 period—a personal military staff attached to the presidency (the *maison militaire*). In addition, there are the separate navy and air force branches, and the very important national security police.

Particular attention is paid to the Kinshasa area, both to ensure the presence of ample repressive forces to stifle any uprising in the capital itself, and to guarantee a multiplicity of units under rival commanders. A good number of the elite units have usually been based near Kinshasa, and given privileged treatment to sustain their morale. In addition, there is the Kinshasa *groupement* command, a sizable detachment of gendarmes, and the presidential security guard. These commands are all held by officers on whose fidelity the president believes he has good reason to rely; a similar trust partly explains the predominance of officers from Equateur noted over the years in the inner core of the army. The system cannot be fully coup-proofed, but a move by a discontented military faction is made very difficult.

The total number of persons serving the FAZ per se is a matter of controversy. Mobutu in 1976 claimed to have 70,000 troops in his armed forces, and confided to foreign military advisors on several occasions that his eventual target was 80,000. The 1970 annual report of the Bank of Zaire cited a figure of 63,200; this was before the 21,000 national police were absorbed. In 1971, House was told by military advisors closely connected with the FAZ that there were 55,000 names on the payroll, and between 45,000 and 48,000 men actually in the ranks—a discrepancy which certainly persisted through the 1970s.[40] Given the number of reliable elements which have been kept in the Kinshasa area to protect the regime itself, and the significant number of the remainder scattered about the country on gendarmery duty, their morale eroded by pay arrearages and supply irregularities, the real number of effective troops available to confront an emergency has not been very great.

Reform and retraining

Security of state and regime inevitably remains a commanding priority in Zaire, as elsewhere. This imperative, however, has come into frequent collision with the recurrent efforts to reform the army and to improve its mediocre level of performance. The most stubborn of all dreams, in the years of Zairian independence, has been that an effective security force is but one retraining program away. Many efforts have been lavished upon the FAZ, yet the problems remain. The dilemma was well illustrated in 1978 by two contradictory events: on the one hand, a new set of French and Belgian military instructors was brought in to form and train new units which could be relied upon to provide security for Kinshasa and the Shaba mineral installations; on the other hand, only a few months earlier, just before Shaba II, more than two hundred of the most promising young officers—nearly 10 percent of the officer corps—had been purged because their political reliability was in question.

A recurrent approach to the reform of the security forces has been the creation of new, elite units with whom a fresh start could be made. Moroccan general Kettani, then with the United Nations peacekeeping force, first proposed a special paratroop unit in August 1960. Israeli advisors played an important part in training the units during the 1960s; the units were comprised exclusively of new recruits, heavily drawn from Equateur and neighboring areas of Bandundu.[41] By 1971 there were five para-commando battalions, organized into a division (known by its acronym, DITRAC). In 1975 the Kamanyola Division was launched, trained with North Korean assistance.

In the wake of Shaba II, a new 21st Brigade was formed under Belgian tutelage, and was based in Shaba. French military advisors organized the 31st Parachute Brigade in Kinshasa; in contrast to the 21st Brigade, which was under Zairian command, French officers were directly incorporated in the command structure of the 31st. (Elements of the 31st, without the French officers, performed respectably when dispatched to Chad in 1981–82 as part of an OAU peacekeeping force, and again in 1983.) At the beginning of the 1980s the Chinese sent about forty advisors to help build a "shock-force brigade" at Kisangani. And in 1982 Israel rewarded Mobutu for his resumption of diplomatic relations by sending advisers for the presidential security force.

The endless reiteration of this pattern suggests that the regime has discovered that one resolution of the dilemma of competence versus control may lie in unending reorganization and reform. The lessons of Shaba I and II suggest an additional motive behind the pattern: the symbolic value, for sustaining an image of invulnerability, of military advisors from powerful external states, whose very presence implies potential armed intervention by the countries they represent should a crisis occur. A U.S. Senate staff report put forward a similar interpretation in 1982:

> One U.S. official noted that Mobutu's power rests in part on the appearance of having powerful friends; thus he may prefer to have French, Belgian, and Chinese military advisers and commanders to well-qualified Zairian commanders. Conspicuous evidence of Western support has a symbolic value which far exceeds the actual number of foreign personnel involved. The "tripwire" presence of these personnel represents the assurance of foreign intervention during a crisis.[42]

Other branches of the armed forces

The Mobutu years have seen a great effort put into diversification of the Zairian military. Whereas the Force Publique of 1960 had been essentially infantry, the FAZ of the 1970s possessed an air force, light armor, and a small navy. Its equipment was moderately sophisticated by African standards.

Yet the costly upgrading of the air force, in particular, has reflected in another way the paradox of the Zairian security establishment: every asset is at once a liability. By 1976 Zaire possessed five Mirage-5 supersonic fighters, with a dozen additional Mirages on order.[43] While Mobutu boasted at the time that he had not paid a cent in cash to France for these excellent aircraft, he referred only to the absence of a down payment. The Mirages were in reality very costly, and one element in the Zairian debt crisis. Sophisticated aircraft require not only a large inventory of spare parts, but also—if permitted to fly—inordinate amounts of fuel; both parts and fuel made a claim upon Zaire's desperately short foreign exchange. A number of Zairian pilots have been qualified to fly the planes, but the logistical systems required to keep the aircraft flying cannot be maintained with Zairian personnel.

The dubious utility of this heavy investment in a high-technology security force was well demonstrated during Shaba I and II. In theory, even Zaire's small number of Mirage jets would have provided total air superiority, and should have permitted the regime to easily decimate the FLNC forces. In fact, the Mirages played virtually no role in these episodes; most were not operational at the hour of necessity. In one twenty-four-hour stretch, two of Zaire's three Canadian Buffaloes were put out of commission by accidents on the ground: one was badly damaged when taxied into a termite hill; the other ran amok when the engines were turned on with full power inside the hangar. In 1981, when remnants of Idi Amin's army provoked disturbances in the Uganda border region in the far northeast, Mobutu was indignant to discover that not a single one of the 5 FAZ C-30 transport planes was operational to ferry in reinforcements; two had crashed while on smuggling runs. The enhanced capability which Zaire acquired through arms purchases was, indeed, a mirage.[44]

Zaire has become wholly dependent on foreign personnel for ground maintenance services for its aircraft. Initially these services were provided mainly by an ostensibly private company, the Western International Ground Maintenance Organization (WIGMO)—in reality a front organization created and staffed by the CIA. WIGMO also had its own fleet of aircraft, which had played an important logistical role during the 1964–65 rebellions. In 1970 WIGMO was sold to Zairian interests (possibly to Mobutu himself), and its name was changed to SODEMAZ (Zairian Upkeep and Maintenance Company).[45] Its mission was the maintenance of all military aircraft, except the jets; SODEMAZ continued to have its own fleet into the 1970s. The jet aircraft were maintained by an Italian firm under contract.

Zaire has no navy in the usual sense; there are only ten miles of sea-coast. However, Zaire has long stretches of river and lake frontier along its borders with Angola, Congo-Brazzaville, Central African Republic, Uganda, Rwanda, Burundi, Tanzania, and Zambia. Diamonds, gold, tea, and other goods are smuggled out of Zaire by water, and black-market transactions in currency and imported goods go both ways. Lake Tanganyika has been a major route for bringing military provisions to insurgents, especially the PRP pocket near Fizi.

When Mobutu visited the United States in 1970, he was told of the swift boat-interceptor system used in Vietnam. Mobutu decided to purchase six of these boats, and in turn President Nixon agreed to provide training for personnel. The Coast, Lake, and River Guard was to be "non-military," and was to be limited initially to operations on Lake Tanganyika. In 1971 the first group of 150 men, former FAZ personnel, finished training in the U.S. and began operations on the lake.[46]

By 1977 the Zairian coast guard had grown to 800 men. The river and lake squadrons possessed thirty patrol craft in all, of seven different types; they were manufactured in the United States, France, and North Korea, and China. Of the thirty, at that time all but twelve were out of commission.[47] In 1978, China sent a group of military advisers to help train the coast guard, as well as two escort vessels to help patrol Zaire's access to the sea.

Police

The police are an ambiguous component in the security equation. State force, in its origins, was purely repressive, designed for hegemony and not the application of law. After World War I, the embryo of a police force somewhat distinct from the army could be found in the division of the army into a garrison force and a gendarme force, the latter under the command of European civil authorities. In 1926 a separate police force was created and also placed at the disposal of the Belgian regional administration. Unlike the army gendarmes, these police were locally recruited and could be utilized for routine order maintenance, as well as for enforcement of colonial law.

At the moment of independence, about 6,000 of the 25,000 troops in the colonial army were assigned to gendarme service. The number of pro-

vincial police fell between 6,000 and 9,000.[48] In addition, local collectivities employed roughly 10,000 police auxiliaries, under command of the
chiefs.

The broad de facto autonomy achieved by the provinces during the
First Republic included full control over the provincial police forces. These
were inflated in size and utilized as provincial armies. One important step
in the recentralization of state power under the New Regime was the removal of control of the police from provincial hands, in December 1966.
Mobutu's legislation authorized a national force of 20,000 policemen,
4,000 brigadiers, 600 subcommissioners, and 400 commissioners and inspectors; since the total number of provincial police had become much
greater than the authorized force, mergers provided the occasion for cull-
ing out unwanted elements. Pius Sapwe, former head of police in secessionist Katanga, was named to head the new national police.

The same centralizing urge was at work in the 1972 decision to abandon the national police formula. The police were merged into the gendarmery by presidential decree. This had the effect of unifying civil law
enforcement, since the national police had been responsible for police services in urban areas, while the gendarmery covered rural areas.

The local dimension of the coercive superstructure deserves mention.
The number of police attached to local collectivities has greatly increased
since 1960. While these men are without professional training, are not
equipped with firearms, and are demoralized by their sporadic pay, at the
most local rural level they are far from a negligible component of the overall repressive apparatus of the state. According to data collected by Schatzberg in 1974 in the Mongala subregion, there was an average of 29 police
per collectivity; if we project this average onto the approximately 1,000
collectivities, we arrive at a rough total of 29,000 collectivity police for
Zaire as a whole.[49]

Note should also be taken of the police power vested in large numbers
of civil administrators. In the exercise of an official function, a functionary
may exercise arrest powers (technically, by holding the warrant of an *Of-
ficier de Police Judiciaire*); those possessing command functions (zone or
subregion commissioners, for example) hold such authority across the
board (*à compétence générale*), while specialized personnel exercise this
power within their sphere of activity (*à compétence restreinte*). An economic
affairs officer may summarily impose a fine on those accused of contraven-
ing price control ordinances; an agricultural officer may levy similar penal-
ties on persons who fail to meet the minimum obligatory planted acreage
requirements.

In the 1970s the *Brigade Disciplinaire* of the JMPR was another local repressive force of some importance. These youths, generally drawn from the ranks of the unemployed and those who had left school, were sometimes furnished uniforms and given a general assignment of "vigilance," which included nocturnal patrolling. If they were lucky, they might receive some payment for their services; alternatively, their authority might permit the extraction of money from the populace as punishment for real or imagined infractions.

The state security apparatus

Our discussion of the coercive apparatus would be incomplete without consideration of the least visible component, the security police. The clandestine nature of the state security organs means that their importance, as instruments of intimidation, is not matched by a corresponding amount of reliable information concerning their operation. At first, state security and intelligence operations were entrusted to a single organ, the Sûreté; in 1975 this was broken into three components, with external and internal wings and a private presidential branch.

The Sûreté came under the control of Nendaka in September 1960. In colonial times it had been an entirely European entity (except for large numbers of Zairian informers on its payroll); there was, accordingly, a nearly complete turnover of personnel with the coming of independence in July 1960. Nendaka, then in close liaison with the CIA, had access to skilled counsel in reconstructing this agency and turning it into a personal fiefdom. With the Sûreté as his base, he became a crucial member of the Binza group.

The security police were a prime concern for Mobutu from the moment of the 1965 coup. Nendaka was shifted from his post and named Minister of Transportation and Communication in the new Mobutu cabinet. Yet even after he ceased to be security director, Nendaka kept one foot in the door; his successor, Colonel Singa, was from the same region, and through him Nendaka continued to exert substantial influence on the police.[50]

It took Mobutu four years to pry the security police completely away from Nendaka. One of the president's tactics was to build up personal secret services outside of the security police, a tactic resisted by Nendaka. The Nendaka hold over the organization was finally ended by his dispatch to Bonn as ambassador in 1969. Colonel Efomi replaced Singa as security police head in August 1969, and established a "new, semi-purged secret police."[51] At this point, the official designation of the organization was changed from Sûreté to the euphemistic Centre National de Documentation.

Continuing instability at the level of the directorship over the next few years reflected Mobutu's determination to retain close personal control. Colonel Efomi lost his job in 1970 and was rusticated to Taiwan as ambassador; Efomi was replaced by Colonel Tukuzu. He in turn served only about a year before being charged with subversion and replaced by Colonel Omba (previously Mobutu's private secretary). Omba then lost his job when he was implicated in the *coup monté et manqué* of 1975.

Following the fall of Efomi, the CND was reorganized into internal and external sections. The external affairs division (renamed the Service National d'Intelligence, or SNI) is small and concerns itself mostly with Zaire's neighbors—especially Congo-Brazzaville, Tanzania, and Angola—and with Zairian exiles and students in Belgium, France, and the United States. The service apparently remains dependent on the United States and Belgium for international intelligence.

Most of the personnel of the CND are attached to the internal affairs division (known since 1980 as the *Centre National de Recherche et d'Investigation*, or CNRI), which is responsible for intelligence and political operations within the country; as of 1971, there were a number of Belgian advisors attached to this service in Kinshasa. The CND's authority to arrest without warrant, hold incommunicado, interrogate, and torture suspects remains one means by which the regime intimidates the population.[52]

The seventh scourge: conclusions

We may now return to the questions that opened this chapter: Why are the armed forces the "seventh scourge" of Zaire? Why is the FAZ at once the indispensable pillar of the state and perhaps its greatest liability? Is the price of security for the state the insecurity of the populace?

The inherent difficulties of the task of assuring security should be recognized. In the post-independence years, political disturbances in all but one of the nine countries bordering on Zaire have spilled over the frontiers, at least momentarily. At one time or another since 1960, supplies or sanctuary for Zairian insurgents have been provided by or through all neighboring states but Central African Republic and Rwanda. The mediocre and deteriorating communications infrastructure makes movement of forces difficult; the vast dimensions of Zaire add to the intrinsic logistical difficulties. Logistics in turn are an enduring weakness of the Zairian security apparatus. Under the best of circumstances, the challenge of performing the normal functions of state coercive forces—protection from outside threat and preservation of domestic tranquility—would be immense.

To this difficulty must be added the doubly negative legacy of history. The colonial Force Publique sustained the hegemony of Bula Matari through its reputation for crushing force, violently and brutally applied at the slightest challenge. The great 1960 mutiny destroyed for a time state control over this implement of intimidation; it was never fully restored, and this fact added new dangers to the utilization of force by the state.

This consideration leads us back to the crucial and unresolved dilemma of control. A unified, professionalized, disciplined, and reliable security force would perhaps better serve the state and be less of a hazard to civil society. Yet for Mobutu the army has been from the outset a political instrument: his power base in the First Republic, his vehicle for seizure of power and rule in the second. One recent analyst has well captured regime preoccupations: "It is the very importance of the military in Zairian *politics* that makes it so dangerous to Mobutu, and it is this threat precisely, the necessary fear of the military, which results in Mobutu's extraordinary efforts to divide, control, manipulate, politicize, and otherwise deinstitutionalize and de-professionalize it."[53]

Within the framework of the patrimonialized state, personal loyalty to the president has become the prime criterion for top military office. It has led to the repeated purges which have cost the armed forces the services of many of their ablest officers. The use of patrimonial devices at the top for fostering personal loyalty has inevitably introduced an element of corruption into the armed forces, which has then had its own ripple effect throughout the structure. The premium on personal loyalty has led to reliance on senior officers with whom the president has ethnoregional affinities; this relationship in turn has generated regional animosities at lower levels of the FAZ, and has reinforced hostility to the army in those regions which see themselves excluded from military leadership (or even from military ranks).

A glance at the composition of the top FAZ leadership in 1980 suggests how strong the Equateur predominance is. The Equateur contingent included Commander in Chief Babia; Chief of Staff Singa Boyenge; Admiral Lomponda, chief of the presidential military staff (*maison militaire*); Gendarmery commander Yeka Mangbau Lowanga; Air Force commander Kikunda Ombala; ground force commander General Boteti Nkanga; FAZ auditor-general Likulia Bolongo; army intelligence chief General Bulozi (married to a sister of Mobutu); and Shaba regional commander Eluki. Reports indicate that 90 percent of the defense ministry personnel were Equateurians.[54]

The security forces are one major dimension of the crisis of the contemporary state. No formula has yet been discovered to make the FAZ a reliable and proficient force for the actual defense of the country, even though diverse training programs have imparted skills to large numbers of individual officers and soldiers. History has yet to repeal Mobutu's stigmatization of the army as the "seventh scourge" of Zairian civil society.

10

Economic Policy during the Mobutu Years

> One no longer works in the Congo. One no longer produces in the Congo. . . . The country is obliged to beg aid abroad. . . . The Congo can no longer feed and clothe its own sons.
>
> Mobutu Sese Seko[1]

The ideological charter of the New Regime included not only the construction of a unified, centralized nation-state, but the restoration of economic order and fulfillment of the manifest destiny of rapid development which its rich natural resource base seemed to promise. As well, the resurrected state would obey the impulse to autonomy by decolonization of its economy. The vocation of political *grandeur*, and its expansive economic designs, placed the revenue imperative at the center of state preoccupations. The resource flow through state channels, internal and external, would have to be sharply increased. The revenue imperative of the state intersected the need of the regime to finance its patrimonial processes of power maintenance and the ambition of the emergent politico-commercial class for a swift accumulation of wealth.

In its consolidation and ascendancy phases, the New Regime appeared to bring these goals within reach. During the state expansion era, in the early 1970s, Zaire embarked on a high-risk, externally financed, mineral-based development strategy, legitimated by the ideological doctrine of economic nationalism; this strategy collapsed following the break in copper prices in 1974. The deepening economic crisis had immediate repercussions in the political realm; the state was unable to meet its own swelling consumption requirements, to provide sufficient resources to finance patrimonial, personalist rule, or to meet the expectations of the dominant politico-commercial class.

In exploring the economic policy of the Mobutu era, we will first examine the stabilization measures undertaken to repair the disarray of the First Republic years. We will then turn to the contest with Belgian colonial capital, and the subsequent opening of Zairian resources to an array of new foreign investors and contractors. The colossal miscalculations in the

276

application of the grand design for a great and prosperous Zaire will be analyzed. Finally, we will consider the decline of the agricultural sector. Two crucial issues of economic policy—the Zairianization and radicalization measures, and the external debts—will be discussed in chapters 11 and 12, respectively.

Stabilization: overcoming the First Republic legacy

The economic toll of the First Republic had been high. Until 1962 there had been no budget at all, and throughout the period public sector financial controls were weak. The GDP, which stood at $1,268 million (1958 prices) in 1959, fell to $1,196 million in 1964.[2] Commercial agricultural output was only 64 percent of the 1959 figure by 1965. Although mineral production had generally held up, there was an important foreign exchange loss through diamond smuggling, which by 1962 had reached an estimated 10 to 12 million carats, or roughly the equivalent in value to the $50 million legal output.[3] Total tonnage of all goods on the four rail lines was by 1965 only 60 percent of the 1959 figure.

By 1961, inflation had gathered momentum; by the time of the coup the real value of the currency, as measured by the parallel market, stood at an index of 741 (1960 = 100). The index rose to 1,250 in 1967, before inflation was finally brought under control. A mild devaluation in November 1961 (the Congo franc went from parity with the Belgian franc to 85 Congo francs for 50 Belgian francs) failed completely. A more comprehensive devaluation scheme in November 1963 did bring a year of respite in 1964, but the ballooning outlays of the Tshombe regime (partly occasioned by liquidation of some salary arrearages and the military costs imposed by the rebellions) quickly brought back the inflationary surge. The latter devaluation introduced a dual exchange rate of 150 francs per dollar on export transactions and 180 per dollar on imports. The differential was a de facto tax which furnished 36 percent of ordinary state revenues in 1964 and 1965.[4] Inflation during this period was essentially caused by disorder in public finance and monetary expansion to cover government deficits; external payments were in relative balance. During the Tshombe spending spree in the year preceding the Mobutu coup, government covered only 60 percent of regular expenditures.[5]

The economic failings of the First Republic were universally recognized and deplored; Mobutu had no difficulty in persuading his audiences on this score. Within two years the Mobutu regime succeeded in repairing

Table 10.1   Government Budgets, 1964–1966 (in millions of Congo francs)

	1964	1965	1966
Ordinary budget expenditure	36,929	55,751	59,939
Ordinary budget revenue	33,588	36,858	56,600
Investment budget expenditure	1,948	3,585	3,420
Investment budget revenue	3,200	3,041	820
Central bank advances	3,500	18,918	8,787

Source: *Congo 1966* (Brussels: Centre de Recherches et d'Information Socio-Politiques, 1967), pp. 446–447.

much of the damage immediately attributable to political disorder and government disorganization. Even before the 1967 stabilization program, the New Regime had brought its budget into balance (see table 10.1). Expenditures were held close to their previous level, while revenues were greatly increased both by better fiscal administration and some new taxes.

The centerpiece of New Regime economic reform efforts was the stabilization plan of June 1967. This far-reaching, comprehensive scheme was designed both to restore a monetary equilibrium and to lay the foundations for long-term development. It sought to halt inflation, to place government finances on a sound and stable basis, to encourage exporters and rural producers, to make possible an end to import controls, to eliminate the commercial rackets built around the licensing system, and to create conditions of confidence which would make long-run development possible.

The obstacles were formidable. Inflation was becoming institutionalized, as table 10.2 indicates. There were important political obstacles to overcome as well. The stabilization plan was closely associated with the central bank technocrats and IMF advisers, and was strongly encouraged by Western embassies. It was viewed with suspicion by the influential group of university-trained intellectuals in the presidency, who found it too much aligned with orthodox Western principles of economic reasoning. It also necessitated a period of public sector wage restraint to allow stabilization to take hold (inflation had been very damaging to civil servants, whose real income had fallen to roughly half of the 1960 level).[6] The commercial class, which had been able to exploit the windfall profits available through the import licensing system and was tributary to and interpenetrated with the political sector, was to lose a highly profitable, if parasitical, mercantile activity.

Table 10.2   Inflation Rate, 1960–1967 (weighted index of retail prices
in Kinshasa stores)

	Index	Exchange rate
June 1960	100.0	$1 = 50 Congo francs
December 1960	112.1	
June 1961	127.5	
December 1961	149.1	$1 = 85 Congo francs
June 1962	157.5	
December 1962	179.8	
June 1963	200.2	
December 1963	261.1	$1 = 150–180 Congo francs
June 1964	380.8	
December 1964	376.9	
June 1965	380.8	
December 1965	425.2	
June 1966	527.0	
December 1966	475.9	
June 1967	584.0	$1 = 500 Congo francs = .50 zaire

Sources: Pierre Dupriez, "La réforme monetaire du 24 juin 1967 en République Démocratique du Congo," *Cahiers Economiques et Sociaux* 6, no. 1 (March 1968): 77; *Congo 1966* (Brussels: Centre de Recherches et d'Information Socio-Politiques, 1967), p. 483.

The reform included a whole package of measures:

1. A roughly 300 percent devaluation
2. Creation of a new monetary unit, the Zaire, equal to 1,000 Congo francs
3. Elimination of the dual exchange rate
4. A sharp increase in taxation of foreign trade
5. A promise of a 40 percent public sector and legal minimum wage rise
6. The end of import licensing
7. The freeing of profit remittances

The currency devaluation was sharp enough to realign the Zaire on its real parallel market value. The new currency unit permitted some camouflage of the scale of devaluation because the Zaire was presented as a money whose unit value was twice that of the dollar. The revenue loss incurred by ending the dual exchange rate was compensated for by new taxes on foreign trade; export levies were at least doubled, with those on the key minerals—copper, diamonds, and cobalt—raised to 40 percent. Overall import tax rates were raised from 12 to 15 percent, with draconian levies of 100 percent on such luxury items as passenger cars and tobacco.

The impact was dramatic. By 1968 the inflation rate fell to 2.5 percent, and the growth rate—negative in 1967—rose to 8 percent.[7] Official wage increases of 25 percent on 1 October 1967, 15 percent on 29 March 1968, 10 percent on 20 June 1969, and 20 percent on 5 December 1970, along with continuing price stability, brought the first real wage rise since early 1961.[8] Public finances were in relative equilibrium by the end of 1967, a balance which was to last for six years.

In general, by 1968 the stabilization operation was clearly a success and contributed decisively to the credibility of the regime, which appeared to possess both the authority and the competence to carry off a difficult and delicate operation. The sacrifices demanded of the wage-earning sector were only temporary, and more than compensated for by the beneficial effects of the end of inflation. The bases for a new economic departure had been laid.

Two significant sectors, however, failed to benefit. The first was the Zairian commercial class, whose competitive advantage over the foreign mercantile sector at this point lay primarily in its political access. When this advantage was lost through the liberalization of imports, many were hard hit. The eclipse of this group in favor of Belgian, Portuguese, and Greek wholesalers led indirectly to the 30 November 1973 Zairianization measures.

In the long run, the missed opportunity to provide benefits to the rural sector was more significant. The end of inflation itself did have some positive impact; Lacroix points out that one consequence of inflation was to draw consumer goods away from the countryside, because under conditions of high demand and rising prices traders could sell their entire stocks at lower costs and higher profits in the towns. Price stability, conversely, meant a renewed flow of consumer items into the countryside.[9] But adjustments in producer prices under the stabilization plan were far too low. Arguments characteristic of the colonial period were invoked to hold down rural incomes. Elasticity of food supply by peasants relative to price was alleged to be low; higher food prices purportedly would endanger real incomes in the urban sector. As Dupriez notes, the price elasticity argument had some validity during the colonial period because "administrative *encadrement* efficaciously replaced economic stimulants."[10] (Less delicately phrased, the Bula Matari state could substitute its densely staffed and coercive agricultural administration for market incentives in a way the post-colonial system could not, for lack of capacity.) In areas such as Bas-Zaire, which had easy access to the urban market and could evade state price regulations, food output for market rose impressively. Overall, however, the stagnation of agriculture, which dated back to 1959, continued.

But the mood by 1968 was bullish. In 1966, the GDP surpassed the pre-independence level for the first time. The new-found economic stability, joined to a number of signal triumphs in the political sphere (defeat of the mercenaries, the Organization of African Unity summit in Kinshasa in 1967), brought new hope and optimism. Stirring thoughts were abroad on what the future might hold in store. (See table 10.3, which shows the tendency toward recovery in output of most commodities by 1969.)

Settling the *contentieux*

With the stabilization of the economy and polity assured, the regime undertook the realization of its rendezvous with abundance. A broad-front strategy was required. A first and indispensable set of measures aimed at extending the political sovereignty of the nation-state into the economic realm. Several major economic issues, collectively known as the *contentieux* with Belgium, confronted the regime from the time it assumed power. These involved the disposition of the colonial debt, the status of charter companies and other corporations in which the colonial state held shares, and the situation of the very large areas in which land or mineral rights had been conceded to colonial corporations but which remained undeveloped.

The issue of the colonial debt had its roots in the ambitious program of public investment undertaken by Belgium under the ten-year plan of 1950. By the postwar years the private sector, favored by a very generous fiscal regime and buoyed by high profits during the commodity boom, was able to finance most of its expansion through reinvestment. Indeed, Governor-General Ryckmans had pointed out with some acerbity in his last annual address that the practice of exempting reinvested profits from taxation provided an extraordinary windfall to the colonial corporations. From 1927 to 1939, the colonial corporations made 15 billion francs in profits, on which their tax payments were only 835 million francs; more than 7 billion francs were protected from taxation altogether by reinvestment.[11]

From 1956 on the colony ran a payments deficit, while the state budget, after long years of surpluses, was in the red. The external debt, which was negligible in 1950, rose rapidly in the final colonial years, reaching $1 billion by independence; debt service payments were 17 percent of the

Table 10.3 Primary Commodity Production, 1959–1980 (in thousands of metric tons, unless otherwise specified)

	1959	1961	1963	1965	1967	1969	1971	1973	1975	1976	1977	1980
Agricultural												
Rice	165	70	60	56	60			120	135			230
Corn	333	205	232	210	260			150	125			500
Coffee	61	64	66	59	60	51	75	67	59	98	64	79
Cotton	60	27	16	6	9	17	18	20	16	85	12	17
Rubber	40	38	38	21	30	33	42	45	29	21	28	20
Palm oil (including kernel oil)	245	207	178	136	179	201	202	140	145			180
Mineral												
Copper	282	295	271	287	321	364	407	489	496	444	481	426
Zinc concentrates	112	156	152	174	183	172	195	156	142			44
Cobalt	8	8	8	7	10	11	15	15	14	16	17	15
Tin	13	7	8	8	8	9	9	8	6	3	5	4
Manganese	193	159	135	176	114	311	329	334	340	201	42	0
Gold (kilos)	10,087	7,268	6,674	2,063	4,758	5,516	5,428	4,157	3,120	2,746	2,434	2,270 (1979)
Diamonds (millions of carats)	15	18	15	13	13	14	13	13	13			8 (1979)

Sources: Banque du Zaire, annual reports, 1967–1975; International Money Fund, internal documents; Africa South of the Sahara: 1976–1977, 6th ed. (London: Europa Publications, 1976); International Bank for Reconstruction and Development, "Economy of Zaire."

1959 operating budget. No payments were made by Zaire during the First Republic years. As leverage on the debt issue, as well as on damage claims arising out of the independence disorders, Belgium retained possession of the portfolio of state holdings in the colonial corporations. The portfolio holdings were valued at 37.5 billion francs in 1960; in the Belgian view they were assets held in escrow against the liability of the 46 billion franc debt.

A first effort at resolving the *contentieux* was made under the Adoula regime. An accord was actually signed in March 1964 which assured that the portfolio would be turned over to Zaire and that the debt liability would be split. In November 1964, the Tshombe government endeavored to sweep away some of the colonial debris by formally dissolving the three charter companies, Comité Special du Katanga (CSK), Comité National du Kivu (CNKi), and Compagnie des Chemins de Fer du Congo Supérieur aux Grands Lacs (CFL). The Belgian private sector reacted with indignation, demanding compensation for the extinction of its rights; the Belgian government backed the demands, refusing to proceed with the debt and portfolio transaction till the charter company issue was settled.

Indeed, the Belgian private claims were so preposterous that a brief examination of their origin and basis will help make clear the frequent irritability of the New Regime in its relations with Belgian capital. In 1891 the Compagnie du Katanga had been formed by friends of Leopold II to finance a reconnaissance mission into Shaba, made urgent by British moves into the area. The company advanced 1 million gold francs for the expedition, and added another 600,000 francs of capital later (worth 100 million contemporary francs). In return, the company was offered as a concession one-third the land surface of Shaba, to be allocated in checkerboard pattern. The cadastral problems of this arrangement made it impractical, so in 1900 the Compagnie du Katanga agreed to unite with the state in forming the CSK; the state's public lands would be joined to those previously conceded to the company.

The CSK, in turn, then conceded an ore-rich tract of 34,000 square kilometers in the upper Zaire (Lualaba), Lufira, and Luapula basins to the newly formed UMHK, whose major private sponsors were the Société Générale de Belgique and Tanganyika Concessions, a British company. In return, the CSK received half of the initial shares of UMHK. Until 1908, CSK actually administered Shaba by delegation; with the coming of Belgian rule, it shed the nuisance and expense of providing bureaucratic services, while retaining the lucrative rights to land and mineral concessions, as well as its UMHK holdings. Though the state held a two-thirds majority on the CSK board of directors, it gave a free hand to the private members directing the commercial operations of the charter company. In 1928, the parent company of the Compagnie du Katanga, the Compagnie Congolaise de Commerce et d'Industrie (CCCI) of Thys, came under the control of the Société Générale as well.

The Compagnie du Katanga, a golden tree which grew from the $2 million seed, yielded phenomenal returns. Ryckmans noted with indignation that the company collected $246,500 (12,250,000 francs) land rents and UMHK dividends in 1939 alone.[12] From 1955 to 1959, the harvest for Compagnie du Katanga was 917 million francs, or nearly ten times its small investment.[13]

With independence on the horizon, a new problem suddenly arose: the new state, juridical successor to the colony, would suddenly become the dominant partner in the CSK, which in turn held 60 percent of the voting shares in UMHK; the latter would thus automatically become a publicly controlled corporation. Another major shareholder was Tanganyika Concessions, with 32 percent, while the Société Générale itself held only 8 percent directly. In practice, the Société Générale, via the Compagnie du Katanga channel, was the dominant influence, given the total passivity of the state.

This intolerable danger (to Belgian capital) of finding UMHK under control of the independent Congolese government was averted in extremis by the expedient dissolution of the CSK by the Belgian government on 27 June 1960. Though the Congo state received back its two-thirds of CSK assets—initially one-third to Kinshasa and one-third to Katanga Province (Shaba)—it lost its potential majority voice (see table 10.4). The post-independence confusion and the Katanga secession left the whole matter in abeyance; so also did the broader *contentieux* dispute, which delayed the effective transfer of the state holdings to the new government.[14]

By the end of 1964, a major obstacle to settlement of the whole *contentieux* question was the demand by the Compagnie du Katanga for reimbursement of its original $2 million plus a share in the CSK portfolio. Though the sum involved was not large, the principle was exceedingly irritating to the Zairian side. The Compagnie du Katanga, after half a century of reclining under the golden tree, watching the fruits drop from time to time into its extended purse, demanded—and got—full reimbursement for the initial cost of the seed.[15]

The CFL originated in a concession made to the Empain group in 1902 to help fulfill the Leopoldian dream of a railway link from the Zaire to the Nile; the Empain group drove a hard bargain, receiving 4 million hectares of transferable land and mineral rights along the eastern frontier, mainly in Kivu. In addition, the state guaranteed 4 percent interest on the 370-million franc capital. The CFL spun off its mining operations, which returned 100 million on a 20-million franc investment from 1935 to 1938 alone; by 1939 it had collected 160 million from the state in guaranteed interest on its less profitable rail operations.[16] As the state held only 25 percent of the shares in CFL, the Belgian government saw no need to dissolve it in 1960, though its land grants, due to expire in 1961, were extended for thirty years by unilateral Belgian action on 17 June 1960.[17] The CFL's compensation claims for assets entirely within Zaire totalled about $80 million (3.2 billion francs).[18] Its concessionary authority was ended in 1965, and in 1974 it was absorbed into the national rail line, Société Nationale des Chemins de Fer Zairois.

The state and CFL set up the most mysterious of the three charter companies, the CNKi, in 1928 in order to encourage Belgian settlement in the temperate Kivu mountain zone. The retroceded CFL lands, plus additional areas from the state domain, initially totalled 12 million hectares. This was eventually reduced to 300,000 hectares of prime land in the Bukavu region. CNKi was intended to finance the necessary infrastructure, in particular roads; it was ultimately able to devolve these costly obligations back upon the state and to retreat into the profitable function of serving as a land office for selling the public domain for the benefit of its shareholders. By the late 1950s, CNKi was viewed as a scandal by African elites and European settlers alike.[19]

The state held a majority of the shares in CNKi, and thus CNKi too, had to be whisked out of existence. The dissolution decree was unilaterally signed by the Belgian government on 30 May 1960; CNKi's private shareholders then reconstituted the company as the Société Belgo-Africaine du Kivu (SOBAKI), which retained control over the small mines CNKi had developed, as well as some other subsidiary private enterprises, CNKi's claims on the public lands were extinguished, for which its private shareholders had the temerity to demand compensation.[20]

The Tshombe government's dissolution of the charter companies in November 1964 had been intended to remove the compensation issue. In the face of strong Belgian reactions (particularly to the unilateral character of the dissolution), Tshombe gave in and acceded to the compensation demands. A compromise was then reached on the colonial debt: Belgium accepted responsibility for the 11 billion Belgian francs it had guaranteed; Zaire took over the 23 billion in Congo francs, which had been devalued by inflation; the 10 billion (Belgian francs) in foreign currency loans were agreed to be a joint responsibility, with Zaire making annual payments of 300 million Belgian francs, and Belgium 250 million.[21] Belgium then turned over the portfolio, which Tshombe exhibited in triumph on his return to Kinshasa. Zaire continued payments until 1971, then ceased to pay; the debt was considered liquidated.

One large fly remained in the ointment, however, which led the Mobutu regime to reopen the entire issue: release of the colonial state holdings in ten companies was held up by the Belgians on the grounds that Zaire had to negotiate the specific terms of the turnover with the private shareholders. Of these, three were substantial: Sabena, Forminière, and the Société des Mines d'Or de Kilo-Moto. The colonial state held 24.8 percent of the votes in Sabena, the Belgian national airline; 55.6 percent in Forminière, which operated the Kasai diamond mines and some forestry enterprises; and 98 percent in the Kilo-Moto gold mines in the far northeast.[22]

In early 1966 rumblings of dissatisfaction with the Tshombe settlement of the *contentieux* began to be heard in presidential circles—one of the first symptoms of the forceful economic nationalist posture which was to emerge. As the regime simultaneously became more hostile to former Prime Minister Tshombe, partly in response to indications of renewed conspiratorial activity on his part, the February 1965 *contentieux* settlement was increasingly perceived as invalid. Because Tshombe is a traitor and a lackey of Belgian capital, ran the reasoning, accords negotiated by him are axiomatically a betrayal of the interests of the Zairian people.[23]

New accords were reached in May 1966, covering some of the disputed issues, but misunderstandings reappeared. In his independence day speech on 30 June 1966 Mobutu, displaying a decisional style which was to flavor the regime, declared: "We have decided, for our part . . . to take concrete actions to settle definitively the *contentieux* at midnight tonight. Our government is determined to take necessary decisions to safeguard the higher interests of the nation."[24] The regime moved at once to fulfill this pledge.

The exceedingly complex Sabena affair was settled by unilateral abandonment of the Zaire state holdings in the Belgian national airline, in return for which Zaire assumed complete control of Air Congo (later Air Zaire), created in 1961 as a Sabena-operated enterprise.[25] Under the original arrangement Zaire had held 65 percent of the Air Congo shares and Sabena 30 percent. Management had been wholly by Sabena; Air Congo had taken over the domestic services formerly covered by Sabena, and shared in the Brussels link. There was also a complex financial interpenetration of the two organisms. Sabena eventually accepted the basic settlement framework Zaire proposed.

Forminière and Kilo-Moto were simply dissolved in July 1966. Kilo-Moto, whose output and work force had been steadily declining, posed no great problem. A new Zairian parastatal was created in place of the colonial company; the private interests, by now small, kept their shares, thus avoiding the compensation issue.

Forminière, once a giant among colonial enterprises, was by this time moribund. Its own diamond mines, scattered through large alluvial deposits in the Tshikapa area, were impossible to exploit in post-independence circumstances; there was no way the company could maintain security over its holdings. Production had totalled 669,000 carats in 1958, though a significant fraction were gemstones. By 1962, mining operations had been suspended. On 25 July 1960 Forminière had created a subsidiary, INTERFOR, to manage its Zairian holdings. Sporadic negotiations with Belgian interests on the status of Forminière assets continued until 1973 when, on 30 November, Mobutu simply took over the subsidiaries of the Forminière family. Some forestry subsidiaries were still operating, of which the Mayombe enterprise, SCAM, was the most important. These were placed under a new Zairian parastatal office. The Forminière dissolution did not arouse much heated controversy, no doubt because of the somber financial prospects for the company. The main private capital holdings in Forminière were those of the Société Générale and the American Ryan–Guggenheim group, each of which held somewhat more than 20 percent. The former had always exercised the dominant influence. The latter had been brought in by King Leopold when the company was launched in 1906 in the hope of stilling agitation in the United States over Congo Free State atrocities.

One other colonial corporation had some of the attributes of a charter company—the Minière du Bécéka. This grew out of the Compagnie du Chemin de Fer du Bas-Congo au Katanga (BCK), renamed in 1952 the Compagnie des Chemins de Fer Katanga-Dilolo-Léopoldville (KDL). The BCK, one of the 1906 companies, was run as a private corporation within the Société Générale family, but its capital was almost all supplied by the state. For much of the time its rates were held so low to encourage its use for copper exports that it operated at a deficit. As part of the inducement which brought it into being, the BCK received extensive prospecting rights along the route it served. In 1919, when diamonds were discovered in Kasai, it transferred its mineral rights to a separate Société Générale subsidiary, the Minière du Bécéka, whose mineral rights extended over an area twice the size of Belgium.

In 1960 the Minière du Bécéka chose to incorporate in Belgium as the Société d'Entreprise et d'Investissement du Bécéka (SIBEKA). Its Zairian operation, centered primarily at Mbuji-Mayi (Bakwanga) and previously managed by Forminière, was reorganized as the Minière de Bakwanga (MIBA), with Forminière dropping from the picture.[26] Zaire was given the right to 50 percent of the profits, though not ownership. Under the New Regime MIBA was stripped of its reserve domains and left with 33,000 square kilometers of a diamond concession. The level of taxation was also sharply increased, reaching more than 40 percent of gross sales, or a figure comparable to the tax on Gécamines. In 1967 the British Diamond Distributors (BRITMOND), a firm tied to the de Beers syndicate, was awarded the right to market the MIBA diamonds, for which service it received close to 25 percent of the gross. In 1974, as part of the radicalization program, the state took 100 percent control of MIBA; in 1978, SIBEKA was brought back in with a 20 percent share.[27]

Another attack upon the vestiges of colonial economic privilege came through the enactment of the Bakajika Law in 1966. To dramatize this act the two houses of Parliament were asked to solemnly vote on it; in July 1966 it was promulgated. The Bakajika Law stipulated that all public land was a domain of the Zairian nation-state, and formally extinguished all land grants and concessionary powers delegated by the colonial state. Corporations were given one month to file claims for confirmation of rights to lands actually developed. Beyond the charter company rights, this law liquidated once and for all the vexatious issue of land concessions held in reserve by colonial corporations. The stake was huge; according to the leading Belgian financial journal, 48 percent of the total land area of Zaire was thus pre-empted.[28] Most companies complied with the one-month deadline for filing claims for developed holdings; these were generally accorded without difficulty.[29] Beneath the nationalist symbolism of this measure lurked the issue of the vast mineral reserves in the UMHK concessions.

The UMHK confrontation

The most melodramatic struggle of all was the combat with UMHK in 1966–67. This epic battle was only a partial and temporary victory for economic nationalism, as the ultimate settlement proved lucrative for UMHK and brought unanticipated costs to Zaire. Yet in the symbolic per-

Table 10.4   Ownership of UMHK, End of 1965

Shareholder	% of shares	% of votes
Zaire	17.95	24.49
Tanganyika Concessions	14.47	20.21
Compagnie Financière du Katanga	8.95	12.24
Société Générale	4.64	6.94
Others	53.99	36.12

Sources: J. Gérard-Libois, "L'affaire de l'UMHK," *Etudes Congolaises* 10, no. 2 (March–April 1967): 3; see also Raymond Mikesell, in Scott R. Pearson and John Dowrie, eds., *Commodity Exports and African Economic Development* (Lexington, Mass.: D. C. Heath & Co., 1974), pp. 180–205.

ceptions of the time the settlement appeared to many in Zaire and Africa to validate the claim of the regime to the Lumumbist heritage of intransigent nationalism.

The UMHK empire was vast. Its core was the complex of copper installations, concentrated in Lubumbashi, Likasi, and especially Kolwezi, which had produced about 300,000 tons of copper by 1965, about two-thirds of it refined. The remaining third, 99 percent blister copper, was exported for final refining by the Société Générale Métallurgique de Hoboken, a UMHK subsidiary whose main business was handling Zairian copper. In addition, UMHK produced in the mid-1960s from 8,000 to 10,000 tons of cobalt, more than half the total amount internationally traded; 174,000 tons of zinc concentrates; and small amounts of precious metals (cadmium, germanium, gold, silver). Until 1960, UMHK had been a major uranium producer; its Shinkolobwe mine, closed just before independence, supplied the ore which produced the first nuclear weapons.

UMHK also controlled an imposing array of subsidiaries, both in Shaba and in Belgium: the Luena coal mines, the hydroelectric infrastructure which supplied the Shaba industrial installations, plants producing sulphuric acid, explosives, and caustic soda, flour mills, and urban property holdings in the copperbelt towns. The marketing of UMHK mineral products was handled by another Société Générale enterprise, the Société Générale des Minerais. In 1965, UMHK assets were valued at 21.3 billion Belgian francs ($430 million). UMHK provided 50 percent of the Zairian state revenues and 70 percent of Zaire's foreign exchange.[30] The ownership structure is indicated in table 10.4.

In 1980 values, the total capital invested in UMHK since its establishment in 1906 has amounted to 5 billion Belgian francs. Its profitability was not assured until the 1920s, but since the recovery from the great depression it has been an extraordinarily lucrative affair. The ore bodies exploited have been exceptionally rich in copper content—from 4 to 6 percent (some as high as 15 percent), or twice the Zambian figure; American producers in the postwar era have been working ore bodies with less than 1 percent.[31] Net profits of UMHK were 31 billion Belgian francs from 1950 to 1959, and 16 billion from 1960 to 1966. In the 1950s, about half the profits were reinvested; all capital expansion since the war has been through internal financing.[32] Though productivity of the labor force was much lower than in Western hemisphere mines, labor unrest was nonexistent; with this factor added to the richness of the deposits, and low taxation rates before the Mobutu era, one can well understand why UMHK stocks were gilt-edged on the Brussels bourse. One can also appreciate why the relationship between the state and UMHK was pivotal to the concept of economic independence.

During the First Republic Zairian political authorities were in far too weak a position to take on UMHK. Until the beginning of 1963, the company operated within the shadow of the Katanga secession, providing nearly all the revenues of the Tshombist state. The advent of the Mobutu regime put Kinshasa for the first time in a position to undertake serious discussions with UMHK concerning the adaptation of its statute to the circumstances of independence.

Beyond publicly asserted economic nationalism, important political motivations inspired the president. As Kamitatu put it in a dissertation on the UMHK nationalization,

> The decision to nationalize UMHK was a political act, deliberately and carefully prepared. Its objective was less, for the decider [the president], the recovery of the economic independence of the Nation, than the consolidation of presidential power, the budgetary underpinning of which was basically constituted by fiscal levies on UMHK. . . .
>
> The second political aspect of nationalization was the presidential determination to remove from UMHK the capacity to offer financial backing to potential political opponents of the regime, in particular Moise Tshombe, considered to be the protege and secular instrument of UMHK.[33]

Initial strategy for economic nationalism was mapped at a meeting in February 1966, attended by key members of the Binza group (Bomboko and Nendaka) Finance Minister (and senior member of the presidential family) Litho Maboti, the quondam intellectual radical Mungul-Diaka, and several anti-Tshombe parliamentarians. A consensus was reached that the state, to achieve its goals, had to acquire control of major new financial resources to provide development funds for supporting Zairian business-men and the rural sector.[34] To achieve these ends some form of takeover of UMHK was indispensable.

The first step toward confrontation was a significant tax hike on turn-over and exports, affecting UMHK above all. Tensions ratcheted one level further in late April 1966 when UMHK raised copper prices without con-sulting Zairian officials. Mobutu rebuked the company sharply, pointing out that the Zambian and Chilean private mining companies had con-sulted their governments before changing prices, while "for us, it is a pri-vate company, furthermore foreign . . . which decides." UMHK could not continue to be a state within a state; Zaire had not only mines, but laws, Mobutu pointed out. Two days later he raised export taxes from 17 to 30 percent, ordered that 10 percent of the minerals produced be deliv-ered to the state as a strategic reserve, and announced a forthcoming law requiring incorporation in Zaire by the end of the year.[35]

As the deadline for incorporation—1 January 1967—neared, nego-tiations centered on a formula for severing UMHK into Belgian and Zairian components. UMHK was prepared to concede to the Zairian state a 50 percent share in Union Minière-Zaire and 17.95 percent in Union Minière-Belgium. The physical installations in Zaire would be vested in the Zairian company, while those overseas would go to the parent com-pany. Management in Zaire was to remain in the hands of the private sec-tor representatives. A critical stumbling block was the distribution of the proceeds of the very large quantity of copper—150,000 tons—already ex-ported from Zaire in a deliberately accelerated fashion, but not yet mar-keted. The UMHK position was that this copper would serve to capitalize Union Minière-Belgium; its value, $150 million, somewhat exceeded the real capitalization of UMHK. Such a view was unacceptable to the Zairian negotiators, although in November 1966 Mobutu indicated his willing-ness to accept the basic formula of a partition of UMHK.

On 8 December 1966, Zaire broke off negotiations and announced that UMHK would simply have to conform to the law requiring incor-poration in Zaire by the end of the month. As the two sides marched to the brink of combat, each mobilized its resources (summarized in table 10.5). The conflict entered its melodramatic stage on 23 December when UMHK announced that it would not transfer its headquarters to Kinshasa. Mo-butu reacted at once, temporarily blocking copper exports, seizing UMHK

Table 10.5   Leverage in the Zaire– UMHK Conflict

UMHK	Zaire
Indispensable technicians	Shaba ore reserves
Technical information on operations and prospecting	Alternative corporate partners
Need of state for foreign exchange and revenue	Sovereignty
7.5 billion BF unsold copper stocks abroad	Belgian desire to avert rupture
Capacity to disrupt marketing through legal harassment	Domestic political support
Belgian diplomatic support	Retaliation on other Société Générale holdings in Zaire
Possible support for Tshombe	American support for regime

bank accounts, and announcing a provisional management board to run the mines. These acts were not nationalization, it was argued at the time; UMHK, by defying Zairian legislation, had placed itself outside the law and had thus abandoned its right to operate. On 1 January 1967, Zaire announced the establishment of a new state-dominated corporation, the Générale Congolaise des Minerais (in 1971 altered to Générale des Carrières et des Mines, or Gécamines). Initially, the state took 60 percent of the shares, while 40 percent was held open for foreign partners. When none were forthcoming, Gécamines became a 100-percent state corporation.

Open economic warfare lasted six weeks after the takeover, as each side sought to actualize its leverage. UMHK gave its staff until 31 January to accept repatriation at the expense of the company or lose their contractual rights. Legal action was threatened against any who might buy the expropriated copper. Strong pressure was brought to bear on the various capital groups that might be enlisted by Zaire as alternatives to UMHK.

On the Zairian side, intensive efforts were made to maintain the production infrastructure intact. UMHK staff were told that twelve months' notice was necessary before they could leave their posts. The Nippon Mining Company and the Banque Lambert in Belgium were approached to take over part or all of the UMHK role as minority partners of the Zairian state.[36] Tanganyika Concessions quickly declined an offer to separate its own interests from those of the Société Générale. The British firm Lonrho, a venturesome (some said buccaneering) organization with extensive African investments, was mentioned as a possible partner.[37] Gestures were also made in the French direction: France had normally bought one-third of the Zairian output, and was the obvious alternative source of French-speaking mining technicians. On Christmas day 1966 Maurice Tempelsman, the New York financier who was Mobutu's confidant and investment collaborator, had received a cable from the president inviting him to come at once to Zaire to take over direction of the copper mines (see the New Copper Investors section below).[38]

These bellicose maneuvers were not designed to bring about total war, which would have been costly to both Zaire and UMHK. On 15 February 1967, an accord was reached. Important symbolic satisfaction was given to Zaire by UMHK acceptance of Gécamines as a state enterprise for the conduct of mining operations in Shaba. Further satisfaction to national dignity came through the exclusion of UMHK altogether from management arrangements for Gécamines; the indispensable management services were to be provided by the Société Générale des Minerais (SOGEMIN), a sister enterprise of the Société Générale family.

The settlement was to prove very profitable for UMHK. SOGEMIN received a management contract for the recruitment of expatriate personnel, the management of the installations, and marketing of the copper. In return, SOGEMIN was to receive 6.5 percent of the sales revenue of Gécamines. Only 1 percent was required to reimburse SOGEMIN itself, so the remainder, in effect, was compensation for UMHK. In addition, Zaire abandoned its claims to shares in Union Minière in Belgium, which was also the major beneficiary of the "pipeline" copper.

In September 1969 this framework was consolidated through formal agreements on a compensation package for UMHK, to be derived from SOGEMIN revenues. SOGEMIN was to receive 6 percent of Gécamines' gross sales revenues for a further fifteen years, after which time compensation would be considered completely paid and the rate would fall to 1 percent. With sales at that time ranging from 9 to 18 billion Belgian francs, depending on price levels, this was a very generous settlement for UMHK—so much so that in 1974 it was agreed that the compensation obligation would be considered fulfilled with a final payment of 4 billion Belgian francs.[39] In fact, UMHK annual reports show that its profits from Zaire were not affected by the nationalization; UMHK earned 8 billion francs from 1960 to 1966, and 8.5 billion from 1967 to 1973.[40]

While it was clear from the outset that UMHK had emerged financially unscathed from the battle, it initially appeared as though the Zairian state as well had achieved significant gains. Zaire was a pacesetter in Third World natural resource takeovers; the takeover of UMHK was the first

Table 10.6   Taxation and Profits of Gécamines (in millions of zaires)

	Net Gécamines profit	Payments to SOGEMIN	As % of Gécamines profit	Tax payments	As % of government budget
1967	17.6	0.9	5.2	69.8	80
1968	12.9	8.9	69	92.1	54
1969	23.9	11.5	48	129.7	61
1970	14.5	17.5	122	132.9	50
1971	17.4	14.4	81	86.5	31
1972	8.9	14.4	162	88.2	31
1973	81.9	21.3	76	168.3	49
1974	15.4			225.8	41
1975				113.6	22

Sources: Kamitatu Massamba, *Le pouvoir à la portée du peuple* (Paris: Maspero, 1977), pp. 515–516; Mulumba Lukoji, "La commercialisation des minérais de la Gécamines," *Zaire-Afrique* 94 (April 1975): 212.

such nationalization in the copper sphere, though others were soon to follow (in Zambia and Chile). Zairian state doctrine aligned itself with emergent Third World economic nationalist ideology; not long after the takeover, the UN General Assembly defined the "full permanent sovereignty of every State over its natural resources and all economic activities" as a constitutive element of the "New International Economic Order."[41] Zairian state control would permit the pace of Africanization to be forced and would break the monopoly on technological knowledge of the European cadres. The state, in the short run, was able to sharply increase its fiscal take from the copper sector. It was able to set aside the cautious production ceilings maintained by UMHK (in tacit accord with other major producers) and to seek greater short-term profit by pricing policies less geared to long-term contracts. (Table 10.6 shows the magnitude of state revenues from Gécamines after nationalization.)

Yet there were unanticipated long-term costs to nationalization which reduced its advantages, especially in the crisis years. In a penetrating analysis of the nationalization, Shafer identifies "loss of risk insulation" as a major hidden liability to the apparent triumph.[42] The instability of state enterprises to maintain the downstream integration employed by multinationals to influence price fluctuations was one factor (though even with wholly private producers the world copper market has always been very volatile). The total failure of CIPEC, the attempted cartel of African and Latin

American copper exporting countries, to gain any leverage over the market was a second factor.

For most of the period from World War II until the 1974 copper price break (the exceptions were a long sag in the late 1950s and a shorter one at the beginning of the 1970s), copper prices had remained relatively high. As insurance against the risk of a sharp fall in prices, private producers generally sold their copper on long-term contracts at prices well below those quoted on the London Metal Exchange. To the Zairian leadership, this practice appeared to be a conspiracy to smuggle profits abroad. The long period of relatively favorable prices lasting into the 1970s, new technologies permitting the working of much lower grade ores (Zairian ore was very high-grade), and perceived high risks in such Third World producing areas as Zaire, Zambia, Chile, or Peru, led to multinational investments in major new capacity in "safe" countries (Australia, Canada, South Africa, the Philippines). The period of relatively high copper prices had led a large number of industrial consumers to switch to aluminum. All of these market trends introduced new risks of volatility into the world copper market, and made more serious the loss of the risk insulation which UMHK's greater skill in playing the international markets had provided.

While the international market situation was becoming more unfavorable, and the silent loss of risk insulation was eroding the Gécamines position, the profitability of the state enterprise was being sapped from within by a substantial increase in its personnel costs. At the managerial level, the number of personnel rose from 2,166 in 1967 to 3,259 in 1980, while total personnel increased from 23,000 to 38,408. Copper production rose from an average of about 300,000 tons earlier to a peak of 464,000 tons in 1975, before falling back to 426,000 tons in 1980. Higher levels of taxation, the illicit diversion of some Gécamines revenue, and—from 1975 on—restrictions on Gécamines' access to foreign exchange, brought about a significant deterioration in its capital infrastructure and compromised its expansion program.

Doubtless the goal of accelerating the Africanization of Gécamines' management was partly achieved, as table 10.7 shows. As growing numbers of Zairian cadres became available in the administrative, accounting, and even medical services, the expatriates withdrew into the technological heart of the enterprise. In November 1973 a Zairian mining engineer, Umba Kyamitala, was named as head of Gécamines. By 1975 Zairians headed the mining, commercial, treasury, and administrative departments of the corporation.[43] They were still a minority on the production commit-

Table 10.7   Africanization of Gécamines Management, 1967–1980
(total managerial personnel: 1974, 2,252; 1980, 3,259)

	1967	1968	1969	1970	1971	1972	1973	1974	1980
African executive personnel	251	547	610	662	720	820	923	1,135	2,249

Sources: Gécamines, *Rapport annuel*, 1974, p. 32; Gécamines, *Rapport annuel*, 1980, p. 31.

tee which made the crucial operational decisions. And in 1983 Umba was removed and replaced by a Belgian manager, Robert Crem.

The greater control of the state over the mineral domain resulted in a determined effort to meet the revenue imperative not only by higher taxation, but also by expanding production. Part of the UMHK reserves could be recuperated and attributed to other partners. The state was able to require an expansion of production levels from Gécamines, which UMHK had always refused. However, the expansion encountered very unfavorable market conditions. By this time copper development projects required a price level of nearly $1 per pound by pay off; since the 1974 price crash, the market has hovered about the $.70 level most of the time.[44]

New Regime projects: the Maluku steel mill

The ambiguous victory in the UMHK confrontation, added to the final settlement of the *contentieux*, greatly enlarged Zaire's sphere of apparent economic sovereignty and set the stage for a new phase in Second Republic development strategy. There were to be three main poles of development: Kinshasa and Bas-Zaire were to be an industrial and energy production zone; the Shaba copperbelt was to greatly expand its mineral output; and Kisangani was to be the pivot of agriculturally based industries. Massive public investment was to go into development of the Inga hydroelectric site in Bas-Zaire and into completion of a national export railway route joining Shaba to the sea. The collaboration of foreign capital was to be solicited for various industrial projects, especially Shaba mineral development. Energy for the latter was to be supplied by high-tension direct transmission lines over the 1,800 kilometers between Inga and the copperbelt.

Political calculations jostled with economic visions in this package. The regime's unfolding ambitions at home and abroad required a rapidly expanding revenue base which could only come from developing the mineral sector. Opening new mines would help to end the monopoly of Belgian capital by bringing in new foreign investors; mineral expansion would require new energy sources. The lingering fear of latent Shaba separatism was an unspoken factor in the decision to tie copperbelt mineral development to power from Inga. When the new infrastructure was complete, the flick of a switch in Kinshasa could cripple the Shaba mining industry and make impossible a resurgence of secession.

The Bakajika Law had cleared the way for new mineral concessions by extinguishing undeveloped colonial claims. By way of positive inducement, a relatively generous investment code was promulgated in 1969, offering exemption from import duties on capital equipment and a five-year holiday from corporate and real estate taxes, as well as from expatriate salaries until production started. The specific content of the investment code perhaps mattered less to foreign capital than by its expressive function as a symbol of Zaire's receptivity to that capital, the appearance of political stability, the apparent success of the 1967 economic stabilization plan, and the impressive potential wealth of the country.[45]

In his address of 12 December 1966, Mobutu had made two specific pledges concerning development projects: production of the first steel in Zaire by 1972, and initiation of the first stage of development at the Inga site by 1968.[46] These pledges were both met. Each was a long-standing scheme, initially mooted during the colonial period.

The steel mill project dated from 1950. Several large and rich iron ore bodies had long been known near Banalia, Isiro, and Ubundu in Haut-Zaire, and Luebo in Kasai. But Zaire was poor in coal, and the domestic market for steel products seemed too small to justify the capital cost. The project was relegated to the list of schemes held in reserve, and to a place among the whispered visions of an African Ruhr, founded on cheap energy, in Bas-Zaire.

In the late 1960s an Italian consulting firm, SICAI, produced lyrical visions of the contribution a steel mill could make to a domestically oriented development program. Its import substitution merits were stressed, and impressive claims were made for its linkage effects.[47] Mobutu, personally committed to the project, never wavered in his determination to see it through. Investors were much more skeptical; while there was no shortage of suitors offering a contractor-financed turnkey project, no foreign capital was tendered for risk on this undertaking. The cost ($250 million) thus had to be borne entirely by the Zairian state; the Italian firms of Finsinder and Societa Italiana Impianta (Italimpianta) and the German firm DEMAG were joint contractors. Construction began in 1972 at Maluku, inconveniently located at some distance from the Zaire River, just beyond the presidential domain of N'Sele, east of Kinshasa. It was completed at a very unfavorable time in 1975.

While the Maluku mill was billed as a major technological achievement of the regime, in reality it proved emblematic of a series of calamitous miscalculations. The assumptions of the SICAI feasibility studies concerning market prospects and production costs were dubious; critics pointed to the financial links between SICAI and the Italian firms participating in the construction of the steel mill and the Inga dam project.[48] There was no possibility of obtaining the immense capital required to develop the internal iron ore deposits at Banalia, Luebo, or elsewhere, so the steel mill had to operate entirely with imported scrap. Production costs per ton proved to be $660 rather than the $450–$480 promised by SICAI, and up to eight times the cost of imported steel.[49] The mill never operated at more than 10 percent of its 250,000-ton capacity; by 1980 it had virtually ceased to operate. It is doubtful that it ever will resume production.

The Inga Dam project

Closely tied to the steel mill was the Inga project, an even older dream. From earliest colonial days the formidable energy potential of the Zaire river had fired the imagination. The river drops 300 meters between Kinshasa and Matadi, and 100 meters within a 12-milometer stretch at the Inga site. The average flow, unusually stable throughout the year, is 42,000 cubic meters per second, surpassed only by the Amazon. As early as 1925 the basic techniques for eventual development of the dams had been devised. Use would be made of dry parallel valleys into which part of the flow could be diverted. The project was abandoned in 1939, but interest was reborn after World War II when for a time there were fears of a Western energy shortage that would affect the possibility of expanding such energy-intensive industries as aluminum. In November 1957 an official announcement was even made that the scheme was to go forward. But the project was stalled by growing political uncertainty, the deteriorating financial situation of the colony, and the conviction that firm commitments for an aluminum plant as client for the energy to be produced were a sine qua non.

The dream of Inga had already been absorbed by the Zairian political elite; as early as September 1960 the new government announced its determination to proceed with the scheme. The First Republic was too fragile to raise the capital required for a project of this scale, but significant planning was done. SICAI was engaged in 1963 to undertake a feasibility study. The central contribution of its very optimistic report was a reconceptualization of the project's purpose. Belgian plans had been shaped by the premises of the colonial economy; the viability of the dam had been linked to an energy-intensive export zone on the coast. SICAI argued the dam development should be firmly tied to domestically centered industrialization, with the steel mill rather than an aluminum plant as centerpiece.[50]

The Mobutu regime was determined that Inga should not be controlled by foreign interests; the commitment to proceed, made almost at once, was primarily financed by the state investment budget ($87 million of an eventual total of $140 million). The arguments for phase I of dam development were solid: Kinshasa was already in a power deficit, with only 80 megawatts available from existing installations on the Inkisi River; no significant industrial expansion in the capital or in Bas-Zaire could occur without additional energy supplies. The proposed steel mill alone would require more than 100 megawatts of the 300 that the first dam (Inga I) would supply. Ground was broken on 1 January 1968, and the first phase was finished in 1972.

Planning at once began for the far more ambitious phase II dam, whose projected capacity was an additional 1,200 megawatts. Though the power was to be as cheap as any in the world, the initial projected cost—$260 million—was twice that of phase I, and clients for the power were not assured.[51] In 1973 the commitment to proceed with Inga II was made, though only 700 megawatts worth of capacity would actually be installed initially; by 1977, this power was available.

Customers, however, were not. The regime anxiously courted aluminum companies for years. In 1969, Kaiser announced plans for a 70,000-ton smelter, to be fed by imported bauxite; this project subsequently evaporated. In 1973–74 an imminent Reynolds commitment was mooted. By 1976–77 hopes for the elusive aluminum project were pinned on Alusuisse; by 1980, Alusuisse (Aluminium Suisse, S.A.) appeared to have confirmed its commitment to build a smelter, but only after playing heavily on Zairian desperation to find any client for its power. The smelter, expected to cost $1 billion, would be assured virtually the lowest power rates in the world. Alusuisse was guaranteed complete and permanent exemption from export duties on the aluminum produced and was given the power to veto any other aluminum project over a ten-year period. These generous advantages were offered in addition to the investment code tax holiday and other inducements. Zaire would also have to make major public investments to create port installations at Banana, on the coast; the cost of these might well reach $900 million. Despite these concessions the Alusuisse project still remained in limbo in 1983.

The struggle to find customers for power led, by the end of the 1970s, to a scheme for a duty-free industrial zone in the vicinity of Inga. Foreign producers would be offered power below cost and exemption from all duties. Such terms might eventually find takers, but offered only limited benefits to the country as a whole.[52]

The giant disaster: Inga-Shaba

Inga II was linked to an even more ambitious project, the 1,800-kilometer power transmission line from the dam to the Shaba grid at Kolwezi. The four existing power stations in Shaba, which produce three-fourths of the national energy total, had a combined capacity of 520 megawatts, already insufficient for Gécamines alone by 1972.[53] The Inga-Shaba project had many critics, particularly in Gécamines circles. It was argued that a $65-million new dam in Shaba could add 250 megawatts to meet immediate needs.[54] There was also some surplus available in Zambia.

There were many serious disadvantages to the Inga-Shaba scheme. The cost was enormous. Though it was initially bid at $260 million (by the American contractors Morrison-Knudsen and Fishback and Moore) for completion in 1977, by 1978 cost overruns had boosted the total to $680 million—a figure which had escalated to a whispered $800 million by 1980, and might well exceed $1 billion. The time required for construction was greatly underestimated, and further delays were created by political disruptions during Shaba I and II; work began in 1973 but was completed only in 1982. Meanwhile, interest payments were due on the huge public debts incurred to finance the project. The technology, although employed in the lines linking Cabora Bassa in Mozambique to South Africa, was unproven, and great uncertainty existed concerning such matters as the magnitude of line losses, vulnerability to lightning damage, and the cost of operating and maintaining complex equipment stretched over vast distances.[55]

In fact, there is every indication that the Inga-Shaba scheme will prove to be a mammoth burden on Zairian society for many years. As one cost overrun succeeded another, the capital charges reached a point where the original presumptions of inexpensive power for new ore processing facilities in Shaba (for concentrating, smelting, and refining) were shattered. The Inga-Shaba line will instead deliver extremely expensive power, which the Zairian state electricity utility will be forced to supply at a loss of Gécamines, the Société de Developpement Industriel et des Mines du Zaire (SODIMIZA), and the Société Minière de Tenke-Fungurume (SMTF) (if and when the latter finally comes on line). Also, management costs were seriously underestimated. Foreign contractors have had to be hired to run the line, and have been paid in foreign exchange. This difficulty led to closure of the line in 1983, at least temporarily, only a few months after its completion.

The scope of the calamity emerges in a revealing exchange between an Export-Import Bank director and U.S. senator Paul Tsongas at 1979 congressional hearings on an additional loan for completion of the scheme:

> Senator Tsongas: Given the shortfall of need for the capacity, how is this ever going to be a paying proposition? . . .
> Mr. [Donald] Stingel [Export-Import Bank Director]: There is no question that for some years the state is going to have to underwrite some of the cost of Inga power for Gécamines. If you include everything in power cost, including the operating cost, the amortization, everything else, we figure . . . the Inga-Shaba line might cost as much as 70 to 80 mills or 15 to 16 cents for copper. That is ridiculously high.[56]

Nor is the cost of power the only problem. Delays in completing the Shaba copper expansion project mean that even by the mid-1980s no more than 50 percent of the Inga Shaba capacity will be used.[57] The line's security is at risk; it passes through regions close to the Angolan border, where disaffection is rife. Indeed, by 1980 one wholly unanticipated danger to the power line appeared: village blacksmiths in regions through which it passes discovered that the pylons were a splendid source of scrap metal.

New copper investors

The most important stake in the investment race that peaked in 1970 was the undeveloped copperbelt deposits. The flurry of contacts with foreign interests, which was designed to create an alternative to UMHK at the peak of the nationalization confrontation, was the prologue to the race for these reserves. One of these overtures matured in 1967 when the Nippon Mining Company received a prospecting permit. Ore was not hard to find, and in 1969 the Société de Développement Industriel et des Mines du Zaire was founded, with Zaire holding 15 percent of the equity (though having no management voice). Production began in 1972, with an initial output of 50,000 tons. The concession area, 36,790,100 square kilometers, was very large; SODIMIZA aimed eventually at producing 200,000 tons annually. The installations for the first mine at Musoshi, on the Zambia frontier, cost $90 million, though the initial capitalization was only $6 million.[58] (The Japanese consortium abandoned operation of its Zairian mines in 1983.)

The Japanese concession was only the beginning. An even richer prize was the copper mountain at Tenke-Fungurume, with a huge deposit of 6 percent ore. First into the fray was the mercantile adventurer Lonrho, which broke ranks with other major Western interests to begin serious discussions with Zairian authorities in 1968, in collaboration with the Japanese combine Nisho Iwai. The Lonrho bait was an offer to link the mining concession to the realization of another nationalist dream: construction of a rail line from Kinshasa to Ilebo, thus completing a national rail link from the capital to Shaba). The cost for the route then favored by Zairian authorities was estimated at from $200 to 300 million. At one point in late 1969 and early 1970 Lonrho appeared to have the inside track.

Lonrho had rapidly expanded its empire in Africa from 1963 on through the aggressive risk-taking of its head, "Tiny" Rowlands, and a strategy of developing intimate and highly personal ties with African leaders. Lonrho cultivated a close relationship with perennial Zairian foreign minister Bomboko, which boomeranged when the latter lost favor in 1969 and fell into disgrace in 1971. The Lonrho-owned *Times of Zambia* offended Mobutu in June 1970 by publishing a highly critical article of the Zairian regime during his official visit to Lusaka. To add insult to injury, the *London Financial Times* shortly thereafter published a statement by a Lonrho executive which indicated that the railway-copper project was in Lonrho's pocket. At about the same time, Lonrho's secret acquisition of a controlling interest in COMINIERE, a Belgian conglomerate with significant Zairian holdings, became generally known both in Zaire and Belgium, further irritating Kinshasa. This combination of factors eliminated Lonrho-COMINIERE from the bidding on the Shaba concession, and provoked legal action in Belgium by other COMINIERE shareholders.[59]

Lonrho's elimination left two main bidders in the competition. Encouraged by the generous settlement of its compensation claims and the warming Zairian relationship with Belgium that was marked by the successful royal visit of King Baudouin in 1970, Union Minière entered the fray as an entity separate from Gécamines. To make its offer more attractive, Union Minière brought in minor American partners—primarily Bethlehem Steel. In August and September of 1970, Union Minière too believed the deal was clinched.[60]

The victory went instead to a consortium stitched together by Maurice Tempelsman of Leon Tempelsman & Son. Maurice Tempelsman had established a diamond-trading office in Kinshasa in 1960. An astute financier with great charm, he had cultivated personal ties with the new political elite and had been an intimate friend of Mobutu from the early days of independence. Tempelsman also had excellent bipartisan political connections in the United States. In the late 1970s he retained on his personal Kinshasa staff Larry Devlin, former CIA station chief in Zaire, and retired colonel John Gerassi, former head of the American military mission to Zaire. With such a web of connections and business acumen to boot, Tempelsman was a prospect for certain success in the personalist world of second republic Kinshasa.[61]

Tempelsman was thus positioned to broker an international consortium which possessed, in addition to its financial solidity and technical capacity, the important political appeal of diversifying mineral development beyond the Société Générale family. The Tempelsman consortium, subsequently incorporated as the Société Minière de Tenke-Fungurume (SMTF), offered a 20-percent interest to the Zairian state in return for the concession. The private partners were American, South African, French, and Japanese.[62]

The SMTF consortium had other attractions relative to the Union Minière combine. The proposed SMTF investment, initially reported to be $300 million, was somewhat higher than the Belgian bid of $240 million. Union Minière had wanted to limit the state holding to 10 percent, and to refine the copper at its Hoboken subsidiary in Belgium; SMTF offered 20 percent, and pledged to build a refinery in Zaire. At least as important as the financial attraction of higher value added to the country was the symbolic value to the regime of a foreign investment which appeared to make greater concessions to the economic sovereignty of Zaire.[63] One significant potential liability of SMTF was the predominantly South African origin of the expatriate technical staff.

In addition to the direct capital investment, the SMTF project involved very high financial requirements. When actual work began in 1972, it was estimated that the cost of an initial production of 100,000 tons would be from $400 to 500 million. The target date for beginning production was set at 1976; by that time it was hoped that inexpensive power from the Inga-Shaba high tension line would be available. By 1975 estimated costs had risen to $650 million, and by 1979 start-up costs were estimated at

$1.2 billion. The prolonged slump in the copper market after April 1974 hit SMTF very hard. Even with the tax holiday offered by the investment code and the richness of the ore body the viability of the scheme was endangered because the sums of capital immobilized were so large. In 1976, after more than $200 million had been expended on site development, SMTF was forced to suspend operations indefinitely while awaiting more favorable market conditions.[64]

Gécamines, for its part, also entered the expansion game. A two-stage development plan was initiated in 1970, designed to raise copper production capacity from 360,000 to 570,000 tons by 1980. The first phase of expansion, primarily internally financed, easily met its production target by 1974. By this time taxation of Gécamines was so heavy that it could no longer finance further development wholly out of its reserves. The second stage was estimated in 1974 to cost $480 million, and was to be partly financed by $220 million in loans. However, the growing Zairian financial crisis from 1975 on, and the Shaba invasions of 1977 and 1978, created serious production dislocations for Gécamines, and the second phase was thrown hopelessly off schedule.[65]

In 1974 the regime took a further step to complete its control over the former UMHK empire by creating the Société Zairoise pour la Commercialisation des Minerais (SOZACOM) to supplant SOGEMIN as the marketing arm of the state. SOGEMIN was given a contract to provide technical assistance to SOZACOM and to undertake construction of $100-million copper refinery near the Maluku steel mill. The refining of 100 percent of Zaire's copper in the country had been a frequently reiterated goal of the regime; it was claimed that the 1974 accord would assure its realization.[66] In practice, as Kamitatu has shown, the new SOZACOM refinery would handle only the 100,000 tons of new output provided by the Gécamines expansion plan. The Hoboken refineries, an enterprise employing 4,000 and subsisting essentially on Zairian copper, would continue to be assured of 300,000 tons annually.[67] SOZACOM quickly ran into difficulties over corruption; its first two directors were jailed for embezzlement in 1977.[68]

Other development projects: multinational manufacturing and public sector expansion

Manufacturing for the domestic market was another attractive area for foreign private investors in the halcyon years of the Mobutu regime. Significant local industry dated from the 1920s, and received a great stimulus from the five years of separation from the metropolitan economy during World War II. In the last two decades of colonial rule manufacturing was the fastest growing economic sector, reaching 8 percent of the GDP by 1958, or four times the comparable Nigerian figure. By the early 1970s manufacturing was about 11 percent of the GDP. The concentration of most manufacturing at Kinshasa and in the copperbelt cities sheltered it from the impact of First Republic dislocations.

The bulk of the new wave of manufacturing investments in the 1969– 72 period fell in the import substitution category.[69] Vehicle assembly plants were created by General Motors, Leyland, and Renault. Goodyear established a $16-million tire factory, which Mobutu claimed would eventually bring in $85 million when promised corollary investments in rubber plantation development were made.[70] Continental Grains opened a flour mill at Matadi in 1972, with start-up costs of $8.5 million, of which 72 percent were bank and supplier credits.[71] The Krupp group provided 15 percent of the $13 million in capital for a palm oil and soap enterprise in Gemena (Equateur); the Zairian state put up 20 percent, and the Moleka group 65 percent (Moleka was a magnate closely tied to the Mobutu family).[72] A German firm built a new cement facility, which entered production in 1974 with a capacity of 350,000 tons; meanwhile, in 1970 the established colonial cement works, Cimenteries du Zaire (CIZA), embarked on an expansion scheme to double its production to 600,000 tons. With a market in 1973 of 420,000 tons, both were destined to produce at a fraction of capacity. Other new factories were built in established fields: breweries, textiles, tobacco.

Several features of this investment surge led to subsequent problems. A number of manufactured products were relatively expensive compared to imports (tires were 40 percent more expensive; textiles, 20–30 percent; passenger cars, 30–40 percent).[73] The proportion of raw materials imported for manufacturing was often very high, causing severe production difficulties when the payments crisis hit in 1974. Frequently there was a significant supplier credit component to construction costs, some of which were liabilities against the Zairian state. Planning problems led to substantial excess capacity in some sectors (cement, matches, vehicle assembly); by 1982 the Goodyear factory was limping along at 18 percent of capacity.[74]

In the miraculous year of 1970 fortune had smiled on petroleum exploration efforts being carried out by Gulf, Mobil, Shell, and Texaco along the coast and in the central basin. Gulf discovered an offshore deposit which entered production in 1975 at a rate of 26,000 barrels a day (by 1980 prices, worth roughly $300 million). But the tax holiday guaranteed by the investment code denied to the state much of the initial benefit from this find. Further, the Italian-built refinery was unable to handle the type of crude being produced, so the entire output had to be exported.

The public sector itself embarked on a major expenditure campaign aimed at expanding the transportation and communication infrastructures. Projects included the development of a deepwater port at Banana (costing perhaps $900 million) which was to be linked to the existing rail net at Matadi (for another $300 million, as well as hundreds of millions more for a bridge at Matadi, completed in 1983). Air Zaire ordered $125 million worth of new aircraft in 1973.[75] Six new cargo vessels were on order in West Germany for the state shipping line, at a cost of DM 190 million.[76] The British contractor Wimpy, in 1974, was charged with a $130-million project to upgrade seven airports. In 1975, French credits provided $85 million for a domestic satellite, to be added to an elaborate $18-million "Voice of Zaire" radio-television complex in Kinshasa. The Chinese supplied a $34-million "people's palace" (a showcase cultural center). Efforts continued to find a contractor and financing for the Ilebo-Kinshasa rail link, which by 1975 was estimated to cost $500 million.[77]

Two overarching results of the vast investment program in the boom years stand out. First, the colossal scale of the outlays, public and private, centering on interrelated copper and energy development and totalling about $3 billion when all the returns are in, has made Zaire's economy tributary to copper to a greatly escalated degree. The copper revenues themselves are largely mortgaged to these investments for years to come, while the survival of the state is ever more tightly bound to copper. Some observers continue to argue that the long-run prospects for copper may be reasonably good; however, for reasons which Prain persuasively documents, copper is exceeded in price volatility among the major internationally traded minerals only by zinc and lead.[78]

Second, although from the first days of the New Regime agriculture has been constantly accorded a leading role, in practice almost none of the investments went into the rural sector. In large measure this was simply by default: when the enormous schemes which constituted the centerpieces of the grand design were served, there was nothing left over for agriculture; nor did foreign investors show any interest in agriculture.

Economic catastrophe

The tidal wave of disaster that struck Zaire with devastating force in 1974–75 arose initially from several conjunctural misfortunes, the most important of which was the break in the copper price in April and May 1974: from an all-time record of $1.40 per pound on the New York market in April 1974 it fell sharply to a low of $.53 in early 1975. Until that point the regime had been quite fortunate in that the period 1967–74 had been one of unusually good copper prices, in historical terms. But the 1974 bust proved to be exceptionally prolonged, with the market below production costs for many producers throughout the world.

Post-1974 prices, expressed in current terms, were apparently not exceptionally low when inflation in the industrial world is taken into account (see figure 10.1); but the real exchange value of copper exports was badly eroded, and by 1977 stood at an all-time low. In 1967, 287,000 tons of copper brought Z 73.8 million; in 1975, 489,000 tons yielded, in contrant prices, Z 67.5 million (expressed in 1966 Zaire values).[79] In 1975, according to the Bank of Zaire, the exchange value of Zairian exports was only half the 1970 rate. Subsequent World Bank data placed the terms of trade index (1970 = 100) at 46.8, 40.0, and 36.2 in 1976, 1977, and 1978, respectively (see table 10.8). Because of the heavy dependency on copper, Zairian terms of trade deteriorated far more sharply than did the average terms for less developed countries as a whole. The loss of purchasing power of Zairian exports in 1975 was no less than $600 million.[80]

The rise in petroleum costs was an additional blow, though later cushioned by compensating exports of Zairian oil, which began in 1976. Nonetheless, by 1977 oil import costs were running at $200 million yearly, or 20 percent of the available foreign exchange—four times the 1973 figure.

The Angolan civil war was a disaster for Zaire not only politically and militarily, but also economically, because of the closure of the Benguela railway in August 1975. The Benguela railway was the shortest, cheapest, and fastest trade route for the Shaba copperbelt. In 1973, 200,000 tons of copper (41 percent of Zairian copper exports), 320,000 tons of exported manganese ore, and 250,000 tons of other merchandise were shipped on the Benguela line.[81] There was no unused capacity on the national route via Ilebo–Kinshasa–Matadi, and the eastern route from Kalemie to Dar-es-Salaam was slow, costly, and hampered by poor connections across Lake Tanganyika and by the congestion of Dar-es-Salaam itself. The Chinese-built Tazara (Tanzania-Zambia) railway was experiencing serious initial operating problems and had no spare capacity. Routes through Mozambique were cut, off leaving as the sole alternative a long and costly route via Zambia and Zimbabwe to South African ports. In addition to being costly, dependence on South African export routes had evident political liabilities.

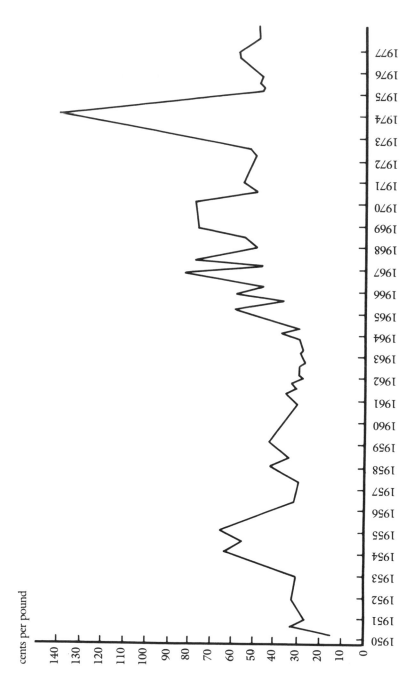

Figure 10.1. Copper Price Movements, 1950–1977 (New York, nearest futures, current prices). *Source: Commodity Yearbook,* 1956 through 1977.

cents per pound

308

Table 10.8 Zairian Terms of Trade, 1967–1975 (1970 = 100)

	Weighted indices of major exports		Overall export price index	Import price index	Terms of Trade
	Mineral	Agricultural			
1967	78.4	99.9	81.7	86.0	95.0
1968	85.7	89.0	85.7	85.1	100.7
1969	102.8	82.4	99.7	88.5	112.6
1970	100.0	100.0	100.0	100.0	100.0
1972	79.5	95.6	82.0	97.8	83.8
1973	108.5	115.8	109.7	128.5	84.7
1974	130.8	168.3	136.5	160.0	85.3
1975	86.9	128.0	93.1	179.8	51.8

Source: Banque du Zaire, *Rapport annuel*, 1975, p. 155.

While these conjunctural blows by a suddenly hostile fate were punishing, they could not alone explain the profound crisis that beset Zaire from 1975 on. The soaring hopes of the early 1970s were suddenly shattered; as they vanished, a full measure of the risk-laden development strategy, hinged to grandiose copper and energy projects, came into view. The deleterious consequences of the systematic corruption besetting the state became more visible, as did the costs of the Zairianization and radicalization adventures (see chapter 11). So also did the impact of policy failings in the agricultural sphere become more apparent.

The agrarian crisis

Agrarian decline was a menace to the underlying health of the polity, and it had begun long before the 1974 disaster. After independence the place of export agriculture in the overall economy had dropped sharply; over time the capacity of the society to feed its swelling urban population was becoming increasingly problematic. With an estimated 36 percent of the population urban by 1980, and nearly half of the population expected to be urban by 1990, the seriousness of the rural crisis cannot be overstated. One conclusion is implacable: many of the agricultural failures have been the unintended yet no less ineluctable consequence of state action.

Yet the agricultural potential of Zaire is impressive. Only 1 percent of the land surface is presently cultivated; though much of the land is not of high potential, nonetheless the productive capacity is far beyond present levels of output. From 1928 to 1959, average annual growth in commercialized agricultural output was 5.35 percent.[82] In 1958, 41 percent of the export value came from the agricultural sector, as compared with 11.2 percent in 1974 (and even less later in the decade). The country easily fed itself before independence, and even exported a small surplus; by 1970 food imports cost $40 million, and by 1977, $300 million.

At the level of official rhetoric the central importance of agriculture is well recognized. In November 1977, agriculture was a central plank in the "Mobutu plan" for economic recovery. But this commitment was translated neither into the practical allocation of state resources nor into policies offering inducements to villagers. In fact, the incentives offered were mainly negative.

In 1973–74, only from 1 to 2 percent of the budgetary outlays went to agriculture, in contrast to the 4–5 percent before independence. Further, 90 percent of these expenditures went toward the salaries of the agricultural administration, whose services to the peasant sector were minimal, in part because it had neither transport to reach cultivators nor resources to offer them. Its major output was statistical tables calculated within its offices; its guesses were aggregated into official national output figures. The excellent research infrastructure created by the colonial administration, generally reputed to be the best in Africa in the 1950s, had lost its function. In the cogent summation of Popelier, agricultural research consisted of "22 inert stations where administration had replaced scientific progress."[83] Neither the state nor private investors found agricultural investment attractive; while agriculture accounted for 15 percent of total investment in 1958, in 1972 the figure was only 3.7 percent.[84]

Even where resources were allocated to agriculture, their impact was doubtful. In 1968, for example, the state set aside a substantial sum for agricultural credit. An elaborate procedure was established for its apportionment, which, according to Mobutu, would be wholly decentralized "so that these funds will not be allocated from the capital for the exclusive profit of those who directly or indirectly can defend their claims in Kinshasa offices."[85] The land rights of the applicant had to be attested by the local chief and countersigned by the zone commissioner. The claim had to provide full details on the farm and data demonstrating how credit would expand output. The local agricultural officer had to make a site visit to evaluate the request, which was forwarded to the regional agricultural director. The zone commissioner had to attach a certificate attesting to the moral integrity of the applicant. The request was then forwarded to Kinshasa for disposition. Given these procedures, it is not surprising that none of the fifty-nine persons in Shaba who applied through these channels received a favorable response. It is true that a number of the requests were ambitious; twenty-four of the fifty-nine applicants asked for $10,000 or more, and one sought $1 million.

There were beneficiaries of the agricultural credit program in Shaba. Some Z 61,884 was accorded to fifteen persons, all of whom introduced their candidacies in Kinshasa, and none of whom were farmers, as far as could be determined. The successful applicants were members of the politico-commercial class. While it is possible that the trucks for which the credit was primarily given transported some farm produce, the program as implemented bore no resemblance to a credit plan for farmers.

Another critical function of the state in sustaining agriculture is the maintenance of a rural road network. Here endemic problems have arisen. Though there have been significant expenditures, their efficacy has been diluted by the difficulty of imposing performance standards on private contractors, and even more by problems entailed in carrying out work through the state public works department (or, after 1971, through the road-building parastatal *Office des Routes*, popularly known as the "Office des Trous"—i.e., office of potholes). It is estimated that the serviceable road network had dwindled from 140,000 kilometers in 1959 to 20,000 by the early 1970s.[86] Though roads had been one of the infrastructural weaknesses before independence as well, and these frequently cited figures somewhat overstate the contrast between colonial times and the present, the impact of the decline has nonetheless been great. Rural transport costs are from 40 to 50 percent higher than before independence, and truck life is no more than 50,000 miles.

The decaying road system helps to explain the immobilization of the state agricultural services. The state vehicle stock swiftly deteriorates. The chronic lack of operating funds means that the state is frequently unable to repair its vehicles when they do encounter breakdowns. In the Shaba region agricultural service in 1972 there were a total of thirty-three vehicles, thirty of which were inoperative. The three usable cars were at regional headquarters in Lubumbashi. Some thirty-nine tractors had been provided to the region, of which only four were in working order.[87]

Agricultural pricing policies

In addition to the regime's inability to deliver positive agricultural services, several of its agricultural policies have had a clearly demonstrated negative impact. Probably the most serious is the pricing policy, which has generated systematic disincentives. The practice of fixing purchasing prices for peasant crops extends far back into the colonial past, a by-product of the regulative Bula Matari mentality. Also a colonial legacy is the tendency to hold down food prices to producers so that urban wages may be held down as well. Over the years, this policy has been justified by three shopworn arguments: the need to sustain the profitability of the industrial sector, to fight inflation, and to curb urban social unrest. But its obvious impact has been to discourage village production and to foster profits in the trading sector. Traders make use of the state-fixed prices to restrict payments they make to villagers, while evading price controls on urban markets when disposing of their purchases. The ability of merchants to enforce price ceilings on peasants is enhanced by the long-standing state policy of according monopolies on buying privileges to public or private intermediaries. Villagers situated close enough to urban markets may evade these regulations and policies, particularly in Bas-Zaire.

The impact of state-determined prices on returns to farmers may be illustrated by early 1970s data for maize and cotton. In the case of maize, farmers were receiving 2 cents per kilo; with average yields of 625 kilos per hectare, an average family maize plot size of .5 hectare, and 75–100 person/days of labor per plot required, the return was only $13, if the entire production could be sold.[88] Cotton returns were quite comparable: with a price in the early 1970s of 12 cents per kilo, yields averaging 200 kilos per hectare, and an average .5 hectare plot size, the peasant could expect a return of $12 for 125 days of family labor committed to cotton output.

The problematic impact of state policy on the peasant also shows up in coffee production. Prices have been kept relatively low, and marketing services have been inadequate. Particularly revealing is the failure of the peasant to share significantly in the extraordinary coffee price surge of 1976–78, recounted below. The state moved to preempt a considerable fraction of this short windfall for itself, and through its action permitted a large part of the remainder to accrue to coffee traders, many of them politicians.

For the peasant producer coffee is a relatively profitable crop. Table 10.9 indicates that returns on labor—the main input for small farmers—is much higher for coffee than it is for most other crops in Zaire. This explains why, in spite of unfavorable state policies, coffee output has actually increased since independence, although it is estimated that as much as 30 percent of it is not purchased.[89]

After a Brazilian frost in 1975 sent coffee prices rocketing to the unprecedented level of $3.30 a pound (up from an average of 60 cents in the

Table 10.9 Returns to Peasant Farm Labor, Northern Zaire, 1973–1974

	Palm oil	Coffee	Cotton (forest)	Cotton (savanna)	Cocoa	Rice	Peanuts
Days labor/person per hectare	1,204.7	3,557.2	225.5	198	1,349.1	454.1	415.6
Yield (kilogram/hectare)	8,580	1,520	400	400	300	1,000	2,700
Price (makuta/kilogram)	0.35	10	6	6	20	4	2
Gross revenue (makuta per person/day)	39.88	68.36	10.64	12.12	71.15	8.80	4.81

Source: Eric F. Tollens, "An Economic Analysis of Cotton Production, Marketing and Processing in Northern Zaire" (Ph.D. diss., Michigan State University, 1975), p. 222.

early 1970s), the price paid to peasants in Zaire for robusta cherry was raised from 9 to 14.3 makuta per kilo in February 1976—the first such price hike since 1972, though the money had lost more than half its value. At the same time, the state added a surcharge of 65 makuta per kilo, which was in addition to an export tax averaging 17.9 percent of the world market value. These calculations make clear the negative impact of state policy upon the coffee growers. The world price went up more than fivefold, while the share permitted to the peasants by the state through the prices it fixed was less than the erosion of buying power by inflation since the previous price rise. It was entirely reasonable that the state capture its portion of the windfall through increased export tax—but the disproportion between the state and peasant shares was striking. Even less justifiable was the failure of the state to stop illegal export rackets, in which some of its top political personnel participated; this leakage in effect transferred benefits from the peasant to the political class. According to official figures, coffee export earnings in 1976 should have totalled 272 million zaires, while the real return was only 80 million; this amounted to an illicit tax of about 1 zaire per kilo.[90] The distribution of returns from the coffee bonanza works out as follows:

Price increase per kilo		Z 3.63/kg.
Peasant price increase	Z .106	
(adjusted to take account of		
weight loss in processing)		
Rise in export tax	Z .65	
Export surcharge	Z .65	
Illicit tax	Z 1.00	
Total		Z 2.406
Balance for marketing intermediaries		Z 1.224

The negative impact of state pricing policies has been equally clear in the palm oil sector. After World War I, and until the 1970s, palm oil had been the most important agricultural export. The industry was based primarily on indigenous palms, spontaneous and planted; Zairians harvested the palm fruits, and export firms processed the fruits and marketed the oil. From the 1930s on some of the foreign firms began to develop improved plantations; these were rapidly expanded during the 1950s, encouraged by a prolonged period of favorable prices.[91] By 1960 there were 220,000 hectares of high-yield plantations, of which one-third had not yet begun to bear.

Much of the palm oil production occurred in the zones most affected by First Republic disorder. Production fell sharply, bottoming in 1965 at little more than half the 1959 level. With the advent of the Mobutu regime, production recovered to 80 percent of its pre-independence peak. A total ·of 20,000 hectares were planted from 1960 to 1970, when new planting was virtually halted.

In 1967 a two-tier pricing system for palm oil had been established. Companies were required to deliver half their production at a fixed price of 69 zaires for the domestic market, while the remainder would be sold abroad at the world market price, which was quite stable during these years at just over 100 zaires per ton. However, production costs varied from 73 zaires per ton of palm oil on the best plantations to 95 zaires per ton for oil produced from wild palm fruits. An export tax of 22.11 percent was levied on the fraction that was exported. Enormous profits went to the commercial intermediaries who were able to acquire domestic palm oil at the fixed price; in Goma in 1976, a ton of palm oil was worth 1,000 zaires.[92]

Although the export value of palm oil doubled in 1974, exports were on an inexorable downward trend by that time. By the second half of 1975 Zaire had to suspend exports to assure a supply for the domestic market, which had expanded from 50,000 tons in 1960 to 181,000 tons in 1971 as a result of explosive urbanization. In September 1975 the domestic price was raised to 145 zaires per ton; the rise failed to compensate for inflation, which had increased production costs to 150–200 zaires per hectare. In 1959, with a total output of palm products at 412,000 tons, Zaire had been the world's second-largest producer; by 1979, the figure had fallen to 110,000 tons.[93]

For the peasants in palm oil production, the low prices and the unreliability of the marketing system were discouraging factors. Further dislocations came from Zairianization and radicalization of the plantations. The Bank of Zaire, in its annual reports, has repeatedly drawn attention to the harmful impact of state policy on the palm oil sector. For the foreseeable future Zaire seems out of the palm oil export market, and there is a serious likelihood that substantial imports may be required. This situation is largely imputable to state action.

For the plantation sector of the rural economy in general there has been a slow rundown of the capital stock and processing installations. The extremely high profitability of plantation enterprises in the 1950s induced rapid expansion, with corporate plantations established in Bandundu, Equateur, and Haut-Zaire, and individual settlers in an arc from Uele to

Kibali-Ituri and the lake regions of Kivu. These plantations were almost wholly devoted to perennial crops, with plantings dating from the 1950s. Thus it was possible to continue exploitation of existing plantings with minimal investment. Until 1973 the corporate structure remained largely unchanged, while a good portion of the individual Belgian settlers sold their farms to Greeks.

A long-term decline of the plantation sector was already in course before 1973. In that year Zairianization compounded the trend with extensive short-term asset-stripping. The Bank of Zaire's 1975 report, analyzing agricultural stagnation, laid emphasis on "the paralysis resulting from the abandonment of a large number of agro-industrial enterprises given to certain Zairians in the framework of the Zairianization measures."[94]

Marketing offices: cotton

One more ingredient was added to the recipe for rural disaster with the emergence in 1972 of state marketing offices to monopolize the purchase of major crops. The creation of the Office National des Fibres Textiles (ONAFITEX)—a cotton board—and the Office National du Café (ONC) in 1972 was followed by eight others at the end of 1973. These boards anticipated the comprehensive set of state marketing offices established under Zairianization.

The birth of ONAFITEX, pacesetter among the state marketing offices, was a logical development in the multifront battle for economic mastery by the state. The inherited structure of cotton production was the very paradigm of the colonial economy. Cotton was an entirely peasant crop; at its production peak in the 1950s some 800,000 peasant households were incorporated in the cotton-centered economy. The expansion of cotton production was closely tied to a 1917 decree under which compulsory cultivation was organized. It was not until the 1930s that output became substantial; production rose from 21,800 tons of seed cotton in 1929 to 132,100 in 1936. In the 1950s output fluctuated between 102,900 tons in 1952 to an all-time record of 180,000 tons (equal to 60,000 tons of lint) in 1959.[95] Coercion was the linchpin of the cotton system; as Lacroix laconically observes, *encadrement administratif* was the major input, in place of material incentives or fertilizer.[96] Enforced by a dense network of agricultural agents employed by the state and the cotton companies, reinforced by the local administration and chiefs (who received a bonus for each kilo produced), exhortation (*propagande agricole*), fines, and prison made the cotton production machinery turn around.

Table 10.10   Comparative State Cotton Prices, 1970 (in
U.S. cents per kilogram)

Zaire	8.62
Central African Republic	10.8
Cameroon	11.52
Benin	10.08
Chad	9.36
Ivory Coast	12.6
Uganda	15.44
Nigeria	17.5
Ethiopia	25.2

Source: Tollens, "An Economic Analysis of Cotton Production,"
p. 65.

A compenetrated structure of parastatal organs and private monopolies handled the processing and marketing of cotton. A parastatal marketing board, COGERCO, financed the crop and marketed it overseas. Private colonial companies, of which the most important was the Société Générale subsidiary COTONCO (Compagnie Cotonnière Congolaise), bought and ginned the cotton in assigned monopoly zones and provided sundry human and economic infrastructural services (seed distribution, feeder-road maintenance, social services, technical advice). The price received by the peasant was a residual, computed after the deduction of all operating costs, profits of the companies and COGERCO, and state export taxes. This system, which transferred all risk to the state—especially to the peasant—and which assured supply by force, induced the extension of cotton cultivation to many areas where its potential for real returns to producers was small, given the high labor requirements. The dice were loaded against the peasant at every turn. He had to pay directly for the regulatory machinery which forced him to grow the cotton (salaries of cotton company agents were deductible as a cost before the peasant's price was fixed). Gin-neries operated on a cost-plus basis, which provided high returns for maximum throughput but no incentive for low operating costs, thus reinforcing the pressure on farmers to grow cotton on marginal land. The farmer was faced with a single buying outlet; further, the railways were permitted to charge unusually high levies on cotton (twice what was charged for manioc). Tollens has found that both before and after independence Zaire almost always paid a lower price for cotton than neighboring countries (table 10.10).[97]

After independence the number of cotton planters dropped substan-

Table 10.11   Returns to Peasants on Main Cash Crops, Gandajika, 1974

	Price (makuta/ kilogram)	Yield per hectare (kilograms)	Days labor/ person per hectare	Gross return per hectare	Return per person/day
Cotton	7	941	180	Z 65.87	.37
Cassava	10	1,700	301	Z 170.00	.56
Corn	15	2,600	156	Z 390.00	2.50

Sources: Tshibangu Banza-Muakula, "La réforme des structures agricoles au Zaire: Cas de l'Office National des Fibres Textiles (ONAFITEX) et la culture cotonnière dans la Zone de Gandajika" (Mémoire de licence, Faculté des Sciences Sociales, Politiques, et Administratives, Université de Zaire, Lumumbashi, 1975), pp. 54–55, 71–73; Agency for International Development, Kinshasa, "Cassava Outreach," 6 July 1978. The Tshibangu date came from local archives and interviews with farmers; the person-per-day data are based upon the AID document.

Note: It should be noted that Gandajika is an exceptionally fertile area, and has access to the Mbuji-Mayi urban market for food crops.

tially, above all in producing areas where yields were lowest. Those producers remaining have been in good measure kept within the cotton production system by the timeworn mechanism of coercion. In an interesting survey carried out by Tollens in about 1972 in two high-yield cotton areas of northern Zaire, 86 percent of the producers indicated that they raised cotton because they were forced to. Some 63.5 percent tilled cotton fields designated for them by local agricultural agents. Disobedience of the cotton regulations still incurred relatively heavy punishment, with fines in the early 1970s averaging Z 3.50 and jail sentences averaging twenty-five days. In addition to the cotton imposition, 83.7 percent of the farmers reported that they had been required to work on road maintenance for an average of six or seven weeks per year, while 41.4 percent had spent an average of ten and a half weeks on conscripted labor for the fields of the chief.[98] Tshibangu, in research carried out in 1974 in Gandajika, one of the highest-producing cotton areas, found that revenues from both manioc and corn were far higher than returns on cotton (see table 10.11).

In the best of circumstances the maintenance of peasant cotton output would have been a heroic struggle. And as with other crops, the pricing policies pursued by the state have constituted another handicap; prices have declined in real terms even if they have risen a little in nominal terms (table 10.12). While the real return on cotton was never high, it has diminished sharply since independence. Popelier, who also interviewed in

Gandajika, records the eloquent explanation of one cultivator for his abandonment of cotton:

> Before independence, profits from my cotton permitted me to buy seven goats; now, I cannot even obtain the value of one. That's why I now grow cassava, which gives me enough to buy four goats.[99]

Under these circumstances, one may well understand why cotton output fell as low as 8,500 tons of lint in 1976, and the number of planters to 350,000. In recent years, except for 1969 and 1970, Zaire has become a net cotton importer; its six textile mills require 20,000 tons of lint to operate at capacity.

The colonial structure for cotton marketing could hardly be sustained in the new context of independence. An initial change occurred in 1962 when a somewhat more restrictive formula for reimbursing operating costs for the private companies was adopted. According to Popelier, this led at once to the systematic falsification of vouchers by the companies to inflate their operating cost figures.[100] The maneuver was well known to the Zairian authorities. Other frictions accumulated when the companies sought to curtail operations outside high-yield zones, whereas Zaire wanted maximum total production. In addition, the regime was convinced that the companies employed an excessive number of high-cost expatriate personnel, and that more vigorous Africanization could lower production costs and permit a rise in producer prices. The companies were further ac-

Table 10.12   Cotton Prices (current prices; makuta per kilo, seed cotton)

	1st quality	2d quality (makuta)
1950	2.50	1
1951	4.5	3
1952–55	5.35	4
1955–60	5.85	4
1960–67	4.5	3
1967–70	5	4
1970–73	6	5
1974	7	5
1975	8	5
1976–77	20	15

Source: Tshibangu, "La réforme des structures agricoles," p. 36, drawn from ONAFITEX files.

cused of defrauding the state of Z 2 million. The companies charged that COGERCO was unable to fulfill its obligation to provide timely crop financing, thereby disrupting buying operations.

This war of attrition led to the sudden creation of ONAFITEX in 1972 to replace the buying operations of both COGERCO and the private companies. Bitter negotiations followed, during which an effort was made to agree on terms for the state to lease the private infrastructure, primarily the aging ginneries. When no accord was reached as the 1972 buying season approached, the government announced that it would requisition the ginneries on its own terms for the short term, and that it would build new ginneries as quickly as possible. The companies were to be permitted to recuperate the functionless and decrepit ginneries; many dated from the 1930s—and all from before 1960.[101] Feelings ran very high, and a number of incidents were reported of sabotage of cotton stocks and plants by disgruntled expatriate personnel.[102]

There was a degree of hope and a surge of good will for ONAFITEX when it began its operations, but the inadequacy of its performance soon dissipated this psychological capital. In Gandajika, Tshibangu found that the new office at once eliminated the quite popular payment of a bonus-in-kind of one kilo of low-grade salt per kilo of cotton, which had added one likuta to the real price. Also abandoned were most of the social activities once carried out by the companies. In 1973 the road-building function carried out by the companies was ceded to the notorious *Office des Routes*, resulting in a cessation of most road maintenance. The number of buying stations diminished, and the ONAFITEX buying agents, demoralized by their low salaries, became susceptible to corruption. Complaints on this score were legion; as one peasant put it, "We are fed up with these buying agents who demand goats, chickens, or bottles of alcohol before buying our produce."[103]

The growing financial and exchange crisis faced by the state from 1974 on added new problems for ONAFITEX. Fuel and spare parts for vehicles and ginneries became hard to obtain. With ginneries down for long periods of time, difficulties in warehousing unginned cotton arose. The loss of middle-level cadres associated with the companies made more difficult the maintenance of the physical plant. By 1974, ONAFITEX was no longer able to gin the full crop and backlogs of unginned cotton built up—a problem which persisted into 1978. Making use of a special presidential donation, ONAFITEX ordered thirty new ginneries for about $1 million, but they have yet to be installed.[104] With domestic cotton not available, and no foreign exchange for imports, the textile mills experienced frequent shutdowns. Although the U.S. Department of Agriculture reported in

1978 that the managerial performance of ONAFITEX was improving—an improvement reflected in a somewhat larger 1977 crop—the viability of existing marketing formulas remains to be demonstrated, as does the capacity of ONAFITEX to substitute incentives for coercion.[105] The available evidence made irresistible the conclusion of Tshibangu: "At least until now, ONAFITEX seems guilty of a number of deficiencies. . . . It is clear that exploitation of the peasant sector, sometimes unconscious, will continue until the authorities take real account of the situation in which the peasants find themselves."[106] The regime finally came to the same conclusion, abolishing ONAFITEX by the end of 1978, and returning to a formula based on cooperation with the former cotton companies. Cotton marketing arrangements appeared to improve; production rose from a low of 16,000 tons in the late 1970s to 40,000 by 1983.

Other agricultural marketing parastatals

The coffee office (ONC) has experienced similar difficulties. It was endowed with a substantial initial capital of $44 million, the disposition of which led to the arrest of the first director. It operated through delegation of its buying rights to local brokers, in many cases political figures. They were granted lucrative cost and profit margins by the ONC, and frequently were able to use the leverage their buying monopoly to pay less than the state-fixed price or to undergrade the coffee purchased. A case study of the ONC office in Beni well documents its operating deficiencies. In 1974, at a time when the peasant was paid 9 makuta per kilo for robusta cherry and 17 makuta for arabica parchment, brokers received a commission officially set at Z 1.10 per kilo of robusta and 1.20 for arabica.[107]

A similar pattern appeared in the *Office National des Céréales* (ONACER), established in early 1974 to handle maize and rice purchases. In the case of maize, planted by an estimated one million farmers, ONACER had an immediate negative impact on marketing, in spite of price rises from about 2 makuta per kilo to 4 makuta in 1974, and to 7.5 makuta in 1975. The expulsion of foreign traders who had previously handled maize marketing created a vacuum that ONACER lacked the capacity to fill; for example, in one area of Kasai Occidental where there was a maize surplus the number of maize buyers fell from fifty-four private traders in 1970 to four Zairian ONACER brokers in 1975. Though one evaluation of ONACER found that its leadership was able, it lacked the financial and organizational structures to cope with marketing of the crop. Thus from 1974 to 1977, when as much as one-third of the desperately short foreign exchange was spent to import food for the cities, large amounts of maize rotted in the countryside.[108] ONACER subsequently set the more modest objective of handling only 20–25 percent of the crop, and permitted a private grain marketing trade to operate.

Of the eleven state marketing offices created in the 1971–74 period, all ran into serious difficulties. In 1978, partly under external pressure from creditors, seven of the agricultural offices were abolished; by 1984 only one (in ranching) was left. In this respect, Zaire has stood out among African states, many of whom find their rural economies stifled by the dead weight of ineffective, extortionate, and often venal agricultural marketing monopolies. No other state to date has dismantled this sector in such a sweeping way.

Other burdens imposed by the state on the rural sector should be noted. The extraordinary fiscal exactions on villagers, and the insecurity created by the deployment of security forces in the countryside are potent disincentives. The pervasive roadblocks encountered on rural roads contribute little to public safety and add considerably to marketing costs, as payments are generally required to pass. One visitor in 1973 counted eighteen roadblocks in the 300 kilometers between Matadi and Kinshasa.[109]

The continuing inability of the state agricultural services to provide support to the farmer must also be noted. The negative legacy of a predisposition towards coercive solutions remains. While there are many functionaries of competence and good will, these characteristics are rarely translated into effective support for villagers. Guy Verhaegen offers a cogent assessment of the limitations of the service: "Unfortunately, the agricultural services have inherited this [colonial] spirit, and still think far too much in terms of imposition (notoriously ineffective), and not in terms of stimulants. . . . They are resented by the populace as an organ of control and constraint."[110]

Agricultural policy is more than simply a weak point in the overall pattern of state action. The rural sector faces a profound and far-reaching crisis that which raises the most fundamental questions about the development and the potential of the state. The balance sheet is not just negative— it is catastrophic.

The crisis of the state and the economy

The decomposition of the state at the center has been marked by a growing loss of control over public finances. From 1967, when the stabilization

Table 10.13   Public Finance, 1970–1977 (in million of zaires, at current prices)

	Government expenditures	Government revenues	Surplus/ deficit
1970	369	343	−26
1971	405	324	−81
1972	431	338	−93
1973	578	429	−149
1974	936	592	−344
1975	604	432	−172
1976	799	486	−313
1977	1,008	699	−310

Sources: Banque du Zaire, *Rapport annuel*, 1975, p. 100; U.S. Department of Commerce, "Foreign Economic Trends and their Implications for the United States, Zaire," June 1978.

plan was implemented, until 1972, overall state operations had been under reasonable control. From 1973 on, public expenditures soared; in 1973 and 1974 revenues also rose (by a lesser amount than expenditures), but when the full impact of the copper price decline was felt, revenues fell sharply. Huge deficits appeared, along with large-scale budget overruns: in 1974 actual outlays for the operating budget were 163 percent of the budgeted figures; in 1975 the figure was 128 percent (see table 10.13).[111]

The state consumes a remarkably high fraction of the GDP, as table 10.14 demonstrates. While to a lesser degree this pattern was also characteristic of the colonial state economy, the proportion of state consumption has increased, and a greater fraction is devoted to the operating budget than to the capital budget. Most of the operating budget goes to remunerate state personnel, a fact which raises questions about productivity.

The once-sturdy currency has been buffeted by all of these trends. Although Mobutu had earlier insisted that his money would never be devalued, both the crisis and the insistence of external patrons left no choice. From the official value of Z 1 = $2 which prevailed from 1967 to 1975, the zaire was devalued six times (in March 1976, February 1978, January 1979, August 1979, February 1980 and mid-1983) to an official exchange rate in early 1980 of Z 1 = $0.34; further reductions devalued it to $0.18 in mid-1981 and less than $0.03 in 1983.

A singular anti-inflation action was undertaken at the end of 1979, when the regime suddenly announced "demonetization" measures. (On the inflation rate, see table 10.15.) The banknotes for 5 and 10 zaires the largest denominations then in circulation, were nullified and had to be ex-

Table 10.14 State Consumption Levels (in millions of zaires, at current prices)

	Commercialized GDP	Government expenditures as % of GDP
1970	857.3	43%
1971	918.5	44%
1972	1,003.4	43%
1973	1,354.2	43%
1974	1,663.4	56%
1975	1,626.0	47%

Source: U.S. Dept. of Commerce, "Foreign Economic Trends and their Implications for the United States, Zaire," June 1978.

Table 10.15 Inflation, 1970–1978

	Inflation rate
1971	8.7%
1972	6.6%
1973	9.3%
1974	30.4%
1975	59.3%
1976	63.3%
1977	58.0%
1978	80.0% (estimate)

Sources: U.S. Dept. of Commerce, "Foreign Economic Trends and their Implications for the United States, Zaire," June, 1978; Kamitatu, *Le Pouvoir à la portée du peuple*, p. 36.

changed for new currency with up to a fixed maximum of 3,000 zaires. Many merchants as well as ordinary citizens held much of their savings in cash, either because of distance from banks or lack of confidence in financial institutions; many of those who lacked access to the centers of power or who were distant from banks lost all their cash savings. The upper echelon of the politico-commercial class either had advance notice of the operation or generally found ways to evade its impact.

In sum, the economic wheel has come full circle under the New Regime. The First Republic had left a legacy of stagnation and dislocation which served as a major justification for the power seizure by the Mobutu regime. During an initial period the Mobutist state succeeded in mastering the elements of dislocation, creating a mood of optimism in the early

1970s. By 1974, what appeared at first to be only momentary conjunctural misfortunes began to lay bare the far-reaching crisis of the state: the destruction of the rural sector, the mortgaging of the future of the society to a costly copper-energy development strategy, and the corrosion of the structures of the public sector. By 1977, negative growth rates had been experienced: 6.1 percent in 1975, 4.3 percent in 1976, 1.9 percent in 1977; negative figures were also recorded for 1978 and 1979. One careful study concluded that by 1980 the GDP was no more in real terms than it had been in 1959, although the population had doubled.[112] The crushing external debt is linked to gigantic projects such as Inga II and Inga-Shaba, which appear to have no early prospect of generating revenue for repayment. The Inga-Shaba line in particular seems certain to incur an operating deficit for many years, even if and when it finally becomes operational. Most of the cost of this many-dimensional catastrophe is shouldered by the mass of the populace. The negative terms of trade between state and society reflect a crisis far more profound than that of 1965—a crisis whose ultimate implications and final resolution evoke the most somber perspectives.

II

Zairianization and Radicalization: Anatomy of a Disaster

> *This 30th of November must be, for us, a decisive turning point in our history. . . .*
> *Zaire is the country which, up till now, has been the most heavily exploited in the world. . . .*
> *That is why, given the constitutional oath to guarantee the total independence of the Republic of Zaire, which I swore before you in this room, I announce to you the great decisions I have taken to put an end to exploitation.*
> *That is why farms, ranches, plantations, concessions, commerce, and real estate agencies will be turned over to sons of the country.*
> *This recuperation of our properties will take place with respect for the property rights of others.*
> *For an equitable compensation for the former owners is foreseen under the control of the state.*
>
> 30 November 1973 speech of
> President Mobutu to the National
> Legislative Council

> *Qui va partager le butin? (Who will divide the loot?)*
> Question posed by a student
> during a public debate on the
> 30 November measures, UNAZA
> Kinshasa campus, December
> 1973

Zairianization: motivating factors

The sweeping measures announced by President Mobutu on 30 November 1973 appeared to be a breathtaking bid for economic independence. Soon to be dubbed "Zairianization," these decisions provided for the seizure of a vast swath of the economy which had remained in foreign hands:

326

most commerce, most of the plantation sector, many small industries, construction firms, transportation, and property-holding enterprises. When Zairianization began to encounter serious difficulties late in 1974, Mobutu plunged even further into the uncharted seas of economic adventure, proclaiming a "radicalization of the Zairian revolution" on 30 December 1974. This set of decisions was a major factor in the contradictions, then the crisis, which engulfed the regime from 1974 on; by 1976, Zairianization and radicalization had been simply abandoned. A careful inquest into these melodramatic reforms and their ultimate failure will illuminate some crucial characteristics of the Zairian state: the contradiction between its expansive ambitions and its practical capabilities, the inner logic of the symbiosis between state and class formation, and the limitations of the personalist, patrimonial structure of power.[1]

A number of motivating factors may be discerned behind these measures. To begin with, Zairianization may be seen as part of a broader African trend toward displacement of foreigners from the commercial sector. In Zaire, as in many other African states, the colonial period had seen the emergence of a mercantile sector, frequently populated by immigrants of Mediterranean or Asian origin, on the margin of the great capitalist enterprises. In Zaire the colonial state had erected a diversity of what Mukenge describes as "blocking mechanisms," which effectively foreclosed all but the most petty trade to Zairians.[2] Though a number of the larger trading houses in Zaire were Belgian, a large fraction of the commercial sector was in the hands of Portuguese (in western Zaire), Greeks, Italians, and Jews (eastern Zaire), and, later, Pakistanis (especially in the Northeast). The familial character of many of these enterprises, and their ready adaptability to irregular forms of commerce (smuggling, foreign exchange traffic), made them quite resistant to Africanization, and also, in many cases, exceedingly profitable. When it became evident in Zaire and elsewhere that this sector would not shrink of its own accord, and potential African rivals (whether of political or mercantile background) began to clamor for full access to trade, a number of states moved to curb immigrant traders, or even to expel them. Between 1968 and 1973 measures to assure the primacy of nationals in commerce and some industrial sectors were taken in Ghana, Sierra Leone, Zambia, Malawi, Uganda, and Nigeria.[3] Of particular importance for Zaire were the indigenization decrees in Nigeria, initiated in 1972; with Mobutu at this juncture grasping for continental leadership, it was uncomfortable to be outflanked in economic self-assertion by the other giant state of tropical Africa. Whatever the excesses of certain states—the erratic economic war of Idi Amin, the displacement of many thousands of alien African traders in Ghana—localization of the secondary and tertiary sectors of African economies seemed to be an idea whose time had come.

We may also see the Zairianization measures as an expression of the state impulse to seek economic autonomy. A commitment to economic nationalism, reflecting this impulse, was enshrined in the MPR ideological cornerstone, the 1967 N'Sele Manifesto. "Economic independence is the essential goal toward which all efforts of the nation must be directed," read the document.

The patrimonialization of power also played its part. The cement of clientage was access to resources. The sudden takeover of this huge zone of the economy offered a vast new pool of goods for patrimonial distribution to deserving members of the political class.

The material ambitions of the politico-commercial class were another critical factor motivating the lunge to Zairianization. The president perhaps viewed the seizure of commercial establishments and plantations as a way of creating a new reserve of prebends to be used for the manipulation and control of the political bourgeoisie; from the perspective of members of this dominant class, forcing open access to these very profitable spheres of ownership offered a decisive opportunity to consolidate their status. Potentially lucrative assets were to be acquired as virtually free goods; the political capital of proximity to power could be thus converted into solid material equity with the promise of effortless accumulation. Among other things, the Zairianization measures were a class action by the politico-commercial bourgeoisie. It was through the trauma of these events that the class character of the state and the regime became fully manifest.

Precursors of 30 November

Though the 30 November announcement took most by complete surprise, there were a number of precursors to the actual event. The tone of official rhetoric relating to economic nationalism had become markedly more strident; in the months before Zairianization references to foreign traders as "bloodsuckers" and "vultures" began to appear in the press. In a speech to a large Kinshasa crowd on 25 November 1972, Mobutu declared that consideration was being given to reserving small- and medium-sized businesses to Zairians; on a Brussels street, he noted, the shops one passes are all owned by Belgians. In the weeks preceding 30 November, the official press began to hint that a forthcoming major presidential address would reveal a dramatic reinforcement of economic independence.

Some specific government measures were also harbingers. On 14 July 1972, taxi and private bus ownership was restricted to Zairians. Particularly in Kinshasa and Lubumbashi, the huge distances and the inadequacy of public transport made such enterprise a risky but very profitable undertaking; it had the further advantage of requiring only a modest sum for entry, and could be managed part-time. In 1971 many thousands of West African traders, whose specialty had been smuggling and contraband, were expelled and their assets confiscated.[4] Most directly, 30 November was foreshadowed by a law of 5 January 1973 which stipulated that the export-import trade, wholesale and retail commerce, and certain commercial services were to be reserved for Zairians.[5]

The 5 January law on commerce provoked a brief flurry of concern, but soon appeared to be stillborn. The Political Bureau, less than a month after publication of the law, decided that foreign traders who were already established in the country were not covered by the legislation. The law made no provision for a compulsory acquisition of foreign firms.[6] While there was a palpable malaise in the foreign business community as a result of the general political atmosphere, the radical verbal positions taken by the regime, and the regime's new-found intimacy with China, there was no sense of imminent cataclysm. Possibly a number of foreign merchants escalated their export of profits through the classic devices of over-invoicing and the use of parallel currency exchanges; but for most business was good in 1973, and their affairs flourished.

The unveiling of Zairianization before the National Legislative Council was a remarkable demonstration of Mobutu's now-total personal rule. In the course of a marathon speech, which included a lengthy historical disquisition on the character of colonial exploitation, Mobutu announced in a few closing paragraphs the broad outline of this extraordinary takeover. No reference was made to the participation in this move of either the Political Bureau or the Council of Ministers; "important decisions have been taken," Mobutu announced, without needing to add that he was the sole author. In the informal constitutionalism of the new order, a presidential speech has force of law. The wisdom, timeliness, or feasibility of the Zairianization measures were totally outside the realm of discourse. There remained only the task of deciding how the concept of Zairianization was to be applied.

Enough public hints concerning the general nature of the measures had been given to alert political elites as to what might be coming. Possibly Mobutu had confided his intentions to the inner circle of presidential courtiers. A confidential joint session of the Political Bureau, Council of Ministers, and deputies had taken place 16 November, in which economic independence was discussed.[7] Yet no evidence has come to light of any careful discussion preceding Zairianization about ways and means of implementation and the probable hazards ahead. In solitary reflection, Mobutu cast the country upon a perilous voyage.

Launching Zairianization

The first announcement was at once sweeping and vague. "Plantations, ranches, . . . commerce" were to come into Zairian hands, but the precise boundaries of these concepts were in no way defined. Indeed, Mobutu paid special tribute in the discourse to Lever Plantations, one of the largest foreign-owned chains. The interests of "good investors"—later defined as those who had brought in capital subsequent to enactment of the 1969 investment code—would be protected and encouraged; their enterprises were exempted from the measures. Those proprietors whose initial capital was loaned by the colonial agency for credit to settlers were expropriated outright; others would be compensated over a ten-year period from the profits of their former businesses.[8]

In interpreting this initial text, considered to be the juridical foundation of Zairianization, some observers understood that Mobutu intended "commerce" to refer only to rural enterprise and the plantation sector. As a Zairian jurist who devoted a four-hundred-page tome to the exegesis of Zairianization and radicalization observed laconically:

> Attentive reading of the presidential speech of 30 November 1973 reveals that only agricultural activities were targetted; these were to be reserved exclusively to Zairians. . . .
> In practice, a very broad interpretation was given to the orders of the chief of state. Thus, along with agricultural activities, commercial and even industrial enterprises were taken from foreigners to be attributed to Zairians.

Other components of the November 30 economic measures we will not consider in detail. A Zairian was named chief executive of Gécamines; charter companies were abolished; a new Zairian shipping line was announced; all motorists, exporters, and owners of commercial and industrial property were required to obtain their insurance through the national insurance parastatal the Société Nationale d'Assurance (SONAS, created in 1967), which was also to take over all real estate agency services. A monopoly on state construction contracts was to be reserved to a newly announced parastatal, the Entreprise Nationale du Construction.[10]

No small part of the enormous confusion which attended the actual attribution of the affected businesses arose because of the absence of a clear legal framework. A hasty ministerial edict was issued with the date of 30 November, which merely presented the Zairianization measures as the application of the law on commerce of 5 January 1973. This edict was supplemented by a paragraph on 10 December 1973 which gave the enterprises concerned three months to liquidate their stocks. On 25 January 1974 another supplementary edict declared that the intention of the liquidation of stocks was merely to have foreign owners turn stocks over to Zairian successors; this was to be accomplished by 1 March 1974. These edicts covered only the commercial enterprises, not plantations, which had not been mentioned in the law of 5 January. On 11 January 1974 a presidential ordinance was promulgated, completing the original ministerial edict. The ordinance is brief enough to quote in full:

> Ordinance-Law 74–019 of 11 January 1974,
> transferring to the State the property of
> certain private enterprises

THE PRESIDENT OF THE REPUBLIC

> Given the Constitution, notably article 14, item 3;
> Given the law 74–001 of 2 January 1974 authorizing
> the President of the Republic to take, in application
> of article 52 of the Constitution, measures having force of law,

ORDERS

> Article 1
> The transfer to the State of the property of agricultural and agro-industrial enterprises, quarries, brickyards, and large commercial units to be determined by the State, which belong either to foreign individuals or corporate entities, or to companies registered in Zaire whose capital is partly or wholly owned by foreigners.

> Article 2
> An equitable indemnity, whose sum will be fixed by the Council of Ministers, to be allocated to the former owners of the enterprises covered

in the previous article, with the exception of owners who benefitted from a loan granted by the *Société de Crédit aux Classes Moyennes et à l'Industrie*, and those who have abandoned their properties.

Settlement of the compensation will be made over a ten-year period, with one year of grace.

Article 3

The present Ordinance-Law is effective 1 December 1973.

> Done at Kinshasa, 11 January 1974
> Mobutu Sese Seko Kuku Ngbendu wa za Banga
> General of the Army[11]

It should be noted that Mobutu lacked the constitutional authority to proclaim the measures of 30 November. Only an ex post facto law enacted on 2 January 1974 offered legal cover for the edicts, which were nonetheless made retroactive to 1 December 1973; such formalities, however, were quite beside the point. More important, the law did not settle all ambiguities concerning which enterprises were to be subject to the measures, and it was wholly silent about who was to succeed to ownership and by what process, and how compensation was to be paid. But no one, whether former owner or potential successor, was much concerned at this time with the fine points of legality; what was central was the practical dynamics of property transfer.

Thus the first public reaction embraced both a sense of melodrama and uncertainty. The whole tone and thrust of the 30 November speech suggested that the president intended his measures as an historic turning point; there was no possibility that they would simply run into the sand, as had the law on commerce of 5 January 1973. But exactly what would come next, who would benefit, and what the impact would be were totally unclear at the time.

The initial response of the Zairian populace was moderately favorable. Certainly the general theme of economic nationalism struck responsive chords. Shopkeepers are rarely popular heroes, especially when they are foreign. One Zairian university student who surveyed a small sample of Lubumbashi residents not long after 30 November, found near unanimity in support of the principle of displacement of foreign traders.[12] Yet the level of animosity felt toward Greeks and Portuguese in Zaire was by no means as sharp as that felt by Ugandans toward Asian traders. Thus, while well received, the measures did not arouse a wave of enthusiasm like that briefly generated by Amin's 1972 economic war. Whatever favorable impact they had was quickly dissipated by the manner of implementation.

The top ranks of the political elite, as potential beneficiaries, obviously found the new mercantile pastures opened up by 30 November a veritable promised land. There was some discreet opposition within the walls, in particular among some senior public servants within the Bank of Zaire and the Finance Ministry, who could foresee the economic risks involved. But these apprehensions were not widely shared; buoyed by the scent of pelf, the politico-commercial class was caught up in the intoxicating conviction that its own prosperity was synonymous with that of society as a whole. The stormy applause which greeted the 30 November speech to the legislature was doubtless strengthened by the tantalizing hints of personal participation in economic independence:

> I do not prevent my collaborators from having, outside their functions, lucrative activities. I even encourage them. But they cannot use these as a pretext for not correctly fulfilling their responsibilities.
>
> As long as they clearly carry out their activities, I can only support them. Otherwise, for example, a legislator who has only his parliamentary duties would be unemployed at the end of his term.
>
> The measures on application of land laws which I have just announced must specifically permit all leaders to be useful to the country and to themselves. . . .
>
> Each year . . . the Department of Agriculture will make a detailed report on the work of the beneficiaries. Those who do not pay well their workers, those who do not make the annual payment to the former proprietors, will have the farms taken away from them and given to others.[13]

An early omen of subsequent public reaction to the political beneficiaries was heard when UNTZA leader Kikonge, in a speech to a gathering of workers, bitterly criticized the prospect of businesses being attributed to the deputies. The deputies, he asserted, did not deserve this favor, and were nothing more than an assortment of chiselling bunglers (*margoulins*). While the Kikonge speech was not reported in the official press, it did cause a minor sensation in Kinshasa and provoked intense corporate indignation among the politicians when the legislature met a few days later.[14]

Implementing the 30 November measures

Though Mobutu perhaps had a very general notion of what was intended by the 30 November measures, there had been virtually no consideration given to the details of application. The difficulties inherent in such sweeping measures were compounded by the total improvisation which characterized implementation. The general content of the measures was at once made known throughout the country by radio, and local administrators had to begin to act on its vague directives. In the weeks that followed the speech contradictory instructions emanated from diverse government offices. The confusion ensuing was increased by the long time it took these to reach the more distant corners of the country—often thirty days or more. Local administrators added their own improvised responses to the daily problems posed by the hasty and ill-digested instructions that eventually made their way outward from the central ministries.[15]

The first administrative preoccupation was to forestall sabotage by the proprietors facing expropriation. Indeed, one justification for the sudden announcement and the absence of detailed preplanning was the necessity of preventing anticipation of the measures and prior liquidation of businesses by foreign merchants and planters. Sabotage was evidently seen as a potential threat particularly from traders, whose capital was primarily tied up in inventory; plantation operators could not quickly liquidate their holdings. On 30 November, Interior Minister Kithima radioed the regional commissioners to be vigilant against subversion attempts. There followed on 2 December an instruction stipulating that foreigners were not to be molested, nor their stores looted. Foreign proprietors were ordered to maintain stocks in their stores.[16]

On 3 December the Council of Ministers met to discuss details of implementation. It was decided that the ministers of Agriculture, National Economy, and Commerce would be asked to complete a census of foreign-owned plantations, small and medium enterprises, and commercial businesses, and to begin receiving applications from aspiring Zairian successors, soon to be known as *acquéreurs*. The first public definition of the potential beneficiaries was provided in a communique from the Information Ministry, which noted that there was "no question of allocating properties . . . to insolvent nationals and even less of creating, in Zaire, a bourgeois class to the detriment of the laboring masses, these measures having been taken with the aim of bettering the living conditions of all Zairian citizens."[17]

The first really detailed instructions went out on 5 December. It was now specified that the turnover of properties would take place over three months. Local administrators were to proceed at once with a census of businesses, and proprietors and a state representative were to jointly establish inventories. Eventual compensation was to be based on the current value of the goods, and would be paid annually over a ten-year period. In a confidential postscript, administrators were told that in reality the takeover by *acquéreurs* should occur within a month.

Meanwhile, diverse measures were taken to prevent proprietors from absconding or stripping assets. Their bank accounts were blocked, though under state supervision they were permitted to make withdrawals for payment of personnel or restocking their enterprises. In fact, many held only small working balances in the banks. An immediate consequence was their ineligibility to receive credit for further orders, as their legal status was in doubt. Many ceased paying their personnel. They were forbidden to ship freight out of the country or to leave before property transfer was completed. At this stage most were waiting to see what expropriation would mean in practice and precisely what the compensation arrangements would be. Premature departure risked de facto abandonment of any subsequent claim. They were bitter, confused, and uncertain about the future; there were some incidents of real sabotage, and a vast web of rumor and innuendo suggesting many more.

During the month of December confusion reigned supreme as to who, in the oft-cited phrase of the Kinshasa student, would share in "the loot." Deputies had been promised on 30 November that they would be beneficiaries, though at first their shares were to be farms, not business houses; they were to be apostles of rural development. At the 11 December legislative session the presidential pledge that they would share personally in "economic independence" was renewed. In the major cities, somewhat apart from the politico-commercial class, there was the growing group of Zairian traders; though prosperity was difficult without political access, many of these persons were not politicians. What was to be their role? What would be the role of the very large ranks of petty bourgeois middle-level functionaries, secondary school teachers, junior army officers, and the like? Was the partition of the external estate to offer new opportunities to them as well?

A plenary session of the top political elite was held on 26 December to address this issue; the Political Bureau, the Council of Ministers, and deputies—roughly 300 persons—attended. A remarkably self-serving set of decisions emerged from this session. Some of the largest agroindustrial and commercial units, seen as "strategic," would become government parastatals. The major plantations and ranches and most large commercial businesses would go to the members of these three organs. "I intend," Mobutu said following the meeting, "to undertake this experiment with my close collaborators." Smaller stores could be allocated to local notables "who have the means and the vocation." The members of the top elite not present at the session saw themselves dealt out of the pelf. It was decided that, in order to maintain their independence and integrity, army officers, judges, functionaries, ambassadors, members of the regional administration, and

chiefs would be excluded. The cake was to be sliced at once; it was announced that the list of allocations would be published by 31 December.

Public reaction was swift and unanimous: universal indignation. The
regime organ *Elima* a week later published a revealing editorial by its editor, Essolomwa:

> In an earlier editorial . . . we had argued the well-founded rationale
> for this experiment, for we thought that the management of these busi-
> nesses was going to be confided to honest and dedicated men, chosen
> within the top three political organs. . . . This experience, we believed,
> would permit the creation of a state organism able to achieve systematic
> control over the means of production and distribution, to guarantee the
> interests of the worker-militant, and to gather the capital necessary for the
> harmonious development of the country.
>
> However, it turned out that the honorable representatives of the three
> supreme bodies had egocentric aims, and nursed the ambition of swallow-
> ing up everything. Some who we encountered had their chests swollen and
> quivered with self-satisfaction over the brilliant victory they had won. . . .
>
> Amongst our businessmen, one could observe a certain fever, since
> they felt themselves suddenly abandoned.
>
> But the greatest reaction came from the popular masses who had fol-
> lowed closely these maneuvers, given that they would be the first victims of
> the failure of the operation. . . .
>
> Opinion of the majority was not favorable to the spirit of the tripartite
> decision, which was labelled as contrary to the MPR slogan: Serve others,
> not yourself.[18]

Immediately following the tripartite decision Mobutu boarded his
presidential boat for a solitary cruise on the Zaire River. His meditations,
and doubtless the echoes of the furious reactions ashore to the crass display
of corporate greed by the top politicians, led him to announce a radical
reversal of the decision in his New Year's message:

> The [tripartite] decision was motivated by our constant concern for a
> policy of a return to the land, and by the desire to try an experiment in this
> domain with the direct collaborators of the Head of State.
>
> . . . In this moment of reflection, I have been led to analyze the deci-
> sion of the tripartite council, and I have concluded that, while legitimate in
> itself, it was nonetheless insufficient to translate the legitimate aspirations
> of our people.
>
> In my speech of 30 November 1973, I considered the people as the
> sole beneficiaries of the measures taken, and not one category of Zairians.
>
> That is why, Head of State that I am, guarantor of the interests of the

people who have elected me, and in my soul and conscience, I have decided that all the economic activities covered by the 30 November measures will be entirely taken over by the State.

For the State is the only institution which represents all the people.

That is why, excepting the case of small-scale commerce which will go to Zairian traders with the means and the vocation, the large commercial concerns, the plantations and farms, the agro-industrial entities, will be taken over by the State. Those citizens who wish to acquire a plantation or a farm will have to buy it from the State, which will determine the conditions and modalities of the cession.[19]

What, in fact, were the meditations of the president aboard the boat? Though it is clear from the 30 November speech that Mobutu intended from the outset that top political cadres would participate in the economic spoils, his first idea seems to have been that through rewards in the rural sector they would form a squirearchy whose dedicated labor of self-improvement would light beacons of rural development. The gift was to have been clearly patrimonial; recipients were to be chosen by the Council of Ministers, with Mobutu presiding, and the allocation of goods was contingent on proper client behavior—the state could summarily reclaim what it had bestowed. The president would appear to have underestimated not only the practical difficulties of implementation, but also the intense pressures generated by the claims of those who saw a once-in-a-lifetime chance to make a fortune. The tripartite council had pushed the president farther than he wanted to go by restricting the huge benefits to the inner ruling circle.

Thus in his New Year's message, momentarily, the president appeared to have taken back what had just been accorded. The state would succeed to the properties sequestered by 30 November and might then sell some of the large farms to worthy citizens. While these noble sentiments fostered some temporary confusion, the uncertainty did not long persist. Nothing more was heard of the role of the state, except as it superintended the division of the spoils. Far from buying properties from the state, *acquéreurs* were to receive them by simple attribution as free goods; beyond that, there was only a hypothetical obligation to compensate former owners from the profits over ten years. Official letters assigning assets read, "You have been allocated . . . ," or simply, "The State authorizes you to take possession. . . ."[20] The triumph of the politico-commercial class was complete.

What then transpired was a tumultuous, disorderly, and profoundly demeaning scramble for the loot. Dossiers were submitted to the three central ministries and to the regional, subregional, and zonal authorities.

At the lower echelons of the hierarchy, the procedure used was closely akin to that employed for the scrutiny of candidates for the legislature in 1970.[21] Aspirant *acquéreurs* had to submit a simple form, providing a basic curriculum vitae, a list of existing properties and shares, a police record, and data on bank accounts, outstanding loans, and commercial experience.[22] The blizzard of administrative circulars subsided; no major new instructions were offered until mid-March. The criteria used for evaluating candidacies—party militancy, personal integrity, solvency, and commercial experience—left ample room for arbitrary preference. As Kumwimba remarked of attributions at Kolwezi, "How can one prove or test the militancy or honorability of a citizen? . . . Zone Commissioners certainly had a large role to play, for it was they who could attest or certify the militancy of such-and-such a citizen. Under these circumstances, it was necessary to be personally known to the administrative authority."[23] The intensity of the competition was suggested by the revelation in the Lubumbashi daily that one regional official had pocketed nearly $25,000 by selling the appropriate application forms.[24]

Actual allocations of the businesses were made for the most part in February and March 1974. Though at first it was stated that the Council of Ministers would make the decisions, in reality several authorities came into play: the ministries of Agriculture, National Economy, and Commerce, the presidency, and the regional commissioners—the latter generally dealing with the less important enterprises. Approximately 2,000 businesses were involved in the distribution.[25]

Although ministers, deputies, and Political Bureau members did not collect all of the major businesses, as they had initially decided, success in the scramble was above all a measure of political influence and proximity to the ultimate sources of power. We have described in chapter 6 the staggering scale of Mobutu's acquisitions under this program. In Equateur, the second-biggest beneficiary was Interior Minister Engulu, who scooped up thirty-five plantations totalling 35,727 hectares. Shaba regional commissioner Duga accumulated enough businesses to gross $100,000 per month in the salad days of Zairianization.

Top regime personnel were served first. Political Bureau members, in keeping with the presidential injunction for a "return to the land," were awarded plantations, and in most instances sought urban businesses as well. Deputies were exempted from the tedious process of transmitting their dossiers through regular channels; their requests were simply submitted to the officers of the National Legislative Council, and they were assured favorable treatment.[26] For those outside the inner ring, the scramble was more arduous and required activating every conceivable link to the attributing authorities—the regional commissioners and the appropriate ministries. Outside of Kinshasa, the dossiers had to be first deposited at the zone level, where an *avis favorable* was required; then crucial lobbying had to be done at the regional capital or Kinshasa, or both. The nature of this process is ably depicted in a series of case studies by Schatzberg; one of these chronicles the successful efforts of a Kasai Luba trader to obtain a business in Lisala, where Kasai Luba traders were rare, but where he was a respected member of the community:

> When the President announced the Zairianization measures, he [the trader] was one of the first to deposit his dossier at the Zone. At least outwardly, he respected the procedure. . . . On other levels, however, he immediately began to lobby intensively for his candidacy. At this time the wife of the Sub-regional commissioner was also a Kasai-Luba. A merchant in her own right, she was President of the Association of Women Merchants in Lisala. A number of informants well-versed in Sub-regional politics believe that the commissioner's wife was active in supporting his candidacy with her husband, himself from Bandundu. Rumors indicate that money changed hands but this remains unconfirmed. As Vice-President of ANEZA [a merchant's association], the Luba trader chaired the delegation from the Mongala which went to Mbandaka [regional capital] to promote the candidacies of Lisala merchants. . . . In Mbandaka the Divisional Chief of the Economic Affairs Bureau was instrumental in presenting recommendations to the regional party committee. Also from the Kasai, there is good, though not conclusive, evidence that this bureaucrat actively supported the candidacy of his fellow Kasaian from Lisala. In any event, Lisala's one Luba trader became the acquirer of a commercial house with several stores in Lisala and Binga valued at ± Z 30,000.[27]

Many applicants who wished to disguise their own candidacies submitted applications through their spouses. A number of spouses were in fact traders in their own right, but wifely applications would (lightly) conceal the real number of businesses a family unit was amassing, or serve as cover for categories of persons such as army officers and civil servants who were at first theoretically excluded from the competition in order to "preserve their neutrality." A number of Portuguese and Greek traders were able to retain their shops by having their Zairian wives (or mistresses) apply as *acquéreurs*; in some cases small businesses were hastily and retroactively ceded to Zairian spouses to exclude the businesses from the distributable pool.

Of the initially proscribed categories of Zairians—army officers, magistrates, ambassadors, functionaries, and regional, subregional, and zone commissioners—the first three derived only limited benefits from Zairianization. Only the very top army officers succeeded in breaching the proscription; most notable among these was the leading mercantile general, Bumba Moaso, then FAZ commanding officer. There are few known instances of magistrates or ambassadors having received businesses, but senior functionaries were well enough placed to assure their own participation. This was particularly true of the politico-administrative cadres of the territorial service. Indeed, at a working meeting of the regional commissioners on 23–26 March 1974, Mobutu retreated from the official proscription of territorial cadres and agreed that regional commissioners could keep one business apiece. The decision was a tardy ratification of what had already occurred; the president himself noted that the commissioners should select one "among the businesses already acquired" and return the others.[28]

The porosity of the proscription of functionaries is illustrated by the attribution process at Kolwezi. The subregional commission which examined the candidacies and inventoried the businesses to be distributed was composed of the subregion's commissioner and economic affairs officers. Some 229 candidacies were recorded, of whom 84 were recommended as *acquéreurs* to the regional commissioner; as Tshiauke observes, the formal criteria of militancy, integrity, and solvency were impossible to appraise on the basis of the written forms, leaving the screening process to be entirely determined by the subjective preferences of the commission, and especially those of the subregion commissioner. In its business inventory the commission astutely overlooked fourteen enterprises, including some large ones; the reasons for the apparent oversight became clear in a confidential letter of 12 February 1974, in which the subregion commissioner solicited the "benevolent intervention" of the regional commissioner in favor of the commission members and some other top functionaries. Tshiauke writes:

> On 15 February 1974, the Sub-regional Commissioner transmitted a list of 14 names, consisting of the wives of the leading functionaries . . . [and suggesting the allocation to them] of the 14 businesses which had been omitted from the official list of suggested distributions by the Kolwezi Sub-region. This authority went so far as to ask the Regional Commissioner to use his influence so that his collaborators would be *rewarded* . . . for everything they had already done and would continue to do for the country. On the top of the list were the names of the wives of the Region authorities, followed by those of the Sub-region authorities of Kolwezi and Lualaba.[29]

Table 11.1   Effects of Zairianization in Lubumbashi

Beneficiaries	No. of businesses acquired	Percentage of businesses allocated
Politicians	69	35.4
Businessmen	67	34.4
Civil servants	9	4.6
Other	50	25.6

Source: David J. Gould, "Underdevelopment Administration and Disorganization Theory: Systematic Corruption in the Public Bureaucracy of Mobutu's Zaire" (Paper presented at the Conference on Political Clientelism, Patronage and Development, Bellagio, Italy, August 1978), p. 56.

The categories of persons who ultimately benefitted from Zairianization is illustrated by the patterns of allocation in two Zairian cities, shown in tables 11.1 and 11.2.

Throughout this phase of the scramble for the mercantile estate in Zaire there was a curious gap between the fictitious world of regime rhetoric, which stressed radical economic nationalism, and the practical reality of class action on a gigantic scale. Mobutu continued to argue that the primary aim of Zairianization was to promote the interests of the Zairian masses, and emphatically not to create a Zairian bourgeoisie; by the time the allocation process had gained momentum in January and February 1974, there was scarcely a person left in Zaire who believed this was true, with the possible exception of some top cadres endowed with special powers of self-deception. At the regional commissioners' conference on 23 March, Interior Minister Engulu, fresh from the arduous labor of stringing together his thirty-five-plantation combine in his native Equateur, solemnly declared that the good reputation of national and regional leaders had to be preserved. He cited as presidential gospel the proposition that party authorities should not violate the "Serve Others, Not Yourself" MPR slogan; thus top collaborators of the president could not benefit from the Zairianized properties.[30]

Ministers, Political Bureau members, regional commissioners, and other politico-administrative cadres were invited by Engulu to renounce businesses they had acquired. It is true that this unwelcome appeal to civic spirit and public morality was softened three days later by the frenetically applauded dispensation in favor of regional commissioners, noted above. The "one man, one business" creed was to reappear from time to time without having any visible impact upon the allocation process—least of all

Table 11.2   Effects of Zairianization in Bumba

Type of business acquired	*Acquéreur*
General commerce, rice mill, saw mill, gas station	Deputy
General commerce	Deputy (alternate)
General commerce and food store	Deputy
General commerce and coffee factory	Kinshasa merchant
General commerce and radio repair	Unknown
General commerce	Assistant regional MPR *animateur* (cheerleader)
General commerce and agricultural trade	Unknown
Garage and butcher shop	JMPR leader
General commerce	Collectivity chief
General commerce	Unknown
General commerce and food store	Party bureaucrat
General commerce	Army general

Source: Michael G. Schatzberg, "Bureaucracy, Business, Beer: The Political Dynamics of Class Formation in Lisala, Zaire" (Ph.D. diss., University of Wisconsin–Madison, 1977), p. 359.

upon the presidential acquisitions; Mobutu was in the process of collecting the sprawling rural domain later incorporated as CELZA. Senior Mobutu clan member Litho, using the cover of the parastatal trading corporation SGA, was likewise using the 30 November measures as a device to vastly expand his commercial empire.

In the Zairianization measures can be seen a bizarre fusion—or confusion—of themes. Three major economic sectors were involved: (1) the commercial sector, extending from the export-import sphere at the top (particularly attractive for its high profits and opportunities for capital export) down through the wholesaling level to the retail sphere; (2) a substantial light industrial sector (food processing, consumer goods), which had rapidly developed since the 1950s, its operations often subsidiary to those of large commercial houses; (3) the plantation sector, including processing facilities for such crops as coffee and palm oil, which were attached to some of the larger units. The law of 5 January 1973 appeared to be aimed only at the first of these, and seemed initially designed to reserve access to this sector to the Zairian mercantile group; it did not include provisions for the expropriation of businesses by the political class. Mobutu himself, in his 30 November address, focussed especially on the third sector as the avenue of fulfillment of the economic nationalist creed. Particularly intolerable to him was the wholesale alienation of the land of the ancestors by foreigners. The social bonds between the political leadership

and the rural mass, in his vision, could be cemented by converting the political elite into a patrimonial gentry, fulfilling a moral obligation to the
ancestors by supplanting foreigners in the management of country estates.
Immersion of the political elite in the daily cares of plantation operation
would focus their energies inward and foster a commitment to overcoming
the rural stagnation which all acknowledged.

Commerce, light industry, and plantations were swept together into a
single pool of distributable assets as application of the 30 November measures proceeded. Mobutu himself concentrated on accumulating plantations, in every region except Kasai Occidental (see table 6.1); most of his
top collaborators respected his enjoinder to "return to the land" by acquiring a plantation or two, but for most competitors in the scramble the primary targets were the commercial and light industrial sectors. While some
vague provisions for compensation to former owners were announced, it is
safe to say that most *acquéreurs* assumed that escape clauses permitted the
businesses to be considered essentially free goods. At the time, it appeared
to those situated to enter the competition like an historic, one-time distribution of goods confiscated by the state—analogous, perhaps, to the
Oklahoma land rush. The themes of a return to the land and mass better-
ment were utterly eclipsed by a turbulent race for assets on a scale which
had few historical precedents.

Disastrous consequences

Although most Zairians were quick to recognize that the benefits of Zairianization would be reserved for only a few and observed the scramble
with a detached cynicism, the disastrous economic consequences of 30 November took some months to become visible. Dislocation of commercial
circuits, shortages, layoffs in Zairianized enterprises, pay arrearages, inflation, tax evasion by *acquéreurs*, abandonment of businesses: these calamities became apparent over the first half of 1974. By mid-year, the security
services of the regime were reporting a flood of angry protests throughout
the country, and *acquéreur* had become a new pejorative category in the
social consciousness, identified with the political class.

Perhaps the most fundamental contradiction created by the 30 November measures was the conflict between the public and private interests of
the top cadres. The state assumed the responsibility for administering the
process of confiscation and the distribution of the assets, ostensibly as
guardian of the interests of society as a whole. The prime beneficiaries,

members of the ruling political class, were expected to use their public capacities to maximize their private gains and at the same time to police the operation so that it truly benefitted the entire populace. The unfolding of these measures, more than any other event, dramatized to civil society the moral vacuum in which the state operated.

The dislocation of commercial circuits became apparent fairly rapidly, although stores had current inventories sufficient to provide a buffer for a few weeks. Under the best of circumstances a period of disruption was inevitable until the issue of proprietorship was sorted out. No bank or supplier credit was available until ownership, and therefore responsibility for debts, was clarified. Beyond this immediate transitional problem, many *acquéreurs* had little or no commercial experience; as businessmen they were poor credit risks for either suppliers or financial institutions. Further complicating the situation were endless disputes about existing debts of the enterprises; a number of *acquéreurs* took the position that they had inherited the assets but that the debts were the responsibility of the former owners.

The legal status of many concerns remained uncertain for a number of months. Parallel processes of allocation at the regional and central ministerial levels resulted in numerous instances of multiple attribution; often more than one *acquéreur* appeared at the gates of the same enterprise with a duly signed letter of designation as the new proprietor. Over time these cases were slowly resolved, generally to the advantage of whomever had the higher-ranking signature on his (or her) attribution letter. In Kolwezi there were eight cases of multiple attribution—about 10 percent of the total.[31]

Many instances of asset-stripping were recorded. In a number of cases, particularly in the retail sector, the *acquéreur* at once proceeded to withdraw the bank deposits and to liquidate the inventory. Other Zairian proprietors soon discovered after a brief effort to operate a business that they had neither the time nor the experience to manage it successfully, and that this task could not be simply delegated to an unemployed close relative. Once impending failure was realized, the rational strategy was swift disposal of the liquid assets and abandonment of the enterprise before the business was taken away for "incompetence." Thus one consequence of Zairianization was a shrinkage of the commercial infrastructure of the country, especially in the hinterland. (Over time, this decline provided new openings for the emergent Zairian merchant class, which did not, for the most part, benefit from the 30 November measures.)

The combined effect of the rupture of the stock supply system and the retrenchment of the trading network was to produce many shortages. As a result, prices rose sharply for many basic commodities, including staple foods. Even before the Zairianization measures were decreed inflation had begun to build again in 1973, reflecting a growing government deficit financed by central bank advances and the rise in costs of some key imports. The oil price rise of 1973–74 in particular coincided with the effects of 30 November. Anticipated inflation and the pattern of dislocation made hoarding an attractive strategy for some *acquéreurs*; hoarding, in turn, was a visible and readily understood cause of inflation, and the combination of shortages and price surges was widely attributed to the 30 November beneficiaries.

As empty shelves and inflation became visible, the reflex of the regime was to announce ever more draconian price controls. Comprehensive price control had been a hallowed tradition from colonial times. The state had long set fixed prices for shops and marketplaces, and for a wide variety of basic goods. A law of 28 March 1961, replacing equivalent colonial legislation, entitled the minister of Economic Affairs (or, by delegation, the regional commissioners) to fix "maximum prices for all products, new or used, and all services." Agents of the ministry, posted at each level of the administrative hierarchy, had plenary powers of search and entry and could demand, without warrant, all business records relative to the operating costs of an enterprise; they could also demand to know the basis for prices charged. As *officiers de police judiciaire*, they had legal authority in economic matters to impose fines or even prison sentences on the spot. This imposing legal power gave great leverage to the functionaries concerned; however, such power by no means translated into effective price control.[32] Given the intervening variable of institutionalized bureaucratic corruption, the price control campaign of 1974 became rather an instrument of enrichment in the hands of the functionaries concerned. Cynicism within this service was already high; for those who failed to partake of the 30 November largesse, the sheer crassness of the Zairianization operation tended to dissipate whatever scruples might remain.

Even in the best of administrative circumstances price control is virtually impossible to sustain when real imbalances of supply and demand exist (unless other devices, such as rationing, are employed). There were many reasons why, in the post-Zairianization situation, the invocation of price control threats was at best a flimsy recourse to the "symbolic uses of politics."[33] Gould reports on one price inspector who conceded that his monthly return from price regulation was $3,000, whereas his official salary was $200.[34] The testimonials of two students, who as interns in the economic affairs department observed the operations of the price control mechanism, illustrate the varied dimensions of the problem:

> The hierarchical authority who is an *acquéreur* will pass the order to the price control services not to inspect his own business, or else to exercise severe control over such-and-such a trader (who is his competitor). . . .
>
> . . . we must note as well that the Economic Affairs functionaries run up against very powerful persons (officers, some high bureaucrats, national deputies, etc.) . . . who call themselves "untouchables." . . .
>
> When such-and-such a price controller notices that a given merchant is guilty of unjustified price rises, he fills out a warrant charging a price contravention, noting the price charged by the trader, and the legal price. The trader must reimburse the state for the illegal profit margin. . . .
>
> The controller presents the warrant with the threat of taking it to the tribunal if the trader does not pay up at once. The phase of negotiations then begins. Fearing incarceration, the merchant proposes a smaller sum, . . . the controller suggests another, and finally there is a compromise. . . . The warrant is ripped up in the presence of the trader, and no echo of the affair remains. If another controller appears in the same shop, the corrupted functionary will intervene to prevent him from acting.[35]

Thus despite repeated threats to *acquéreurs* who contravened the established prices, the immunity of the more powerful (the "untouchables") on the one hand and the corruption of the regulative machinery on the other assured that the state was totally unable to dam the tides of inflation.

Sheer managerial problems were another grossly underestimated difficulty. Characteristic of the naive optimism on this score was the organization by the UNAZA Lubumbashi campus of a three-day colloquium for *acquéreurs* in early 1974; the implication was clear that the colloquium would suffice to impart basic commercial knowledge.

The bulk of the *acquéreurs* were in one way or another full-time employees of the state; management of a business was seen as a mere sideline. While taxis or urban rental property could be handled on a part-time basis, a major commercial undertaking could not. A widespread practice was to assign a close relative or client to the daily management of such enterprises; the *acquéreur* feared, with good reason, that he would not be able to control the cash flow or profits unless a director with personal ties to him was overseeing the operation.[36] Similar logic is found behind the frequent practice of using spouses as proprietors. These persons generally were not up to their tasks. All the technical aspects of operating a business—cost control, stock maintenance, management of inventory, profit margin calculations, handling of a work force, bookkeeping, and the like—were beyond the ken of many, if not most, *acquéreurs*.

One solution, employed by a number of the larger *acquéreurs*, was either to retain the former expatriate managers or to hire new ones. This was the formula generally employed by Mobutu for the management of CELZA enterprises. Regional Commissioner Duga, in Shaba, gave a completely free hand to his managers, asking only his cut at the end of the month. In the case of businesses taken over by powerful *acquéreurs*, the arrangement could well be profitable for both the *acquéreur* and the foreign manager; to operate with the patronage of a top political figure was to be ensured of prompt and favorable passage of documents through the most tortuous administrative labyrinth. The "Ali-Baba" formula, however, had evident disadvantages. For the *acquéreur* who delegated managerial authority, it was often exceedingly difficult to know whether his European collaborator was taking more than the agreed cut. A number of European traders found working under this formula an intolerable restraint. For the public, the practical effect was higher prices resulting from the significant inflation of the cost of business management; the European would seek to maintain his earnings at close to the former level, and the *acquéreur* would anticipate a hefty return as well.

In the agricultural sector several paralyzing problems occurred. In the case of a number of plantations, the permanent crops, plantation stores, and processing facilities were separately distributed, thus creating interminable difficulties when it came to breaking up what had once been integrated operations. Following the failure of this formula, some plantations were assigned to the sundry national agricultural offices; when these in turn proved to be wholly unequipped to staff and capitalize them, they were often reattributed to individuals. Many plantations had large labor forces; their *acquéreurs* thus at once faced the necessity of meeting payrolls, without access to the necessary liquidity to meet these obligations.

In sum, the mismanagement and incompetence of the *acquéreur* class as a whole was widely conceded by August 1974, and by 1975 had become official orthodoxy. The overpowering sense of the failure of the Zairianized sector was reflected in quite forthright denunciations in commentaries by the Bank of Zaire, which were normally staid and understated. The broader Zairian economic crisis was largely imputable to the "poor management" by the *acquéreurs*, "who for the most part demonstrated negligence, incompetence, and greed." The plantation sector had been largely paralyzed by "the abandonment of a large number of agro-industrial enterprises attributed to certain Zairians within the framework of the Zairianization measures."[37]

A major problem was also caused by the layoffs of workers in a number of Zairianized businesses, often in order to offer jobs to unemployed members of the kinship and ethnic clientele of the *acquéreur*. Although beginning in December 1973 there were repeated official warnings to *acquéreurs* that forbade the dismissal of personnel, the practice was widespread.[38] Bitter letters of protest from dismissed employees began to shower down upon the administration and UNTZA. The union, for its part, was angered by the refusal of many *acquéreurs* to turn over to UNTZA the dues collected from the workers.[39]

A variant of the layoff occurred with respect to salesmen or shop managers for businesses consisting of several outlets. In these cases unwanted salesmen could be frozen out by failing to supply their particular shops, thus drying up their commissions. The mood of the moment is captured in a bitter letter of resignation written by one such salesman-manager in Lisala, who had held his post since 1957:

> Now that the whites have left . . . their firms have been given to you, our Zairian brothers, with the idea that we will be well treated, . . . but it is the contrary. A Zairian treats his Zairian brother completely like a slave.
>
> You always want to give merchandise only to the three stores which are run by your brothers and brother-in-law and if I want to make a requisition for merchandise which arrived you always create a quarrel. . . . Go see, the three stores run by your brothers are always filled with merchandise; come to my place . . . and there is a big difference.[40]

An unforeseen consequence of Zairianization was the near cessation of tax payments from the sectors affected. Though taxes on the mining sector and export-import duties were by far the most important state revenue sources, taxation of the commercial sector (taxes on income and turnover, as well as excise charges) was significant.[41] The European proprietors had generally met their fiscal obligations, doubtless with some evasion, partly because of the leverage afforded the state by their precarious position as foreigners. For the new Zairian owners, the tax disputes initially concerned income taxes for 1973, which fell due on 31 March 1974. *Acquéreurs* took the position that the former owners were liable for taxes of the previous year, while the latter maintained that their dispossession automatically annulled any fiscal claims. But the *acquéreurs* also declined to pay the current excise and turnover taxes that were due. One student who served as intern has described his attempt to collect the tax due on advertising:

In some cases, *acquéreurs* tried to distract us with conversation and joshing, or accepted the summons without obeying it.

. . . In other instances the *acquéreur* who had a relative or friend in the administration accepted the summons, but passed it on to his kinsman . . . who complained [to the authorities] about the nuisance being caused. . . .

. . . Others simply refused to pay the tax. They told us . . . to collect the tax first from the shops we had skipped that belonged to politico-administrative cadres. . . .

. . . During an entire day of work, when we should have collected Z 800, we took in only 15. . . .

. . . From this experience, we can say that only the poor merchants, who have no political support, paid.[42]

A final problem, which came to loom much larger when the full force of the economic crisis hit, was the absence of any meaningful provision for compensation. As we have seen, it was at first announced that a former owner would be repaid over a ten-year period from the profits of the enterprise, provided that the expropriated proprietor remained in Zaire to help the new owner during this period. Compensation was to be based on the declared value of the assets at the time of the state inventory. In reality this deceptively simple formulation was inadequate and unworkable.

One obvious defect was that no provision was made for the terms on which the former owner would stay on during the ten-year period; by this formula the *acquéreur* could evade compensation obligations by the simple expedient of paying no salary to the ex-proprietor, or expelling him from the living quarters often attached to the commercial premises. By the time regulations governing property transfers were tardily published on 6 September 1974, months after the transfers had taken place, the obligation to remain for the ten-year repayment period had been dropped.[43] However, the date for the first compensation payments was pushed back till January 1976, by which time Zairianization was being abandoned. Another flaw was the lack of provision for bankruptcy—as we have seen, a quite frequent outcome of expropriation. For the commercial sector, where assets were primarily the value of inventory, the compensation issue was not a fundamental problem. But among light industries and agroindustrial enterprises capital assets could be substantial; owners were certain to battle hard for compensation, and to enlist the support of their respective governments.

As public reaction grew more and more hostile to the manner in which the 30 November measures had been carried out, and as their multiple negative consequences were felt, various expedients were used to deflect the protest. On 22 March 1974 the president announced the creation of an appeals commission to hear complaints from former owners and others concerning the attribution process. This commission was quietly disbanded without, so far as is known, adjudicating any claims. Regular promises were made to publish the full list of *acquéreurs*, but the roster was never made public.

By mid-year 1974 the official press had begun to print open attacks on the *acquéreurs*. *Elima* on 21 May declared that "the majority of the *acquéreurs* . . . have no concern whatsoever for the well-being of the population." On 21 June, *Elima* denounced the "treason of Zairian businessmen," calling for the "unmasking and pillorying of the 'untouchables.'" In a major address to the party ideological institute on 15 August 1974, Mobutu was even more forthright:

> With a few rare exceptions, and I stress the word "rare," the manner in which the attribution and transfer of properties has occurred is a veritable scandal for most MPR cadres.[44]

The last months of 1974 saw some improvement in the operation of a certain number of Zairianized enterprises; some of the shortages resulting from the rupture of stocks at the time of the takeover became less acute. Still, mass resentment directed at the *acquéreurs* continued to intensify. The extravagant consumption standards of many *acquéreurs* was reflected in a surge of luxury imports. Symptomatic was a dramatic rise in demand for the ultimate status symbol, the Mercedes-Benz, which retailed for $50,000. On the anniversary of the Zairianization measures Mobutu bitterly announced that Zaire had broken all African records for Mercedes imports in 1974.[45] The *Guide* was by this time groping for a dramatic new gesture with which to disentangle the regime from the economic and political nightmare that 30 November had become.

Fuite en avant: radicalization

In December 1974, suddenly abandoning announced plans for an official visit to the Soviet Union, Mobutu made a hastily arranged visit to China and North Korea. Although there is no evidence that either host country offered any advice to Mobutu on the pathway out of the morass, he appeared to have been deeply impressed by the contrast between the disarray and distress at home and what he perceived as the sense of revolutionary discipline in China and, especially, North Korea. There revolution apparently had exorcised the demons of inflation and unemployment which were still ravaging Zaire. The solution: a *fuite en avant* (escape by advance) through all-out "radicalization of the revolution."

On his return from Asia the president summoned the Political Bureau for a two-day meeting aboard the presidential boat. After a frequently stormy session, on 30 December the Political Bureau announced the adoption of a ten-point "radicalization" program; this was essentially the product of presidential meditation on the ailments afflicting Zairian society, viewed in light of the transcendental visions gathered on his journeys to the future that worked. The new program was cast in Old Testament language. Ten *fléaux* (scourges, plagues) ravaging Zairian society were identified, and a remedy proposed for each (see table 11.3). The ten scourges did indeed add up to a recognizable portrait of the problems of contemporary Zaire, though many Zairians privately noted the absence from the list of the regime itself. The remedies, however, seemed inadequate to the challenge, and in practice soon vanished.

These themes were further embellished by the president in a fiery discourse on 4 January 1975. The food shortage would be overcome by the mobilization of agricultural brigades. Unemployment would be liquidated by the end of the year. Inflation was "a malady inherent in the capitalist system"; its abolition required only a state-decreed price rollback and the nationalization of commerce so that mercantile services could be provided by the state, which did not require a profit. "I am declaring war on the bourgeoisie," he proclaimed; "it is unthinkable that I, who have battled relentlessly against the 300 Belgian families who have exploited our country, could tolerate having 300 Zairian families substitute themselves for the Belgians." "MPR cadres," he concluded, "have your hands clean, and your conscience at rest in working for the people and only for the people." Radicalization, for Mobutu, was a "revolution in the revolution. From now on, we will completely change the system," pursuing "a revolution . . . which has not been accomplished anyplace else." Private initiative could be encouraged in small and medium enterprises, but "major economic initiatives remain the exclusive domain of the State."[46]

In the flurry of pronouncements which attended this short-lived "revolutionary moment" a number of additional measures were decreed. All communities were to construct nursery schools, which were to begin operation in September. Employers (including government agencies) were to provide free school uniforms for all dependents of their employees. Zairians were to repatriate their overseas bank holdings and turn their property

Table 11.3   Radicalization: The Ten Scourges and Their Remedies

Scourge	Remedy
1. Liberty confused with license: saying and writing no matter what; disrespect for authority; pornography; drugs; multiplicity of political parties	Discipline; fidelity to Mobutu; designation of the places which marked the life of the president as sites for pilgrimage
2. Agricultural crisis; food imports	Raise food output; cooperatives; roads; green zones around cities; fertilizer; price stabilization funds; abundance
3. Unemployment	Plan labor market; register the unemployed; training
4. Inflation, inherent in the liberal economy	Orient production and consumption; promote heavy industry to remove causes of inflation
5. Consumption society; enrichment of a few individuals	Reinforcement of import controls
6. Education lacking authenticity; an underemployed, delinquent youth	Obligatory civic service in agricultural labor; military training; political education for secondary school graduates; requiring favorable civic service reports and military certification for admission to universities; return to Zaire of all children in primary and secondary schools abroad, and removal of children from consular schools within Zaire; suppression of theology faculties, and religious school networks; attachment of JMPR to the presidency; training of JMPR cadres by the party ideological institute
7. Costly and unproductive army	Army to participate in agricultural programs; more political education for army
8. Social injustice; appropriation of large businesses by private individuals	State to take over all construction, large production, and distribution units, all building material factories, large public transport firms; foreign firms under investment code to be exempted

Table 11.3, continued

Scourge	Remedy
9. Social problems	Abolition of Ministry of Social Affairs; assignment of all social functions to Mrs. Mobutu
10. Individualism and egoism	Political Bureau members to turn over to state all businesses acquired through 30 November measures, or those they had previously obtained; members to devote themselves to agricultural activities; all MPR party cadres to turn over to state all 30 November businesses

Source: Yabili Asani, *Code de la Zairianisation* (Lumumbashi: Editeur "Mwanga Ilůlů," 1975), pp. 111–114.

holdings abroad over to the state, which would use them to house Zairian diplomatic missions. To all on the scene, the senses were overpowered by this stunning succession of revolutionary initiatives.

Radicalization: economic dimensions

For one frenzied month, radicalization appeared to be a bewildering reality. Ferocious attacks on the new bourgeoisie filled the columns of the official press. *Elima* warned that the people would return a harsh verdict on the "anti-revolutionary behavior of certain top-ranking political figures." "Many party cadres," it thundered, "distinguish themselves by their mercenary behavior, which borders on dishonesty and anarchy, in the exercise of their functions," adding that the official behavior of most regime officials daily worsened.[47] The editors "frenetically" saluted the abolition of economic liberalism and the consumption society to halt inflation; there was no inflation, it was said, in China and North Korea.[48] On a verbal level, the war on the bourgeoisie had indeed been launched, and many *acquéreurs* were fearful. Rumors circulated that certain leading businessmen, who felt their mercantile kingdoms were to be destroyed, had committed suicide (though no such cases were ever verified). A leading Lubumbashi *acquéreur*, also a member of Parliament and a university official, summoned intimates for a late-night session and confided, head in hands, that he was a ruined man (happily for him, the apprehension was false).

The momentary panic felt by the *acquéreurs* was created by the characteristic vagueness of the measures. Political Bureau members were enjoined to surrender the businesses they had gained through Zairianization, as well as those they had acquired on their own hook. All MPR party cadres were required to turn back to the state their Zairianized businesses, and to confine their activities to the agricultural sphere. But what were "agricultural activities"? And did this measure mean that plantations and agro-industrial enterprises were excluded from radicalization? (It may be recalled in this connection that the Mobutu CELZA empire consisted exclusively of plantations.) Who, exactly, were "party cadres"? A narrow interpretation might have limited this group to those holding posts of command in the party-state; but the term had often been applied in a broader sense to everyone who held any public post whatsoever. In mid-January 1975 a Political Bureau member visited Lubumbashi to explain the content of the measures to an anxious audience of the local elite; everyone down to the humblest messenger was a "party cadre," he declared, to the stupefaction of his listeners. Some public statements also conveyed the impression that all party cadres, in the extended sense, had to abandon all their businesses, not just those acquired through Zairianization.

In early January 1975 the Political Bureau and the Council of Ministers dutifully applied themselves to defining the economic scope of radicalization. It began to become clear that the prime target of radicalization would be a vast array of larger businesses, mostly Belgian-owned, which had not been covered by the measures of 30 November; on 8 January, the Political Bureau announced the creation of a series of commissions to oversee the various sectors of the economy that were to come under state control. These included transport, petroleum, mines, agriculture and ranches, metallurgy, hotels, breweries and soft drink processing, construction and quarrying, banks and financial institutions, printing and publishing (diverse industries), and food-processing.

At the same time it was announced that a commission for further study of the measures was being created, to be chaired by Political Bureau member Nzondomyo Lingo and to consist of four ministers and the governor of the central bank. Its principal task was "to define the best method for distinguishing between small and medium businesses, and large enterprises." The Political Bureau members, the communique announced, had turned over to the president a list of their own businesses; with no doubt unintended irony, the communique concluded with the statement that

Mobutu had "thanked them, and turned the lists over to the party secretary to be filed in the party archives."[49]

The distinction between small and large production units was shortly to constitute the escape hatch for most *acquéreurs*. The shift in the focus of radicalization from stripping the November 30 bourgeoisie of its newly acquired assets to an assault on the (primarily Belgian) industrial sector dating from the colonial era was signalled by a presidential speech before a Kinshasa meeting of the African-American Institute on 21 January 1975. "Total independence" was the goal; Zaire, "guided by Mobutism, not Marxism," remained "neither on the left nor on the right." It had to be understood that the state would no longer tolerate the behavior of "corporations that have operated in Zaire since the colonial period, but which have functioned in our country without bringing anything in return, and which have, in spite of creating capital reserves for amortization, never invested or modernized their capital equipment." Such industries now operated with outmoded equipment and archaic management techniques. "We believe that, 15 years after our independence, perpetuation of colonial exploitation in a politically independent country is henceforward inadmissible."[50]

This subtle but decisive shift in emphasis was not at once picked up by regime propaganda organs. The following day *Elima* again lambasted the *acquéreurs*, declaring that through Mobutu's decision to have the state "recapture control of all the Zairianized enterprise . . . the vast joke the new *acquéreurs* have wanted to play on the country is once and for all ended."[51]

The fears of the 30 November beneficiaries were more specifically allayed when Mobutu summoned the Kinshasa citizenry to a mass meeting on 4 February 1975. "We have misunderstood each other," he declared to the businessmen present. His aim had not at all been to strip the politico-commercial class of its assets, but only to induce it to invest in the country. Those who had many houses in the country were free to keep them; but it was wrong to invest capital in overseas property. Even if the capital had been accumulated by embezzlement, it could be retained if invested at home, especially in rural areas.[52] The bloodless war on the bourgeoisie was all but over.

In February some gaping loopholes were blasted through the radicalization program. The extended concept of the identity of party cadres had totally disappeared. Small enterprise, which was exempted from radicalization, was defined as a business having a turnover of Z 1 million—a spacious tent which could shelter most businesses, especially given the fungibility of business accounting, the possibility of splitting firms into smaller units, and the like. Businesses acquired by spouses and relatives were also exempt. In fact, only a small number of Zairianized enterprises were taken away from their *acquéreurs*.

But the foreign-owned industrial sector was another matter; the war became deflected onto approximately 120 companies dating from the colonial period. Affected were textile mills, breweries, cigarette factories, cement works, and construction firms, among others. Those firms of colonial origin which had made post-1969 investments acquired the immunity of the investment code, though in fact few of the old Belgian firms had done so.

The crowning blow to the initially defined purposes of radicalization came on 15 March 1975 when a list was published of "delegates-general" who were to be placed in charge of the new radicalized sector. The roster was a veritable who's who of old-line politicians, including such standbys as Nendaka, Bolikango, Diomi, Ngalula, Sakombi, Kandolo, and Mushiete. The upper layer of the state bourgeoisie had converted the January war on itself into a March preemptive strike against a formerly untouched sector of the economy.

The disruptive effects of Zairianization were now extended into even more important spheres of the economy. Though the delegates-general did not acquire ownership of these enterprises, they did gain the authority to divert company resources to private ends.[53] For example, the Equateur party stalwart named to head the newly reorganized and nationalized railway network (SNCZ) transferred substantial operating funds to his private bank account, summarily fired numerous Belgian cadres, used the company jet for weekends in Europe with female consorts, and ordered a Versailles-style redecoration of his home. Within a few months the dislocation of the railway was so serious that Mobutu had to fire his client and bring back a Belgian manager, at a salary exceeding $200,000.[54]

For the Zairianized enterprises of 30 November a fictitious and inoperative set of compensation arrangements had been announced. For enterprises subject to radicalization, no public statement regarding the status of previous owners was ever made; the state had simply assumed managerial control over the 120 companies in the person of delegates-general. The Greeks, Portuguese, and Pakistanis who had been the major losers in the 30 November reform had received little effective support from their home countries, which had no leverage in Zaire. For the Belgians who were prime victims of radicalization the situation was quite different, particularly as radicalization coincided with the crisis phase of the new order.

Toward retrocession

In March 1975 the Belgian office that provided export insurance suspended all guarantees for shipments to Zaire. Parent companies of firms confiscated under Zairianization and radicalization, which often were major suppliers for their subsidiaries, cut off all credit.[55] International banks which had been major lenders since 1970 began to be aware by the spring of 1975 that repayment problems existed. By September 1975 the eighty-odd Kinshasa-based state corporations had incurred debts of $552 million (including $100 million in tax arrearages, $60 million in inter-enterprise debt, $72 million in domestic bank credit, and $68 million in debts to foreign banks and suppliers).[56]

Disaster crowded in upon the regime from all sides. The bankrupt state had no choice but to appeal to its public and private creditors for salvation. By late 1975, virtually no one beyond the narrowing group of beneficiaries challenged the conclusion that Zairianization had been a total fiasco, and that radicalization had added insult to injury. One Zairian observer, evaluating this experiment in early 1976, noted that the beneficiaries of radicalization had all been either politicians or politically-connected businessmen: "The distribution of economic activities taken from foreigners affected only a tiny minority of the population. . . . It was inconceivable to ask this minority . . . which pursued the maximization of its own monetary profit to pursue at the same time the maximization of social profit."[57]

After a first round of contacts with his creditors and the IMF, Mobutu established a stabilization committee in November 1975; under his own direction, it was composed of the ministers of Finance and Portfolio, the head of the presidential secretariat, and the governor of the Bank of Zaire. Very quickly, on 25 November, a first "retrocession" formula was announced; it provided for a return of 40 percent equity in foreign-owned radicalized or Zairianized enterprises. Important exceptions were made for petty trade, plantations without processing facilities, Zairian-owned radicalized businesses, and those that had been first Zairianized and then radicalized.[58]

This formula was judged insufficient by most foreign ex-proprietors, and left Zaire liable for a very large compensation bill. The bill has never been fully calculated, but its scale is suggested by the fact that radicalization affected most Belgian-owned enterprises in the country, whose value was estimated at $700 million. By September 1976 a much more far-reaching retrocession (or "deradicalization," as it came to be called) was decided upon, by which former owners regained up to 60 percent equity, but were obligated to find Zairian buyers (over a period of several years) for 40 percent of the ownership. Though small businesses and plantations well-managed by their *acquéreurs* were excluded, the revised retrocession scheme did permit a large-scale return of enterprises to former owners. Indeed, many regarded the 60 percent formula as a 100 percent return in view of the delay permitted for finding Zairian participants. At the same time, the compensation issue was essentially settled. It was agreed, in the case of those preferring compensation to a return to Zaire, that the Belgian government would advance the compensatory sum to aggrieved Belgian nationals over a ten-year period, while the Zairian state would reimburse Belgium, in Belgian francs, over a twenty-year period. While this humiliating abandonment of the Mobutu masterstrokes of Zairianization and radicalization was accepted by Zaire with reluctance, there was really no choice. Private and public creditors alike insisted on elimination of both the mismanagement and compensation issues as a sine qua non. If any reinforcement of the retrocession measures was required, the pivotal position of the Belgian state and the private sector among the ranks of the creditors gave decisive leverage.

On 3–4 February 1977 "clarifications" of the retrocession measures were issued, providing for total restitution of radicalized properties; Zairianized businesses would only be given back if mismanagement were demonstrated. Mismanagement was subsequently defined operationally as cessation of activity, embezzlement, failure to maintain bookkeeping records, or nonpayment of taxes. For disputed cases retrocession commissions were constituted, composed of regional commissioners (themselves major *acquéreurs*), members of the Chamber of Commerce (ANEZA), economic affairs officers, and local bank representatives. By April 1978 more than three-quarters of the expropriated businesses in Lubumbashi had been retroceded, most without contest. Among the forty-six contested cases in the same region, by May there had been thirteen retrocessions, eight "arrangements" between former owners and *acquéreurs*, six unresolved cases, and nineteen retentions by *acquéreurs*.[59]

Many were quick to note that the presidential CELZA empire was long exempted from retrocession. It was only in early 1978 that Mobutu agreed to return 51 percent equity to the former owners, after considerable external pressure had been exerted. The baffling gap between the public morality preached with apparently genuine conviction by the president and his private behavior, which so greatly damaged the external and domestic credibility of the regime, was once again in evidence.

Other declared aspects of economic radicalization, which were to have formed part of the ephemeral war on the state bourgeoisie, were never applied. There is no recorded example of overseas real property being turned over to the state by the political-commercial class; least of all were the extensive presidential holdings abroad disturbed. Nor is there any known instance of foreign bank accounts being repatriated; their Zairian holders had no more confidence in the Zairian economy at that juncture than did foreign interests.

Radicalization: social dimensions

The radicalization program included not only economic measures, but a series of social projects. The ten scourges Mobutu set out to remedy included such undoubted evils as unemployment, inadequate schooling, insufficiently developed civic consciousness, juvenile delinquency, and insufficient social services, among other items. The curative powers of the treatments prescribed, unfortunately, was no match for the ailments diagnosed. (Table 11.3 lists the scourges and the proposed remedies.)

Indeed, few of the proposed remedies were even tried, and those that were performed dismally. No cooperatives were created, and food output continued to stagnate. There was a brief effort to force the urban unemployed to register at town halls. Few were naive or foolish enough to do so, rightly suspecting that such a step would guarantee forced repatriation to their villages—or worse, conscription into one of the stillborn agricultural brigades or the youth corps, to till public farms to provide food for cities.

The plan for obligatory civic service took several months to die, and spread panic among members of the graduating secondary school class, estimated to number about 20,000. It was announced that the army would take in hand the organization and supervision of these young people; however, there was quiet but firm opposition to the plan within the FAZ hierarchy, which at the same time had been called upon to prepare for participation in the Angolan civil war. An army of 70,000 was housed in facilities built for 24,000; it had no means of housing or feeding 20,000 more, let alone the means to cope with the multitude of problems that would arise in attempting to control a turbulent set of young people bitterly resentful of their conscription. Army officers well remembered the difficulties the FAZ had experienced when students were conscripted in 1971–72.

Not only were the students affected; their families also were deeply concerned about the civic service scheme. Parents of daughters destined for assignment to military camps wondered what criteria would be used for the "militancy" certification that would be required for further study, and what kind of sexual leverage this requirement would offer to soldiers and party officials involved.

The suppression of the religious school networks was made effective for the 1975–76 school year and was implemented, with the unhappy effects most had anticipated. This measure was also quietly abandoned in 1976. In the end, Zairian access to the Belgian, French, and American consular schools was permitted to continue. The high fees charged by these schools restricted access to offspring of the politico-commercial class (as well as to foreign children). The announced repatriation of Zairian children studying in Europe (estimated at several thousand) was never enforced.

The promise to provide school uniforms disappeared almost as soon as it was made, perhaps partly because the cost of this measure would have been charged to the *acquéreurs*. The nursery school construction project did linger on for several months; occasional communiques announced that local communities would devote their *salongo* communal labor to this project.[60] Yet even if citizens were prepared to turn out on Saturdays for "voluntary" labor, funds were not available for tools and building materials, and the skilled labor infrastructure necessary for the erection of buildings—even buildings of dried-mud bricks—was lacking.

Not the least astonishing of the remedies was the prescription for scourge number nine, vaguely stated as "social problems." These were to be overcome by abolition of the Ministry of Social Affairs and the transfer of all responsibilities in this field to the president's wife. Mrs. Marie-Antoinette Mobutu had a forceful personality and a mind of her own; as one example, she refused to drop her baptismal name in favor of an "authentic" one. She had devoted considerable energies to supporting medical installations and the well-being of women and children. Many whispered doubts were expressed about her ability to manage such a large sphere of state activity, however inadequately it was then being carried out. Even though she had the important asset of speaking with the voice of the president, she lacked administrative experience, and had an imperfect command of French, the bureaucratic language. Another privately voiced objection was that this new authority would give her personal control over the substantial social security pension fund. These uncertainties were soon removed; the measure was quickly and quietly abandoned.

The fiasco evaluated

In sum, the Zairianization and radicalization measures represented the final, audacious thrust of regime expansion. Zairianization was a self-confident lunge for economic independence, while radicalization was a desperate gamble, an attempt to confront the accumulating troubles of Mobutism ascendant. Viewed as drastic surgical operations to amputate foreign domination over a huge swath of the economy, the measures were truly revolutionary. Arguably this was the most sweeping and comprehensive set of nationalizing measures yet undertaken in independent Africa (excluding those situations in which European owners simply fled, as in Algeria and Angola).

Yet these measures were at once denatured by the character of the Mobutist state and class control of the regime. The pathology of personalized power meant that the measures were conceived and dictated by the president alone, with little attention paid to the difficulties of realization. The country would accordingly embark upon the most momentous changes having neither clear blueprint nor legal framework, nor indeed continuing presidential support. Presidential proclamation of radical but only loosely defined sets of measures triggered a turbulent response, whereby the confused improvisation of those charged with applying the decrees never quite caught up with the economic disorders unleashed.

The consequences were in all respects calamitous. The politico-commercial class illuminated both its greed and its parasitic character; it drew off enormous wealth through the confiscated assets placed at its disposition by the state. In the process, it dislocated an economy which under any circumstances would have been severely buffeted by the fall of copper prices, the rise of oil and other import costs, and the export bottlenecks resulting from the Angolan civil war.

Taken together, Zairianization, radicalization, and retrocession laid bare essential characteristics of the Mobutist state. The internal hegemony of the politico-commercial class, and its capacity to transform the ideology of state autonomy and economic nationalism into a weapon for its own material aggrandizement, were now completely clear. The president, in orchestrating the seizure of foreign assets, sought to exploit the takeover process as a patrimonial instrument for the further consolidation and extension of his personal power. Both the dominant class and the president were undermined by the infirmities of the state which was their instrument of accumulation; the nationalizing measures proved so economically disruptive that, however much they served the interests of the politico-commercial class and the president, they could not be sustained. At that point yet another aspect of the New Regime, to which we turn in the next chapter, came into view: its ultimate dependence upon external interests. When the dislocations engendered by Zairianization and radicalization coincided with a broader economic crisis, Western creditors were in a position to insist, as a fundamental condition for any assistance to the virtually bankrupt Zairian state, that these measures be undone through retrocession.

In this episode three widely-disseminated images of the Zairian state jostle for recognition: the state as patrimonial domain of the personalist ruler; the state as executive committee of the ruling class; the state as dependent instrument of the Western capitalist order. Each of the three has elements of validity; none can stand on its own. Both patrimonial aspiration and class action were involved in the initial Zairianization. Radicalization in its initial form was a presidential effort to restore patrimonial initiative and curb the politico-commercial class, whose naked greed was deflating the legitimacy of the regime. But the dominant class soon succeeded in denaturing the radical thrust of the remedies to the ten scourges. External capital interests and Western powers, however horrified they were at Zairianization and radicalization, were powerless to block these measures. Only when their utter failure, combined with a general weakening of Zaire's economic position, forced the regime to turn to its external patrons for financial relief was Western leverage strong enough to impose a rollback of the measures.

Economic radicalization, then, was a nearly mortal self-inflicted wound. Zaire careened from a position of African leadership to abject dependence upon its creditors. Its most significant bankruptcy, however, was in the eyes of its citizenry; the real degree of legitimacy acquired in the ascendancy and expansion phases eroded almost to the vanishing point.

12

Zaire in the International Arena

Zaire, as a territorial entity, was created in 1885 by the international (then European) community, at the Berlin Congress. From 1885 to 1908, as the Congo Free State, it was held under the personal sovereignty of King Leopold II, with no other formal link with Belgium than the common monarch. In his dying days, in 1908, Leopold bequeathed his sprawling African estate to Belgium, which transformed the territory into a *chasse gardée*, with other external influences largely excluded. Then, with the breakdown of the decolonization formula in 1960, Zaire suddenly became a cold war battleground, with a number of forces competing for political influence and the United Nations and its peacekeeping forces holding the ring. The United States played a dominant role. In the Mobutu years the character of external relationships began to change. Especially from 1974 on, the Zairian state found itself enmeshed in a new kind of external bondage, this time much more economic in nature. The tributary relationship to Western states and economic institutions which emerged in the late 1970s seemed much more durable in character than the political dependency of the first republic.

In examining the international dimension of Zairian politics, our primary concern is with Zairian diplomacy. It is not our object to unravel the motivations that shaped the actions of those external forces which impinged upon the Zairian political process. We seek rather to record their impact, and to explore Zairian action in the international realm, the objectives that governed its choices, and the mechanisms by which external vectors became embedded in the Zairian political economy.[1]

First Republic background

It will be recollected that the First Republic was a period of pervasive international involvement in Zairian politics. A number of factors explain the scope of involvement: the drama and hopes generated internally and

abroad by the abrupt surge to independence; the fragility of Zaire's domestic political formations, compounded by the immediate loss of control
over the bureaucratic and coercive apparatus of the state, which compelled
all political figures to eagerly solicit external backing; the discrediting of
Belgium as a result of its partial support for the Katanga secession and its
armed intervention in a number of Zairian localities, which precluded a
bilateral metropolitan-colonial framework of the kind often used in precarious decolonizations (Cameroon, Djibouti); the ferocity of cold war rivalries, joined to the limited understanding on the part of both Soviets and
Americans of the determinants of Zairian internal politics; the lofty dream
of UN officials (particularly Hammarskjold) of using the Congo crisis as
an opportunity to enlarge and validate the peacekeeping role of the world
body. Little by little, the impact of these factors began to fade, despite the
momentary resurgence of external involvement during the rebellions of
1964–65.

The phenomenon of omnipresent, intruding entourages of foreign advisors surrounding nearly all politicians had greatly diminished by 1965.
Despite the valuable contributions made by civilian UN programs in particular sectors, the disappointments of the UN operations led to resumed
reliance on Belgium as the major source of expatriate personnel. Although
Belgian–Zairian ties remained permeated by ambivalence, the passions
and distrusts of 1960 had subsided. While cold war rituals retained their
power, and renewed crises—such as the rebellions—revived cold war responses, still "communism" was so transparently not a real force in Zaire
that arguments about "communist penetration" carried little conviction
among Westerners, even among the American people, at whom these
claims were particularly directed. On the Soviet side, there was a parallel
mood of disenchantment, even cynicism, concerning radical African nationalism; the vaunted concept of the "non-capitalist path to development," applied with some enthusiasm in 1960 in Ghana, Guinea, and
Mali, was quietly shelved at this time by Moscow.[2]

The dependency of the First Republic was mainly political; economic
interest played only a secondary role. The Shaba mining interests, in particular UMHK, did give encouragement and support to the Katanga secession, but soon found themselves immersed in a crisis over which they had
little influence. The largely Belgian private capital interests in Zaire had
practically no leverage in the UN policy arena; while the Société Générale
group had important influence in Belgium, it had little capacity to shape
the direction of a cold war strategic debate. The "Katanga lobby" in the
United States found one congressional voice in Senator Thomas Dodd of

Connecticut, and was a minor nuisance, but it was never taken seriously by the foreign policy establishment. Multinational capital and the international banks saw little attraction in unstable, disorganized First Republic Zaire.

External actors during the First Republic operated in good part through the recruitment of Zairian political allies. The game of influence was thus subject to abrupt changes. The formless nature of Zairian politics gave free rein to reversals of alliance; the quest for access was highly competitive. The presence of a particular advisor in a politician's entourage did not mean that his advice was heeded, but only that his foot was in the door.

Durable influence depended upon the capacity to deliver reliable support over time, as well as palatable advice. The most resilient connection during these years—between the caucus of key leaders known as the Binza group and the American embassy—was founded upon a mutuality of interests [3] Both wished a stable, moderate regime, and were fearful of the Lumumbist bloc domestically and of Soviet diplomacy externally. The alliance was between unequal partners, but each side had its own leverage; the Binza group could not easily have sustained its influence without the American backing available to it, while no alternative channels of strategic access could have supplanted this Zairian caucus for the Americans.

External legitimation of the New Regime

The whole fabric of external relationships was transformed during the Second Republic. The greater authority and internal cohesion of the state permitted a new and much more active role on the international scene for a time. The rapid affirmation of personal rule also changed the parameters of external access. The only really decisive point of contact was with the presidency.

In the short run, the consolidation of the political authority of the New Regime somewhat reduced the permeability of the polity to external influences, and diminished its need for continuous external backing. The rebellions were shattered, a large swath of the political spectrum co-opted into the government coalition, and elements of the radical intelligentsia absorbed into the presidential staff. These factors permitted Zaire to momentarily define an international role of its own rather than being a mere object of external pressures.

The climate in Africa was propitious. Though the insurgents had enjoyed substantial sympathy, particularly after the November 1964 Belgo–

American intervention in Kisangani, their leaders—Christophe Gbenye, Gaston Soumialot, and Nicolas Olenga—had discredited themselves by their murderous rivalries and mutual denunciations.[4] Nkrumah observes that consideration was given to inviting the exiled revolutionaries to be Zairian representatives at the October 1965 OAU summit in Accra, until news came in August of the Gbenye-Soumialot fracture.[5]

One of Mobutu's first acts on coming to power was to dispatch a former Lumumba follower, Marcel Lengema, to Accra to explain and justify the coup. Nkrumah's explanation of his own willingness to accept the Mobutu regime offers revealing insight into the early diplomatic success of the New Regime in Africa:

> Until his "coup" of November 1965, Mobutu's role . . . had not been such as to commend him to progressive African opinion. . . . There has also never been much doubt about Mobutu's special leaning towards the western powers. He had demonstrated his partisanship towards the west by his intense hostility to Lumumba. . . .
>
> . . . his western supporters warned Mobutu against leaning unduly towards Kasavubu. They even went so far as to drop a calculated hint that the Katangese gendarmes and white mercenaries would rise in revolt if Mobutu did this. The western supporters thus left no stone unturned in their efforts to prop up Tshombe against President Kasavubu. . . .
>
> However, Congolese patriots spearheaded by the *Front Démocratique Congolais* were not unmindful of these moves and maneuvers. Secret and delicate negotiations were going on between them and Mobutu as to the best means of circumventing and eclipsing the maneuvers of Tshombe and his foreign mentors. . . . It was therefore agreed that Mobutu with the support of the FDC should intervene by a military coup so as to forestall the attempts being made . . . to install Tshombe as President.[6]

Nkrumah, shortly before he himself was overthrown, was thus prepared to accept and support the Mobutu regime if it would commit itself to nonalignment and a pro-African policy. With the Unilateral Declaration of Independence (UDI) of the white regime of Ian Smith in Rhodesia and the growing liberation struggle in the Portuguese territories, the elimination of Tshombe and the installation in Kinshasa of any effective regime with a reasonably African perspective permitted removal of the endless Congo crisis from the agenda so that energies could be directed to the more urgent struggles in southern Africa.

During its first months in power the regime succeeded in dispelling many of the widespread suspicions about its basis and its sources of support. An authoritative Belgian study, after reviewing various reports of external influence and the roles of foreign advisors, concluded:

> It seems clear that on political problems, beyond normal consultation . . . President Mobutu did not seek inspiration from European advisors; he consulted and listened to nationalist Congolese elements, especially university graduates not compromised with the former regime; he discussed problems with his intimates such as . . . Kande . . . Litho . . . Bomboko . . . Tshisekedi . . . and Nendaka.[7]

The nationalist image of the regime was reinforced during 1966–67 by a series of gestures: relations with Portugal were severed in October 1966 because of Portuguese colonial intransigence in Angola; Lumumba was rehabilitated and declared a national hero; the Bakajika Law, and especially the UMHK struggle, conveyed a sense of the combative assertion of Zairian economic rights, as did the frequently strained relations with Belgium. All of these factors helped set the stage for the regime's full acceptance by the African family of nations—an approval symbolized at the 1966 OAU summit by the acceptance of Kinshasa's invitation to host the 1967 OAU meetings. Such approval in turn guaranteed that the fragmented remnants of the rebellion would be denied sympathy and sanctuary. With the elimination of the Tshombist threat in 1967, the New Regime was relatively secure at home and abroad, and no longer required sustained and continuous backing.

Zairian diplomacy in expansion

By 1968, Zairian diplomatic ambitions had begun to expand. A place of respect was already assured; the time for larger dreams was at hand. The first major initiative, in 1968, was the proclamation of a "Union of States of Central Africa" (UEAC) linking Zaire, the Central African Republic, and Chad; it was hoped that the union of three would form a pole of attraction for others. Given the dismal record of African attempts at unions of sovereign states (other than that of Tanganyika and Zanzibar), it seems unlikely that this missile ever could have lifted more than a few inches from the launching pad. However, the French apparently saw the proclaimed union as the serious threat to the Customs Union of Central African States (UDEAC, composed of the territories of former French Equatorial Africa and Cameroon). Their emissaries prevailed upon then-President Bokassa to withdraw the Central African Republic from UEAC, which then limped along for several years as a combine of Zaire and Chad, even though these states had no common border.

Though this initiative did not prosper, others were more successful. In 1969 a final compensation deal with UMHK cleared the way for the participation of the World Bank and foreign investors in Zairian development. The new investment code, the stabilized economy, and the treasure trove of minerals gave Mobutu an attractive dossier. Over the following year he undertook a pilgrimage to the major capital centers of the world: Japan, France, Germany, and the United States. In Washington, in August 1970, he received a cordial welcome and warm endorsement from President Nixon. The National Press Club and other audiences learned with interest that the term "nationalization" did not even exist in the Zairian lexicon. From the point of view of Mobutu and his collaborators, diversification of capital sources would increase Zaire's leverage in its dealings with Belgian corporate interests, and would also give a wider range of industrial states some stake in the welfare of Zaire (and, an unspoken corollary, of its regime).

Mobutu also offered himself on the African scene as a skilled conciliator of diplomatic conflicts among African states. He proposed his services as intermediary to repair the tense relations between Tanzania and Uganda in 1971 following the Obote overthrow, and was instrumental in the establishment of a formal relationship between Amin and Nyerere (though this was not to prove a lasting accomplishment). He also actively mediated disputes between Burundi and Tanzania concerning border violations by Burundi forces (see chapter 9). He offered his services in 1970 to reconcile Nigeria with the four states which had recognized Biafra. In 1971 he was a member of the OAU team of sage elder statesmen charged with ending the Israeli occupation of Egyptian territory, though this conflict was too intractable to succumb to Mobutu's mediatory skills.[8]

Beyond mediation and the stalking of investors, Mobutu embarked on a remarkably ambitious program of diplomatic travel. In 1970 he visited ten other African states; in 1972, there were state visits to Togo, Gabon, Ethiopia, Tanzania, and, above all, Guinea. The triumphant reception accorded Mobutu by Sékou Touré, one of his most vehement critics of yore, was particularly important; Mobutu was not just tolerated in Guinea, but welcomed with deference in this symbolic capital of radical African nationalism.[9] Shortly after his return from Conakry, Mobutu greeted eight chiefs of state at an MPR congress. In 1973 Mobutu spent no fewer than

150 days outside Zaire, visiting twenty-six countries, including fourteen in Africa.[10]

Active regional diplomacy was based on intimate personal relationships with other heads of state. Regular tripartite consultations were held with Habyalimana of Rwanda and Micombero of Burundi. In the 1972–75 period there were also frequent triangular summits with Nyerere and Kaunda, largely devoted to conversations about southern Africa. Mobutu gave strong backing to Idi Amin in his quest for African recognition, and opposed the transfer of the 1971 OAU summit conference from Kampala. This amity was sealed by the renaming of two Ugandan–Zairian border lakes; former Lakes Edward and George became Lakes Mobutu and Amin.

During the early phases of the New Regime the only neighboring state with which relations were periodically troubled was Congo–Brazzaville. Kinshasa did not easily forgive Brazzaville for its roles as rebel headquarters and base for insurgent training during the 1964 rebellions. Amity had barely been resumed when relations were again poisoned by the Mulele affair; Brazzaville was angered by the summary execution of the former guerrilla leader after he had left Brazzaville under an amnesty guarantee. A new crisis broke in 1972 when Zaire provided arms and sanctuary for insurgents led by Ange Diawara, whose small maquis was eliminated in early 1973.[11] Through the entire period support for opposing Angolan factions by the two capitals (the FNLA by Kinshasa, the MPLA by Brazzaville) was a constant source of tension. Despite all of these irritants, Mobutu and Ngouabi developed a close personal relationship; close relationships were also maintained with Ngouabi's successors.

The Mobutist diplomatic offensive was extended to the Arab world in 1973–75. Mobutu played a very active role in the Afro–Asian summit in Algiers in September 1973. In his United Nations speech of 4 October 1973 he stunned the General Assembly by solemnly announcing the rupture of diplomatic relations with Israel. Arab states, in return, accorded him the unusual honor of inviting him to observe the November Arab summit as the sole non-Arab participant. He then followed up with a major swing through the Middle East, including visits to Libya, Egypt, Saudi Arabia, Kuwait, the United Arab Emirates, and (non-Arab) Iran. While Mobutu's hope to obtain a guaranteed oil supply at concessional prices failed, these overtures did bear fruit later when Morocco, Egypt, Sudan, and Saudi Arabia were among his strong supporters during the 1977 and 1978 Shaba invasions. Earlier, Libya had become a financial participant in the second phase of the Gécamines expansion program.

The swelling diplomatic ambitions of the regime went well beyond an active regional role. At the extravaganza organized to mark the sixth anniversary of the coup in 1971, the regime proclaimed the goal of making Zaire a "great international power."[12] In the Third World context, this more expansive dream encountered the serious handicaps of Zaire's close Western associations and its investment campaign in the West. Though nonalignment was Zaire's officially stated diplomatic ideology, and figured prominently in the 1967 N'Sele Manifesto, in practice the most widely recognized diplomatic yardstick was the pattern of Zaire's linkages to the two major cold war protagonists. And though Mobutu could point to frequently vexed relations with the former metropole, ties with the United States were consistently intimate.

Symbolic affirmation of nonalignment through at least normalized relations with the Soviet Union was made difficult by the legacy of the First Republic years. Mobutu and the Soviets had good reason to distrust each other. From the president's standpoint, the Soviet Union had given consistent backing to his opponents (even if this support was more verbal than material): Lumumba in 1960, the rebels in 1963–65. Moscow, in its official commentaries on the Mobutu takeover, described him as an instrument of Belgian and American monopolies, borne to power by a "colonial-racist armed rabble."[13] The Soviets were wary about his intimate American ties and CIA links.

Though the more radical members of Mobutu's entourage had urged swift normalization of relations with the Soviet Union and with China in order to project an "anti-imperialist" image, it was not until April 1968 that the Soviet Embassy was opened for the first time in the Mobutu era. There were repeated incidents which kept relations with the Soviets frosty. In 1970 four Soviet diplomats were expelled for "subversion," and in 1971 some twenty Soviet-bloc officials were declared persona non grata after being accused of complicity in student disturbances on the university campus at Kinshasa. Moscow is the only major world capital to which Mobutu has not paid a state visit; in November 1974 an official journey to the USSR was announced for December, but it never took place.[14]

Credentials of nonalignment through closer links to the Soviet Union were thus difficult to obtain. By 1972, however, new opportunities were opening on the Chinese side as Peking emerged from the diplomatic paralysis of the cultural revolution. Chinese policy perspectives in the 1970s changed markedly from those of the early 1960s, when significant aid was provided to insurgent forces. Hostility toward Soviet diplomacy now enjoyed the higher priority; correct relations between states were the rule.

From Mobutu's perspective, there were other facilitating factors in following the Chinese pathway to nonalignment. The triumphant Nixon visit to China in 1972 meant that bridges to China no longer encountered American hostility. There were also significant shifts in Sino–Soviet relations with neighboring Brazzaville. When ideological radicalism had become regime doctrine in Congo–Brazzaville following the ouster of the Youlou government in August 1963, Chinese diplomacy at first had gained the upper hand—a predominance which was reaffirmed in the 1968–72 period. But the Chinese were implicated in the Diawara conspiracy in late 1972 and lost favor with the Brazzaville authorities. Privileged relationships with Kinshasa became as useful to Peking as they were to Mobutu.[15]

Thus the stage was set for Mobutu's spectacular state visit to China in January 1973; there he was received with full honors in what to much of Third World opinion at that time was still the heartland of world revolution. The *People's Daily* in Peking, six years earlier, had found it "fantastic" that "Mobutu, the degenerate betrayer of the Congolese people and murderer of Lumumba, has now, as if by magic, made himself look like a different man, waving the banner of the Congolese national hero Lumumba."[16] That fantastic transformations are indeed possible was demonstrated when Mobutu returned with Chinese benediction, a commitment for $100 million in economic aid for agricultural development, and pledges of arms and instructors for the Angolan liberation movement favored by Mobutu. During 1973 and 1974 the Chinese ambassador to Kinshasa enjoyed privileged access to Mobutu, and was believed by many in the diplomatic community to be Mobutu's most trusted diplomatic confidant. These links were apparently not used by the Chinese to influence Zairian domestic policy, but they did play a valuable part in projecting an image of Mobutu as a leader now closer to the Third World mainstream.

Pre-crisis relations with the United States

The doctrine of nonalignment did not, of course, require active hostility to the West; for most of the period of Mobutu's quest for leadership relations with the United States remained warm. But the nature of the links changed in important ways. With external and internal threats all but eliminated by 1967, the saliency of the military-intelligence connections with the U.S. sharply diminished. According to an American diplomatic source cited by Weissman, CIA political payments to Mobutu had ceased by the end of the 1960s.[17] By 1970 American aid programs in Zaire were being sharply cut back on the grounds that the inflow of commercially negotiated public and private capital sufficed.

From 1969 to 1973 the most important Zairian–American political tie was personalized through the exceptional intimacy between the president and Ambassador Sheldon Vance. The latter, a career diplomat, became a faithful advocate in Washington of the New Regime. He was deeply impressed by Mobutu's accomplishments in creating what seemed to be a unified, stable, and prosperous country, and he encouraged Mobutu's aspirations to regional leadership.[18] Vance was also a persuasive emissary to the financial community, arguing the case for the attractive investment opportunities in Zaire.

Relationships did cool in 1974–75, after the departure of Ambassador Vance in late 1973. His replacement, Deane Hinton (subsequently ambassador to El Salvador, 1981–83), arriving in early 1974, never was able to establish a cordial working rapport with Mobutu. According to diplomatic sources, Hinton was too blunt in expressing apprehension about the direction of the radicalization program of the regime; nor did he find it easy to sugarcoat his conversations with the admiring expressions of deferential flattery which by this time were de rigueur for all who dealt personally with the president.

By this time there were clear hints of Mobutu's displeasure with Ambassador Hinton. The president chose the occasion of the Kinshasa meeting of the African-American Institute in January 1975 to launch an unusual attack on American policy in Africa, which he stigmatized as "a policy of the status quo." The United States, Mobutu declared, "had done nothing for the liberation of Africa from colonialism and apartheid," and, "in certain cases, the United States had even worked against African interests." He deplored the nomination of Nathaniel Davis, former ambassador to Chile, as U.S. assistant secretary for African affairs; by extension this was also an attack on Hinton, who had served in Chile during the Allende period.[19]

A virtual rupture with the United States occurred in June 1975 when Mobutu accused the CIA of plotting his overthrow, and even his "physical elimination." This bizarre episode, which saw the arrest of eleven Zairian general officers and some civilians and the condemnation in absentia of former Central Bank head and Binza group member Ndele, remains obscure in motivation.[20] American diplomatic sources insist that no convincing evidence was ever supplied to document Mobutu's allegations; even within Zaire, where earlier activities of the CIA were well known among the intelligentsia, the charges were generally disbelieved. The juxtaposition is striking between these conspiracy allegations and imminent publication in the United States of findings of parallel inquiries into CIA activities by an executive commission headed by Vice-President Nelson Rockefeller and a congressional committee chaired by Senator Frank Church of Idaho. Mobutu may well have had reason to fear that his name would be publicly mentioned in one of the reports, in particular in connection with possible CIA involvement in the Lumumba assassination. In any event, Mobutu was not specifically fingered by these commissions. Stockwell offers a different explanation, suggesting the officers concerned were CIA contacts, and that Mobutu wished all such linkages to pass through him.[21] When he made his allegations, Mobutu also insisted that Hinton be withdrawn as ambassador.

U.S. secretary of state Kissinger was reported to have been irritated by the gesture of rupturing relations with Israel and infuriated by Mobutu's attacks on American policy and the Davis appointment. Kissinger had not always attached much weight to Mobutu or to Zaire; the first two volumes of his memoires contain but a single, passing reference to Mobutu. But by June 1975 the United States was well along the path to major covert intervention in the Angolan civil war, and it was imperative to improve relations with Mobutu. Hinton was recalled without a whimper, and the master arm-stroker Vance was hurriedly dispatched to repair relationships. A new ambassador, Walter Cutler, was designated—with Mobutu's approval—and the charge of a CIA plot quietly disappeared from presidential rhetoric.[22]

The ambivalent ties with Belgium

Relations with Belgium fluctuated widely. After the crisis surrounding the UMHK nationalization, hostilities—intense at that juncture—slowly faded. Later in 1967, Foreign Minister Pierre Harmel decided to partly disengage the state from the frictions between Belgian capital and Mobutu. The private sector, he reasoned, had ample leverage to defend its interests without constant political intervention by the Belgian government; the state would henceforward focus on social, cultural (and, presumably, political) linkages.[23] By 1968 a thaw was evident in the attitude of Belgian corporations: the Fédération des Entreprises Belges publicly appealed for new investment in Zaire, while the repatriation of profits of Belgian firms in Zaire was again permitted. Mobutu paid his first visit as president to Belgium in 1968; this was followed by the final settlement with UMHK in early 1969. The new honeymoon was symbolized by heavy Belgian participation in the first Kinshasa international trade fair (Fikin), which was deliberately scheduled between 30 June (Zairian independence day) and 21 July (Belgian independence day). The apogee of amity was reached in mid-1970 when King Baudouin again toured Zaire, receiving a welcome as warm as that of 1955. A new chill set in shortly thereafter when UMHK lost out to the Tempelsman consortium in the bidding on major new copper concessions (September 1970), and four Belgian officials of the Société Congolaise de Banque (SOCOBANQUE) were jailed on charges of currency fraud and tax evasion (March 1971). In early 1971, a short-lived ceiling was placed on Belgian imports; Mobutu had grumbled that Belgian capital deliberately abstained from new investment. The battle between Mobutu and the Catholic Church in 1971–72 offended Belgian Christian Democratic milieux, adding to the chill.

A new phase of relative cordiality opened later in 1972. Belgium was quite pleased to see Zaire sever its connections with the French-dominated Organization Commune Africaine et Malgache (OCAM), into which Tshombe had taken Zaire in 1965. But the measures of 30 November 1973 were a new blow; and in March 1974 Mobutu all but severed relationships because the Belgian government refused to seize Jules Chomé's anti-Mobutist volume, *L'ascension de Mobutu* (see chapter 6). The Zairian press agency, AZAP, suggested that the basic issue was whether "there existed friendship between Zaire and Belgium or not." The radicalization measures, which hit Belgian interests much harder than Zairianization, rubbed salt in the wounds. Yet Belgium by this time had sufficient experience with Mobutu's susceptibilities to simply hunker down and wait for better days. By late 1975 the deepening crisis had forced Mobutu to again seek reconciliation.

The French—and other—connections

France evinced sporadic but growing political interest in Zaire, especially during the presidency of Giscard d'Estaing (1974–81). Paris valued Zaire's 1965 adhesion to OCAM, and was correspondingly disappointed when Mobutu pulled out in 1972. Zaire, as the largest officially French-speaking African state, had evident cultural attractions, and France supplied Zaire with a significant number of teachers, especially at the university level. The alchemy of highly personal ties and profitable economic partnership during Giscard's presidency produced a period of unusually close Franco-Zairian relationships. Giscard paid Mobutu the honor of a state visit in August 1975, at a time when Zaire badly needed such a mark of high-level respect. The following year France landed a contract for a national telecommunications system, which was bitterly opposed by other Western creditors as a costly extravagance. The Voice of Zaire thus acquired one of the world's most advanced domestic satellite communications facilities. When it was completed in 1980, sums committed to this scheme exceeded $500 million, by some estimates. Perhaps coincidentally, the major contractor, Thomson CSF International, was then headed by Philippe Giscard d'Estaing, cousin of the French president. Another cousin, François Giscard d'Estaing, was chairman and chief executive of the Banque Française du Commerce Exterieur, which provided a large share of the financing.[24]

France was also Zaire's major supplier of costly military equipment (Mirage jets, Panhard tanks, Puma helicopters). French equity investment was a mere $20 million; a new textile plant in Kisangani was the biggest single undertaking.[25] Against this background, the muscular French military and diplomatic support for the Mobutu regime during Shaba I and II takes on new meaning.

During the 1970s other Western powers played a distinctly secondary role in Zaire. West Germany was a significant participant in the investment field, though the noisy Zairian press releases concealed a quite modest real capital influx. The German combine Klockner–Humbolt–Deutz announced in May 1974 that it would lead a consortium of German interests, holding a 49 percent share in an association with Zaire, in developing some twenty projects in the northeastern part of the country, including iron ore deposits in Banalia and methane gas in the Lake Kivu area. A total investment of $400 million was mentioned, but very little of this moved beyond the drawing board.[26] A German-sponsored cement works was built in Bas-Zaire, where a long-standing factory simultaneously expanded its capacity. Krupp interests had a small equity in the Combinat Industriel de Gemena, primarily a Zairian-financed turnkey project involving various agricultural processing schemes for palm oil and cotton.

Overall, what stands out about the early 1970s is the aggressiveness of the Zairian pursuit of regional leadership and Third World recognition. The regime was sufficiently strong politically and healthy financially to define its own priorities. Still, its diplomatic options, even in its thrust for a

Third World orientation and real nonalignment, were not fundamentally at variance with Western interests, though they frequently were in conflict with particular Belgian aims.

Diplomacy of the Angolan crisis

The issue which draws together all the diplomatic threads of the pre-crisis epoch was the Angolan civil war. The Mobutu strategy in this situation was a bold gamble, for very high stakes. Its ultimate failure had far-reaching costs, and finally unravelled the whole fabric of New Regime diplomacy (on the military aspects of this affair, see chapter 9).

The coup in Portuguese in April 1974 transformed the parameters of southern African politics.[27] The Angolan liberation struggle, hampered by the entrenched divisions among the three major insurgent movements—MPLA, FNLA, and UNITA—was stalemated. Suddenly with the coup some form of independence became an imminent possibility. Mobutu was determined to help broker the transition.

Since 1960 Zaire had maintained close ties with the FNLA, whose ethnic base was located in the northwestern Angolan areas bordering Zaire. Many of the FNLA leadership, including its head, Holden Roberto, had lived in Kinshasa most of their lives. Roberto had quasi-kinship ties with Mobutu through his second wife, who came from the same village as Mobutu's first spouse (though they were not sisters, as many reports held). The FNLA was permitted guerrilla camps on Zairian territory.

In contrast, Zairian relations with the Marxist-oriented MPLA were consistently hostile. Since 1963 the MPLA's main external headquarters had been in Congo–Brazzaville. The MPLA guerrilla effort was seriously complicated by the persistent Zairian denial of transit rights to soldiers moving from the Congo–Brazzaville rear bases into Angola.

Overlying this pattern of relations was the broader, global set of linkages. The FNLA had received episodic CIA support, which resumed after the Portuguese coup. The Soviet Union had been an important patron of the MPLA, although that relation was in abeyance in April 1974. The new-found Zairian–Chinese intimacy of 1973, and the reinforced anti-Soviet pattern of Chinese diplomacy, led to a substantial Chinese military and diplomatic commitment to the FNLA in 1973. Once the Portuguese coup brought Angolan independence into view, the dominant African diplomatic position was that only a coalition among the three major liberation movements could effect a peaceful transition and insulate Angola from the cold war.

While formally supporting the OAU position, Zairian diplomacy in reality aimed at a different outcome: the exclusion of the MPLA from the Luanda formula. Achievement of this goal would assure an Angolan regime closely tied to Zaire and attuned to Zairian aspirations at that peak moment of state expansion, and would enable Zaire to play a role as regional hegemon. There might also be opportunities to split off from Angola the oil-rich Cabinda enclave, separated from the rest of Angola by a narrow strip of Zairian territory (a game also played, for a time, by Congo–Brazzaville). Cabinda might move more directly into the Zairian orbit; Cabinda separatist movements were available for the support of this scheme. The Zairian strategy was also motivated by the fear of being sandwiched between two socialist-oriented states with close Soviet ties—Angola and Congo–Brazzaville.

In 1974, when the Mobutu strategy took form, Zaire held what looked like a number of trump cards:

1. The FNLA, with approximately 2,000 guerrillas inside Angola and 10,000–12,000 in Zairian camps, had the largest extant military force

2. The new Chinese alliance, plus the potent Chinese animosity toward the MPLA, could be utilized to rapidly augment FNLA armament; by mid-year a large flow of Chinese equipment to the FNLA camps was in progress

3. The MPLA was at that time splintered, and one of its factions might be (and was) wooed away

4. The acute hostilities between UNITA and the MPLA, resulting from lethal competition between their respective forces in eastern Angola, opened possibilities of eventual Zairian links to UNITA

5. One of the Cabinda separatist groups, based in Kinshasa, was subject to Zairian direction

6. While Zambia and Tanzania could not be expected to support the FNLA, they might well be attracted to some coalition that included parts of the MPLA and UNITA

7. The United States had a long-standing antipathy to the MPLA and could be counted upon to mount an effort to block its bid for power, once the issue acquired policy visibility in Washington

8. The Zairian armed forces, whose continued weakness had not yet been exposed by Shaba I and II, could ultimately be employed on the side of the FNLA; Zairian territory was within easy striking distance of Luanda

9. South Africa was disposed to assure a clandestine flow of military supplies to UNITA and the FLNA to prevent an MPLA triumph

History invalidated many of these assumptions. The FNLA and Zairian forces proved unreliable in the decisive phases of the civil war. The Soviet Union, unwilling to see an easy American and Chinese triumph and perceiving its own opportunity to project power, began accelerating arms deliveries to the MPLA in early 1975. The unforeseen and decisive military intervention of Cuba began with the arrival of advisors in the summer of 1975; then followed military units during the crucial phases of the civil war in November and December 1975.[28] Meanwhile, the swift exposure of CIA involvement, and especially the full-scale invasion of Angola by South African military units in October 1975, led to OAU backing for the MPLA. By mid-1975, sensing the risks were becoming too high, the Chinese had tiptoed away from the civil war.

Diplomatically as well as militarily, the defeat could hardly have been more complete for Zaire. The MPLA was installed in Angola, buttressed by a strong Soviet–Cuban presence; the South African and CIA interventions had swung African opinion solidly behind the MPLA, and legitimated the Soviet–Cuban role. The vision of an Angolan triumph that would confirm Zaire as hegemonic regional power had thus become the nightmare of an embattled Zaire, again cast into diplomatic isolation, anew the pariah state of tropical Africa. This disaster, great as it was, was soon eclipsed by the relentless onslaught of the economic crisis.

Diplomacy of bankruptcy

The first public tip-off of the impending crisis was the suspension of export insurance guarantees by the Belgian *Office Ducroire* in the spring of 1975. Soon thereafter Zaire began to fall behind in debt repayments; this was publicly revealed by the *Wall Street Journal* on 20 October 1975. At this juncture, with the United States deeply embroiled in partnership with Zaire in the Angolan civil war, an effort was made to provide a bailout of the Zairian government through a special $60 million infusion (one-third each from Export-Import Bank, Public Law 480, and AID credit).[29] At that time State Department sources privately agreed with the Mobutu argument that the Zairian financial problem was purely short term and had been primarily provoked by the fall in copper prices; it sufficed to throw up a bailey bridge over the turbulent but narrow torrent of insolvency to help Zaire across to the abundance lying on the far shore.

Zaire had quietly made its first gestures toward fending off bankruptcy in the spring of 1975. Mobutu approached Irving Friedman, Citibank vice-president, who had developed a personal relationship with him while serving as an IMF official. Friedman had been a major artisan of the hefty Citibank commitment to Zaire; from 1972 to 1974, with an office established in Kinshasa, Citibank and its affiliates in Paris and London helped to arrange loans of $164 million, or 59 percent of all private bank borrowing by Zaire.[30] Mobutu was anxious to obtain a reprieve on the debt without passing through the IMF, to which he had a strong antipathy; its conditions were likely to be too stringent, and he had privately pledged in 1967 that he would never again commit himself to following the fund's prescriptions.[31]

Citibank, however, was not willing to go along with such a scheme; Friedman was convinced that IMF involvement was indispensable. By 1975 ninety-eight banks worldwide held Zairian debts totalling $887 million, of which about $500 million was not guaranteed. The claims were about equally divided among American, European, and Japanese banks. When payments gradually stopped during 1975, the banks began to make inquiries; to their dismay, it was exceedingly difficult to discover just what Zaire's financial situation was.

By the fall of 1975, Mobutu had no choice but to invite an IMF team and to enter into discussions about drawing the relatively easy first tranche of credit to which members were entitled. The IMF was flabbergasted to discover that no one in Zaire knew exactly what the debt was; borrowing had been undertaken through various channels, by diverse government bodies and parastatals, and the Bank of Zaire had no comprehensive data.

Recourse to the IMF inquisition was forced not only by the insistence of private and public creditors, but also by Zaire's dependency on imports. A large fraction of urban food supplies, especially in Kinshasa, was imported. Petroleum products were another crucial drain (especially after 1973). The mines required a continuous flow of machinery, fuel, and supplies; they were obligated to pay expatriate personnel partly in foreign exchange. The industrial sector was even more dependent on imported materials.

Mobutu did explore all other conceivable avenues of potential support, especially among the Arab states. Some of the oil sheikhdoms responded, well after Western banks had locked their doors. In July 1975 a Beirut bank lent Z 6.2 million, and in December 1975 Kuwait and the United Arab Emirates advanced Z 24.7 million.[32] These sums fell far short of the need.

The vise was closing. The ninety-eight banks involved in loans to Zaire, most of whom had entered via syndicates and without close scrutiny of the Zairian situation, were thoroughly alarmed; the recent failures of the Franklin Bank in New York and United States Bank in San Diego had raised questions as to the soundness of the loan structure of a number of American banks. Though no one bank had a very large exposure of un-guaranteed credit to Zaire, the enormous surge of private bank lending to developing countries in the early 1970s had created a number of potential default situations (in Turkey, North Korea, Brazil, Argentina, among others).[33] According to Citibank officials, in late 1975 a significant number of the banks involved felt the Zairian circumstances so unpromising that they preferred to simply declare the default rather than accept the precedent of open-ended and unlimited rescheduling.

Until 1975, former Ambassador Vance testified to a U.S. Senate committee, "Mobutu had thought . . . [Zairians] would be able, through their own austerity measures and their relationships with the . . . several major creditor nations . . . , to resolve their problems without turning to the IMF." Mobutu, with earlier accolades still ringing in his ears, had little idea how low his credit had fallen. In a revealing exchange in an October 1975 Senate hearing, Senator Richard Clark of Iowa asked what credit rating Zaire had with the Export-Import Bank, noting that ratings fell into four categories: a, b, c, and d. A State Department spokesman responded that "nobody is in 'd' anymore, because it is such a low rating." On further checking, it subsequently was revealed that Zaire's rating was, indeed, in the unmentionable "d" category.[34]

In short, Mobutu found that all roads led to the IMF. The private banks insisted on such an approach, believing that only through intervention by the fund could sufficient external leverage be assured to enforce economic policies which offered some hope of recovering their loans. The United States, in spite of Mobutu's allegations of a CIA plot, was still seeking generous IMF treatment for Zaire. Ambassador Vance explained the velvet-glove strategy he favored for winning Mobutu to the IMF formula:

> In our judgement, the most effective way to negotiate with the Government of Zaire . . . to assure that they would turn to the most appropri-

ate way of resolving their financial problems . . . was in view of our prior relationships with Zaire . . . to indicate our supportive attitude and at the same time obtain this commitment from the President.

There is . . . an important psychological difference . . . between our offering to be helpful without condition but at the same time seeing that in the course of friendly discussions that they moved in the direction of the IMF as opposed to going in and saying, look, we will help you only if you make an approach to them. . . . The results are the same.[35]

In March 1976 an initial agreement was reached with the IMF, providing for a first tranche standby credit worth $47 million. Zaire agreed to a 42 percent devaluation of its currency, a limit of 20 percent on wage increases, and a sharp curtailment in government expenditure. This accord gave what a State Department spokesman termed "the IMF 'Good Housekeeping' seal of approval . . . which will enable a cross-section of private and public creditors to help [Zaire]."[36]

The accord cleared the way for a debt-rescheduling meeting involving the public creditors in June 1976; participants, dubbed the "Paris Club," were the United States, Canada, Japan, West Germany, France, Italy, Great Britain, Belgium, the Netherlands, Sweden, and Switzerland. Zaire skillfully played upon divergences within the creditor group to win a relatively favorable rescheduling plan; France in particular supported an indulgent stance at this juncture. Payment on some 85 percent of the outstanding public debt would be postponed for three years, then stretched out over seven additional years. Zaire pledged to pay the remaining 15 percent due immediately (a promise that was not kept).

The private banks, dismayed by the Paris Club terms, met for the first time in June 1976 to devise a common strategy. At that time Zaire was nearly a year behind in payments. On this occasion, fortified by the relative success with the Paris Club, Bank of Zaire director Sambwa Pida demanded a rescheduling of payments over fifteen years. Citibank countered with a proposal for $300 million in new short-term credit for the purchase of equipment essential to generating a cash flow sufficient for loan repayment; credit would be given on condition that arrears be paid and fiscal reforms instituted. The proposal's basic object, according to a financial writer, was to make it possible for Zaire to "use its scarce cash resources to continue paying us back and get their house in order. We wanted to keep the pressure on Zaire and control the use of their funds."[37] It was argued that the rescheduling route had dangerous precedent-setting implications.

In November 1976 an agreement was reached between Zaire and the banks; they joined in what became termed the "London Club." The key features of the accord were a pledge by Zaire to pay at once outstanding interest (about $40 million), to begin making payments on arrears on principal by March 1977 ($51 million was repaid by January 1977), and to accept the IMF program necessary for eligibility for the more stringent second tranche. Citibank, in return, pledged that if the terms were met it would make its "best effort" to syndicate a new $250 million loan, both to facilitate debt repayment and to permit imports of critical supplies for productive enterprises.

In March and April 1977, with great reluctance, the IMF agreed to a second tranche—a $52.2 million standby arrangement, and a $32.8 million loan. But the report of an IMF team which visited Zaire in February 1977 was very critical. While Zaire kept the agreement on holding wage increases to 20 percent, it did not restrict the budget deficit, which soared to a record Z 313 million—12 percent of GDP. The balance of payments deficit, $156 million, was far greater than had been estimated; poor copper prices, and the leakage of foreign exchange through venal coffee export rackets, SOZACOM, and other mechanisms each played a part. At this time Citibank officials estimated that Gécamines, the Bank of Zaire, and the presidential brotherhood each controlled about one-third of the total foreign exchange.[38]

The IMF second tranche agreement apparently cleared the way for Citibank to put together its $250 million loan. However, the eighty-day war of Shaba I suspended these efforts. Hardly had the dust settled after the war when Mobutu fired Bank of Zaire director Sambwa for "errors of judgement." Sambwa was the chief line of access for the bankers; further, the sins imputed to the dismissed director were partly tied to his efforts to plug the venal exchange hemorrhage.

Citibank made a substantial effort to syndicate the promised new loan, but encountered great difficulties. Many banks, for various reasons, were not interested in extending their commitment to Zaire. Indeed, Citibank's own syndication department would not cooperate.[39] Zaire, by the end of 1977, concluded that Citibank could not raise the loan.

By 1977 the old illusion in Zaire and the West that the economic crisis was a passing epiphenomenon had been thoroughly dispelled. The result, in 1977–78, was a curious mixture of temporizing and of escalating demands for reforms, yet no real willingness on the part of either public or private external lending agencies to extend major new commitments. A consultative Group for Zaire came into being, joining to the Paris Club the two international agencies most heavily involved in Zaire—the IMF and the World Bank. Zaire was asked to provide an integrated program for development which could serve as a basis for new credit. The response, unveiled in November 1977 at the MPR party congress, was cut of classic Mobutu cloth, as the terms used in the president's announcement suggest:

> Given that I am the guarantor of the well-being of the Zairian people, I propose to you a RECOVERY PLAN, which I call, without demagoguery, the MOBUTU PLAN, because, not only have I conceived it, but further, I intend to personally apply it and see to its success.[40]

At this point there literally was no Mobutu Plan, in the sense of a document setting forth Mobutu's conception. What eventually emerged from the Ministry of Planning was a call for $1 billion in new foreign aid, bolstered by a vague collation of pious aspirations such as better transport, higher agricultural production, decentralized decision-making, and improved administration. As administrative reshuffles, redrawn organizational charts, and verbal affirmations of beneficent intent were aging nags which had done innumerable laps around the racetrack of Mobutist rhetoric before, the credibility of this new program was nil.

Though the savage curtailment of imports (and the failure to repay many debts) did produce a short-lived improvement in the balance of payments in 1977, the trade position deteriorated again in 1978. The 1977 budget deficit was again Z 321.7 million, or 32 percent of the total budget, and a comparable shortfall was in prospect for 1978.[41] Inflation and shortages continued unabated.

By the end of 1977 the IMF had rescinded Zaire's eligibility for higher tranche credit, noting that the country was not meeting arrears, and that indeed it had no notion of what Zaire was doing. Zaire in 1978 had all but stopped paying its debts; only $50 million was reimbursed. By the end of 1978 delinquent payments amounted to at least $800 million and were increasing by $125 million per quarter.[42] By this time international creditors had adopted a new approach: they insisted that Zaire, in effect, place its key financial organs into receivership. The IMF was charged with recruiting a team of experts to assume direction of the Bank of Zaire; the team leader, Erwin Blumenthal, was a former head of the international department of the German Bundesbank. Blumenthal soon earned the nickname of "Bula Matari" when in November and December 1978 he embargoed foreign exchange to some fifty companies tied to members of the politico-commercial class—including seven members of the Political Bureau and, most prominently, Mobutu's relative Litho. A Belgian team was to take over management of the Customs Service, notoriously riddled with corruption, yet responsible for collecting the greater part of state revenues. To square the circle, external personnel were obtained to control the Finance Ministry. The IMF long balked at recruiting among treasury (as opposed to central bank) personnel, and for a time it was believed that France would supply these experts. Finally, in early 1979, the IMF did recruit a Turk for strategic placement in Finance.

The international team of plumbers recruited to plug leaks in the country's resource flows faced an uphill struggle. The presence of "Bula Matari" did for a time make some difference. But Blumenthal's embargo soon developed leaks of its own, and by the fall of 1979 he had left in disgust. His replacement, former IMF official Mamadou Touré of Mauritania, was more diplomatic in his approach to his functions (yet even Touré lasted only two years).

In 1980 there was a momentary interlude of improvement in Zaire's external payment situation; in addition, inflation slowed somewhat. A brief rise in copper prices was part of the explanation, as was the impact of the Mobutu demonetization scheme (see chapter 10). Blumenthal wryly suggested another explanation: "Mobutu," he wrote in a confidential report, "was almost constantly abroad, and the new Prime Minister, Minister of Finance, and central bank director were able to work without constraint."[43] In mid-1981 this temporary improvement led to another—and larger—IMF advance of approximately $950 million. Soon thereafter Zaire was again out of compliance with the agreement, and by 1982 further advances had again been cut off.

In 1983 Zaire managed to come to a new accord with the IMF, which won him another advance and further respite from his creditors, who by now were much more worried about the debts of Argentina, Mexico, and Brazil than they were about those of Zaire. In each successive accord the Fund had tried to seal holes that had been discovered in the failure of preceding agreements. On this occasion, Mobutu was required to float his currency, which immediately fell from an official rate of six zaires per dollar to about thirty-to-one. The currency float, Fund officials hoped, would make impossible foreign exchange rackets which had made large sums for leading members of the politico-commercial class. Not formally linked to the accord, but nonetheless related to it, was the replacement of Zairian Gécamines director Umba by a veteran Belgian manager. Gécamines was to market most of its metal production, assuring it a more regular flow of foreign exchange to finance its machinery, spare parts, and other required imports. SOZACOM, the corruption-ridden mineral marketing parastatal, was largely cut out of metal exports. Diamond purchasing offices were established to buy diamonds produced by small diggers, to halt exchange loss through smuggling.

The ephemeral character of previous accords inevitably raised questions about the durability of the 1983 agreement. By this time many of Zaire's creditors had come to share Blumenthal's harsh verdict. At each point of renegotiation Mobutu could be counted upon to promise a new set of financial reforms; once past the immediate crisis, the old routines would return. The regime, Blumenthal concluded, "counted on the generosity of its creditors for an indefinite rescheduling of their loans." There was, however, "no—I repeat no—possibility on the horizon that the numerous creditors of Zaire will recover their funds." The root cause "which destroys all possibilities" of recovery was "the CORRUPTION of the ruling group." [44]

The economic imbroglio involved complex interrelationships among private creditors, international financial institutions (the IMF and the World Bank), and Western governments, each of which had somewhat different objectives. The private banks wanted controls placed over the Zairian economy so that they could recover their loans; alone, they lacked the leverage to achieve this. The IMF was an indispensable mechanism, yet the IMF was not enough; as Friedman of Citibank put it, "the IMF really doesn't care if the private banks are repaid." [45] The IMF, at the bottom line of its mandate, had to see Zaire return to a situation in which the management of its currency and its foreign exchange made it a reliable participant in international trade. The Fund did not see protection of the interests of private banks as a major goal, nor did it believe that hand-in-glove collaboration with the banks was feasible; indeed, one Fund official argued that the lending policies pursued by the private banks were frequently "frustrating." [46] Western states, while also concerned about debt recovery, had more political motivations; the warm spot which Mobutu had earned over the years, and fears of an anti-Western alternative regime, were more important than the money owed. In fact, neither international, state, nor private lenders had any ultimate means to collect their debts. External actors were in a curious position; they could neither afford to see Mobutu fall politically nor fail economically. This situation, in spite of the desperate dimensions of the crisis, gave Mobutu some room to maneuver. By 1977 it had become fairly clear that Western creditors would not, in practice, declare a default. The disadvantages of this route were multiple. Long and costly litigation would be necessary, including efforts to seize Zairian assets abroad as part of the liquidation process. The bulk of the private bank debt

Table 12.1   Zaire's External Public Debt, 1972–1977 (millions of U.S. dollars)

	1972	1973	1974	1975	1976	1977
Total outstanding, including undisbursed	714.9	1,750.8	2,876.9	3,008.3	3,305.6	3,543.3
Private creditors	468.4	1,209.9	1,818.0	1,896.2	2,000.0	2,054.3
Suppliers	225.6	442.0	564.5	622.2	645.1	671.9
Private financial institutions	237.8	762.7	1,247.6	1,268.6	1,349.0	1,376.0
Multilateral institutions	85.5	101.3	136.6	284.7	349.8	367.6
IBRD	2.5	1.5	0.5	100.0	100.0	100.0
IDA	54.0	63.5	73.5	125.5	176.0	194.0
Bilateral official lenders	161.1	439.5	722.3	827.4	955.8	1,121.4
Total outstanding, disbursed only	544.2	862.3	1,294.6	1,655.1	2,168.8	2,639.3
Private creditors	389.9	677.8	983.0	1,172.3	1,462.8	1,658.4
Suppliers	188.0	246.5	325.8	347.4	425.3	505.9
Private financial institutions	197.0	426.1	651.3	819.5	1,031.6	1,146.0
Multilateral institutions	30.4	50.0	60.4	79.1	116.8	179.8
IBRD	2.5	1.5	0.5	11.8	32.4	56.4
IDA	8.4	16.3	26.3	37.8	54.6	87.0
Bilateral official lenders	123.8	134.5	251.3	403.7	589.1	801.2

Source: Guy Gran, "Zaire 1978: The Ethical and Intellectual Bankruptcy of the World System," *Africa Today* 25, no. 4 (October–December 1978): 18.

carried public guarantees, but the precise circumstances in which state authorities would agree to bring these into play were not entirely clear. Thus by 1978 there was a tacit standoff, punctuated by the ongoing ritual of stabilization programs and rescheduling discussions. The whole situation was unprecedented in the international politics of debt; it had become a surrealistic theater whose underlying humbug was elaborately camouflaged by symbolic exchanges. (Data on the structure of the Zairian external debt are presented in tables 12.1 and 12.2.)

Political aspects of crisis phase diplomacy

In the political realm, Zaire pulled far back from the aggressive nonalignment of 1973–75. While Zairian and American motivations in the Angola affair were not identical, their close collaboration reduced the momentary estrangement of 1974–75. At the same time, Zaire played an active role in

Table 12.2   Debt Service Obligations, 1978–1983
            (millions of U.S. dollars)

	1978	1979	1980	1981	1982	1983
Debt service	477.1	471.9	482.9	421.9	392.3	341.4
Private creditors	392.7	366.9	367.5	299.9	266.1	213.6
Multilateral institutions	15.8	23.6	22.0	23.3	23.3	22.9
Bilateral lenders	68.6	81.4	93.4	98.7	103.0	105.0
Amortization	325.7	324.9	347.0	304.3	291.7	260.1
Interest	151.4	147.0	135.9	117.6	100.7	81.3

Source: Gran, "Zaire 1978," p. 19, based on World Bank debt tables.

Third World forums in opposing the rash of resolutions that called Zionism a form of racism, which were being assiduously promoted by Arab states in every conceivable international gathering. Ambassador Vance, pleading the Mobutu cause before the Clark Senate subcommittee in October 1975, urged not only the "basic commonality of attitudes and policies in foreign affairs," but Mobutu's "recent rather gallant opposition to efforts of the Arab states at the Lima non-aligned conference to reverse the thrust of anti-Israeli sentiment in Africa."[47] A marked reduction in Zairian bellicosity on southern African questions resulted not only from collaboration with South Africa in the Angola civil war, but also from new dependence on South Africa for credit for consumer imports and for an export route for copper after closure of the Benguela railway in August 1975.

In an apparent effort to secure a West German commitment to the survival of the regime, Mobutu entered into a politically controversial accord, damaging to his relations with neighboring states, with a private German rocket firm. A remarkable contract was signed by Mobutu on 26 March 1976 with the Orbital Transport and Raketen A.G. (OTRAG), which granted the company virtual sovereignty over a 150,000-square-kilometer tract in northeastern Shaba that was to be used as a rocket-launching base.[48] By the terms of the contract, OTRAG was accorded "the right to possess and use the territory without restriction for the purpose of launching missiles into the atmosphere and into space . . . and to take all measures which, in the opinion of OTRAG, are related directly, indirectly or otherwise." The rocket firm thus acquired the right to displace populations and to operate as a law unto itself in a huge area of the country.[49] Just why this extraordinary concession was ever granted remains a mystery. The Zairian state apparently received some rental from OTRAG, and the possibility in sharing in the ultimate profits of this speculative venture. Hull alleges that Mobutu received 47 percent of the profits of the OTRAG aviation subsidiary which transported materiel to the Shaba site.[50]

More sinister interpretations were placed upon the transaction when its terms were revealed by the leftist journal *Afrique Asie* in August 1977. Apparently planted by East European intelligence services, allegations were made that the OTRAG venture was really a cover for a cruise missile test site, or even a base for nuclear weapon development in collaboration with South Africa. The OTRAG affair became a cause célèbre throughout Africa and caused acute embarrassment to West Germany; partly as a result of pressure from Bonn, the contract was cancelled in 1979.[51] In reality, the OTRAG project appears to have been simply a commercial undertaking aimed at developing an inexpensive launching technique for earth satellites. Many experts consider its technology to have been dubious; indeed, at a public launch in the presence of Mobutu and foreign journalists, the OTRAG missile veered off the launching pad and fizzled to an ignominious crash nearby.

Mobutu was able to make some use of the warm spot developed in some Middle Eastern hearts during his overtures to the Arab world in 1973, even though he then drew back from the anti-Israel campaign. He succeeded in persuading Saudi Arabia, Egypt, and Morocco that he was a solid rampart against Soviet expansion in tropical Africa. These Arab connections, aside from providing occasional cash injections outside the IMF straitjacket (Saudi Arabia lent an additional $60 million in early 1978), were to prove of inestimable value during the Shaba crises of 1977 and 1978.

In his dealings with the United States, Mobutu was able to invoke his long record of intimate liaison both through conventional diplomatic channels and through the CIA, despite the contretemps of 1974–75. The change of administration in January 1977 clearly weakened Mobutu's position; the key figures in U.S. African policy formulation—Richard Moose, Anthony Lake, Andrew Young, and Donald McHenry—did not share the earlier perception of Zaire as the linchpin of African stability, and were skeptical of the Mobutu regime. Their African diplomatic strategy relied on developing effective working relationships with states closer to the African mainstream (Nigeria and Tanzania in particular) than Zaire had become. There was also strong skepticism concerning Zaire in Congress, especially in the House Subcommittee on Africa.

The new American ambivalence to the relationship was laid bare during the Shaba I incursion. Mobutu had promptly accused not only Angola but also Cuba and the Soviet Union of instigating, arming, and equipping the invaders. The American response, officially described as "limited and measured," was a sharp disappointment to Mobutu, consisting as it did mainly of an acceleration of the supply of military equipment already in the pipeline.

Shaba II, in May 1978, brought much more direct American military support. The scale of the Soviet–Cuban intervention in Ethiopia just before Shaba II supplied new arguments for globalists in the U.S. policy community, who argued that Shaba II bore the hallmark of Soviet machinations and required direct confrontation.

The general Western reaction to Shaba II was swifter than it had been to the earlier invasion, though it was divided. The most unequivocal support came from France. The French Foreign Legion and Belgian paratroopers received American air transport support. Mobutu once again placed heavy stress on allegations of Soviet and Cuban complicity in the invasion. This time President Carter publicly echoed the charges, only to retreat from them in late June when it became evident that the CIA was unable to document them.[52]

If the surprising diversity of actors who sprang to the defense of Zaire demonstrated the skill of Mobutu in making a virtue of his very vulnerability, it also widened the scope of reform proposals emanating from the partners of Zaire, particularly the United States. By July 1978 strong pressure was being exerted to induce a rapprochement with Angola. This was accomplished by August; both Angola and Zaire found advantage in reducing arms flows and curtailing sanctuary. Beginning in 1977, political liberalization was also added to the agenda of reform strictures; this was met by Mobutu by the organization of elections for the Political Bureau and Parliament in November 1977. Finally, military reform was added to the list because of the utter unreliability of the FAZ when faced with even small challenges. By late 1978 France and Belgium were each at work developing new brigades, following the by-now well-worn pattern of dealing with the awesome disabilities of the extant armed forces by forming new units outside the existing structure.

The pressure for reforms had slackened by 1980, and Mobutu was able to quietly shelve those he found inconvenient. He privately argued to American representatives that they had failed to keep their end of the bargain; he could only accept the political risk of liberalizing the system if substantial new resources became available to him for managing it. What was offered by public and private American and other Western sources fell far short of his requirements. Further, as the 1980 American electoral campaign unfolded, the prospect opened of a new administration whose central foreign policy theme was the construction of an anti-Soviet "strategic consensus" in all directions. Mobutu was a willing recruit for such enterprises. Thus by the early 1980s the campaign to overcome the Zairian crisis through economic and political reforms, under American guidance and encouragement, had run completely into the sands.

Throughout the late 1970s consistent French support, symbolized by the intimate Giscard–Mobutu relationship, provided Mobutu crucial room to maneuver. In debt renegotiations, in supplying military equipment, in organizing foreign troops to repulse the FNLC, Giscard proved a reliable ally. Mobutu ably played upon not only his personal ties and upon contracts profitable for French interests, but also upon the susceptibility of Paris to the argument that Zaire was the second-largest French-speaking country in the world. The election of François Mitterrand in 1981 produced a moment of panic as Socialist Party Africanists had been sharply critical of the Mobutu regime. The organization of the 1982 Franco–African summit in Kinshasa symbolized Zairian success in retaining the assurance of French backing.

Belgium was a more prickly partner. Successive weak and divided governments in Brussels reflected the hostility of important segments of Belgian public opinion, particularly in left Flemish milieux. The dispatch of Belgian paratroopers to Kolwezi in 1978 was bitterly divisive; some Flemish ministers were still arguing against the dispatch of the troops after they were already airborne.[53]

In its African diplomacy, Zaire has never again been able to regain the standing briefly achieved in the early 1970s. Nonetheless, Mobutu did recover from the nadir in relationships that marked the aftermath of the Angolan fiasco. The rapprochement with the Luanda regime facilitated a return to at least formally correct relations within Africa. The regime ceased to be subject to the open derision which had been reflected in 1977 in President Nyerere's thinly disguised reference to "corrupt dictators." In 1981 Zaire was able to secure African bloc support for election to a UN Security Council seat. Its troops were part of an OAU peacekeeping force in Chad in 1981–82, and returned, at bilateral invitation, in 1983. However, the residual costs of the Angolan adventure were illustrated in the rebuff given by members of the Southern African Development Coordination Conference (SADCC) to Zairian overtures to join this group, which had been formed after Zimbabwe gained independence to collaborate on reducing dependence on South Africa.

The riddle of Zairian dependency

The character of the dependent Zairian relationship to the international arena was a series of interlocking riddles. The crisis had utterly voided the regime's legitimacy at home, and through exposure of its infirmities and derelictions had destroyed its credibility abroad. Yet the external world had become heavily implicated in the patchwork of expedients that kept the state lurching forward. The IMF became more heavily immersed in the internal processes of coping with the Zairian payments crisis than it had ever been in the internal processes of other countries. The private creditors silently endured a default in payments. But external support was at best half-hearted. The flaws of the new order were too deep-seated for ready remedy. The alternatives were unclear, and there was considerable uncertainty as to whether a new regime would, or indeed could, repair the corroded apparatus of the state.

In its ascendant and expansionist phases the Mobutist state, with its internal hegemony assured, sought to expand its autonomy, pursue a vocation of regional leadership, and enlarge the opportunities for accumulation by its dominant politico-commercial class. The rendezvous with multinational capital and international finance, deemed necessary to achieve these goals, yielded a transaction whose logic has been categorized by Verhaegen as "technological imperialism."[54] Long-term returns on capital investment were uncertain because of the possibility of economic dislocations (inflation, monetary crises) or political misfortunes (disorders, coups, nationalizations). The sale of technology to Zaire in the form of management services, turnkey factories, patents, and the like, had potent attractions: in Verhaegen's terms, "It produces an immediate profit, safe from political and economic risks . . . taken at the time of sale, before production and independent of profitability" of the enterprise; profit is "all the higher because the technology is complex, costly, fragile and not adapted to the real needs of development and to the conditions of society."[55]

The circle was closed, Verhaegen argues, by the coincidence of interest between the supplier of technology and the hegemonic class within Zaire. The growing technocratic class of university-trained functionaries, most of whom sought employment in public or private bureaucracies, found that "a part of their revenue depends on the 'coefficient' of corruption which they can derive from technological transactions."[56] Indeed, the major participants in this process—foreigner and Zairian alike—transferred abroad as many of their liquid assets as possible, which suggests that they shared an underlying lack of confidence in the future of the country. The evident solution for financing development projects was for the state to borrow the capital, thus shouldering the risks, while the foreign technology purveyors and the politico-commercial class divided the immediate gain.

The pattern of capital transfer to Zaire was, of course, directly related to the debt issue. The regime, committed to the copper-energy strategy, wished a central role for the state. Private banks, awash in Eurodollars and then petrodollars in the early 1970s, were in a phase of aggressive lending to less developed countries, all the more because these loans frequently carried high interest rates and often were largely guaranteed by Western governments. Many Western firms were more interested in supplying their services than in staking their own capital. The confluence of these factors led to the monumental debt crisis, which in turn placed the state in a condition of permanent mendicity.

Not all external forces promoted the borrowing formula. IMF officials were skeptical of the direction of the Zairian economy from the early days of the capital rush, but the solid Zairian position in exchange balances during most of the early 1970s gave no leverage to the Fund, whose advice Mobutu was disinclined to consider in any case. The World Bank expressed influential opposition to some of the capital investment schemes, and particularly to Inga-Shaba and the Ilebo–Kinshasa railway. In 1972 the American Embassy solicited a report on Zaire from development economist Wolfgang Stolper, who had earlier been involved in Nigerian planning. His conclusions were "on the somber side"; he warned of the potential liabilities of the Inga II and Inga-Shaba projects, though by this time the Zairian decisions to proceed with them were irreversible. He also pointed out the dependency-creating effects and doubtful prospects of the Maluku steel mill.[57]

The end result of the apparent investment boom, far from leading to the promised abundance for 1980, resembled the "tragedy of the commons." External lenders and contractors, the Western states supporting the Zairian development scheme, and the politico-commercial class in intense pursuit of its short-term advantages, wound up destroying the means of their livelihood.

Some analysts (and many Zairians) see in this tragic outcome the implacable workings of "dependency."[58] In their cruder form, these interpretations require one to impute conscious purpose and causal force to a vast anthropomorphic abstraction such as the "world capitalist system." In the Zairian case one would further have to believe in truly perverse motivations on the part of capital and contract purveyors in order to conclude that they find the present crisis desirable. Creditors of Zaire face slender prospects of recovering their loans. Most of the import substitution factories built in the 1970s have fared poorly, and the $250 million sunk in the SMTF project is a dead loss for the foreseeable future. More broadly, the decay of the state and the deterioration of the public economy have created conditions in which it is impossible for international capital to profit from the Zairian resource base.

From another perspective, the new set of external economic linkages with Western capital and states that were formed during the ascendancy and expansion phases constructed tributary bonds which still pervade the external policy concerns of Zaire. The debt and its ramifications is a daily preoccupation. Successive improvisations must be managed, and the desperate scramble to somehow sustain the flow of goods indispensable to the minimal functioning of the economy dominates Zairian diplomacy.

Zaire is by no means unarmed in these transactions. Mobutu has had several kinds of resources to bring to dealings with stronger powers. The pursuit of policies (through image construction or votes in international forums) in conformity with the broader foreign policy goals of the stronger partner is one such bargaining counter whose value was raised to the extent that for a time Zaire enjoyed secondary influence over smaller states in the region. Overt hostility to the Soviet Union was a device that offered significant gratification simultaneously to the Chinese and the Americans. Over the years Mobutu has also played with impressive skill upon the somewhat different objectives and orientations of its major external partners. France, for example, is influenced by cultural policies and the incorporation of Zaire into a set of francophonic states with close European (and French) ties. Belgium is preoccupied with its economic involvement in Zaire and accords less priority to global perspectives. For United States policy makers economic factors have played their part (especially access to minerals), but more important are Zaire's regional influence and significance and the overall strategic value of the country from a global perspective. Chinese interest in Zaire is heavily conditioned by anti-Soviet goals, while the Soviet Union would evidently prefer a strongly anti-Western regime in Kinshasa. Figure 12.1 summarizes our judgements of the fluctuating relations of Zaire with the most salient international actors.

Within important limits, there are possibilities for profiting from these divergences. During the various negotiations occasioned by the bankruptcy crisis, Mobutu—whose bargaining position was exceedingly weak—none-

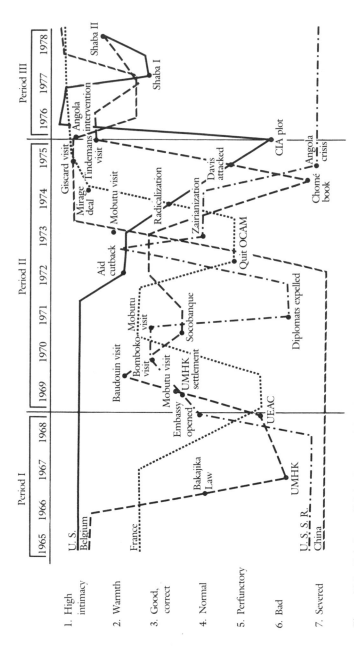

Figure 12.1. Relations of Major Powers with Zaire, 1965–1978

394

theless showed keen insight into the differing degrees of severity of the conditions required by Western partners. France was usually the soft underbelly of the phalanx of creditors.

Mobutu manages to transform the very weakness of Zaire into an asset for the survival of his regime. He has astutely sustained the "Mobutu or chaos" thesis, which unfailingly brings Western powers to his rescue when push finally comes to shove. The more enfeebled the regime, the more "Mobutu or chaos" becomes a live issue. By repressing, dividing, and co-opting potential opposition, the regime has succeeded in preserving near total uncertainty abroad as to what the contours of an alternative regime would be or how it might come into being. There is, accordingly, no way to really test the "Mobutu or chaos" formula. For Western states, a radical anti-imperial regime that sought a Soviet alliance, the dissolution of the state into warring factions (on the Chad model), or the disintegration of Zaire into several small entities are all exceedingly unpalatable scenarios. The capital at stake, the significance to Western economies of Zairian resources—especially cobalt—and the turbulence which might be unleashed throughout central and southern Africa by any of these three scenarios make Western chanceries unwilling to accept a serious risk of such alterations in the African geopolitical landscape. The risk is probably very small; Mobutu's ultimate trump card is the impossibility of calculating it. Thus even though few believe that the incumbent regime has the will or the capacity to overcome the current crisis, Zairian diplomacy extracts reluctant and limited but nonetheless sufficient backing whenever the regime is in mortal peril.

Meanwhile, Zairian civil society is a helpless spectator. It is called upon to shoulder the cost of the transactions between the state and its external political partners and economic creditors. The hegemony of the state and the survival of its incumbent rulers will be assured by the external forces, as state and regime are the sole guarantors of their interests. The apparent passivity of civil society in the face of its unending series of misfortunes is rooted in part in the consequent conviction of its powerlessness.

13

Conclusion: Crisis of the Zairian State

We are all responsible, whoever we may be, and we must awaken our consciences. A profound discouragement comes over each of us. . . . We no longer react to the misery, the corruption at all levels, to the shameful exploitation of the poor, the greed of the rich, and the degradation of the respect due to each human being.

Monsignor Kabanga,
Archbishop of Lubumbashi[1]

The nature of the Mobutist state

In its early years, from 1965 to 1973, the New Regime pursued a state-building strategy which closely conformed to the behavioral imperatives of state reason sketched in chapter 1.[2] The unchallenged hegemony of the state was reasserted, fusing the models of the absolutist Leopoldian bureaucratic autocracy and the post-colonial unitary, nationalist, one-party African state. The security imperative was pursued through the elimination of unreliable Katanga gendarme and mercenary elements in the armed forces, the suppression of competing provincial paramilitary formations, the construction of a proficient state security agency, and the maintenance of linkages with external protectors. Enlarged state autonomy was sought through a diversification of external patrons (China, conservative Arab states, France, as well as the United States and Belgium), and by chipping away at the entrenched positions of colonial capital (through the Bakajika Law, UMHK nationalization) while soliciting a multiplicity of new Western multinational and bank connections. An earnest search for legitimation was undertaken by creating a new ideological doctrine for the state (nationalism, authenticity, ultimately "Mobutism"), by weaving together the inherited image of the Bula Matari state's technocratic efficacy with new inspirational designs for grandiose development ("Objectif 80"), and by projecting the regime as the institutionalization of the Zairian nation (through the MPR). The revenue imperative of the state was to be met by sharp increases in fiscal impositions on the colonial corporate sector

396

(which had been very lightly taxed by the Bula Matari state), a silent perpetuation of the crushing panoply of fiscal extraction devices imposed upon the peasantry, and by drawing in major new resources from abroad through loans, aid, and investments as well as by mortgaging the rich natural resource base.

Parallel to these institutional transformations were important alterations in the basic nature of the state. As the framework of European hegemony, the African colonial state operated through a parsimonious alien bureaucracy whose costs could be met through internal resources, particularly before 1945 when its functions were largely limited to security and extraction. Tshibumba, in his "colonie belge" paintings, captured its essence; impersonal, institutionalized, and unchallengeable force was the ultimate basis of the colonial state, and gave it tacit legitimation.

The effort to design an institutionalized post-colonial state through a transfer of the constitutional apparatus of the European state failed in most African states, but nowhere more dramatically than in Zaire during the *pagaille* era. The political forces unleashed by the demise of the Bula Matari state could not be managed and manipulated by a restoration of its institutional framework alone. Incumbent rulers in the African post-colonial state, including Zaire, constructed a set of patrimonial linkages by which their ascendancy over the political class was maintained. The state was not simply a set of institutions of governance; it was a system of personal rule.

The resurrected state of the New Regime thus had a dual character: formally institutionalized, in party and administration, but informally patrimonial and personal.[3] Mobutu from the outset used the analogy of chief and followers, joined in a quite personal bond of rulership. There was a progressively more explicit personalization of the state, whose apotheosis was constitutional enshrinement of "Mobutism" as the national ideology, and which was expressed by an imposing array of praise-names for the president: "Guide," "Timonier" (helmsman), "President-Fondateur," "Mulopwe" (emperor, with overtones of divinity), and finally even "Messiah." What began as a collegial alliance of former Lumumbists, the Binza group, the top military command, and young, often radical university graduates gradually became an assemblage of courtiers doing the bidding of the presidential monarch. This design, executed with methodical skill, required the progressive clientelization of erstwhile colleagues. Autonomous power bases of influential First Republic personalities were sapped. Systematic rotation of high office was practiced. As a co-optative resource, a pool of vacant high offices was sustained through the continuous pensioning of former collaborators into lucrative business opportunities, in return for their quiet retirement from key positions. The sanction for not cooperating in elite circulation was imprisonment on corruption, nepotism, or subversion charges, or exile. Access to high rank in all state agencies depended upon presidential favor; this was exercised by direct designation at the top levels, while presidential scrutiny and veto applied at intermediate levels. By the 1970s those in high office understood very well that only presidential grace kept them there, and that the principle of rotation was unlikely to leave them in place very long. An occupational hazard of high office was vulnerability to charges of nepotism, corruption, or disloyalty; the prison gate was too close to permit incurring presidential disfavor by deviation from the norms of faithful clientage.

Patrimonialism increasingly defined the relationship between the state and civil society. A politico-commercial class crystallized around the organs of state power, and in turn depended upon the hegemony of the state for both its security and its accumulation. The main sources of recruitment for this new class were First Republic politicians and the new generation of university graduates, who by the end of the 1960s were becoming numerous. In certain respects, this social group was a veritable service class. Continuity in proximity to power, either through holding public office or pursuing private business sheltered by state favor, was ultimately contingent on *fidelité au Guide*, or some intermediary patron. Service rendered to the system was the price of entry; opposition by deed or even word ran the risk of loss of class standing. Thus, although the politico-commercial class had become an entrenched category in Zairian society, its individual membership was in constant flux. Within this group existed an inner core of persons with especially close kinship, ethnoregional, or personal ties to the president; variously known as the "presidential brotherhood" or the "untouchables," they were able to conduct their mercantile affairs in blatant disregard of normal legal regulations. Those at the lower end of the politico-commercial class enjoyed much less leeway. Overall, the character of the state could not be understood apart from this internally hegemonic group.

The regime, as the years wore on, also took on an ethnoregional coloration. Though the politico-commercial class as a whole was reasonably representative, in geographic terms, power at the inner core was exercised by a more narrowly defined group, of Equateur and Lingalaphone background, who had particularly close affinities with the president. This relationship was particularly visible at the top of the security apparatus (in the FAZ and CND). Mobutu told a *Jeune Afrique* reporter in 1973 that he regarded national integration as his most important achievement; at that time there was some justification for his claim.[4] In the crisis years, however, not only did the ethnoregional core of the regime become more apparent, but distrust of regions where disaffection was believed to be particularly intense escalated.

Crisis and decline of the state

The era of state decline, brought on by the crisis that began in 1974, thrust to the fore new questions concerning the nature of the state and the ultimate implications of its decay. As the realization grew that the crisis was endemic and not just a passing phase, doubts emerged about its capacity for rational behavior and its ability to serve—depending on one's theoretical perspective—the interests of development, capitalism, or the ruling class. The state might become simply an insecure predator upon civil society, a debt collector for external creditors.

We would suggest that an important part of the pathology of state decay is expressed by three processes: shrinkage in the competency, credibility, and probity of the state. In considering each of these it should be borne in mind that the state is an exceedingly complex social formation, institutional matrix, and ideological domain. Decline is not a single process or an absolute condition; rather, it consists of corrosion which occurs unevenly in different portions of the state.

The decline of competence refers to the growing inability of the state to relate material means to policy ends. We have illustrated this process in our chapters on administration, the security forces, economic policies, and (particularly) Zairianization and radicalization. State agencies become involuted mechanisms, mainly preoccupied with their own reproduction. Their formal activity tends to become symbolic and ritualistic.

Deflation in credibility brings a loss of belief by the citizenry in the capacity of the state to perform its accustomed functions. The Bula Matari state, however negatively it was viewed, had undeniable credibility, which is reflected still in the frequent, perversely nostalgic conversational references by rank and file Zairians to the orderly conditions of *le temps des belges*, when the trains ran on time. State credibility was seriously compromised during the *pagaille* years, but then apparently was restored in the early Mobutu years. The erosion of credibility resumed with a vengeance in the decline era. A mood of utter cynicism regarding the state now pervades the populace. Less than a *pagaille*, the state has become an irrelevancy. Its armed forces, while dangerous to the unwary or unarmed, are visibly unable to contend with any armed challengers, unless reinforced by foreign cadres. The state is unable to maintain its transport and health infrastructures, or to sustain the value of its currency. Any activity carried out by the state is assumed by its citizenry to malfunction. Vanishing credibility is far more apparent on the periphery than in the center; everywhere, however, its absence shapes the basic assumptions and expectations of civil society.

The third vector of decay, the decline in probity, is manifest in Zaire in the systemization of corruption. From the petty venality entailed in survival among the lower echelons to kleptocracy at the summit, corruption is presumed in transactions with the state—enrolling a child in school, visiting a public clinic, passing a police roadblock. The extraordinary fortunes accumulated by Mobutu and some of the inner ring of collaborators are internationally notorious, and do not escape the notice of the average citizen. Without any public morality in the exercise of state power, it is hard for the state to sustain the legitimacy necessary for routine functioning.

Overconsumption by the state

The nature and scope of state consumption is a central dimension of the unending crisis. In Zaire and elsewhere expenditures of the African colonial state rose very rapidly during the terminal decade. These went primarily into welfare infrastructure and investment in public development. The prolonged postwar commodity boom, and some aid from metropolitan budgets, made such state expansion possible. Much of the agricultural commodity price rise was withheld from the peasantry and collected as state rent. The Bula Matari state was in full fiscal crisis when Zaire became independent.

With the resurrection of the state, the dynamic of increased expansion resumed in Zaire, with state expenditures reaching the extraordinary level of 59 percent of the GDP by 1974. Equally important was the change in the composition of expenditures. Actual developmental investment shrank to a small fraction—from 30 percent of the GDP in the late 1950s to 4 percent in 1977 (according to IMF data). Welfare outlays became concentrated in a single sector: education (a point to which we will return). The greater part of state expenditures were devoted to remuneration of its personnel—in other terms, to the reproduction of its own structure. Most state consumption in the crisis years has been accounted for by three items: financing patrimonialism, the security forces, and the school system.

Add to this pattern of expenditures the huge overhanging liability of the external debt, on which episodic payments are made, and the revenue crisis comes into full view. Internally the revenue gap is closed, after a fashion, by inflation, with its hidden fiscal impact. Externally the deficit is covered by the diverse expedients considered in the preceding chapter, and by the state's inability to supply domestic markets with critical goods, thereby creating attendant dislocations in both production and consumption.

Payment of state personnel inevitably has first claim on state resources. After this deduction, and after Gécamines and the presidency have extracted their quotient, precious little remains for all other state functions. Thus schools and clinics are without basic supplies, roads cannot be repaired, and state vehicles cannot be maintained.

State consumption, under the patterns set by the Mobutu regime by the early 1970s, was financed by a combination of high revenues from exceptionally favorable copper prices and the large inflow of loans and, to some extent, investments from external sources. Since 1974 a depressed copper market has shrivelled the fiscal returns from Gécamines, and virtually no new external funds have been in prospect. A corresponding reduction in state consumption has proven difficult to achieve. Neither education nor defense funds can be easily slashed. The very weakness of the regime doubtless increases the upward pressure on patrimonial expenditures to purchase the fidelity of a sustaining number of the politico-commercial class. The latter shows no signs of slackening its demands for accumulation through privatization of public resources.

During the 1970s the burden placed upon the public economy by venal diversion of state resources and external borrowing was enormous. Corrupt drainage of public resources in one form or another was probably at least $5 billion over the decade; much of this found its way abroad, and was lost to the Zairian economy. The external debt rose from almost nothing in 1970 to $5 billion by the early 1980s; what makes this figure painful is that so little has been incurred for projects having any possibility of amortization. Indeed several, like Inga-Shaba, involve large deficits on current operations. (One is reminded of the nineteenth-century borrowing patterns by the Ottoman state, Egypt, Tunisia, and Morocco, placed in receivership or worse for decades because—by one careful estimate—no more than 5 percent of the borrowed funds were used for productive investments.)[5] Taking these two items together, we have a loss to the Zairian economy amounting to roughly a quarter of the recorded gross national product.

The uneven nature of decline

Decline is not an absolute condition or a uniform process. In fact, the very metaphorical expressions of "rise" and "decline" that we have employed to frame our analysis run the risk of creating images which are more comprehensive and categorical than the conditions they are intended to describe. Decline is a central tendency among many complex processes. It is much more evident in some aspects of state operations than in others. Those segments of the state apparatus most crucial to its survival receive priority attention, and may continue to function with relative effectiveness.

The security police is generally believed to be an efficacious instrument, exempt from the overall decline in competency.[6] The services of the presidency have excellent personnel and have first call on the resources of the state. As a general axiom, one may suggest that state decay is least evident in the center, and grows increasingly conspicuous the farther one journeys toward the periphery. In Zaire, the high concentration of material resources and human skills in the capital permits partial functioning at the center of state agencies, while the provincial arms of the same agencies are paralyzed.

It should not be imagined that the regional administration has vanished from the scene. Far from it; visit a zone headquarters, and the offices will have their full complement of personnel. They deliver little by way of services to civil society, and lack the capacity to execute any complex development project. But they do have the ability to maintain a preemptive order by forestalling any direct threats to the authority of the state. Since funds from above arrive fitfully, state personnel have developed the knack of foraging on local society to secure the minimum funds required to assure their own reproduction over time. And they are able to organize the occasional ceremonial functions which ritualize the continued existence of the state as a normative hegemonical institution, as they did in 1984 through the organization of the unopposed presidential campaign of Mobutu, which terminated in a triumphantly unanimous reelection.

The sphere of education is a source of some of the greatest Zairian paradoxes. A large part of the school system seems to be in a condition of advanced decay; buildings are derelict, and even the most basic equipment (chairs, tables, books) is lacking. Much of the teaching staff is totally demoralized. Yet the system continues to operate and to produce "output." The yield of the schools, measured by the number of pupil units processed, continues to expand. End-of-the-year examinations are held, and young Zairians work their way upward through the system.

Part of the explanation of this paradox lies in the contribution of the organizational resources of the churches, which operate an important fraction of the primary and secondary schools. Beyond the church contribution, we may discern the tremendous importance of the mobility myth embodied in the school system (see chapter 4). The clientele of the educational system constitute a potent force for the maintenance of its structures, insisting that its annual rites of passage be respected. If need be, they will feed the teachers and supply the indispensable minimum of pedagogical materials in order to keep alive the hope of their own social ascension. They also keep afloat a highly visible state function, and so help to preserve residues of state legitimacy.

The external arena sets important limits on the state decline process. The formal machinery of international relations provides settings in which the appearance of the state is nurtured: Zairian membership in the UN Security Council, the dispatch of Zairian military units to Chad as a peacekeeping force, state visits by Mobutu to major capitals. As we have argued in chapter 12, the international system has a major stake in sustaining the state and in propping up the Mobutu regime because they are the indispensable guarantors of international economic and strategic interests in Zaire.

Another factor which on occasion has countered decline processes has been the ability of the state withdraw from some of its worst mistakes. The very concentration of decisional authority in the presidency, along with the lack of ideological constraint upon its choices, have sometimes facilitated retreat from disaster. One example was the abandonment of Zairianization and radicalization by 1976; another was the liquidation of all but one of the state agricultural marketing offices created in the early 1970s.

The state as an idea remains intact. Whatever one may think of its present form or rulers, no one doubts that the state is a natural part of the Zairian social order. So deeply rooted is this notion that the state is taken for granted both as empirical fact and normative expectation.

The idea of state is ritualized in innumerable ceremonies, small and large, from the daily flag-raising in front of each administrative headquarters to the presidential electoral campaigns (1970, 1977, 1984), with their vast deployment of fanfare and pageantry. The banal artifacts of everyday life—coins, banknotes, stamps, party buttons worn by officials—image the state. In its days of decline, with shrinkage in the effective scope of state governance, the persistence of its theatrical aspects stands out, evoking the model of the classical Indic state portrayed by Geertz, "pointed not toward tyranny, whose systematic concentration of power it was incompetent to effect, and not even very methodically toward government, which it pursued indifferently and hesitantly, but rather toward spectacle, toward ceremony."[7] The image of political order theatricalized in its ritual performances combines notions of an ascendant Zairian state of earlier times and idealized visions of the powerful and dynamic modern nation-state constructed from the global cosmos of exemplary states. However great the gap between the ceremonialized image and the practical reality of the Zairian state in the early 1980s, the magnetic force of the model in the social imagination should not be underestimated.

The response of civil society

All of these factors may set some outer limits on decline. They do not lessen the costs placed upon civil society (excepting that small segment that benefits from the present circumstances). The question arises as to what responses are available to civil society.

Generalized discontent has not translated into open opposition. The regime has been adept at forestalling opposition through a panoply of tactics. Co-optation has been used with particular skill; each new slate of Political Bureau or Council of Ministers members contains spectacular examples of the "recuperation" of prominent individuals known to be disaffected, or identified with the external opposition. Each new amnesty brings home from exile some major leaders.[8] The constant stream of recuperations has been a main element in fostering division and distrust among the exiled opposition; who can be sure what trusted associate is not in secret negotiation with the regime for dramatic re-entry into the Mobutist orbit?

Repression and intimidation share the other side of the coin. Overt criticism of Mobutu himself has never been acceptable; more veiled criticism of regime policies may be tolerated, depending on the context. Persistent and public articulation of hostility to the regime exposes the individual to diverse reprisals: domicile search or muscular interrogation by the CND, loss of position, legal charges of corrupt or nepotistic actions.

Organized opposition within Zaire is by definition excluded; the MPR has the exclusive monopoly on political space.

Within the country, latent opposition is universal; manifest opposition is almost nonexistent. Private disaffection with the regime penetrates even the ranks of its major internal beneficiary, the politico-commercial class. Yet however weak the state has become in certain respects, it retains the ability to prevent the active organization of resistance.

A fluctuating set of political personalities and organizations operates from European bases, mainly in Belgium. The persistent divisions and factional disputes among them, their remoteness from Zaire itself, and the absence of a leader of unchallengeable standing and authority all weaken such external opposition, which represents a nuisance rather than a serious threat to the regime.[9]

The most important response by civil society is withdrawal into a plethora of survival activities. The decay of the state has opened up new economic and social space, which is being rapidly organized into parallel markets. The vitality of these mechanisms demonstrates not only the creative energies of civil society, but also the possibility of survival. If one took only measurements from the public economy (real urban wages, for example), not only impoverishment but starvation would be indicated; but while the impoverishment of large segments of the populace is real, so also is their survival. Compared to such African capitals as Dar-es-Salaam, Maputo, and Luanda, in the early 1980s Kinshasa appears prosperous.

The importance of the parallel economy has only recently become evident, and its social and political implications are not clear. In the short term, the vigorous development of these markets supplies insulation for civil society against the costs of state decay. Over a longer term, they may generate their own social and even political structures, and so challenge the hegemony of the state.

In any case, the parallel markets are suggestive of hidden reservoirs of rejuvenative capacity in Zaire. The potential natural wealth of the vast country remains, a tantalizing hint of the possibility of happier times. Zaire as well has abundant human talent; the decline of state competence is not to be confused with the skill potential of its employees.

The operation of the system is such as to devalue individual proficiencies. Yet one encounters in the state structure a number of individuals who, with a most resilient idealism, deliver their best efforts. Indeed, until the early 1970s there was reason to believe that there was a gradual improvement in the effectiveness of the state. But by the late 1970s demoralization was disheartening even the most dedicated, thus forcing most public servants to direct their efforts to assuring the survival of their kin.

"No condition is permanent," runs a popular African aphorism. There is wisdom as well as solace in this proverb; the decline of the Zairian state cannot be perpetual, even though its end is not in sight. Perhaps we need to turn to Ibn Khaldun and Polybius to understand contemporary Zaire: both rise and decline are, to the classical mind, parts of an inevitably cyclical pattern of history.

Notes

Index

Notes

Chapter 1

1 Terminological difficulties arise from the change in the name of the country from Congo to Zaire in 1971, from changes in the names of provinces and cities, and from the requirement, in 1971, that persons drop their Christian forenames in favor of Zairian postnames. We will use names current in the early 1980s, and where identity requires clarification we will indicate former names of persons and places upon first mention of the current name.

2 For a perceptive analysis of Tshibumba and other urban folk artists, see Ilona Szombati-Fabian and Johannes Fabian, "Art, History, and Society: Popular Art in Shaba, Zaire," *Studies in the Anthropology of Visual Communication* 3 (1976). Johannes Fabian recorded twenty-five hours of interviews with Tshibumba in Swahili, in which the artist explains his own understanding of his paintings.

3 Fabian and Fabian, "Art, History, and Society," p. 15.

4 Alexandre Passerin d'Entreves, *The Notion of the State* (Oxford: Clarendon Press, 1967).

5 Charles Tilly, ed., *The Formation of National States in Western Europe* (Princeton: Princeton University Press, 1975); see especially Tilly's introductory essay, pp. 3–83.

6 Sheldon S. Wolin, *Politics and Vision* (Boston: Little, Brown and Co., 1960), pp. 265–266.

7 Shlomo Avineri, *Hegel's Theory of the Modern State* (Cambridge: Cambridge University Press, 1972). This concept of the state is expressed in the *Philosophy of Right*. In the *Phenomenology of Mind* the state is a slightly less exalted idea. There the state is represented as "objective mind," which makes possible the pursuit of the "absolute mind" (philosophy, art, and religion).

8 In their 1848 *Manifesto of the Communist Party*. This, of course, is not the only concept of state encountered in Marx. In *The Class Struggles in France* (1850) and *The Eighteenth Brumaire of Louis Bonaparte* (1852) the state appears as an autonomous mechanism regulating conflict in a crisis situation where no class enjoys clear hegemony. In *The Civil War in France* (1871) and *A Critique of the Gotha Program* (1875), Marx analyzes the nature of the state in the transition to socialism. One Marxist scholar, Bob Jessop, identifies six different usages of the

state concept in Marx: "Recent Theories of the Capitalist State," *Cambridge Journal of Economics* 1, no. 1 (1977): 353–373.

9 In "Politics as a Vocation," reprinted in H. C. Gerth and C. Wright Mills, eds., *From Max Weber* (New York: Oxford University Press, 1958), p. 78.

10 Woodrow Wilson, *The State* (1898; Boston: D. C. Heath, 1918).

11 R. M. MacIver, *The Modern State* (1926; London: Oxford University Press, 1964), p. 22.

12 Arthur F. Bentley, *The Process of Government* (Chicago: University of Chicago Press, 1908).

13 David Easton, *A Systems Analysis of Political Life* (New York: John Wiley & Sons, 1965).

14 Theodore J. Lowi, *The End of Liberalism* (New York: W. W. Norton, 1969).

15 Leon N. Lindberg, ed., *Stress and Contradiction in Modern Capitalism: Public Policy and the Theory of the State* (Lexington, Mass.: Lexington Books, 1975). See also the special issue on "The State," *Daedalus* 108, no. 4 (Fall 1979); J. P. Nettl, "The State as a Conceptual Variable," *World Politics* 20, no. 4 (1968): 559–592; Robert Solo, "The Need for a Theory of the State," *Journal of Economic Issues* 11, no. 2 (June 1977): 379–385.

16 David A. Gold, Clarence Y. H. Lo, and Erik Olin Wright, "Recent Developments in Marxist Theories of the Capitalist State," *Monthly Review* 17, no. 5 (October 1975): 29–43, and 17, no. 6 (November 1975): 36–51; Bob Jessop, *The Capitalist State: Marxist Theories and Methods* (New York: New York University Press, 1982).

17 Ralph Miliband, *The State in Capitalist Society* (London: Camelot Press, 1969). Miliband is generally labelled an "instrumentalist."

18 Nicos Poulantzas, *State, Power, Socialism* (London: NLB, 1978). Poulantzas is probably the most influential member of the "relative autonomy" school, and reflects the French "structuralist" school of Marxism. His rejection of "historicism" and "empiricism" makes his paradigm singularly abstract; it is striking that, though Poulantzas is widely cited by those examining the Third World state, no author, to our knowledge, has endeavored to apply his conceptual system as a whole.

19 Claus Offe, "Political Authority and Class Structure: An Analysis of Late Capitalist Societies," *International Journal of Sociology* 2, no. 1 (Spring 1972): 73–108; James O'Connor, *The Fiscal Crisis of the State* (New York: St. Martin's Press, 1973).

20 See the valuable theoretical discussions in Alfred Stepan, *The State and Society: Peru in Comparative Perspective* (Princeton: Princeton University Press, 1974); Jean-François Bayart, *L'Etat au Cameroun* (Paris: Presses de la Fondation Nationale des Sciences Politiques, 1979).

21 Stephen R. Graubard, in his preface to the special issue on "The State," *Daedalus* 108, no. 4 (Fall 1979): viii.

22 Gianfranco Poggi, *The Development of the Modern State* (Stanford: Stanford University Press, 1978), pp. 1–15.

23 Theda Skocpol, *States & Social Revolutions* (Cambridge: Cambridge University Press, 1979), pp. 25–32.

24 Kenneth H. F. Dyson, *The State Tradition in Western Europe* (New York: Oxford University Press, 1980), p. 206. The Dyson study is particularly valuable for drawing together the French and German, as well as the Anglo-American, state theories. He argues that the continental and Anglo-American traditions sharply differ because of the far more profound impact of state on law, philosophy, and culture on the continent.

25 The history of this doctrine is comprehensively reviewed by F. H. Hinsley, *Sovereignty* (London: C. A. Watts, 1966); and Bertrand de Jouvenal, *On Sovereignty: An Inquiry into the Political Good* (Cambridge: Cambridge University Press, 1957).

26 Rupert Emerson, *From Empire to Nation* (Cambridge: Harvard University Press, 1960), pp. 95–96.

27 Hans Kohn, "Nationalism," in *International Encyclopedia of the Social Sciences* (New York: MacMillan Co. and Free Press, 1968) 11: 63–70.

28 Gerth and Mills, eds., *From Max Weber*, p. 79.

29 Dyson, *The State Tradition*, p. 108.

30 John M. Cammett, *Antonio Gramsci and the Origins of Italian Communism* (Stanford: Stanford University Press, 1967), pp. 190–191; Christine Buci-Glucksmann, *Gramsci et l'Etat* (Paris: Fayard, 1975).

31 Jurgen Habermas, *The Legitimation Crisis* (Boston: Beacon Press, 1973), p. 49.

32 Gerth and Mills, eds., *From Max Weber*, p. 82.

33 Ruth Leger Sivard, *World Military and Social Expenditures 1982* (Washington: World Priorities, 1982), p. 5.

34 Michael Howard, "War and the Nation-State," *Daedalus* 108, no. 4 (Fall 1979): 101–110; Hedley Bull, *The Anarchical Society* (New York: Columbia University Press, 1977).

35 Stephen D. Krasner, *Defending the National Interest* (Princeton: Princeton University Press, 1978), p. 12.

36 Eric A. Nordlinger, *On the Autonomy of the Democratic State* (Cambridge: Harvard University Press, 1981). Nordlinger perhaps weakens his argument by insisting on viewing the state as the set of public actors which staff its institutions.

37 Jessop, *The Capitalist State*.

38 Talcott Parsons, "Some Reflections on the Place of Force in Social Process," in Harry Eckstein, ed., *Internal War* (New York: Free Press of Glencoe, 1964), pp. 33–70.

39 Karl Marx, "The German Ideology," in Robert C. Tucker, ed., *The Marx-Engels Reader* (New York: W. W. Norton, 1972), p. 136. The original was drafted in 1844.

40 Habermas, *Legitimation Crisis*, pp. 36–37.

41 Gabriel A. Almond and G. Bingham Powell, Jr., *Comparative Politics: A Developmental Approach* (Boston: Little, Brown and Co. 1966), p. 195.

42 Robert H. Bates, *Markets and States in Tropical Africa* (Berkeley: University of California Press, 1981).

43 O'Connor argues that the capitalist state faces an endemic crisis caused by the tension between revenue need for legitimation expenditures (welfare) and resources required for public and private accumulation: *The Fiscal Crisis of the State*.

44 Note that our concept of civil society differs from the classical Gramsci view, which defines it as the infrastructure of social institutions and associations which are neither purely economic nor governmental. Without such associational structuring, civil society, for Gramsci, is "gelatinous" in character, as in czarist Russia. On the civil society issue, we are grateful for having had the opportunity to consult the manuscript by Evelyne Stephens and John Stephens, "Democratic Socialism in Jamaica: The Political Movement and Social Transformation in Dependent Capitalism," forthcoming.

45 This point has some parallels in the arguments of Poulantzas, *State, Power, Socialism*, pp. 93–120.

46 On these themes, see Reinhard Bendix, *Kings or People* (Berkeley: University of California Press, 1978).

47 Harold R. Isaacs, *Idols of the Tribe* (New York: Harper & Row, 1975); A. L. Epstein, *Ethos and Identity* (London: Tavistock Publications, 1978).

48 Joseph Rothschild, *Ethnopolitics* (New York: Columbia University Press, 1981); Donald Rothchild and Victor Olorunsola, eds., *State Versus Ethnic Claims: African Policy Dilemmas* (Boulder: Westview, 1982); Crawford Young, "Patterns of Social Conflict: State, Class, and Ethnicity," *Daedalus* 111, no. 2 (Spring 1982): 71–98; Crawford Young, *The Politics of Cultural Pluralism* (Madison: University of Wisconsin Press, 1976).

49 See Frederick B. Pike and Howard Wiarda, eds., *The New Corporatism: Social-Political Structures in the Iberian World* (Notre Dame, Ind.: University of Notre Dame Press, 1974), especially the seminal contribution of Philippe Schmitter, "Still the Century of Corporatism?," pp. 84–131; Stepan, *State and Society*.

50 A provocative literature has emerged around this theme; see Stanley B. Greenberg, *Race and State in Capitalist Development* (New Haven: Yale University Press, 1980); John Cell, *The Highest Stage of White Supremacy* (Cambridge: Cambridge University Press, 1982); George N. Fredrickson, *White Supremacy* (Oxford: Oxford University Press, 1981).

51 Paul Brass makes this point with particular force in his introduction to a forthcoming work, under his editorship, with the provisional title *Ethnic Groups and the State* (London: Croon Helm).

52 This point finds illustration in the elegant Graham Allison typology of modes of conflict within the state: *Essence of Decision: Explaining the Cuban Missile Crisis* (Boston: Little Brown, 1971).

53 The model of state elaborated by Anthony Giddens is particularly effective in integrating the institutional and human actor aspects of the state: *A Contemporary Critique of Historical Materialism,* vol. 1, *Power, Property and the State* (Berkeley: University of California Press, 1981), especially pp. 49–68. See also Robert Fossaert, *La société,* 5 vols. (Paris: Editions du Seuil, 1977–1980); Henri Lefebvre, *De l'état,* vol. 1, *L'état dans le monde moderne* (Paris: Union Générale des Editions, 1976). From the standpoint of legal philosophy, a similar notion may be found in Hans Kelsen, *General Theory of Law and State* (New York: Russell & Russell, 1961), pp. 182–200.

54 Gabriel Almond, Mervin Chodorow, and Roy H. Pearce, eds., *Progress and Its Discontents* (Berkeley: University of California Press, 1982).

55 Philip Mason, *A Matter of Honour* (New York: Holt, Rinehart, and Winston, 1974), pp. 13–24.

56 George Balandier, "La situation coloniale: approache theorique," *Cahiers Internationaux de Sociologie* 11 (1951): 44–79.

57 William B. Cohen, "The French Colonial Service in French West Africa," in Prosser Gifford and Wm. Roger Louis, eds., *France and Britain in Africa* (New Haven: Yale University Press, 1971), p. 504.

58 Peter Kilby, *Industrialization in an Open Economy: Nigeria 1945–1966* (Cambridge: Cambridge University Press, 1969), p. 9.

59 Eritrea, for example, finally balanced its budget from local resources only in 1928: Stephen Longregg, *A Short History of Eritrea* (1945; Westport, Conn.: Greenwood Publishers, 1954), p. 132.

60 Pierre Ryckmans, *Dominer pour servir* (Brussels: Edition Universelle, 1948).

61 Albert Sarraut, *La mise en valeur des colonies françaises* (Paris: Payot, 1923), p. 19, quoted in D. Bruce Marshall, *The French Colonial Myth and Constitution-Making in the Fourth Republic* (New Haven: Yale University Press, 1973), p. 44.

62 For a comprehensive treatment and bibliography on this subject, see Prosser Gifford and Wm. Roger Louis, eds., *The Transfer of Power in Africa* (New Haven: Yale University Press, 1982).

63 For a masterful synthesis and critique of the literature on the African state, see John Lonsdale, "States and Social Processes in Africa: A Historiographical Survey," *African Studies Review* 24, nos. 2/3 (June/September 1981): 139–225.

64 This model, particularly applicable to the southern cone of Latin America in the 1960s and 1970s, is associated with Guillermo O'Donnell; for an extended discussion of his work, a rebuttal, see David Collier, ed., *The New Authoritarianism in Latin America* (Princeton: Princeton University Press, 1979). Among other recent contributions, see especially Amos Perlmutter, *Modern Authoritarianism* (New Haven: Yale University Press, 1981); James M. Malloy, ed., *Authoritarianism and Corporatism in Latin America* (Pittsburgh: University of Pittsburgh Press, 1977); Juan L. Linz, "Totalitarian and Authoritarian Regimes," in Fred I. Greenstein and Nelson Polsby, eds., *Handbook of Political Science* (Reading, Mass.: Addison-Wesley Co., 1975) 3: 175–411.

65 Robert H. Jackson and Carl G. Rosberg, *Personal Rule in Black Africa* (Berkeley: University of California Press, 1982), pp. 17–19.

66 S. N. Eisenstadt and Rene Lemarchand, eds., *Political Clientelism, Patronage and Development* (Beverly Hills: Sage Publications, 1981).

67 Goran Hyden, *Beyond Ujamaa in Tanzania* (Berkeley: University of California Press, 1980).

68 Carl J. Friedrich, cited in Nettl, "State as a Conceptual Variable," p. 565.

69 We are thinking here of such mechanistic and doctrinaire versions as those of Andre Gunder Frank, *Capitalism and Underdevelopment in Latin America*, rev. ed., (New York: Monthly Review Press, 1969).

70 Lusibu Zala N'kanza, "The Social Origins of Political Underdevelopment in the ex-Belgian Congo (Zaire)" (Ph.D. diss., Harvard University, 1976), pp. 232–234, 390. Sigbert Axelson argues that the term goes back to the sixteenth century, with a somewhat different meaning: *Culture Confrontation in the Lower Congo* (Falköping, Sweden: Gummessons, 1970), p. 203. See also F. F. Boutinck, "Les deux Bula Matari, *Etudes Congolaises* 13, no. 3 (July 1969): 83–97.

71 The Bula Matari concept is intriguingly illustrated in a song propagated by colonial organs:

Kala kala Boula Matari wa Belji (bis)   Since the Bula Matari of the (bis)
Abongisi na nguya na ye ye ye   Belgians reorganised your village,
Mokili oyo oh oh oh   Your whole country
Ava Congo civilise (bis)   Has been civilized

Nienga 'cha Niengo, "Le role de la propagande dans la politique en République du Zaire" (Mémoire de licence, Faculté des Sciences Sociales, Politiques et Administratives, Campus de Lubumbashi, Université Nationale du Zaire, 1977), p. 44. The concept lives on in contemporary discourse; when Erwin Blumenthal of the International Monetary Fund imposed an audacious ban on the granting of import licenses to a number of leading mercantile figures with close presidential ties in 1978, he at once acquired the popular nickname of "Bula Matari."

72 Ruanda-Urundi, acquired by Belgium as a mandated territory after World War I, would have been incorporated as well but for its distinctive international legal status. Until 1956 it was still widely assumed that Rwanda and Burundi would form part of a decolonized Congo.

73 Jean Stengers, *Belgique et Congo: élaboration de la Charte Coloniale* (Brussels: La Renaissance du Livre, 1963).

74 Mulambu Muvulya, "Le régime des cultures obligatoires et le radicalisme rural au Zaire (1917–1960)" (Doctoral diss., Université Libre de Bruxelles, 1974).

75 On the colonial state, see especially Jean Stengers, "The Congo Free State and the Belgian Congo," in L. H. Gann and Peter Duignan, eds., *Colonialism in Africa 1870–1960* (Cambridge, Cambridge University Press, 1969) 1: 261–292; Roger Anstey, *King Leopold's Legacy* (London: Oxford University Press, 1969); Jean Stengers, "La Belgique et le Congo," in *Histoire de la Belgique Contempo-*

raine (Brussels: La Renaissance du Livre, 1974); Crawford Young, *Politics in the Congo* (Princeton: Princeton University Press, 1965), and the references cited therein.

76 René J. Cornet, *La bataille du rail* (Brussels: Editions L. Cuypers, 1947).

77 On these issues, see Neal Ascherson, *The King Incorporated* (London: George Allen & Unwin, 1963); Jean Stengers, *Combien le Congo a-t-il couté à la Belgique?* (Brussels: Academie Royale des Sciences d'Outre Mer, Sci. Mor. et Pol., n.s., T. 11, fasc. 1, 1957).

78 S. E. Katzenallenbogen, *Railways and the Copper Mines of Katanga* (Oxford: Clarendon Press, 1973).

79 Jean-Philippe Peemans, "Le rôle de l'état dans la formation du capital au Congo pendant la période coloniale (1885–1960)," *Etudes et Documents* (Louvain, Belgium: Institut pour d'Etude des Pays en Développement, Université de Louvain, 1973).

80 One important exception to state passivity was its involvement in the Kilo-Moto gold mines in the far northeast. These were initially exploited as a state monopoly. By the 1920s, however, the state found that it could not command the technical skills or geological expertise to expand production at the desired rate. In 1926, in return for a quite small equity participation of $2 million, a private combine was awarded management rights over the gold mines. The role of gold as a currency reserve for both the colony and the metropole gave the state a direct interest in this mining operation that went beyond its interest in other mineral developments. Even after management was turned over to the private sector, the state continued to take a more direct role in the basic decisions on production and investment at Kilo-Moto than it did in the cases of UMHK, Forminière, and other mining corporations in which it held equity. See the impressively documented dissertation by Bakonzi Agayo, "The Gold Mines of Kilo-Moto in Northeastern Zaire, 1905–1960" (Ph.D. diss., University of Wisconsin–Madison, 1982).

81 Mulambu, "Le régime des cultures obligatoires," p. 96.

82 Pierre Piron and Jacques Devos, *Codes et Lois du Congo Belge*, 8th ed. (Brussels: Maison Ferdinand Larcier, 1960) 2: 211.

83 Ibid.

84 Edouard Bustin, *Lunda under Belgian Rule* (Cambridge: Harvard University Press, 1975).

85 Jan Vansina, "Les Kuba et l'administration territoriale de 1919 à 1960," *Cultures et Développement* (4, no. 2 (1972): 275–326.

86 The interpretation of the *mission civilisatrice* by the Catholic church was not necessarily the same as that desired by the state. The mission objective was above all the creation of Christian communities, which at times placed the missions in conflict with the state and its productionist concept of progress. As one early example, during the Free State days Leopold II wished the use of French promoted, and held a vaguely assimilationist view of the final objective of the *mis-*

sion civilisatrice. The Catholic missions resolutely opposed the monarch on this score, wanting to use only African languages in such schooling as they felt necessary for evangelization at that time. The missions were also lukewarm at first on industrial education, and did not see themselves as suppliers of subaltern personnel for the state. The mission community, isolated from the pernicious influences of dissolute traders, was the ideal for many in the early years. See Barbara A. Yates, "*The Missions and Educational Development in Belgian Africa, 1876–1908*" (Ph.D. diss., Columbia University, 1967).

87 Professor Munzadi Babole, personal communication. Not all observers agree on the question of white missionaries and Bula Matari; not only did mission interests at times diverge from those of the state, but many missionaries did not follow the Bula Matari role model.

88 Mary Douglas, *The Lele of the Kasai* (London: Oxford University Press, 1963), p. 259.

89 See the reactions of liberal governor-general Pierre Ryckmans, *Dominer pour servir*, pp. 16–28.

90 Pierre Ryckmans, *Etapes et jalons* (Brussels: Maison Ferdinand Larcier, 1946), pp. 211–225.

91 Stengers, "La Belgique et le Congo," p. 397.

92 *Le Congo Belge* (Brussels: Inforcongo, 1959) 2: 60, 82; Joseph Segers, "L'économie congolaise hier, demain, aujourd'hui," *Documents pour l'Action* 3, no. 15 (May–June 1963): 146–152.

93 Antoine Rubbens, in *Dettes de guerre* (Elisabethville: Editions de l'Essor du Congo, 1945), pp. 142–143.

94 *Congo 1959* (Brussels: Centre de Recherche et d'Information Socio-Politiques, 1959), pp. 10, 15.

95 Ibid., pp. 18–19.

96 Mobutu Sese Seko, *Mobutu: Discours, allocutions, et messages 1965–1975*, (Paris: Editions J. A., 1975) 1: 20–21.

97 Mobutu Sese Seko, speech of 25 November, 1977, mimeo.

98 *Le Monde*, 28 July 1981, p. 4.

99 For valuable theoretical analyses of the Amin regime, see especially E. A. Brett, "Relations of Production, the State and the Ugandan Crisis," *West African Journal of Sociology and Political Sciences* 1, no. 3 (January 1978): 249–283; John Saul, "The Unsteady State: Uganda, Obote, and General Amin," *State and Revolution in Eastern Africa* (New York: Monthly Review Press, 1979), pp. 350–390.

100 Timothy M. Shaw, "Beyond Underdevelopment: The Anarchic State in Africa" (Paper presented at the annual meeting, African Studies Association, Washington, D.C., December 1982), p. 2.

101 Robert H. Jackson and Carl G. Rosberg, "Why Africa's Weak States Persist: The Empirical and the Juridical in Statehood," *World Politics* 35, no. 1 (October 1982): 1–24.

102 For examples, see Robert I. Rotberg, *Haiti: The Politics of Squalor* (Boston: Houghton Mifflin Co., 1971); Martin Weinstein, *Uruguay: The Politics of Failure* (Westport, Conn.: Greenwood Press, 1975); Josef Silverstein, *Burma: Military Rule and the Politics of Stagnation* (Ithaca: Cornell University Press, 1977).

103 Naomi Chazan, *An Anatomy of Ghanaian Politics: Managing Political Recession, 1969–1982* (Boulder: Westview Press, 1983).

104 Ibid., pp. 334–335.

Chapter 2

1 From a speech given in Brussels in November 1974; reproduced in *Remarques Africaines*, no. 454 (1 January 1975): 9. Mpinga was subsequently prime minister, from 1977 to 1979.

2 For the Tshombe perspective, see Moise Tshombe, *Quinze mois du gouvernement au Congo* (Paris: Table Ronde, 1966); Ian Colvin, *The Rise and Fall of Moise Tshombe* (London: Leslie Frewin, 1968).

3 Other key members of the Binza group were Mobutu, central bank director Albert Ndele, Interior Ministry general secretary Damien Kandolo, and Bomboko Lokumba. For more detail, see Crawford Young, *Politics in the Congo* (Princeton: Princeton University Press, 1965) pp. 379–380. Binza was the name of the prosperous Kinshasa suburb where the group held its caucuses.

4 The First Republic was always an orphan in African affairs, at first because of its widely publicized disorders and bitterness in radical states over the ouster and murder of Lumumba. Zairian standing in Africa was again weakened by the 1964–65 rebellions and events related to them, especially the use of mercenaries and Belgian-American paratroop operations in Kisangani and Isiro. Tshombe personally was a controversial figure in African affairs, and was viewed by a number of African leaders as an instrument of imperialism. By late 1965 the lethal rivalries among rebel Zairian factions, staged in several African capitals (Algiers, Cairo, Khartoum, and Kampala) had cost the armed opposition its modest reservoir of diplomatic support. The Kasavubu gestures (both in content and timing) thus found a very receptive audience among African leaders. According to some sources, Kasavubu was pressed in private conversations with other African leaders at the OAU summit to get rid of Mobutu as well as Tshombe.

5 For a full analysis of the vote, see *Congo 1965* (Brussels: Centre de Recherche et d'Information Socio-Politiques, 1966). This pattern first became evident in the Lumumba investiture vote in June 1960; though members of his cabinet represented parties holding 94 percent of the seats, only 54 percent voted to confirm the government.

6 Cléophas Kamitatu, *La grande mystification du Congo-Kinshasa* (Paris: Maspero,

1971), p. 120. Moju'ongway Untuube was subsequently to serve as minister of the interior from 1967 to 1970, fall from grace on embezzlement charges, and rise phoenixlike to the post of prime minister in 1981–82.

7 Ibid., p. 135.

8 Madeleine G. Kalb, *The Congo Cables* (New York: Macmillan Publishing Co., 1982), p. 364. According to Kalb, there were some American officials who were sympathetic to this scheme at the time, though it was firmly vetoed by Assistant Secretary of State for African Affairs G. Mennen Williams.

9 *Congo 1965*, p. 409. (Daniel) Monguya Mbenge, however, claims that the first Mobutu session with the army high command aimed at charting the coup took place in April 1965: Monguya, *Histoire secrète du Zaire* (Brussels: Editions de l'Esperance, 1977).

10 Stephen Weissman, "The CIA and U.S. Policy in Zaire and Angola," in Rene Lemarchand, ed., *American Policy in Southern Africa: The Stakes and The Stance* (Washington: University Press of America, 1978), p. 394.

11 Devlin was Kinshasa CIA station chief from 1960 to 1962 and from 1965 to 1968. Former CIA agent John Stockwell, in his exposé of his Angolan experience, makes a passing reference to Devlin, "shuffling new governments like cards, finally settling on Mobutu as President." Stockwell had earlier served a tour in Zaire, and would have been in a position to know; however, this intriguing passage lifts the veil no further on the exact nature of the CIA role in the coup. See John Stockwell, *In Search of Enemies* (New York: W. W. Norton, 1978), p. 136.

12 Not long after the coup, Godley was, in effect, declared persona non grata by Mobutu on the grounds that he had been too closely associated with Tshombe. This has led to some speculation as to whether Ambassador Godley and the CIA station might have been working at cross-purposes in the maneuvering associated with the coup.

13 Kamitatu, *La grande mystification*, p. 160. Kamitatu was to have been offered the Foreign Ministry, and might have accepted, but the nomination was vetoed by the American and Belgian embassies, which blamed Kamitatu for the "turn to the left" in Zairian diplomacy: *Congo 1965*, p. 419.

14 See the excellent analysis of the functioning of Parliament by Maurice Lovens in *Congo 1966* (Brussels: Centre de Recherche et d'Information Socio-Politiques, 1967), pp. 169–208.

15 Mobutu Sese Seko, *Mobutu: Discours, allocutions, et messages, 1965–1975* (Paris: Editions J. A., 1975) 1: 26.

16 Kinshasa had become a separate capital district when new provinces were created in 1962–63; the Mobutu changes somewhat extended its area and elevated its status. Because in most respects the capital district of Kinshasa had the same structure and administrative characteristics as the other eight provinces, subsequently rebaptized "regions," we will henceforward refer to "nine regions."

17 The same pattern of presidential hegemony reappeared when the post of prime minister was reestablished in 1977.

18 *Congo 1966*, pp. 19–20. The purported church influence was funneled through Mulamba's relative, Msgr. T. Bakole, then vice-rector of Lovanium. Mulamba was also very popular with the troops. His Kasai origin likewise was a factor in the criticism; Mobutu was fearful of the growing number of Kasaian officers in the armed forces.

19 Quoted in Kamitatu, *La grande mystification*, p. 176. Kamitatu recounts a conversation with Mobutu before his power seizure, in which the latter described entrapment devices he used to check on the loyalty of his officers. He would enlist the cooperation of military attaches at friendly embassies to draw out the officers' grievances and their potential interest in conspiracy (p. 167). Whether or not this precise tactic was used, there were certainly informer networks everywhere, and the hint of anti-regime action, as opposed to routine grumbling, was dangerous. Kamitatu himself was arrested as an accessory to the Pentecost Plot, and sentenced to five years in prison; by some reports, he nearly attended the meeting at which the four victims were seized, but was tipped off at the last minute.

20 The Guevara episode in Zaire has now been documented by quasi-official Cuban sources; see John Seiler, ed., *Southern Africa since the Portuguese Coup* (Boulder: Westview Press, 1980), p. 31.

21 See, for example, the early reactions to the New Regime in *Remarques Africaines*, then a Brussels-based organ of far left opinion. The strident denunciations of "Monsieur Tiroir-Caisse" evidently facilitated a surprisingly benevolent evaluation of the Mobutu regime in this anti-imperialist journal, widely read by students at the time.

22 The phrase is used in the first official Chinese assessment of the Mobutu takeover: *Congo 1965*, p. 455.

23 Colvin, *Rise and Fall*, pp. 228–232.

24 Bodenan, after spending the period 1957–66 in prison, joined the shadowy entourage of Jacques Foccart, the *eminence grise* of Gaullist African clandestine diplomacy. He succeeded in infiltrating the Tshombe group, and reportedly lured Tshombe to his fate with a promise of a lucrative financial transaction. To the embarassment of Foccart, Bodenan returned to France full of swagger about his feat; he was silenced, and placed in cold storage. In 1975 Bodenan reemerged on the margins of the Cabinda secession affair; in November 1979 he was arrested by Belgian police on swindling charges: *Jeune Afrique* 1,009 (7 May 1980).

25 As it is impossible to imagine that the sordid assortment of hijackers involved in this episode acted on their own, most observers have assumed that the kidnapping involved a more extensive clandestine operation by some private or public group. It is doubtful that Zairian security services had the capacity to mount the complex operation on their own, though it is easily conceivable that they could have purchased the professional services of a private European criminal ring. But the complexity of the operation implied an extensive network, and the capacity to operate with impunity in Europe, especially in Spain and

Switzerland, suggests the hand of some intelligence service. Various sources have suggested that the CIA, the KGB, or the French SDECE were authors of the kidnapping; while intriguing circumstantial evidence is available for each of these hypotheses, no definitive version has yet emerged. For an excellent resumé of the different versions, see *Congo 1967*, (Brussels: Centre de Recherche et d'Information Socio-Politiques, 1968), pp. 337–346. Tshombe's biographer, Colvin, tends to believe that the CIA was at least an accessory: *Rise and Fall*, pp. 239–253. Weissman, a careful student in CIA activity in Zaire, does not include the Tshombe kidnapping in the comprehensive catalogue of CIA deeds; René Lemarchand, however, does claim that the CIA was "largely responsible," though he does not cite his evidence: Lemarchand, ed., *American Policy in Southern Africa*, p. 358. Monguya, a Tshombe supporter, blames both the CIA and a French group associated with Jacques Foccart; the death of Tshombe, Monguya implies, was by poisoning, arranged by Mobutu with the aid of Maître Jacques Vergès, who was assigned by Algerian authorities as attorney for Tshombe. Vergès, who had briefly served as a legal advisor to Lumumba in 1960, was the son of a Communist deputy from Réunion, and very active in far left Parisian circles before moving to Algiers: Monguya, *Histoire secrète*, pp. 126–127.

26 *Congo 1967*, p. 25.

27 Ibid., p. 28. The Kongo, numerous in Kinshasa, occupy the area from the capital westward to the Atlantic coast.

28 According to an official then in charge of the Kinshasa voting.

29 *Congo 1967*, pp. 30–31. Kasongo was part of the editorial team that produced *Congo 1967*.

30 Tshisekedi suffered a second eclipse in 1981, when he played a leading role among thirteen parliamentarians who signed a document cataloguing the corruption and dereliction of the regime; he and others were arrested.

31 Regime opponents, especially in Bas-Zaire, hoped Kasavubu might eventually break his silence. See the obituary by André Guery, "Kasa-Vubu, Président de l'Abako," *Remarques Africaines* 334 (20 April 1969): 185–188. Monguya claims that Kasavubu was poisoned—a rumor frequently encountered in Zaire—but offers no evidence: *Histoire secrète*, p. 147.

32 The text of the N'Sele Manifesto may be found in *Etudes Congolaises* 10, no. 3 (May-June 1967): 66–79. See also Oscar Manwana, "Le role des syndicats au Zaire," *Zaire-Afrique* 65 (May 1972): 265; *Congo 1967*, pp. 167–182.

33 On university politics, see Ilunga Kabongo, "Quelques considérations sur l'Université Nationale du Zäire et la dynamique politique Zairoise" (Paper presented to the Rockefeller Foundation conference on the African university and development, Bellagio, Italy, August 1978); Bernadette Lacroix, "Pouvoir et structures de l'Université Lovanium," *Cahiers du CEDAF* 2/3 (1972); Galen S. Hull, "Nationalization of the University in the Republic of Zaire" (Ph.D. diss., Northwestern University, 1974); Jean-Claude Willame, in Donald A. Emmer-

son, ed., *Students and Politics in Developing Nations* (New York: Frederick A. Praeger, 1968), pp. 37–60.

34 Hull, "Nationalization of the University," p. 105. See also the perceptive "thick description" of these episodes in Jan Vansina, "Mwasi's Trials," *Daedalus* 111, no. 2 (Spring 1982): 49–70.

35 Mobutu, *Discours, allocutions, et messages* 2: 42–43.

36 E.-Xavier Ugeux, "La diplomatie agissante de Mobutu," *Remarques Africaines* 427 (16–30 September 1973): 10–12.

37 Note the difference between Mobutu's inaugural presidential address on 5 December 1970 (*Discours allocutions, et messages*, 2: 68–69) and speeches from late 1972 on in the same collection.

38 Nigeria, then seen by Mobutu as Zaire's chief rival on the African scene, had embarked on "Nigerianization" of its economy in 1972.

39 "Les relations entre l'Eglise et l'Etat au Zaire," *Etudes Africaines du C.R.I.S.P.* 145 (28 December 1972): 3. See also the useful article by Kenneth Lee Adelman, "The Church State Conflict in Zaire. 1969–1971," *African Studies Review* 18, no. 1 (April 1975): 102–116.

40 Adelman, "The Church-State Conflict," p. 112.

41 Office of Internal Health, U.S. Department of Health, Education, and Welfare, "Syncrisis: The Dynamics of Health, XIV: Zaire" (Washington, 1975), mimeo.; Agency for International Development, "Basic Family Health Services," Zaire Project 660–0067, 15 December 1975.

42 "Les relations entre l'Eglise et l'Etat," p. 21.

43 Adelman, "The Church-State Conflict," p. 106.

44 Quoted, ibid., p. 107.

45 This controversy smoldered on, and resurfaced in surprising ways. In November 1977, when Cardinal Malula conducted a memorial mass for Mobutu's late first wife, he again offended by referring to her as "Marie-Antoinette." It appears that Mrs. Mobutu never did take on an "authentic" name.

46 Mpinga Kasenda and David J. Gould, *Les réformes administratives au Zaire (1972–1973)* (Kinshasa: Presses Universitaires du Zaire, 1975). Some observers believe this law was in retaliation for the opposition of some leading chiefs to the abortive proposal to acclaim Mobutu as "Life President" at the 1972 MPR congress.

47 Mpinga and Gould, *Les réformes administratives*, p. 133.

48 In a much-remembered address to the Institut Royal des Relations Internationales, in November 1974; reported in *Remarques Africaines* 454 (January 1975): 9.

49 Though the deputies were elected, until 1977 they were submitted to voters as a single slate, approved by the Political Bureau and, in reality, by Mobutu. See "Le régime presidentiel au Zaire," *Etudes Africaines du C.R.I.S.P.* 144 (20 December 1972): 27.

50 Kamitatu Massamba, *Le pouvoir à la portée du peuple* (Paris: Maspero, 1977), p. 24.

51 Monseigneur Kabanga, "Je suis un homme," Archeveché de Lubumbashi, March 1976, pp. 5–7.

52 *Salongo*, 1 August 1972.

53 Mobutu, *Discours, allocutions, et messages*, 2: 571. The impact of this war was quickly diluted by a speech on 1 February 1975, when Mobutu assured the bourgeoisie that their property in the country was safe, even if acquired "with money you have stolen, for many of you are not very smart in that regard." Mobutu's public speeches were generally extemporaneous and delivered in Lingala; the subsequent official printed transcripts, in French, were cleansed of such embarrassing passages.

54 It should be added that these defiant gestures by the deputies were perhaps influenced by Mobutu's announcement that their previously generous stipends were to be pared to an allowance covering only the brief periods when the legislature was actually sitting. The assembly was shortly thereafter dissolved pending new elections in November 1977.

55 Nguza, a Lunda, was accused of prior knowledge of the March 1977 invasion by insurgents based in Angola. He had been in touch with J. B. Kibwe, a well-known Shaba political figure with contacts in the insurgent camp, who was the former finance minister of Katanga and the first Zairian head of the board of directors of Gécamines. Both posts were lost as a result of corruption charges, and Kibwe had subsequently gone into exile. His contacts with Nguza were to negotiate terms for his return, and were authorized by Mobutu at the time. By 1978 Nguza was out of prison, and soon back in office; in 1980 he was named prime minister, but he went into exile and opposition in April 1981. See his autobiographical account, Nguza Karl-i-Bond, *Mobutu ou l'incarnation du mal zairois* (London: Rex Collings, 1982).

56 A fascinating private report on this episode by a Zairian Catholic priest, which we had an opportunity to consult, shows that the movement was led by one Kasongo, a Tetela healer recently arrived in the region. As has so often been the case, the movement did become a vehicle for externalizing secular discontents, and its assemblies did defy local officials, even capturing a Belgian priest and killing one functionary. Army reinforcements that were sent in required local chiefs to identify and deliver sect followers guilty of defiance of authority; many of those delivered were killed. As time went on, it became possible for the accused to ransom themselves with substantial payments as soldiers came to realize the mercantile potential in the repressive campaign.

57 We may interpret this reception as above all a mark of the deep resentments felt by many over Zaire's desperate socioeconomic circumstances. Thus any humiliation of the regime was to be welcomed. This is not to say that many hoped that the FLNC per se would seize power, but rather than its action would trigger the collapse of the regime. Within the Lunda zone itself, reaction was ambivalent; however strong the antipathy to the regime was, people were reluctant to commit themselves totally to a movement whose prospects for success were

uncertain, and they correctly anticipated that brutal retaliation would face those who exposed themselves if the national army returned. The FLNC, in turn, was enraged by the ambiguity of the support, in 1977, of a number of Lunda notables, especially members of the family of the Mwaant Yav (paramount chief). Several members of Mwaant Yav's family were killed by the FLNC when it withdrew from the area. At the same time, retreating FLNC tried to force a large number of Lunda notables to accompany them back to Angola, and an unsuccessful attempt was made to capture Lunda royal regalia. On recent Lunda politics, see J. Jeffrey Hoover, "*Ant ni Antw*: Ruund Chiefs and People" (Paper presented at the annual meeting of the African Studies Association, Houston, November 1977); and Edouard Bustin, *Lunda under Belgian Rule* (Cambridge: Harvard University Press, 1975).

58 While there can be no doubt that Luanda, Havana, and Moscow desired the overthrow of the regime, only part of the armament of the FLNC was of Soviet fabrication, and no Cuban participants were captured. The evidence advanced by Zairian and some American officials was generally circumstantial: such plans could only have originated in Havana or Moscow, the FLNC had access to Soviet arms and the like. President Carter publicly chastised the Soviets and Cubans for their alleged role, then had to back down to the charge that the Cubans should have prevented the second invasion. In fact, Cuba had informed U.S. diplomatic representatives when the invasion occurred that it had no connection with the event, and indeed had tried to prevent the operation when it learned of the plan in April 1978. The *New York Times* of 11 July 1978 reviews this controversy.

59 See, for example, Daniel Bonehill, "La dépendance et la fragilité," *Le Monde Diplomatique*, June 1978; Jean Rymenam, "Comment le régime Mobutu a sapé ses propres fondements," *Le Monde Diplomatique*, May 1977. For an expose by a Zairian journalist, see Buana Kabwe, *Citoyen Président* (Paris: Editions L'Harmattan, 1978).

60 Kamitatu, *Le pouvoir à la portée du peuple*, pp. 8–9.

Chapter 3

1 Among the most important recent studies dealing with contemporary urbanization are Benoit Verhaegen et al., *Kisangani 1876–1976* (Kinshasa: Presses Universitaires du Zaire, 1975); Valdo Pons, *Stanleyville* (London: Oxford University Press, 1969); J. S. La Fontaine, *City Politics: A Study of Leopoldville, 1962–63* (Cambridge: Cambridge University Press, 1970); Nzongola Ntalaja, "Urban Administration in Zaire: A Study of Kananga, 1971–73" (Ph.D. diss. University of Wisconsin–Madison, 1975); Kajika Lupundu Jérôme, "Les manifestations de la solidarité dans une ville négro-africaine (Lubumbashi: République de Zaire)" (Doctoral diss., Université de Paris-V,

1972). For older sources, see the references in Crawford Young, *Politics in the Congo* (Princeton: Princeton University Press, 1965); Joseph Houyoux, *Budgets ménagers, nutrition et mode de vie à Kinshasa* (Kinshasa: Presses Universitaires du Zaire, 1973).

2 Michael G. Schatzberg, "Bureaucracy, Business, Beer: The Political Dynamics of Class Formation in Lisala, Zaire" (Ph.D. diss., University of Wisconsin–Madison, 1977), p. 10.

3 Office of Internal Health, U.S. Department of Health, Education, and Welfare, "Syncrisis: The Dynamics of Health, XIV: Zaire" (Washington, 1975), mimeo., pp. 85–119.

4 Interview with Mobil Oil executives, New York, 17 April 1978.

5 International Bank for Reconstruction and Development, *Zaire: Current Economic Situation and Constraints* (Washington, 1980), p. 17. A similar pattern continued in 1979: *New York Times*, 4 February 1979.

6 Léon de St. Moulin, "Kinshasa," *Revue Française d'Etudes Politiques Africaines*, September 1971, pp. 51–56.

7 J. Ph. Peemans, "The Social and Economic Development of Zaire since Independence: A Historical Outline," *African Affairs* 74, no. 295 (April 1975), p. 168.

8 Michael G. Schatzberg, "Islands of Privilege: Small Cities in Africa and the Dynamics of Class Formation" (Paper presented at the Conference on the Small City and Regional Community, Stevens Point, Wis., March 1978); see also Schatzberg's contribution in Aidan Southall, ed., *Small Urban Centers in Rural Development in Africa* (Madison: African Studies Program, University of Wisconsin–Madison 1979), pp. 297–312.

9 Houyoux, *Budgets ménagers*, p. 24.

10 The figure 230,000 is no doubt significantly inflated by fictitious names on the education payroll, the salaries for which might be pocketed by sundry principals and functionaries. Gould makes the probably exaggerated claim that two-thirds of the education payroll could be attributed to phantom teachers; the real figure is likely to be well short of that extreme. Mobutu himself, in arguing the case for his economic reform program in a 1978 Paris press conference, noted that fictitious teachers on the payroll represented a major source of potential budgetary savings. See David J. Gould, *Bureaucratic Corruption and Underdevelopment in the Third World: The Case of Zaire* (Elmsford, N.Y.: Pergamon Press, 1980), p. 72.

11 De St. Moulin, "Kinshasa," p. 50

12 Schatzberg, "Bureaucracy, Business, Beer"; Schatzberg, "Islands of Privilege."

13 The importance of this little-understood portion of the urban economy was first given sustained examination in International Labour Organization, *Employment, Incomes and Equality in Kenya* (Geneva: International Labour Organization, 1972).

14 Houyoux, *Budgets ménagers*, p. 27. There is some evidence that this pattern has ceased to be so prevalent, as one measure taken by some employers to mitigate

the impact of inflation in the face of state-imposed wage freezes (made under international pressure) has been to reclassify positions or accelerate promotions, as the following table illustrates. However, this action has far from compensated for deteriorating real wages.

DISTRIBUTION OF GOVERNMENT EMPLOYEES BY SALARY SCALE

Range of monthly salary (zaires)	January 1977 Numbers employed	%	January 1978 Numbers employed	%
0–99	280,912	86.2	262,252	67.9
0–25	37,523	11.5	29,745	7.7
26–55	166,206	50.9	86,776	22.5
56–75	68,777	21.2	45,607	11.8
75–99	8,406	2.6	100,124	25.9
100–199	37,913	11.6	91,787	23.7
200 and over	7,036	2.2	32,475	8.1

Source: International Bank for Reconstruction and Development, *Zaire: Current Economic Situation and Constraints*, (Washington: 1980), p. 22.

15 Schatzberg, "Bureaucracy, Business, Beer," p. 232.

16 Overseas Liaison Committee, American Council on Education, *Survey of Education in the Democratic Republic of the Congo* (Washington, 1969), p. 67.

17 Houyoux, *Budgets ménagers*, p. 243.

18 Nzongola, "Urban Administration," p. 94. See also Susanne Comhaire-Sylvain, *Femmes de Kinshasa hier et aujourd'hui* (Paris: Mouton, 1968); Joan La Fontaine, "The Free Women of Kinshasa: Prostitution in a City in Zaire," in J. Davis, ed., *Choice and Change: Essays in Honor of Lucy Mair* (London: Athlone Press, 1974), pp. 89–113. Only relatively prosperous males can afford a mistress or concubine, or even to visit prostitutes; thus the expansion in the number of young females is linked in part to the emergence of a politico-commercial class.

19 Nzongola, "Urban Administration," p. 77.

20 Verhaegen, et al., *Kisangani*, 1: 50.

21 Robert H. Bates, *Rural Responses to Industrialization: A Study of Village Zambia* (New Haven: Yale University Press, 1976).

22 E. Ndongala, "Mutations structurelles de l'economie traditionelle dans le Bas-Congo sous l'impact de la colonisation et de la decolonisation," *Cahiers Economiques et Sociaux* 4, no. 1 (March 1966): 23. See also Etienne Van Hecke, "Structure agraire et habitat au Bas Congo," *Etudes Africaines du C.R.I.S.P.*, T. A. 106–107 (1970).

23 Weka Engango a Ngola, "L'état d'exception de Bumba" (Mémoire de Licence, Faculte des Sciences Sociales, Politiques et Administratives, Campus de Lubumbashi, Université Nationale du Zaire, 1975), pp. 28–31.

24 Interviews with Minière de Bakwanga (MIBA) executives, Mbuji-Mayi, June 1967.

25 Kanyinda Lusanga, "Les institutions socio-politiques traditionelles et les institutions politique modernes au Zaire" (Doctoral diss., Université Catholique de Louvain, 1974), pp. 66–67.

26 David Merrill Ewert, "Freire's Concept of Critical Consciousness and Social Structure in Rural Zaire" (Ph.D. diss., University of Wisconsin–Madison, 1977), p. 170.

27 Ibid., pp. 177–178.

28 Ibid., p. 177. The collectivity and the locality were the lowest echelons of Zairian administration (see chapter 8). Headed by chiefs, they corresponded to the "native administration" structure of colonial times.

29 Fremont A. Regier, "Ownership, Participation in Planning, Administration and Operation of a Rural Development Project, Nyanda, Zaire" (Ph.D. diss., University of Wisconsin–Madison, 1977), p. 34.

30 International Bank for Reconstruction and Development, "The Economy of Zaire," (1975) 2: 16.

31 Ewert, "Freire's Concept," p. 171.

32 Catharine Newbury, "Ebutumwa Bw'emiogo: The Tyranny of Cassava—A Women's Tax Revolt in Eastern Zaire" (Paper presented at the Annual Meeting, Canadian Association of African Studies, Quebec, May 1983). The protest took the form of a series of demonstrations before local government buildings.

33 The "rural radicalism" thesis of Zairian nationalism was first argued, in lucid fashion, by Herbert Weiss, *Political Protest in the Congo* (Princeton: Princeton University Press, 1967).

34 On the rebellions, see in particular Benoit Verhaegen, *Rébellions au Congo*, 2 vols. (Brussels: Centre de Recherche et d'Information Socio-Politiques, 1966, 1969); Renée Fox et al., "La deuxième indépendence: étude d'un cas: la rébellion au Kwilu," *Etudes Congolaises* 8, no. 1 (January-February 1965): 1–35; Crawford Young, "Rebellion and the Congo," in Robert Rotberg and Ali Mazrui, eds., *Protest and Power in Black Africa* (New York: Oxford University Press, 1970), pp. 968–1,011; Thomas Turner, "Peasant Rebellion and Its Suppression in Sankuru, Zaire," *Pan African Journal* 7, no. 3 (1974).

Chapter 4

1 The parable, of recent origin, was recorded by Vwakyanakazi Mukohya during his dissertation research in Butembo, Kivu, in 1980–81, and reproduced in his doctoral dissertation, "Traders in Butembo" (University of Wisconsin–Madison, 1982).

2 This point is developed at greater length in Crawford Young, "Patterns of Social Conflict: State, Class, and Ethnicity," *Daedalus* 111, no. 2 (Spring 1982): 76–85.

3 While ethnicity has an "objective" dimension (the observable linguistic, religious and other identity-related characteristics of an individual or group), understandings of both analyst and participant of this form of collective representation tend to be based upon subjective self-identifications.

4 For an example of an alternative approach, which argues in the Marxist vein for mode of production as key determinant, see Dennis L. Cohen, "Class and the Analysis of African Politics: Problems and Prospects," in Dennis L. Cohen and John Daniel, eds., *Political Economy of Africa* (London: Longman, 1981), pp. 85–111.

5 Stanislaw Ossowski, *Class Structure in the Social Consciousness* (New York: Free Press of Glencoe, 1963), p. 38.

6 Michael G. Schatzberg, *Politics and Class in Zaire* (New York: Africana Publishing Co., 1980), p. 79.

7 Georges N. Nzongola, "The Bourgeoisie and Revolution in the Congo," *Journal of Modern African Studies* 8, no. 4 (December 1970): 511–530. In his current work, Nzongola's views on class have significantly evolved from those expressed in this article.

8 Christian Coméliau, *Fonctions économiques et pouvoir politique* (Kinshasa: Institut de Recherches Economiques et Sociales, 1965), pp. 75–100.

9 Jean Lacroix, *L'industrialisation au Congo* (Paris: Mouton, 1966), p. 200.

10 Renee Fox et al., "La deuxième indépendance: étude d'un cas: la rébellion au Kwilu," *Etudes congolaises* 8 (January-February 1965): 18–19; Benoit Verhaegen, *Rébellions au Congo*, 2 vols. (Brussels: Centre de Recherche et d'Information Socio-Politiques, 1966, 1969) 1: 101–136. Pierre Mulele, who briefly served as education minister in the Lumumba government, June-September 1960, was the most ideological of the rebel leaders of 1963–65. The insurgency he directed in Kwilu was the first episode in this wave of rural rebellion. He fled into exile when the uprising lost momentum, then was lured back to Kinshasa in 1968 by an amnesty plea. He was at once arrested, tried by a military tribunal for high treason, and summarily executed. See the invaluable biography by Herbert Weiss, "Mulele," in Charles-André Julien et al., eds., *Les Africains* (Paris: Editions Jeune Afrique, 1977) 6: 161–189. The Mulele categories show the impact of a long visit to China in about 1962.

11 This thesis is expounded in B. Verhaegen, "Transferts de technologie ou impérialisme technologique? Le cas du Zaire," *Cahiers du CEDAF*, nos. 5–6 (1981), pp. 93–102.

12 David J. Gould, *Bureaucratic Corruption and Underdevelopment in the Third World: The Case of Zaire* (Elmsford, N.Y.: Pergamon Press, 1980).

13 Jean Rymenam, "Comment le régime Mobutu a sapé ses propres fondements," *Le Monde Diplomatique*, May 1977. See also J. Rymenam, "Classes sociales, pouvoir et économie au Zaire," *Genève-Afrique* 18, no. 1 (1980): 41–54. Rymenam is a pseudonym for a leading student of Zairian politics.

14 Mukenge Tshilemalema, "Businessmen of Zaire: Limited Possibilities for Capi-

tal Accumulation under Dependence," (Doctoral diss., McGill University, 1974), pp. 351–354.

15 Michel Merlier, *Le Congo de la colonisation belge à l'indépendance* (Paris: Maspero, 1962).

16 The full implications of this point are developed in David B. Abernethy, "Bureaucratic Growth and Economic Decline in Sub-Saharan Africa" (Paper presented at the annual meeting, African Studies Association, Boston, December 1983).

17 Union Minière du Haut Katanga, *Rapport annuel*, 1966; Gécamines, *Rapport annuel*, 1974, 1980.

18 Coméliau, *Fonctions économiques*, pp. 80–81, gives an excellent analysis of these groups.

19 Interviews with MIBA executives in Mbuji-Mayi, June 1967.

20 Janet MacGaffey, "Class Relations in a Dependent Economy: Businessmen and Businesswomen in Kisangani, Zaire" (Paper presented at the Annual Meeting, African Studies Association, Bloomington, Ind., October 1981).

21 Colin Legum, ed., *Africa Contemporary Record, 1974–1975* (London: Rex Collings, 1975), p. B607.

22 Legum, ed., *Africa Contemporary Record, 1975–1976*, p. B508.

23 Lacroix, *L'industrialisation au Congo*, p. 211; J. Ph. Peemans, "The Social and Economic Development of Zaire since Independence: A Historical Outline," *African Affairs* 74, no. 295 (April 1975): 168.

24 René Dumont, *L'Afrique Noire est mal partie* (Paris: Editions du Seuil, 1962), p. 66. In a different setting, a similar view had been expounded by Milovan Djilas, *The New Class* (New York: Frederick A. Praeger, 1968).

25 A particularly influential article stressing this category is Claude Meillassoux, "A Class Analysis of the Bureaucratic Process in Mali," *Journal of Development Studies* 6, no. 2 (January 1970): 97–110.

26 Joel Samoff, "Class, Class Conflict, and the States: Notes on the Political Economy of Africa" (Paper presented at the Annual Meeting, African Studies Association, Houston, November, 1977), p. 23.

27 The colonial administration did at times seek to interest the church missions in providing instruction to sons of chiefs, with a view to increasing the efficiency of these appendages of the colonial state. The few abortive ventures in schools for sons of chiefs foundered before Catholic reticence. Future chiefs were believed by many missionaries to be bound for polygamous marriages, and were viewed as not necessarily the best material on which to erect Christian communities.

28 *Livre Blanc: Apport Scientifique de la Belgique au développement de l'Afrique Centrale* (Brussels: Académie Royale des Sciences d'Outremer, 1962) 1: 154.

29 C. Guebels, *Relation complète des travaux de la Commission Permanente pour la protection des indigènes* (Elisabethville: Centre d'Etudes des Problems Sociaux Indigènes, 1953).

30 For a useful discussion of the *évolué*, see Roger Anstey, "Belgium's Role in the Congo and the Aspirations of the Evolué Class," in L. H. Gann and Peter Duignan, eds., *Colonialism in Africa 1870–1960* (Cambridge: Cambridge University Press, 1970) 2: 194–225.

31 We are indebted to Yamvu Makasa for correction of our own earlier interpretations on this point; in Crawford Young, *Politics in the Congo* (Princeton: Princeton University Press, 1965), pp. 197–200, it was argued that *évolué* status was an automatic correlate of educational level.

32 *Dettes de Guerre* (Lubumbashi: Editions Essor du Congo, 1965), pp. 128–129.

33 Mukenge, "Businessmen of Zaire," pp. 203–204.

34 Young, *Politics in the Congo*, p. 201.

35 Merlier, *Le Congo*, p. 188.

36 Joan Vincent, *An African Elite: Big Men in a Small Town* (New York: Columbia University Press, 1968).

37 J. Jeffrey Hoover, "Ant ni Antw: Ruund Chiefs and People" (Paper presented at the Annual Meeting, African Studies Association, Houston, November 1977).

38 Mukenge, "Businessmen of Zaire," p. 261.

39 Ibid., pp. 274–281.

40 Ibid., pp. 326–331. On the Indonesian parallel, we are indebted to Donald Emmerson, personal communication. On the impact of inflation in general, see Institut de Recherches Économiques et Sociales, *Indépendance, inflation, développement* (Paris: Mouton, 1968).

41 Mukenge, "Businessmen of Zaire," pp. 228–234.

42 Peemans, "Social and Economic Development," pp. 148–179.

43 Indeed, this process had begun long before. The failure of independence to bring the mass benefits promised by *évolué* politicians in 1960, and the widespread public recognition of the politico-commercial class in formation, led to the violent assaults upon *intellectuels* (white-collar state personnel, teachers, and the like) during the 1964–65 rebellions.

44 This is not the only connotation acquired by *citoyen*. One may hear a high-status person declare that something is "only for the *citoyens*," or just for common folks.

45 Michael G. Schatzberg, analyzing dossiers of candidates for party nomination for legislative seats in the Mongala subregion in the 1970 elections, offers convincing documentation: "Bureaucrats, Business, Beer: The Political Dynamics of Class Formation in Lisala, Zaire" (Ph.D. diss., University of Wisconsin–Madison, 1977), pp. 291–297.

46 These relations bear some resemblance to the "transnational class" interpretation argued by Sklar in the Zambian case: Richard L. Sklar, *Corporate Power in an African State* (Berkeley: University of California Press, 1975), p. 201. For a comparison of the Zairian bourgeoisie to Sklar's "transnational class," see

Thomas Turner, "Class Conflict in Zaire" (Paper presented to the annual meeting, American Political Science Association, Washington, September 1979).

47 For an excellent treatment of this point, see Nzongola Ntalaja, "The Continuing Struggle for National Liberation in Zaire," *Journal of Modern African Studies* 17, no. 4 (December 1979): 595–614.

48 Benoit Verhaegen, "Impérialisme technologique et bourgeoisie nationale au Zaire," in C. Coquéry-Vidrovitch, ed., *Connaissance du Tiers Monde* (Paris: Union Générale d'Editions, 1978), pp. 347–379; David J. Gould, "From Development Administration to Underdevelopment Administration," *Cahiers du CEDAF*, no. 6 (1978), p. 34.

49 Vwakyanakazi, "Traders in Butembo."

50 MacGaffey, "Class Relations." Other evidence on the emergence of the mercantile class may be found in Schatzberg, *Politics and Class in Zaire*; Bakonzi Agayo, "The Gold Mines of Kilo-Moto in Northeastern Zaire, 1905–1960" (Ph.D. diss., University of Wisconsin–Madison, 1982); and Bianga Waruzi, "Peasant, State, and Rural Development in Postindependence Zaire: A Case Study of 'Réforme Rurale' 1970–1980 and Its Implications" (Ph.D. diss., University of Wisconsin–Madison, 1982). For a parallel process in Nigeria, see Adrian Peace, "Prestige, Power and Legitimacy in a Modern Nigerian Town," *Canadian Journal of African Studies* 13, no. 2 (1979): 25–51.

51 Sklar, *Corporate Power*, p. 201.

52 Mukenge, "Businessmen of Zaire," p. 222.

53 Coméliau, *Fonctions économiques*, p. 74.

54 Nicos Poulantzas, *Classes in Contemporary Capitalism* (London: NLB, 1975), pp. 194–201.

55 Frank Parkin, *Class Inequality and Political Order* (London: NLB, 1975), p. 3; see also the excellent discussion in Schatzberg, "Bureaucrats, Business, Beer," pp. 73–75 and passim.

56 Ngoyi Makita et al., "Les étudiants et les élèves de Kisangani (1974–1975): Aspirations, opinions et conditions de vie," *Cahiers du CEDAF*, nos. 7–8 (1977), p. 100.

57 Survey conducted by the authors.

58 Schatzberg provides impressive documentation of the mechanisms of what he terms "rural exploitation": "Bureaucrats, Business, Beer," pp. 169–220.

59 Ibid. It is worth noting that the collectivity personnel, a quite numerous category nationwide, are not included in the public sector employee totals in table 3.8.

60 Mukenge, "Businessmen of Zaire"; Joseph Houyoux, *Budgets ménagers, nutrition et mode de vie à Kinshasa* (Kinshasa: Presses Universitaires du Zaire, 1973); Paul Raymaekers, *L'organisation des zones de squatting* (Paris: Editions Universitaires, 1964); H. Mpinga, "La coexistance des pouvoirs 'traditionnel' et 'moderne' dans la ville de Kinshasa," *Cahiers Economiques et Sociaux* 2 (March 1969): 67–90. See also H. Knoop, "Some Demographic Characteristics of a

Suburban Squatting Community of Leopoldville," *Cahiers Economiques et Sociaux* 4, no. 2 (June 1966): 119–150.

61 See Peter C. W. Gutkind, "The Energy of Despair: Social Organization of the Unemployed in Two African Cities: Lagos and Nairobi," *Civilisations* 17, nos. 3–4 (1967).

62 Raymaekers, *L'organisation des zones de squatting*, pp. 132–135, 144, 152, 171, 189, 197. See also Marc Ross, *The Political Integration of Urban Squatters* (Evanston: Northwestern University Press, 1973).

63 Raymaekers, *L'organisation des zones de squatting*, p. 117.

64 Nzongola, "The Bourgeoisie and Revolution," p. 521.

65 Mpinga, "La coexistance." This is also documented by Margaret Turner in her forthcoming dissertation on housing in Lubumbashi (University of Wisconsin–Madison).

66 Most notably G. Arrighi and J. S. Saul, *Essays on the Political Economy of Africa* (New York: Monthly Review Press, 1973). Saul later retreated from this position.

67 Robin Cohen, in Peter Gutkind and Emmanuel Wallerstein, eds., *The Political Economy of Contemporary Africa* (Beverly Hills: Sage Publications, 1976), p. 165. Cohen himself rejects the "labor aristocracy" term.

68 Mwabila Malela, "Prolétariat et conscience de classe au Zaire" (Doctoral diss., Université Libre de Bruxelles, 1973), p. 7.

69 Ibid., p. 188.

70 A. Lux, personal communication, April 1969.

71 We are indebted to Bogumil Jewsiewicki for important details concerning these events; his brilliant contribution to Zairian social and economic history is only beginning to make itself felt. See his "La contestation sociale et la naissance du prolétariat au Zaire au cours de la première moitié du XXᵉ siecle," *Canadian Journal of African Studies* 10, no. 1 (1976): 47–70.

72 Mwabila, "Prolétariat et conscience de classe," p. 14.

73 Jean-Louis Lacroix, "Le rôle de l'industrie dans le développement économique général," *Zaire-Afrique* 61 (January 1972): 12.

74 Benoit Verhaegen, "Paradoxes zairoises" (Paper presented at the Annual Meeting, Canadian Association of African Studies, Quebec, May 1983), p. 2.

75 Ilunga Kabongo, "Baffling Africa or the Dying Gasps of a Discourse" (Paper presented at the Conference on African Crisis Areas and United States Foreign Policy, Los Angeles, March 1983), p. 8.

76 Anthony Oberschall, "On the Political Economy of Zaire" (Paper presented at the Annual Meeting, African Studies Association, Bloomington, Ind., October 1981), p. 11.

77 Ilunga, "Baffling Africa," pp. 10–11.

Chapter 5

1 Crawford Young, *Politics in the Congo* (Princeton: Princeton University Press, 1965), pp. 232–272; Crawford Young, *The Politics of Cultural Pluralism* (Madison: University of Wisconsin Press, 1976), pp. 163–215; Thomas Turner, "Congo-Kinshasa," in Victor A. Olorunsola, ed., *The Politics of Cultural Sub-Nationalism in Africa* (Garden City, N.Y.: Anchor Books, 1972); Thomas Turner, "L'ethnie tetela et le MNC/Lumumba," *Etudes Congolaises* 12 (October-December 1969): 36–57. Some portions of this discussion are drawn from Crawford Young, "Ethnic Politics in Zaire" (Paper presented at the Annual Meeting, African Studies Association, Houston, November 1977).

2 The speech is reprinted in *Etudes Zairoises* 2 (September-October 1973): 79–102.

3 This point is argued as the central defining characteristic of ethnicity in the influential statement by Fredrik Barth, ed., *Ethnic Groups and Boundaries* (Boston: Little, Brown and Co., 1969), pp. 9–39.

4 A. L. Epstein, *Ethos and Identity* (London: Tavistock Publications, 1978), p. xi.

5 See the various contributions in Abner Cohen, ed., *Urban Ethnicity* (London: Tavistock Publications, 1974).

6 This distinction has recently become recognized in the theoretical literature; see Charles Keyes, ed., *Ethnic Change* (Seattle: University of Washington Press, 1981). Among recent major works, Joseph Rothchild, *Ethnopolitics* (New York: Columbia University Press, 1981), and Nelson Kasfir, *The Shrinking Political Arena* (Berkeley: University of California Press, 1975), represent the instrumentalist approach, while such works as Harold R. Isaacs, *Idols of the Tribe* (New York: Harper & Row, 1975), and John Armstrong, *Nations before Nationalism* (Chapel Hill: University of North Carolina Press, 1982), exemplify primordialist orientation.

7 Raymond Apthorpe, "Does Tribalism Really Matter?" *Transition* 7, no. 6 (October 1968): 18.

8 G. Vanderkerken, *L'ethnie Mongo*, 2 vols. (Brussels: Institut Royal Colonial Belge, 1944).

9 Edmond Verhulpen, *Baluba et balubaïsés du Katanga* (Antwerp: Editions de l'avenir belge, 1936); Kanyinda Lusanga, "Les institutions socio-politiques traditionelles et les institutions politiques modernes au Zaire" (Doctoral diss., Université Catholique de Louvain, 1974), p. 25. The thesis of Kabasela Mpinda, consulted in draft form, makes the same argument (prepared for submission to the Lubumbashi campus, Université Nationale du Zaire).

10 See in particular the careful study by Benoit Verhaegen and E. de Bethune, "Consultations électorales et élections au Congo, 1957–1969," *Cahiers Economiques et Sociaux* 3, no. 3, (1965): 247–289.

11 A voluminous literature has grown up around the phenomenon of urban ethnicity in Africa; for a recent statement and full references, see Cohen, ed., *Urban Ethnicity*.

12 Ilunga Mbuya Kabongo, "Ethnicity, Social Class and the State in the Congo, 1960–65: The Case of the Baluba," (Ph.D. diss., University of California–Berkeley, 1973), pp. 299–306.

13 These factors accounted for 30 of the MNC/L's 33 national seats, and 80 of its 92 provincial seats. For details on the 1960 elections, see Gérard-Libois and Verhaegen, *Congo 1960* (Brussels: Centre de Recherche et d'Information Socio-Politiques, 1961) 1: 136–266; W. J. Ganshof van der Meersch, *Fin de la Souveraineté belge au Congo* (Brussels: Institut Royal des Relations Internationales, 1963). For an extended analysis of the Tetela-Kusu zone electoral returns, see Thomas Turner, "A Century of Political Conflict in Sankuru" (Ph.D. diss., University of Wisconsin–Madison, 1973).

14 On the Kongo, see *ABAKO 1950–1960* (Brussels: Centre de Recherche et d'Information Socio-Politiques, 1963); Laurent Monnier, *Ethnie et intégration régionale au Congo* (Paris: Editions Classiques d'Expression Française, 1970).

15 Herbert Weiss, *Political Protest in the Congo* (Princeton: Princeton University Press, 1967); *Parti Solidaire Africain (P.S.A.)* (Brussels: Centre de Recherche et d'Information Socio-Politiques, 1963).

16 Jules Gérard-Libois, *Katanga Secession* (Madison: University of Wisconsin Press, 1966).

17 On the provincial fragmentation, see B. Verhaegen, "Présentation morphologique des nouvelles provinces," *Etudes Congolaises* 4, no. 4 (1963): 1–25, and the five volumes by J. C. Willame (with L. Monnier), *Les provinces du Congo: structure et fonctionnement* (Kinshasa: Institut de Recherches Economiques et Sociales, 1964–1965).

18 Aidan Southall, "The Illusion of Tribe," *Journal of Asian and African Studies* 5, nos. 1–2 (1970): 44.

19 The term is borrowed from Armstrong, *Nations before Nationalism*.

20 These points are more fully discussed in Young, *The Politics of Cultural Pluralism*, pp. 44–49, 181–189. See also Rothschild, *Ethnopolitics*, pp. 67–100; Brian Weinstein, *The Civic Tongue* (New York: Longman, 1983), pp. 62–78.

21 See, for example, the historical charter for the Lunda, in Jeffrey Hoover, "The Seduction of Rwej: Reconstructing Lunda History (The Nuclear Lunda; Zaire, Angola, Zambia)" (Ph.D. diss., Yale University, 1978). Note that large-scale historical kingdoms usually incorporate diverse linguistic groups; Jan Vansina, *The Children of Woot* (Madison: University of Wisconsin Press, 1978), documents the multi-ethnic character of the Kuba state.

22 Two examples of ideological contributions by Zairian intellectuals are Lusibu Zala N'kanza, "The Social Origins of Political Underdevelopment in the ex-Belgian Congo (Zaire)" (Ph.D. diss., Harvard University, 1976) on the Kongo, and Kanyinda, "Les institutions socio-politiques traditionnelles," on the Luba.

23 This program is reminiscent of the strategies analyzed by Kasfir, *The Shrinking Political Arena*.

24 Nzongola Ntalaja, "Urban Administration in Zaire: A Study of Kananga, 1971–73" (Ph.D. diss., University of Wisconsin-Madison, 1975), demon-

strates the vacuous nature of these councils. They were restored in the 1977 "democratization."

25 There were still some channels open for ethnic patronage in the bureaucracy; each minister had a personal "cabinet," which tended to be a repository for ethnic clients. In 1974 ministers were officially prohibited from designating co-ethnics to these slots, but the practice persisted.

26 Kajika Lupundu Jérôme, "Les manifestations de la solidarité dans une ville négro-africaine (Lubumbashi: République de Zaire)" (Doctoral diss., Université de Paris-V, 1972), pp. 261–273. Cultural meanings of the Kalela dance on the Zambian copperbelt, where it is particularly well-known and popular, are elucidated by J. Clyde Mitchell, *The Kalela Dance* (Manchester: University of Manchester Press, 1958).

27 Michael G. Schatzberg, "Bureaucracy, Business, Beer: The Political Dynamics of Class Formation in Lisala, Zaire" (Ph.D. diss., University of Wisconsin–Madison, 1977), pp. 229–260, 324–403; Edward Kannyo, "Political Power and Class-Formation in Zaire: The 'Zairianization Measures,' 1973–75" (Ph.D. diss., Yale University, 1979).

28 Joseph Greenberg, *The Languages of Africa* (Bloomington: Indiana University Press, 1966), p. 9; Jan Vansina, *Introduction à l'ethnographie du Congo* (Kinshasa: Editions Universitaires du Congo, 1966), pp. 27–33.

29 H. Burssens, *Les peuplades de l'entre Congo-Ubangi* (Tervuren, Belgium: Musée Royal de l'Afrique Centrale, 1958), pp. 13–15.

30 B. Verhaegen, "Les associations congolaises à Léopoldville et dans le Bas-Congo avant 1960," *Cahiers Economiques et Sociaux* 8, no. 3 (September 1970): 403.

31 The more whimsical translation often encountered—"cock who leaves no hen intact"—is apparently incorrect.

32 On the national language issue, see Bokamba Eyamba, "Authenticity and the Choice of a National Language, the Case of Zaire," *Studies in the Linguistic Sciences* 6, no. 2 (Fall 1976); W. J. Samerin, "Colonization and Pidginization on the Ubangi River," *Journal of African Languages and Linguistics* 4 (1982): 1–42; J. Fabian, "Missions and the Colonization of African Languages: Developments in the Former Belgian Congo," *Canadian Journal of African Studies* 17, no. 2 (1983): 165–188.

33 Monganga Pili, "Esprit d'intégration nationale chez les étudiants du Campus de Lubumbashi" (Mémoire de licence, Faculté des Sciences Sociales, Politiques et Administratives, Université Nationale du Zaire, 1974), pp. 118–127.

34 Ibid., p. 111.

35 Walter M. Rideout et al., *Survey of Education in the Democratic Republic of the Congo* (Washington: Overseas Liaison Committee, American Council on Education, 1969), p. 60. We may note in passing that some intellectuals, especially those from groups that feel victimized by the quota system, place the blame for the quota system on this document, which warns of sociopolitical dangers arising from regional imbalances in educational access.

36 Tshivuadi Katamba, "La participation des étudiants zairois à la politique" (Mémoire de licence, Faculté des Sciences Sociales, Politiques et Administratives, Université Nationale du Zaire, Lubumbashi, 1974), pp. 164–167.

37 The classic statements on this tie remain those of René Lemarchand, "Political Clientelism and Ethnicity in Tropical Africa: Competing Solidarities in Nation-Building," *American Political Science Review* 66, no. 1 (March 1972): 68–90; James Scott, "Patron-Client Politics and Political Change in Southeast Asia," *American Political Science Review* 66, no. 1 (March 1972): 91–113. For a more recent recapitulation of patron-client theory, see S. N. Eisenstadt and René Lemarchand, eds., *Political Clientelism, Patronage, and Development* (Beverly Hills: Sage Publications, 1981).

38 Valuable evidence on this issue is offered by Robert M. Price, *Society and Bureaucracy in Contemporary Ghana* (Berkeley: University of California Press, 1975).

40 Data for this paragraph are drawn from Muteba Kazadi, "L'agent public zairois et la question du tribalisme actuel" (Mémoire de licence, Faculté des Sciences Sociales, Politiques et Administratives, Université Nationale du Zaire, Lubumbashi, 1974), pp. 110–111.

41 Pierre van den Berghe, "Ethnicity: The African Experience," *International Social Science Journal* 23 (1971): 507–518.

42 Worth nothing here is the interaction between corruption and clientelism. Ethnic nepotism is, of course, a contravention of official administrative norms, and in this sense it is corrupt. But in the monetary meaning of corruption—the sale for private gain of a public service—kinship affinity is an alternative to financial payment. Roughly speaking, the less able the seeker of a government service is to activate a social obligation based on personal affinity, the heavier will be the payment required for the service. Even where some affinity has been established a payment may be necessary as well, perhaps discounted by the proximity of the relationship (as suggested by the answer of the last two respondents).

43 Martin Kilson, *Political Change in a West African State* (Cambridge: Harvard University Press, 1966), p. 88.

44 Kajika, "Les manifestations de la solidarité," pp. 228–240. Adrian Peace makes a similar argument for Nigeria, documenting processes by which client claims may be avoided: "Prestige, Power and Legitimacy in a Modern Nigerian Town," *Canadian Journal of African Studies* 13, no. 2 (1979): 25–51.

45 Tshilemalema Mukenge, "Businessmen of Zaire: Limited Possibilities for Capital Accumulation under Dependence" (Doctoral diss., McGill University, 1974), pp. 305–324.

46 Claude Meillassoux, *Anthropologie économique des Gouro de Côte d'Ivoire* (The Hague: Mouton, 1964); Emmanuel Terray, *Marxism and 'Primitive' Societies* (New York: Monthly Review Press, 1972).

47 Hugues Bertrand, *Le Congo* (Paris: François Maspero, 1975), pp. 64–91. For another interesting Marxist treatment, see John Saul, *The State and Revolution in Eastern Africa* (London: Heinemann, 1979), pp. 391–423.

48 Mwabila Malela, "Pour une relecture de la sociologie à la lumière de la théorie de la dépendance," in V. Y. Mudimbe, ed., *La dépendance de l'Afrique et les moyens d'y rémedier* (Paris: Berger-Levrault, 1980), pp. 266–267.

49 Bogumil Jewsiewicki, "Quelques reflexions préalable à une analyse historique des pratiques et de l'idéologie de l'ethnicité au Zaire" (Paper presented at the Annual Meeting, Canadian Association of African Studies, Quebec, May 1983).

50 Michael G. Schatzberg, *Politics and Class in Zaire* (New York: Africana Publishing Company, 1980), p. 173.

Chapter 6

1 Cited in Colin Legum, ed., *Africa Contemporary Record, 1970–1971* (London: Rex Collings, 1971), p. B288.

2 The term "patrimonialism" was first systematically applied by J. C. Williame, *Patrimonialism and Political Change in the Congo* (Stanford: Stanford University Press, 1972).

3 For a useful resumé of the Weberian concept, see Reinhard Bendix, *Max Weber: An Intellectual Portrait* (Garden City, N.Y.: Doubleday & Co., 1962), pp. 334–360.

4 Nguza Karl-i-Bond, *Mobutu ou l'incarnation du mal zairois* (London: Rex Collings, 1982), p. 38.

5 E.-Xavier Ugeux, "Marathon dans la brousse zairoise," *Remarques Africaines*, nos. 432–433 (December 1973), p. 18.

6 *Zaire-Afrique* 91 (January 1975): 25. One can understand why the Catholic church regarded these pretensions at quasi-divination as verging on sacrilege.

7 In a January 1976 conference in Brussels, reported by *Remarques Africaines*, 477 (15 January 1976): 8.

8 Watilaninwa Yaya, "Une approche générale sur le rôle du charisme au Zaire sous la deuxième République" (Mémoire de licence, Faculté des Sciences Sociales, Politiques et Administratives, Université Nationale du Zaire, Campus de Lubumbashi, 1974), p. 71. This study offers an interesting review of the various aspects of official "charisma."

9 Jules Chomé, *L'ascension de Mobutu* (Brussels: Editions Complexe, 1974; originally published by Maspero in France). Chomé had authored numerous polemical works on the First Republic; this book owed its notoriety to the affair of state Mobutu made of it.

10 Interviews with officials of some of the companies involved (Petrofina, Mobil, B. P., Shell, and Texaco). Oil exploration concessions were not affected by this nationalization. Petrozaire, a parastatal concern, initially did a competent job of supplanting the foreign oil companies in the marketing of oil products; however, it fell prey to the inherent logistical problems of managing distribution over so far-flung a territory, and to the black market operations of its own per-

sonnel, which had been opened up by the persistent shortages resulting from the inability to pay for sufficient oil to meet domestic demand. In 1978 a settlement was reached with the companies, by which they resumed Zairian marketing, and the state purchased at a generous price a 40–51 percent share in their holdings (except for those of B. P., which chose to abandon its small assets in the easterrn frontier regions).

11 Francis Monheim, *Mobutu, l'homme seul* (Brussels: Editions Actuelles, 1963), provides the most complete biographical details on Mobutu's early life. This admiring portrait has been widely criticized for its sycophantic tone. Aside from the Chomé volume, *L'ascension du Mobutu*—also polemical—printed biographic information on Mobutu is scattered. There is an enormous reservoir of oral anecdotal material in circulation, most of which is unverifiable, however entertaining. We have restricted ourselves, in using oral (interview) data, to information we were able to validate from more than one source. For details on Mobutu's role in First Republic politics, we refer the reader to the standard sources on this period, particularly the annual documentary studies published by the Brussels Centre de Recherche et d'Information Socio-Politiques (C.R.I.S.P.), *Congo 1960* through *Congo 1965*.

12 The extravagant outlays on the reconstruction of Gbadolite have been denounced by regime opponents. In 1978 the Gbadolite infrastructure was enhanced by a handsome mausoleum erected by Mobutu for his deceased wife. The remoteness of the locale, and necessity to air-freight in most building materials, made these projects both expensive and difficult.

13 Monheim, *Mobutu*, p. 22. This tale stands in interesting contrast to an anecdote told by Kenneth Kaunda of his youthful encounter with a lion while bicycling down a rural path. The beast blocked his way; he slowly advanced up on it, ringing his bicycle bell, and finally shaking his lifted bicycle at the lion. This last gesture accomplished its purpose; the lion scurried away. The anecdote serves parallel allegorical purposes, exemplifying courage. Kaunda notes, "To my great surprise the fear that had been haunting me quickly gave way to a feeling of strength and boldness." The contrast in political style of the two leaders is well illustrated in these two tales. (Kenneth Kaunda, *Zambia Shall Be Free* [London: Heinemann, 1962], p. 54.)

14 Representative of the scurrilous anti-Mobutu tracts alleging Mama Yemo had been a prostitute was the following parody on the national anthem, "La Zairoise," circulated in Lubumbashi in June 1976:

"La Zairoise"

(true version)	(student version)
Zairians, living in rediscovered peace,	Zairians, living in entrenched madness,
United people, we are Zairians;	All is finished, we are at bay;
Let us go forward, proud and dignified.	Forward, proud, yet covered with
A great people, a people forever free.	indignity,
	An insane people, a people forever
	intoxicated.

"La Zairoise" (*continued*)

(true version)	(student version)
Tricolored flag, light in us the sacred flame, Which binds us to our ancestors and our children, Peace, justice, and work; Peace, justice, and work.	Tricolored flag, remind us of the spilt blood, Which builds our country into chaos, Peace, injustice, and corruption; Peace, injustice, and corruption.
Tricolored flag in the wind, which revives the ideal, Which links us to our ancestors and our children, Peace, justice, and work; Peace, justice, and work.	Tricolored flag in the wind, which revives party dances, Which link us to the prostitute Yemo, Peace, injustice, and corruption; Peace, injustice, and corruption.

15 Monheim, *Mobutu,* p. 25.

16 Monguya Mbenge, *Histoire secrète du Zaire* (Brussels: Editions d'Esperance, 1977), p. 160.

17 Monheim, *Mobutu,* pp. 29–31. Marie-Antoinette Mobutu, to whom Mobutu was married in 1955, was only fourteen when their first child was born.

18 Ibid., p. 31. Mobutu did enter into more amicable relationships with the Catholic church in Belgium, and he went through a religious marriage ceremony in 1959.

19 Maurice Tempelsman, scion of an Antwerp diamond-trading family which had moved to New York before World War II, remained a Mobutu confidant over the next two decades; see the "New copper investors" section of chapter 10. In 1974 Devlin retired from CIA service (after tours in Laos and Washington) and became the $100,000-per-year personal representative of Tempelsman in Kinshasa: Legum, ed., *Africa Contemporary Record, 1975–1976,* p. B514. Devlin had no known background in the diamond or metal sectors in which Tempelsman was interested; what was purchased for this hefty salary was evidently his personal access to Mobutu. At the same time, Devlin continued to function as an intelligence channel; according to a former U.S. deputy assistant secretary of state who visited Zaire in 1979, Devlin was "the true representative of the United States Government in President Mobutu's eyes," having much better access than the ambassador. The same source reported that embassy personnel believed that "Devlin had complete access to classified Government files long after he left the Government": *New York Times,* 6 December 1981.

20 See Chomé, *L'ascension de Mobutu,* and the several references he cites, pp. 69–71. Professor A. A. J. Van Bilsen, in a personal communication, indicates that he personally warned Lumumba that Mobutu was working as an informer. Lumumba responded that he already was aware of this, and that it was innocent activity designed to bring in some badly needed extra income. We should add that the network of part-time informers was enormous. *Kongo dia Ngunga,* on

11 April 1961, devoted several pages to a list of informers discovered in Belgian records.

21 See the intriguing analysis, "Poids socio-politiques des ressortissants de l'Equateur à Kinshasa," *Courrier African du C.R.I.S.P.*, T.A. 84 (8 November 1968).

22 Monheim, *Mobutu*, p. 117.

23 Cléophas Kamitatu, *La grande mystification du Congo-Kinshasa* (Paris: Maspero, 1971), p. 82.

24 Adversaries of Mobutu would later argue that he was a central figure in making this decision; see Chomé, *L'ascension de Mobutu*, pp. 100–109. For the most detailed account of the Lumumba assassination, see G. Heinz and H. Donney, *Patrice Lumumba: ses 50 derniers jours* (Brussels: C.R.I.S.P., 1966). The polemics over who precisely was responsible for what in the Lumumba slaying cannot be resolved here; clearly all those in the inner councils of power in Kinshasa at the time, as well as those external interests—especially American and Belgian—which weighed heavily in Kinshasa calculations, had at least foreknowledge of and encouraged the decision to deliver the former prime minister to Katangan authorities. On the CIA role, see Madeleine G. Kalb, *The Congo Cables* (New York: Macmillan Publishing Co., 1982), pp. 189–196.

25 Monheim, *Mobutu*, pp. 36, 49.

26 *Miso Gaa*, 8 August 1975. See also *Afrique-Asie*, 252 (9 November 1981), for additional detail on Mobutu's real property holdings in Europe. Nguza, in his September 1981 congressional testimony, noted that Mobutu owned "eight houses and two castles" in Brussels; he also listed property holdings in Paris, Lucerne, Ndjamena, Abidjan, and Dakar. In the Senegalese capital, Mobutu owned three hotels that were managed for him by his Senegalese diviner, who was evidently a reliable business partner as well as a counsellor on the occult and the supernatural. In this testimony Nguza described in chilling detail the torture he experienced in 1977 when he was dismissed as foreign minister and sentenced to death for "high treason" after a summary trial. Mobutu, according to Nguza, threatened to shoot him personally, but was dissuaded by then-Prime Minister Mpinga and senior Political Bureau member Ileo. During Nguza's subsequent interrogation by security personnel, a metal tube was inserted in his penile shaft, through which jets of air were introduced, rupturing a number of blood vessels and causing intense pain. Electrical shocks were applied to his testicles at the same time. (Subcommittee on Africa, Committee on Foreign Affairs, House of Representatives, *Political and Economic Situation in Zaire—Fall 1981*, 97th Cong., 1st sess., 15 September 1981, pp. 17–20.)

27 A photocopy of the act of incorporation is found in Monguya, *Histoire secrète*, pp. 221–222.

28 Comité Zaire, *Zaire: Le dossier de la recolonisation* (Paris: Harmattan, 1978), pp. 124–134.

29 Testimony of Nguza Karl-i-Bond, in Subcommittee on Africa, *Political and Economic Situation in Zaire*, p. 4. When senior Mobutu kinsman Litho died in

1982, litigation over succession to assets in the United States revealed that their value was $1 billion. The U.S. television program "Sixty Minutes," in a presentation on Zaire on 4 March 1984, advanced an estimate of $5 billion for the Mobutu fortune.

30 Ibid., p. 6.

31 Ibid., p. 7.

32 Barry Cohen, "L'ébauche d'une stratégie occidentale," *Le Monde Diplomatique*, July 1978.

33 Juan L. Linz, "Totalitarian and Authoritarian Regimes," in Fred I. Greenstein and Nelson Polsby, eds., *Handbook of Political Science* (Reading, Mass.: Addison-Wesley Co., 1975) 3: 240.

34 Willame, *Patrimonialism*.

35 Stanislav Andreski, "Kleptocracy as a System of Government in Africa," in Arnold J. Heidenheimer, ed., *Political Corruption* (1970; New Brunswick, N.J.: Transaction Books, 1978), pp. 346–357.

36 David J. Gould, *Bureaucratic Corruption and Underdevelopment in the Third World: The Case of Zaire* (Elmsford, N.Y.: Pergamon Press, 1980).

37 On the delegitimizing impact of such a perception, see the compelling analysis of Jorge Dominguez concerning pre-Castro Cuba, *Cuba: Order and Revolution* (Cambridge: Harvard University Press, 1978).

38 Mabika Kalanda, *La remise en question* (Brussels: Editions "Remarques Africaines," 1967), p. 149.

39 Ilunga Kabongo, "Baffling Africa or the Dying Gasps of a Discourse" (Paper presented at the Conference on African Crisis Areas and United States Foreign Policy, Los Angeles, March 1983), pp. 9–10.

Chapter 7

1 *Congo 1965* (Brussels: Centre de Recherche et d'Information Socio-Politiques, 1966), pp. 411–412.

2 *Congo 1965*, pp. 413–414.

3 The official history of the MPR gives the date of 12 December 1965 for the creation of the CVR; *Histoire du Mouvement Populaire de la Révolution* (Kinshasa: Institut Makanda Kabobi, 1975), p. 109.

4 *Congo 1966* (Brussels: Centre de Recherche et d'Information Socio-Politiques 1967), pp. 38–39.

5 Communique published in *Le Progrés*, 11 January 1966, reproduced in *Congo 1966*, p. 40.

6 *Congo 1966*, pp. 44–45.

7 *Congo 1966*, p. 72.

8 "Résolutions du seminaire," reprinted in *Congo 1966*, p. 72.

9 Thomas Turner, "Peasant Rebellion and its Suppression in Sankuru," *Pan African Journal* 7, no. 3 (1974): 204.

10 *Congo 1967* (Brussels: Centre de Recherche et d'Information Socio-Politiques, 1968), pp. 94–107.

11 *Le Soir* (Brussels), reprinted in *Congo 1967*, p. 103.

12 *Histoire du Mouvement Populaire de la Révolution*, p. 41.

13 Lissanga Egala, "L'impact du Mouvement Populaire de la Révolution sur l'administration publique zairoise" (Mémoire du licence, Faculté des Sciences Sociales, Politiques, et Administratives, Université Nationale du Zaire, Campus de Lubumbashi, 1975).

14 Kithima bin Ramazani, "Recueil des directives à l'usage des secrétaires permanents" (ca. 1978). In the early 1980s the insistence on party supremacy over the state, which had become subdued by the late 1970s, was revived.

15 *Histoire du Mouvement Populaire de la Révolution*, p. 44.

16 *La Dépêche*, Lubumbashi, 26 September 1967.

17 *La Tribune* (Kinshasa), 10 October and 17 October 1967. Shabani retorted that "only . . . Mobutu was competent" to judge him.

18 *Histoire du Mouvement Populaire de la Révolution*, p. 46.

19 Ibid., p. 75.

20 P. Demunter, "Les relations entre le mouvement étudiant et le régime politique congolais, le Colloque de Goma," *C.R.I.S.P.*, T.A., no. 126 (30 April 1971).

21 *Histoire du Mouvement Populaire de la Révolution*, p. 46.

22 Demunter, "Les relations entre le mouvement étudiant et le régime," p. 7.

23 Ibid.

24 *Histoire du Mouvement Populaire de la Révolution*, p. 46; Michael G. Schatzberg, "Fidelité au Guide: J.M.P.R. in Zairian Schools," *Journal of Modern African Studies* 16, no. 3 (1978): 417–431.

25 Schatzberg, "Fidelité au Guide," pp. 430–431.

26 Oscar Manwana, "Le rôle des syndicats du Zaire," *Zaire Afrique* 65 (May 1972): 265; see also *Congo 1967*, pp. 167–182.

27 J. Ngoie, "Situation salariale au République Démocratique du Congo (1966–1970)," *Cahiers Economiques et Sociaux* 8, no. 2 (June 1970): 216.

28 Mwabila Malela, "Prolétariat et conscience de classe au Zaire" (Doctoral diss., Université Libre de Bruxelles, 1973), p. 226.

29 Kay Lawson, ed., *Political Parties and Linkage* (New Haven: Yale University Press, 1980), p. 3.

30 Michael G. Schatzberg, *Politics and Class in Zaire* (New York: Africana Publishing Co., 1980), p. 112.

31 Interviews by Thomas Turner, Kinshasa, 1971; see also Turner, "A Century of Political Conflict in Sankuru" (Ph.D. diss., University of Wisconsin-Madison, 1973), pp. 448–454.

32 The case of a young Zairian professor at the Free University of the Congo in Kisangani is illustrative. His wife had been given the two ballots and told that green stood for peace and prosperity, while red stood for disorder. The professor himself simply was handed a green ballot.

33 *Mwanga*, Lubumbashi, 17 October 1975.

34 "Discours du Citoyen Mobutu Sese Seko, Président-Fondateur de Mouvement Populaire de la Révolution, Président de la République, prononcé le 1er juillet 1977 à N'sele après les événements du Sud-ouest Shaba," mimeographed.

35 Ibid., pp. 4–5.

36 On the alleged massacres, see "Les massacres de Katekelayi et de Luamela (Kasai oriental)," *Politique Africaine* 2, no. 6 (May 1982): 72–106; on the parliamentarians' revolt, see "Lettre ouverte au Citoyen Président-Fondateur du Mouvement Populaire de la Révolution, Président de la République par un groupe de parlementaires," *Politique Africaine* 1, no. 3 (September 1981): 94–140; Dikonda wa Lumanyisha, *Massacrer pour gouverner* (Liege, Belgium: Club Travail et Développement, 1983).

An episode revelatory of the political style of the regime occurred not long after the massacres. At a nearby secondary school students and teaching staff were warned by the zone commissioner to use caution in speaking about the massacre to any foreign investigators who might appear. One student asked whether the zone commissioner meant to forbid them from telling what they knew. After a moment's hesitation, he answered that they should of course speak truthfully; he added, however, that if they did have certain knowledge they must have been on the scene when the incidents occurred. If they were present, they must have been clandestine diamond diggers, and as such subject to arrest. (Brian Digre, personal communication, 15 May 1984; Digre attended the meeting.)

37 Dikonda, *Massacrer pour gouverner*, provides a detailed account of the action of the thirteen parliamentarians. The thirteen were Kibassa Maliba, Ngalula Mpanda Njila, Kyungu wa ku Mwanza, Lumbu Maloba Ndida, Makanda Mpinga Shambuyi, Dia Onken a Mbel, Kasala Kalamba Kabuadi, Lusanga Ngiele, Biringanine Mukaruka, Kanana Tshiongo a Minanga, N'goy Mukendi, Kapita Shabangi, and Tshisekedi wa Mulumba.

38 On the political thought of First Republic leaders, see Jean Van Lierde, ed., *La pensée politique du Patrice Lumumba* (Paris: Editions Présence Africaine, 1963); René Lemarchand, "Patrice Lumumba," in Walter Skurnick, ed., *African Political Thought: Lumumba, Nkrumah and Touré* (Denver: Social Service Foundation and Graduate School of International Studies, 1968), pp. 13–64; Loka ne Kongo, "La pensée politique de Kasa-Vubu" (Mémoire de licence, Faculté des Sciences Sociales, Politiques, et Administratives, Université Nationale du Zaire, Campus de Lubumbashi, 1974).

39 Otto Klineberg and Marisa Zavalloni, *Nationalism and Tribalism among African Students* (Paris: Mouton, 1969), pp. 28–51. The other countries surveyed were Senegal, Ghana, Nigeria, Ethiopia, and Uganda. The symbolic exploitation of Lumumbist and nationalist themes was foreshadowed by, and possibly influenced by, actions taken by the short-lived insurgent "People's Republic" in Kisangani in 1964; the rebel leaders renamed the monuments to Belgian monarchs after nationalist leaders, and replaced European street names with African ones.

40 Manwana Mungonga, *Le Général Mobutu Sese Seko parle du Nationalisme Zairois Authentique* (Kinshasa: Editions Okapi, n.d. [1972?]), p. 116.

41 Mobutu Sese Seko, *Mobutu: Discours, allocutions, messages et 1965–1975* (Paris: Editions J.A., 1975) 2: 100–101.

42 Ibid., pp. 104–105.

43 Mulumba Lukoji, "Le premier Congrès ordinaire du Mouvement Populaire de la Révolution," *Zaire-Afrique* 67 (August-September 1972): 409–414.

44 Ironically, *Zaire* had also been the title of a 1732 Voltaire play, whose theme was symbolically prophetic. "Zaire" was a beautiful maiden who grew up in bondage to the King of Jerusalem, with whom she fell in love. Her lost brother then appeared on the scene to inform her of her noble birth. She then faced an agonizing choice between her birthright and her dependent love for the Saracen King. *Zaire* was dedicated by Voltaire to an English merchant, a choice felt bizarre and tasteless by many in the Parisian salons. (Voltaire, *Zaire*, edited by Eva Jacobs [London: Hodder and Stoughton, 1975.])

45 Placide Tempels, *Bantu Philosophy* (Paris: Editions Présence Africaine, 1948). For details on the work of Tempels, see Johannes Fabian, *Jamaa* (Evanston: Northwestern University Press, 1971). Tempels was vigorously attacked by an older generation of missionaries who believed the African cultural heritage worthless; he attracted great attention from African intellectuals, as evidenced by the publication of French and English editions of his study by Présence Africaine. The general thrust of his conclusions received the tribute of confirmation by subsequent philosophical studies by African scholars; see, for example, Willie Abraham, *The Mind of Africa* (Chicago: University of Chicago Press, 1962).

46 Mabika Kalanda, *La remise en question* (Brussels: Editions "Remarques Africaines," 1967), pp. 150–151.

47 Jan Vansina, *Introduction à l'ethnographie du Congo* (Kinshasa: Editions Universitaires du Congo, 1966), p. 10.

48 Manwana, *Le Général Mobutu*, p. 19.

49 Ibid., pp. 75–76. The "life force" concept was a central argument.

50 Ibid., pp. 85–86.

51 N. Tutashinda, "Les mystifications de l'Authenticité," *La Pensée* 175 (May-June 1974): 68–81; Nzongola Ntalaja, "The Continuing Struggle for National Liberation in Zaire," *Journal of Modern African Studies* 17, no. 4 (December 1979): 595–614.

52 E. U., "Idées forces du Mobutisme," *Remarques Africaines* 477 (15 January 1976): 8, reporting a Brussels lecture by Nguza Karl-i-Bond.

53 Mobutu, *Discours, allocutions, et messages* 2: 527–528.

54 Mpinga Kasenda, "Le Mobutisme," *Remarques Africaines*, 451 (1 January 1975): 8–12.

55 There were some real similarities between the regime of Kim Il Sung and the vision Mobutu had for Zaire. Kim, like Mobutu, was a political figure who

catapulted to power through a military role; likewise, he had only a modest formal education. From 1955 on, the regime had developed an intensive personality cult around Kim, who was referred to as the infallible genius who had rethought Marxism-Leninism and Korean traditions. The Kim entourage was composed of a set of close, loyal followers whose fate was bound up with him; the state apparatus was managed by a subservient technocrat class which had supplanted the old 1945 generation of Communist politicians. Social discipline was the watchword, manifested for the visitor by imposing displays of mass gymnastics, as well as a Korean version of *animation*. Through this discipline the ills of inflation and unemployment had been banished. One of the practical consequences of Mobutu's 1974 trip was the shipment to Zaire of large quantities of the collected works of Kim Il Sung, a particularly tedious compendium of banalities which was found in succeeding months on the desks of officials throughout Zaire.

56 Arnold Strickon and Sidney Greenfield, *Structure and Process in Latin America: Patronage, Clientage, and Power Systems* (Albuquerque: University of New Mexico Press, 1972).

57 Schatzberg, *Politics and Class in Zaire*, pp. 109–110.

58 Herbert Weiss, personal communication; Schatzberg, personal communication.

Chapter 8

1 Nor can it be said that the central bureaucracy is given satisfactory treatment in the existing literature, which is dominated by the public and administrative law perspectives. Main works include Serge A. Vieux, *L'administration zairoise* (Paris: Berger-Levrault, 1974); Mpinga-Kasenda and David J. Gould, *Les réformes administratives au Zaire, (1972–73)* (Kinshasa: Presses Universitaires du Zaire, 1975); Mpinga Kasenda, *L'administration publique du Zaire* (Paris: A. Pédone, 1973).

2 Mpinga, *L'administration publique*, p. 135.

3 Crawford Young, *Politics in the Congo* (Princeton: Princeton University Press, 1965), pp. 10–11, citing Raymond Leslie Buell, *The Native Problem in Africa* (New York: Macmillan, 1928) 2: 466; Philip Woodruff [Mason], *The Men Who Ruled India*, 2 vols. (London: Jonathan Cape, 1953) 2: 300.

4 Nzongola Ntalaja, *Urban Administration in Zaire: A Study of Kananga, 1971–73* (Ph.D. diss., University of Wisconsin-Madison, 1975).

5 *Année Politique au Congo* (Kinshasa: Office National de le Recherche et du Développement, 1970), p. 15.

6 "Discours du Citoyen Mobutu Sese Seko, Président-Fondateur du Mouvement Populaire de la Révolution, Président de la République, prononcé le 1ᵉʳ juillet 1977 à N'sele après les événements du Sudouest Shaba," mimeographed, p. 7.

7 Thomas M. Callaghy, "State Formation and Absolutism in Comparative Perspective: Seventeenth Century France and Mobutu Sese Seko's Zaire" (Ph.D. diss., University of California–Berkeley, 1979), p. 325.

8 Speech of Interior Minister Kithima bin Ramazani, 29 January 1973, reprinted in Mpinga and Gould, *Les réformes administratives*, p. 126.

9 Quoted by Thomas M. Callaghy, "State Formation and Centralization of Power in Zaire: Mobutu's Pre-Eminent Public Policy" (Paper presented at the Annual Meeting, African Studies Association, Boston, November 1976), p. 19.

10 Schatzberg's interviews with administrative personnel in Lisala in the mid-1970s show what high importance was attached to providing a solid educational opportunity for one's offspring: Michael G. Schatzberg, *Politics and Class in Zaire* (New York: Africana Publishing Co., 1980), pp. 33–58.

11 Mayo-Mokelo Justin, "Instabilité dans les institutions communales de la ville de Kisangani (ex-Stanleyville), 1958–1968" (Mémoire de licence, Faculté des Sciences Economiques et Sociales, Université Libre du Congo, 1971), pp. 28–86.

12 Mpinga, *L'administration publique*, pp. 238–239.

13 Nzongola, *Urban Administration*, p. 47.

14 Jan Vansina, *Introduction à l'ethnographie du Congo* (Kinshasa: Universitaires du Congo, 1966), p. 17.

15 For exhaustive detail, see J. Magotte, *Les circonscriptions indigènes* (La Louvière, Belgium: Imprimerie Louvièroise [1952]).

16 Vundowe T'Angambe Pemako, "Le processus de l'intégration des autorités traditionnelles dans l'administration moderne de la République du Zaire (de 1885 à 1972)" (Doctoral diss., Université Catholique de Louvain, 1973), p. 185.

17 J. D. Mobutu, *Les paroles du Président* (Leopoldville: Editions du Léopard, 1968), p. 19.

18 Vundowe, "Le processus de l'intégration," pp. 329–340.

19 Commissaire d'Etat aux Affaires Politiques, "Note aux Citoyens Commissaires de Région (tous) relative à la réforme de l'organisation territoriale et administrative," 22 January 1973.

20 Commissaire d'Etat aux Affaires Politiques aux Commissaires de Région (tous), Instruction no. CAB/25/00/0280 of 8 August 1974.

21 Interviews with personnel of Regional Divisions of Political Affairs, Lubumbashi and Bukavu, 1974–1975.

22 Tshoya K., "Les collectivités de la zone de Dilolo sous l'Ordonnance-loi No. 73/015, du 15 janvier 1973" (Mémoire de licence, Faculté des Sciences Sociales, Politiques, et Administratives, Université Nationale du Zaire, Lubumbashi, 1975); Lualaba Sub-Region archives, Kolwezi.

23 Onotamba P., "La collectivité Ngandu-Wuma face à la réforme administrative du 5 janvier 1973" (Mémoire de licence, Faculté des Sciences Sociales, Politiques, et Administratives, Université Nationale du Zaire, Lubumbashi, 1975).

24 Tshoya, "Les collectivités de la zone de Dilolo."

25 Tshibanda Kabongo, "La modernisation differenciée: le cas des Baluba de Kabondo-Dianda, un sous-groupe de l'ethnie Luba du Shaba (Zone de Bukama)" (Mémoire de licence, Faculté des Sciences Sociales, Politiques, et Administratives, Université Nationale du Zaire, Lubumbashi, 1975), appendix.

26 Vundowe, "Le processus de l'intégration," pp. 271–285.

27 Maeda identifies eight major objectives which the *ujamaa* rural development strategy tried to accomplish: (1) establishment of self-governing communities, (2) better use of rural labor, (3) taking advantage of economy of scale to increase production, (4) dissemination of new values, (5) avoidance of exploitation, (6) increasing the standard of living of the peasants, (7) mobilization of people for national defense by using the villages as paramilitary organizations, and (8) facilitation of national planning. Justin H. J. Maeda, "Popular Participation, Control and Development: A Study of the Nature and Role of Popular Participation in Tanzania's Rural Development" (Ph.D. diss., Yale University, 1976), pp. 163–165.

28 Ombala Osombo W'ombala, "Le regroupement de villages dans la Zone de Lodja: avantages politiques, socio-économiques et difficultés de realisation" (Mémoire de licence, Faculté des Sciences Sociales, Politiques, et Administratives, Université Nationale du Zaire, Lubumbashi, 1975).

29 David and Catharine Newbury, personal communication; Bianga Waruzi, "Peasant, State and Rural Development in Postindependent Zaire: A Case Study of Réforme Rurale 1970–1980 and its Implications" (Ph.D. diss., University of Wisconsin–Madison, 1982). The Newburys have carried out extensive research in rural eastern Kivu over the past decade.

30 *Congo 1965* (Brussels: Centre de Recherche et d'Information Socio-Politiques, 1966), pp. 438–459.

31 Richard Vengroff, in *Development Administration at the Local Level: The Case of Zaire* (Syracuse: Maxwell School of Citizenship and Public Affairs, Syracuse University, 1983), a study originally carried out for the United States Agency for International Development, endeavors to present his findings in a positive light. However, a careful reading of his survey data (gathered from local officials in Bas-Zaire, Bandundu, and Haut-Zaire) provides additional evidence on the seriousness of Zairian administrative shortcomings. Incentives for hard work were found to be "almost non-existent" (p. 38), and much of the energies of field officers were channelled into the preparation of reports whose empirical content was small, and whose aim was "to provide 'information' which superiors want to hear" (p. 44).

32 Nzongola, *Urban Administration*, pp. 109–216.

33 Margaret Turner, doctoral dissertation on the politics of housing in Lubumbashi, in progress (University of Wisconsin–Madison).

34 Diombamba Miala, "Summary Considerations on the Program for Training Local Administrative Cadres in Zaire" (Washington: United States Agency for International Development, 1980), p. 2, cited in Vengroff, *Development Administration*, p. 4.

35 Nzongola, *Urban Administration*, passim; Schatzberg, *Politics and Class in Zaire*, pp. 59–82.
36 See the contributions of James Scott, Colin Leys, and Joseph R. Nye in Arnold J. Heidenheimer, ed., *Political Corruption* (New York: Holt, Rinehart, and Winston, 1970).
37 David J. Gould, "Underdevelopment Administration and Disorganization Theory: Systemic Corruption in the Public Bureaucracy of Mobutu's Zaire" (Paper presented at conference on Political Clientelism, Patronage and Development, Bellagio, Italy, August 1978), pp. 19–35.
38 Ibid., p. 7. See also David J. Gould, *Bureaucratic Corruption and Underdevelopment in the Third World: The Case of Zaire* (Elmsford, N.Y.: Pergamon Press, 1980).
39 David J. Gould, in Guy Gran, ed., *Zaire: The Political Economy of Underdevelopment* (New York: Praeger, 1979), p. 102.
40 For further detail, see Crawford Young, "Zaire: The Unending Crisis," *Foreign Affairs*, 57, no. 1 (October 1978): 169–185.
41 Gould, in Gran, ed., *Zaire*, pp. 96–97.
42 Michael G. Schatzberg, "Islands of Privilege: Small Cities in Africa and the Dynamics of Class Formation" (Paper presented at the Conference on the Small City and Regional Community, Stevens Point, Wisconsin, 30–31 March 1978).
43 Gould, *Bureaucratic Corruption*. A similar theme runs through the contributions to Gran, ed., *Zaire*.

Chapter 9

1 "Discours du Citoyen Mobutu Sese Seko, Président-Fondateur du Mouvement Populaire de la Révolution, Président de la République, prononcé le 1ᵉʳ juillet 1977 à N'Sele après les événements du Sud-ouest Shaba," mimeographed, p. 3.
2 Mobutu, "Discours du Président de la République du Zaire devant le Conseil Législatif, le 4 janvier 1975," mimeographed, pp. 13–14; *Elima*, 31 December 1974.
3 Arthur House, "The Congolese Security Capacity: Center of the Coalition," manuscript, p. 1.
4 "Deux mois après l'opération 'dragon rouge' à Stanleyville; entretiens en Afrique avec C. Gbenye et ses compagnons du M.N.C.-Lumumba," *C.R.I.S.P.*, T.A., no. 61 (18 February 1967), p. 3.
5 Maonyesho Lulela W'Etunda, "La rébellion de 1964 dans le Territoire de Fizi" (Mémoire de licence, Faculté des Sciences Sociales, Politiques, et Administratives, Université Nationale du Zaire, Lubumbashi, 1974), pp. 91–93.
6 *Congo 1966* (Brussels: Centre de Recherce et d'Information Socio-Politiques, 1967), pp. 345–355.
7 This account of the 1967 mutinies and their aftermath is based on *Congo 1967*

(Brussels: Centre de Recherche et d'Information Socio-Politiques, 1968), pp. 351–392.

8 House, "The Congolese Security Capacity," pp. 52–53.

9 René Lemarchand and David Martin, *Selective Genocide in Burundi* (London: Minority Rights Group, 1974), pp. 14–15. Mobutu presumably became involved because Micombero had been helpful during the 1967 mercenary revolt, and especially because Zairian rebel remnants were allied with the Hutu.

10 The MPLA, FNLA, and UNITA were the three main contenders for power in post-independence Angola. The MPLA drew its internal support from the urban intelligentsia, mulattoes, and the Luanda hinterland (especially the Mbundu). The FNLA strength was primarily among the Kongo in northern Angola, while UNITA backing was concentrated in south central Angola, especially among the large Ovimbundu group. The MPLA leadership employed Marxist-Leninist language, and drew external support especially from the Soviet Union and Cuba. The FNLA, and subsequently UNITA (by 1975), received assistance from the United States. The differing sources of external support intensified their rivalries, and gave the appearance of greater ideological divergence among them than really existed.

11 Kamitatu Massamba, *Le pouvoir à la portée du peuple* (Paris: Maspero, 1977), pp. 21–24.

12 Some have claimed that entry of Zairian troops came earlier; LeoGrande states that 1,200 Zairian soldiers crossed the Angolan border in March 1975: William M. LeoGrande, "Cuban-Soviet Relations and Cuban Policy in Africa," in Carmelo Mesa-Lago and June S. Belheim, eds., *Cuba in Africa* (Pittsburgh: Center for Latin American Studies, University of Pittsburgh, 1982), p. 23.

13 *New York Times*, 30 January 1976.

14 For an excellent analysis of the FLNC, see Jean-Claude Willame, "Contribution à l'étude des mouvements d'opposition au Zaire: Le F.L.N.C.," *Cahiers du CEDAF* 6 (1980).

15 *Washington Post*, 25 March 1977.

16 Pierre Sergent, *La Légion saute sur Kolwezi* (Paris: Presse de la Cité, 1978), p. 18.

17 The best account of these events is Jean-Claude Willame, "La seconde guerre du Shaba," *Enquêtes et Documents d'Histoire Africaine* (Louvain, Belgium; 1978).

18 Our interviews, Lubumbashi, October 1978; *Quarterly Economic Review*, Economist Intelligence Unit, 4th quarter 1978, p. 4.

19 International Bank for Reconstruction and Development, *Zaire: Current Economic Situation and Constraints* (Washington, May 1980), p. 67.

20 Msgr. Kabanga, "Je suis un homme," Archeveché de Lubumbashi, March 1976, p. 7.

21 Confidential personal communication, 1981.

22 On the mercenaries, see: "Les mercénaires dans l'histoire du Congo (1960–1967)," *C.R.I.S.P.*, T.A. no. 74–75, (26 February 1968), pp. 13–14; Frédéric

J. Van de Walle, *Ommegang* (Brussels: Livre Africain, 1970); Mike Hoare, *Congo Mercenary* (London: Hale, 1967).

23 House, "The Congolese Security Capacity," p. 24.

24 Ibid., p. 25.

25 See *Congo 1965* (Brussels: Centre de Recherche et d'Information Socio-Politiques, 1966), pp. 411–412, for the text.

26 Ibid., p. 413.

27 Mobutu speech to 2d ordinary congress of MPR, November 1977, typescript, p. 6.

28 *Salongo*, 16–17 November 1972.

29 General Molongya Mayikusa, "Le militaire et la révolution," speech given at the Institut Makanda Kabobi, 8 May 1975, mimeographed, pp. 15, 23.

30 According to one interpretation of this affair, senior army officers were furious at the amnesty offer conveyed by Foreign Minister Bomboko to Mulele, then in Brazzaville. In this thesis, the officers seized Mulele after his return on their own initiative and insisted on an immediate court-martial on treason charges, to be followed by swift execution. Mobutu, in Morocco on an official visit, only acquiesced after the fact, labelling Mulele a "war criminal" (House, "The Congolese Security Capacity," p. 45).

31 Anecdotes belittling the limited educational attainments of Bobozo are legion. According to Monguya, a representative of the Common Market asked the general what he thought of the "Marché Commun"; Bobozo replied, ". . . Il y a beaucoup de marchés communs à Kinshasa: le marché de Saint-Jean, le marché centrale . . . beaucoup trop de marchés." On arrival at Brussels for an official visit, the Belgian military delegation received Bobozo at the foot of the plane's ramp, saying, "Enchanté, mon général. Nous espérons que votre voyage s'est bien déroulé." The general responded, "Mon Colonel, moi, le Général, je ne chante pas. Rochereau et Franco qui chantent, sont restés au Congo." (Monguya Mbenge, *Histoire secrète du Zaire* [Brussels: Editions de l'Esperance, 1977], pp. 40–41).

32 General Massiala was killed in a mysterious helicopter crash in September 1975. Many believed he had been lured aboard by a false tale that he was needed at once in connection with a family crisis in his home region of Bas-Zaire. His sudden death, which followed close on the heels of the sacking of half of the general officers after the *coup monté et manqué* of June 1975, produced bitter hostility within the army, already badly divided over the Angolan adventure. General Ingila, one of the Compagnons de la Révolution who signed the 1965 act of power seizure, and later a thorn in Mobutu's side, perished in an accident in 1976.

33 House, "The Congolese Security Capacity," p. 46.

34 Ibid., p. 30.

35 *Africa Research Bulletin*, 1–31 August 1977.

36 Agence Zairoise de Presse, 12 July 1977.

37 *Salongo*, 20 August 1975; *Jeune Afrique*, 12 September 1975. Another version of this episode is provided by John Stockwell, who asserts that those implicated were CIA agents: *In Search of Enemies* (New York: W. W. Norton, 1978), p. 44.

38 *New York Times*, 18 March 1978; *Africa Research Bulletin* 1–28 February 1978, p. 4,754.

39 Center for Development Policy, "Open Letter to the Citizen Mobutu Sese Seko, President of Zaire, from Thirteen Members of Parliament" (Washington, 6 October 1982), p. 42.

40 House, "The Congolese Security Capacity," pp. 24–25.

41 Ibid., p. 29. Senate Committee on Foreign Relations, *Zaire*, July 1982, 97th Cong., 2d sess., p. 5.

43 In addition, the FAZ possessed 13 Aermacchi MB 326 GB armed yet trainers, 5 C-130 Hercules turboprop transports, 18 Alouette and SA 330 Puma helicopters, 23 SIAI-Marchetti SF.260 MC basic trainers, and some smaller craft. A dozen additional Mirages and three Buffalo transports were being acquired from Canada. (*Statesman's Year-Book 1977–78* [New York: St. Martin's Press, 1977], p. 1,502.)

44 Another example of the difficulty of maintaining the sophisticated equipment was the high accident rate among the helicopters. The Puma top rotor, under certain conditions, is prone to become unstable and may sever its own tail, sending the craft into an ignominious descent to self-destruction. The C-130 wrecks were partly caused by grossly overloading them with illicit merchandise; see the testimony by Nguza Karl-i-Bond, House Committee on Foreign Affairs, Subcommittee on Africa, *Political and Economic Situation in Zaire—Fall 1981*, 15 September 1981, 97th Cong., 1st sess., pp. 12–13.

45 According to House, Mobutu was reported to be the principal owner: "The Congolese Security Capacity," p. 33.

46 Ibid., p. 44; U.S. Agency for International Development, AID Public Safety Report, 1973 & 1974.

47 *Statesman's Year-Book 1977–78*, p. 1,502.

48 House, "The Congolese Security Capacity," p. 9, cites 6,000, while U.S. Agency for International Development, "Police Mission Survey" (1963), p. 7, gives the figure of 8,927 Zairian police and 272 Belgian police commissioners.

49 Michael G. Schatzberg, *Politics and Class in Zaire* (New York: Africana Publishing Co., 1980), p. 68. The same source shows that in the town of Lisala the collectivity police had a hypothetical salary of Z 3,283.58 per year during the 1968–74 period, but were actually paid an average of Z 2,131.36 per annum: p. 70.

50 House, "The Congolese Security Capacity," p. 41.

51 Ibid.

52 As one example of a CND operation, in Lubumbashi in March 1975 there suddenly appeared in town a goon squad, dubbed the "gorillas," who sowed terror among the population. After a few weeks of seemingly random intimidation,

the gorillas vanished as suddenly as they had appeared. Some additional detail on CND operations may be found in Amnesty International, *Human Rights Violations in Zaire*, (New York, 1980); and Michael G. Schatzberg, "The Long Arm of the Law: Insecurity, Instability, and the Political Police in Zaire" (Paper presented at the Annual Meeting, International Studies Association, Cincinnati, March 1982).

In addition to the CND (CNRI), SNI, and presidential security service, there are other agencies performing security police functions. Attached to the Gendarmerie (now a branch of the army) are security units, scattered through the country (Brigade Spéciale de Recherches et de Surveillance). Army headquarters also has a special security and intelligence branch. Numerous instances of torture by various security agencies, brutal interrogations, disappearances, and rustication to villages are recorded in the Amnesty International documentation.

53 Michael Shafer, "United States Military Assistance to Zaire" (Paper presented at the Annual Meeting, African Studies Association, Washington, November 1982), p. 11.

54 *Africa Confidential* 21, no. 25 (10 December 980): 2. Nguza, in his September 1981 congressional testimony, provided extensive evidence of Equateurian domination at the top: House Committee on Foreign Affairs, Subcommittee on Africa, *Political and Economic Situation in Zaire*, pp. 44–46.

Chapter 10

1 Speech of 12 December 1965, in *Mobutu: Discours, allocutions, et messages* (Paris: Editions J. A., 1975) 1: 22.

2 Banque du Zaire, *Rapport annuel*, 1967, p. 36.

3 Théophile Lukusa, "Situation économique et financière du Congo en 1965 et en 1966," *Etudes Congolaises* 10, no. 3 (May-June 1967): 12.

4 Pierre Dupriez, "La réforme monetaire du 24 juin 1967 en République Démocratique du Congo," *Cahiers Economiques et Sociaux* 6, no. 1 (March 1968): 71–99.

5 Lukusa, "Situation économique," pp. 2–24. For a detailed analysis of the inflation phenomenon, see Institut des Recherche Economique et Sociales, *Indépendence, inflation, développement* (Paris: Mouton, 1968).

6 Dupriez, "La réforme monetaire," p. 77. This, of course, presumes functionaries held comparable positions. Those who had enjoyed major promotions were far ahead.

7 Banque du Zaire, *Rapport annuel*, 1968–1969, p. 30.

8 Joseph Houyoux, *Budgets ménagers nutrition et mode de vie à Kinshasa* (Kinshasa: Presses Universitaires du Zaire, 1973) pp. 29–30.

9 Jean-Louis Lacroix, "Le rôle de l'industrie dans le développement économique général," *Zaire-Afrique* 61 (January 1972): 12.

10 Dupriez, "La réforme monetaire," p. 93.

11 Pierre Ryckmans, *Etapes et jalons* (Brussels: Maison Ferdinand Larcier, 1946), p. 216.

12 Ibid., p. 212.

13 Pierre Joye and Rosina Lewin, *Les trusts au Congo* (Brussels: Société Populaire d'Editions, 1961), pp. 211–212. See also Jean-Luc Vellut, "Les bassins miniers de l'ancien Congo Belge. Essai d'histoire économique et sociale (1900–1960)," *Cahiers du CEDAF* 7 (November 1981).

14 Jules Gérard-Libois, *Katanga Secession* (Madison: University of Wisconsin Press, 1966), pp. 48–49.

15 *Congo 1964* (Brussels: Centre de Recherche et d'Information Socio-Politiques, 1965), pp. 512–513.

16 This also was noted with bitterness by Ryckmans, *Etapes et jalons*, p. 212.

17 Joye and Lewin, *Les trusts au Congo*, p. 295.

18 Jacques Ceulemans, "Matabiche, Bwana," *Remarques Congolaises et Africaines* 236 (17 February 1965): 3–5.

19 See the highly critical analysis by Bukavu journalist Paul Masson, who termed it a monster hated by all: *Dix ans de malheurs au Kivu* (Brussels: Max Arnold, 1970) 1: 15–19.

20 Joye and Lewin, *Les trusts au Congo*, pp. 294–295.

21 *Congo 1965*, (Brussels: Centre de Recherche et d'Information Socio-Politiques, 1966), p. 293.

22 Full details on the ownership structure and all other aspects of the Zairian gold mines are found in the excellent study by Bakonzi Agayo, "The Gold Mines of Kilo-Moto in Northeastern Zaire, 1905–1960" (Ph.D. diss., University of Wisconsin–Madison, 1982). See also note 80 to chapter 1.

23 *Congo 1966* (Brussels: Centre de Recherche et d'Information Socio-Politiques, 1967), p. 146.

24 Ibid., p. 151.

25 For a full account, see "Contribution à l'étude des relations Sabena–Air Congo 1960–1968," *Etudes Africaines du C.R.I.S.P.*, T.A., nos. 90–91 (March 1969).

26 On the Mbuji-Mayi mines, see the valuable study by Mulumba Lukoji, "La 'MIBA': Société Minière de Bakwanga," *Zaire-Afrique* 88 (October 1974): 479–494. See also Joye and Lewin, *Les trusts au Congo*, pp. 223–226.

27 In 1981, the relationship with BRITMOND came to a temporary end when Zaire severed its relationships with the de Beers Central Selling Organization, a private diamond marketing cartel. Zairian diamonds were to be marketed by SOZACOM, a parastatal under direct presidential control. Tempelsman reportedly made an urgent trip to Kinshasa in March 1981 to head off this rupture; remarkably, Mobutu refused to see his old and intimate friend. While the Zairian effort to outflank the de Beers cartel was courageous, it was also risky; a huge Australian mine came on line in 1982, and is expected to place 20 million carats of industrial diamonds on the market (or three times the 1981 Zairian

official output). Diamond prices are likely to remain under great pressure: *Washington Post*, 11 November 1981. In 1983, Zaire returned to the de Beers fold: *Wall Street Journal*, 7 July 1983.

28 *Echo de la Bourse*, 24 August 1970.

29 Mulumba Lukoji, "La Générale des Carrières et Mines du Zaïre," *Zaire-Afrique* 81 (January 1974): 10–11.

30 J. Gérard-Libois, "L'affaire de l'UMHK," *Etudes Congolaises* 10, no. 2 (March-April 1967): 1–4; Joye and Lewin, *Les trusts au Congo*, pp. 217–222.

31 Sir Ronald Prain, *Copper: The Anatomy of an Industry* (London: Mining Journal Books, 1975), pp. 14–27.

32 Joye and Lewin, *Les trusts au Congo*, p. 218; *Unité*, February-March 1970.

33 Kamitatu Massamba, "Problématique et rationalité dans le processus de nationalisation du cuivre en Afrique Centrale: Zaire (1967) et Zambie (1969)" (Doctoral diss., Institut d'Etudes Politiques de Paris, 1976), p. 181.

34 Ibid., pp. 182–183.

35 Gérard-Libois, "L'affaire de l'UMHK," p. 12.

36 Ibid., pp. 22–23.

37 A Tory prime minister once labelled Lonrho "the unacceptable face of capitalism." For an exposé of Lonrho, see Suzanne Cronjé, Margaret Ling, and Gillian Cronjé, *Lonrho: Portrait of a Multinational* (Hammondsworth, Middlesex: Penguin Books, 1976).

38 Kamitatu, "Problématique et rationalité," pp. 219–224; on Tempelsman, see the portrait by Leon Dash, *Washington Post*, 31 December 1979.

39 *African Contemporary Record*, 1974–75, p. B612; *Unité*, February-March 1970.

40 Kamitatu Massamba, *Le pouvoir à la portée du peuple* (Paris: Maspero, 1977) pp. 120–121.

41 U.N. General Assembly, "Declaration and Action Programme on the Establishment of a New International Economic Order," 6 May 1974(e).

42 Michael Shafer, "Capturing the Mineral Multinationals: Advantage or Disadvantage?" *International Organization* 37, no. 1 (Winter 1983): 91–117.

43 Mulumba, "La Générale des Carrières," p. 13.

44 Shafer, "Capturing the Mineral Multinationals," p. 104.

45 Mulumba Lukoji, "Le code des investissements zairois," *Zaire-Afrique*, 85 (May 1974): 275–284; interviews with World Bank, Export-Import Bank, Citibank officials, April 1978.

46 *Discours, allocutions, et messages* 1: 28–29.

47 Reflecting the SICAI view is the very optimistic article by Rutebingwa Ndakiwa, "La sidérurgie de Maluku," *Zaire-Afrique*, 96 (June-July 1975): 339–348.

48 J. C. Willame, "Le saga d'Inga. Quelques réflexions sur les pratiques de transferts de technologie au Zaire," *Cahiers du CEDAF* 5–6 (1981): 103–110; A. Huybrechts et al., *Du Congo au Zaire 1960–1980* (Brussels: Centre de Recherche et d'Information Socio-Politiques, 1981), p. 275.

49 Ernest J. Wilson III, "The Political Economy of Public Corporations in the En-

ergy Sectors of Nigeria and Zaire" (Ph.D. diss., University of California–Berkeley, 1978), p. 492.

50 J. L. Lacroix, "Inga," *Etudes Congolaises*, 10, no. 1 (January-February 1967): 1–72; René Beeckmans, "Inga, grandiose réalisation d'un utopie," *Zaire-Afrique*, 69 (November 1972): 537–543; *Salongo*, 23–26 November 1972.

51 By 1975, the Inga II total cost was estimated at $360 million, though only four of the eight projected turbines were to be installed initially: *Salongo*, 31 March 1975.

52 Paul Serlon, "Les ressorts d'un système axé sur la survie," *Le Monde Diplomatique*, 330 (September 1981): 16–17.

53 The four dams and their megawatt capacities are: Seku (ex–Le Marinel), 276; Nzilo (ex-Delcommune), 120; Mwadingusha (ex-Francqui), 77; Koni (ex-Bia), 47: Alan Rake, "Zaire Economic Survey," *African Development*, September 1972, p. 6.

54 Wilson, "The Political Economy of Public Corporations," p. 593. A Gécamines study for the World Bank in 1970 argued that this dam could meet needs at least until 1980, and could be completed by 1973. Zambian power was even cheaper, but was held to involve unacceptable political risks. Also opposing the Inga-Shaba choice was the most qualified Zairian expert, Professor F. Malu, who undertook a major study of Zairian energy options.

55 Willame, "Le saga d'Inga," pp. 106–108.

56 Senate Committee on Banking, Housing, and Urban Affairs, Subcommittee on International Finance, *U.S. Loans to Zaire*, 96th Cong., 1st sess., 24 May 1979, p. 7. The Export-Import Bank now estimates that, for a fifty-year period, Inga-Shaba power will cost four times as much as existing electricity: Willame, "Le saga d'Inga," p. 108.

57 Subcommittee on International Finance, *U.S. Loans to Zaire*, p. 4.

58 Mulumba Lukoji, "La SODIMIZA; un consortium international minier," *Zaire-Afrique* 70 (December 1972): 581–592. The Japanese output was exported as concentrate; they had a large smelting and refining infrastructure which they preferred to keep employed by importing 36 percent concentrate, rather than 99 percent blister or 99.9 percent refined copper: Prain, *Copper*, pp. 75–77.

59 *Le Soir*, 30 October 1971; *Echo de la Bourse*, 4–6 September 1970, 5 October 1970, 28 April 1971; *Special*, 2 September 1970; *West Africa*, 28 February 1970. Lonrho subsequently regained good grace in 1973 by appointing Litho Maboti to the board of directors of the Lonrho-Zaire subsidiary. A Litho portrait adorns the London board room: Cronjé, Ling, and Cronjé, *Lonrho*, pp. 42–44.

60 *Pourquoi Pas*, 20 August 1970, 24 September 1970, 8 October 1970; *Jeune Afrique*, 1 December 1970.

61 Leon Dash, in the *Washington Post*, 31 December 1979, suggests that the Tempelsman influence extended to exercising a voice in the selection of Robert

Oakley as U.S. ambassador for Zaire in 1979—an inference that was denied in Washington. According to a diplomatic source quoted by Dash, both Tempelsman and Mobutu have reaped "substantial earnings from the gem diamond trade," which some believe to be the major source of the fortune accumulated by the president while in office.

62 The original partnership breakdown was Amoco Minerals (a Standard of Indiana subsidiary), 28%; Charter Consolidated (South African and British, linked to the Oppenheimer interests), 28%; Mitsui (Japanese), 14%; Omni Mines (French), 3.5%; Bureau de recherches géologiques et minières (French), 3.5%; Leon Tempelsman & Son, 2%. Standard of Indiana became increasingly discontented with the delays and escalating capital costs of the SMTF project by 1976; by late 1979 it had bailed out, selling its 28 percent share to the French interests. According to sources close to the transaction, the French interests had initially been offered a small share to prevent them from causing trouble. When Amoco Minerals withdrew, they became, with the Oppenheimer subsidiary Charter Consolidated, the main partners. Tempelsman challenged the French acquisition in the Zairian courts in a heated struggle which brought presidential intervention from France. After angry charges of bribery of the judiciary, Tempelsman was called off by Mobutu.

63 *Jeune Afrique*, 1 December 1970; *Africa Contemporary Record*, 1975–76, B519–520; interviews with Tempelsman and Wesley Cohen, April 1978. Cohen, then a Yale University doctoral candidate, has invaluable data on American investments in Zaire, to be incorporated in a forthcoming study.

64 Needless to say, these unforeseen delays in bringing the mines into profitable operation were not welcome in the boardrooms of the capital interests involved. The *Wall Street Journal*, 26 May 1979, reports in a feature story on Standard of Indiana that company executives cited the Zaire venture as a prime example of a major mistake: "'The company threw a lot of money into overseas ventures that didn't produce a good return,' one company analyst conceded. 'He recalls numerous firings of executives blamed for the mistakes.'"

65 Gécamines, *Rapport annuel*, 1980.

66 Mulumba Lukoji, "La commercialisation des minerais de la Gécamines," *Zaire-Afrique* 94 (April 1975): 209–220.

67 Kamitatu, *Le pouvoir à la portée du peuple*, pp. 119–120. The Hoboken refinery has some special technological capacities, in particular the ability to recover rare precious metals (gold, silver, germanium, cadmium) present in small quantities in blister copper ingots.

68 Because SOZACOM's directors were named by the president, the revenue flows involved in marketing the Gécamines mineral output were also brought within reach of the presidency. A *Wall Street Journal* reporter, Jonathan Kwitny, was told that of the $104 million SOZACOM received monthly from mineral sales, $40 million was theoretically returned to Gécamines, but that half of this was corruptly diverted: *Wall Street Journal*, 26 June 1980.

69 See the excellent inventory in Jean-Claude Willame, "La secteur multinational au Zaire," *Cahiers du CEDAF*, 1 (1980).

70 *Special*, 12 September 1970.

71 *Epanza*, 16 June 1973. Continental Grain's Zairian subsidiary, Minoterie de Matadi, had a running dispute with the trading conglomerate Société Générale d'Alimentation (SGA), run by Mobutu confidant and relative Litho. Continental Grain was promised it could supply the whole domestic market; subsequently Litho received a monopoly for flour imports: *Salongo*, 31 December 1972–1 January 1973.

72 *Salongo*, 5 October 1972.

73 International Bank for Reconstruction and Development, "The Economy of Zaire" (1975) 2: 58. See also Willame, "Le secteur multinational au Zaire."

74 Elise Forbes Pachter, "The Economic Component of U.S.-Zaire Relations" (Paper presented at the Annual Meeting, African Studies Association, Washington, November 1982), pp. 20–21.

75 *African Development*, February 1974.

76 *Salongo*, 20 November 1974.

77 *Africa Contemporary Record*, 1974–75, B613–614. The Ilebo-Kinshasa rail link also posed difficult choices as to route. The shortest and cheapest route, Ilebo–Bandundu–Kinshasa (857 kilometers), had the handicap of passing through the poorest and most sparsely inhabited region, with low agricultural potential. The alternatives, Kananga–Tshikapa–Masi–Manimba–Kenge (1,420 kilometers), and Kananga–Tshikapa–Southern Kwango–Lukisi (1,360 kilometers), served regions of high agricultural potential but involved many more bridges, two or three times the cost, and construction time of nine years instead of six: *Tribune Africaine*, 20 March 1970; Kamitatu, *Le pouvoir à la portée du peuple*, pp. 113–114.

78 Prain, *Copper*, pp. 101–103.

79 Daniel Van der Steen, "Echanges économiques extérieures du Zaire: dépendance et développement," *Cahiers du CEDAF*, 4–5 (1977): 10.

80 International Bank for Reconstruction Development, *Zaire: Current Economic Situation and Constraints* (Washington, May 1980), pp. 26–27.

81 *Africa Contemporary Record*, 1975–76, p. B517. Zairian copper and manganese are also indispensable for the Benguela railway, built by Tanganyika Concessions. Although its reopening was several times announced by Angola, by 1980 normal traffic had not yet resumed.

82 Huybrechts et al., *Du Congo au Zaire*, p. 191.

83 G. H. Popelier, "Nature et évolution de l'agriculture zairoise," *Cahiers du CEDAF*, 6 (1977): 9. On the colonial agricultural research network (INEAC), see René J. Cornet, *Les phares verts* (Brussels: Editions Cuypers, 1965).

84 Popelier, "Nature et évolution," p. 8.

85 Mali-Kidogo Chakali Muranga, "Politique agricole et service de l'agriculture au Shaba" (Mémoire de licence, Faculté des Sciences Sociales, Politiques, et Administratives, Université Nationale du Zaire, Lubumbashi, 1974), p. 62.

86 Kaninda Kasongo, "Contribution à la recherche sur l'économie des transports dans les pays de l'Afrique Noire (exemple du Zaire)" (Doctoral diss., University of Bordeaux, 1973), p. 28.

87 Mali-Kidogo, "Politique agricole," pp. 68–69.

88 These calculations are based upon data from internal AID documents.

89 Popelier, "Nature et évolution," p. 22.

90 "Le café et l'économie zairoise," cited by Professor Kawatu Bualum, *Elima*, 4 November 1977.

91 See the officially sponsored study of the largest palm oil enterprise: Charles Wilson, *The History of Unilever*, 2 vols. (London: Cassell & Co., 1954). The Unilever palm oil operation in Zaire only became really profitable from World War II on.

92 Popelier, "Nature et évolution," pp. 22–29. See also the rather unsatisfactory account in M. K. K. Kabala Kabunda, "Unilever in Zaire," in Carl Widstrand, ed., *Multi-National Firms in Africa* (Uppsala: Scandinavian Institute of African Studies, 1975), pp. 303–322.

93 Huybrechts et al., *Du Congo au Zaire*, p. 192.

94 Banque du Zaire, *Rapport annuel*, 1975, p. xvi.

95 Tshibangu Banza-Muakula, "La réforme des structures agricoles au Zaire: Cas de l'Office National des Fibres Textiles (ONAFITEX) et de la culture cotonnière dans la Zone de Gandajika" (Mémoire de licence, Faculté des Sciences Sociales, Politiques, et Administratives, Université Nationale du Zaire, Lubumbashi, 1975), p. 10. On the development of cotton in Zaire, see especially A. Brixhe, *Le coton au Congo Belge*, 3d ed. (Brussels: Ministère des Colonies, 1958); B. Van de Walle, *Essai d'une planification de l'économie agricole congolaise* (INEAC, Série Technique no. 61, 1960); Eric F. Tollens, "An Economic Analysis of Cotton Production, Marketing and Processing in Northern Zaire," (Ph.D. diss., Michigan State University, 1975).

96 Lacroix, "Le rôle de l'industrie," p. 20.

97 Tollens, "An Economic Analysis of Cotton Production," p. 48.

98 Ibid., pp. 173–181.

99 Popelier, "Nature et évolution," p. 33.

100 Ibid., p. 30. Popelier cites documentation collected by Guy Verhaegen, a rural economist who has devoted years of research to Zairian agricultural development. There can be no doubt as to the reliability of the Verhaegen evidence; see, inter alia, his excellent article "Le développement de l'agriculture paysanne au Zaire," *Zaire-Afrique* 76 (June-July 1973): 345–360.

101 For fuller detail, see *Echo de la Bourse*, 6 July 1972, 11 July 1972.

102 *Le Soir*, 11–12 May 1972.

103 Tshibangu, "La réforme des structures agricoles," p. 68. Bifuko Baharanyi in his 1974–76 field research in the Ruzizi plain found identical problems: "The Study of Management of Rural Development in Zaire: The Cases of the National Board for Fibres and Textiles (ONAFITEX) and the Agro-Pastoral

Project in the Ruzizi Valley (1968–1975)" (M.A. thesis, University of Dar-es-Salaam, 1977).

104 Tollens, "An Economic Analysis of Cotton Production," p. 115. According to Benoit Verhaegen, all but one of these ginneries disappeared in the ports of arrival: "Transferts de technologie ou impérialisme technologique? Le cas du Zaire," *Cahiers du CEDAF*, 5–6 (1981): 98.

105 Foreign Agricultural Service, American Embassy, Kinshasa, Annual Cotton Report, 1 September 1977.

106 Tshibangu, "La réforme des structures agricoles," pp. 90–91.

107 Enungo Kahindo-Dalau, "De l'Office des Produits Agricoles du Kivu (OPAK) à l'Office National du Café (ONC): Quelques considérations comparatives sur la fonctionnement administratif" (Mémoire de licence, Faculté des Sciences Sociales, Politiques, et Administratives, Université Nationale du Zaire, Lubumbashi, 1975), pp. 57–58 and passim.

108 Agency for International Development, "Grain Marketing," 12 December 1975.

109 Joseph Boute, "Demographic Trends in the Republic of Zaire," *Munger African Library Notes*, December 1973, p. 20.

110 G. Verhaegen, "Le développement de l'agriculture," p. 347.

111 Banque du Zaire, *Rapport annuel, 1975*, pp. 111–113.

112 Huybrechts et al., *Du Congo au Zaire*, p. 184. For an overview of the economy in the late 1970s, see also Kabuya Kalala and Kikassa Mwanalessa, *Stabilisation économique et financière au Zaire* (Kinshasa: Centre d'Etudes pour l'Action Sociale, 1980).

Chapter 11

1 Of particular value for this chapter is the research by Michael G. Schatzberg in Lisala, in *Politics and Class in Zaire* (New York: Africana Publishing Co., 1980); and by Edward Kannyo in Lubumbashi, in "Political Power and Class-Formation in Zaire: The 'Zairianization Measures,' 1973–75" (Ph.D. diss., Yale University, 1979). We also benefitted from the collaboration of two UNAZA students who devoted their *mémoires de licence* to the 30 November measures: Kumwimba Kabongo, "Approche sur les aspects administratifs des mesures économiques du 30 Novembre 1973 (Cas de Lubumbashi)" (Mémoire de licence, Faculté des Sciences Sociales, Politiques, et Administratives, Université Nationale du Zaire, Lubumbashi, 1975); Tshiauke Mukongo, "Les problèmes administratifs des mesures économiques du 30 Novembre 1973 (Cas de la Sous-Région de Kolwezi)" (Mémoire de licence, Faculté des Sciences Sociales, Politiques, et Administratives, Université Nationale du Zaire, Lubumbashi, 1975).

2 Mukenge Tshilemalema, "Businessmen of Zaire: Limited Possibilities for Capi-

tal Accumulation under Dependence" (Doctoral diss., McGill University, 1974).

3 Kannyo, "Political Power."

4 *Africa Contemporary Record*, 1971–72, p. B526. Estimates of those expelled ran as high as 38,000. West African traders held businesses throughout the country, even in smaller centers. A number of these expropriated assets passed into the hands of politicians, foreshadowing the 30 November pattern.

5 The text of this law may be found in Yabili Asani, *Code de la Zairianisation* (Lubumbashi: Editeur "Mwanga-Hebdo," 1975), pp. 111–114.

6 Kannyo, "Political Power"; Mulumba Lukoji, "Les Lois du 5 janvier 1973 sur le commerce et les petites et moyennes entreprises zairoises," *Zaire-Afrique*, 74 (April 1973): 221–238.

7 *Elima*, 17 November 1973.

8 The Société pour le Crédit au Colonat, a parastatal that operated in the postwar period, had primarily offered financing to individual plantation operators.

9 Lukombe Nghenda, *Zairianisation, radicalisation, retrocession en République du Zaïre* (Kinshasa: Presses Universitaires du Zaïre, 1979), p. 15.

10 Unrelated to the 30 November measures, but almost simultaneous with them, was the sudden seizure of foreign oil company marketing assets (Shell, Mobil, Petrofina, Texaco, and BP); see chapter 6.

11 Yabili, *Code de la Zairianisation*, pp. 119–120. Article 14, item 3 of the constitution permits the state to expropriate private property, with equitable compensation; article 52 permits the legislature to delegate full legislative power to the president.

12 Tshiauke, "Les problèmes administratives," p. 75.

13 *Compte-rendus analytiques*, Conseil Législatif National, 30 November 1973, pp. 45–46.

14 Ibid., 11 December 1973.

15 For some intriguing detail, see Michael G. Schatzberg, "Bureaucracy, Business, Beer: The Political Dynamics of Class Formation in Lisala, Zaire" (Ph.D. diss., University of Wisconsin–Madison, 1977), pp. 332–333.

16 We rely here on a valuable chronology established by Michael G. Schatzberg, based upon the administrative archives pertaining to 30 November measures at Lisala (typescript; hereafter cited as Schatzberg chronology).

17 Schatzberg chronology.

18 *Elima*, 3 January 1974.

19 Ibid.

20 Lukombe, *Zairianisation*, p. 15.

21 This process is given superb treatment by Schatzberg, "Bureaucracy, Business, Beer," pp. 288–309.

22 Yabili, *Code de la Zairianization*, pp. 120–121.

23 Kumwimbe, "Approche sur les aspects administratifs," pp. 130–131.

24 *Taifa*, 3 April 1974.

25 David J. Gould, "Underdevelopment Administration and Disorganization

Theory: Systematic Corruption in the Public Bureaucracy of Mobutu's Zaire"
(Paper delivered at the conference on Political Clientelism, Patronage and Development, Bellagio, Italy, August 1978), p. 56.
26 Schatzberg, "Bureaucracy, Business, Beer," p. 352.
27 Ibid., p. 351.
28 Schatzberg chronology.
29 Tshiauke, "Les problèmes administratives," p. 132.
30 Schatzberg chronology.
31 Tshiauke, "Les problèmes administratives," p. 135.
32 The sweeping powers of price control may be seen in the legislative text, Pierre
Piron et al., *Supplément au Code Congolais: Législation de la République Démocratique du Congo* (Brussels: Maison Ferdinand Larcier, 1970) 3: 716–717.
33 A concept developed especially by Murray Edelman, *Politics as Symbolic Action:
Mass Arousal and Quiescence* (Chicago: Markham Publishing Co., 1971).
34 Gould, "Underdevelopment Administration," p. 46. Data provided by Gould
on visible property (automobiles) owned by members of other economic regulatory services (Customs and Tax Collection) illustrate the same problem:

REGIONAL FINANCE OFFICIALS' CAR OWNERSHIP
(Sixth Bureau: Customs Verification, Shaba Region, 1977)

Position	Monthly salary (zaires)	Cars owned	1977 value (zaires) New	Used
Office head	115	Renault 17	8,000	6,000
		Mustang	10,000	7,000
		VW	7,000	4,000
		Pickup truck	10,000	7,000
		Kombi	12,000	8,000
Office worker	90	Mercedes	30,000	15,000
Office worker	90	Renault 4	7,000	4,000
Temporary worker	36–66	Fiat station wagon	10,000	4,000
(Third Bureau: Tax Collection)				
Office head	115	Toyota	10,000	7,000
Collection agent	90	VW	7,000	4,000
Accountant	72–90	Peugeot 404	12,000	8,000
Cashier	36–66	Peugeot	12,000	8,000
Clerk	22–26	Ford Capri	9,000	6,000
Clerk	22–26	Fiat	8,000	6,000

35 Kumwimba "Approche sur les aspects administratifs," p. 70. Schatzberg offers
similar evidence in "Bureaucracy, Business, Beer," pp. 252–254.
36 For example, the vice-rector of the Lubumbashi campus of UNAZA assigned a
teaching assistant from his region to control his newly acquired enterprises.
37 Banque du Zaire, *Rapport Annuel* 1975, pp. xvi, xx.

38 Kumwimba, "Approche sur les aspects administratifs," pp. 85–89; Tshiauke, "Les problèmes administratives," pp. 184–185; Schatzberg, "Bureaucracy, Business, Beer," p. 376.

39 Tshiauke, "Les problèmes administratives," p. 185.

40 Schatzberg, "Bureaucracy, Business, Beer," p. 378.

41 Bank of Zaire, IMF, and World Bank figures do not break down state revenue data in such a way as to make possible precise calculations of the sums involved. All observers agree, however, that *acquéreur* tax evasion was general.

42 Tshiauke, "Les problèmes administratives," pp. 148–149.

43 For the text of the regulations, see Yabili, *Code de la Zairianization*, pp. 124–127.

44 *Discours, allocutions, et messages* 2: 529.

45 *Elima*, 1 December 1974.

46 Yabili, *Code de la Zairianization*, pp. 138–142.

47 *Elima*, 3 January 1975.

48 Ibid., 7 January 1975.

49 Ibid., 9 January 1975.

50 *Discours, allocutions, et messages* 2: 580–583.

51 *Elima*, 22 January 1975.

52 Speech of 4 February 1975 (typescript). Delivered in Lingala, the speech included many key phrases which were deleted from the official version subsequently distributed in French.

53 It was indicative of the many flaws in the radicalization program that the radicalized corporations suddenly found themselves in a juridical void. The delegates-general apparently had plenary powers, but no definition was given to them, nor were the boards of directors initially promised ever designated. Confusion in corporate authority structures was heightened by the well-publicized installation of JMPR units within major economic enterprises; these units appeared to supplant the official UNTZA, and to claim significant prerogatives within the factory. On the juridical aspects of radicalization, see Lukombe, *Zairianisation*, pp. 39–41.

54 Gould, "Underdevelopment Administration," p. 64.

55 Kikassa Mwanalessa, "La stabilisation des enterprises zairianisées et radicalisées," *Zaire-Afrique* 102 (February 1976): 95.

56 World Bank, "Economic Conditions and Prospects of Zaire," Report no. 1407–ZR, 13 April 1977.

57 Kikassa, "Stabilisation des entreprises," p. 94.

58 Mulumba Lukoji, "Le programme de redressement de l'économie zairoise (suite)," *Zaire-Afrique* 114 (April 1977): 205–221.

59 Gould, "Underdevelopment Administration," pp. 66–67.

60 President Mobutu, after returning from his state visit to China in January 1973, announced the following month that henceforward all Zairian adults would be expected to contribute a half-day of voluntary labor on Saturdays, to

be devoted to community and public works projects. *Salongo*, a Lingala term connoting communal collaboration, was the label given for this Saturday obligation, evidently stimulated by Mobutu's observations in China. During the first weeks there was widespread participation, but problems quickly became apparent. Organizing and utilizing this labor, even if freely given, was a formidable task. Most useful projects required tools of some sort, which citizens could not be required to provide. Mines and factories at once protested the loss of production time, and their work forces were exempted. But the state employees—for whom Saturday morning was part of the work week—were not exempted; over time, as observance of *salongo* became more and more sporadic, the impact tended to be the elimination of Saturday hours in government offices as employees claimed to be busy with *salongo* tasks. There were occasional efforts to revive *salongo*, of which the nursery school project was an example. In some times and places useful work was accomplished, but national implementation of such an ambitious scheme was beyond the capacity of state or party.

Chapter 12

1 Some portions of this chapter, in abbreviated form, appeared in Crawford Young, "Zaire, The Politics of Penury," *SAIS Review* 3, no. 2 (Winter-Spring 1983): 114–130. There is a very large literature available on this chapter's topic; the C.R.I.S.P. series of yearbooks, published in Brussels by the Centre de Recherche et d'Information Socio-Politiques from 1960 to 1965, stands at the head of the list. Other valuable works include Cathryn Hoskyns, *The Congo since Independence* (London: Oxford University Press, 1965); Thomas Kanza, *Conflict in the Congo* (Baltimore: Penguin Books, 1972); Ghislain Kabwit, "The Evolution of the Congo Foreign Policy from 1960–1970: A Case Study in Determinants Influencing the Making of Foreign Policy" (Ph.D. diss., American University, Washington, 1975); Stephen R. Weissman, *American Foreign Policy in the Congo, 1960–1964* (Ithaca: Cornell University Press, 1974); Arthur House, *The U.N. in the Congo* (Washington: University Press of America, 1978); Rajeshwar Dayal, *Mission for Hammerskjold* (Princeton: Princeton University Press, 1976); Paul-Henri Gendebien, *L'intervention des Nations Unies au Congo, 1964–1965* (Paris: Mouton, 1967); Ernest Lefever, *Crisis in the Congo* (Washington: Brookings Institution, 1965); Kwame Nkrumah, *Challenge of the Congo* (New York: International Publishers, 1967); Madeleine G. Kalb, *The Congo Cables* (New York: Macmillan Publishing Co., 1982).

2 For extended analyses of shifting Soviet assessments of African development, see Robert Legvold, *Soviet Policy in West Africa* (Cambridge: Harvard University Press, 1970); Christopher A. Stevens, *The Soviet Union and Black Africa* (London: Macmillan, 1976). The "national democracy" theme began to re-emerge in Africa in the 1970s.

3 On the Binza group, see chapter 2 and note 3 to that chapter.

4 For a sample of their statements, see *Congo 1966* (Brussels: Centre de Recherche et d'Information Socio-Politiques, 1967), pp. 424–426.

5 Nkrumah, *Challenge of the Congo*, p. 286. Gbenye was the head of the short-lived (August-November 1964) people's republic insurgent regime in Kisangani, proclaimed at the peak of the wave of rebellions which broke out at the end of 1963 and continued into 1965; Soumialot was the effective political leader on the ground in insurgent zones in eastern Zaire; Olenga was the military commander of the insurgent army. By 1965 all three had fled into exile; they became engaged in angry and public recriminations, which by the time of the October 1965 OAU summit had cost the rebels their remaining external support. For detail on the rebellions, see especially Benoit Verhaegen, *Rébellions au Congo*, 2 vols. (Brussels: Centre de Recherche et d'Information Socio-Politiques, 1966, 1969); Crawford Young, "Rebellion and the Congo," in Robert Rotberg and Ali Mazrui, eds., *Protest and Power in Black Africa* (New York: Oxford University Press, 1970), pp. 968–1,011; Renée Fox et al., "La deuxième indépendance: étude d'un cas: la rébellion au Kwilu," *Etudes Congolaises* 8, no. 1 (January-February 1965), pp. 1–35.

6 Nkrumah, *Challenge of the Congo*, pp. 288–289.

7 *Congo 1966*, p. 17.

8 Jeannick Odier, "La politique étrangère de Mobutu," *Revue Française d'Etudes Politiques Africaines* 120 (December 1975): 25–41.

9 *Jeune Afrique*, 620 (25 November 1972), reports that discussions were held on linking exploitation of Guinean bauxite to development of an aluminum complex near Inga.

10 Odier, "Politique étrangère," pp. 25–26.

11 Charles K. Ebinger, "External Intervention in Internal War: The Politics and Diplomacy of the Angola Civil War," *Orbis*, 20, no. 3 (Fall 1976): 680.

12 *Africa Contemporary Record*, 1971–1972, p. B520.

13 From Izvestia, cited in *Congo 1965*, p. 455.

14 *Agence Zairoise de Presse*, 13 November 1974.

15 Ebinger, "External Intervention," p. 680.

16 Quoted in Alan Hutchinson, *China's African Revolution* (London: Hutchinson, 1975), p. 148. On the Chinese role in Zaire, see also Bruce Larkin, *China and Africa* (Berkeley: University of California Press, 1971); Warren Weinstein, ed., *Chinese and Soviet Aid to Africa (New York: Praeger, 1975); Alvin Z. Rubinstein, ed., Soviet and Chinese Influence in the Third World* (New York: Praeger, 1975).

17 Stephen Weissman, "The CIA and U.S. Policy in Zaire and Angola," in René Lemarchand, ed., *American Policy in Southern Africa: The Stakes and the Stance* (Washington: University Press of America, 1978), pp. 393–394.

18 Ibid., p. 395. The *New York Times*, 4 January 1976, cited a "high State Department official" (the usual euphemism for Secretary of State Kissinger) as expressing the desirability of bolstering Zaire "in the hope that it could extend its hegemony throughout the continent." Diplomats posted in Zaire at the time

report that Vance would not permit negative analyses of the Mobutu regime to be transmitted to Washington. After his retirement, Vance joined the law firm representing the Zaire government.

19 Mobutu Sese Seko, *Mobutu: Discours, allocutions, et messages* (Paris: Editions J. A., 1975) 2: 577–578. Mobutu, of course, was not then aware of Davis's real perspectives on Africa; see Nathaniel Davis, "The Angola Decision of 1975: A Personal Memoir," *Foreign Affairs*, 57, no. 1 (Fall 1978): 109–124.

20 Ndele by this time was pursuing graduate studies at Yale University.

21 John Stockwell, *In Search of Enemies* (New York: W. W. Norton, 1978), p. 44. Devlin, by then Tempelsman representative in Kinshasa, was asked in August to intercede with Mobutu to secure the release of the generals, several of whom received death sentences.

22 *Elima,* 17 June 1975, carried the full official account of the *coup monté et manqué.*

23 Comité Zaire, *Zaire: Le dossier de la recolonisation* (Paris: Harmattan, 1978), pp. 172–173.

24 See the remarkable exposé on the Giscard d'Estaing family empire by Jonathan Kwitny, *Wall Street Journal,* 23 April 1981. On Franco-Zairian relations, see also M'Kola Kalubi, "Les relations franco-zairoises de 1960 à 1978," *Afrique et l'Asie Modernes,* 122 (1979): 30–49.

25 Comité Zaire, *Zaire,* pp. 192–196.

26 Comité Zaire, *Zaire,* p. 117.

27 The best source on the complex history of the Angolan nationalist movements is John Marcum, *The Angolan Revolution* (Cambridge: MIT Press, 1969, 1979). On the sequence of events during this confusing period, see Davis, "Angola Decision"; Stockwell, *In Search of Enemies;* John A. Marcum, *"Lessons of Angola,"* *Foreign Affairs,* 54, no. 3 (April 1976): 407–415; Colin Legum, "The Soviet Union, China and the West in Southern Africa," *Foreign Affairs,* 54, no. 4 (July 1976): 745–762; Mohammed A. El-Khawas and Barry Cohen, eds., *The Kissinger Study of Southern Africa* (Westport, Conn.: Lawrence Hill & Co., 1976); House Committee on International Relations, Subcommittee on Africa, *United States-Angolan Relations,* testimony of Gary Bender, 95th Cong., 2d sess., 1978; John Seiler, ed., *Southern Africa since the Portuguese Coup* (Boulder: Westview Press, 1980).

28 For an excellent resumé of the Cuban dimension, see Carmelo Mesa-Lago and June S. Belkin, eds., *Cuba in Africa* (Pittsburgh: Center for Latin American Studies, University of Pittsburgh, 1982).

29 Senate Committee on Foreign Relations, Subcommittee on Africa, *Security Supporting Assistance for Zaire,* 95th Cong., 2d sess., 24 October 1978. See also the excellent article by Emma Rothschild, "The Politics of Debt," *New York Review of Books,* 23, no. 11 (24 June 1976): 25–32.

30 "Citibank in Zaire," Harvard Business School case study, typescript.

31 David Alexander, "Debt Rescheduling by LDC's: A Case Study of Zaire," Harvard University, 1977, typescript.

32 Mulumba Lukoji, "Le programme de redressement de l'économie zairoise (suite)," *Zaire-Afrique*, 114 (April 1977): 206.

33 Citibank, the most heavily involved in Zaire, had less than $30 million in unguaranteed loans outstanding to Zaire, and less than $120 billion altogether, according to a Citibank vice-president: personal communication, March 1979.

34 Senate Committee on Foreign Relations, *Security Supporting Assistance for Zaire*, pp. 11–16.

35 Ibid., p. 13.

36 Ibid., p. 14.

37 N. Belleveau, "Heading Off Zaire's Default," *Institutional Investor* (March 1977), p. 23.

38 "Citibank in Zaire."

39 Ibid.

40 Speech to Second MPR Congress, Kinshasa, November 1977 (typescript).

41 There were some significant changes in government revenue and expenditure patterns during these years. Government expenditure as a fraction of GDP did decrease from the extraordinary 59 percent figure of 1974 (which exceeded expenditures of even the most advanced welfare states of Western Europe) to the (still high) figure of 37 percent in 1977. This above all reflected the sharp contraction of government capital expenditure. However, large deficits persisted because government revenues, mostly derived from foreign trade, also fell sharply. Imports were curtailed, which diminished fiscal proceeds from them; the state was forced to rebate a large fraction of the Gécamines export taxes (60 percent in 1977) to leave the company sufficient operating liquidity. International Bank for Reconstruction and Development, *Zaire: Current Economic Situation and Constraints* (Washington, 1980), pp. 55–71.

42 Guy Gran, "Zaire 1978: The Ethical and Intellectual Bankruptcy of the World System," *Africa Today* 25, no. 4 (October-December 1978): 23.

43 "Le rapport Blumenthal & annexes," *Info Zaire*, 36 (October 1982): 5.

44 Ibid., pp. 6, 9, 26.

45 Quoted in "Citibank in Zaire."

46 C. Reich, "Why the IMF Shuns a 'Super' Role," *Institutional Investor*, September 1977, p. 35, quoted in "Citibank in Zaire."

47 Senate Committee on Foreign Relations, *Security Supporting Assistance to Zaire*, p. 33.

48 *Afrique-Asie*, 8 August 1977, published the full text of this extraordinary document, which had been stolen from the safe of the Zairian Embassy in Bonn, presumably by East German intelligence services, and leaked to *Afrique-Asie*. See also Allen F. Roberts, in Guy Gran, ed., *Zaire, The Political Economy of Underdevelopment* (New York: Praeger, 1979) pp. 213–235.

49 Roberts, in Gran, ed., *Zaire*, p. 214.

50 Galen Hull, in Gran, ed., *Zaire*, p. 280.

51 Later in 1979 OTRAG acquired a base in Libya, and was soon accused by American intelligence services of planning sales of military rockets to radical

Arab states. By the end of 1981 the peripatetic company had pulled out of Libya, again under West German government pressure: *New York Times*, 27 December 1981.

52 Castro, on 17 May, had informed the chief American diplomat in Havana that Cuba had no role in the invasion, and had indeed tried to dissuade the FLNC from invading when Cubans learned of the plan in April. While Cubans, East Germans, Soviets, and Angolans may well have provided some help to the FLNC, it is most likely that the initiative for the attack came from its leader, M'Bumba: *New York Times*, 11 July 1978. M'Bumba consistently rebuffed efforts of other Zairian opposition groups to tie his movement to a broader political effort, and indeed on at least two occasions arranged for their emissaries to be jailed in Luanda: Jean-Claude Willame, "La seconde guerre du Shaba," *Enquêtes et Documents d'Histoire Africaine* (Louvain, Belgium, 1978), pp. 170–175.

53 Willame, "La seconde guerre," pp. 186–195.

54 Benoit Verhaegen, "Universities, Social Classes and Economic Dependency" (Paper presented at the Conference on the African University and Development, Bellagio, Italy, August 1978).

55 Ibid.

56 Verhaegen, "Universities, Social Classes, and Economic Dependency."

57 Wolfgang Stolper, "Report to Ambassador Vance and Acting Director Kelly on Certain Problems of the Zairian Economy," Kinshasa, 5 September 1972. Stolper's objections, and those of some other embassy staff, were overridden by the resolute optimism of Ambassador Vance.

58 In recent years a vast literature has accumulated on the theme of dependency, which attributes to the unequal economic relationships between Western capitalist states and Third World countries the causes of underdevelopment. In its extreme forms, as in the works of Andre Gunder Frank, international capitalism becomes a *deus ex machina* generating underdevelopment, and "lumpenbourgeois" regimes foster the persistence of this relationship. Over the years, a number of distinct themes have emerged in the dependency literature; various writers have laid particular stress on one or another aspect of the asymmetrical economic relationship: trade, capital, aid, technology, or debts. Others have suggested more nuanced applications of the dependency perspective; particularly influential among these analysts has been the work of Fernando Cardoso, who argues the possibility of "associated-dependent" development. Among the more influential works in this field, we may note Andre G. Frank, *Development and Underdevelopment in Latin America* (New York: Monthly Review Press, 1968), and later works by Frank; Arghiri Emmanuel, *Unequal Exchange* (New York: Monthly Review Press, 1972); Fernando Cardoso, "Associated-Dependent Development: Theoretical and Political Implications," in A. Stepan, ed., *Authoritarian Brazil* (New Haven: Yale University Press, 1973); Osvaldo Sunkel, "Big Business and Dependency," *Foreign Affairs*, 50, no. 3 (April 1972);

Henry Bernstein, ed., *Underdevelopment and Development: The Third World Today* (Baltimore: Penguin Books, 1972); Celso Furtado and T. dos Santos, "Dependency Theory: A Reassessment," *Latin American Perspectives*, 3, no. 4 (special issue, Fall 1976); Peter C. W. Gutkind and Immanuel Wallerstein, eds., *The Political Economy of Contemporary Africa* (Beverly Hills: Sage Publications, 1976); Colin Leys, *Underdevelopment in Kenya* (Berkeley: University of California Press, 1975); Samir Amin, *Unequal Development* (New York: Monthly Review Press, 1976), and other works. For critiques, see James A. Caporaso, ed., "Dependence and Dependency in the Global System," *International Organization*, 32, no. 1 (special issue, Winter 1978); Neil R. Richardson, *Foreign Policy and Economic Dependence* (Austin: University of Texas Press, 1978). Recent works on Zaire substantially influenced by the dependency perspective include David J. Gould, *Bureaucratic Corruption and Underdevelopment in the Third World: The Case of Zaire* (Elmsford, N.Y.: Pergamon Press, 1980); Gran, ed., *Zaire*; Ghifem Jacques Katwala, "Bureaucracy, Dependency and Underdevelopment in Zaire" (Ph.D. diss., University of California-Berkeley, 1979); Daniel Van der Steen, "Le Zaire malade de sa dépendance extérieure," *Genève-Afrique*, 18, no. 1 (1979): 121–131.

Chapter 13

1 Monseigneur Kabanga, "Je suis un homme," pastoral letter for Lent, Archeveché de Lubumbashi, March 1976.

2 Thomas M. Callaghy, treating this period, offers an intriguing comparison of state-building in Zaire to that in seventeenth-century France in "State Formation and Absolutism in Comparative Perspective: Seventeenth Century France and Mobutu Sese Seko's Zaire" (Ph.D. diss., University of California–Berkeley, 1979).

3 Relevant to this point is the insightful article by Peter Ekeh, "Colonialism and the Two Publics in Africa: A Theoretical Statement," *Comparative Studies in Society and History*, 17, no. 1 (1975): 91–112.

4 Cited in Kenneth Lee Adelman, "The Influence of Religion on National Integration in Zaire" (Ph.D. diss., Georgetown University, 1975), p. 8.

5 The calculations were made with particular relation to the Ottoman state by Charles Issawi, *An Economic History of the Middle East and North Africa* (New York: Columbia University Press, 1982), p. 63.

6 Michael G. Schatzberg, "The Long Arm of the Law: Insecurity, Instability, and the Political Police in Zaire" (Paper presented at the Annual meeting, International Studies Association, Cincinnati, March 1982).

7 Clifford Geertz, *Negara: The Theatre State in Nineteenth-Century Bali* (Princeton: Princeton University Press, 1980), p. 13.

8 For example, a 1983 amnesty brought home two leaders of exile opposition organizations—Mungul Diaka and Mbeka Makosso.

9 On the opposition groups, see the excellent analyses by Jean-Claude Willame, "Divisions et faiblesses d'une opposition privée de strategie politique," *Le Monde Diplomatique*, 330 (September 1981); Willame, "Contribution à l'étude des mouvements d'opposition au Zaire: le F.L.N.C.," *Cahiers du CEDAF*, 6 (1980); Benoit Verhaegen, "Les mouvements de libération en Afrique: Le cas du Zaire en 1978," *Genève-Afrique*, 17, no. 1 (1979): 173–181.

Index

ABAKO (Alliance des Bakongo), 40, 143,
153, 234, 235
ABAKO 1950–1960 (Centre de Recherche
et d'Information Socio-Politiques,
1963), 433
Abernethy, David B.: "Bureaucratic Growth
and Economic Decline in Sub-Saharan
Africa" (paper, 1983), 428
Abraham, Willie: *The Mind of Africa* (University of Chicago Press, 1962), 443
Acquereur. *See* Class
Actualités Africaines (African Weekly),
175, 187
Adelman, Kenneth Lee: "The Church-State
Conflict in Zaire: 1969–1971," *African
Studies Review* 18, no. 1 (1975), 421;
"The Influence of Religion on National
Integration in Zaire" (Ph.D. diss.,
Georgetown University, 1975), 467
Administration: reform failure, 232–44.
See also Belgian Administration; Regional
Administration; Rural Administration;
Chieftaincy; Urban Administration
Adoula, Cyrille, 47, 52, 58
Africa Confidential 21 (10 December
1980), 451
Africa Contemporary Record (1971–1972),
459, 463; (1974–1975), 453, 456;
(1975–1976), 455, 456
Africa Research Bulletin (August 1977),
449; (February 1978), 450
African Development (February 1974), 456
Africanization: bureaucracy, 106; local
churches, 109
Afrique-Asie 252 (9 November 1981), 439;
(8 August 1977), 465
Afrique Chrétienne (Catholic weekly), 68

Afro-Asian summit (Algeria, 1973), 369
Agence Zairoise de Presse (12 July 1977),
449; (13 November 1974), 463
Agriculture: policies in Congo Free State,
34–35; prices, 91; shipments, 92;
palm oil, 92–93, 314–15; quotas, 94;
Belgian planters after World War II, 108;
Kisangani industry development, 296; investment, 306; potential, 309–10; crises,
309–11; administration, 310; research
decline, 310; credit program, 310–11;
land rights, 310–11; pricing policies,
311–12, 314–16; plantations, 315–16;
cotton, 316–21; grain and rice, 312–
22; policy, 322
Agricultural Boards. *See* ONACER (maize
and rice); ONC (coffee); ONAFITEX;
COGERCO
Aircraft, 269
Air Force, 269–70. *See also* Military
Air Zaire (national airline): 306; labor
problems, 131
Alexander, David: "Debt Rescheduling in
LDC's: A Case Study of Zaire" (typescript, Harvard University, 1977), 464
Algeria: mentioned, 26
Allison, Graham: *Essence of Decision: Explaining the Cuban Missile Crisis* (Little,
Brown, 1971), 412
Almond, Gabriel A., and G. Bingham
Powell, Jr.: *Comparative Politics: A Developmental Approach* (Little, Brown,
1966), 413; with Marvin Chodorow and
Roy H. Pearce (eds.): *Progress and Its Discontents* (University of California Press,
1982), 413
Aluminum, 298; plant, 299

Alusuisse (aluminum smelter), 299–300
Amin, Idi: Ugandan interests, 17; mentioned, 369
Amin, Samir: *Unequal Development* (Monthly Review Press, 1976), 467
Amnesty International: *Human Rights Violations in Zaire* (New York, 1980), 451
Anany, Jérôme (defense minister), 56
Andreski, Stanislav: "Kleptocracy as a System of Government in Africa," in Arnold J. Heidenheimer (ed.), *Political Corruption* (Transaction Books, 1978), 440
ANEZA (National Association of Business), 192, 358
Angola: pro-Tshombe mercenaries, 188; Zaire's military involvement in, 254; Cuban army involvement in, 254, 255; factions within, 369, 389
Angolan Civil War: Zaire's involvement in, 72, 253–54; FLNC, 256, 376–78; Cabinda Separatist movement in, 377; results of, 378; Soviet-Cuban involvement in, 378; mentioned, 253
Anstey, Roger: "Belgium's Role in the Congo and the Aspirations of the Evolué Class," in L. H. Gann and Peter Duignan (eds.), *Colonialism in Africa 1870–1960*, (Cambridge University Press, 1970), 429; *King Leopold's Legacy* (Oxford University Press, 1969), 414
Anti-Colonialism: awareness of, 37–41; mentioned, 110
Apthorpe, Raymond: "Does Tribalism Really Matter?" *Transition* 7, no. 6 (1968), 432
Arabs: Afro-Arab relations, 138, 388
Armstrong, John: *Nations before Nationalism* (University of North Carolina Press, 1982), 432, 433
Army. *See* FAZ; Military
Arrighi, G., and J. S. Saul: *Essays on the Political Economy of Africa* (Monthly Review Press, 1973), 431
Art: urban folk, "Colonie belge," 3; Tshibumba Kanda-Matula, 3
"Article 15," 228

Ascherson, Neal: *The King Incorporated* (George Allen & Unwin, 1963), 415
Authenticity, concept of, 43, 65; opposition to, from Catholic Church, 68; in form of address and dress, 117; cultural ideologies, 148; cultural heritage, 212–13, 214; building of, 213; criticism of, 215
"Authentic Congolese Nationalism": mentioned, 208
"Authentic Zairian Nationalism": mentioned, 210
Authoritarianism: African, 27; Latin American, 27
Autonomy: state, 15–16
Avineri, Shlomo: *Hegel's Theory of the Modern State* (Cambridge University Press, 1972), 409
Axelson, Sigbert: *Culture Confrontation in the Lower Congo* (Gummessons, 1970), 414
AZAP (Zairian Press Agency), 374

Babia Zongbi Malobia (general), 265, 274
Baka regiment, 250
Bakajika Law (1966), 288, 297, 367
Bakole, Msgr. T., 419 n18
Bakonzi Agoyo: "The Gold Mines of Kilo-Moto in Northeastern Zaire, 1905–1960," (Ph.D. diss., University of Wisconsin-Madison, 1982), 415, 430, 452
Balandier, Georges: "La situation coloniale: approche théorique," *Cahiers Internationaux de Sociologie* 11 (1951), 413
Bamba, Emmanuel (finance minister), 56
Banana: proposed aluminum port in, 300; deep water port in, 306
Bangala, Alphonse (colonel), 56
Bangala, Madame (market woman), 128
Bankruptcy: in Zaire, 71–72, 357; Angola, 77; crisis, 378–86. *See also* International Monetary Fund
Banks: World Bank, 29, 75, 132, 307, 368, 392; Bank of Zaire, 132, 357, 382; Bank of Kinshasa, 179; Mobutu's holdings, 181; Citibank, 379, 380, 382, 385, 465 n33; Export–Import, 380; private

bank loans to Zaire, 380–381. *See also* International Monetary Fund

Banque du Zaire: *Rapport Annuel* (1967), 451; (1968–69), 451; (1975), 457–58, 460

"Bantu wisdom": mentioned, 214

Barth, Fredrik (ed.): *Ethnic Groups and Boundaries* (Little, Brown, 1969), 432

Bates, Robert H.: *Markets and States in Tropical Africa* (University of California Press, 1981), 412; *Rural Responses to Industrialization: A Study of Village Zambia* (Yale University Press, 1976), 425

Baudouin (King of Belgium), 63, 302, 374

Bayart, Jean-Francois: *L'Etat au Cameroun* (Presses de la Fondation Nationale des Sciences Politiques, 1979), 410

Beeckmans, René: "Inga, grandiose realisation d'une utopie," *Zaire-Afrique* 69 (1972), 454

Beer: consumption of, 88

Behavior: European model of, 111–12

Belgium: administrators, 3–4; Mobutu coup, 52; colonial party, 111; regional administration by, 222–24; economic settlement, 285; government, 285; involvement in Zairianization, 357; discrediting, 364; intervention in Kisangani, 365–66; Belgo American relations, 373–74, 390; involvement with radicalization, 456–57

Belleveau, N.: "Heading Off Zaire's Debt," *Institutional Investor* (1972), 465

Bemany, Alberic (Mobutu's father), 173

Bendix, Reinhard: *Kings or People* (University of California Press, 1978), 412; *Max Weber: An Intellectual Portrait* (Doubleday & Co., 1962), 436

Bentley, Arthur F.: *The Process of Government* (University of Chicago Press, 1908), 410

Berlin Congress (1884–1885), 23, 363

Bernstein, Henry (ed.): *Underdevelopment and Development: The Third World Today* (Penguin Press, 1972), 467

Bertrand, Hugues: *Le Congo* (François Maspero, 1975), 435

Bethlehem Steel, 303

Biafra, 368

Bianga Waruzi: "Peasant, State, and Rural Development in Postindependent Zaire: A Case Study of 'Réforme Rurale' 1970–1980 and Its Implications," (Ph.D. diss., University of Wisconsin-Madison, 1982), 430, 446

Bifuko Baharanyi: "The Study of Management of Rural Development in Zaire: The Cases of The National Board for Fibers and Textiles (ONAFITEX) and the Agro-Pastoral Project in the Ruzizi Valley (1968–1975)" (M.A. Thesis, University of Dar-es-Salaam, 1977), 457–58

Bintu, 200

Binza group: Belgian and American influence on, 165; mentioned, 60, 417 *n3*

Bisengimana, Rema, 167

Black Arrows, 255

Black market: growth in 1970's, 120

Blumenthal, Erwin (IMF official), 384–85

Bo-boliko, 200

Bobozo Salelo (army commander), 154, 174, 264

Bodenam, Francis, 58, 419 *n24*

Bokamba Eyamba: "Authenticity and the Choice of a National Language, the Case of Zaire," *Studies in the Linguistic Sciences* 6, no. 2 (1976), 434

Bokassa (president of Central African Republic), 367–68

Bolikango Akpolobako (Jean): Equateur political, 52; ouster, 56; Liboke movement, 153

Bomkoko Lokumba (Justin): member Binza group, 54; foreign affairs minister, 58; member Political Bureau, 60–61, 206; mentioned, 302

Bonehill, Daniel: "La dépendance et la fragilité," *Le Monde Diplomatique* (1978), 423

Bontinck, F. F.: "Les deux Bula Matari" *Etudes Congolaises* 13, no. 3 (1969), 414

Bosango (general), 264

Boteti Nkanga (ground force commander), 274

Bourgeoisie. *See* Class

Boute, Joseph: "Demographic Trends in the Republic of Zaire," *Munger African Library Notes* (1973), 458

Boyenge, Singa (Alexandre): security chief, 60; chief of staff, 274

Boyoko (Citizen), 196

Brass, Paul: *Ethnic Groups and the State* (Croon Helm, forthcoming), 412

Brett, E. A.: "Relations of Production, the State and the Ugandan Crisis," *West African Journal of Sociology and Political Sciences* 1 (1978), 416

British Diamond Distribution (Britmond), 288

Brixhe, A.: *Le coton au Congo Belge* (Ministère des Colonies, 1958), 457

Buana Kabwe: *Citoyen President* (Editions L'Harmattan, 1978), 423

Buci-Glucksmann, Christine: *Gramsci et l'Etat* (Fayard, 1975), 411

Buell, Raymond Leslie: *The Native Problem in Africa* (Macmillan, 1928), 444, 466

Buganda chiefs, 24

Bukavu: mercenary led revolt in, 251–53

Bula Matadi. *See* Bula Matari

Bula Matari: use of force by, 30–31, 185, 274; hegemony of, 32, 274; extraction of taxes by, 97; relations to chiefs, 239; mentioned, 35, 36, 39, 40, 76, 78, 79, 133, 221, 234, 312, 396, 400

Bull, Hedley: *The Anarchical Society* (Columbia University Press, 1977), 411

Bulozi (army intelligence chief), 274

Bumba: rice production in, 92

Bumba Moaso (brigadier-general), 154, 264–65, 340

Burssens, H.: *Les peuplades de l'entre Congo-Ubangi* (Musée Royal de l'Afrique Centrale, 1958), 434

Bustin, Edouard: *Lunda under Belgian Rule* (Harvard University Press, 1975), 415, 423

Butembo group, 120

Callaghy, Thomas M.: "State Formation and Absolutism in Comparative Perspective: Seventeenth Century France and

Mobutu Sese Seko's Zaire," (Ph.D. diss., University of California-Berkeley, 1979), 445, 467; "State Formation and Centralization of Power in Zaire: Mobutu's Pre-eminent Public Policy" (paper, 1976), 445

Cammett, John M.: *Antonio Gramsci and the Origins of Italian Communism* (Stanford University Press, 1967), 411

Caporaso, James A. (ed.): "Dependence and Dependency in the Global System," *International Organization* 32, no. 1 (special issue, 1978), 467

Cardoso, Fernando: "Associated-Dependent Development: Theoretical and Political Implications," in A. Stepan (ed.), *Authoritarian Brazil* (Yale University Press, 1973), 466

Cassava: trade in, 114

Carter, Jimmy (U.S. President), 389

Cell, John: *The Highest Stage of White Supremacy* (Cambridge University Press, 1982), 412

CELZA (Cultures et Elevages du Zaire), 179, 347, 358

Cement production, 305

Center for Policy Development: "Open Letter to the Citizen Mobutu Sese Seko, President of Zaire, From Thirteen Members of Parliament" (Washington, 1982), 450

Central African Republic, 273

Centre National de Documentation (CND), 66, 166, 273

Centre National de Recherche et d'Investigation (CNRI), 273

Centres extra-coutumiers (African townships), 230

Ceulemans, Jacques: "Matabiche, Bwana," *Remarques Congolaises et Africaines*, 236 (1965), 452

CFL (Chemin de Fer du Congo Supérieur aux Grands-Lacs), 283, 285

Charter companies, 34, 283, 285

Chazan, Naomi: *An Anatomy of Ghanaian Politics: Managing Political Recession, 1969–1972* (Westview Press, 1983), 417

Chiefs and chieftaincy: diminution of, 69;

Luba, 92; legal of Rwanda and Burundi, 111; as petty gentry, 126; authenticity of, 211–12; Belgian classification of, 233; post-independence, 233; Belgian reforms and, 234; anti-chief measures, 234–35; involvement in secessionist movements, 234–35; and political parties, 235–36; 1968 reorganization of, 236; *tribunaux de paix*, 236; reforming by, 236–40; selection process of, 237; role of incumbent in, 237; transfer of, 237–38; "customary," 238; "administrative," 238, 428*n27*; mentioned, 22, 35, 36

China: support of Tanzanian rebels, 57; military advisers, 270; Mobutu's visit to, 350, 370; economic aid to Zaire, 370; relations with Zaire, 370, 376; relationship with FNLA, 376; alliance with Zaire in Angolan civil war, 377

Chipenda, Daniel (MPLA dissident), 253

Chomé, Jules: *L'ascension de Mobutu* (Editions Complexe, 1974), 436, 438, 439

Christian missions: 26, 37; Catholic evangelism, 32; role in education, 38, 111, 125; rural, 90; expatriates, 108–9

Churches: Catholic, status of, 66–68; Archbishop Kabanga pastoral letter, 72; Zairian clergy, 109; missionaries, 112; priestly status, 121; Mobutu relations, 175, 374, 415*n86*, 416; Kimbanguist, 66, 121; Protestant, 66, 121

Citibank, 379, 380, 382, 385*n33*, 465

"Citibank in Zaire": Harvard Business School (typescript), 464–65

Cities: growth of, 79–85, 89; emigration from rural areas, 90, 98; division of, 230. *See also* Urbanization

Civil society: response of, 404–6; 412*n44*

Clark, Richard (U.S. Senator), 380

Class: society and consciousness of, 18; Butembo parable, 100; merchant, 100; concept of, 101–2, 130, 135; stratification, 102–10; formation, 104; bureaucratic, 110; national bourgeoisie, 110; politico-commercial, 110–20, 398; Belgian colonial policy on, 111; chiefs' role in Belgian state, 111, 112; *évolué*,

111–14; in Kasanga, 113; intellectual, 113–15; mobility, 114; subsistence, 114; acquereur, 114–17, 122, 334, 337, 338, 344, 345, 347–49; powers of, 115, 130; mercantile, 115–16, 120–21; concept of *citoyen*, 117; ruling, 117; loss of prestige of, 119–20; metropolitan bourgeoisie alliance with West, 119–20; military purges, 121; concept of bourgeoisie, 122–23; sub-bourgeoisie, 122–27; university graduates in government, 123; teachers, 124–25; informal sector, 127–29; *jeunesse désoeuvrée* (unemployed young men), 128; rural, 129, 130; working, 129–33; involvement in strikes, 130; relational concept, 131–32; social mobility, 133–35; structural changes, 135–37; in New Regime, 152; sociopolitical, 162–63; Zairianization, 337–38; press attacks, 350, 354, 355; consequences of, 361, 398

Clientage: in social mobility, 135

Close, Dr. William (Mobutu's doctor), 167

CNK: (Comité National du Kivu), 283, 285

Coast Guard, 270

Cobalt: Mobutu's sale of, 181, 182; UMHK production, 289; mentioned, 76

Coffee: exports, 61, 76; Kivu, 92; prices, 312, 314; plantations, 312

COGERCO (parastatal marketing board), 317, 320

Cohen, Abner: *Urban Ethnicity* (Tavistock Publications, 1974), 432

Cohen, Barry: "L'ébauche d'une stratégie occidentale," *Le Monde Diplomatique* (1978), 440

Cohen, Dennis L.: "Class and the Analysis of African Politics: Problems and Prospects," in Dennis L. Cohen and John Daniel (eds.), *Political Economy of Africa* (London: Longman, 1981), 427

Cohen, Robin: in Peter Gutkind and Emmanuel Wallerstein (eds.), *The Political Economy of Contemporary Africa* (Beverly Hills: Sage Publications, 1976), 431

Cohen, William B.: "The French Colonial Service in French West Africa," in Prosser Gifford and William Roger Louis (eds.),

Cohen, William B. (*continued*)
France and Britain in Africa (Yale University Press, 1971), 413
Collier, David (ed.): *The New Authoritarianism in Latin America* (Princeton University Press, 1979), 413
Colonial administration, 24–25; organization of, 223; lack of outside controls on, 223; influence of on contemporary Zaire, 223; New Regime's application upon Zaire, 223–24
Colonial charter: with Belgium, 32
Colonialism, 22–23
Colonie belge, 3–8; urban folk art, 3; comparison to first years of Mobutu, 30
Colvin, Ian: *The Rise and Fall of Moise Tshombe* (Leslie Frewin, 1968), 419
Comeliau, Christian: *Fonctions économiques et pouvoir politique* (Institut de Recherches Economiques et Sociales, 1965), 427–28
Comhaire-Sylvain, Susanne: *Femmes de Kinshasa hier et aujourd-hui* (Mouton, 1968), 425
COMINIERE (Belgian conglomerate), 302
Comité National du Kivu (CNKi), 283
Comité Special du Katanga (CSK), 283
Comité Zaire: *Zaire, Le dossier de la recolonisation* (Harmattan, 1978), 439, 464
Commerce, 329
Commissaire d'Etat aux Affaires Politiques (22 January, 1973), 445
Commissaire d'Etat aux Affaires Politiques aux Commissaires de Région (tous) (8 August 1974), 445
Communications: satellite, 306, 375; Voice of Zaire, 375
Compagnie Congolaise de Commerce et de l'Industrie (CCCI), 284
Compagnie du Chemin de Fer du Bas-Congo au Katanga (BCK), 287
Compagnie du Chemin de Fer du Congo Supérieur aux Grands Lacs (CFL), 283–84
Compagnie des Chemins de Fer Katanga-Dilolo-Léopoldville (KDL), 287
Compagnie du Katanga, 283–84
Compte-rendus analytiques (30 November 1973), 459

CONACO (Convention Nationale Congolaise), 49
"Congo crisis," 7
Congo Free State: state ascendancy, 7, 363; Leopold II, 31
Congo-Brazzaville: Marxist ideology, 161; mentioned, 369, 376; relationship with U.S.S.R., 370; mentioned, 6, 363
Congo 1959 (1959), 416
Congo 1960 (1961), 433
Congo 1964 (1965), 452
Congo 1965 (1966), 417, 418, 419, 440, 449, 452
Congo 1966 (1967), 418, 419, 440, 447, 452, 463
Congo 1967 (1968), 420, 441, 447, 463
Conscience Africaine group, 40
Constitution: Kananga (1964), 49; of 1967, 59; of 1974, 69–71
Consumption: expatriates, 109–10
Continental Grains: Matadi flour mill, 305
Contentieux: major economic issues with Belgium, 281–88; Tshombe settlement, 296
"Contribution à l'étude des relations Sabena-Air Congo 1960–1968," *Etudes Africaines du C.R.I.S.P.*, nos. 90–91 (March 1969), 469
Cooptation: Mobutu's use of, 56–57
Copper: price fluctuations of, 43, 71; Shaba I and Shaba II invasions, 73, 74–75; sale of for Mobutu, 181; UMHK, 290; cartel attempts, 94–95; development during Second Republic, 296; deposits and development, 301–4; Japanese investment, 301–2; refining plants, 304; prices, 304, 306, 307, 323, 382, 395–96; concessions, 374
Cornet, René J.: *La bataille du rail* (Editions L. Cuypers, 1974), 415; *Les phares verts* (Editions L. Cuypers, 1965), 456
Corporations: in Congo Free State, 33–34; in Second Republic, 107; charter companies, 283; colonial debt, 284; private claims with independence, 284; colonial, 286, 287; Forminière, 287, 288, Minière du Bécéka, 287; Sabena, 286–87; Société des Mines d'Or de Kilo-Moto,

286–87; Minière de Bakwanga (MIBA), 288; Société d' Entreprise et d'Investissement du Bécéka (SIBEKA), 288; British Diamond Distributors (Britmond), 288; and land divestiture, 288

Corruption: effect on state, 45, 75–77, 400–402; in palm oil distribution, 93; in politico-commercial class, 116; and natural resources, 246; in regional administration, 246; in state payroll system, 246; systemic, 246–47; and land divestiture, 288; in industry, 309; systemization of, 399

COTONCO (Compagnie Cotonnière Congolaise), 317

Cotton: pricing policy, 312; Office National des Fibres Textiles (ONAFITEX), 316; colonial peasant production and marketing of, 316–17; production and pricing of since independence, 317–19; ginneries, 320

Coup: Mobutu, 52–53, 1965 army proclamation, 186

Coup attempts. *See* Military

Coup monté et manqué, 265

CPP (Convention People's Party of Ghana), 217

Cronjé, Susanne, Margaret Ling, and Gillian Cronjé: *Lonrho: Portrait of a Multinational* (Penguin Books, 1967), 453, 454

CSK (Comité Special du Katanga), 283

CSLS (Conféderation des Syndicats Libres du Congo), 199

Cuba: involvement in Angolan civil war, 72, 75

Cultural pluralism, 18–19, 152

Currency devaluation. *See* Economics

Currency reform, 171

Customs Union of Central African States (UDEAC), 367

Cutler, Walter (U.S. Ambassador to Zaire), 373

CVR (Corps des Volontaires de la République), 186–88, 189, 190, 194, 199

Dash, Leon: (*Washington Post,* 31 December 1979), 453

Davis, Nathaniel: "The Angola Decision of 1975: A Personal Memoir," *Foreign Affairs* 57, no. 1 (1978), 464

Davister, Pierre (editor, *L'Avenir*), 175

Dayal, Rajeshwar: *Mission for Hammerskjold* (Princeton University Press, 1976), 462

de Banzy (Mobutu pseudonym), 175

de Beers, 288

Debt: 1976, 75–77; colonial, 281, 284; non-repayment of, 283; Belgian, 285; repayments to Belgium, 286; energy development in Inga-Shaba, 300–301; external, 325, 401; 1975, 357; Arab support, 380; 1977, 382–83; 1980, 378–86; capital transfer, 392

Decolonization, 26–30

Deficits, 323

Deflation. *See* Economics

de Gaulle, Charles: French interests, 17

"Demonetization" measures, 323

Denard, Bob, 250, 251

d'Entreves, Alexandre Passerin: *The Notion of the State* (Clarendon Press, 1967), 409

de Jouvenal, Bertrand: *On Sovereignty: An Inquiry into the Political Good* (Cambridge University Press, 1957), 411

Demunter, P.: "Les relations entre le mouvement étudiant et le régime politique congolais, le Colloque de Goma," *C.R.I.S.P, T.A.,* 126 (1971), 441

Dependency, 29, 393–95; theory of, 44; patron-client, 158; Zaire, 391–95

"Deradicalization." *See* Retrocession.

de St. Moulin, Léon: "Kinshasa," *Revue Française d'Etudes Politique Africaines* (1971), 424

Dettes de Guerre (Editions Essor du Congo, 1945), 429

Devaluation. *See* Economics

Development: strategy in Second Republic, 296–97. *See also* Communications; Economic Development; Minerals; Resources; Transportation

Developmentalism: African state ideology, 29; "objectif 80," 63

Devlin, Lawrence (CIA official), 53, 176, 303, 418n11

Diamonds: Kasai Oriental, 92; Forminière, 107, 108, 287; MIBA managers, 107,

Diamonds (*continued*)
108; trade network, 108; sale for Mobutu, 181, 452*n27*, mentioned, 76
Diawara conspiracy, 371
Dikonda wa Lumanyisha: *Massacrer pour gouverner* (Club Travail et Développement, 1983), 442
Diombamba Miala: "Summary Considerations on the Program for Training Local Administrative Cadres in Zaire," (*U.S. Agency for International Development*, 1980), 446
Diplomacy: expansion, 367–71; Mobutu and Arab states, 369; and Angola, 376–78; and economics, 378–86; and politics, 386–90
District urbain, 230
Djilas, Milovan: *The New Class* (Frederick A. Praeger, 1968), 428
Dodd, Thomas (U.S. senator), 364
Dominguez, Jorge: *Cuba: Order and Revolution* (Harvard University Press, 1963), 416
Douglas, Mary: *The Lele of the Kasai* (Oxford University Press, 1963), 416
Drama, Louis (president of Equateur): MPR party rivalry, 191–92
Duga (Shaba regional commissioner), 338
Dumont, René: *L'Afrique Noire est mal partie* (Editions du Seuil, 1962), 428
Dupriez, Pierre: "La réforme monétaire du 24 juin 1967 en République Démocratique du Congo," *Cahiers Economiques et Sociaux* 6, no. 1 (1968), 451, 452
Dyson, Kenneth H. F.: *The State Tradition in Western Europe* (Oxford University Press, 1980), 411

Easton, David: *A Systems Analysis of Political Life* (John Wiley and Sons, 1965), 410
Ebinger, Charles K.: "External Intervention in Internal War: The Politics and Diplomacy of the Angola Civil War," *Orbis* 20, no. 3 (1976), 463
Echo de la Bourse (24 August 1970), 453; (4–6 September 1970), 454
Economic development: concession grants, 65–66; Inga Dam project, 298–300

Economics: cycles, 30; linkages with West, 104–6; private sector, 107–8; 1967 rescheduling and repayments, 107–8, 116; political-commercial, 115–16; deflation, 116, 131, 381; 1967 and 1976, 153; 1967–83, 322–23; black market growth, 120; payments, 136; underground, 136–37; stabilization, 277; 1968, 281; GDP, 277; nationalization of resources, 288; catastrophe, 306, 309; 1967, 83, 322–23; analysis, 324–25; 30 November 1976 policy implementation, 326–27, 330–33, 333–45; nationalism, 328; price controls, 345–56; payments to corporations, 378–86; devaluation, 379; 1975 crisis, 379, 401; balance of payments, 382–83; deflation, 399. *See also* Debts; Inflation
Edelman, Murray: *Politics as Symbolic Action: Mass Arousal and Quiescence* (Markham Publishing Co., 1971), 460
Education: post World War II, 38–39; school age population, 87; expansion and women, 88; access to, 111; Western intellectual class, 113–14; 117–18, 135; UNAZA staff, 121; stratification, 133–35; of Mobutu, 174; restructure of higher, 197–98; private, 360; decline of state education, 402–3
Efomi (Head of Security Police), 56–57, 60, 272
Eisenstadt, S. N., and René Lemarchand (eds.): *Political Clientelism, Patronage and Development* (Sage Publications, 1981), 414, 435
Ekeh, Peter: "Colonialism and the Two Publics in Africa: A Theoretical Statement," *Comparative Studies in Society and History* 17, no. 1 (1975), 467
Election: 1960, 144–45; 1970–1982, 201–4; 1977, 389
Elima: (3 January 1974), 459; (17 November 1973), 459; (1 December 1974), 461; (3 January 1975), 461; (7 January 1975), 461; (9 January 1975), 461; (22 January 1975), 461; (17 June 1975), 464
El-Khawas, Mohammed A., and Barry Cohen (eds.): *The Kissinger Study of*

Southern Africa (Lawrence Hill & Co., 1976), 464

Emerson, Rupert: *From Empire to Nation* (Harvard University Press, 1960), 411

Emmanuel, Arghiri: *Unequal Exchange* (Monthly Review Press, 1972), 466

Empain group, 33, 284

Employment, 87, 89, 129–33; *évolué*, 112; clerical and intellectual, 116

Employment, Incomes and Equality in Kenya (International Labor Organization, 1972), 424

Energy: hydroelectric, 296; Inga dam, 298–300

Engels, Friedrich, 9

Engulu Baanga (interior minister), 34, 226, 227, 228, 330, 341, quoted in *Zaire Afrique 91*, 436

Enterprise Nationale de Construction, 331

Enungo Kahindo-Dalau: "De l'Office des Produits Agricoles du Kivu (OPAK) à l'Office National du Cafe (ONC): Quelques considérations sur la fonctionnement administratif," (Mémoire de license, Université Nationale du Zaire, Lubumbashi, 1977), 458; Conference remarks, *Remarques Africains 477* (1976), 436

Epanza (16 June 1973), 456

Epstein, A. L.: *Ethos and Identity* (Tavistock, 1978), 412, 432

Equateur group, 398

Equateurians: 153–54; UNAZA-Lubumbashi resentment against, 156–57; in military, 274–75

Ethiopia: Mobutu's state visit to, 368

Ethnic nepotism, 435*n42*

Ethnicity: in First Republic, 41–42; relation to class, 101; effect of, on labor, 131; concepts of, 138, 140, 157–63; mobilization and competition, 140–48; political impact of, 142–48; rural-urban, 144; in 1960 elections, 144–45; ethno-regional, 146–47; New Regime, 149–52; regional, 152–57; in Second Republic, 155–57; rural, 162, 427*n3*; mentioned, 78

E. U.: "Idées forces du Mobutisme," *Re-*

marques Africains 477 (1978), 433, 443

Evolué. See Class

Ewert, David Merrill: "Freire's Concept of Critical Consciousness and Social Structure in Rural Zaire," (Ph.D. diss., University of Wisconsin-Madison, 1977), 426

Expatriates, 106–10

Export-Import bank, 380

Fabian, Johannes: *Jamaa* (Northwestern University Press, 1971), 413; "Missions and the Colonization of African Languages: Developments in the Former Belgian Congo," *Canadian Journal of African Studies* 17, no. 2 (1983), 434

Fabians (students of Zairian urban art), 6

Factories, 305

FAZ (Forces Armées Zairoises): field performance of, 126; officer corps, 154, 274–75; combat record of, 248, 249–58; FNLA military units, 254; defeat of in Angola, 254–55; resistance of to FLNC, 256; limitations of during Shaba I, 256–57; general performance of, 259–62; Mobutu's political control of, 266–67; reform efforts of, 267–68; foreign assistance to, 268. *See also* Military

Fédération des Entreprises Belges, 373

FGTK (Fédération Générale des Travailleurs Kongolais), socialist labor union, 199

First Republic: *pagaille* state, 41–42; patrimonialism, 165; Mobutu, 178; unions in, 199; foundations of, 363–65; economic reform efforts in, 271–81, 417*n4*; mentioned, 208, 222, 260, 397, 398

Fizi-Baraka, 57

FLEC (Frente de Libertação do Enclave de Cabinda), 254

FLNA (Frente Nacional de Libertação de Angola), 253–54; involvement in Angolan Civil War, 377–78

FLNC (Front pour la Liberation Nationale du Congo), 75, 255–57

Food: production of, 89–90, 92; prices of, 93–94; shortage of, 351

Force Publique, 260, 261, 274

Fossaert, Robert: *La Société*, 5 vols. (Editions du Seuil, 1977–1980), 413

Fox, Renée (et al.): "La deuxième indépendance: étude d'un cas: la rébellion au Kwilu," *Etudes congolaises* 8, no. 1 (1965), 427, 463

France: mining interests in Zaire, 293; Franco-Zairian relations, 374–75, 390

Frank, Andre Gunder: *Capitalism and Underdevelopment in Latin America*, rev. ed., (Monthly Review Press, 1969), 414, 466

Fredrickson, George N.: *White Supremacy* (Oxford University Press, 1981), 412

French Foreign Legion, 258

French Revolution: influence on nation formation, 8

French West Africa, 24

Friedrich, Carl J.: in Nettl, "State as a Conceptual Variable," 414

Friedman, Irving (Citibank vice president), 379, 385

Furtado, Celo and T. dos Santos: "Dependency Theory: A Reassessment," *Latin American Perspectives* 3, no. 4 (1976), 467

Gabon: Mobutu's state visit to, 368

Gangs: urban, 128

Gbadolite (Mobutu ancestral village), 173

Gbenye, Christophe (leader of Kisangani rebellion), 366

Gécamines (Générale des Carrières et de Mines): employees, 107; work environment of, 122; health services provided by, 158–59; relation to presidency, 167; cash flow, 181; formation of, 292–93; management of, 295–96; energy requirements of, 300, 301; copper production by, 304; foreign exchange of, 382, 384; mentioned, 369

Gécamines, *Rapport annuel* (1974), 428; (1980), 428, 455

Geertz, Clifford: *Negara: The Theatre State in Nineteenth-Century Bali* (Princeton University Press, 1980), 467

Gemena, 174

Gendebien, Paul-Henri: *L'intervention des Nations Unies au Congo, 1964–1965* (Mouton, 1967), 462

General Motors: vehicle assembly plants, 305

Gérard-Libois, Jules: *Katanga Secession* (University of Wisconsin Press, 1966), 433, 452; "L'affaire de l'UMHK," *Etudes Congolaises*, 10, 2 (1967), 453

Gérard-Libois, Jules, and Benoit Verhaegen: *Congo 1960* (Centre de Recherche et d'Information Socio-Politiques, 1969), 433

Gerassi, John (American military mission head), 303

Germany: economic involvement in Zaire, 375

Gerth, H. C., and C. Wright Mills (eds.): *From Max Weber* (Oxford University Press, 1958), 410, 411

GDP (Gross domestic product). See Economics

Ghana: state decay, 44–45

Giddens, Anthony: *A Contemporary Critique of Historical Materialism*, vol. 1, *Power, Property and the State* (University of California Press, 1981), 413

Gifford, Prosser, and William Roger Louis (eds.): *The Transfer of Power in Africa* (Yale University Press, 1982), 413

Giscard d'Estaing, François, 375

Giscard d'Estaing, Philippe, 375

Giscard d'Estaing, Valéry (president of France), 374, 375

Godley, McMurtrie (U.S. Ambassador to Zaire), 53, 418n12

Gold, David A., Clarence Y. H. Lo, and Erik Olin Wright: "Recent Developments in Marxist Theories of the Capitalist State," *Monthly Review*, 17 (1975), 410

Goodyear tire plant, 305

Gould, David J.: *Bureaucratic Corruption and Underdevelopment in the Third World: The Case of Zaire* (Pergamon Press, 1980), 424, 427, 467; "From Development Administration to Underdevelopment Administration," *Cahiers du CEDAF*, 6 (1978), 430; in Guy Gran (ed.), *Zaire: The Political Economy of Underdevelopment*, (Praeger, 1979), 447; "Underdevelopment Administration and

Disorganization Theory: Systemic Corruption in the Public Bureaucracy of Mobutu's Zaire," (paper, 1978), 447, 459, 460, 461

Gramsci: civil society, 412 *n44*

Gran, Guy: "Zaire 1978: The Ethical and Intellectual Bankruptcy of the World System" *Africa Today* 25, no. 4 (1978), 465, 467

Goma colloquium, 197

Graft, 124, 183. *See also* Corruption

Grain: production, 321

Graubard, Stephen R.: Preface to the Special Issue on "The State," *Daedalus* 108, no. 4 (1979), 410

Greenberg, Joseph: *The Languages of Africa* (Indiana University Press, 1966), 434

Greenberg, Stanley B.: *Race and State in Capitalist Development* (Yale University Press, 1980), 412

Guebels, C.: *Relation complète des travaux de la Commission Permanente pour la protection des indigènes* (Centre d'Etudes des Problems Sociaux Indigènes, 1953), 428

Guery, André: "Kasa-Vuba, Président de l'Abako," *Remarques Africaines*, 334 (20 April 1969), 420

Guevara, Ernesto "Che," 57

Guinea: Mobutu's state visit to, 368

Guinea-Bissau, 26

Gutkind, Peter C.: "The Energy of Despair: Social Organization of the Unemployed in Two African Cities: Lagos and Nairobi" *Civilisations* 17, nos. 3, 4 (1967), 431; and Immanuel Wallerstein (ed.): *The Political Economy of Contemporary Africa* (Sage Publications, 1976), 467

Habermas, Jurgen: *The Legitimation Crisis* (Beacon Press, 1973), 411, 412

Habyalimana (President of Rwanda), 369

Hammarskjold, Dag, 364

Harmel, Pierre (Belgian Foreign Minister), 373

Health Services: through churches, 67; in urban areas, 82; in rural areas, 91; Gécamines, 158–59

Hegel, G. W. F.: sovereignty theory, 8–9

Hegemony: concepts of, 13, 16; and new

African states, 29; administrative role, 69

Heinz, G., and H. Donnay: *Patrice Lumumba: ses 50 derniers jours* C.R.I.S.P., (1966), 439

Hinton, Deane (U.S. Ambassador to Zaire), 372–73

Hinsley, F. H.: *Sovereignty* (C. A. Watts, 1966), 411

Histoire du Mouvement Populaire de la Révolution (Institut Makanda Kabobi, 1975), 440, 441

Hoare, Mike: *Congo Mercenary* (Hale, 1967), 449

Hobbes, Thomas, 8

Hoboken: copper refineries in, 304

Hoover, J. Edgar, 20

Hoover, J. Jeffery: "Ant ni Antw: Ruund Chiefs and People," (paper, 1977), 423; "The Seduction of Rwej: Reconstructing Lunda History (The Nuclear Lunda; Zaire, Angola, Zambia)" (Ph.D. diss., Yale University, 1978), 433

Hoskyns, Cathryn: *The Congo Since Independence* (Oxford University Press, 1965), 462

House, Arthur: "The Congolese Security Capacity: Center of the Coalition," (manuscript), 447, 448, 449; *The U.N. in the Congo* (University Press of America, 1978), 462

Housing, 115

Houyoux, Joseph: *Budgets ménagers, nutrition et mode de vie à Kinshasa* (Presses Universitaires du Zaire, 1973), 424, 425, 430, 451

Howard, Michael: "War and the Nation-State," *Daedalus* 108, no. 4, (1979), 411

Hull, Galen S.: "Nationalization of the University in the Republic of Zaire" (Ph.D. diss., Northwestern University, 1974), 420, 421; in Guy Gran, *Zaire, The Political Economy of Underdevelopment*, 465

Humphrey, Hubert (U.S. Vice President), 1968 Zairian visit, 197

Hutchinson, Alan: *China's African Revolution* (Hutchinson, 1975), 463

Huybrechts, A. (et al.): *Du Congo au Zaire 1960–1980* (Centre de Recherche et l'In-

Huybrechts, A. (et al.) (*continued*)
formation Socio-Politiques, 1981), 453,
456, 457, 458
Hyden, Goran: *Beyond Ujamaa in Tanzania*
(University of California Press, 1980),
414

Ideology: state, 16; "developmentalism,"
29; authenticity, 65; radicalization,
65–66; Zairianization, 65–66; deviationism in 1974 constitition, 70;
Mobutism, 70, 168–73, 397; cultural,
148; New Regime, 185–89; CVR, 188;
MPR, 190–91; foundation of Zairian
state, 208–17
Identities: colonial impact, 140–42; language, 140–42; urban, 143; components, 148. *See also* Ethnicity
Ilona Szombati-Fabian and Johannes Fabian: "Art, History, and Society: Popular
Art in Shaba, Zaire," *Studies in the Anthropology of Visual Communication*,
3 (1976), 409
Ilunga Mbuya Kabongo: "Baffling Africa
or the Dying Gasps of a Discourse,"
(paper, 1983), 431, 440; "Ethnicity, Social Class and the State in the Congo,
1960–65: The Case of the Baluba,"
(Ph.D. diss., University of California–
Berkeley, 1973), 433; "Quelques considérations sur l'Université Nationale
du Zaire et la dynamique politique
Zairoise," (paper, 1978), 420
Imports: import-export duties, 95; 1961
and later, 115–16; Mercedes-Benz, 118,
350; food, 300
Independence: preparation conference with
Belgium, 176
Indonesia: commercial conditions in,
115–16
Inflation: 1973–80, 71–72; 1961, 115;
1967 and 1973, 132; 1973, 345
Inforcongo (Belgian propaganda agency),
175
Inga dam: electric power, 296–97; genera-
tion, 298–300
Inga-Shaba transmission lines, 300–301
International Bank for Reconstruction and

Development: *Zaire: Current Economic
Situation and Constraints* (1980), 424,
456, 458, 465; "The Economy of Zaire,"
(1975), 426, 456
Institut de Recherches Economiques et Sociales: *Indépendance, inflation, développement* (Mouton, 1968), 429, 451
Institut Makanda Kabobi: Mobutu lecture
at, 216
International Monetary Fund (IMF): 1975
stabilization, 357; 1975 debt crisis, 379;
Zairian agreement, 380–81; 1977 and
1978, 383; mid-1981 loan, 384; 1983
agreement, 384–85; debt agreement for
repayment, 385–86; mentioned, 75,
132, 391, 392
International relations, 403
Investment: foreign capital in minerals,
297, 298, 299–300, 300–306; manu-
facturing, 304; agriculture, 310
Iron: deposits, 297, 298
Isaacs, Howard R.: *Idols of the Tribe*
(Harper & Row, 1975), 412, 432
Islam: mentioned, 14, 26
Issawi, Charles: *An Economic History of the
Middle East and North Africa* (Columbia
University Press, 1982), 467
Israel: Mobutu's break with, in diplomatic
relations, 138, 369

Jackson, Robert M., and Carl G. Rosberg:
Personal Rule in Black Africa (University
of California Press, 1982), 414; "Why
Africa's Weak States Persist: The Empirical and Juridical in Statehood," *World
Politics* 35, no. 1 (1982), 416
Japan: involvement in copper concessions,
301–2
Jessop, Bob: *The Capitalist State: Marxist
Theories and Methods* (New York University Press, 1982), 410; "Recent Theories
of the Capitalist State" *Journal of Economics* 1, no. 1 (1977), 410, 411
Jeune Afrique, (7 May 1980), 418, 419;
(12 September 1975), 450; (1 December
1970), 454, 455; (25 November 1972),
463
Jeunesse du Mouvement Populaire de la

Révolution (JMPR). *See* Political Movements and Parties

Jewsiewicki, Bogumil: "La contestation sociale et la naissance du prolétariat au Zaire au cours de la première moitié du XX siècle," *Canadian Journal of African Studies* 10, no. 1 (1976), 431; "Quelques reflexions préalable à une analyse historique des pratiques et de l'idéologie de l'ethnicité au Zaire" (paper, 1983), 436

Joye, Pierre and Rosina Lewin: *Les Trusts au Congo* (Société Populaire d'Editions, 1961), 452, 453

Kabala, Kabunda, M. K. K.: "Unilever in Zaire," in Carl Widstrand (ed.), *Multi-National Firms in Africa* (Uppsala: Scandinavian Institute of African Studies, 1975), 457

Kabanga, Monseigneur: "Je suis un homme," (Archeveché de Lubumbashi, 1976), 442, 448, 467

Kabesela Mpinga: (thesis in draft form, Université Nationale du Zaire), 432

Kabwit, Ghislain: "The Evolution of the Congo Foreign Policy from 1960–1970: A Case Study on Determinants Influencing the Making of Foreign Policy," (Ph.D. diss., American University, 1975), 462

Kabuya Kalala, and Kikassa Mwanalessa: *Stabilisation économique et financière au Zaire* (Centre d'Etudes pour l'Action Sociale, 1980), 458

Kaiser Aluminum: smelter, 299

Kajika Lupundu Jérôme: "Les manifestations de la solidarité dans une ville négro-africaine (Lubumbashi: République du Zaire)" (Doctoral diss., Université de Paris-V, 1972), 423, 434, 435

Kalb, Madeline G.: *The Congo Cables* (Macmillan Publishing Co., 1982), 418, 439, 462

Kamanda wa Kamanda (Grégoire), 56, 61–62, 187–88

Kamanyola: division, 170, 268

Kambimbi, Baudouin, 195

Kamitatu (Cléophas), 49, 51, 54, 76, 290, 418 *n13*; *La grande mystification du Congo-Kinshasa* (Maspéro, 1971), 417, 419, 439

Kamitatu Massamba: *Le pouvoir à la portée du peuple* (Maspéro, 1977), 421, 448, 453; "Problématique et rationale dans le processus de nationalisation du cuivre en Afrique Centrale: Zaire (1967) et Zambie (1969)" (Doctoral diss., Institut d'Etudes Politiques de Paris, 1976), 453

Kananga: 1964 constitution, 49, 89, 243

Kande Zamuleta (Jean-Jacques), 54

Kaninda Kasongo: "Contribution à la recherche sur l'économie des transports dans les pays de l'Afrique Noire (exemple du Zaire)," (Doctoral diss., University of Bordeaux, 1973), 457

Kanyinda Lusanga: "Les institutions socio-politiques traditionelles et les institutions politiques modernes au Zaire," (Doctoral diss., Université Catholique de Louvain, 1974), 426, 432, 433

Kannyo, Edward: "Political Power and Class Formation in Zaire: The 'Zairianization Measures,' 1973–1975," (Ph.D. diss., Yale University, 1979), 434, 458, 459

Kanza Nsenga, 116

Kanza, Sophie (Lubio Zala n'Kanza), 193

Kanza, Thomas: *Conflict in the Congo* (Penguin Books, 1972), 462

Kapend, Joseph (father of Moise Tshombe), 114

Kasavubu, Joseph (president of Zaire): Tshombe rivalry, 49–51; end of presidency, 52; U.S. support, 53; death, 62; mentioned, 41, 42, 55, 208

Kasfir, Nelson: *The Shrinking Political Arena* (University of California Press, 1975), 432, 433

Kasongo Nyembo (Shaba Luba chief), 211

Katanga: defacto autonomy, 31; minerals, 33; mutiny, 58, 249; secession, 255, 260–61, 290, 364; lobby in U.S., 364

Katwala Ghifem Jacques: "Bureaucracy, Dependency, and Underdevelopment in Zaire," (Ph.D. diss., University of California–Berkeley, 1979), 467

Katzenellenbogen, S. E.: *Railways and the*

Katzenellenbogen, S. E. (*continued*)
Copper Mines of Katanga (Clarendon
Press, 1973), 415
Kaunda, Kenneth: *Zambia Shall be Free*
(Heinemann, 1962), 437
Kawantu Bualum: "Le café et l'économie
zairoise," *Elima* (1977), 457
Kelson, Hans: *General Theory of Law and
State* (Russell & Russell, 1961), 413
Kettani, General, 268
Keyes, Charles (ed.): *Ethnic Change* (Uni-
versity of Washington Press, 1981), 432
Kibassa-Maliba (MPR youth leader),
195, 196
Kibassa Mwanalessa: "La stabilisation des
enterprises zairianisées et radicalisées,"
Zaire-Afrique, 102 (1976), 461
Kikonge (UNTZA leader), 200, 333
Kilby, Peter: *Industrialization in an Open
Economy: Nigeria 1945–1966* (Cambridge
University Press, 1969), 413
Kilson, Martin: *Political Change in a West
African State* (Harvard University Press,
1969), 435
Kimba, Evariste, 50, 52, 56
Kinshasa: riots in, 40; resource concentra-
tion of, 81–85, 87; growth of, 92, 127;
strikes in, 130–31; centralization of po-
litical power in, 155; Mama Yemo hospi-
tal, 174; Bank of, 179; status of, 231,
418*n16*; Fikin trade fair, 374
Kinship, 160
Kisangani: capture of capital, 49; commer-
cial enterprises, 120–21; mutiny, 250–
51; development, 296
Kissinger, Henry (U.S. Secretary of State),
373
Kithima bin Ramazani: executive secretary,
MPR, 192; education minister Goma
Colloquium, 197–98; Interior Minister,
334; mentioned, 200; "Recueil des directives à l'usage des secrétaires permanents," (ca. 1978), 441; speech
29 January 1973 in Mpinga and Gould,
*Les réformes administratives publique de
Zaire*, 445
Kivu rebellion, 249
Klineberg, Otto, and Marisa Zavalloni: *Na-
tionalism and Tribalism among African
Students* (Mouton, 1969), 442
Klocker-Humbolt-Deutz (German business
consortium), 375
Knoop, H.: "Some Demographic Charac-
teristics of a Suburban Squatting Com-
munity of Leopoldville," *Cahiers Eco-
nomiques et Sociaux*, 2 (1966), 430
Kohn, Hans: "Nationalism," vol. 1, *Inter-
national Encyclopedia of the Social Sciences*
(Macmillan Co. and Free Press, 1968), 411
Kongo dia Ngunda (April 1961), 411
Krasner, Stephen D.: *Defending the National
Interest* (Princeton University Press,
1978), 411
Krupp: palm oil and soap, 305
Kumwimba Kabongo: "Approche sur les
aspects administratifs des mesures écono-
miques de 30 Novembre 1973 (Cas de
Lubumbashi)," (Mémoire de licence,
Université Nationale du Zaire, Lubum-
bashi, 1975), 458, 459, 460, 461
Kwitny, Jonathan: *Wall Street Journal* (23
April 1981), 464

Labor: colonialization, 22–23, 35–36;
UNTZA strikes, 74; aristocracy theory,
129; organizations, 130; uprising and
strikes, 130–31; First Republic, 199;
productivity in mines, 290
Lacroix, Bernadette: "Pouvoir et structures
de l'Université Lovanium" *Cahiers du
CEDAF*, 2/3 (1972), 420
Lacroix, Jean-Louis: *L'industrialisation au
Congo* (Mouton, 1966), 427; "Le role de
l'industrie dans le développement écono-
mique général," *Zaire-Afrique*, 61
(1972), 428, 431, 451; "Inga," *Etudes
Congolaises* 10, no. 1 (1967), 454, 457
La Dépêche (Lubumbashi, 1967), 441
La Fontaine, Joan S.: *City Politics: A Study of
Leopoldville, 1962–1963* (Cambridge Uni-
versity Press, 1970), 423; "The Free
Women of Kinshasa: Prostitution in a
City in Zaire," in J. David (ed.), *Choice
and Change: Essays in Honor of Lucy Mair*
(Athlone Press, 1974), 425
Languages: European retention of in de-

colonization, 27; referring to whites, 31; Swahili, 79–80; Lingala, 79–80, 153; selected and standardized, 140–41; Mongo, 141; standardization of Kikongo, 148; Sudanic group, 152; Bantu, 152; Lumumba fluencies, 154; Mobutu's use of Lingala, 154–55; Second Republic, 155–56

Larkin, Bruce: *China and Africa* (University of California Press, 1971), 463

Latin America: authoritarianism in, 27

La Tribune (10 and 17 October, 1967), 441

L'Avenir (Kinshasa Journal), 175

Laws: 27 April 1962, 146–47; 20 January 1978 (Law 78–001), 232; 12 March 1969 (Law 69–012), 236; 5 January 1973 (Law 73–015), 236, 329, 337, 342; Law 73–250, 237, 238, 342; 11 January 1974 (Law 74–019), 331–32

Lawson Kay, (ed.): *Political Parties and Linkage* (Yale University Press, 1980), 441

Lefebre, Henri: *De l'état*, vol. 1, *L'état dans le monde moderne* (Union Générale des Editions, 1976), 413

Lefever, Ernest: *Crisis in the Congo* (Brookings Institution, 1965), 462

Legal dependency: new African states, 29

Legal system: state role, 14

Legitimacy, state, 16

Legum, Colin (ed.): *Africa Contemporary Record 1974–75* (Rex Collings, 1975), 428; *Africa Contemporary Record 1970–71* (Rex Collings, 1971), 436; "The Soviet Union, China and the West in Southern Africa," *Foreign Affairs* 54, no. 4 (1976), 464

Legvold, Robert: *Soviet Policy in West Africa* (Harvard University Press, 1970), 462

Lemarchand, René (ed.): *American Policy in Southern Africa: The States and the Stance* (University Press of America, 1981), 420; "Patrice Lumumba," in Walter Skurnick (ed.), *African Political Thought: Lumumba, Nkrumah and Touré*, (Denver: Social Service Foundation and Graduate School of International Studies, 1968), 442; "Political Clientelism and Ethnicity

in Tropical Africa: Competing Solidarities in Nation-Building," *American Political Science Review*, 66 (1972), 435; and David Martin: *Selective Genocide in Burundi* (Minority Rights Group, 1974), 448

Le Monde: Zaire series, 172

Lengema, Marcel, 366

LeoGrande, William M.: "Cuban-Soviet Relations and Cuban Policy in Africa," in Carmelo Mesa-Lago and June S. Belheim (eds.), *Cuba in Africa* (Center for Latin American Studies, University of Pittsburgh, 1982), 448

Leopold II (King of Belgium), and Congo Free State, 31–34; mentioned, 6, 22, 287, 363

Le Progrès (11 January 1966), 440

Le Soir (11–12 May 1972), 457; (30 October 1971), 454

"Les relations entre l'Eglise et l'Etat au Zaire," *Etudes Africaines du C.R.I.S.P.*, 145 (28 December 1972), 421

Lever plantations, 330

Leyland Motors: vehicle assembly plant, 305

Leys, Colin: in Arnold J. Heidenheimer (ed.): *Political Corruption* (Holt, Rinehart, and Winston, 1970), 447; *Underdevelopment in Kenya* (University of California Press, 1975), 467

Liberalization: effects of on rural and urban society, 232

Liboke lya Bangala: ethnic movement, 150, 153

Libre Belgique (Belgian Catholic daily), 68

Libya: Mobutu state visit to, 369

Lindberg, Leon, N.: *Stress and Contradiction in Modern Capitalism: Public Policy and the Theory of the State* (Lexington Books, 1975), 410

Likulia Bolongo (FAZ auditor-general), 274

Lingalaphone group, 398

Linz, Juan L.: "Totalitarian and Authoritarian Regimes," in Fred I. Greenstein and Nelson Polsby (eds.), *Handbook of Political Science* (Addison-Wesley Co., 1975), 413, 440

Lissanga Egala: "L'impact du Mouvement Populaire de la Révolution sur l'administration publique zairoise," (Mémoire du licence, Université Nationale du Zaire, Lubumbashi, 1975), 441

Litho Maboti: holdings, 181–82, 342–43; CVR activity, 188; mentioned, 52, 167, 206

Litigation: African treaty rights, 25

Livre Blanc: Apport Scientifique de la Belgique au développement de l'Afrique Centrale (Académie Royale des Sciences d'Outrement, 1962), 428

Loka ne Kongo: "La pensée politique de Kasa-Vubu," (Mémoire de licence, Université Nationale du Zaire, Lubumbashi, 1974), 442

Lomami-Tshibamba, Paul, 38

Lomponda, Admiral (chief of presidency military staff), 274

"London Club," 75, 382

Longregg, Stephen: *A Short History of Eritrea* (Greenwood Publishers, 1954), 413

Lonrho: African investments, 292; copper investment strategy, 302

Lonsdale, John: "States and Social Processes in Africa: A Historiographical Survey," *African Studies Review* 24, nos. 2, 3 (1981), 413

Lovanium University: state assumption of, 67–68; refuses admission to Lumumba, 112; student demonstrations, 198; mentioned, 62

Lovens, Maurice: *Congo 1966* (Centre de Recherche et d'Information Socio-Politiques, 1967), 418

Lowi, Theodore J.: *The End of Liberalism* (W. W. Norton, 1969), 410

Luba-Kasai: movement to Mbuji-Mayi, 80; ethnicity, 142–44; university quotas, 155

Lubumbashi: administrative services, 80; traders, 114; 1940 labor uprising, 130; ethnic groups, 150; mentioned, 80, 260

Lukombe Nghenda: *Zairianisation, radicalisation, retrocession en République du Zaire* (Presses Universitaires du Zaire, 1979), 459

Lukusa, Théophile: "Situation économique et financière du Congo en 1965 et en 1966," *Etudes Congolaises* 10, no. 3 (1967), 451

Lulua Frères: ethnic group, 143; in elections, 144; loss of influence, 150

Lumumba, Patrice: symbols used by Mobutu, 53, 150–51; class and education, 112; ethnic support, 145; New Regime, 150–51; languages used, 154; relationship with Mobutu, 169, 176–78; assassination, 172; 1960 army mutiny, 177; mentioned, 41, 50–51, 61, 183, 208, 366

Lunda, 390

Lundula, Victor (army commander-in-chief), 177, 261

Lutula, Eugene (member of Political Bureau), 203

Lux, A.: study of forestry workforce, 130; personal communication, 431

Mabika, Kalanda: tribute to Placide Temples, 213; *La remise en question* (Editions "Remarques Africaines," 1967), 440, 443

MacGaffey, Janet: "Class Relations in a Dependent Economy: Businessmen and Businesswomen in Kisangani, Zaire," (paper, 1981), 428

Machiavelli, Nicolo: mentioned, 8

MacIver, R. M.: *The Modern State* (Oxford University Press, 1964), 410

Maeda, Justin H. J.: "Popular Participation, Control and Development: A Study of the Nature and Role of Popular Participation in Tanzania's Rural Development," (Ph.D. diss., Yale University, 1976), 446

Magotta, J.: *Les circonscriptions indigènes* (Imprimerie Louvièroise, 1952), 445

Mahamba, Alexandre (Minister of Mines and Energy), 56

Maize: policy, 312

Mali-Kidogo Chakali Muranga: "Politique agricole et service de l'agriculture au

Shaba," (Mémoire de licence, Université Nationale du Zaire, Lubumbashi, 1974), 456

Malloy, James M. (ed.): *Authoritarianism and Corporatism in Latin America* (University of Pittsburgh Press, 1977), 413

Maluku Steel Mill, 296–98, 305

Malula, Cardinal, 67, 68

Manwana Mungonga: *La Général Mobutu Sese Seko parle du Nationalisme Zairois Authentique* (Editions Okapi, 1972), 443

Manufacturing: under colonial rule, 304–5; for domestic market, 305

Manwana, Oscar: "Le rôle des syndicats du Zaire," *Zaire-Afrique*, 65 (1972), 441

Manzikala (governor of Katanga), 255

Maonyesho Lulela W'Etunda: "La rébellion de 1964 dans le Territoire de Fizi," (Mémoire de licence, Université Nationale du Zaire, Lubumbashi, 1974), 447

Marcum, John: *The Angolan Revolution* (MIT Press, 1969, 1979), 464; "Lessons of Angola," *Foreign Affairs* 54, no. 3 (1976), 464

Marlière, 175

Marx, Karl: ruling class theory, 16, 44; "The German Ideology," in Robert C. Tucker (ed.) *The Marx-Engels Reader* (W. W. Norton, 1972), 411; mentioned, 9, 10

Marxism: classic theory on petty bourgeoisie, 122–23

Marxism-Leninism: in African states, 28; social classes, 102–3

Marxists: political theories, 10; state theory, 11; MPLA, 367

Mason, Philip: *A Matter of Honour* (Holt, Rinehart, and Winston, 1974), 413

Massiala Kinkela (senior army officer, 1972–75), 154, 264, 449n32

Masson, Paul: *Dix ans de malheurs au Kivu* (Max Arnold, 1970), 452

Matadi: 1945 dockworkers uprising, 130

Mayo-Mokelo Justin: "Instabilité dans les institutions communales de la ville de Kisangani (ex-Stanleyville), 1958–

1968," (Mémoire de licence, Université Libre du Congo, 1971), 445

Meillassoux, Claude: "A Class Analysis of the Bureaucratic Process in Mali," *Journal of Development Studies* 6, no. 2 (1970), 428; *Anthropologie économique des Gouro de Côte d'Ivoire* (Mouton, 1964), 435

Mercedes-Benz, 118, 133, 350

Mercenary-led revolts: in 1967, 251–53

Merchants: subsistence, 114. *See also* Class

Merlier, Michel: *Le Congo de la colonisation belge à l'indépendance* (Maspero, 1962), 428

Mesa-Lago, Carmelo, and June S. Belkin (eds.): *Cuba in Africa* (University of Pittsburgh, 1982), 464

MIBA (Minière de Bakwanga): managers, 107, 108; 1974 state control, 288; mentioned, 122. *See also* Diamonds

Micombero (President of Burundi), 369

Miliband, Ralph: *The State in Capitalist Society* (Camelot Press, 1969), 410

Military: intervention, 53, 136; officer class and purges, 121, 265–66; wages, 125–26; disaffection, 126; troops in Leopoldian state, 260; role in New Regime, 262–67; commanders-in-chief, 264–65; infrastructure, 266; diversification, 268–70; suppliers, 375; mentioned, 52. *See also* Army; FAZ

Minerals: Katanga, 33; rights in Shaba and Maniema, 34; tin production, 34; Bakajika Law, 209, 288, 297, 367; nationalization, 288–89; development, 296–97; mentioned, 59. *See also* Diamonds; Copper; Cobalt

Minière de Bakwanga (interviews, 1967), 426. *See also* MIBA

Mining: operation, 285

Miso Gaa (8 August 1975), 439

Mission civilisatrice, 26, 31, 37, 415n86

Mission schools, 121

Mitchell, J. Clyde: *The Kalela Dance* (University of Manchester Press, 1967), 434

Mitterand, François (President of France), 390

M'Kola Kalubi: "Les relations franco-

M'Kola Kalubi (*continued*)
zairoises de 1969 à 1978," *Afrique et l'Asie Modernes*, 122 (1979), 464
MNC (Mouvement Nationale Congolaise), 40
MNC/L (Mouvement Nationale Congolaise, Lumumba wing), 217, 234, 235
Mobility: class, 144; social, 133–35
Mobutu, Marie-Antoinette (wife of Mobutu Sese Seko), 360
Mobutu Sese Seko (Joseph Désire): 1965 coup, 7, 51–53, 186–87; presidency, 20–21, 59; first years of reign, 30; speeches, 42, 64, 73–74, 125, 189, 216, 328–29, 335, 336–37, 350, 355, 368, 369, 372; First Republic, 42–43; political strategy, 53, 61; power consolidation, 54–60; cabinet changes, 61; institutionalization of party, 62–63; Catholic Church, 66–68; powers in 1974 constitution, 69–71; travels abroad, 72, 175, 350–51, 368–70; involvement in Shaba mining invasions, 73–74; MPR party congress, 74; 1977–1980 reforms, 76; biographical information, 79, 152–54, 172–78; rural policies, 98–99; Mercedes-Benz imports, 118; 1973–1982 break with Israel, 138; ethnic strategy with New Regime, 149–52; patrimonial presidency, 165–68; direct contact with people, 170–71; policy formations, 171–72; personal wealth, 177–82, 343, 440*n*29; dualism, 190–91; youth and student movements, 196–99; election candidate, 202–4; "democratization" of 1979 electoral process, 204–6; end to democratization, 207; state funds diversion, 207; "Mobutu pragmatism," 216–17; nationalism, 220; policy towards chiefs, 232–40; and military, 248–49, 260, 261–62, 264, 265; and security police, 272; involvement in mineral development, 291, 299–300; attack in *Times of Zambia*, 302; personal rule, 329, 361, 397; "idea of commerce," 330; and Zairianization, 336–37, 343, 355; foreign and African diplomacy, 367–71; as Third World leader, 370–71;

attacks upon U.S., 372–73; Angola civil war strategy, 376–78; Recovery Plan, 383–86; and rise of state, 391, 396–99; "chaos" thesis, 395; opposition to, 404–5; mentioned, 6, 17; (speech, quoted in *Le Monde*, 28 July 1981), 416; *Mobutu: Discourses, allocutions, et messages 1965–1975* (Editions J.A., 1975), 416, 418, 421, 422, 443, 453, 464; (speech, 25 November 1977), 416, 449; *Les paroles du Président* (Editions du Léopard, 1969), 445; (speech, *Etudes Zairoises*), 2 (1973), 432; "Discours du Citoyen Mobutu Sese Seko, President-Fondateur du Mouvement Populaire de la Révolution, Président de la République, prononcé le 1ᵉʳ juillet 1977 à N'Sele après les événements du Sub-ouest Shaba," (mimeographed) 447; "Discourses du Président de la République du Zaire devant le Council Législatif, le 4 janvier 1975," (mimeographed, 1975), 447; 4 February 1975, typescript, 461; (speech 1977), 465
Mobutism: ethnoregional politics, 154; as cult, 170–71; approval of, 215; as presidential doctrine, 215–16; retreat from, 217; nationalism, 220; as national ideology, 397; mentioned, 43, 208, 216
Moju'ongway Untuube (Joseph Nsinga), 51
Molongya Mayikusa (general): "Le militaire et la révolution (mimeographed, 1975), 449; mentioned, 263
Mondja-Nganda: village regrouping, 240–41
Monganga Pili: "Esprit d'intégration nationale chez les étudiants du Campus de Lubumbashi," (Mémoire de licence, Université Nationale du Zaire, 1974), 434
Mongo: concept of Mongohood, 141–42; political activity, 145
Monguya Mebenge (Daniel): *Histoire secrète du Zaire* (Editions de l'Espérance, 1977), 418, 420, 438, 439, 449
Monheim, Francis: *Mobutu l'homme seul* (Editions Actuelles, 1963), 437, 438, 439

Monnier, Laurent: *Ethnie et intégration regional au Congo* (Editions Classiques d'Expression Française, 1970), 433
Moral Rearmament, 167
Moroccan army: in Shaba, 258
Mozambique, 26
Mpinga Kasenda (prime minister, 1977–79), 150; "La coexistence des pouvoirs 'traditionnel' et 'moderne' dans la ville de Kinshasa," *Cahiers Economiques et Sociaux*, 2 (1969), 430; *L'administration publique du Zaire* (A. Pedone, 1973), 444, 445; "Le Mobutisme," *Remarques Africaines*, 451 (1975), 443; and David J. Gould, "Les reformes administratives au Zaire (1972–1973)," 421, 444; speech, reproduced in *Remarques Africaines*, 454 (1975), 417, 421
MPLA (Movimento Popular de Libertação de Angola), 376, 377
MPR (Mouvement Populaire de la Révolution (MPR). *See* Political movements and parties
Mukamba, Jones (governor of Equateur): MPR party rivalry, 191–92
Mukenge Tshilemalema: "Businessmen of Zaire: Limited Possibilities for Capital Accumulation under Dependence," (Doctoral diss., McGill University, 1972), 427, 459
Mulamba Nyunyi wa Kadima (Leonard), 53–54, 55–56, 57, 150, 262
Mulambu Muvulya: "Le régime des cultures obligatoires et le radicalisme rural au Zaire (1917–1960)," (Université Libre de Bruxelles, 1974), 414
Mulele, Pierre, 427*n10*; uprising (1963–64), 103–4
Multinational corporations: political-commercial class, 119; payments, 136; mentioned, 29, 110
Mulumba Lukoji: "Le premier Congrès ordinaire du Mouvement Populaire de la Révolution," *Zaire-Afrique* 67 (1972), 443; "La 'MIBA': Société Minière de Bakwanga," *Zaire-Afrique* 88 (1974), 452; "Le code des investissements zairois," *Zaire-Afrique* 35 (1974),

453; "La Générale des Carrières et des Mines du Zaire," *Zaire-Afrique* 81 (1974), 453; "La SODIMIZA: un consortium international minier," *Zaire-Afrique* 70 (1972), 454; "La commercialisation des minerals de la Gécamines," *Zaire-Afrique* 94 (1975), 455; "Les Lois de 5 janvier 1973 sur le commerce et les petites et moyennes enterprises zairoises," *Zaire-Afrique* 74 (1973), 459; "Le programme de redressement de l'économie zairoise (suit)," *Zaire-Afrique* 114 (1977), 461, 465
Mungul-Diaka (Bernardin), 54, 58, 61
Muslims, 66
Muteba Kazadi: "L'argent public zairois et la question du tribalisme actuel," (Mémoire de licence, Université Nationale du Zaire, Lubumbashi, 1974), 435
Mwabila Malela: "Prolétariat et conscience de classe au Zaire," (Doctoral diss., Université Libre de Bruxelles, 1973), 431, 441; "Pour une relecture de la sociologie à la lumière de la théorie de la dépendance," in V. Y. Mudimbe (ed.), *La dépendance de l'Afrique et les moyens d'y rémedier*, 436

Names: elimination of Christian, 68
Nande: vegetable marketing in, 121
Nation: definition of, 13, 28
Nation-state: concept of, 7; Zairian concerns, 39; New Regime, 149; social framework, 162
National bourgeoisie, 110
National economic model. *See* Zairianization
Nationalism: rise of African, 26–27, 39, 208–9; Zaire in New Regime, 367–68
National Legislative Council, 204, 206
National School of Administration, 229
Navy, 270. *See also* Military
Ndele, A., 60–61
Ndolonga, E.: "Mutations structurelles de l'économie traditionelle dans le Bas-Congo sous l'impact de la colonisation et de la decolonisation," *Cahiers Economiques et Sociaux* 4, no. 1 (1966), 425

Négritude, 210

Nendaka Bika (Victor), 49, 51, 54, 58, 60, 61, 206, 272

Netherlands: welfare state, 10

Neto Agostino (MPLA leader), 253

Nettl, J. P.: "The State as a Conceptual Variable," *World Politics* 20, no. 4 (1968), 410

Newbury, Catharine: "Ebutumwa Bw'emiogo: The Tyranny of Cassava—A Women's Tax Revolt in Eastern Zaire," (paper, 1983), 424

Newbury, David and Catharine (personal communications), 446

New York Times, The: (11 July 1978), 423; (4 February 1979), 424; (6 December 1981), 438; (30 January 1976), 448; (18 March 1978), 450; (4 January 1976), 463; (27 December 1981), 466; (11 July 1978), 466

New Regime: establishment, 60–63; social networks, 159; territorial administration, 224–29; military roles, 262–67; economic stabilization, 278–81; inflation, 278; economic reform measures, 279; currency devaluation, 279; foreign trade taxes, 279–80; failure of economic benefits, 280; MIBA, 288; consolidation of political power, 365; nationalism, 367–72; diplomacy, 367; regional diplomacy, 368–71, 396; mentioned, 43, 209

Ngbandi: original boundaries, 152–53; Ngbandihood, 153–54

Ngoie, J.: "Situation salariale au République Démocratique du Congo (1966–1970)," *Cahiers Economiques et Sociaux* 8, no. 2 (1970), 441

Ngouabi, M. (president of Congo-Brazzaville), 369

Ngoyi Makita (et al.): "Les étudiants et les élèves de Kisangani (1974–1975): Aspirations, opinions et conditions de vie," *Cahiers du CEDAF* nos. 7–8 (1977), 430

Nguza, Karl-i-Bond: treason trial, 74; foreign minister, 166–67; prime minister, 181; *Mobutu ou l'incarnation du mal zairois* (Rex Collings, 1982), 422–36; testimony, U.S. House of Representatives, House Committee on Foreign Affairs, Subcommittee on Africa, *Political and Economic Situation in Zaire—Fall 1981*, 15 September 1981, 97th Congress, 1st sess., 450; quoted in *Remarques Africaines* 177, (January 1976), 436

Nigeria, 327

Nippon Mining Company: interest in UMHK, 292, 301–2

Nixon, Richard (U.S. President), 64, 270, 368

N'Kanza, Dolumingu: (president UGEC), 187–88; arrest, 197

N'Kanza, Lusibu Zala (Sophie Kanza), member Political Bureau, 193; "The Social Origins of Political Underdevelopment in the ex-Belgian Congo (Zaire)," (Ph.D. diss., Harvard University, 1976), 414, 433

Nkrumah, Kwame: *Challenge of the Congo* (International Publishers, 1967), 462

Nonalignment, 370

Nordlinger, Eric A.: *On the Autonomy of the Democratic State* (Harvard University Press, 1981), 411

N'Sele Manifesto (May 1967), 190–91, 198, 199–200, 209–10, 370; text reprinted in *Etudes Congolaises* 10, no. 3 (1967), 420

N'Sengi Biembe (Gaston): editor of *Actualités Africaines*, 187; president of CVR, 190

Nsinga, Joseph. *See* Moju'ongway Utuube

Nyerere, Julius (President of Tanzania), 369, 390

Nye, Joseph: in Arnold J. Heidenheimer (ed.): *Political Corruption* (Holt, Rinehart, and Winston, 1970), 447

Nzondomyo Longo (Political Bureau member), 354

Nzongola, Georges N. "The Bourgeoisie and Revolution in the Congo," *Journal of Modern African Studies* 8, no. 4 (1970), 427, 431

Nzongola Ntalaja: "The Continuing Struggle for National Liberation in Zaire," *Journal of Modern African Studies* 17, no. 4 (1979), 440, 443; "Urban Administration in Zaire; A Study of Kananga, 1971–1973," (Ph.D. diss., University of Wisconsin-Madison, 1975), 423, 425, 433, 444, 445, 446, 447

OAU (Organization of African Unity): first summit conference, 27; Chad, 46; Accra summit, 50, 366; Kinshasa summit, 59–60, 367; 1966 summit, 367; peacekeeping force in Chad, 390
Oberschall, Anthony: "On the Political Economy of Zaire," (paper, 1981), 431
Obote, A. M., 368
OCAM (Organisation Commune Africaine et Malgache), 374
O'Conner, James: *The Fiscal Crisis of the State* (St. Martin's Press, 1973), 410, 412
Occult revenue, 123–24, 126
Odier, Jeannick: "La politique étrangère de Mobutu," *Revue Française d'Etudes Politiques Africaines*, 120 (1975), 463
O'Donnell, Guillermo in David Collier (ed.): *The New Authoritarianism in Africa* (Princeton University Press, 1979), 413
Offe, Claus: "Political Authority and Class Structure: An Analysis of Late Capitalist Societies," *International Journal of Society* 2, no. 1 (1972), 410
Oil: price increases, 71; imports, 83–84; nationalization of, 172; production and exploration of, 305–6; costs, 307
Olenga, Nicolas (leader of Kisangani rebellion), 366
Omba, Colonel (head of security police), 273
Ombala Osombo W'ombala: "Le regroupement de villages dans la Zone de Lodja: avantages politiques, socio-économiques et difficultés de realisation," (Mémoire de licence, Université Nationale du Zaire, 1975), 446
ONACER (Office National des Cereales), 321
ONAFITEX (Office National des Fibres Textiles), 316, 320–21
ONC (Office National du Café), 316, 321
Onotamba, P.: "La collectivité Ngandu-Wuma face à la réforme administrative du 5 janvier 1973," (Mémoire de licence,

Université Nationale du Zaire, Lubumbashi, 1975), 445
Ossowski, Stanislaw: *Class Structure in the Social Consciousness* (Free Press of Glencoe, 1963), 427
OTRAG (Orbital Transport and Raketen A. G.): rocket base, 387–88
Overseas Liaison Committee: *Survey of Education in the Democratic Republic of the Congo* (American Council on Education, 1969), 425

Pachter, Elise Forbes: "The Economic Component of U.S.–Zaire Relations" (paper, 1982), 456
Palm oil: Kwilu, 92–95; Krupp investment in, 305; policy and prices, 314–15; exports, 315
"Paris Club," 75, 381
Parkin, Frank: *Class Inequality and Political Order* (NLB, 1975), 430
Parliament: loss of power, 55–56; 23 March 1967 dissolution, 189
Parsons, Talcott: "Some Reflections on the Place of Force in Social Process," in Harry Eckstein (ed.), *Internal War* (Free Press of Glencoe, 1964), 411
Parti Solidaire Africain (P.S.A.): (Centre de Recherche et d'Information Socio-Politiques, 1963), 433
Patrimonialization: in Zaire, 28, 30, 60, 165–68, 337; Max Weber's theory of, 165; presidency, 167–68; investments, 182; institutionalization of, 183; Political Bureau, 193; state, 274; of power, 328
Patron-Client: networks, 157–59; kinship relationships, 160
Patronage, 116, 149–50
Peace, Adrian: "Prestige, Power and Legitimacy in a Modern Nigerian Town," *Canadian Journal of African Studies* 13, no. 2 (1979), 430, 435
Peemans, J. P.: "Le rôle de l'état dans la formation du capital au Congo pendant le période coloniale (1885–1960)," *Etudes et Documents* (Université de Louvain, 1973), 415; "The Social and Economic Development of Zaire since Indepen-

Peemans, J. P. (*continued*)
dence: A Historical Outline," *African Affairs* 74, no. 295 (1975), 424, 428, 429
Pentecost Plot: to overthrow Mobutu regime, 56–57; mentioned, 166
Perlmutter, Amos: *Modern Authoritarianism* (Yale University Press, 1981), 413
Petroleum: price rises, 71, 304, 307; consumption, 83–84; exploration, 305
Petrozaire, 436n10
PGD (Parti Démocratique de Guinée), 217
Piron, Pierre, and Jacques Devos: *Code et Lois de Congo Belge* (Maison Ferdinand Larcier, 1960), 415; (et al.) *Supplément au Code Congolais: Législation de la République Démocratique du Congo* (Maison Ferdinand Larcier, 1970), 460
Pike, Frederick B., and Howard Wiarda (eds.): *The New Corporatism: Social-Political Structures in the Iberian World* (University of Notre Dame Press, 1974), 412
Plantations: CELZA, 179; system and decline, 315–16; Lever, 330; sector, 343, 347–48
PNP (Parti National du Progrès), 145, 149, 186
Poggi, Gianfranco: *The Development of the Modern State* (Stanford University Press, 1978), 411
"Poids socio-politiques des ressortissants de l'Equateur à Kinshasa," *Courrier African du C.R.I.S.P., T.A.*, 84 (1968), 439
Police: during Belgian regional administration, 270; during First Republic, 271; civil administration, 271; powers and civilian government, 271–72
Political Bureau: formation of, 190; members and benefits, 192–93; youth groups, 196; 1970 election candidate selection, 202–3; election, 205–6
Political cadres, 354
Political commercial class. *See* Class
Political movements and parties: Conscience Africaine group, 40; Mouvement National Congolaise (MNC), 40; Alliance des Bakongo (ABAKO), 40, 143, 153, 234, 235; federalism, 40–41; pluralism,

41; Mouvement Populaire de la Révolution (MPR), 43, 54; Convention Nationale Congolaise (CONACO), 49; diplomacy by Mobutu, 55, 149; Union Générale des Etudiante Congolais (UGEC), 56, 187, 197; Fizi-Baraka, 57; Jeunesse du Mouvement Populaire de la Révolution (JMPR), 62; in Catholic seminaries, 68; control through military units, 69; 1974 Constitution and, 70, 192; Front pour la Libération Nationale du Congo, 75, 235, 256, 257; 1977 elections and Campaign, 118–19; candidate pools, 142–43; Parti National du Progrès (PNP), 145, 149, 186; youth organization and strategy, 157; membership in, 165–66; Corps des Volentaires de la République (CVR), 186–88, 189, 190, 194, 199; formation of, 186–89; single-party politics, 189–93; and Mobutu, 190–91; in provinces, 191–92; first extraordinary congress, 192; legitimacy of, 195–99, 217–19; candidate selection, 202; Mouvement Nationale Congolaise, Lumumba wing, (MNC/L), 217, 234, 235; party mission, 217; party models in China and North Korea, 218; function of, 219; political retreat, 219; ideology, 219–20; Parti Solidaire Africain (PSA), 235; Popular Revolutionary Party (PPR), 250; brigade disciplinaire, 272
Political networks, 175–76
Pons, Valdo: *Stanleyville* (Oxford University Press, 1969), 423
Popelier, G. H.: "Nature et évolution de l'agriculture zairoise," *Cahiers du CEDAF* 6 (1977), 456, 457
Portugal, 255; coup, 253, 376; relations with Zaire, 366–67
Poulantzas, Nicos: *State, Power, Socialism* (NLB, 1978), 410
Power: personalization of, 168–72. *See also* Mobutism
PRP (Popular Revolutionary Party), 250
Prain, Sir Ronald: *Copper: The Anatomy of an Industry* (Mining Journal Books, 1975), 453, 454, 456
Presidency: power under Mobutu, 55;

powers in 1974 constitution, 70–71; cost of patrimonialism, 168. *See also* Mobutism

Price ceilings: agriculture, 312

Price, Robert M.: *Society and Bureaucracy in Contemporary Ghana* (University of California Press, 1975), 435

Prisons, 97–98

Private sector. *See* Economics

Promontorio, Victor, 79

Provinces: reorganization, 55; divisions, 81

PSA (Parti Solidaire Africain), 235

Public Services: state, 14

Quota system: in university admission, 155

Radicalization: 1975, 117; educational policies, 118; ten point program, 351–53; economic dimensions of, 353–56; targets of, 354; definition of small enterprise, 355–56; shift in focus, 355; definition of foreign-owned enterprises, 356; "delegates-general," 356; social impacts, 359–60; effectiveness, 359, 362; evaluation, 361–62; Belgium interests, 374; mentioned, 65, 66

Railways. *See* Transportation

Rake, Alan: "Zaire Economic Survey," *African Development* (1972), 454

Raymaekers, Paul: *L'organisation des zones de squatting* (Editions Universitaires, 1964), 430, 431

Rebellions: Haute-Zaire, 259. *See also* Shaba I rebellion

Regier, Fremont A.: "Ownership, Participation in Planning, Administration and Operation of a Rural Development Project, Nyanda Zaire," (Ph.D. diss., University of Wisconsin-Madison, 1977), 426

Regime d'exception, 54

Regional administration: colonial, 221; failure of reform, 242–45; corruption, 246–47; mentioned, 402

Reich, C.: "Why the IMF Shuns a 'Super' Role," *Institutional Investor* (September 1977), 465

Renault vehicle assembly plant, 305

Resource development: Africa, 25–26; Congo wild rubber, 33. *See also* Diamonds, Copper, Minerals

Retrocession, 357–59

Revenue: state, 16–17. *See also* Economics, State

Reynolds Aluminum, 299

Rhodesia: mentioned, 366

Rhodes, Cecil, 22

Rice, 321

Richardson, Neil R.: *Foreign Policy and Economic Dependence* (University of Texas Press, 1978), 467

Rideout, Walter M. (et al.): *Survey of Education in the Democratic Republic of the Congo* (American Council of Education, 1969), 434

Roads: rural, 91, 93; food distribution, 96; agricultural use, 311; building and maintenance by cotton companies, 320

Roberto, Holden (FNLA leader), 253, 376

Rockefeller Foundation: technical assistance to Zaire, 107

Ross, Marc: *The Political Integration of Urban Squatters* (Northwestern Press, 1973), 431

Rotberg, Robert I.: *Haiti: The Politics of Squalor* (Houghton Mifflin, 1971), 417

Rothchild, Donald, and Victor Olorunsola (eds.): *State Versus Ethnic Claims: African Policy Dilemmas* (Westview, 1982), 412

Rothschild, Emma: "The Politics of Debt," *New York Review of Books* 23, no. 11 (1976), 464

Rothschild, Joseph: *Ethnopolitics* (Columbia University Press, 1981), 432, 433

Rousseau, Jean Jacques: Sovereignty theory, 8

Rowlands, "Tiny": development strategy, 302

Rubbens, Antoine: in *Dettes de guerre* (Editions de l'Essor du Congo, 1945), 416

Rubber: wild, 32–34; plantations, 305

Rubinstein, Alvin Z. (ed.): *Soviet and Chinese Influence in the Third World* (Praeger, 1975), 463

Rulers: authority and power of, 28

Rural administration: chieftancy, 232–36

Rural population: out migration, 90–99

Rutebingwa Ndakiwa: "La siderurgie de Maluku," *Zaire-Afrique* 96 (1975), 453

Rwanda, 273

Rykmans, Pierre (Belgian governor-general): UN speech, 38; *Dominer pour servir* (Editions universelle, 1948), 413; *Etapes et jalons* (Maison Ferdinand Larcier, 1946), 416, 452; mentioned, 25, 39, 281

Rymenam, Jean: "Class sociales, pouvoir et économie au Zaire," *Genève-Afrique* 18, no. 1 (1980), 427; "Comment le régime Mobutu a sapé ses propres fondements," *Le Monde Diplomatique* no. 1 (1977), 423, 427

SADCC (Southern African Development Conference), 390

Salongo, (1 August 1972), 422; (16–17 November 1972), 449; (31 March 1975), 454; (5 October 1972), 456; (20 November 1974), 456

Sambwa Pida (director, Bank of Zaire), 381

Samerin, W. M.: "Colonization and Pidginization on the Ubangi River," *Journal of African Languages and Linguistics* 4 (1982), 434

Samoff, Joel: "Class, Class Conflict, and the State: Notes on the Political Economy of Africa" (paper, 1977), 428

Sanctions: political under Mobutu, 166. *See also* Economics

Sarraut, Albert: French colonial minister, 25–26; "La mise en valeur des colonies françaises," in D. Bruce Marshall, *The French Colonial Myth and Constitution-Making in the Fourth Republic* (Yale University Press, 1973), 413

Saul, John: "The Unsteady State: Uganda, Obote and General Amin," in *State and Revolution in Eastern Africa* (Monthly Review Press, 1979), 416, 435

Savimbi Jonas (UNTA), 253

Schatzberg, Michael G.: in Aidan Southhall (ed.), *Small Urban Centers in Rural Development in Africa* (African Studies Program, University of Wisconsin-Madison,

1979), 424; "Islands of Privilege: Small Cities in Africa and the Dynamics of Class Formation," (paper, 1978), 424, 447; "Bureaucracy, Business, Beer: The Political Dynamics of Class Formation in Lisala, Zaire," (Ph.D. diss., University of Wisconsin-Madison, 1977), 424, 425, 429, 434, 459, 460, 461; *Politics and Class in Zaire* (Africana Publishing Co., 1980), 427, 436, 441, 444, 445, 447, 450, 458; "Fidelité au Guide: J.M.P.R. in Zairian schools," *Journal of Modern African Studies* 16, no. 1 (1978), 441; *Schatzberg chronology*, (typescript), 459, 460; "The Long Arm of the Law: Insecurity, Instability, and the Political Police in Zaire" (paper, 1982), 451, 467

Schmitter, Philippe: "Still the Century of Corporatism?" in *The New Corporatism: Social-Political Structure in the Iberian World* (University of Notre Dame Press, 1974), 412

Schools: role in colonial Africa, 26; religious, 67, 68; fees, 95–96; Mobutu's attendance and expulsion, 174; mentioned, 87, 91, 109

Scott, James: "Patron-Client Politics and Political Change in Southeast Asia," *American Political Science Review* 66, no. 4 (1972), 435; in Arnold J. Heidenheimer (ed.) *Political Corruption* (Holt, Rinehart, and Winston, 1970), 447

Schramme, Jean, 251–52

Second Republic: external relationships, 365–67; mentioned, 221

Security: state, 15, 272–73; African, 29; weaponry, 29–30; urban, 90; rural, 90

Security police: forces in urban areas, 128; heads of, 272–73; involvement in 1965 coup, 272; and CIA, 272; mentioned, 402

Segers, Joseph: "L'économie congolaise hier, demain, aujourd'hui," *Documents pour l'Action* 3, no. 15 (1963), 416

Seiler, John (ed.): *Southern Africa since the Portuguese Coup* (Westview Press, 1980), 419, 464

Sékou Touré (president of Guinea), 368
Sergent, Pierre: *La Légion saute sur Kolwezi* (Presse de la Cité, 1978), 448
Serlon, Paul: "Les ressorts d'un système axé sur la survie," *Le Monde Diplomatique,* 330 (1981), 454
Shaba: resource concentration, 34, 83–84; chiefs, 238
Shaba I rebellion, 255–57; Shaba II rebellion, 257–58; American response to Shaba I, 388–89; Shaba II and FAZ, 257; Arab support, 369; rebellion impact on energy development, 300; rocket base, 387; American support in Shaba II, 389; mentioned, 196, 249
Shabani, Andre (secretary, youth affairs), 195, 196
Shafer, Michael: "United States Military Assistance to Zaire" (paper, 1982), 451; "Capturing the Mineral Multinationals: Advantages or Disadvantages?" *International organization* 37, no. 1 (1983), 453
SGA (Société Générale d'Alimentation), 342
Shaw, Timothy M.: "Beyond Underdevelopment: the Anarchic State in Africa" (paper, 1982), 416
SIBEKA (Société d'Entreprise et d'Investissement du Beceka), 288
SICA (Italian consulting firm); Maluku steel mill, 297, 298; Inga Dam project, 299
Silverstein, Joseph: *Burma: Military Rule and the Politics of Stagnation* (Cornell University Press, 1977), 417
Singa, Boyenge (Alexandre): security chief, 60, 272; chief of staff, 274
Sivard, Ruth Leger: *World, Military and Social Expenditures 1982* (World Priorities, 1982), 411
Siwa dio Banza (union leader), 200
Sklar, Richard L.: *Corporate Power in an African State* (University of California Press, 1975), 429
Skocpol, Theda, *States and Social Revolutions* (Cambridge University Press, 1979), 411
Smith, Ian: mentioned, 366

SMTF (Société Minière de Tenke-Fungurume), 303–4
Smuggling, 87
SNI (Service Nationale d'Intelligence), 273
SOBAKI (Société Belgo-Africain du Kivu), 285
Socialist Party Africanists, 390
Société Générale de Belgique: mentioned, 283, 284, 364
SOCOBANQUE (Société Congolaise de Banque), 374
Solo, Robert: "The Need for a Theory of State," *Journal of Economic Issues* 11, no. 2 (1977), 410
Soumialot, Gaston (leader of Kisangani rebellion), 366
South Africa: involvement in Angolan civil war, 72, 378
Southall, Aidan: *Small Urban Centers in Rural Development in Africa* (African Studies Program, (University of Wisconsin, 1979), 424; "The Illusion of Tribe," *Journal of Asian and African Studies* 5, nos. 1–2 (1970), 433
Sovereignty, 12–13, 16–17, 36
Soviet Union: involvement in Angolan civil war, 72, 75; African political involvement, 364; embassy opening, 370; mentioned, 350
SOZACOM (Société Zairoise pour le Commercialisation des Minerais), 18, 304, 384–85, 455n68
Spécial (Belgian weekly), 175; (2 September 1970), 454; (12 September 1970), 456
Spinola (president of Portugal), 253
Squatters, 127–28
Stanley, Henry, 31, 32
"The State," Special Issue *Daedalus* 108, no. 4 (Fall, 1979); 410
State: colonial Africa, 7, 22–26; concept, 7–22; definitions, 8–12; "welfare," 10; as territorial entity, 12–13; concept of nation state, 13; sovereignty, 13; hegemony, 13–14, 15; organization of, 13–14; ideology, 14, 16; legal systems, 14; revenue implications, 14–17; security, 15; autonomy, 15–16; legitimacy, 16, 185; agriculture policy, 17; fragmentation

State (*continued*)
within, 19–20; interstate relationships, 21; African new authoritarian, 27; patrimonialization of power, 28; *pagaille*, 43, 45, 104; decay, 44; three-class layers, 105
Statesman's Year-Book 1977–1978 (St. Martin's Press, 1977), 450
Steel: plant development, 296–98
Stengers, Jean: *Belgique et Congo: élaboration de la Charte Coloniale* (La Renaissance du Livre, 1963), 414; "La Belgique et le Congo," in *Histoire de la Belgique Contemporaine* (La Renaissance du Livre, 1974), 414, 416; "The Congo Free State and the Belgian Congo," in L. H. Gann, and Peter Duignan (eds.), *Colonialism in Africa, 1870–1960* (Cambridge University Press, 1969), 414; *Combien le Congo a-t-il coûté à la Belgique?* (Académie Royale des Sciences d'Outre Mer, 1975), 415
Stepan, Alfred: *The State and Society: Peru in Comparative Perspective* (Princeton University Press, 1974), 410, 412
Stephens, Evelyne, and John Stephens: "Democratic Socialism in Jamaica: The Political Movement and Social Transformation in Dependent Capitalism," (forthcoming), 412
Stereotypes: ethnic, 143; mentioned, 140
Stevens, Christopher A.: *The Soviet Union and Black Africa* (Macmillan, 1976), 462
Stockwell, John: *In Search of Enemies* (W. W. Norton, 1978), 418, 450, 464
Stolper, Wolfgang, 32; "Report to Ambassador Vance and Acting Director Kelly on Certain Problems of the Zairian Economy," (Kinshasa, 1972), 382, 466
Strickon, Arnold, and Sidney Greenfield: *Structure and Process in Latin America: Patronage, Clientage, and Power Systems* (University of New Mexico Press, 1972), 444
Strikes: 1976 Shaba and Kinshasa, 74, 131; 1962 Kinshasa, 130; 1941 Lubumbashi, 130; 1945 Matadi, 130; 1976 Air Zaire, 131; 1961 SNCZ, 131
Student associations, 62. *See also* Political movements and parties

Student unrest and demonstrations, 197
"Sultanism," 182–83
Sunkel, Osvaldo: "Big Business and Dependency," *Foreign Affairs* 50, no. 3 (1972), 466
Sûreté, 272
Sweden: welfare state, 10

Taifa, (13 April 1974), 459
Tanganyika Concessions: mentioned, 283, 284
Tanzania: Mobutu's state visit to, 368
Taxes: colonial Africa, 23; agriculture, 94–95; school, 96; penal, 96; indirect, 97; diamonds, 288; UMHK, 288; payments, 348–49; colonial corporate sector, 396–97
Teachers: 1960–1980, 124–25
Technology: in Zaire, 104; and energy development, 300
Tempels, Placide: *Bantu Philosophy* (Editions Présence Africaine, 1948), 443
Tempelsman consortium, 374
Tempelsman, Maurice (financier), access to Mobutu, 171, 176; involvement with copper, 293; involvement with Inga-Shaba, 303; mentioned, 179
Terray, Emmanuel: *Marxism and "Primitive" Societies* (Monthly Review Press, 1972), 435
Territorial administration: historic, 221–23; Belgian model, 222–27; regional commissions, 227–32. *See also* Chiefs, Colonial Administration, Regional Administration, Urban Administration
Tetela-Kusu: ethnic group, 150–51
Third World: autonomy in state, 15–16
Tilley, Charles (ed.): *The Formation of National States in Western Europe* (Princeton University Press, 1975), 409
Tin: production of, 34
Togo: Mobutu's state visit to, 368
Tollens, Eric F.: "An Economic Analysis of Cotton Production, Marketing and Processing in Northern Zaire," (Ph.D. diss., Michigan State University, 1975), 457, 458
Toure, Mamadou (IMF official), 384

Touré, Sékou (president of Guinea): mentioned, 41

Towns: rapid growth of, 230. *See also* Urbanization

Trade: import-export after 1961, 115; copper, 307; in commercial sector, 343

Trade unions, 62

Traders: income and wealth of, 114; in urban centers, 132; payments to villages, 312; in colonial period, 327; expulsion, 329; foreign, 332; Zairianization, 339; mentioned, 108

Transportation: railways, 32–34; 284–85, 296, 302, 306, 307; air, 286–87

Tribalism: denunciation of, 138–39; New Regime, 149, 150

Tribune Africaine (20 March 1970), 456

Tripartite decision, 336

Tshiauke Mukongo: "Les problèmes administratifs des mesures économiques du 30 Novembre 1973 (Cas de la sous-Région de Kolwezi)" (Mémoire de licence, Université Nationale du Zaire, 1975), 458–61

Tshibanda Kabongo: "La modernisation differenciée: le cas des Baluba de Kabondo-Dianda, un sous-groupe de l'ethnie Luba du Shaba (Zone de Bukama)," (Mémoire de licence, Université Nationale de Zaire, 1975), 446

Tshibangu Banza-Muakula: "La réforme des structures agricoles au Zaire: Cas de l'Office National des Fibres Textiles (ONAFITEX) et de la culture contonnière dans la Zone de Gandajika," (Mémoire de licence, Université Nationale du Zaire, 1975), 457, 458

Tshibumba Kanda-Matula (urban folk artist), 3; political conditions expressed in art, 6–7; colonial belge, 30; mentioned, 31, 37

Tshilemelema Mukenge: "Businessmen of Zaire: Limited Possibilities for Capital Accumulation under Dependence," (Doctoral diss., McGill University, 1974), 435

Tshipola, Ferdinand (Colonel), 250

Tshisekedi, E., 61; 420*n*30

Tshivuadi Katamba: "La participation des étudiants zairois à la politique," (Mémoire de licence, Université Nationale du Zaire, 1974), 435

Tshombe, Moise: political career of, 42, 47–50, 57–58; and copper strikes, 75; leader of Katanga secession, 114; attempted return to power by, 251; plot, 251; conspiracy, 261; charter companies, 283; 1967 threat, 367; mentioned, 250, 277; *Quinze mois du gouvernement au Congo* (Table Ronde, 1966), 417

Tshoya K.: "Les collectivés de la zone de Dilolo sous l'Ordonnance-loi No. 73/015, du 15 janvier 1973," (Mémoire de licence, Université Nationale du Zaire, 1975), 445

Tsongas, Paul (U.S. senator), 301

Tukuzu (head of security), 273

Turner, Margaret: work in progress (University of Wisconsin-Madison), 446

Turner, Thomas: "Peasant Rebellion and Its Suppression in Sankuru, Zaire," *Pan African Journal* 7, no. 3 (1974), 426, 440; "Class Conflict in Zaire," (paper, 1979), 430; "L'ethnie tetela et le MNC/Lumumba," *Etudes Congolaises* 12 (1969), 432; "Congo-Kinshasa," in Victor A. Olorunsola (ed.), *The Politics of Cultural Sub Nationalism in Africa* (Anchor Books, 1972), 432; "A Century of Political Conflict in Sankuru," (Ph.D. diss., University of Wisconsin, 1973), 433, 441

Tutashinda, N.: "Le mystifications de l'Authenticité," *La pensée*, 175 (1974), 443

UDI (Unilateral Declaration of Independence), 366

UEAC (Union of States of Central Africa), 371

Uganda: Obote overthrow in, 368

UGEC (Union Générale des Etudiants Congolais), 56, 187, 197

Ugeux, E.-Xavier: "La diplomatie agissante du Mobutu," *Remarques Africaines*, 427 (1973), 421; "Marathon dans la brousse zairoise," *Remarques Africaines*, 432–33 (1973), 436

UMHK (Union Minière du Haut Katanga): nationalization, 59, 288–96; copper, 61; corporate personnel, 107; mineral resources, 288–89; subsidiaries, 289; assets division, Zaire and Belgium, 291–92; Inga–Shaba bid, 302–3; settlement with Mobutu, 374; *Rapport Annual* (1966), 428; mentioned, 283, 284

UNARCO (Union of Nationalists of Revolutionary Africa), 189

UNAZA (Université Nationale du Zaire), staff, 121; mentioned, 62, 229

Unemployment, 127, 351

UNESCO (United Nations Educational, Scientific and Cultural Organization), 209

UNITA (Uniaõ Nacional para la Independência Total de Angola), 376

Unite, February-March 1970, 453

United Nations: Article 73, 38; military forces in Zaire, 1960–64, 47–48; technical assistance in Zaire, 1960–64, 106–7; security force in Zaire, 107; peacekeeping force in Zaire, 260; and Congo crisis, 364; mentioned, 363

United Nations General Assembly: "Declaration and Action Programme on the establishment of a New International Economic Order," (6 May 1974), 453

United Nations Security Council: seat for Zaire, 390, 403

United States: constitution, 9; military, 49; on Zairian realignment, 1965, 50; and Adoula regime, 52; support for Mobutu, 57; logistical support, Shaba I and II, 75; "Pre-crisis" Zaire relations and aid, 371–72; decline of Zaire relations, 372–73; and Angolan civil war, 376; Zairian relations, Angolan civil war, 377, 380; "bailout" of Zairian government, 378–79; relations with Zaire during debt crisis of 1975, 380; ambivalence toward Zaire, 1978, 388–89; 1980 relations with Zaire, 389–90

United States, Agency for International Development, "Basic Family Health Services," Zaire Project 600–0067 (15 December 1975), 421; AID Public

Safety Report, 1973 and 1974, 450; "Grain Marketing," (12 December 1975), 458

United States, Central Intelligence Agency (CIA): relations, Mobutu, 51; role in Mobutu coup, 53; involvement in Angolan civil war, 72, 378; Mobutu connection to Lumumba assassination, 172; security police, 272; payments, 371; plot to overthrow Mobutu, 372–73; mentioned, 388, 389

United States Congress, House of Representatives: Subcommittee on Africa, Committee on Foreign Affairs: "Political and Economic Situation in Zaire—Fall 1981," 97th Congress, 1st sess., 15 September 1981, 439, 440; "Political and Economic Situation in Zaire—Fall 1981," 97th Congress, 1st sess., 15 September 1981, testimony by Nguza, 451; Committee on International Relations, Subcommittee on Africa, *United States–Angolan Relations*, testimony of Gerald Bender, 95th Congress, 2nd sess., 1978, 464

United States Congress, Senate: Committee on Foreign Relations, *Zaire*, 97th Congress, 2nd sess., July 1982, 450; Committee on Banking, Housing and Urban Affairs, Subcommittee on International Finance, *U.S. Loans to Zaire*, 96th Congress, 1st sess., 24 May 1979, 454; Committee on Foreign Relations, Subcommittee on Africa, *Security Supporting Assistance for Zaire*, 95th Congress, 2nd sess., 24 October 1978, 464, 465

United States, Department of Agriculture: cotton management, 320–21

United States, Department of Health, Office of International Health, "Syncrisis: The Dynamics of Health, XIV: Zaire," (mimeo), 421, 424

United States, Foreign Agricultural Service, American Embassy, Kinshasa, *Annual Cotton Report*, (1 September 1977), 458

UNTZA (Union Nationale des Travailleurs Zairois), 199–201

Uranium: Shinkolobwe mine, 289

Urban administration: Kisangani, 230; 1967 constitution, 231; subregions, 231; Kinshasa, 231; lack of autonomy, 232

Urban communes: role in elections, 142–43; land plot allocations, 143; mentioned, 230

Urban councils: dismantling of, 149

Urban ethnicity, 139, 142–44

Urban growth, 80–90, 230

Urban workers, 129, 130, 133

Urbanization, 78–90, 127

UTC (Union des Travailleurs Congolais), Catholic-inspired labor union, 199

Vance, Sheldon (United States ambassador to Zaire), 372, 373, 380, 387

Van der Berghe, Pierre: "Ethnicity: The African Experience," *International Social Science Journal* 23 (1971), 435

Vanderkerken, Georges (provincial governor), political concept of Mongohood, 141–42; *L'ethnie Mongo*, 2 vols. (Institut Royal Colonial, 1944), 432

Van der Steen, Daniel: "Echanges économiques extérieurs du Zaire; dépendence et développement," *Cahiers du CEDAF* 4–5 (1977), 456; "Le Zaire malade de sa dépendance extérieure," *Genève-Afrique* 18, no. 1 (1979), 467

Van de Walle, B.: *Essai d'une planification de l'économie agricole congolaise* (INEC, 1960), 457

Van de Walle, Frederic J.: *Ommegang* (Livre Africaine, 1970), 449

Van Hecke, Etienne: "Structure agraire et habitat au Bas Congo," *Etudes Africaines du C.R.I.S.P.*, T.A. 106–7 (1970), 425

Van Lierde, Jean (ed.): *La pensée politique du Patrice Lumumba* (Editions présence Africaine, 1963), 442

Vansina, Jan: "Les Kuba et l'administration territoriale de 1919 à 1960," *Cultures et Developpment* 4, no. 2 (1972), 415; "Mwasi's Trials," *Daedalus* 111, no. 2 (1982), 421; *The Children of Woot* (University of Wisconsin Press, 1978), 433; *Introduction à l'ethmographie du Congo* (Editions Universitaires du Congo,

1966), 434, 443, 445

Vehicle assembly plants, 305

Vellut, Jean-Luc: "Les bassins miniers de l'ancien Congo Belge. Essai d'histoire économique et sociale (1900–1960)," *Cahiers du CEDAF*, 7 (1981), 452

Vengroff, Richard: *Development Administration at the Local Level: The Case of Zaire* (Syracuse University, 1983), 446

Verhaegen, Benoit, on economic bourgeoisie, 120; schools as mobility myths, 135; on Ngbandi, 153; (et al.): *Kisangani 1876–1976* (Presses Universitaires du Zaire, 1975), 423, 425; *Rébellions au Congo*, 2 vols. (Centre de Recherche et d'Information Socio-Politiques, 1966, 1969), 127, 163; "Transferts du technologie ou imperialisme technologique? Le cas du Zaire," *Cahiers du CEDAF*, 5, 6 (1981), 427, 458; "Impérialisme technologique et bourgeoisie nationale au Zaire," in C. Coquery-Vidrovitch (ed.), *Connaissance du Tiers Monde* (Union Generale d'Editions, 1978), 430; "paradoxes zairoises" (paper, 1983), 431; and E. de Bethune, "Consultations électorales et elections au Congo, 1957–1969," *Cahiers Economiques et Sociaux*, 3, 3 (1969), 432; "Présentation morphologique des nouvelles provinces," *Etudes Congolaises*, 4, 4 (1963), 433; "Les associations congolaises à Leópoldville et dans le Bas-Congo avant 1960," *Cahiers Economiques et Sociaux*, 8, 3 (1970), 434; "Universities, Social Classes and Economic Dependency" (paper, 1978), 466; "Les mouvements de libération en Afrique: Le cas du Zaire en 1978," *Genève-Afrique* 17, 1 (1979), 468

Verhaegen Guy: "Le développement de l'agriculture paysanne au Zaire," *Zaire-Afrique*, 76 (1973), 457, 458

Verhulpen, Edmond: *Baluba et balubaisé du Katanga* (Editions de l'avenir belge 1936), 432

Vietnam War, 11

Vieux, Serge A.: *L'administration zairoise* (Berger-Levrault, 1974), 444

Village regrouping, 240–42; New Regime policy and attitudes towards, 240; Mondji-Ngandu collectivity, 240–41; Watambulu Collectivity, 241; Olemba collectivity, 241; policy application, 241–42; Tanzanian experiment, 241–42

Vincent, Joan: *An African Elite: Big Men in a Small Town* (Columbia University Press, 1968), 429

"Voice of Zaire" (radio, TV), 306, 375

Voltaire: *Zaire* Eva Jacobs, ed. (Hodder and Stoughton, 1975), 443

Voting process, 143–44

Vundowe T'Angambe Pemako: "Le Processus de l'intégration des autorités traditionnelles dans l'administration moderne de la République de Zaire (de 1885 a 1972)," (Doctoral diss., Université Catholique de Louvain, 1973), 445, 446

Vwakyanakazi Mukohya, "Traders in Butembo," (Ph.D. diss., University of Wisconsin-Madison, 1982), 426, 430

Wages: employment, 85; legal minimum, 87–88; management, 107; cadres, 122; First Republic sub-bourgeoisie, 123; public sector, New Regime, 123–24; teacher, 124–25; military, 125–26; urban, 127; labor, 131, 132–33; agriculture, 312

Wall Street Journal, (7 July 1983), 453; (26 May 1979), 455; (26 June 1980), 455

Washington Post, (25 March 1977), 448; (11 November 1981), 453

Watilaninwa Yaya: "Une approche générale sur le rôle du charisme au Zaire sous la deuxième République," (Mémoire de licence, Université Nationale du Zaire, 1974), 436

Weber, Max: theory on state power, 9–10; social closure theory, 123; patrimonialism theory, 165; mentioned, 14

Weber, Max: "Politics as a Vocation," in H. C. Gerth and C. Wright Mills (eds.) *From Max Weber* (Oxford University Press, 1958), 410

Weinstein, Brian: *The Civic Tongue* (Longman, 1983), 433

Weinstein, Martin: *Uruguay: The Politics of Failure* (Greenwood Press, 1975), 417

Weinstein, Warren (ed.), *Chinese and Soviet Aid to Africa* (Praeger, 1975), 463

Weiss, Herbert: *Political Protest in the Congo* (Princeton University Press, 1967), 426, 433; "Mulele" in Charles-André Julien et al. (eds.), *Les Africains* (Editions Jeune Afrique, 1977), 427; *Parti Solidaire Africain (P.S.A.)* Centre de Recherche et d'Information Socio-Politiques, 1963), 433

Weissman, Stephen R.: "The CIA and U.S. Policy in Zaire and Angola," in René Lemarchand, (ed.), *American Policy in Southern Africa: The States and the Stance* (University Press of America, 1978), 418, 463; *American Foreign Policy in the Congo, 1960–64* (Cornell University Press, 1974), 462

Weka Engango a Ngola, "L'état d'exception de Bumba," (Mémoire de licence, Université Nationale du Zaire, 1975), 425

Welfare state: African colonial, 26; Congo Free State, 38

West Africa, (28 February 1970), 454

Western International Ground Maintenance Organization (WIGMO), 269

West Germany: Zairian relations, 375; economic involvement in Zaire, 375, 387–88

Willame, J. C. (with L. Monnier): *Les provinces du Congo: structure et fonctionnement* (Institut de Recherches Economiques et Sociales, 1964–65), 433; *Patrimonialism and Political Change in the Congo* (Stanford University Press, 1972), 436, 440; "Le saga d'Inga. Quelques réflexions sur les pratiques de transferts de technologie au Zaire," *Cahiers du CEDAF* 5–6 (1981), 453, 454

Willame, Jean-Claude: in Donald A. Emmerson (ed.), *Students and Politics in Developing Nations* (Frederick A. Praeger, 1968), 420–21; "Le secteur multinational au Zaire," *Cahiers du CEDAF* 1, (1980), 456; "La seconde guerre du Shaba," *Enquêtes et Documents d'Histoire Africaine* (Belgium, 1978), 448; "Contri-

bution à l'étude des mouvements d'op- position au Zaire: Le F.L.N.C.," *Cahiers du CEDAF* 6 (1980), 448, 468; "Divi- sions et faiblesses d'une opposition privée de strategie politique," *Le Monde Diplo- matique* 330 (September 1981), 468
Wilson, Charles: *The History of Unilever*, 2 vols. (Cassell & Co., 1954), 457
Wilson, Ernest J. III: "The Political Econ- omy of Public Corporations in the En- ergy Sectors of Nigeria and Zaire," (Ph.D. diss., University of California- Berkeley, 1978), 453–54
Wilson, Woodrow: state theory, 10; *The State* (D. C. Heath, 1918), 410
Wolin, Sheldon S.: *Politics and Vision* (Little, Brown, 1960), 409
Women: education and jobs, 88–89; cultivators taxes, 96; employment oppor- tunities for, 127; N'kanza, Lusibu Zala, Political Bureau, 193; spouses, business allocation applications, 339
Woodruff, Philip (Mason): *The Men Who Ruled India*, 2 vol. (Jonathan Cape, 1953), 444
World Bank: "Economic Conditions and Prospects of Zaire," (Report No. 1407– ZR, 13 April 1977), 461. *See also* Banks

Yabili, Asani: Code de la Zairianisation (ed- iteur "Mwanga-Hebdo," 1975), 459, 461
Yaka state, 233
Yates, Barbara A.: "The Missions and Edu- cational Development in Belgian Africa, 1876–1908," (Ph.D. diss., Columbia University, 1967), 416
Yeka Mangbau Lowanga (Gendarmery commander), 274
Yemo, Marie-Madeline (mother, Mobutu), 173–74, 437*n14*
Young, Crawford: "Patterns of Social Conflict: State, Class, and Ethnicity," *Daedalus* 111, no. 2 (Spring 1982), 412, 426; *The Politics of Cultural Pluralism* (University of Wisconsin Press, 1976), 412, 432, 433; *Politics in the Congo* (Princeton University Press, 1965), 412, 417, 424, 429, 432, 444; "Rebellion and

the Congo," in Robert Rotberg and Ali Mazrui (eds.), *Protest and Power in Black Africa* (Oxford University Press, 1970), 426, 463; "Ethnic Politics in Zaire," (paper, 1976), 432; "Zaire: The Unend- ing Crisis," *Foreign Affairs* 57, no. 1 (1978), 447; "Zaire, The Politics of Pen- ury," *SAIS Review* 3, no. 2 (1983), 462
Youth: political movements, 194–99

Zaire-Afrique, 91 (January 1975), 436; 69 (November 1972), 454; 70 (December 1972), 454
Zaire, Bank of, 132, 357, 382
Zaire: Post-colonial, 6, 397; growth of, 30–37; First Republic, 41–43; decline of state, 42–46, 71–77, 119, 136; inter- national role and linkages, 46; post- colonial conditions for change, 47–54; OAU and Kinshasa, 59–60; expansion of, 63–71; state dependency and eco- nomics, 135–36; *Le Monde* series on, 172; legitimating myths of, 208–17; cul- tural heritage of, 211–12; GDP, 211 212, 277, 323–25, 281, 400; diplomatic expansion of, 365–71; conflict with Congo-Brazzaville, 369; relations with Third World, 375–76; strategy in An- golan civil war, 376 78; diplomatic rela- tions, 386–90; Mobutist state, 396–99; expenses, 400–401
Zairianization: traders, 108, 335–36; mili- tary exclusion, 264, 340; announcement of, 326; importance of Nigeria, 327–28; national economic model for Mobutu, 327–32; economic autonomy, 328; for- eign firms' reaction to, 329; 1969 invest- ment code of, 330; Mobutu's idea of commerce, 330; legal framework of, 331–32; popular response to, 332–33; implementation of 30 November mea- sures, 333–43; compensation, 334; benefits and consequences for those af- fected, 346–47, 349; political cadres, 335–37; land scramble, 337–38; re- wards, 338–39; role of spouses, 339; ob- jectives of, 341; economic sectors in, 342; public vs. private interests, 343–

Zairianization (*continued*)
  44; consequences of, 343–50; asset-
  stripping, 344; commercial, 344; managerial problems, 346–47; agriculture,
  347; plantation sector, 347–48; layoffs,
  348; tax collections, 348; public reaction
  to, 349–50; mentioned, 37, 66
Zairian Upkeep and Maintenance Company, 269
Zimbabwe: decolonization of, 26

DESIGNED BY MIKE BURTON
COMPOSED BY G&S TYPESETTERS, AUSTIN, TEXAS
MANUFACTURED BY THOMSON-SHORE, INC., DEXTER, MICHIGAN
TEXT AND DISPLAY TYPE ARE SET IN GALLIARD

Library of Congress Cataloging in Publication Data
Young, Crawford, 1931–
The rise and decline of the Zairian state.
Includes bibliographies and index
1. Zaire—Politics and government—1960–   .
2. Mobutu Sese Seko, 1930–   . I. Turner, Thomas
1939–   . II. Title.
DT658.25.Y68   1985   967.5′103   84-40204
ISBN 0-299-10110-X